1 and 2 Timothy

CLINTON'S
BIBLICAL LEADERSHIP
COMMENTARY SERIES

Apostolic Leadership Picking Up the Mantle

J. Robert Clinton, D. Miss., Ph. D.

ISBN No 978-1-932814-03-3

Table of Contents

Articles—Table of Contents

Leadership Articles[1]

---

[1] Throughout the commentary Articles listed with numbers are included with this commentary and refer to the numbered articles listed above. Some articles, without numbers occur in other commentaries. I will be publishing a series called, **Clinton's Leadership Encyclopedia**, which will contain all the articles in all the leadership commentaries. Those articles not included in this commentary will be available also there. Some of the articles included here were written later, some time after the 1,2 Timothy commentary was already done. But in reviewing all of the leadership articles I felt that some were very appropriate to Paul's ministry with the Ephesian church. In any case, I introduce each article with a short paragraph telling how the article is relevant to the Ephesian ministry. All of these articles were revised at least somewhat for this issue of the 1,2 Timothy Leadership Commentary.

(This page is deliberately left blank.)

Abbreviations

Bible Books

Genesis	Ge	Nahum	Na
Exodus	Ex	Habakkuk	Hab
Leviticus	Lev	Zephaniah	Zep
Numbers	Nu	Haggai	Hag
Deuteronomy	Dt	Zechariah	Zec
Joshua	Jos	Malachi	Mal
Judges	Jdg	Matthew	Mt
Ruth	Ru	Mark	Mk
1 Samuel	1Sa	Luke	Lk
2 Samuel	2Sa	John	Jn
1 Kings	1Ki	Acts	Ac
2 Kings	2Ki	Romans	Ro
1 Chronicles	1Ch	1 Corinthians	1Co
2 Chronicles	2Ch	2 Corinthians	2Co
Ezra	Ezr	Galatians	Gal
Nehemiah	Ne	Ephesians	Eph
Esther	Est	Philippians	Php
Job	Job	Colossians	Col
Psalms	Ps	1 Thessalonians	1Th
Proverbs	Pr	2 Thessalonians	2Th
Ecclesiastes	Ecc	1 Timothy	1Ti
Song of Songs	SS	2 Timothy	2Ti
Isaiah	Isa	Titus	Tit
Jeremiah	Jer	Philemon	Phm
Lamentations	La	Hebrews	Heb
Ezekiel	Eze	James	Jas
Daniel	Da	1 Peter	1Pe
Hosea	Hos	2 Peter	2Pe
Joel	Joel	1 John	1Jn
Amos	Am	2 John	2Jn
Obadiah	Ob	3 John	3Jn
Jonah	Jnh	Jude	Jude
Micah	Mic	Revelation	Rev

Other

BAS	**Basic English Version**
CEV	**Contemporary English Version**
fn	footnote(s)
KJV	King James Version of the Bible
LB	**The Learning Bible—Contemporary English Version**
NEB	**New English Bible**
NLT	**New Living Translation**
N.T.	New Testament
O.T.	Old Testament
Phillips	**The New Testament in Modern English**, J.B. Phillips
TEV	**Today's English Version** (also called Good News Bible)
Vs	verse(s)

(This page is deliberately left blank.)

List of Tables for the 1,2 Timothy Leadership Articles

List of Tables for the 1,2 Timothy Leadership Articles

List of Figures for the 1,2 Timothy Leadership Articles

(This page is deliberately left blank.)

Introduction

This leadership commentary on 1,2 Timothy is part of a series, **Clinton's Leadership Commentary Series.** For the past 17 years I have been researching leadership concepts in the Bible. As a result of that I have identified the 25 most helpful Bible books that contribute to an understanding of leadership. I have done fourteen of these commentaries to date and am continuing on the rest. I originally published eight of these leadership commentaries in a draft manuscript for use in classes. But it became clear that I would need to break that large work (735 pages) into smaller works. The commentary series does that. 1,2 Timothy is part of that series of smaller books that give leadership insights.

This is a leadership commentary, not an exegetical commentary. That means I have worked with the text to see what implications of leadership it suggests.

A given commentary in the series is made up of an *Overview Section,* which seeks to analyze the book as a whole for historical background, plan, theme, and fit into the redemptive story of the Bible. In addition, I identify, up front, the basic leadership topics that are dealt with in the book. Then I educe leadership observations, guidelines, principles, and values for each of these leadership topics. This *Overview Section* primes the reader to look with leadership eyes.

Then I present the *Commentary Proper.* I use my own translation of the text. I give commentary on various aspects of the text. A given context, paragraph size, will usually have 3 to 4 comments dealing with some suggestions about leadership items.

The *Commentary Proper* suggests *Leadership Concepts* and connects you to leadership articles that further explain these leadership concepts. The emphasis on the comments is not exegetical though I do make those kinds of comments when they are helpful for my leadership purposes.

The *Leadership Articles* in the series carry much of what I have learned about leadership in my years of ministry. In one sense, these articles and others in the series are my legacy. I plan to publish all of the articles of the total series in a separate multi-volume work, **Clinton's Encyclopedia of Biblical Leadership Insights,** which will be updated periodically as the series expands. A leader at almost any level of leadership can be helped greatly by getting leadership perspectives from these articles.

I also include a *Glossary* which lists all the leadership concepts labeled in the comments.

I have already done a study of each book in the Bible from a leadership standpoint and have identified and written up a number of leadership topics for each book. This analysis is captured in my book, **The Bible and Leadership Values.**

In an age of relativity, we believe the Bible speaks loudly concerning leadership concepts offering suggestions, guidelines, and even absolutes. We, as Christian leaders, desperately need this leadership help as we seek to influence our followers toward God's purposes for their lives.

I want to give my special thanks and acknowledgement of Brian Dowd's work in compiling this commentary and its articles. Brian did a superb job of pulling all the loose ends together and thus enabled me to publish this work as a single commentary. Brian's work involved taking the material from its original publishing as part of the eight book single volume commentary and putting the material all together as a single commentary. Thanks Brian.

J. Robert Clinton
Summer 2006

Preface

Every Scripture inspired of God is profitable for leadership insights (doctrine), pointing out of leadership errors (reproof), suggesting what to do about leadership errors (correction), and for highlighting how to model a righteous life (instruction in righteousness) in order that God's leader (Timothy) may be well equipped to lead God's people (the special good work given in the book Timothy to the young leader Timothy) .
(2 Timothy 3:16,17—Clinton paraphrase—slanted toward Timothy's leadership situation)

The Bible--a Major Source of Leadership Values and Principles

No more wonderful source of leadership values and principles exists than the Bible. It is filled with influential people and the results of their influence—both good and bad. Yet it remains so little used to expose leadership values and principles. What is needed to break this *leadership barrier*? Three things:

1.   A conviction that the Bible is authoritative and can give leadership insights
2.   Leadership perspectives to stimulate our findings in the Bible—we are blind in general to leadership ideas and hence do not see them in the Bible.
3.   A willful decision to study and use the Bible as a source of leadership insights

These three assumptions underlie the writing of this leadership commentary series. **1,2 Timothy—Apostolic Leadership Picking Up The Mantle**, is one of a series of books intended to help leaders cross the *leadership barrier*.

Leadership Framework

Perhaps it might be helpful to put the notion of leadership insights from 1,2 Ti in the bigger picture of leadership in the Bible. Three major leadership elements give us our most general framework (cross-culturally applicable as well) for categorizing leadership insights. The study of leadership involves:

1.   **THE LEADERSHIP BASAL ELEMENTS** (The *What* of Leadership)
   a. leaders
   b. followers
   c. situations

In 1,2 Timothy we will see:
   a. *leaders*— like Paul, Timothy, Priscilla, Aquila, and Onesiphorus.
   b. *followers*— The church at Ephesus, as a whole, are the followers in this book. Remember this is the church that Paul released to those elders in Acts 20. The leadership influence of Paul was intended for the whole church, not just only for Timothy—Paul's representative.
   c. *situations*— In 1,2 Timothy we will see that Paul was addressing several problems including some heresies creeping into the church. That church was

15-20 years old, and hence facing the problems of a church of that age: a tendency toward nominality, contextualization issues, application of the Gospel to social problems, truth and heresy, folks straying from their Christian commitment, and leadership selection. We are not clear exactly on the heresies being dealt with. There are four lines of heresy suggested in 1Ti (See fn 1:3,4,6,7; 2:12; 4:3,7; 6:4,5,20) but not taught clearly. There is something to be learned from this. Enough information is not given to deduce the exact heresies (at least from an orthodoxic standpoint). But the results of these heresies are described. So while we may not know the exact teaching involved in the heresy we can see what it does to people and the church. Hence, we can take a look at our own teaching and others too and see what are the results of our teaching. Heresy is concerned with truth—both its content and its behavioral implications. We can be heretical both in what we believe and what we practice. The heretical practices (disrupting the church, hypocritical leadership, failure to submit to leadership, teaching to gain finances, the selection of leaders—partiality shown, the failure to discipline, the evident criticism coming from the society as it judged Christianity) were more in focus than the actual teaching. Rest assured, the Ephesian people knew the content of these teachings.

2. **LEADERSHIP INFLUENCE MEANS** (The *How* of Leadership)
   a. *individual means*—this concept involves identifying leadership styles of individual leaders influencing the situation. In 1,2 Ti Paul is influencing both the church and his representative consultant, Timothy. With Timothy he is very close. Paul is a mentor. In fact, he models several mentoring styles including: contemporary model, counselor, teacher, and spiritual guide. In 1, 2 Timothy we see that Paul uses several leadership styles in getting at these problems in the Ephesian church. Though *apostolic*, Paul does not come down using that style openly. But it is clear he expects them to listen and follow what he says. *Maturity appeal* is certainly evident, especially in 2 Ti. The *father-initiator* style is always lurking behind his advice, as well. But one special leadership style is seen here. This is one of only two times we see Paul demonstrating the special leadership style, *indirect conflict*. See especially the comments on 1 Tim 1:20. Spiritual discernment and warfare are involved—more than likely without direct confrontation of the parties involved. This is an example of power ministry, so desperately needed to demonstrate God's intervention. This is a rare illustration. Paul doesn't include *indirect conflict* often. Paul's leadership styles in 1,2 Ti are not as overt as in 1,2 Co. But they are there by implication.

   b. *corporate means*—this refers to organizational structures or group pressures that influence followers in a corporate sense. Paul recognizes the importance of the body of elders that are leading the church. His advice to Timothy was certainly read and picked up by the existing elders.

3. **LEADERSHIP VALUE BASES** (The *Why* of Leadership)
    a. *cultural*
    b. *theological*

In 1,2 Timothy we will see several outward indications that flow from Ephesian values. At least two of the potential heresies flow right out of the culture's religious views. Paul's reference to Jesus as the one mediator is written to confront the Ephesian religious practices in the temple. The prohibition of abusive authority concerning women most likely flows right out of the culture. The Ephesian culture as well as religious views are alive and well throughout both books.

It is through using these major leadership elements—leaders, followers, and situations—that we are able to analyze leadership throughout the whole Bible. Using these major notions we recognize that leadership, at different time periods in the Bible, operates sufficiently different so as to suggest leadership eras—that is, time periods within which leadership follows more closely certain commonalities than in the time preceding it and following it. This allows us to identify six such eras in the Bible.

Six Bible Leadership Eras

The six leadership eras include,

1. **Patriarchal Era**

2. **Pre-Kingdom Era**
    A. Desert Years
    B. The War Years
    C.   The Tribal Years

3. **Kingdom Era**
    A. United Kingdom
    B. Divided Kingdom
    C. Southern Kingdom

4. **Post-Kingdom Era**
    A. Exilic
    B. A Foothold Back in the Land

5. **Pre-Church Era**

6. **Church Era**

We are here.

Preface

For each of these major eras we are dealing with some fundamental leadership questions.[2] We ask ourselves these major questions about every leadership era. Usually the answers are sufficiently diverse as to justify identification of a unique leadership era.

Where does 1,2 Timothy fit?

The books of 1,2 Timothy fit in the sixth leadership era, *The Church Era*. It is a pioneering time in which the Gospel is spreading to the Gentile world. Churches have been started in about 5 separate city/town locations in Asia Minor, and Greece. The churches are new. The one at Ephesus could be around 15-20 years old.[3]

What do 1,2 Timothy say?

Before we can look at leadership insights from 1,2 Ti we need to be sure that we understand why they are in the Scriptures and what they are saying in general. Having done our homework, hermeneutically speaking, we are free then to go beyond and look for other interpretative insights—such as leadership insights. But we must remember, always, first of all to interpret in light of the historical times, purposes of, theme of, and structure of the each of these epistles. Let's look at 1 Ti first in terms of Paul's organization of the book and his thematic intent and hoped for purposes. Then we will do the same three items for 2 Ti.

There is a lack of well integrated structural sections in this book, 1 Ti. It is written by an older person—who throws in asides (certain of his words and phrases will remind him of important things he has learned in the past—and he will divert to include them). There is a purpose statement which loosely integrates every thing that is said. See 1Ti 3:14,15.

Structure			
	I.	(Ch 1,2)	Paul's Advice on Major Problems in the Church
	II.	(Ch 3)	Paul's advice on Local Leadership Selection
	III.	(Ch 4)	Paul's Personal Advice to Timothy on How to Handle Himself
	IV.	(Ch 5)	Paul's Advice on Social Problem on Widows
	V.	(Ch 6)	Paul's Miscellaneous Exhortations

The overall thematic intent could be represented by a subject, which permeates all of what God is doing through the book of 1 Ti and several ideas about that subject. These ideas are tied to the structure just given above. Here is my analysis of such a theme.

Theme **Leading God's People, As Model Representatives Of God's Truth,**

- requires confrontation against false doctrines and practices,
- involves selection of quality local leadership,
- demands personal development as a leader, and
- outworks itself in meeting social needs for the believers.

---

[2] The six questions we use to help us differentiate between leadership eras includes: 1. What is the major leadership focus? 2. What are the influence means used? 3.What are the basic leadership functions? 4. What are the characteristics of the followers? 5. What was the existing cultural forms of leadership? 6. Other? I comment on each of these in the **Clinton's Encyclopedia of Biblical Leadership Insights.**

[3] See **Article *11*.** *Ephesian Church—Its Time-Line.*

Preface

Purpose

It is always difficult to synthesize statements of purpose when the author does not directly and **explicitly** give them. In the case of 1 Tim, Paul does state one general purpose. See 1Ti 3:14,15 for that stated purpose.

> 1 Ti 3: 14 These things I am writing to you hoping to come to you shortly: 15 But if I am delayed, you will know how you should handle yourself the house of God, which is the church of the living God, the pillar and ground of the truth.[4]

In addition to that stated purpose it is likely from seeing the issues being dealt with in the letter to assume that several of the following were also purposes.

- to give Timothy advice on numerous church problems including:
  -confronting false doctrine and troublesome leaders propagating it,
  -instruction on church prayers,
  -selection criteria for overseers and deacons,
  -spiritual disciplines,
  -Timothy's lack of boldness,
  -how to properly rebuke in the church,
  -handling of support of widows,
  -financial support of church elders,
  -accusations against elders,
  -attitudes of slaves,
  -attitudes toward money,
  -Timothy's personal conduct,
  -giving.
- to encourage Timothy to confront the problems,
- to encourage Timothy to develop personally and warn him against the consequences of failure to develop,
- to model several mentoring styles including: contemporary model, counselor, teacher, spiritual guide,
- to show the complexity of leading a church which has the truth of the Bible as its central controlling guidelines.

---

[4] 2 (3:15 truth) This great truth statement forms the basis for my thematic subject for the whole book of Timothy—Leading, God's People, As Model Representatives of God's Truth. That is what Paul is repeatedly emphasizing to Timothy. See again my full statement of the theme. The church, here basically a local church, is God's foundational means for teaching, clarifying, and living out truth before the world.

Preface

Now on to 2 Ti, a follow-up letter, written not too long after 1 Ti and shortly before Paul was to die. One way of analyzing the structure, that is, the way that Paul organizes his material to accomplish his purposes, in 2 Ti would be:

Structure

I.	(Ch 1-2:13)	Exhortations to Persevere and Select Leaders to Carry On in Ministry
II.	(Ch 2:14-26)	Warnings for the Newly Selected Leaders to Aid Them in Persevering
III.	(Ch 3:1-17)	Persevering in Difficult Days Ahead
IV.	(Ch 4:1-8)	End Result of Persevering—A Good Finish
V.	(Ch 4:9-18)	Personal Matters

Again, the overall thematic intent could be represented by a subject, which permeates all of what God is doing through the book of 2 Ti and several ideas about that subject. Here is my analysis of such a theme.

Theme

Persevering In A Ministry
- should be done to meet God's approval,
- will require the suffering of hardships,
- involves the modeling of righteous living, and
- necessitates the proper use of God's word.

It is likely that some of the following were certainly the purposes of this letter.

Purposes
- to summon Timothy to his side,
- to encourage Timothy during these tough days in the Roman empire,
- to give his farewell advice (on numerous issues),
- to highlight the need for transparency in a mentoring relationship (see 3:10,11),
- to give an inspirational model of a leader finishing well,
- to pass the torch of leadership to Timothy (giving continuity),
- to transfer the stewardship of the Word to Timothy.

Having done our overview of the book, hermeneutically speaking, we can now focus on leadership issues seen in 1, 2 Ti.

Approach To 1,2 Timothy In Perspective

With this background in mind, we can now proceed to the leadership commentary including its *General Reflection, Leadership Lessons, Commentary Notes, Articles,* and *Glossary.*

Today, we live in the Church Leadership Era.[5] It is not difficult to place ourselves back hundreds of years into the 6th leadership era—Church Leadership. Though quite removed from us in time and certainly culturally, we can still identify with Paul and his church planting ministry. Most of us have studied well the New Testament. We are relatively familiar with the Acts and the Pauline epistles. So then, when Paul deals with church problems, such as the problems in Ephesus, we are eager to learn about the problems. We want to see how Paul dealt with them. We want to learn about his solutions. For we live in the church leadership era. We will be facing these exact same problems or some similar to them. Paul will model for us both how to deal with church problems and actually give us some answers—at least when we are dealing with the same problems. Paul also demonstrates how to sponsor a leader and pass the mantle to that leader. We are seeing a great leader, Paul, passing off the scene and knowingly committing part of his ministry to a younger leader, Timothy. Understanding Paul's apostolic farewell with this heresy prone church at Ephesus is a must for present day leaders.

Suggested Approach for Studying The 1,2 Ti Leadership Commentary

Read through the overview to get a general feeling for what 1 Ti is about. Note particularly the *Theme* of the book and its *Plan* for developing that theme, i.e., the outline for developing that theme. Then note the various purposes I suggest that the book of 1 Ti is seeking to accomplish. Then read through each of the leadership topics that I suggest are in 1 Ti. This is all preparation for the first reading of the text.

Read the text of 1 Ti, preferably at one sitting, without referring to any of the commentary notes. Just see if you can *see what of the overview information* and the *leadership lessons* are suggested to you as you read the text.

Then reread the text, probably a chapter at a time and note the comments I give.[6] From time-to-time, go back and read a leadership lesson again when it is brought to your mind as you read the text and the commentary. Also feel free to stop and go to the **Glossary** for explanation of leadership terms suggested by the commentary. And do the same thing with the **Articles.** The articles capture what I have learned about leadership over the years as I have observed it, researched it, and taught it. It is these articles that will enlighten your

---

[5] See **Article,** *26. Leadership Eras In The Bible— Six Identified;* This is probably an important prerequisite for you before approaching the commentary.

[6] From time-to-time in the comments, we will use the abbreviation SRN. SRN stands for Strong's Reference Number. Strong, in his exhaustive concordance, labeled each word in the Old Testament (dominantly Hebrew words but also some Aramaic/Chaldean) and New Testament (Greek words mostly) with an identifying number. He then constructed an Old Testament and New Testament lexicon (dictionary). If you have a **Strong's Exhaustive Concordance** with lexicon, you can look up the words we refer to. Many modern day reference works (lexicons and word studies and Bible Dictionaries and encyclopedias) use this Strong's Reference Number.

leadership understanding. Obviously because of the uniqueness of the book, dealing primarily with apostolic problem solving dealing with a local church ministry, there will be some hopefully helpful leadership articles.

After finishing your whole study on 1 Ti then move on to 2 Ti and repeat the same procedure described above. You will be saddened to see this great leader finish his ministry. And finish it well, he did. And 2 Ti reveals how Paul passes the mantle to Timothy urging him, advising him, and encouraging him to pick up the apostolic ministry.

Further Study

I have provided some *note space* at the conclusion of the textual comments, for both books, where you can jot down ideas for future study. Have fun as you work through 1,2 Ti, and by all means learn something about *apostolic leadership selection and transition.* Let these two books inspire your own leadership selection, development and transition as you minister for God during this church leadership era.   And also learn the important lesson of learning vicariously by studying other leaders' lives.[7] Paul is exemplary in his modeling for church leaders. It was deliberate. And it was impactful then and can be impactful now.

The overview follows. It gives a summarized version of the hermeneutical background studies for 1 Ti. Later I will repeat the same thing for 2 Ti.

---

[7] The old adage, *experience is the best teacher* is true, **if you learn from it**. Personal experience is a great way to learn. But in terms of leadership, you will never have enough time to learn, *by personal experience alone*, all you need to know for your leadership. I suppose that is why God gave us the leadership mandate—Hebrews 13:7,8. He emphatically reminds us that vicarious learning is crucial for our leadership. And we have three whole books (Job, Habakkuk, Jonah) in the Bible devoted exclusively to illustrating God's shaping of leaders. And that is their main purpose for being in the Bible. Paul's leadership is in view throughout the church leadership era. We can learn leadership practices vicariously from his model.

Overview Of 1 Timothy

BOOK	1 Timothy	**Author: Paul**

Characters   Those mentioned or involved: Paul, Timothy, Hymenaeus, Alexander

Who To/For   To Timothy, a protégé of Paul, who is helping advise church leaders in Ephesus

Literature Type   A personal letter with powerful advice backed by years of experience

Story Line   Paul had helped found the church in Ephesus (Ac 19). It became an indigenous church. Later he met with the elders of this church in a stop over on his trip back to Jerusalem (Ac 20). At that time he warned them of problems that would arise in the church. Later he also wrote an epistle to them (along with the ones to Colosse and Philemon). At that time there were no major problems as witnessed by the general nature of the letter. Several years later the problems he warned about have arisen. He sends Timothy to try to minister to the situation and advise the church elders. Timothy runs into a number of problems which he does not know how to handle. This epistle is written to Timothy to help him in that situation.

Structure   There is a lack of well integrated structural sections in this book. It is written by an older person—who throws in asides (certain of his words and phrases will remind him of important things he has learned in the past—and he will divert to include them). There is a purpose statement which loosely integrates every thing that is said. See 1Ti 3:14,15.

    I.   **(Ch 1,2)**   **Paul's Advice on Major Problems in the Church**
   II.   **(Ch 3)**   **Paul's advice on Local Leadership Selection**
  III.   **(Ch 4)**   **Paul's Personal Advice to Timothy on How to Handle Himself**
  IV.   **(Ch 5)**   **Paul's Advice on Social Problem on Widows**
   V.   **(Ch 6)**   **Paul's Miscellaneous Exhortations**

Theme **Leading God's People, As Model Representatives Of God's Truth,**
- requires confrontation against false doctrines and practices,
- involves selection of quality local leadership,
- demands personal development as a leader, and
- outworks itself in meeting social needs for the believers.

Key Words   godliness (8), good (three different Greek words) (23), conscience (4), doctrine (8), teach, teacher (7)

Key Events   none in focus

Purposes   See 1Ti 3:14,15 for a stated purpose.

- to give Timothy advice on numerous church problems including:
    -confronting false doctrine and troublesome leaders propagating it,
    -instruction on church prayers,
    -selection criteria for overseers and deacons,
    -spiritual disciplines,
    -Timothy's lack of boldness,
    -how to properly rebuke in the church,
    -handling of support of widows,
    -financial support of church elders,
    -accusations against elders,
    -attitudes of slaves,
    -attitudes toward money,
    -Timothy's personal conduct,
    -giving.
- to encourage Timothy to confront the problems,
- to encourage Timothy to develop personally and warn him against the consequences of failure to develop,
- to model several mentoring styles including: contemporary model, counselor, teacher, spiritual guide,
- to show the complexity of leading a church which has the truth of the Bible as its central controlling guidelines.

Why Important
Church leadership is desperately needed at all times. This book gives advice and warning to church leaders on the necessity for their own personal development and for how to go about problem solving. It shows that the true function of the church is the proclamation of the truth in the world about it. And the leader of the church must have as a true function the exposition, application, and modeling of that truth. The leader(s) is/are key. He/she/they must be loyal to truth, consistent in outward life and inner life, and maintaining a learning posture personally.

Where it Fits
In the redemptive drama Timothy occurs in Part II Salvation proclaimed and chapter 4, the church. Throughout this era God is inviting people everywhere (Ac 15:14) to be reconciled to Himself. His instrument for this is the church. When churches are started, where ever they are, there will always be a need for leadership. There will always be problems both within the personal life of the leaders and in the congregation. The problems in the church are part of the reason for existence of leaders. They must be confronted. Problems in the church will not be solved without a leader who is developing. This book, addresses leadership issues at a specific church in a specific culture. Yet its advice is broad enough to be multi-culturally acceptable—certainly in the

problem solving methodology if not the actual solution. This book is also peculiar in that it is addressing the problem of indigenous leadership which needs help. How can an outside consultant be accepted by them, have authority with them and be useful to them yet without destroying their indigeneity? Such is the task Paul faces in writing and giving leadership information to Timothy.

1Ti, 2Ti, and Tit are primary books on leadership for the Church Leadership Era. They are written by Paul toward the end of his ministry. He has accumulated much wisdom in his ministry of church planting and leadership development. The problems being faced in these church situations will be repeated throughout the Church Leadership Era. Leaders today can profit greatly by learning about leadership from them.

General Reflections

The church leadership era spans from the time of Paul's ministry right on up to the present. Anything that contributes to an understanding of leadership for this era scratches where today's leaders itch. First Timothy is such a book. In fact, I consider it to be the most important leadership book in the N.T. It was written to a young church leader, sent on a special leadership mission, trying to solve problems in an indigenized church with its own leadership in its unique cultural situation. That church was 15-20 years old, and hence facing the problems of a church of that age: a tendency toward nominality, contextualization issues, application of the Gospel to social problems, truth and heresy, folks straying from their Christian commitment, and leadership selection.

Paul was an experienced missionary. He was near the end of his 33 years of ministry experience. He had faced almost all of these problems or similar ones before. He had personally mentored Timothy over 10 or so years—on-the-job training. He knew the difficult task young Timothy would have as a young leader coming into a church with its own older leadership in place. And so Paul gave him his best advice. This is a mellowed Paul, a wise Paul, and a Paul concerned for a young leader and a young church. And so we benefit from Paul's advice and solutions to this specific church situation. We, with young Timothy, listen and reflect on and apply these truths to our own leadership situations. We may not have exactly the same problems as this church. So the exact solutions may not fit us. But the dynamic principles underlying the solutions, the processes used in arriving them, and the leadership wisdom of this book are foundational. We have much to learn from these things.

The book itself is an example of distance mentoring. Paul demonstrates what mentoring is all about. Mentoring is a relational experience in which one person, the mentor, empowers another person, the mentoree via a transfer of resources—in this case mostly ideation—wisdom and advice. It is an outstanding example of a mentor who is a contemporary model, a mentor sponsor, a mentor counselor, a mentor teacher and a mentor spiritual guide.

1Ti also illustrates several of the leadership genre from which we gain leadership information. It contains biographical information about Paul's life and has several direct leadership contexts. Its actual theme is a leadership theme so that it is also an outstanding example of the genre, book as a whole. It is a great source of leadership information. It provides us an example of a value driven leader. See **Articles**, *38. Mentoring, an Informal Training Model; 47. Paul—Mentor For Many; 26. Leadership Eras in the Bible—Six Identified; 71. Value Driven Leadership; 28. Leadership Genre—Seven Types.*

1 Timothy—Key Leadership Lessons/Topics

1. MENTORING.

Experienced leaders need to be mentoring others and all leaders need mentoring. All leaders will need various kinds of mentoring help throughout their leadership time-line. They will need help from those more experienced and further along in life and ministry (called upward mentoring). They will need help from peers who are roughly at the same place in life and ministry (called lateral mentoring). They will benefit from mentoring others less mature than themselves (called downward mentoring). Paul's ministry to Timothy demonstrates five of the nine mentor roles that mentors can take with mentorees: mentor sponsor, spiritual guide, teacher, counselor and contemporary model. These roles of course require a special relationship between mentor and mentoree. Paul had that with Timothy. See **Articles**, *69. Timothy, A Beloved Son in the Faith; 47. Paul— Mentor For Many; 38. Mentoring, An Informal Training Model; 7. Constellation Model, Mentoring Relationships.*

Leadership Principles/ Values Suggested by this concept:
  a. Older mature Christian leaders ought to have several life-long mentorees who they will help over a lifetime to reach their potential in leadership. Paul did. See **Article**, *43. Paul—And His Companions.*
  b. Christian leaders will need balancing relationships with others so as to have healthy growth over a lifetime (upward, lateral and downward mentoring).
  c. Personal mentoring relationships allow for change of character and *intimate meddling* of the right sort.
  d. Mentoring is one of the five enhancement factors identified with leaders who finish well.

2. GIFTEDNESS.

Giftedness can be imparted by mature Christian leaders. Giftedness needs to be motivated and developed. Aspects of a leader's giftedness can be neglected, grow cold, and be ineffective. See 1Ti 4:14 for Paul's admonition. See also 2Ti 1:6. However, recognize how little giftedness is emphasized in 1Ti compared to character. See *List Idiom* for selection of leaders (fn ch 3 vs 2 describes a list item) and the many pieces of advice to Timothy about character. See also 1Co **Key Leadership Insights**, *Topic— Giftedness.* See **Articles**, *63. Spiritual Gifts, Giftedness, and Development; 2. Apostolic Functions; 31. Leadership Selection.*

Leadership Principles/ Values Suggested by this concept:
  a. As part of the leadership selection process, apostolic leaders should impart spiritual gifts to emerging leaders.
  b. Leaders can neglect use of some spiritual gift and hence be less effective in their ministry.
  c. Giftedness must be developed.
  d. Giftedness should receive less stress in leadership selection and development than character building.

3. BALANCE—Between Developing and Achieving

Effective leaders maintain a balance between personal development and ministry productivity. Being and Doing must be kept in balance throughout a leader's life. It is clear that Paul saw both as important to Timothy. See 1Ti 4:16. Covey's P + PC (productivity + production capability) balance is in focus here. Covey Covey (see his 7 Habits...listed in the bibliography) says that efforts toward productivity must be balanced by efforts to develop the production capability. Paul says it more succinctly: Timothy "watch yourself and your ministry (1 Ti 4:16)."

<u>Leadership Principles/ Values Suggested by this concept:</u>
   a. Ministry essentially flows out of being where being is made up of a complex number of items including: intimacy with God, giftedness, personality, gender, character, destiny, values accrued.
   b. An unbalanced situation (either overly concerned with productivity or overly concerned with developing production capability) can be withstood for special intense times but not over the long haul.
   c. Of the two, productivity or production capability, most leaders err on the side of productivity and tend to bypass developing production capability.
   d. Leaders who lead with a developmental bias will be concerned with this important balance and will stress character development and giftedness development.

4. DISCIPLINE.

Discipline of leadership must be done carefully and upon good evidence (1Ti 5:19,20). The best antidote to this is proper leadership selection and on-going development. Nevertheless this will be an on-going problem and must be done and done properly with a view to redeeming the leader and protecting the church. Leaders need to be disciplined carefully for reputation and character are at stake and can ruin leadership. Discipline must occur after investigation and upon reliable evidence. Leaders who fail need to be rebuked publicly in church in order to warn the church, maintain credibility for high standards of leadership, and as a basis for recovery. Cover-ups hurt everybody both leaders and people.

<u>Leadership Principles/ Values Suggested by this concept:</u>
   a. Avoid prejudging a situation without careful investigation.
   b. Avoid backing off from confrontation because the leader under question has power, prestige, and reputation.
   c. Leaders ought to be disciplined with a view toward recovery.
   d. Failures in leadership which are covered up and then brought to light do much more damage than if the issue were faced publicly initially.
   e. Leadership credibility for all Christian leaders suffers when leaders are caught in on-going sinful behavior.

5. COMPLEXITY—LEADERSHIP PROBLEMS

Leadership is very complex. A major focus, that is, an on-going function that leaders must perform is problem solving: doctrinal—attacks from without and within, which will split the believers and woo some away, problems of integrity (conscience), problems of character, problems of hypocrisy in public worship and in leadership, submission, problems from men and women, practical financial problems (support of leaders and support of needy people in the church), subtle inroads of culture that weaken the gospel, contextualization balance, leadership selection, loss of heart for ministry, lack of leaders developing themselves, lack of confronting problems by leaders, unusual emphases which over balance Christian practice, social problems in the church, finances in the church, wrong views toward stewardship of resources, etc. The interesting thing about some of these problems is that Paul foresaw them years earlier (see his talk to the Ephesian elders, Ac 20:29,30). One of the Major Macro Lessons seen across the entire six leadership eras is the complexity macro: *Leadership is complex, problematic, difficult and fraught with risk—which is why leadership is needed.*

Leadership Principles/ Values Suggested by this concept:

    a. Leaders must expect heresy both as to belief (orthodoxy) and practice (orthopraxy) to arise both from within the church and without it.

    b. Integrity, as reflected in a pure conscience, should be the goal of every leader for himself or herself personally (Ac 24:16).

    c. Leadership should take hope; problems can be solved. Wise mentors, i.e. examples of Biblical, historical, and contemporary leaders show this to be true.

    d. Teaching should be judged by its effects on people (their character and behavior) probably even more so than by its content. Notice the descriptions of the content of heretical teaching are not given clearly in 1Ti but the results are often given.

    e. Contextualization, while stressing being relevant to given cultures, must also recognize the negative effect of cultures upon truth (beliefs and practices).

    f. People will stray from the faith (due to false teaching, consciences being overridden and made ineffective, sexuality pressures, love for power and money). People must be warned of these things.

    g. Practical problems (like widows in need of financial help) can be worked out based on principles.

    h. Leadership selection must be based primarily on character.

6. LEADERSHIP GUIDELINES.

Patterns or guidelines for local church leadership in this specific church include:

1) a knowledge of what leadership is not and what it is. Paul shows that local leadership is not: controversial teachers of laws that bind people; hypocritical people using ministry as a means of financial gain. He shows that it is a plurality, yet a strongly led plurality—Timothy's role was directive and corrective. He was to inspire, correct, and move this leadership and church toward correcting its problems.

2) qualifications for leaders which include character and conscience. Paul's list of qualifications focuses on integrity and deals mainly with character not giftedness. At least three kinds of leaders are seen in this specific local church situation: elders (overseer—two kinds—ruling and word gifted, and some both), lesser leaders (SRN 1249 deacons) those in the process of emerging and learning to serve), and roving apostolic function (Timothy—probably regional influence). Notice that a good or clear conscience is stressed as fundamentally important in a leader (see 1:5,18-20, 3:9, 4:1,2). Early ministry is where foundational character is solidified. Timothy is urged to solidify his

inner life in this regard and warned of the consequence of not doing so. Controversial teaching should be avoided—stick to the fundamentals—notice the *truth-asides* that Paul inserts—all are core and central to Christianity (1:15; 2:3,4,5,6; 3:1; 3:16; 4:9, 10; 6:15).

3) Strong local church leadership is not incompatible with plurality. Frequently strong leadership is associated only with authoritative structures. And frequently weak task oriented leadership is associated with plurality. This does not have to be.

4) Emphasis on selection is maturity in character, not riches, position, or ability. Selection of good potential/emerging leaders with character is the best preventive for avoiding bad leaders that later must be disciplined.

5) Testing and time is involved in selection of local leadership. Too quick a selection is warned against as leading to pride and problematic leadership.

6) The spirituality factors of external testimony and inner character in the leader's life must be kept in balance. Reputation without is crucial to a leader; a leader can sway followers and deceive them—but usually a bad character is recognized by non-followers external to the situation. Personal inward growth in a leader is a must and should lead to and be consistent with outward behavior.

7) Gender and Leadership issues are treated in 1Ti. This is a male dominated culture. Paul honors that while at the same time leaving room for female leadership. The list idioms give both male and female leadership character traits that should be present in a leader. The 1Ti 2:12 passage is not a passage preventing women from teaching but a passage dealing with women who are disrupting the church with a heretical teaching that is probably splitting families. Below is my paraphrase which is seeking to follow the flow of heretical problems in the church.

My Interpretive Paraphrase—1 Timothy 2:9-15:

9-10 Likewise, women in the public services, should behave with proper decorum. They should dress modestly, not showy like prostitutes. Their inner beauty is what should be seen. Such beauty of character as befits a Christian woman—that should be the real attire. 11 They should not be disruptive in the services. Don't let them interrupt with questions. Maintain an orderly service. 12-15 This doctrine about sexual things which is splitting families and threatening to blow up the church must stop. Don't permit such teaching. The women there are being deceived just as Eve was. Nevertheless, the results of their disastrous efforts can be overcome if they will return to the Lord and live dedicated godly lives.

Leadership Principles/ Values Suggested by this concept:
   a. Character is crucial to leadership.
   b. A Spirit controlled conscience is the norm for a leader.
   c. Varying levels of church leadership and differing roles (probably based on giftedness) is to be expected in local churches. The varying levels should be part of an overall leadership selection process.
   d. A plurality of leadership can be used in a local church.
   e. Plurality of leadership does not mean a lack of strong leadership. Plurality is not identified with consensus.
   f. A foundational emphasis underlying leadership selection is the identification of integrity, character, and traits of exemplary being and behavior in a culture.

Leadership in a local church should be above criticism (as to character) by the surrounding culture.

g. Lower levels of leadership allow for a time of testing of younger leaders.

h. Females are not barred from leadership in 1Ti.

7. FINANCES.

Finances can be a blessing and a curse. Having or not having wealth is not the issue. It is the stewardship of resources that is the major issue. What they are used for is what is significant. There are dangers of having financial resources—they can subtly turn away trust from God to trust in the resources. Paul admonishes to use resources well.

Leadership Principles/ Values Suggested by this concept:

a. Money can not be trusted as a source of power or security.

b. Money must be appreciated as coming from God.

c. The use of money to bring enjoyment is valid.

d. Money ought to be a strong power base useful to do good for people.

e. Learning to use money wisely for God's kingdom work will allow a person to experience a reality in their Christian life.

8. SPIRITUAL WARFARE.

Paul gives several pieces of advice and cautions concerning spiritual warfare which can be generalized as follows:

1) Spiritual warfare is a natural part of the ministry. Paul doesn't make a big thing over it nor does he avoid it. He simply assumes spiritual warfare as part of the cause of the problems that Timothy faces.

2) Maintain balance with regard to spiritual warfare. Paul does not see spiritual warfare as the cause of everything. On the other hand, natural causes are not the source of everything either. Paul does not even advocate some special means of dealing with it other than use of truth and righteousness. He does not attack the spirit world directly nor does he give any special instructions about it (Perhaps that is because he had already done this in his letter to the Ephesian church). His inclusion of spiritual warfare is not in focus; it is subtly woven into the normal discussion. (see 1:18-20, 3:6, 3:7, 4:1).

3) Paul has spiritual authority to discipline indirectly. (See 1:18-20—where Paul disciplines indirectly, handing over to Satan).

4) Paul identifies areas of Satanic involvement: doubt and matters of conscience, pride, deceptive teaching and lustful indiscipline. See also **Daniel, Key Leadership Insights—Topic, Supernatural Emphasis.**
See also **Article, 65. *Spiritual Warfare, Two Extremes to Avoid*; 64. *Spiritual Warfare— Satan's Tactics.***

Leadership Principles/ Values Suggested by this concept:

a. Every leader needs to know about and be able to deal with spiritual warfare problems in the church.

b. Righteous living, a sincere faith, a prayerful life, and a pure conscience are tools with which a leader has to offset spiritual warfare.

    c. Apostolic leaders can take authority over spiritual warfare problems and deal with them indirectly by speaking a word of faith about the issue.

    d. Doubt, matters of conscience, pride, deception and indiscipline with regard to sexuality are areas in which spiritual forces can gain toe holds (called hooks) and eventually lead a person to stray from the faith.

9. LEADERSHIP PROBLEMS—HERESY (orthodoxic and orthopraxic)

There are four lines of heresy suggested in 1Ti (See fn ch 1, vs 3,4,6,7; ch 2, vs 12; ch 4, vs 3,7; ch 6, vs 4,5,20) but not taught clearly. There is something to be learned from this. Enough information is not given to deduce the exact heresies (at least from an orthodoxic standpoint). But the results of these heresies are described. So while we may not know the exact teaching involved in the heresy we can see what it does to people and the church. Hence, we can take a look at our own teaching and others too and see what are the results of our teaching. Heresy is concerned with truth—both its content and its behavioral implications. We can be heretical both in what we believe and what we practice. The heretical practices (disrupting the church, hypocritical leadership, failure to submit to leadership, teaching to gain finances, the selection of leaders—partiality shown, the failure to discipline, the evident criticism coming from the society as it judged Christianity) were more in focus than the actual teaching. Rest assured, the Ephesian people knew the content of these teachings.

Leadership Principles/ Values Suggested by this concept:

    a. Heresy is not limited to what we believe. What we practice is just as important. A given leader may be orthodoxic as to tenets agreed to but still be heretical because of practice and life style which will draw criticism (character wise) from the surrounding culture.

    b. Be as clear as the Bible is clear; nothing more, nothing less, nothing else. A leader must learn to live with ambiguity if the Bible is ambiguous on an issue.

I. (Ch 1, 2)   Paul's Advice on Major Problems in the Church
Chapter 1

1 Paul,[8] an apostle of Jesus Christ by the commandment[9] of God our Savior, and the Lord Jesus Christ, which is our hope; 2 Unto Timothy,[10] my own son[11] in the faith: Grace, mercy, and peace, from God our Father and Jesus Christ our Lord.

3 I urged you[12] to stay on at Ephesus,[13] when I went to Macedonia, that you might order some to stop teaching false doctrine.[14] 4 Neither should they pay attention to fables and endless genealogies, which produce arguments, rather than God's plan for growth which comes by faith.[15]

---

[8] Paul authored 13 epistles. See **Article**, *68. Time-Lines, The Apostle Paul.*

[9] Paul had a strong sense of appointment to ministry from God. This conviction is part of his sense of destiny. See also 1:12, 2:7 and other salutations: Ro 1:1; 1Co 1:1; 2Co 1:1; Gal 1:1; Eph 1:1; Col 1:1; 1Ti 1:1; 2Ti 1:1; Tit 1:1. See fn 1:12; 2:7 for a summary. See *sense of destiny*, **Glossary**. See **Article**, *42. Paul—A Sense of Destiny.*

[10] Timothy's name occurs 31 times in the N.T. Timothy should be studied as an example of how a next generation leader is trained and transitioned into ministry. Timothy's last mention in Heb 13:23 is instructive. He, a respected leader, has just been let out of prison. See **Articles**, *45. Paul The Developer; 69. Timothy A Beloved Son in the Faith*

[11] Other references showing the closeness of relationship between Paul and Timothy include: 1Ti 1:2,18; 2Ti 1:2; 2Ti 2:1; Php 2:22. See also Tit 1:4 and Phm 1:10 where Paul uses this relational phrase with Titus and Onesimus. Paul believed in personal ministry.

[12] This whole epistle represents Paul's activity as a mentor sponsor. Paul is giving Timothy his own personal backing for undertaking the ministry at Ephesus. See also **Key Lessons, 1** *Timothy—Topic: Mentoring.* See *mentor sponsor*, **Glossary**. See **Article**, *47. Paul—Mentor for Many.*

[13] The church at Ephesus was an indigenized church with its own leadership at this point in time. Timothy was sent in as a consultant on Paul's behalf to straighten up several heresies that were present in it. He really needs the credibility and status that Paul had with this church. Paul seeks to give it through this letter. See *indigenized church*, **Glossary**. See **Articles**, *2. Apostolic Functions; 11. The Ephesian Church—Its Time-Line.*

[14] Heresy refers to deviation from the standard in what is believed and/or what is practiced. In this book, there are at least four lines of heresy that Paul is dealing with. See also 1:3,4,6,7; 2:12; 4:1-5; 4:7; 6:3,4 for other mention of heresies and the basic antidote for them in 1Ti 3:15. See **Key Lessons, 1** *Timothy—Topic:* Leadership Problems. See *heresy*, **Glossary**.

[15] Heresy number 1. Commentators are not exactly clear on what this heresy is but Dean Alford is inclined to believe it is the seeds of what became in the 2nd century, Gnoticism. Probably it has to do with applying the law wrongly to Christians (see vs 7). Paul gives here one of its results—producing argumentative people.

5 Now the purpose for this strong command is to produce love that comes from a pure heart, and a clean conscience,[16] and a genuine faith.[17] 6 From which some having swerved have turned aside unto foolish talking. 7 They want to be teachers of the law; yet not understanding what they say, nor what they strongly affirm.[18] 8 But we know that the law is good, if a person use it legitimately. 9 We know this, that the law is not made for righteous people, but for: the lawless and disobedient, for the ungodly and for sinners, for unholy and profane, for those who kill fathers and mothers and murderers in general, 10 for male prostitutes, for homosexuals, for men who traffic in slaves, for liars, for perjurers, and for anything else that goes against healthy teaching 11 which is in harmony with the glorious gospel of the blessed God, which was entrusted to me.

12 And I thank Christ Jesus our Lord, who has strengthened me. He considered[19] me faithful, putting[20] me into the ministry; 13 Who was before a slanderer, and a persecutor, and insolently abusive (toward Him or His church). But I was shown mercy, because I did it ignorantly in unbelief. 14 But the Lord gave much grace to me and faith and love which is in Christ Jesus.[21]

---

[16] Paul uses *conscience* (SRN 4893), some 21 times—four times in this epistle. Ministry flows out of being. Being is a complex diversity consisting of at least: intimacy with God, character, giftedness, gender, personality, destiny, learned values. Conscience, reflects the inner life governor of character. Leadership must have a moral foundation. Evidently those teaching the heresies did not have such a foundation. Conscience can be ineffective (4:2). See also 1Ti 1:19; 3:9; 4:2 for other references to conscience. See *conscience*, **Glossary**. See **Article**, *6. Conscience, Paul's Use of in 1,2 Ti.*

[17] Motivation, why a leader does something, i.e. the underlying *leadership value*, is as important as the doing of it. Note Paul's value. *True teaching ought to result in people who have love, a pure heart and a genuine faith.* He is contrasting this result with the first heresy and its results—argumentative people. See *leadership value*, **Glossary**.

[18] Paul is describing more about heresies here. See also: 1:3, 4, 6, 7; 2:12; 4:1-5; 4:7; 6:3,4 and the basic antidote to heresies in 1Ti 3:15 and accompanying fn with comments on heresy.

[19] The word *considered* (SRN 2233) is a word denoting one who leads. The connotation of this phrase implies, *"He saw leadership potential in me, a faithful leader, and hence appointed me for ministry."* This is a statement about leadership selection. See *leadership selection*, **Glossary**. See **Article** *31. Leadership Selection.*

[20] *Putting* (SRN 5087) carries the sense of appointing or ordaining. See also 1:1 *apostle by the commandment of God* and other Pauline salutations which all stress this concept: Ro 1:1; 1Co 1:1; 2Co 1:1; Gal 1:1; Eph 1:1; Col 1:1; 1Ti 1:1; 2Ti 1:1; Tit 1:1. Leaders need a strong sense of God's calling for their lives if they are to persevere and be effective over a lifetime. *See sense of destiny,* **Glossary**. See **Article**, *42. Paul—A Sense of Destiny.*

[21] In this personal testimony section, 1:12-16, Paul is transparent. He tells it like it is, the negative side of his background, but also shows how God worked through it, the positive side. Leaders who model must be transparent and vulnerable. See **Article**, *48. Paul— Modeling As An Influence Means.*

15 This is a reliable saying,[22] and worthy of full acceptance.[23] "Christ Jesus came into the world to save sinners," of whom I am chief. 16 In spite of this, I was shown mercy, for this reason, that in me as a prime example, Jesus Christ might demonstrate forbearance, as a model to those who later would come to believe on him to life everlasting.

17 Now unto the King eternal, immortal, invisible, the only wise God, be honor and glory for ever and ever. Amen.[24]

18 This command I am entrusting to you, son Timothy. It is based on the prophecies[25] which were given about you. These words should encourage you to fight on bravely.[26] 19 Keep faith and a clear conscience, which some having failed to listen to, have shipwrecked their faith. 20 Two such are Hymenaeus and Alexander; whom I have delivered unto Satan,[27] that they may learn not to speak evil of God.[28]

---

[22] Paul repeats this strong lead-in three times: 1:15; 3:1; 4:9. It is his equivalent of Jesus' use of *Verily, Verily*. Both are attention getters that seek to tell the listener—this is important stuff, believe it, hear it, listen up.

[23] When Paul repeats the strong truth assertion, sometimes he puts in a doxological or other truth statements (1:17; 2:3-6; 3:16; 6:15, 16). While not all things can be known for certain there are core truths that can be asserted strongly and must be proclaimed by the church (see 3:15).

[24] This is one of those statements which sounds like a doxology. See also 3:16; 6:15, 16 for other core doxological truths.

[25] Here, *prophecies*, and 2Ti 1:6, *laying on of hands*, are indications of how the divine and human side of leadership selection intersect. Paul here gives affirmation of Timothy's leadership both to encourage Timothy and to give credibility in the eyes of the Ephesian elders. Prophecies are often used by God to engender a sense of destiny. See also 2Ti 1:6 where Paul uses this same kind of incident to exhort Timothy to grow and continue in ministry. See *leadership selection, mentor sponsor*, **Glossary**. See **Article**, *31. Leadership Selection.*

[26] This is a strong exhortation. The repetitive idiom showing the superlative, war...war (verb and noun forms) has been captured. War a good warfare = fight bravely. See *superlative idiom, capture*, **Glossary**.

[27] Paul interweaves spiritual warfare into his flow of thought. See also 3:6, 7; 4:1 for other references to Satan.

[28] Paul is demonstrating here a special leadership style, *indirect conflict*. Spiritual discernment and warfare are involved—more than likely without direct confrontation of the parties involved. This is an example of power ministry, so desperately needed to demonstrate God's intervention. This is a rare illustration. Paul doesn't include indirect conflict often. One other occurrence is in 1Co 5:5. See *leadership style, indirect conflict, power gifts, power ministry*, **Glossary**. See **Articles**, *2. Apostolic Functions*; *49. Pauline Leadership Styles.*

Chapter 2

1 Consequently, I strongly urge that, first of all, requests to God, prayers, intercessions, and giving of thanks, be made for all people.[29] 2 Do so for kings, and for all that are in authority, that we may lead a quiet and peaceable life in all godliness and seriousness. 3 For this is good and acceptable in the sight of God our Savior, 4 who would wish for all people to be saved, and to come unto the knowledge of the truth. 5 For there is one God, and one mediator[30] between God and mankind, the man Christ Jesus,[31] 6 who gave himself a ransom for all, to be testified in due time.[32] 7 And this is why I was established[33] as a preacher, and an apostle. I speak the truth in Christ, and lie not; a teacher of faith[34] and truth to the Gentiles.

8 Therefore I desire that men pray every where, lift up holy hands, without anger and argumentative attitudes.[35]

9 In like manner also, that women dress themselves in modest clothing, with regard

---

[29] Paul uses four different words to describe prayer: *requests* (SRN 1162) meaning petitions for needs; *prayers* (SRN 4335) prayer directed toward God; *intercessions* (SRN 1783) meaning intimate conversation with God; *thankful prayers* (SRN 2169) thankfulness given to God. Paul models what he asks of others. See **Articles**, *25. Jesus—Five Leadership Models in the Gospels*; *46. Paul—Intercessor Leader; 52. Prayer Macro Lesson.*

[30] For other references to the mediator concept, see Gal 3:20; Heb 8:6; 9:15; 12:24.

[31] This could well be directed at the heresy underlying 1Ti 2:12 since mediation via temple prostitutes was part of the Ephesian religious scene.

[32] This is another one of those truth asides which Paul drops in. See also 1:17; 2:3-6; 3:16; 4:10; 6:15,16.

[33] Note 2:7 established. Again, this is an assertion of divine assignment from God. *Established* (SRN 5087) carries the sense of appointing or ordaining as was seen in *putting in* 1:12. See also 1:*1 Apostle by the commandment of God* and other salutations. Leaders need a strong sense of God's calling for their lives if they are to persevere and be effective over a lifetime. In 2Co this is identified as a Pauline leadership value called *divine appointment. Leaders ought to be sure that God appointed them to ministry situations.* See *divine appointment,* **Glossary**.

[34] Faith is here used as a figure of speech, a metonymy (one word substituted for another). Faith is substituted for Christian truth and emphasizing, that which is believed by faith. Paul's calling in ʾolved contextualizing the Christian faith to the Gentile scene. See *contextualization, metonymy,* **Glossary**.

[35] Holy hands, is a metonymy for lives made holy by the Gospel. This is a public symbolic act of worship. The public church service was being disrupted by arguments from men (vs 8), by distractive attire by women (vs 9), and by disorderly conduct by women (vs 11). This is part of the results flowing from heresy 1 (1:4). Paul addresses these, primarily, by what ought to be done, rather than what ought not to be done. See also 1:4 where this heresy is alluded to. See *heresy, metonymy,* **Glossary**.

for others and careful restraint;[36] not with unusual hairdos calling attention to themselves, or gold, or pearls, or expensive clothing. 10 But with good works, which are fitting for women professing godliness. 11 A woman should learn in an orderly manner.[37] 12 But I do not permit a woman to teach, that is, to use upsetting doctrines involving men,[38] (especially in a disruptive way). 13 For Adam was first formed, then Eve. 14 And Adam was not deceived, but the woman being deceived was in the wrong.[39]
15 Nevertheless, the results of their (women at Ephesus) disastrous efforts can be overcome[40] if they will return to the Lord and live dedicated godly lives.[41]

---

[36] They must disassociate themselves from showy attire often associated with prostitutes and pagan religious situations.

[37] *Hesuchia* translated in the **KJV** by *silence* (SRN 2271) is best translated by orderly manner. The word silence in English primarily denotes being quiet not speaking whereas the Greek word, *hesuchia*, denotes orderliness of manner, a proper decorum.

[38] The connotative emphasis is not on the teaching but on what the teaching is doing. A heretical teaching is doing something there in the church. See also 1:3,4, 6, 7; 2:12; 4:1-5; 4:7; 6:3,4 and the basic antidote for heresy in 1Ti 3:15. See *heresy*, **Glossary.**

[39] The implication being that the women at Ephesus are being deceived by this heresy, whatever it is.

[40] Women are not saved by bearing children as the **KJV** seems to indicate as this would go against all that Paul has ever taught about salvation being by faith. In my opinion, here the sense is not of personal salvation but of remedying the situation at Ephesus.

[41] Heresy 2 is also unclear but is at the heart of the vs 12 warning. Some women are teaching something disruptive. Chapter 2:9-15 is a difficult passage to translate. The two words, *hesuchia* translated in the **KJV** by *silence* (SRN 2271) and *authentein* = *usurp authority* (SRN 831), a one time only occurring word (*hapax legomena*) are the crux of the problem. The word silence in English primarily denotes being quiet, i.e. not speaking, whereas the Greek word, hesuchia, denotes orderliness of manner, a proper decorum. Authentein did not take on its authoritative connotation until after N.T. times. In N.T. times and prior, it had to do with murderous behavior with some sexual connotations. I have tried to give an interpretive paraphrase which takes into account the book as a whole and the heresies being promulgated in Ephesus. (**See Key Leadership Lessons** *Topics— Leadership Guidelines; Gender and Leadership* for the interpretive paraphrase). This is definitely not a prohibition against a woman teaching but a correction of wrongful behavior and influence via teaching. Remember, Priscilla is a teacher (Ac 18:26ff) and is at Ephesus (2Ti 4:19). See *heresy*, **Glossary.** See **Key Leadership Lessons—1 Timothy,** *Topic: Leadership Guidelines, Gender and Leadership.* See **Article,** *20. Gender and Leadership.*

II. (Ch 3) Paul's Advice on Local Leadership Selection

Chapter 3

1 This is a reliable saying,[42] "If anyone aspires to leadership oversight, that one desires a good work."[43] 2 Such a church leader then must be exemplary in moral conduct:[44] e.g. the husband of one wife,[45] calm and collected in spirit, discreet, modest, a hospitable person, able to teach;[46] 3 not a drunkard, not belligerent, not one open to shady deals for money. Other qualities include: one who is gentle, not hotheaded, not money-hungry;[47] 4 ruling well one's own household, having obedient and reverent children. 5 For if anyone can not rule a household, how can that person take care of the church of God?

---

[42] This is another one of those strong truth assertion lead-ins. See also 1:15; 3:1; 4:9.

[43] Notice the anyone (**KJV** any man). Note also there is a place for holy ambition. On the one hand, leadership should not be sought for the wrong reasons of promoting self, etc., but it also should not be avoided when one is gifted and called to it. It is honorable service to God. See **Articles**, 20. *Gender and Leadership; 50. Pauline Leadership Terms in the New Testament; 67. Starting Point Plus Process.*

[44] This is apparently a list idiom in which the initial item on the list is the main assertion and other items illustrate or clarify the primary item. If so, then the major leadership trait is integrity, a moral characteristic implying consistency of inner and outer life. The items on the list would then illustrate in the Ephesian culture what moral character, integrity, looks like. So then these items in themselves are not necessarily universal characteristics for a leader but are indicative of what moral character and integrity looks like in this culture. The obligatory item is inner integrity, moral character. Paul concludes this small section in vs 7 by returning to this important idea to reemphasize it. This is repeated in descriptions of the lesser leader lists described in vs 8-10, 11-13. Note especially vs 8 and 11. See *list idiom*, **Glossary.**

[45] This has been interpreted in various ways. I don't think it is talking about polygamy or being married only once (otherwise it would rule out Paul and Timothy as leaders, who were unmarried) or more than once. I think it is talking about a character trait, one who has loyalty—a one wife kind of man. This fits more in line with the whole list and the situation at Ephesus. This is also a strong interpretation of a number of Greek scholars and some modern translators—see Peterson's **Message** (*committed to his wife*).

[46] The same word, give here as *able to teach*, is used in 2Ti 2:24 describing one who *can gently explain*. I think here the emphasis is not on teaching as a gift but the ability to gently explain—again emphasis on character not gifting. This is also another prohibition against an argumentative style.

[47] A leader who is in ministry for money (that is, money-hungry) can easily be led into lack of financial integrity. Lack of integrity with finances, specifically, and money matters, in general, is identified as one of the six major barriers to finishing well. See **Article**, *17. Finishing Well- Six Major Barriers.*

6 Not a new believer,[48] who can easily become proud[49] and condemned by the devil.[50] 7 But instead, a good reputation with outsiders; lest reproach allow entrapment by the devil.

8 Similarly a lesser church leader[51] should have good character, not deliberately deceptive with words, not a drunkard, not one open to shady deals for money. 9 One who has a clear understanding of the deep things of the faith with a clear conscience.[52] 10 Primarily, these men should be carefully scrutinized; they should minister well, being above board in their ministry. 11 Similarly, women leaders[53] should have good character, not prone to slander others, marked by restraint in satisfying desires, can be trusted with anything. 12 Let those who minister[54] be faithful spouses,[55] ruling their children and their own households well. 13 For they that have ministered well are making progress toward leadership and gain great boldness in the faith which is in Christ Jesus.[56]

14 These things I am writing to you hoping to come to you shortly: 15 But if I am delayed, you will know how you should handle yourself the house of God,[57] which is the

---

[48] This vs implies a major leadership selection principle. Don't put an inexperienced Christian into leadership too soon. Let that one grow in the things of the Lord and in ministry tasks that will lead into leadership. Follow the Lk 16:10 principle. See also 1Ti 5:22, *lay hands hastily*. See *Lk 16:10 principle, ministry tasks*, **Glossary**.

[49] Pride (inappropriate and self-centered) which leads to a downfall is one of six major barriers to finishing well. Pride as a barrier is usually associated with successful leaders but here we see it associated with a very young leader. Pride can hit all leaders. As a leader, there is a dynamic tension that must be maintained. We must have a healthy respect for our selves, and yet we must recognize that we have nothing that was not given us by God. He is the one who really enables ministry. See **Article**, *17. Finishing Well— Six Major Barriers.*

[50] This is one of several vs which indicate spiritual warfare. Paul does not overemphasize this nor does he avoid it. He simply weaves it in where it fits. See also 1:18-20, 4:1. See *spiritual warfare*, **Glossary**. See **Article**, *64. Spiritual Warfare— Satan's Tactics.*

[51] The word here (**KJV** deacon) is translated the majority of times by minister (20 times) (SRN 1249). It probably referred to a lesser leader, like a house church or small group leader, being supervised by an elder. See **Article**, *50. Pauline Leadership Terms.*

[52] For other references to conscience, see 1Ti 1:19; 3:9; 4:2.

[53] I agree with Peterson on this translation, as opposed to wives, **KJV**.

[54] This probably carries the force of a third person imperative (must minister).

[55] This follows Peterson's rendering and is based on the character quality of loyalty and perseverance represented by a "one wife kind of person," one of the interpretations for the husband of one wife that I suggested in fn 1Ti 3:2.

[56] This is the Pauline statement of the Lk 16:10 little/big principle. See *Lk 16:10 principle*, **Glossary**.

[57] Again, Paul, as a mentor sponsor, gives backing to Timothy's ministry.

church of the living God, the pillar and ground of the truth.[58] 16 And with great assurance we know that great is the mystery of godliness: God was manifest in the flesh, justified in the Spirit, seen of angels, preached unto the Gentiles, believed on in the world, received up into glory.[59]

III. (Ch 4) Paul's Personal Advice to Timothy on How to Handle Himself

Chapter 4

1 Now the Spirit is clearly saying, that in the latter times some will withdraw themselves from the faith, listening to misleading spirits, and the teaching of evil spirits.[60] 2 These hypocritical leaders speak lies, having their conscience seared with a hot iron.[61] 3 They forbid marriage. They command abstinence from meats.[62] God has created meat to be received with thanksgiving by believers who know the truth. 4 For every creature of God is good, and nothing to be refused, if it be received with thanksgiving: 5 For it is consecrated by the word of God and prayer.

6 If you remind the believers of these things, you will be a good minister of Jesus Christ, (showing you have been) well nourished in the words of faith and of genuine teaching that you have followed. 7 But avoid godless legends and old wives' fables.[63]

---

[58] This great truth statement forms the basis for my thematic subject for the whole book of Timothy—Leading, God's People, As Model Representatives of God's Truth. That is what Paul is repeatedly emphasizing to Timothy. See the **Overview of 1 Timothy** for the full statement of the theme. The church, here basically a local church, is God's foundational means for teaching, clarifying, and living out truth before the world.

[59] This is another one of those doxological truth statements. This one paints the whole Gospel story in concise terms. For other references, see 1:17; 3:16; 4:10; 6:15, 16.

[60] 1 Jn 4:1-3 similarly says test the spirits—a metonymy, one word substituted for another to which it is related for emphasis. It means test the teaching (spirits, source of the teaching, is substituted for the teaching) of the people giving the teaching to see if they are being influenced by misleading spirits. So too here. These false teachers are leaders who are taking people astray. See also 1:3,4, 6, 7; 2:12; 4:1-5; 4:7; 6:3,4 and the basic antidote in 1Ti 3:15. See *metonymy*, **Glossary**.

[61] This additional reference to conscience shows it can become unreliable (seared = hardened to truth) if false teaching is accepted. Conscience alone is not a totally reliable guide, but a spirit controlled conscience is. However, one should not violate conscience—a basic principle. Here Paul shows that a person's conscience can become dead to truth and hence can not function as a governor of the inner life. For other references on conscience see 1Ti 1:19; 3:9; 4:2.

[62] Heresy 3 is more explicit than heresies 1 and 2. The false teachers are forbidding marriage (probably promoting the abstinence of sexual relations) and abstinence of meat. They also (vs 7) are teaching something akin to heresy 1(1:4). See *heresy*, **Glossary**.

[63] What the godless legends and *old wives' fables* (probably an idiomatic phrase) are is unknown. But the overall message is clear. Paul is saying here, don't get sidetracked. Focus on spiritual things. For other references to heresy, see also 1:3,4, 6, 7; 2:12; 4:1-5; 4:7; 6:3,4 and the basic antidote in 1Ti 3:15. See *heresy*, **Glossary**.

Instead exercise your mind in godly things. 8 For physical exercise is advantageous somewhat but exercising in godliness[64] has long term implications both for today and for that which will come. 9 This [is] a reliable saying,[65] and worthy of full acceptance. 10 To this end we both work hard (at ministry) and are criticized for it, because we trust in the living God, who offers salvation to all human beings, and fulfills it in those that believe.[66]

    11 Declare strongly these things and keep on teaching them.[67] 12 Stop letting them put you down because of your youthful age; but instead be a model for believers, in word, in your lifestyle, in love, in spirit, in faithfulness, and in purity.[68] 13 Till I come, give attention to public reading of the Scriptures,[69] to persuasive explanation (on them), and to teaching (of them).[70] 14 Don't keep on neglecting your spiritual gift, which was given to you by prophecy in conjunction with the laying on of the hands of the leaders.[71]

---

[64] Comparative study of effective leaders who finished well unearthed five factors which enhanced their perseverance and good finish. One of those was the presence of spiritual disciplines in the life. See **Articles**, *15. Finishing Well—Five Factors Enhancing (Perspective, Repeated Renewals, Disciplines, Learning Posture, Mentoring);61. Spiritual Disciplines—And On-Going Leadership.*

[65] This truth lead-in (see also 1:15; 3;1; 4:9) emphasizes that leaders, committed to a Gospel ministry will be criticized for it. Sometimes an older person gets sidetracked for a moment and puts in something in the conversation not necessarily going with the flow. And frequently the aside comment will be important in terms of something from their past—like Paul throws in these aside comments.

[66] Paul gives here another doctrinal truth. Note how many of these truths are rooted in the basic notion of salvation. See also 2:3-6; 3:16; 4:10; 6:13. I have used Alford's exposition on this troublesome *apparently universal salvation phrase.* See KJV.

[67] This passage, 4:11-15, is one of the best of many examples in 1Ti of Paul's role of a *mentor counselor* and *mentor spiritual guide.* He is personally giving advice to Timothy about his own spiritual life and ministry. Paul demonstrates in this book four mentor roles: mentor sponsor, mentor counselor, mentor spiritual guide and mentor teacher (in that priority order). See also 1Ti 6:11-14. See *mentor, mentor counselor, mentor spiritual guide, mentor sponsor, mentor teacher,* **Glossary.**

[68] Modeling is the dominant way a young leader will gain respect among older believers. Notice that this modeling is primarily of character qualities, not giftedness. See *modeling,* **Glossary.**

[69] This word for reading implies the public reading of Scriptures. See Ac 13:15; 2Co 3:14; 1Ti 4:13.

[70] Paul gives good advice for structuring public ministry. He asserts a threefold formula for ministry: public reading of truth, explanation of it and application of it. Most public services in churches today have public reading of truth and may or may not have explanation of it but do not have any application of it. Application is hopefully left to the hearer. What is needed is a Spirit-led ministry time where the application of the Scripture is at least as much emphasized as the communication of it (the explanation).

[71] Note two things. Giftedness can be imparted by mature leaders and giftedness should be developed and used for God. A developmental perspective on life is a great boon to a leader who wants to finish well. Impartation of gifts is one apostolic function. See **Articles**, *2. Apostolic Functions; 9. Developing Giftedness, Paul's Advice to Timothy; 21. Impartation of Gifts... ; 25. Jesus—Five Philosophical Leadership Models in the Gospels (Stewardship Model especially);63. Spiritual Gifts, Giftedness and Development..*

15 Keep on meditating[72] on these things; give yourself wholly to them.[73] Then your progress[74] will be recognized by all. 16 Watch yourself. Watch your teaching.[75] Continue in these things: for in doing this you will keep yourself from danger and those that listen to you.

IV. (Ch 5) Paul's Advice— Social Problem, Widows

Chapter 5

1 Don't rebuke an elderly man, but appeal to him as a father; Treat the younger men as brothers and 2 the elder women as mothers and the younger women as sisters, with all purity.[76]

3 Take care of widows that are really widows. 4 But if a widow has children or grandchildren, they should take care of her as their religious duty. This will also repay their parents and grandparents: for that is good and acceptable before God. 5 Now she that is a widow indeed, and forsaken, depends upon God, and continues in bringing her needs and prayers night and day (to him). 6 But the widow that lives for pleasure is dead while she is living. 7 Strongly urge what I am saying that widows may be beyond criticism.[77] 8 But if any provide not for his own, and most of all, for those of his own family, that one has denied the faith, and is worse than a non-believer.

---

[72] *Meditating* (SRN 3191) means not only to ponder and think about but also to attend to, to practice. A much stronger word than our word for meditate.

[73] *Give yourself wholly to them* is an admonition to focus or to put it negatively, don't get sidetracked. It is easy for a leader to get sidetracked on the many things that clamor for attention. For Timothy it would be trying to argue with the holders of the heresies. Paul's admonition is to practice spiritual disciplines, model godliness, teach the positive truth and apply it.

[74] *Progress* (SRN 4297), is a developmental perspective.

[75] This is Paul's equivalence of modern day (1990s) leadership theorist, S. Covey's P + PC balance (product, product capability). Paul is saying and I think the order is important: take care of yourself, your own life. Be what you should be. And then take care of your ministry. Do what you should do. Being plus doing are both in focus. Ministry flows out of being. If being lacks, then ministry will too, eventually.

[76] Illicit sexual relationships is a major barrier to finishing well. Many U.S. church leaders have fallen due to illicit sexual relationships (both married leaders and single leaders). This advice is good for all leaders. See **Article**, *17. Finishing Well, Six Major Barriers.*

[77] Paul is concerned throughout the book for how a Christian or a Christian leader is perceived without. See also 3:2, 7, 10; 4:12; 5:7,12, 14; 6:1 for emphasis on outward testimony.

9 Don't put a widow on the widow's list who is younger than sixty. Further she should having been a loyal wife[78]— 10 A reputation for good works. She should have brought up her children well. She should have lodged strangers, and she should have washed the saints' feet. She should have assisted those in deep trouble. She should be a good worker.

11 But the younger widows refuse (to put on the list): for when they have strong desires to marry[79] they turn away from Christ. 12 They are judged,[80] because they have rejected their first faith. 13 Further they idle away their time, wandering about from house to house; and not only idle, but gossiping and minding others' business saying things which they ought not. 14 I would prefer that the younger women marry, bear children, manage their households, give no opportunity for opponents to speak reproachfully 15 For some are already turned aside after Satan.[81] 16 If any Christian woman has relatives who are widows, she must take care of them, and keep the church from being burdened; It should take care of widows who are alone and needy.[82]

17 Church leaders that are exercising good leadership should be evaluated as worthy of double pay— especially the ones who are working hard teaching the word.[83] 18 For the scripture says, Don't muzzle the ox that is treading out the corn.[84] And, The laborer is worthy of his reward.[85] 19 Don't listen to an accusation against a leader unless it is

---

[78] This is probably a list idiom. See fn 3:2. See other lists: 3:2-7; 3:8-10; 3:11-13. But note again that Paul is concerned throughout the book for how a Christian or a Christian leader is perceived without.

[79] This word feel *strong desires* (SRN 2691) means have sexual impulses. Implication being they will turn away from Christ and follow these desires. This could be part of the problem of 1Ti 2:12.

[80] They are *judged* (SRN 2917), i.e. found guilty, already condemned. By who is unclear. But the idea is probably that the surrounding society criticizes them (and hence casts a bad light on Christianity). See other vs on criticism or above reproach before others: 3:2,7,10; 4:12; 5:12,14. Remember Paul is saying that the church (3:15,16) represents truth to those around them.

[81] This is the negative way of stating *turn away from Christ* in vs 11. Spiritual warfare is involved.

[82] This is a social problem that the Ephesian church faced. While we as a church may not face this exact problem it is instructive to note how Paul advises solving it.

[83] Two implications are worth noting. (1) Leaders should be recompensed for their ministry. Those doing exceptional ministry, especially word oriented ministry should be amply rewarded. (2) There are differing functions of elders—ruling, teaching.

[84] See Dt 25:4 and 1Co 9:9. Paul knows and uses his O.T. *See Bible centered leader*, **Glossary**.

[85] Note that the first quote comes from Dt 25:4 and the second from Lk 10:7. Both are considered authoritative Scripture.

backed by two or more witnesses.[86] 20 Those leaders that are sinning rebuke[87] before[88] all, that others also may fear.

21 I solemnly testify before God, and the Lord Jesus Christ, and the elect angels, in order that you keep these things without prejudging and showing partiality to some.[89] 22 Don't hastily lay hands on any person for leadership, neither be partaker of other's sins: keep yourself pure.[90]

23 Don't only drink water, but use a little wine for your stomach and for your frequent illnesses.[91]

24 Some people's sins are transparent— easily providing evidence for judgment almost right away. But some (sins of people) only become apparent after time. 25 In a similar way good works (of some) are easily seen; and even those not so easily seen can not be hidden for long.[92]

---

[86] This is an important leadership principle. Accusations against leaders must be carefully examined. There should be strong confirmation where wrongdoing is involved. Note also in vs 20 that those found in the wrong should be publicly rebuked. This serves as part of the disciplinary action to restore the leader and to warn others. It also serves to guard the credibility of leadership. Today both of these guidelines are avoided. Frequently, accusations which are unfounded are given which destroy a leader even if later proved wrong. And very seldom is there public discipline of a leader found in the wrong.

[87] *Rebuke* (SRN 1651) implies to expose, find fault with, convict and carries the connotation of bringing shame.

[88] Those who are accused (vs 19) and *found to be wrong* (SRN 264) are to be publicly censured (SRN 1799).

[89] Several leadership problems are implied here. They are serious—note the solemn oath, I *strongly testify* (SRN 1263) preceding the admonition *to keep these things* (SRN 5442). This is actually a word describing someone who is closely watching or guarding a prisoner lest he escape. When applying Scriptural principles to leaders vs 17 and 18, concerning finances; vs 19 potential accusations against leaders; vs 20 public censure) Paul knows there is a tendency to prejudge without really finding out the facts, *prejudge* (vs 21 SRN 4299), a form of cover up. There is also a tendency to *show partiality* (SRN 4346), that is, give in to leaders who have power. This is not theoretical. Timothy is going to have to apply this to some elders in Ephesus who are teaching heresy. Paul knows Timothy does not like to confront.

[90] Emerging leaders should be tried before putting them into leadership. It is unclear what the phrase *"partakers of others sins"* means unless it means that putting an untried and proven leader into leadership makes one liable for the problems they will cause.

[91] This is humorous. It is as if Paul knows that these strong admonitions to confront leaders at Ephesus is going to cause Timothy anxiety and worry. Take it easy Timothy. Have some wine and calm down.

[92] Is this a postscript comment on choosing leaders hastily and on judging leaders? Otherwise, why include it here?

VI. (Ch 6) Paul's Miscellaneous Exhortations

Chapter 6

1 Slaves, under the yoke,[93] must consider their own masters deserving of proper respect, that the name of God and [his] teaching not be spoken evil of.[94] 2 Those (slaves) who have Christian masters—Don't despise them because they are believers, instead serve them well knowing that they, believers you love, benefit from your service. These things teach and urge strongly.[95] 3 If anyone teaches differently, and doesn't agree with this solid teaching, true teaching right from our Lord Jesus Christ, which flows from godliness, 4 then that one is proud, knows nothing, and has an unhealthy focus on questions and argumentative things.[96] This leads to envy, strife, slander, evil suspicions, 5 as well as useless occupation of people whose minds are corrupt.[97] They are no longer concerned with truth but using religion to make money.[98]

6 But a godly life with contentment[99] is riches indeed. 7 For we brought nothing into this world, and it is certain we can carry nothing out.

---

[93] This is essentially a third person imperative—note the translation, must. This is a powerful metaphor describing a slave. To such a one this command would seem very difficult. See *metaphor*, **Glossary** and **Article**, *13. Figures and Idioms.*

[94] Another reference to criticism from without—and its impact on the Christian testimony of the Church—the pillar and foundation of truth. See 3:2, 7, 10; 4:12; 5:12, 14, 6:1 for references to outward testimony.

[95] From this strong admonition, one can easily surmise that another problem in the church had to do with slaves who were believers causing problems for their masters, some of whom must have been believers. It is interesting that Phm, written only shortly after this letter, and after Paul had personally met Onesimus, shows much more empathy for the slave situation and takes it a step further than this.

[96] See also 1:3,4, 6, 7; 2:12; 4:1-5; 4:7; 6:3,4 and the basic antidote in 1Ti 3:15 for other references to heresy and its results.

[97] This is heresy 4, described loosely as teaching that is not in harmony with Christ's teaching—or maybe referring to slaves being submissive to masters. Its results are described (questioning; argumentative; leading to strife, slander, evil suspicions, money hungry leaders). See *heresy*, **Glossary.**

[98] In fn 1Ti 3:3 (money problems), fn 1Ti 3:6 (pride), and fn 1Ti 5:2 (illicit sexual relationships) I mentioned three of the six barriers commonly seen as those which waylay leaders from finishing well. Here money is mentioned again. Two others are hinted: family problems—the character traits for leaders states that positively leaders must rule their families well (3:4,5, 12)—and plateauing (4:14). The only barrier missing is abuse of power. See **Article**, *17. Finishing Well—Six Major Barriers.*

[99] *Contentment* (SRN 841) refers to an inner attitude satisfied with its lot, an inner sufficiency. *Riches* (SRN 4200) translates a word meaning source of gain, or a means to gain, or gain). *Indeed* (SRN 3173) simply means great or a lot. The idea being, there is an inner source of satisfaction that a godly person has which is far better than worldly riches.

8 So we should be content to have the food and clothing we need. 9 But those that set their hearts on becoming rich, can be easily trapped by foolish and harmful desires, which lead to ruin and destruction. 10 For the love of money is the root of all evil. Some have sought this and have strayed from the faith,[100] and suffered deep grief because of it.[101]

11 But you, man of God,[102] avoid these traps. Pursue a life of integrity, holiness, faith, love, steadfastness, gentleness. 12 Struggle well[103] in your Christian life as you appropriate and realize the Christian life[104] you committed yourself to before many witnesses.[105] 13 I am strongly commanding you—in the presence of God, who gives life to all things, and Christ Jesus, who stood on his convictions before Pontius Pilate—[106] 14 That you guard and obey my words to you. Do so with exactness so that no one can reproach you at the appearing[107] of our Lord Jesus Christ.[108] 15 At that time He will prove (who is) the rightly honored and only Sovereign Ruler, the King of kings, and Lord of lords. 16 He alone has immortality, existing in a heavenly brightness that is inaccessible to a human being. No one has seen, nor can see God. To him be honor and dominion forever. Amen.[109]

17 Command those who are rich in this world's things, not to be proud, nor to trust in uncertain riches, but in the living God who supplies us generously with all things to enjoy;

---

[100] *Strayed from the faith* is a repeated theme. See also 1:6, 20; 5:11, 15; 6:10. This is a major problem that pastors and apostolic workers will face—especially in situations of radical conversions.

[101] This desire for money (or the power it can bring) can easily sidetrack a leader or a Christian follower.

[102] This is a beautiful example of Goodwin's Expectation Principle. Paul gives a powerful word of affirmation, man of God, what a compliment— only Moses, Samuel, Shemaiah, Elijah, Elisha, David, Hanan—are described by these words. He then challenges Timothy with doable goals. He does not challenge him to achieve but to be—something well within his grasp. See *Goodwin's Expectation Principle*, **Glossary,**

[103] The repetitive idiom showing the superlative, struggle...struggle (verb and noun forms) have been captured. Both words are words used of an athlete competing well in the games—a disciplined struggle. We get our English word agony and agonize from these Greek words. Realizing eternal life in its qualitative sense in the here and now involves struggle as well as rest. See *capture, superlative idiom*, **Glossary.**

[104] See Php 2:12 for the same idea of appropriating with effort and with God's backing. See also **Article**, *12. Fear And Trembling- The Right Attitude.*

[105] A strong motivational principle occurs here. *Public committals on major decisions form a touchstone.*

[106] This is another one of those doctrinal as. les.

[107] This is another of those motivational causes—the return of Christ and accountability. For other references see also: Php 1:6; 2:16; 4:1; Heb 13:17.

[108] This is the first time in 1Ti that Paul refers to one of his strong leadership values, *Leaders will ultimately give an account for their ministries.* This passage, 6:11-14 is another of the great passages in which Paul is acting as a spiritual guide mentor. See 4:11-15.

[109] This is another truth aside—a doxology type. See also 3:16; 6:15, 16.

18 Tell them to do good and to be rich in good works, ready to give to others, and ready to share. 19 Invest in their real future and thus really grasp what eternal life is.[110]

20 Dear Timothy, guard what has been entrusted to you.[111] Avoid worldly and fruitless discussions and false tenets of "so called science."[112] 21 Some have followed these and have strayed from the faith.[113] Grace[114] be with you. Amen. <<[The first to Timothy was written from Laodicea, which is the major city of Phrygia Pacatiana.]>>[115]

---

[110] In this passage 6:17-19 lies the true use of money as power: (1) It can not be trusted in; (2) It must be appreciated as from God; (3) It is to be enjoyed; (4) It is to be used to do good—i.e. good works; (5) It is to be shared with others who need it; (6) Its generous use in these ways will help one having these resources to experience some of what eternal life really is. *In giving away, we get that which can not be taken away.*

[111] Leadership responsibility seen as an entrustment—A repeated theme. See also 1:11,18; 4:14. See **Article**, *10. Entrustment- A Leadership Responsibility.*

[112] Paul closes by coming back to his warning about heresy. See *heresy*, **Glossary**.

[113] This is the final appearance of this repeated *theme—danger of turning away from Christianity.* See also 1:6,20; 4:16; 5:11,15; 6:10.

[114] Grace as used in 1Ti, 2Ti and Tit is the enabling presence of God in a life so as to cause that one to persevere victoriously. See *grace*, **Glossary**.

[115] This note occurs on some manuscripts.

(This page is deliberately left blank.)

For Further Leadership Study

General

If you were a young leader sent into a church with all kind of problems you would be glad to have a wise mentor who could advise you. And not only one who could advise you but one who was respected by the church leaders. You would not only want his advice but his backing. And that is just what we have with Paul and Timothy. This book should be studied in depth by every church leader and younger emerging leader. If you are a younger leader you need to find a Paul. And if you are a Paul you need to be reaching out to younger leaders.

Suggestions for Further Study

1. Study the mentoring roles that Paul works on in his relationship with Timothy as illustrated in this book. What empowering tasks of a spiritual guide, coach, counselor, teacher, sponsor, or contemporary mentor are illustrated?
2. What to Paul are core doctrines that must be foundational to a local church? See his asides on doctrinal truth and his emphasis to Timothy. How would your own list differ?
3. Which of the qualifications for leaders are specific to this situation? Which can be generalized and seen in other local church cultural situations in the New Testament? How do you know?
4. 1 Ti 2:11-13 (entire context is 1-14) should be studied as a cultural problematic issue regarding women and abuse of authority. This is not a general admonition against women in leadership but a specific cultural issue being dealt with—the issue is abuse of authority and influencing the church improperly. Forming a major doctrine on an unclear text dealing with a problem issue is questionable (like excluding women in ministry because of this text).
5. Giftedness development and impartation of gifts suggested in this letter need further comparative study in other Pauline letters and in fact across other leader's ministry.
6. Both the harvest and shepherd models of philosophy are in view in this letter. However, due to the development of the church the emphasis is more on the shepherd model—internal nurture and problem solving. But see the subtle emphasis in the truth asides toward harvest model thought.
7. Two principles of discipline are highlighted: the Principle of Validity (Is it true?), the Principle of Public Discipline (the value of warning). Both of these need to be studied for wider confirmation. What other principle is in view (hint: redemptive)?
8. Issues of conscience must be addressed in leadership. Paul gives here some basics but much more needs to be done with conscience. What is seen about the conscience in 1Ti?
9. The model for plurality needs to be traced to other situations for wider confirmation. Is this one of several configurations or the ideal? Is it culturally suggested? What other models are allowable?

10. Can a leader's personality be changed? Timothy does not seem to be very confrontational (Titus does seem to be so). In this situation Paul knows that confrontation is a must. Paul seems to think that Timothy can become confrontational, and more authoritative. Do these kind of assumptions hold for other leaders in Scripture? Can bold authoritative leaders become gentle? Can gentle leaders become bold?

Special Comments

This major book contributing to leadership is a must for personal study and application and for teaching for the church. It should fundamentally affect a leader's ministry in the Church leadership era.

Personal Response

1.   What is the most significant leadership insight you have gained from your study of 1Ti?

2.   What one idea from this study can you put into practice in your own leadership? How?

3.   Immediate Application: List an idea from this study that you can share with someone today?

        a. Idea:

        b. Who?:

Your Observations.

You may want to jot down important insights you want to remember. You may wish to note follow-up intents.

(This page is deliberately left blank.)

BOOK　　　　　　　　　**2 Timothy**　　　　　　　　**Author: Paul**

Characters　　Those mentioned include Paul, Timothy, Onesiphorus, Demas, Crescens, Titus, Luke, Tychicus, Carpus, Alexander, Priscilla, Aquila, Erastus, Trophimus, Eubulus, Pudens, Linus, Claudia.

Who To/For　To Timothy, a protégé of Paul, who is helping advise church leaders in Ephesus.

Literature Type　　A personal letter with powerful advice backed by years of experience and pointing to the need to finish well.

Story Line　　Paul had helped found the church in Ephesus (Ac 19). It became an indigenous church. Later he met with the elders of this church in a stop-over on his trip back to Jerusalem (Ac 20). At that time he warned them of problems that would arise in the church. Later he also wrote an epistle to them (along with the ones to Colosse and Philemon). At that time there were no major problems as witnessed by the general nature of the letter. Several years later the problems he warned about have arisen. He sends Timothy to try to minister to the situation and advise the church elders. Timothy runs into a number of problems which he does not know how to handle. Paul writes an epistle to Timothy to help him in that situation. That is 1Ti. Now after a period of time, Paul sensing that his end is near writes a second time to Timothy. These last words are powerful because they are just that. They reflect the fruit of a life that counted.

Structure

I.	(Ch 1-2:13)	**Exhortations to Persevere and Select Leaders to Carry On in Ministry**
II.	(Ch 2:14-26)	**Warnings for the Newly Selected Leaders to Aid Them in Persevering**
III.	(Ch 3:1-17)	**Persevering in Difficult Days Ahead**
IV.	(Ch 4:1-8)	**End Result of Persevering—A Good Finish**
V.	(Ch 4:9-18)	**Personal Matters**

Theme Persevering In a Ministry
- should be done to meet God's approval,
- will require the suffering of hardships,
- involves the modeling of righteous living, and
- necessitates the proper use of God's word.

Key Words　　faith, faithful (11); good (6); grace (5)

Key Events   An O.T. spiritual authority event is alluded to—see 3:8, Jannes and
Jambres who opposed Moses; Paul's first trial which did not go too well.

Purposes

- to summon Timothy to his side,
- to encourage Timothy during these tough days in the Roman empire,
- to give his farewell advice (on numerous issues),
- to highlight the need for transparency in a mentoring relationship (see 3:10,11),
- to give an inspirational model of a leader finishing well,
- to pass the torch of leadership to Timothy (giving continuity),
- to transfer the stewardship of the Word to Timothy.

Why Important

This is the most personal of all of Paul's letters (possible exception, 2 Corinthians). In the midst of his trial at Rome (his first hearing had not gone well) he writes Timothy. Most likely you would expect details as to what happened in the trial and the possible outcomes. But you hear little of that. For Paul is concerned about the church and about Timothy. The letter is filled with that personal concern. Its advice is based upon personal experience. These are the final words of a leader. And they both reveal in his own model and what they say that which is the essence of one who would exercise leadership as a minister for God. 2Ti reveals what true ministry is. It describes a true minister of Jesus Christ. Leaders are gifted by the Holy Spirit for ministry and must guard that good deposit by using it and developing themselves to use it. But leaders are not only gifted, they must also experience the enabling grace of God in life, that is, they must be able to appropriate God's enablement in every kind of situation. Character is crucial both for the minister and for the people to whom ministered. Development in holiness is a priority. The Word of God must be known thoroughly and applied to life and ministry. As regards the Word, three marks describe a leader who finishes well. They must: 1. know the Word thoroughly and 2. use it appropriately, and 3. must pass on the stewardship of the Word to others. The stewardship of the Word is crucial. Leaders must pass on to others the responsibility to know and use God's Word. No Christian leader will last long unless he or she abides in the Word. And their work will not abide long after them if they have not passed on the stewardship of the word. Leaders must be diligent—have initiative and discipline to get things done. Finally, leaders must persevere and finish well. All of the above is what Paul did and what he admonished Timothy to do and what comes to us as the abiding message of 2Ti.

Where it Fits

This is the last of the Pauline epistles. In the redemptive drama it occurs in Chapter 4, The Church. Messiah has come. The foundational work at the Cross has been done. Peter, the gatekeeper has ushered people into the Church, and manifested the Kingdom during this era. Paul the master builder now builds upon that foundation. To Paul is given the task of establishing the church; he will outline its form, its essentials, and its leadership requirements. To John will come the task of restoring that church—renewing it, calling it back to its essentials. But it is Paul who tells us what the church is, what ministry is, and what a leader of that church must be and do. 2Ti occurs at the end of Paul's lifetime, about two-thirds way through the first century. It carries the essence of what leadership is all about and it demonstrates what it means for a leader to finish well. No present church or para-church leader can fail to thoroughly grasp this book and still hope to minister well.

In terms of the six leadership eras, 2Ti occurs in the church leadership era, the sixth and present era in which leaders today are also living. Paul, the architect of church forms and functions, has modeled for present leaders what it means to minister in the church over a lifetime and finish well. Leaders today can not say that they have not seen leadership at its complex best. Paul has showed this.

General Reflections

The church leadership era spans from the time of Paul's ministry right on up to the present. Paul wrote 1,2 Ti to a young church leader. Timothy had been sent on a special leadership mission, trying to solve problems in an indigenized church at Ephesus. This church had its own leadership in its unique cultural situation. That church was 15-20 years old, and hence facing the problems of a church of that age: a tendency toward nominality, contextualization issues, application of the Gospel to social problems, truth and heresy, folks straying from their Christian commitment, and leadership selection. The book, 1Ti, deals more with the problems Timothy was facing in the church and with Timothy's own personal needs. The book, 2Ti, the final book written by Paul, concentrates less on the heresies in that church. It focuses primarily on three things: Leadership selection, encouragement for Timothy personally and personal news about Paul as he finishes his ministry. It is the outstanding book in the Bible from the standpoint of a leader finishing well. All the characteristics of a good finish are indicated in this little book. It is clear that Paul feels he is passing the torch on to Timothy.

2 Timothy—Leadership Lessons/Topics

1. FINISH WELL.

This book demonstrates what it means to finish well in a ministry. Paul is the classic N.T. case of a leader finishing well. Christ is still Lord of His life. He is ministering looking for the return of Christ. All six characteristics of a good finish are indicated. (a) His relationship with God via Christ is still warm and personal. (1Ti 4:17). (b) He evinces a learning posture (1Ti 4:13). (c) He has been shaped by the Holy Spirit over his lifetime into the image of Christ. That is, he demonstrates Christ-likeness (1Ti 4:16). (d) He lives by Biblical convictions, his faith intact (2Ti 4:7). (e) He is leaving behind a legacy. His ultimate contributions include those associated with saint, stylistic practitioner, mentor, pioneer, writer, promoter. See *mentor, pioneer, promoter, saint, stylistic practitioner, ultimate contribution, writer,* **Glossary.** See **Article,** *35. Legacy— Leaving One Behind.* (f) A destiny has been accomplished—finished his course (2Ti 4:7). You can be sure that his advice to Timothy comes out of one who has done those things himself. He is a pace setter whose advice should be heeded. 2Ti 4:1-8 is a great inspirational passage on finishing well. Every leader should read this passage every so often just to be refreshed and to remember what it means to *begin with the end in mind.* Modeling of what it means to finish well tops the list of contributions from this book. Paul is the architect of the Christian Church as we know it. How did Christianity work out for him? His failure would probably have torpedoed the whole church leadership era. But his great finish caps off a triumphant ministry and gives all leaders of this era hope and a challenge to do likewise. He has finished his task with honor. Peterson interprets Paul's final words, "All that's left now is the shouting—God's applause!" And we who are in leadership today shed a tear and applaud loudly as we read this great leader's finish.

Leadership Principles/ Values Suggested by this concept:

a. Present ministry should always be seen in the light of a whole life of ministry and particularly the end of ministry—a good finish. A good thought question, "In what way is my present shaping circumstances going to affect my finish?"
b. One's sense of destiny guides toward and highlights a good finish.
c. A leader's character is tested and shown for what it is by a major crisis. (Paul shines here.)
d. An anticipation of the Lord's return is a major motivating factor for a leader to minis er well and finish well.
e. Recognition of giving an accountability for one's ministry is a second motivating factor for a leader to minister well and finish well.
f. A leader does not have to fear injustice in God's appraisal of ministry. He/she can confidently know that God will interpret and evaluate life and ministry with mercy, accuracy and justice.

2. MINISTRY PRAYER PRINCIPLE.

Paul illustrates the ministry prayer principle first seen in Moses and highlighted in Samuel's ministry. *If God has called you to a ministry then He has called you to pray for that ministry.* Paul's mentoring of Timothy was a major emphasis of his ministry. It needed to be bathed in prayer. And Paul did that (2Ti 1:3). He practiced what he preached (1Th 5:17). This simple responsibility is, in seed form, the very core of the priestly ministry philosophy model given for leadership in full blown form in Heb. See **Articles**, *25. Jesus' Five Leadership Models: Shepherd, harvest, Steward, Servant, Intercessor; 46. Paul The Intercessor Leader.*

Leadership Principles/ Values Suggested by this concept:
    a. Leaders are responsible for praying for their ministries.
    b. Leaders who pray for their ministries will often deepen their burden for those ministries.

3. PRAYER ENCOURAGEMENT PRINCIPLE.

Jesus first demonstrates this principle in Luke 22:31-34. He tells Peter that he has prayed for him and that he will make it through the trying time that is to come. This basic motivational principle can be stated as, *A leader should pray specifically and personally for those in his/her ministry and tell them of those prayers.* This is a great motivator. And the more specific it is, the more it will motivate. Paul prays continually for Timothy (2Ti 1:3). And you can be sure he prayed along the lines of the advice he gave Timothy. Paul knew Timothy's weaknesses and strengths very well.

Leadership Principles/ Values Suggested by this concept:
    a. A leader should pray personally for those in his or her ministry.
    b. A leader should seek God for specific prayers for those in his or her ministry.
    c. A leader should tell those in his or her ministry about those prayers and thus encourage them to believe also that God will answer those prayers.
    d. One of the best ways a leader can demonstrate love is by following this prayer encouragement principle.

4. GIFTEDNESS DEVELOPMENT.

Giftedness development is highlighted in this book. Christian leaders must constantly keep in balance doing and being. We must produce in our ministry. But we must also develop the production capability. We must develop ourselves. Both our production and our production capability must be developed. Giftedness can be and must be developed or atrophy sets in (1:6). Gifts can be imparted (1:14) by those having spiritual authority. They should be used with gifted power (1:7). Self-discipline is needed both to develop and use giftedness (1:7 and 4:1-5). See *gifted power, giftedness set, Stewardship Model, spiritual gift*, **Glossary**. See **Articles**, *25. Jesus' Five Leadership Models: Shepherd, Harvest, Steward, Servant, Intercessor.* (especially the Stewardship Model); *63. Spiritual Gifts, Giftedness and Development.*

<u>Leadership Principles/ Values Suggested by this concept:</u>
a. The stewardship model requires development of giftedness in general, which includes spiritual gifts as well.
b. The stewardship model points out a leader will be accountable for developing every resource he/she has.
c. A leader should develop knowledge, skills, and other perspectives which will enable giftedness to be used with effectiveness.
d. One apostolic function involves the impartation of gifts as God directs.
e. Gifts should be exercised with gifted power, that is, by faith in the Holy Spirit's empowerment of that giftedness. See *gifted power*, **Glossary**.

5. ULTIMATE ACCOUNTABILITY.

Christian leaders minister always with a conscious view to ultimate accountability to God for their ministry. Paul was conscious of a future day in which God would hold him and others accountable for their actions (see 1:16, 4:8, 4:14). This is more fully developed in 2Co and 1, 2Th but is affirmed in many epistles. See especially He 13:17.

<u>Leadership Principles/ Values Suggested by this concept:</u>
a. Leaders will be held accountable for their ministry efforts.
b. Leaders will be rewarded for their positive achievements in ministry.
c. A final accountability is one motivating factor for a leader.
d. God will be a just evaluator of a leader's ministry efforts.

6. LEADERSHIP SELECTION.

Effective leaders see leadership selection and development as a priority function in their life. This is one of seven major leadership lessons seen in effective leaders. See **Article**, *29. Leadership Lessons—Seven Major Lessons Identified.* Paul here (2:2, 2:14ff) advocates top-down recruitment of potential leaders. The selection criterion focuses on three major qualities: (1) being faithful, (2) being teachable, and (3) having the ability to pass on to others that which has been life changing for them.

<u>Leadership Principles/ Values Suggested by this concept:</u>
a. Leadership selection and development is a responsibility of a leader.
b. Faithfulness, being teachable, and ability to pass on to others should be the focus of one's selection criteria.
c. Emerging leaders should be taught how to handle correctly God's written word.
d. Emerging leaders should be taught the importance of the written word as a source of leadership insights.

7. FOCUS.

To persevere in ministry, a leader must have a single-minded focus. 2:1-4, 10, 15, 21; 3:16,17; 4:7. Life and its many problems can encumber and entangle so as to sidetrack one from a disciplined life that counts for Christ. See especially the soldier analogy, 2:3,4 and the athlete analogy, 2:5, fn 2:2, as well as the notion of Paul finishing his course, fn 4:7, fn. See his persevering attitude in Acts 20:24. See *focused life*, **Glossary**. See **Articles**, *18. Focused Life; 42. Paul—A Sense of Destiny.*

<u>Leadership Principles/ Values Suggested by this concept:</u>
   a. Effective leaders increasingly move toward a focused life as God reveals information on the four focal issues: life purpose, effective methodology, major role, and lasting legacies.
   b. Disciplines are necessary for persevering in ministry over a lifetime.
   c. A leader's sense of destiny is a primary factor in determining focus.
   d. A leader can persevere, can focus and can finish well. Paul has modeled this for us.

8. FINANCIAL PRINCIPLE.

A leader's ministry is worthy of remuneration. This is not a big thing with Paul. But a leader who is effective should not be ashamed of reward for having done effective ministry. (2:6,7)

<u>Leadership Principles/ Values Suggested by this concept:</u>
   a. Leaders deserve remuneration for effective ministry.
   b. Leaders need not be ashamed of this fact but should assume it as a God-given resource.

9. BIBLE-CENTERED MINISTRY.

An effective leader who finishes well must have a Bible-centered ministry. 2Ti 2:15 and 3:16, 17 give the keynotes on a Bible-centered ministry. It is a God ordained requirement. It brings confident ministry (litotes = not ashamed). It is a matter of integrity (correctly handling). It will change life and ministry (3:16, 17). See *Bible Centered Leader*, **Glossary**. See **Article**, *5. Bible Centered Leader*.

<u>Leadership Principles/ Values Suggested by this concept:</u>
   a. Leaders should strive to handle the word correctly in their ministry so as to be approved of God.
   b. A leader who handles the word of God correctly gains confidence in his/her leadership ability.
   c. The Bible is an authoritative source for getting leadership insights and other teaching appropriate for ministry.
   d. The Bible is an authoritative source for pointing out leadership errors.
   e. The Bible is an authoritative source for suggesting what to do about correcting leadership errors.
   f. The Bible is an authoritative source for giving models of righteousness that leaders can follow.
   g. The Bible is an authoritative source for fully equipping a leader for leadership ministry.
   h. A leader should seek to become a Bible centered leader.

10. GENTLENESS.

Gentleness, rather than argument, is a major influence means for a leader to affect change. There are few gentle leaders. Such a one stands out. Gentle persuasion is a major tool for a change agent. See 2Ti 2:22-26.

Leadership Principles/ Values Suggested by this concept:
   a. Leaders with spiritual authority depend heavily upon persuasion as a strong influence means.
   b. Gentleness is a primary trait of a leader who wants to persuade (as opposed to one who wants to prove he/she is right).
   c. A leader is one who influences toward God's purposes. This is the bottom line for assessing leadership influence means.

11. OPPOSITION.

Effective leaders should expect opposition to their ministry—especially on issues of truth they teach. Forewarned is forearmed. However, major on the majors. See 2Ti 2:22-26 and 3:8. A major macro lesson observed by comparative study of all six of the leadership eras warns that *leadership is complex, problematic, difficult and fraught with risk—which is why leadership is needed.* Nowhere is this seen more than when a leader faces opposition. Paul warned of opposition in this very church in Ac 20:29, 30. He points out that this opposition will come from within the church, even among its leaders, and from without the church. In 2Ti he directly identifies a typical outward opposition, Alexander the coppersmith, and indirectly inward opposition, 2Ti 3:13 (more clearly seen in 1Ti with all the heresies identified).

Leadership Principles/ Values Suggested by this concept:
   a. A leader should expect opposition to ministry.
   b. Opposition can come from within or without.

12. MODELING/TRANSPARENCY.

Transparency in modeling God's enabling grace in a life and ministry provides an effective base for influencing followers toward maturity. Paul was conscious of his own life as being a model for others and used it deliberately as such. He shared the ups and downs and always the need for the grace of God to enable one in the midst of them. See 2Ti 3:10-14. See especially 2Ti 4:6-8. See also **Key Leadership Insights—Philippians**, *Topic: Modeling*.

Leadership Principles/ Values Suggested by this concept:
   a. A leader should proactively use modeling to influence followers.
   b. A leader who i. finishing well, and hence who is modeling that, has a strong power base to influence followers.
   c. Transparency which also includes vulnerability, along with God's enablement in a situation is a most powerful influence means.

13. ADVENT OF CHRIST.

The return of Christ was a major motivating factor of Paul's leadership. He advocates this for all leaders (all those who love his appearing). See 2Ti 4:7,8. See also John's emphasis (1Jn 3:1-3). See **Article**, *40. Motivating Factors for Ministry*.

Leadership Principles/ Values Suggested by this concept:
   a. A leader should use Christ's return as a personal motivating factor for life and ministry. One evidence of a leader's consciousness of Christ in a life or ministry is a love for the return of Christ.
   b. Leaders should make explicit the motivating factors in their ministry.

14. LEARNING POSTURE.

Effective leaders maintain a learning posture all during their lives. This is one of the seven major leadership lessons identified about effective leaders. "And the books, Timothy, don't forget the books!" speaks reams about Paul (2Ti 4:13). How leaders learn varies from culture to culture. It is clear in studying Paul's life that he learned from a variety of sources: the Scriptures, from shaping experiences in life, from people, from his formal and informal training, from revelation from God for specific situations.

Leadership Principles/ Values Suggested by this concept:
   a. A leader should develop a learning posture.
   b. A leader should expand the sources from which he/she learns and expand the means to learn.
   c. The major antidote to plateauing in a ministry is a good learning posture (not actually seen in 2Ti but observed in life about those having a good learning posture).

15. BALANCE IN SPIRITUAL WARFARE

As in 1Ti Paul demonstrates balance in viewing leadership issues, problems, and situations. He neither identifies everything as being caused by Satanic influence (note his description of being opposed by Alexander and his deliverance from death). Nor does he exclude spiritual warfare as a cause. Note his explanation in 2Ti 2:26, caught in the Devil's trap.

Leadership Principles/ Values Suggested by this concept:
   a. People blinded to the truth are one evidence of spiritual warfare and Satanic influence.
   b. Gentle persuasion and using the word correctly are major means of combating spiritual warfare where folks are blinded to truth.

I. (Ch 1-2:13) Exhortations to Persevere And Select Leaders to Carry On in Ministry

Chapter 1

1 Paul,[116] an apostle of Jesus Christ by God's design,[117] to proclaim the promised life which is in Christ Jesus, 2 To Timothy, my dearly beloved son.[118] May you have Grace, mercy, and peace, from God the Father and Christ Jesus our Lord.

3 I thank God, whom I serve with a pure conscience[119] just as my ancestors did.[120] Unceasingly I remember you in my prayers night and day.[121] 4 I remember your tears as

---

[116] Paul authored 13 epistles. This was the last one. See **Time-Lines, The Apostle Paul**.

[117] In all of his writings, Paul had a strong sense of appointment to ministry from God. See also 1:11. This conviction is part of his sense of destiny. See also 1Ti 1:12; 2:7 and other Pauline salutations: Ro 1:1; 1Co 1:1; 2Co 1:1; Gal 1:1; Eph 1:1; Col 1:1; 1Ti 1:1; 2Ti 1:1; Tit 1:1. Leaders need a strong sense of God's calling for their lives if they are to persevere and be effective over a lifetime. See *sense of destiny*, **Glossary**. See also **Article**, *42. Paul—A Sense of Destiny*.

[118] Timothy's name occurs 31 times in the N.T. He was Paul's closest mentoree. Paul used this very intimate description with three younger leaders. See 1Ti 1:2,18; 2Ti 1:2; 2Ti 2:1; Php 2:22. See also Tit 1:4; Phm 1:10. Timothy's last mention in Heb 13:23 is instructive. He, a respected leader, has just been let out of prison. See *mentor*, **Glossary**. See **Articles**, *43. Paul—and His Companions; 45. Paul—Developer Par Excellence; 69. Timothy A Beloved Son in the Faith*.

[119] Paul uses *conscience* (SRN 4893) some 21 times. Ministry flows out of being. Being is a complex diversity consisting of at least: intimacy with God, character, giftedness, gender, personality, destiny, learned values. Conscience reflects the inner-life governor of character. Leadership must have a moral foundation. See also 1Ti 1:5, 19; 3:9; 4:2 for references to conscience. See **Article**, *6. Conscience, Paul's Use of...*

[120] Paul had a clear conscience that what he was doing, following Jesus, the Messiah, was true to the tradition of his Jewish ancestors. Messianic Jews today have this same conviction.

[121] Paul follows his own medicine (1Th 5:17 pray without ceasing). His mentoring relationship with Timothy was considered a ministry by him. So that he illustrates here the macro lesson on prayer first seen in Abraham's ministry in the *Patriarchal Leadership Era*, in Moses' ministry in the *Pre-kingdom Leadership Era* and identified most strongly in Samuel's ministry (see 1 Sam 12:23). The macro lesson stated is: *Leaders called to a ministry are called to intercede for that ministry.* This macro lesson occurs in all six leadership eras in the Bible. See *macro-lesson*, **Glossary**. See **Article**, *36. Macro Lesson—Defined*.

we parted.[122] I really want to see you for that would bring me joy. 5 I recall your sincere faith, which your grandmother Lois had, and your mother Eunice had. I am persuaded[123] that faith is still in you.[124] 6 Because of this I am reminding you, fan the flame of your God-given spiritual gift, which you received when I laid hands on you.[125] 7 For God has not given us a fearful spirit. Instead He has given us power, love, and self-discipline. 8 Don't be ashamed then of witnessing for our Lord, nor ashamed of me, his

---

[122] Paul talks here from the heart. He is illustrating one of his strongest leadership values. *A leadership value is an underlying assumption which affects how a leader behaves in or perceives leadership situations. Paul felt ministry ought to be very personal.* Stated more generally for all leaders, *Leaders should view personal relationships as an important part of ministry, both as a means for ministry and as an end in itself of ministry.* In his epistles Paul names almost 80 people by name—most of whom he ministered to or ministered with or in some way ministered to him. Note especially that one of the major reasons for leaders failing in ministry situations has to do with relationships. See *leadership value*, **Glossary**. See **Articles**, *43. Paul—and His Companions; 51. Pauline Leadership Values.*

[123] This is a beautiful example of Goodwin's Expectation Principle. Paul gives strong words of affirmation, *unfeigned* (SRN 505) faith—meaning a sincere and pure faith—and *persuaded* (SRN 3982), meaning absolutely convinced. He then challenges Timothy to use that faith courageously (see vs 7) by reminding him of a past benchmark, the impartation of gifting. Goodwin's Expectation Principle states *that a younger leader tends to live up to the genuine challenge given by an older leader whom he/she respects.* See *Goodwin's Expectation Principle, spiritual benchmarks*, **Glossary**. See **Article**, *60. Spiritual Benchmarks.*

[124] Timothy comes from a *foundational heritage pattern.* This means, that growing up, he had background and teaching about God and his ways. He had modeled for him what it meant to follow God. His mother and grandmother were students of the O.T. which enabled them to embrace Christ as Messiah when Paul and his team came through there. Modeling is one of the more important influence means. See **Key Leadership Lessons—Topic 12. MODELING/TRANSPARENCY**. See *modeling*, **Glossary**. See **Articles**, *48. Paul—Modeling As An Influence Means; 19. Foundational Patterns—Four Identified.*

[125] Three important leadership observations are implied here. (1) Giftedness can be imparted. (2) Giftedness can be ignored or not used and hence it atrophies. (3) On the other hand one can develop or use with zeal a gift and see it more productive. This complex metaphor *stir up the flame (gift)* indicates just that, that a gift can be developed or used with power. See *metaphor*, **Glossary**. See **Articles**, *2. Apostolic Functions; 63. Spiritual Gifts, Giftedness Development.*

prisoner.[126] Instead suffer hardship[127] for the gospel as God gives you strength to do so. 9 He has saved us, and called us with a holy calling—not because of anything we had done, but in line with his own purpose and grace, which was given us in Christ Jesus before the world began. 10 And now this has been clarified for us by the coming of our Savior Jesus Christ, who has defeated death, and has made evident to us everlasting life through the gospel.[128]

11 So I was divinely chosen[129] as a preacher, and an apostle, and a teacher.[130] 12 For this reason I am suffering in prison.[131] Yet I am completely confident.[132] For I know

---

[126] This is a prison epistle. (c.f. Eph, Php, Col, Phm, 2Ti). A most striking thing about this is that Paul is facing a major trial. This was his second major imprisonment and turned out to be his final one. He was martyred. And yet you get no griping, moaning or complaining out of him. Note here Paul's indication of the sovereignty of God in his life. He is a prisoner for Christ, note *his prisoner*, not a prisoner of the Roman Empire. He consistently was able to perceive God's overriding providence in his life even with negative things. See also Php 1:12; 4:11,12. When a leader responds to life's situations this way, he/she will be shaped toward God's purposes. The inability to see shaping activities from a sovereign mindset will be the undoing of many leaders. See *sovereign mindset*, **Glossary**. See **Articles**, *44. Paul—Deep Processing*; *58. Sovereign Mindset*.

[127] Suffering is a repeated theme with Paul. He constantly warns believers that they are called to this. See Php 1:29; 2Ti 1:12; 2:3, 9; 4:5. Evidently Timothy learned this well. See Heb 13:23.

[128] This is one of those doctrinal asides. See also 1Ti 1:17; 2:3-6; 3:16; 4:10; 6:15,16 and 2Ti 1:9,10; 2:8,19.

[129] The heart of a ministry that is effective begins here. This is a statement of a *leadership committal*—a response to God's call on a life for leadership. It is a sense of destiny experience, a spiritual benchmark, which a leader can always look back to and be bolstered in ministry. This is a repeated theme with Paul—divine calling; See also 1Ti 1:1,12; 2:7. See *leadership committal, sense of destiny*, **Glossary** . See **Article**, *60. Spiritual Benchmarks*.

[130] Three spiritual gifts are implied here: exhortation, apostleship, teaching. All three are word gifts. Exhortation is the most common of the word gifts. All leaders have at least one word gift in their gift-mix—the set of spiritual gifts they use in ministry. In fact, Paul had a relatively large gift-mix. *See apostleship, exhortation, gift-mix, love gifts, power gifts, spiritual gift, teaching, word gifts*, **Glossary**.

[131] This is another occurrence of the repeated theme, suffering. See others: 2Ti 1:12; 2:3,10; 4:5.

[132] This is an example of a *litotes/ tapenosis*, a negative emphatic figure of speech—being used by Paul to emphasize something, to really make a point. The actual words are *I am not ashamed*. Something is diminished in order to emphatically stress just its opposite. e.g. not ashamed of the Gospel in Ro 1:16 means emphatically—completely confident in the Gospel. Paul here is completely confident that the *"leadership trust"* given him will be preserved until it is completed. See *capture, entrustment, figure, invincibility principle, litotes-tapenosis*, **Glossary**. See **Article**, *13. Figures and Idioms*.

whom I have believed, and am persuaded that he is able to keep that which was entrusted to me until that day.[133] 13 Hang on to my model of right teaching, which you understood from me. Do so in faith and love which is yours in union with Christ Jesus. 14 Guard carefully[134] what was entrusted to you with the help[135] of the Holy Spirit who lives within us.

15 You know that everyone, Christians in Asia[136] deserted me—including Phygellus and Hermogenes. 16 May the Lord give mercy to Onesiphorus and his family.[137] For he frequently encouraged me and was not ashamed because I was in prison. 17 But, when he was in Rome, he searched until he found me. 18 May the Lord reward him specially in that day.[138] You know how much he did for me at Ephesus.

Chapter 2

1 As for you, my son, be strong through the special enablement[139] that is in Christ Jesus.

---

[133] Paul viewed his leadership ministry as something entrusted to him—a leadership stewardship—that he was to use and fulfill. He also recognized that God would protect him in the carrying out of that trusteeship until it was finished. Finally, he knew he would have an accounting for it (*That Day*). One could not have this view nor the confidence about it without a strong sense of destiny—including a major leadership committal. See *accountability, entrustment, leadership committal, sense of destiny,* **Glossary**. See **Article**, *10. Entrustment—A Leadership Responsibility.*

[134] *Guard carefully* (SRN 5442). This is actually a word describing someone who is closely watching or guarding a prisoner lest he escape.

[135] *With the help* translates the Greek word (SRN 1223). Its sense here is *by means of.* This shows the delicate balance in union life. We are responsible to act, behave, believe; yet we do it by means of or in the strength of the Holy Spirit. See also the concept *of divine mentor* introduced in Jn 14 and 16. See **Article**, *70. Union Life.* See also fn Php 1:19.

[136] The Roman province of Asia (we would call it Asia minor today).

[137] Paul repeats this theme of accountability often: 1:16; 4:8,14; See also Php 1:6,10; 2:16; 4:1 fn 1:6; 4:1. Note here that kind acts by believers will be rewarded. Nothing will be lost of our work for God, be it seemingly small or seemingly big. Particularly will love-gifted people receive their rewards—which are so often overlooked today. See *accountability, love gifts,* **Glossary**.

[138] Not only will leaders be held accountable and rewarded or the opposite but also lay leaders and followers. Onesiphorus is one of the great unsung heroes. Here we have the gift of helps or mercy in action. Where would leaders be without people who care and support via the love cluster of gifts. See *helps, mercy, love gifts,* **Glossary**.

[139] The Greek word here is grace, (SRN 5485). Paul uses this in 1Ti, 2Ti and Tit in the sense of the *enabling presence of God in a life* so as to cause that one to persevere victoriously. See *grace,* **Glossary**.

2 And the things that you have heard from me, confirmed by many witnesses,[140] commit to trustworthy people, who will be competent to teach others also.[141]

3 So endure hardness,[142] as a good soldier of Jesus Christ. 4 If you go on a military expedition you can't get enmeshed in civilian life or you won't please your commanding officer. 5 And if a person competes to win an athletic crown, that one follows the rules or else will not be crowned. 6 A hard working farmer ought to be the first to enjoy the harvest. 7 Consider these analogies and the Lord will help you understand them.[143]

8 Remember that Jesus Christ, a descendant of David, was raised from the dead—that's my gospel[144] 9 Because I preach this I have been treated as a criminal and put in prison. But the word of God can not be imprisoned. 10 For this reason I take patiently this suffering[145] in order that those God has chosen can come to know the salvation and eternal glory which is in Christ Jesus.

---

[140] This, *confirmed by many others,* avoids the cultic-like things that can be passed on from a strong leader who otherwise unchecked might sway people to heretical teaching and practices.

[141] This is a great leadership selection and development verse. *Commit* (SRN 3908) means to entrust. Leadership is an entrustment which should be passed on, entrusted to others. One of the seven major leadership lessons derived from comparative study of leaders who finished well involves this principle. *Effective leaders view leadership selection and development as a priority function in their ministry.* The Navigators have always used this verse to challenge leaders to develop other leaders. They note the four generations involved: Paul, Timothy, trustworthy ones, others. See **Articles,** *10. Entrustment—A Leadership Responsibility; 29. Leadership Lessons—Seven Major Lessons Identified.*

[142] Note again this repeated theme, suffering for Christ. See also 2Ti 1:12; 2:3,10; 4:5. I am going to repeat this little reminder at every incident because we as leaders need to know this experientially.

[143] I think these three analogies are applied directly to Timothy's situation. The *soldier illustration* is a warning for Timothy not to get sidetracked (this is repeatedly admonished in 1Ti also); the *athlete illustration* warns that it will take discipline to pull off the ministry. Timothy must maintain integrity (play by the rules) as he faces the Ephesian problems. The *farmer illustration* probably goes to the heart of the lack of financial support for Timothy. No leader likes to have to push his or her own situation where finances are concerned. 1Ti 5:17,18 also dealt with this. Timothy was not being supported. Paul says, "You need to be."

[144] This is an important doctrinal aside which treats the very heart of Paul's gospel—Jesus' resurrection from the dead. For other spontaneous doctrinal utterances see also 1Ti 1:17; 2:3-6; 3:16; 4:10; 6:15,16 and 2Ti 1:9,10; 2:8,19.

[145] Paul knew that his imprisonment, though a real example of suffering, was not the end of his ministry. He could endure it because he knew even his imprisonment was being used by God. The word would go forth. See also 2Ti 1:12; 2:3,8,12; 4:5 for other mentions of suffering.

11 This is a reliable saying:

> Since we have died with him,
> we shall also live with him:
> 12 If we continue enduring hardship,[146]
> we shall also rule with him:
> if we deny him, he also will deny us:
> 13 If we are unfaithful, he remains faithful:
> he cannot be false to himself.[147]

II. (Ch 2:14-26)   Warnings for the Newly Selected Leaders To Aid Them in Persevering

14 Remind all of these things. Solemnly order them in the presence of the Lord not to argue over useless words which destroy the listeners.[148] 15 Make every effort[149] to win[150] God's approval,[151] a worker who does not need to be ashamed—[152] one who handles

---

[146] If you are a leader you will suffer, sooner or later. Again recognize this important, repeated warning. See: 2Ti 1:12; 2:3,10; 4:5.

[147] This is another doctrinal aside. See also See also 1Ti 1:17; 2:3-6; 3:16; 4:10; 6:15,16 and 2Ti 1:9,10; 2:8,19. All leaders need core doctrinal truths which are part of them and come out spontaneously from time-to-time.

[148] See 1Ti 1:3,4,6,7; 2:12; 4:1-5; 4:7; 6:3,4 and basic antidote in 1Ti 3:15. See also heresy fn 1Ti 1:3,4; 2:5,6,12,13,15; 4:3,7; 6:4. In all of these we are reminded of the importance of heresy and its disrupting influence in the church.

[149] 2Ti 2:15 is a crucial leadership verse, one of the most important pieces of advice that Paul gives in the whole epistle. This phrase *make every effort* (SRN 4704) translates one Greek word, which carries with it the sense of time—hasten or hurry to—and the notion of diligent effort. Leaders are people who have a sense of urgency and a desire to achieve.

[150] *To win* (SRN 3936) is used in the sense of presenting to God one's ministry for His approval. This is a major Pauline leadership value dealing with motivation for ministry. One's ministry, especially ʹith regard to using the word correctly, should be done primarily for the Lord's approval. See **Article**, *40. Motivating Factors for Ministry.*

[151] *Approval* is a picture word, (SRN 1384), bringing to mind, for a Greek reader familiar with Athens, a person of integrity who would not accept counterfeit coins, i.e. coins not up to the standard weight. This practice of passing less than the standard coin was wide spread. See *integrity*, **Glossary**.

[152] *Not ashamed* (SRN 422) carries the sense of can't be put to shame, i.e. allowing no cause for anyone to criticize one's ministry of the word.

correctly the word of truth.[153] 16 But avoid ungodly useless discussions that lead to more and more ungodliness.[154] 17 That kind of teaching will spread like an incurable disease.[155] Hymenaeus and Philetus are like this. 18 They have strayed from the truth,[156] saying that the resurrection is past already. They have destroyed the faith of some. 19 But God's foundational truth stands unshakable, having this guarantee; The Lord knows those who are his. Those who claim to belong to Christ must turn away from wrong doing.[157]

20 But in a large house there are not only gold and silver utensils, there are also wood and clay utensils. Some are for special occasions and others for regular use. 21 A person remaining pure[158] will be a utensil dedicated for special occasions for God's special purposes. Such a one is prepared for every good work.[159] 22 Avoid[160] the passions of youth. Instead seek eagerly to have in your life righteousness, faith, love, and peace, along with all those who with pure hearts cry out to the Lord for his help.

---

[153] *Handles correctly*, (SRN 3718), is a compound word meaning: (1) to cut straight to the point, like a surgeon's quick and accurate incision; (2) to follow along a straight path, not deviate. It means an accurate use of the word. This underlies my third concept of a Bible Centered leader: *has grasped the intent of Scriptural books and their content in such a way as to apply them to current situations*. In every generation this admonition is needed again. Leaders who know and use their Bibles well with integrity are in demand. See *Bible centered leader*, **Glossary**. See **Article**, *72. Vanishing Breed*.

[154] This admonition against heretical teaching is strongly contrasted to what has just been said about handling truth correctly. Here is a negative illustration of what not to do. See *heresy*, **Glossary**.

[155] We get our word gangrene from this Greek word (SRN 1044). It denotes an infectious spreading which is incurable.

[156] This is a repeated theme—danger of turning away from Christianity (1Ti 1:6,20; 4:16; 5:11,15; 6:10; 2Ti 2:18, 3:8). Leaders today are not aware of just how many are turning away—see especially 2nd generation Christians of ethnic churches. Paul warns us about this.

[157] This doctrinal aside is a subtle warning on the difficulty of discerning who is and who are not really Christians. See also 1Ti 1:17; 2:3-6; 3:16; 4:10; 6:15,16 and 2Ti 1:9,10; 2:8,19.

[158] This is another of Paul's repeated themes, purity of heart (along with purity of conscience). He reemphasizes this again in the very next verse, see vs 22. And note his appeal toward a select group of people who want purity of heart. Timothy must have been moved. See also 1Ti 1:5; 3:9; 2Ti 1:3; 2:22; Tit 1:15 (three occurrences).

[159] This word, (SRN 2090), a past perfect, (that is, prepared in the past with continuous aftermath in the future) and carries the sense of *having been prepared for every good work*. This is one of two times in which Paul talks about a leader being prepared to every good work. Here the emphasis is on character, purity. In the other passage, 2Ti 3:17 the emphasis is on knowing the word of God and having its impact in one's life—the second concept of a Bible Centered leader: *who personally has been shaped by Biblical values*. See *Bible centered leader*, **Glossary**. See **Article**, *72. Vanishing Breed*.

[160] *Avoid* (SRN 5343) translates the complex metaphor, run away from or flee. One is reminded of Joseph literally doing this—Gen 39. See *metaphor* **Glossary**. See **Article**, *13. Figures and Idioms in the Bible*.

23 But avoid foolish and ignorant discussions which lead to quarrels. 24 The Lord's servant must not quarrel; instead be gentle unto all, skillfully teaching and being patient, 25 gently instructing those opponents. Perhaps God will give them opportunity to repent and see the truth.[161] 26 Then they may come to their senses and escape the devil's trap[162] who has caught them and has them doing whatever he wants.

III. (Ch 3:1-17) Persevering in Difficult Days Ahead

Chapter 3

1 Realize this. In the last days[163] there will be very difficult times. 2 For people will be extremely self-centered, greedy, boastful and conceited; they will scoff at God, be disobedient to parents, unthankful, wicked. 3 They will be unkind, merciless, slanderers and have no self-control; they will be savage, hating what is good. 4 They will be traitors, reckless, filled with pride; they will love pleasure more than God. 5 They may have the outward form of our religion but miss its real power. Avoid these kind of people. 6 Some of these get into homes and win the confidence of women who are burdened with guilt for their sins. 7 These women are looking for something—some new truth—but they never find it. 8 Now as Jannes and Jambres withstood Moses, so do these teachers also resist the truth: depraved minds, having abandoned[164] the faith. 9 But they won't get far. Everyone will see their stupidity just like Jannes and Jambres.

---

[161] The amazing thing about this admonition is *who it comes from*. God has done a marvelous transforming work in Paul's heart over the years. Here, he is one who gently instructs in order to win by persuasion his opponents. In earlier years, he was argumentative and brusque only basically caring that he was right and his opponents wrong. Gentle leaders who can persuade are one of the great needs of the hour. A leader should be transformed over the years by the shaping work of the Holy Spirit so as to demonstrate the fruit of the Spirit. For Paul's transformation into a more gentle leader, see also, the *introductory discussion given* in the Philemon Leadership Commentary under the heading, **Philemon As A Source of Leadership Topics**. Especially note the remarks on Paul becoming more gentle.

[162] This is the only occurrence of spiritual warfare in 2Ti. Note it has to do with people blinded, not open to the truth. But see also 1Ti 1:18-20; 3:6; 3:7; 4:1 and fn 1Ti 3:6. See also **Key Leadership Lessons— 1 Timothy**, *Topic: Spiritual Warfare*. See **Articles**, *64. Spiritual Warfare—Satan's Tactics; 65. Spiritual Warfare— Two Extremes to Avoid.*

[163] Evidently Paul was describing the times Timothy was to face since he was warning him about them. But the last days is used theologically to refer to the end times. If these things were true for Timothy almost 2000 years ago, how much more for our own days, so much closer to the end times. See *last days*, **Glossary.**

[164] This is again a repeated theme—the danger of turning away from Christianity. See also 1Ti 1:6, 20; 4:16; 5:11,15; 6:10; 2Ti 2:18, 3:8. It is interesting that Paul, dominantly a harvest model leader should be so interested in this pastoral function of keeping and maturing believers. Evidently in his long experience of apostolic ministry he saw that much more than just reaping must be done. See *harvest model, shepherd model,* **Glossary.**

10 But you fully know my teaching, my lifestyle, my purpose in life, my faith, my steadfastness, my love, my endurance.[165] 11 I was persecuted at Antioch, at Iconium, at Lystra; I endured those persecutions. Yet the Lord delivered me out of them. 12 And indeed all who will live godly lives—in union with Christ Jesus— will suffer persecution. 13 But evil people and impostors will go from bad to worse. They will deceive others, and they will be deceived themselves.[166] 14 But, as for you, stay with that which you have experientially learned. You are confident of it because you know who you have learned it from.[167] 15 From early childhood[168] you have known the holy scriptures.[169] They have given you the wisdom to accept salvation through faith which is in Christ Jesus. 16 Every scripture inspired by God is profitable[170] for teaching, for reprimand, for correction, for leading one to righteous living.[171] 17 That a person of God

---

[165] This, vs 3:10-17, is one of the great passages on a mentoring relationship. Here you have the mentor, Paul, describing a very personal, open, transparent, vulnerability in his mentoring with Timothy. The mentoring types of teacher, counselor, and contemporary model are reflected in this intense passage, appealing to Timothy. *See mentor, mentor counselor, mentor model, mentor teacher,* **Glossary.** See **Articles,** *38. Mentoring—An Informal Training Model; 45. Paul—Developer Par Excellence.*

[166] Any leader can be blindsided by self-deception. One of Paul's antidotes is to recognize good models who have experientially confirmed truth for you (verse 14). When you differ from them you are in danger of self-deception. See *contemporary model, modeling,* **Glossary.**

[167] Trustworthy models are needed early on in the life of a developing leader. This is particularly true when transitioning into ministry and/or when facing a new situation. But it is also true that leaders will need various kinds of mentoring all of their lives. comparative case studies have shown that effective leaders will have from 10-25 important mentoring experiences throughout their lifetime. See *mentor,* **Glossary.**

[168] The foundational heritage pattern is referred to here, highlighting one of its advantages (vs 15). Also one who is familiar with the Scriptures, even just the facts of them, has a jump start on learning the Scriptures for use in ministry once the call of God on a life is received. See *heritage pattern,* **Glossary.**

[169] Paul is here referring to the O.T. Scriptures which can be expanded today to include the N.T. Scriptures as well. See *Bible centered leader,* **Glossary.** See **Article,** *72. Vanishing Breed.*

[170] *Profitable* (SRN 5624) comes from a word meaning used to advantage or having an advantage.

[171] This verse has as its intent, not the doctrine of the inspiration of Scripture, but that every inspired (God breathed) Scripture has usefulness for equipping Timothy for his leadership (and by extension other leaders). See *Bible centered leader,* **Glossary.** See **Article,** *72. Vanishing Breed.*

may be equipped, completely ready[172] to do well.[173]

IV. (Ch 4:1-8) End Result of Persevering--A Good Finish

Chapter 4

1 In the presence of God and the Lord Jesus Christ,[174] who shall judge the living and the dead when he appears to set up his kingdom,[175] I strongly urge you with these admonitions: 2 Publicly proclaim[176] the word; be persistent[177] whether the time is right for it or not. Patiently convince, admonish, and encourage with your teaching. 3 For the time will come when they will not endure wholesome teaching. Instead, following their

---

[172] This is an instance of the superlative (i.e. repetitive idiom) being used. *Completely ready* (SRN 1822) is a combination of two words, one an intensifying preposition and a root word which is a derivative of *equipped*, (SRN 739). So what we have here is equipped, thoroughly equipped, that is, really, really equipped. I captured it using *equipped, really ready.* My concepts 1 and 2 of the Bible centered leader flow from this verse: (1) whose leadership is being informed by the Bible and (2) who personally has been shaped by Biblical values. See *Bible centered leader, capture, superlative idiom,* **Glossary.**

[173] Seeing that this admonition is given to a leader in a leadership situation, I do not think I am far wrong to paraphrase this passage as follows. *Every Scripture inspired of God is profitable for (1) leadership insights* (doctrine), *(2) pointing out of leadership errors* (reproof), *(3) suggesting what to do about leadership errors* (correction), *(4) for highlighting how to model a righteous life* (instruction in righteousness) *in order that God's leader* (Timothy) *may be well equipped to lead God's people* (the special good work given to the young leader Timothy). (Clinton paraphrase—slanted toward Timothy's leadership situation).

[174] This is a strong oath-like reference to authority which reinforces the giving of the strong command. See Also 2Ti 2:14; 1Ti 6:13; 1Ti 5:21.

[175] This is another doctrinal aside—giving a kingdom truth. See also 1Ti 1:17; 2:3-6; 3:16; 4:10; 6:15,16 and 2Ti 1:9,10; 2:8,19.

[176] The words *publicly proclaim,* (SRN 2784), mean to proclaim after the manner of a herald, always with the suggestion of formality, seriousness and an authority which must be listened to and obeyed. Heralds were sent to make governmental announcements and as such were treated as authoritative represents of the higher governmental officials. The word preach is often used to translate this word. The spiritual gift most associated with this word is exhortation. See *exhortation, spiritual gift,* **Glossary.**

[177] *Be persistent,* (SRN 2186), carries the idea of pay attention to and be ready for. It is used to describe rain that suddenly falls unexpectedly. Whether the time is right or not translates two words back to back, seasonably or unseasonably. It is an emphatic way of saying, seize every opportunity to proclaim the word of God.

own desires they will find teachers who tell them what they want to hear. 4 And they will turn away from listening to the truth and heed fictitious teaching. 5 But you be discreet about these things. Endure hardships.[178] Preach to win others to Christ.[179] Demonstrate fully[180] what your ministry is all about.

6 As for me, I am ready to be sacrificed.[181] The time for me to depart this life is near. 7 I have run a good race.[182] I have fulfilled my God-given destiny.[183] I still have my faith intact.

---

[178] Evidently Paul knew that repetition is the key to retention. Here he reminds us again that suffering will happen, be prepared for it. See also: 2Ti 1:12; 2:3,10; 4:5.

[179] Literally, do the work of an evangelist. Normally evangelism would be a vested spiritual gift that some leaders have. A leader can, however, always expect God to provide the necessary gifts to get the job done. Sometimes this will happen through others. Sometimes the leader, himself/herself will have that gift. At other times, they may not have the gift permanently but are enabled to do what is needed for a time—a gifted pattern called *role enablement*. It is not clear that Timothy had this as a vested gift. See *evangelism, role enablement, spiritual gift, vested gifts,* **Glossary**.

[180] Literally, *fulfill your ministry*, (SRN 4135) means to carry out to the fullest or make it very clear with convincing persuasion.

[181] *Ready to be sacrificed*, (SRN 2235 and SRN 4689) literally means *already being poured out as a drink offering*, a special sacrificial offering in the Levitical law. It is used here, figuratively, to describe one whose blood is poured out in a violent death for the cause of God. Paul really knew his death was at hand. A drink offering. See also Php 2:17 where Paul refers to this same offering in terms of his sacrificial service for the Philippians. Sacrificial service is at the heart of shepherd leadership. See *shepherd model*, **Glossary**.

[182] Literally, this is *the good struggle I have struggled*, a use of the superlative repetitive idiom. The two words for struggle are the noun form and verb form from which we derive our words agony and agonize and refer to an Olympic athlete who is disciplining himself for a marathon or other event.

[183] Fulfilled my destiny, literally I have finished or completed (SRN 5758) a perfect action, i.e. already done it with on going results, my course (SRN 1408). Course, used three times in the New Testament, refers to life's destiny, the pathway set before one to do. The destiny pattern usually follows a threefold pattern: destiny preparation, destiny revelation, and destiny fulfillment. This idea of already completing it is the use of a certainty idiom, the prophetic past. It is so certain that he speaks of it in the past tense as if it had already happened. See Ac 20:24 where Paul states his desire to finish his course. See also, Ac 13:25 where the same word refers to John the Baptist's having finished his course. See *certainty idiom, destiny preparation, destiny fulfillment, destiny revelation, prophetic past, sense of destiny,* **Glossary**. See **Articles**, *8. Destiny Pattern; 42. Paul—A Sense of Destiny.*

8 And now for my prize, a crown of righteousness. The Lord, the righteous judge, will award it to me at that day.[184] And not to me only, but unto all those who eagerly await[185] his return.[186]

V.   (Ch 4:9-18) Personal Matters

9 Do your best to come to me soon. 10 For Demas, pursuing the things of this world, has deserted me[187] and gone to Thessalonica. Crescens went to Galatia and Titus is gone to Dalmatia. 11 Only Luke is with me.[188] Take Mark,[189] and bring him with you: for he will be helpful to me in my ministry. 12 I sent Tychicus to Ephesus. 13 The coat

---

[184] Again we see Paul's value, *A leader will give accountability for ministry at that day.* Eternal rewards are a motivating factor for a leader. Note also his remark about a righteous judge. He knows that he is now being tried by judges who are not necessarily just ones. But he knows that God will judge correctly. This is the nearest thing you will get to a complaint from Paul, with his sovereign mindset. This repeated theme, accountability occurs frequently: 1:16; 4:8,14; See also Php 1:6,10; 2:16; 4:1 fn 1:6; 4:1. See *accountability, leadership value, sovereign mindset,* **Glossary.** See **Article,** *58. Sovereign Mindset.*

[185] This is one of the great motivating factors behind a leader's ministry. Stated as a value, *A leader ought to be motivated to lead well in anticipation of the Lord's return.* This was a major value with M.R. DeHaan one of the great Radio Bible Teachers in the 20th Century—A remark, **PERHAPS TODAY!**, referring to 1 Th 4:16, emphasized its importance is on his tombstone. See **Article,** *40. Motivating Factors for Ministry.*

[186] Vs 4:6-8 show that Paul finished well. He is the classic case of a N.T. church leader finishing well. All six characteristics of a good finish are seen: (1) vibrant personal relationship with God; (2) have a learning posture; (3) Christ-likeness in character; (4) live by Biblical convictions; (5) leave behind ultimate contributions; (6) fulfill a sense of destiny. One of the major leadership contributions of 2Ti is this challenge to finish well, which Paul models. See *modeling,* **Glossary. Article,** *16. Finishing Well—Six Characteristics.*

[187] The implication is, *abandoned the faith,* turning away from Christianity—a repeated theme. This is a strong word, deserted me. And it is a strong word for us today. Few leaders finish well. See 1Ti 1:6, 20; 5:11,15; 6:10; 2Ti 2:18, 3:8.

[188] This is the last reference to Luke who authored Lk and Ac. Luke was developed by Paul on his traveling team. Note in these closing words how Paul's value of personal relationships in ministry stands out. Notice the personal names throughout the epistle: Demas, Crescens, Titus, Luke, Mark, Tychicus Carpus, Prisca, Aquila, Onesiphorus, Erastus, Trophimus. Eubulus, Pudens, Linus, Claudia. See **Article,** *43. Paul—And His Companions.*

[189] This is evidence of a heart change in Paul—See Paul's argument in Ac 15:37-41 with Barnabas about John Mark. Probably a heart change in John Mark as well. It is good to see a leader who can continue to grow. Paul was such a leader. He is a much gentler leader now, at the end of his life, than when he first began his cross-cultural ministry with Barnabas and John Mark.

that I left at Troas with Carpus, when you come, bring it. And my books, and papers, bring them.[190]

14 Alexander the coppersmith[191] did me much harm; the Lord will reward him for what he has done.[192] 15 You be careful of him. He has fiercely opposed our message.

16 At my first defense no one stood with me; all deserted me. May God not hold it against them.[193]17 In any case, the Lord stood with me, and strengthened me[194] so that I might fully preach the full message to the Gentiles.[195] I was delivered from a certain death. 18 And the Lord will deliver me from every evil attack. He will bring me safely into his heavenly kingdom.[196] To Him be glory for ever and ever. Amen.

---

[190] This is one of the evidences of Paul's maintaining a learning posture. A learning posture is one of the six characteristics of a leader finishing well. It is also one of the five factors enhancing a good finish. See *learning posture*, **Glossary**. See **Articles**, *15. Finishing Well—Five Factors Enhancing; 16. Finishing Well—Six Characteristics.*

[191] Paul not only liberally sprinkles in people he has personal relationships with in ministry but also names of those opposing the ministry. One of the sometimes surprising things which makes ministry so difficult and complex is this fact of fierce opposition. Notice, Paul does not attribute it to Satan, though that is probably true.

[192] Paul here extends accountability, in a final, ultimate sense to non-believers, as well as believers and leaders. Evidently this repeated theme of accountability is very important to a leader: See 1:16; 4:8,14; See also Php 1:6,10; 2:16; 4:1 fn 1:6; 4:1.

[193] This is evidence of Christ-likeness in his life, one of the six characteristics of finishing well. Paul first saw this, years before, when he held the coats of those stoning Stephen. See Ac 7:58,59. Now Paul follows that model. See *modeling*, **Glossary**. See **Article**, *16. Finishing Well—Six Characteristics.*

[194] This is an instance of the shaping activity that in leadership emergence theory is called *divine affirmation*. God in some special way gives inner confirmation at a needy time. All leaders need such affirmation from time-to-time. See *divine affirmation*, **Glossary**.

[195] This is one of the indications of Paul's fulfilling his destiny, one of the six characteristics of finishing well. Ananias proclaimed long ago, Ac 9:15,16, that part of Paul's destiny would be to witness before the Gentiles and kings and to suffer for Christ. Paul has lived out that destiny revelation. See *destiny fulfillment, sense of destiny*, **Glossary**. See **Article**, *16. Finishing Well—Six Characteristics.*

[196] See fn 2Ti ch 1, vs12. This is another reference to the notion of leadership entrustment and protection of it till done. See *invincibility principle*, **Glossary**.

19 Greet Prisca and Aquila[197] for me and the family of Onesiphorus. 20 Erastus has stayed at Corinth. I left Trophimus at Miletum since he was sick.[198] 21 Try to get here before winter. Eubulus, Pudens, Linus, and Claudia all send their greetings to you along with other brothers and sisters.

22 The Lord be with your spirit. Grace be with you.[199] Amen.

<<The second epistle unto Timotheus, ordained the first bishop of the church of the Ephesians, was written from Rome, when Paul was brought before Nero the second time.>>[200]

---

[197] This is a leadership team, wife and husband, involved in hosting several house churches. Prisca, also called Priscilla seems to be the lead person (mentioned first in the majority of listings of their names). They, with Priscilla probably in the lead, grounded Apollos in the Gospel truths (see Ac 18:26). Priscilla is teaching in this church, most likely. Another indication that 1Ti 2:12 is not prohibiting women from teaching or leadership but is dealing with a heretical teaching. Paul has the highest regard for this couple, see Romans 16:3,4. See **Article**, *20. Gender and Leadership*.

[198] Paul had healed before, using supernatural healing. So this seems a clear indication that not all folks can be healed. Certainly Paul would have healed him were it the case that all people can be divinely healed.

[199] These are the last words we have from Paul. Note they concern grace. The Greek word here is *grace*, (SRN 5485). Paul uses this in 1Ti, 2Ti and Tit in the sense of the enabling presence of God in a life so as to cause that one to persevere victoriously. See fn 2:1 where I translate grace by special enablemeı ˙. It is interesting to see that all three great church leaders, Peter, Paul, and John close their writing ministry with words about grace. And all three seem to use it in the sense of the *enabling presence of God*. A leader will not make it to the end without knowing experientially this grace—the enabling presence of God. See *grace*, **Glossary**.

[200] This occurs in at least one manuscript. If true Timothy must have learned about this grace spoken of. And the Ephesians must have eventually recognized his leadership. See also Heb 13:23.

For Further Leadership Study

General

2Ti is dominantly a leadership book so that everything in it is important. All the articles referred to should be read. Words should be looked up in the **Glossary**. Other references listed in the comments should be looked up. **The Key Leadership Lessons** should be studied thoroughly and even be expanded upon.

Suggestions for Further Study

1. Study each of these lessons given in the **Key Leadership Lessons—2 Timothy** and then study each one comparatively throughout Paul's life both for validation and development.
2. Paul finished well. He is the classic N.T. leader who finished well. Using the six characteristics of finishing well, identify other leaders in the Bible who finished well. There are less than 20.
3. Paul's mentor-mix includes spiritual guide, teacher, counselor, coach, contemporary model and sponsor. Using these six categories, identify passages under each category which illustrate a mentoring function of that category. You should probably do this exercise across both 1Ti and 2Ti.
4. Take any one of the repeated themes of 2Ti and study it in depth across Paul's ministry: a. conscience; b. suffering; c. abandoning the faith; d. doctrinal asides; e. doxologies.
5. Study the book of Ac for illustrations of Paul's use of spiritual warfare. Study also Eph 6:10-20 as a core passage on Pauline Spiritual Warfare guidelines.

Special Comments

As is the case with 1Ti and Tit, this is a book about leadership. Its basic ideas should permeate a ministry philosophy. Emerging leaders need to immerse themselves in it until they see, feel, believe, and engraft its values.

Personal Response

1. What is the most significant leadership insight you have gained from your study of 2Ti?

2. What one idea from this study can you put into practice in your own leadership? How?

3. Immediate Application: List an idea from this study that you can share with someone today?

   a. Idea:

   b. Who?:

Your Observations.

You may want to jot down important insights you want to remember. You may wish to note follow-up intents.

Relevance of the Article to 1,2 Timothy

This article was written primarily for the 1,2 Co commentary. Two of Paul's core passages on judgment occur in the Corinthian letters—1 Cor 3 and 2 Cor 5. But Paul also emphasizes repeatedly in 1,2 Ti that leaders would have to give an account for their influence. See especially his triumphant closing remarks in 2 Ti 4:6-8 and Leadership Topics on finishing well and ultimate accountability.

1. Accountability—Standing Before God As A Leader

Introduction

What do the following biblical quotes have in common?

> 27 Each person is destined to die; and then they will be judged by God. Heb 9:27

> 10 That at the name of Jesus every knee should bow, of those in heaven, and of those on earth, and those under the earth. 11 Further, every tongue will confess that Jesus Christ is Lord, to the glory of God the Father. Php 2:10, 11

> 10 For we must all stand before Christ and be judged. We will each receive what we deserve for what we have done in these bodies,—whether good or bad. 2Co 5:10

How does the following quote, which is similar, differ?

> 17 Obey your leaders. Follow what they say. They diligently watch out for your spiritual welfare since they must give an account of their ministry to God. Give them occasion to lead with joy as they see you obeying. Otherwise they lead with lack of joy. And that doesn't help you either. Heb 13:17

The first three passages, two by Paul, and one by the author of Heb talk about the general notion of accountability. All people will be held accountable before God for their lives and what they did with them. But the Heb 13:17 passage narrows this accountability to leaders in particular. It avers that leaders will give an account to God for their ministry efforts.

Paul has an underlying value regarding accountability and his ministry efforts.

> **Leader's actions must be restrained by the fact they will ultimately give an account to God for their leadership.**

Paul operates always with a view that he will answer to God for his leadership influence.

Accountability

This value is seen as a motivating factor in Paul's ministry to the Philippians and the Corinthians. Paul, in 1Co and 2Co, more than any other of his books shows his awareness of this very important leadership value. In 1,2Co he uses this notion to clear his character of the accusations against him. He reveals his honesty before God, declares his responsibility to God, and in general claims a clear conscience before God concerning his leadership actions. Motivations, decisions, and explanations in general are all weighed in light of God's appraisal of them. Paul was an accountable leader—constantly reminding his readers that he was aware of God's awareness and judgment of his actions as a leader.[201] Two leadership observations arising from this notion of accountability include:

a. Leaders must be restrained by the fact that they will ultimately give an account to God for their leadership actions.
b. Leaders show burden for a ministry by recognizing their accountability to God for it.

Stewardship Model

Jesus teaches with authority this general notion of accountability. The stewardship model is a philosophical model which is founded on the central thrust of several accountability passages, that is, that a leader must give account of his/her ministry to God. These accountability parables include: Mt 20 Laborers in the Vineyard; Mt 24 The Waiting Servants; Mt 25 The Ten Virgins; Mt 25 The Ten Talents; Lk 16 The Worldly Wise Steward; Lk 19 The Pounds. Paul and the author of Heb build on Jesus' teaching in such passages as: Ro 14:11,12; 1Co 3:5-9,12-15; 4:1-5; 2Co 5:10; Php 2:10,11; Heb 9:27, 13:17; Jas 3:1; 1Pe 5:1-4.

Some of the basic values which underlie the Stewardship Model include:

1. God holds a leader accountable for leadership influence and for growth and conduct of followers. A leader must recognize this accountability.
2. Leaders must recognize an ultimate accounting of a leader to God in eternity for one's performance in leadership.
3. Leaders should recognize that they will receive rewards for faithfulness to their ministry in terms of abilities, skills, gifts and opportunities. This is one motivating factor for leading.
4. Leaders ought to build upon abilities, skills, and gifts to maximize potential and use for God.
5. Leaders ought to know that they frequently must hold to higher standards than followers due to "the above reproach" and modeling impact they must have on followers.

Paul exemplifies these Stewardship Model values in his ministry.

Conclusion

Leaders should be aware of giving accountability to God for their ministry. Such a value can change day-to-day ministry. Such a value maintained over a lifetime is a springboard to a good finish for a leader. Such a value is greatly needed, especially by strong leaders.

See **Articles**, 25. *Jesus—Five Leadership Models: Shepherd, Harvest, Steward, Servant, Intercessor; 51. Pauline Leadership Values; 41. Motivating Principles—Pauline Influence; 2. Apostolic Functions.*

---

[201] See especially 1Co 1:8; 3:13,15; 4:5; 2Co 1:14,23; 2:18; 4:2; 5:10; 11:31; 12:19; Php 1:6,10; 2:16. For other references see 2Th 2:2; 1Ti 5:19,20; 2Ti 1:16; 4:8,14.

Relevance of the Article to 1,2 Timothy

This article was written primarily for use with the Titus commentary. However, it is helpful for us to recognize the three phases of apostolic ministry and to see the Ephesian ministry as third Phase work. See function 5 Combat Heresy (both orthodoxy and orthopraxy). Heresy refers to deviation from a standard, whether in belief (orthodoxy) or practice (orthopraxy). e.g. In 1Ti both are present in the Ephesian church (as prophesied in Ac 20:30). This article along with the two following articles details thinking about apostolic work. You will see that Paul was performing a number of these apostolic functions with the Ephesian church, but especially combating heresy.

2. Apostolic Functions

Introduction

What do apostles do? Comparative studies in Ac, 1,2Ti and Tit reveal a number of functions that are symptomatic of apostles. But before looking at what apostles do perhaps it is in order to examine some characteristics of apostolic workers such as giftedness, power bases used, leadership styles and leadership models. This will lay a good foundation for understanding apostolic functions.

Apostolic Giftedness

All apostolic workers have spiritual gifts as the focal element of their giftedness set.[202] But what spiritual gifts? First of all, an apostle in this technical sense being examined in this article, is one who has the gift of apostleship. Second, such leaders are often multi-gifted and include various power and word gifts. The below definitions refer to giftedness seen in apostles.

Definition   The <u>gift of apostleship</u> refers to a special leadership capacity to move with authority from God to create new ministry structures (churches and para-church groups) to meet needs and to develop and appoint leadership in these structures. **Its central thrust is Creating New Ministry.**

Definition   <u>Power gifts</u> refer to a category of spiritual gifts which authenticate the reality of God by demonstrating God's intervention in today's world. These include: tongues, interpretation of tongues, discernings of spirits, kinds of healings, kinds of power (miracles), prophecy, faith, word of wisdom, word of knowledge.

Definition   <u>Word gifts</u> refer to a category of spiritual gifts used to clarify and explain about God. These help us understand about God including His nature, His purposes and how we can relate to Him and be a part of His purposes. These include: teaching, exhortation, pastoring, evangelism, apostleship, prophecy, ruling, and sometimes word of wisdom, word of knowledge, and faith (a word of). All leaders have at least one of these and often several of these.

---

[202] <u>Giftedness set</u> refers to natural abilities, acquired skills, and spiritual gifts which a leader has as resources to use in ministry. <u>Focal element</u> refers to the dominate component of a giftedness set—either natural abilities, acquired skills, or spiritual gifts.

Frequently, in addition to power gifts which authenticate and validate an apostle's ministry, an apostle will have the gift of faith—which enables a strong projection of vision on others.[203]

What Power Bases Enforce Apostolic Functions?

Apostles use various power bases[204] to enforce their leadership influence. While, most would recognize spiritual authority as the ideal, they frequently use other forms since they often are dealing with immature followers in new works. A prioritized list of power forms seen in apostolic ministry would include personal authority, competent authority, coercive authority, induced authority—all laced with a sense of spiritual authority. Networking power often buttresses power used by apostolic workers.

What Leadership Styles Flow From the Power Bases?

Apostles frequently use highly directive leadership styles. A prioritized list of leadership styles seen in apostolic ministry includes: apostolic style, father-initiator, father-guardian, confrontation, indirect conflict, obligation persuasion, imitator. Highly indirect styles are used basically only with loyal trusted leaders.

What Leadership Models Dominate Apostolic Work?

Apostolic workers dominantly are driven by values underlying the stewardship model and the harvest model. Apostolic workers have a strong sense of calling and desire to accomplish for God. And for the most part this is directed toward the outward functions of the Great Commission as seen in the Harvest model. Servant, Shepherd, and Intercessor models are less seen in apostolic ministries.

Apostolic workers are dominantly task-oriented leaders with strong inspirational leadership. Usually apostolic workers lack relational leadership skills and must depend on others to supplement this or suffer the consequences of conflict, confrontation, and large back doors in their ministry as emerging workers leave them.

What Are Some Apostolic Functions?

Table 1, 2 Tim 2-1 below lists seven major headings for apostolic functions observed in the N.T. Church Leadership Era. While there may be other apostolic functions these at least are highlighted in the Ac and epistles. I subsume a number of minor apostolic functions under these higher level categories.

Table 1,2 Ti 2-1. Apostolic Functions

Function	N.T. Indication	Description/Explanation
1. Start New Ministries	Paul and Barnabas, Ac 13; Paul Ac 16, 18	Paul and Barnabas inaugurate the missionary movement. Paul breaks open a new work in Europe and other new works in Asia. These are usually creative new approaches to ministry which challenge traditional approaches. Power ministry is often used to validate the apostle's ministry and authenticate God's existence, power, and presence. When starting new ministries whether churches, movements, organizations, apostolic workers attract followers due to their personality, competency, and power seen in ministry. Paul tried to start indigenized churches.[205] Most apostolic workers are driven by values underlying the Harvest Leadership model, though these values may be implicit.

[203] Apostolic workers are strong leaders who use highly directive leadership styles. Those with the gift of faith obtain vision from God and can exercise strong inspirational leadership to motivate and recruit to the vision. They attract followers to their cause.

[204] Wrong sees power in terms of a power holder, a power subject and the means the power holder uses to gain compliance from the power subject. Power base deals with the means. Force, Manipulation, Authority, and Persuasion are the general categories containing various power bases.

[205] An indigenized church has its own leadership from its own people and is organized to survive independently of outside leadership from other cultures and operates with appropriate forms, rites, and ministry fitting to its own culture.

2. Appoint Leaders	Paul and Barnabas do (1st missionary trip). Paul does this on all his missionary trips. Titus did this in Crete. Timothy does this in Ephesus.	Apostolic workers raise up leadership including selecting, developing and giving training that will develop these workers; they impart gifts as Paul did with Timothy; they appoint leaders in works. In fact, the basic message of Titus (and in 1,2Ti) concerns leadership selection and appointment. The basic message of the book of Tit (Setting The Church In Order involves the appointing of qualified leaders, requires leaders who are sound in teaching and who model a Christian life style, and necessitates leaders who exhort others to practical Christian living.) exemplifies this apostolic function and function.
3. Establish Works	Paul does this in Phillipi, Corinth, Ephesus, Rome and Crete.	Apostolic workers are concerned that ministries they have begun mature in the faith. They will send workers to solve problems, help develop leaders, and teach and help followers mature. They will send helpful materials. They will exert influence through relationships to keep works going and growing. But establishing is secondary to creating new works. See the book of Tit.
4. Intercede for Works, both new and old	Paul does this for the churches he established.	Paul had a real burden for the churches he founded and worked with. *Beside outward circumstances pressing me, there is the inward burden, i.e. the anxiety and care, I feel daily for all the churches.* 2Co 11:28. Almost all apostolic leaders will have many values of the Intercessor Leader Model and will feel the responsibility of prayer for the works they associate with.
5. Combat Heresy[206] **(both orthodoxy and orthopraxy)**	Paul does this somewhat in Corinth and Crete and much in Ephesus. See also the Jerusalem conference, Ac 15.	1Ti is the comprehensive example of this apostolic function (four lines of heresy dealt with). Paul deals with potential heresy both in orthopraxy and orthodoxy. The practice of Christianity as well as the beliefs of Christianity can be heretical. Apostles are concerned with this. And apostles and "so-called apostles" themselves, frequently not accountable to others, can easily be the source of heresy. See 1,2Co.
6. Resource New Ministries and Old Ones	Paul and Barnabas Ac 11; Paul in 1Co, 2Co.	Apostolic workers raise finances for workers like Paul did for Timothy (1Co 16, 1Ti), Stephanus (1Co 16). They help out old works in special need. Paul had the Philippian church giving to other churches. He had Corinthian churches giving to needs in Jerusalem. They also provide workers to help out in situations like Timothy, Titus, etc. Part of the resourcing includes knowledge, wisdom and findings from related experience. They also help those with resources understand both their freedom and responsibility to use these for the kingdom (1Ti).
7. Test New Ministries for Validity	Barnabas Ac 11	Barnabas is sent on a ministry task from the apostles in Jerusalem to test the Christianity in Antioch. Titus' ministry tasks had somewhat of this flavor in Crete as well.

Conclusions

Apostolic functions involve the critical job of expanding ministry into new situations. Most apostolic workers identify strongly with values of the *Harvest Leadership model*. Without this expansion Christianity would die. Apostles exhibit strong gifts and strong leadership. Along with this strength goes the corresponding weakness of independence. Interdependence is needed—especially for accountability. Most apostolic workers do not have accountability for their ministries and hence abuses of power and heresies, both orthodoxic and orthopraxic, occur. A strong task-oriented leadership bias by most apostolic workers

---

[206] Heresy refers to deviation from a standard, whether in belief (orthodoxy) or practice (orthopraxy). e.g. See 1Ti where both are present in the Ephesian church (as prophesied in Ac 20:30).

often lacks the needed balance of a relational leadership bias. Apostolic workers tend to build empires which they over control in a micro-managing manner. Needed is the indigenization function modeled by Paul, a very strong apostolic worker, which releases leadership and allows new leadership to function. But hats off to apostolic workers! They carry out the Great Commission. They want to reach the world!

See *gifts of healings; discernings of spirits; exhortation; evangelism; faith; prophecy; ruling; teaching; word of knowledge; word of wisdom; coercive authority; competent authority; induced authority; personal authority ; spiritual authority; leadership styles; apostolic style; father-initiator; father-guardian; imitator; confrontation style; indirect conflict; obligation persuasion; harvest model, stewardship model, shepherd model, servant model, intercessor model;* **Glossary.** See **Articles,** *25. Jesus-Five Leadership Models: Shepherd, harvest, Steward, Servant, Intercessor; 9. Developing Giftedness; 62. Spiritual Gift Clusters; 63. Spiritual Gifts, Giftedness, and Development. 49. Pauline Leadership Styles; 71. Value Driven Leadership.* See For **Further Study Bibliography,** Clinton's **Coming to Conclusions on Leadership Styles**.

Relevance of the Article to 1,2 Timothy
This article was written primarily for use with the Titus commentary. In reviewing the Ephesian ministry, it can be seen that it is apostolic functions 5,6, and 8 introduced in this article, which are being highlighted.

3. Apostolic Functions—Comparison of Titus and Timothy

Introduction

In a previous article I identified 7 apostolic functions.[207] As I worked on the Titus leadership commentary I identified a new function that stood out because of the Cretan situation. I also identified three phases of apostolic ministry.[208] So this article is written not only to update the former article but also to compare which of these functions is seen in Titus ministry on Crete and Timothy's ministry in Ephesus and to draw out some comparative observations. All of the apostolic functions are seen in Paul's various ministries which addressed different issues in all three phases of apostolic ministry.[209]

Apostolic Functions Updated

Below in Table 1,2 Ti 3-1 are given the previous 7 apostolic functions and the new function seen in Titus, function 8—Contextualization.

Table 1,2 Ti 3-1 Apostolic Functions--Paul's, Timothy's and Titus

Function	Apostolic Thrust	Supplementary Gifts
1. Start New Ministries	pioneer new work	evangelism, power gifts
2. Appoint Leaders	leadership selection	basically an apostolic gifting function; sometimes word of knowledge, word of wisdom
3. Establish Works	leadership development; edification ministry with believers	teaching, exhortation, ruling
4. Intercede for Works, both new and old	release spiritual power in situations	faith, discernings of spirits, sometimes word of knowledge or word of wisdom
5. Combat Heresy[210] (both orthodoxy and orthopraxy)	correct and stabilize a deteriorating situation	exhortation, prophecy, teaching
6. Resource New Ministries and Old Ones	resource apostolic ministries; give help to needy church situations	not clear
7. Test New Ministries for Validity	authenticate God's work	not clear
8. Contextualize[211] the Gospel to Cross-cultural Situations	apply truth to complex cultural situations	teaching, exhortation, sometimes prophecy

---

[207] See **Article**, *2. Apostolic Functions*.
[208] See **Article**, *4. Apostolic Giftedness—Mulitple Gifted Leaders*.
[209] Paul does have ministry in all three but dominantly in phase 1 ministries.
[210] Heresy refers to deviation from a standard, whether in belief (orthodoxy) or practice (orthopraxy). e.g. See 1Ti where both are present in the Ephesian church (as prophesied in Ac 20:30).
[211] See **Article**, *Basic Contextualization Principles*.

Comparison of Timothy and Titus's Apostolic Ministries

Three phases of apostolic ministry will work on differing apostolic functions:

Phase   I.   Ground Breaking Apostolic Work (like Paul and Barnabas in Thessalonica)
Phase II.   Edification Work (like Titus in Crete)
Phase III.   Corrective Work (like Timothy in Ephesus)

Table 1,2 Ti 3-2 Comparison of Apostolic Functions--Timothy and Titus

Function	Apostolic Thrust	Seen In Ministry
1. Start New Ministries	pioneer new work	neither
2. Appoint Leaders	leadership selection	seen in both
3. Establish Works	leadership development; edification ministry with believers	seen in both
4. Intercede for Works, both new and old	release spiritual power in situations	Paul models this in Timothy and commands Timothy to do so. Not seen in Titus.
5. Combat Heresy[212] (both orthodoxy and orthopraxy)	correct and stabilize a deteriorating situation	Timothy is combating at least 4 lines of heresy; Titus 2.
6. Resource New Ministries and Old Ones	resource apostolic ministries; give help to needy church situations	Paul does this in Titus. Titus does to (also did this at Corinth) gives Timothy advice on doing this in Ephesian situation.
7. Test New Ministries for Validity	authenticate God's work	neither
8. Contextualize the Gospel to Cross-cultural Situations	apply truth to complex cultural situations	Titus must do this. Cretan cultural has many values degrading from Christian testimony

Conclusion

Timothy does apostolic functions 2, 3, 4, 5 and 6. Titus does apostolic functions 2, 3, 5, 6 and 8.

Timothy's situation was complex because it involved turning around a situation that had developed over 20 years. A major problem involved turning the leadership around—getting rid of leaders who were involved in heresy—both orthodoxic and orthopraxic. Four lines of heresy had to be combated.

Titus ministry was complicated in that he had to introduce values into a Cretan culture which had many counter values. His was a primitive situation in which new believers had a relatively small church base to work from. He too had to do leadership selection—to get leaders of integrity to help him model the needed changes.

Here is an observation on both their ministries. Neither were using or admonished to use power gifts. However, both were admonished to use the gifts they had with power—dominantly teaching, exhortation, and probably prophetical gifts.

Apostolic ministries will vary due to local cultural situations and gifting of the apostolic leaders as well as the type of apostolic ministry being done, Phase 1, or 2, or 3.

---

[212] Heresy refers to deviation from a standard, whether in belief (orthodoxy) or practice (orthopraxy). e.g. See 1Ti where both are present in the Ephesian church (as prophesied in Ac 20:30).

Relevance of the Article to 1,2 Timothy

This article was written primarily for use with the Titus commentary. However, the Ephesian ministry illustrates Apostolic giftedness as Paul deals with the heresies in the church. Teaching, exhortation, discernings of spirits are seen with regard to the Ephesiah church.   This article delves into that concept of apostolic giftedness. One can easily appreciate the multiple giftedness of Paul in dealing with the problematic situations he faced in the churches as they spread into the Gentile world.

4. Apostolic Giftedness—Multiple Gifted Leaders

Introduction

Breaking open new ground, like planting a church in a cross-cultural situation, will require a number of gifts. This can be done by a team which has the necessary gifts comprising the total needed in the situation.[213] One of the gifts needed for such new work is the apostleship gift. Another is the gift of evangelism. Sometimes power gifts will be needed in order to authenticate the work as being of God. As the work begins to succeed other gifts will be needed like teaching, exhortation, and pastoring. As a work ages it usually experiences ecclesiastical entropy—plateauing or worse, diverting from truth. Prophetical gifts, teaching gifts and exhortation gifts are desperately needed to embrace and correct this situation. Examples in the New Testament show apostolic ministries arising to help in all these situations.

Usually an apostolic leader will have multiple gifts, a gift-mix.[214] Teammates will come along side to provide other needed gifts, the apostolic support gifts.[215] In reading any of the Pauline epistles[216] or especially leadership books like Titus or 1, 2 Timothy or the book of Acts one needs an understanding of apostolic giftedness in order to read with an enlightened perspective. Such a perspective might also help to prevent certain excesses in apostolic ministries which may lead to leaders not finishing well. This article gives a quick overview of apostolic giftedness. Three phases of apostolic ministry will need differing sets of gifts:

Phase I.	Ground Breaking Apostolic Work (like Paul and Barnabas in Thessalonica)
Phase II.	Edification Work (like Titus in Crete)
Phase III.	Corrective Work (like Timothy in Ephesus)

---

[213] Different sets of gifts will be needed in different situations. More on this later.

[214] *Gift-mix* refers to the set of spiritual gifts that a leader is exercising at a given time in his/her ministry. the broader term is *giftedness set* which includes natural abilities, acquired skills and spiritual gifts. In this article, we are restricting ourselves to spiritual gifts. See **Article, 9.** *Developing Giftedness*. See *spiritual gifts, gift-mix, giftedness set,* **Glossary**, each of the individual spiritual gifts named in this article.

[215] From 1973 to 1983 I did Biblical research on *spiritual gifts* and taught on spiritual gifts in a number of teaching roles. I published a book, **Spiritual Gifts**, which defined the gifts, from an exegetical and comparative study of them in the New Testament. From 1983 to 1993 we (my son began helping me in the research) did empirical research on giftedness in leaders. Around 500 contemporary leaders were studied. Out of that research came our present understanding of giftedness, a broader and more comprehensive treatment of how a leader operates. Of special interest was the whole notion of developing spiritual gifts. This research is written up **in Unlocking Your Giftedness** and forms the basis for much of this article.

[216] Paul's epistles should be studied not only for content but to see what Paul is doing and how he is doing it. Paul exercises apostolic ministry throughout his missionary career. An understanding of apostolic ministry and its giftedness is instructive for appreciating Paul's leadership.

Leaders--Word Gifted

Apostleship, prophecy, evangelism, pastoring and teaching are often called the leadership gifts. Because of their nature and function, the exercising of these gifts are directly connected to exercising leadership influence. Some would not call these gifts but would call them offices. Because of the way that these gifts are listed in Ephesians 4, it is easy to see how this viewpoint is formed. In the Ephesians 4 passage, we believe that Paul is using metonymy as he wrote the text on spiritual gifts. We believe that he is referring to individuals who are gifted in apostleship, prophecy, evangelism, pastoring and teaching not just to apostles, prophets, evangelists, pastors and teachers who hold that office in the church.[217]

Is it possible to operate with these gifts without the *office* or official position? We believe that it is possible. In fact, we have observed many leaders operating in these gifts without the *official* title or position. Often, those positions were not available to these individuals because of things like denominational tradition, gender issues, or certain types of circumstances in their past. The fact that they were not in the position didn't stop them from exercising the leadership influence associated with the gift.

It is primarily these leadership gifts that have responsibility for maturing the body. Evidently they were needed to mature the church as described in Ephesians 4. Even if you don't believe them to be gifts you can ask yourself the question, what did each of these offices contribute to the maturing of the body? Even if the offices don't exist officially today, what functions did they represent? These functions will be needed today to mature the body. So what are these functions? They are essentially the thrust of certain spiritual gifts. Those central thrusts are essentially the functions that are needed to mature the body. Look at them!

1. The Apostolic Function-- **CREATING NEW MINISTRY**

2. The Prophetic Function-- **TO PROVIDE CORRECTION OR PERSPECTIVE ON A SITUATION**

3. The Evangelistic Function-- **INTRODUCING OTHERS TO THE GOSPEL.**

4. The Pastoring Function-- **CARING FOR THE GROWTH OF FOLLOWERS.**

5. The Teaching Function-- **TO CLARIFY TRUTH**

And to these we have added two other influence gifts—exhortation and ruling.

6. The Exhortive Function-- **TO APPLY BIBLICAL TRUTH**

7. The Ruling Function-- **INFLUENCING OTHERS TOWARD VISION.**

It is our contention that God is still following the Ephesians 4 mandate of equipping the body and developing it toward maturity. And these kinds of functions are still needed.

---

[217] We have some difficulties with the whole idea of these being just offices. What is the office of pastor? What kind of gifts would a person in that office have? What is the office of teacher? What kind of gifts would a person in that office have? What is the office of evangelist? What kind of gifts would a person in that office have? What is the office of prophet? What kind of gifts would a person in that office have? What is the office of Apostleship? What kind of gifts would a person in that office have? Why would these offices be in the church? If to equip and lead the body to maturity is that not needed today? Has the church reached the full maturity described in Ephesians 4 so that we can do away with these offices and the gifts entailed in them? Why would some of them disappear and not all of them? Are just some of them needed to take the body to maturity?

Implications

1. All seven of the functions listed above are needed to bring a balanced maturity to the body.

2. In general, over an extended time, no one of the functions should be overemphasized to the exclusion of others.

3. For a given contextual situation and for a given time, one or more of the functions may need to be overemphasized to meet crucial needs.

Phase I Apostolic Ministry--Initial Breakthroughs

The Acts of the Apostles traces Paul's pioneering ministry in a number of places including Cyprus, Iconium, Lystra, Derbe, Phillipi, Thessalonica, Berea, Athens, Corinth, and Ephesus. In these pioneer ministries Paul demonstrates apostolic gifting supplemented with various power gifts (word of knowledge, working of powers, gifts of healings, discernings of spirits, faith) to authenticate divine backing and various word gifts (dominantly teaching and exhortation with evangelism, occasionally prophecy) to start the edification process. Paul was very multi-gifted and needed to be since he is basically ushering in the church leadership era. He is an exemplar.

In the initial stages of a new work, power gifts validate the word gifts and bring about breakthroughs. Various word gifts initiate the growth process.

Phase II Apostolic Ministry--Edification Breakthroughs

Once a work gets going, apostolic leadership will usually transition leaders from the local setting in to do the edification work (especially pastoral gifting and ruling) needed to stabilize the embryonic work. In some situations, where much contextualization of the Gospel is needed, apostolic leadership will be necessary to get edification breakthroughs. This was the case for Titus in Crete. We do not know for certain Titus' giftedness set. But we do know that the demands that Paul gave him required strong teaching and exhortation gifts as well as the ruling gift. His apostolic gift gave him authoritative backing to contextualize the Gospel into the Crete situation with its values so counter to living out Gospel truth.

Phase III. Apostolic Ministry--Correction Breakthroughs

Timothy's work in Ephesus exemplifies apostolic ministry that is corrective in nature. The Ephesian church had stagnated, in fact, deteriorated following along the lines of Paul's prophetic warning to given to them in Acts 20. It was about 20 years old and had its own indigenous leaders at the time Timothy is sent in to correct the situation.[218] A number of heresies (orthopraxic and orthodoxic) needed to be countered. Timothy did this. Again we do not know for certain what Timothy's gift-mix was but we do know what was needed in addition to apostleship: teaching, exhortation, prophecy.

Apostleship Functions And Giftedness Needed

Elsewhere in two articles,[219] I have described some apostolic functions. Below in Table 1,2 Ti 4-1 I list these functions and suggest the apostleship gift and supplementary gifts needed to probably carry out the functions.

Table 1,2 Ti 4-1 Apostolic Functions and Supplementary Gifts

Function	Apostolic Thrust	Supplementary Gifts
1. Start New Ministries	pioneer new work	evangelism, power gifts
2. Appoint Leaders	leadership selection	basically an apostolic gifting function; sometimes word of knowledge, word of wisdom

---

[218] See **Article**, *11. Ephesian Church—Its Time-Line.*
[219] See **Articles**, 2. *Apostolic Functions*; *3*. Apostolic *Functions—Comparison of Titus and Timothy.*

3. Establish Works	leadership development; edification ministry with believers	teaching, exhortation, ruling
4. Intercede for Works, both new and old	release spiritual power in situations	faith, discernings of spirits, sometimes word of knowledge or word of wisdom
5. Combat Heresy[220] (both orthodoxy and orthopraxy)	correct and stabilize a deteriorating situation	exhortation, prophecy, teaching
6. Resource New Ministries and Old Ones	resource apostolic ministries; give help to needy church situations	not clear
7. Test New Ministries for Validity	authenticate God's work	not clear
8. Contextualize the Gospel to Cross-cultural Situations	apply truth to complex cultural situations	teaching, exhortation, sometimes prophecy

In the following discussion I will suggest a basic core that is usually seen throughout apostolic ministry. Then I will show how it may be modified to fit the three phases of apostolic ministry. At this point, having discussed the apostolic functions and related giftedness, I want to suggest that frequently apostolic leaders easily recruit people to come alongside and work with them in an apostolic ministry. Such team members will usually be drawn for two very different reasons. Two patterns discovered in our giftedness research describes these reasons:

    1. The Like-Attracts-Like Pattern
    2. The Needs Pattern

The *like-attracts-like pattern* is a general giftedness pattern very helpful to a leader in assessing leadership selection and development. It asserts that potentially gifted emerging leaders are attracted to leaders because of gifts which they already have in potential or will receive. *The Needs Pattern*, much more rarely seen, asserts that emerging leaders recognize some glaring omissions in an apostolic leader in terms of giftedness and are drawn to help solve those needs. These emerging leaders have the needed gifts to supplement and support the apostolic ministry.

Definition   <u>Apostolic support</u> gifts refer to gifts that are needed in an apostolic work and are supplied by leaders drawn to the ministry.

This relieves the pressure on a given apostolic leader. Such a leader then does not have to have all the gifts needed in a situation.

Apostleship Giftedness--The Core

    We can display a person's gift-mix and show the relationship between the various spiritual gifts that he/she operates in.[221] All leaders we have studied are multi-gifted. In our research we have commonly seen that certain gifts frequently supplement other gifts. Below I give the core Venn diagram for an apostolic worker. Then I modify it to fit the three phases of apostolic work.

---

[220] <u>Heresy</u> refers to deviation from a standard, whether in belief (orthodoxy) or practice (orthopraxy). e.g. See 1Ti where both are present in the Ephesian church (as prophesied in Ac 20:30).

[221] These are called Venn diagrams. See chapter 9 in **Unlocking Giftedness** for a detailed explanation of a Venn diagram and guidelines for constructing.

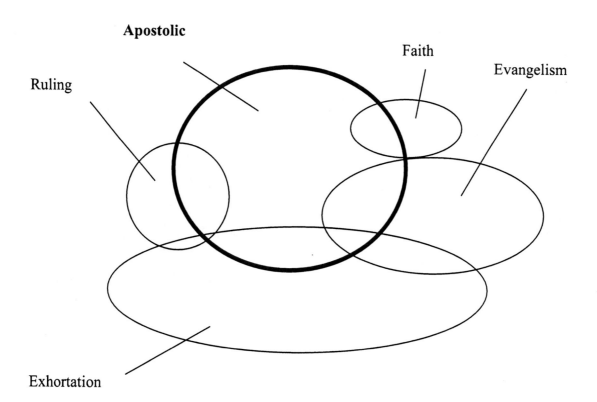

Figure 1,2 Ti 4-1. Venn Diagram--Apostolic Core

Of course in team situations, one or more of the gifts shown in the apostolic core may be dominantly supplied to the situation by some other team member. Frequently, in our giftedness research, the gift of faith accompanied the apostleship gift—especially in Phase 1 ministry.

For a Phase 2 ministry, like Titus' ministry in Crete, the apostolic core would be modified somewhat. The evangelism gift would usually be dropped off. In its place would be the teaching gift. Again, any of the peripheral gifts could be supplied by a team member. The *faith gift* may or may not be seen. The *ruling gift* takes on more of an influence as indicated by the larger bold faced line. Actually the book of Titus indicates a strong exhortation and teaching gift is needed.

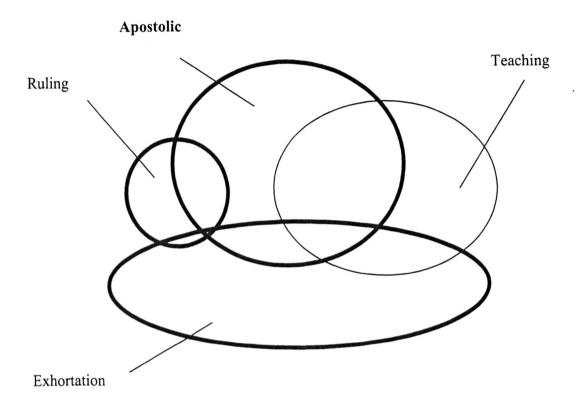

Figure 1,2 Ti 4-2. Venn Diagram--Apostolic Core Modified for Phase 2

For a Phase 3 ministry like Timothy's ministry in Ephesus, the core would be modified again.

Figure 1,2 Ti 4-3. Venn Diagram--Apostolic Core Modified for Phase 3

Notice the strong exhortation and/or prophetic gift. This is needed to correct the drift from known truth or practiced truth and to regain momentum. The teaching gift has to take on heightened use due to the clarification of heresy. The ruling gift drops off somewhat since there is indigenous leadership in place. However, leadership selection is usually needed to transition in leaders that can get the situation back on track. Old leaders, those immersed in the heresy and the stagnation will probably have to be moved on. The apostolic function of appointing leaders will be really needed.

Conclusion

Paul, Timothy, and Titus model for us apostolic ministries. Paul was powerfully multi-gifted as can easily be demonstrated from Luke's historical narrative in Acts. The gift-mix of Timothy and Titus is not demonstrated. But from the functions they had to perform in their ministries, certain things about gifts can be inferred.

Perspective is needed on apostolic ministry and apostolic giftedness. In the fervor of a powerful movement, like the present day emphasis on apostolic leaders, it is easy to be carried away pragmatically by tides that tug away from Biblical anchors. This article is a start to analyzing apostolic ministry and giftedness. The varying gift needs in terms of the basic three phases provides some anchors.[222] The concept of apostolic support gifts, another anchor, takes some of the pressure off of an apostolic worker. They do not have to have it all.

---

[222] In terms of the barriers to finishing well it is easy for present day apostolic ministries to fall into the traps of five of the six barriers: abuse of power, financial impropriety, family neglect, sexual impropriety, pride. This basically relates to lack of accountability of powerful apostolic leaders.

Relevance of the Article to 1,2 Timothy

Paul demonstrates in his Ephesian ministry several aspects of a Bible Centered leader. See leadership topic 9 and the nine references to a Bible Centered Leader in the commentary on 1,2 Ti. Paul strongest Bible Centered leadership emphases is his impactful teaching. He expects this letter to impact Timothy's ministry and the Ephesian church. We do well to heed Paul's example of a Bible Centered Leader. Problematic leadership will always test one's grasp of God word and its use for those situations. And God will instruct us through many of the examples of the Bible, both Old and New Testaments.

5. Bible Centered Leader

Introduction

Where would you go in the O.T. if you wanted to look at a description of a Bible centered leader? Where would you go in the N.T. if you wanted to look at material about a Bible Centered Leader. Here is where I would go.

Table 1,2 Ti 5-1. Bible Centered Material O.T./ N.T.

| Old Testament | Psalm 1, 19, 119 |
| New Testament | 2 Timothy |

Glance quickly at Psalm 1 and feel its impact about how important it is to base a life on God's word.[223]

1. O, how happy is the person
    who hasn't based his conduct on the principles of the ungodly
    Nor taken his stand in the way of sinners,
    Nor taken his place with an assembly of scoffers!

2. But it is in the law of the Lord that he takes his delight;
    And on His law he keeps thinking day and night.

3. And he will be like a tree planted by the side of streams of water,
    That yields its fruit in its season;
    Its leaves also do not wither;
    And whatsoever he attempts, succeeds

4. Such is not the case with the ungodly,
    But they are like the chaff which the wind scatters.

5. Because of this, the ungodly will not be able to maintain themselves when the judgment comes,
    Nor sinners, with righteous people.

6. For the Lord watches over (knows intimately) the way of the righteous;
    But the way of the ungodly is headed toward destruction.

What is A Bible Centered Leader? According to this passage, Psalm 1, given above here is a definition.

---

[223] An adaptation of Leupold's work. See **For Further Study Bibliography** section.

Definition   A <u>Bible centered leader</u>[224] is one who:
1. Gets his/her counsel on life matters from other Bible centered leaders.
2. Delights in the Word of God and lets it permeate his/her soul.
3. Will persevere joyfully and with stability through out life (figure of tree/ rooted deep in water).
4. Will be watched over by God and will prosper. That is the bent of the life.

Now glance at two passages taken from 2Ti. These were given to a relatively young leader, Timothy, probably in his early 30s. I have reversed the order of these passages so you can see the challenge first and then the appropriate response next.

2 Timothy 3:16,17 The Guarantee
Every Scripture inspired of God is profitable for teaching, for setting things right, for confronting, for inspiring righteous living, in order that God's leader be thoroughly equipped to lead God's people.

That is quite a challenge for any leader. My response to that choice and one which is encouraged by Paul himself is:

2 Timothy 2:15 The Proper Response to the Guarantee
Make every effort to be pleasing to God, a Bible Centered leader who is completely confident in using God's Word with impact in lives.

From these two passages and from reading 1Ti and 2Ti in general, I would define a Bible centered leader as,

Definition   A <u>Bible centered leader</u> is one who:
1. studies the word of God in order to use it confidently and proficiently, and
2. recognizes that inspired Scripture will equip him/her for a productive leadership ministry.

A Bible Centered Leader Defined
Here is my own definition, derived from a comparative study of several Bible characters and numerous passages stating the importance of the **Word of God**.

Definition   A <u>Bible Centered leader</u>
- refers to a leader whose leadership is informed by Biblical leadership values,
- has been shaped personally by Biblical values,
- has grasped the intent of Scriptural books and their content in such a way as to apply them to current situations,
- and who uses the Bible in ministry so as to impact followers.

Note carefully the meaning of each of the concepts:

---

[224] I am using Bible loosely to mean what is known of God's word; I realize the Psalmist was limited in terms of how much of God's word was available. I also am assuming that a Bible centered leader is first of all a person centered in God. The word of God becomes a central part of centering one self in God. So I am not talking about some one who is simply technically proficient in knowing the Word but one whose life is centered in God and as such wants to hear from God.

Table 1,2 Ti 5-2. Bible Centered Leader Components Explained

Concept	Meaning
Bible centered	A person who is centered on God and recognizes that hearing from God involves seeing the Word of God as being very important.
Leadership informed from the Bible	Recognizes that the Bible itself will have much to say about leadership (one thrust of the words equipped to lead in 2Ti 3:16,17). Further, it means recognizing leadership issues from the Bible like that which is given in the Biblical Leadership commentary series and **The Bible and Leadership Values.**
Has been shaped personally by Biblical values	The Bible has been used by God to change the life of the leader. That is one reason such a leader can use it confidently. He/she knows it has life changing power in it.
Has grasped the intent of Scriptural books and their content in such a way as to apply them to current situations,	A thorough understanding of books in the Bible allows for the application of dynamic principles where they fit current situation.
Uses the Bible in ministry so as to impact followers	The Bible contains authoritative truth. When used it will change lives.

Conclusion

Take comfort in the **Guarantee** and **Your Response** to it.

2 Timothy 3:16,17 The Guarantee
Every Scripture inspired of God is profitable for teaching, for setting things right, for confronting, for inspiring righteous living, in order that God's leader be thoroughly equipped to lead God's people.

2 Timothy 2:15 Your Response To the Guarantee
Make every effort to be pleasing to God, a Bible Centered leader who is completely confident in using God's Word with impact in lives.

Become a Bible Centered leader. It will take a lifetime of discipline. But it is worth it. It will revolutionize your life and ministry.

See **Article**, 72. Vanishing Breed; Daniel—Exemplar of a Learning Posture.

Relevance of the Article to 1,2 Timothy

This article was written primarily for explanation of Paul's remarks on conscience in 1,2 Ti. Those uses were compared to Paul's other use of conscience elsewhere. Conscience is one of the factors of beingness. My leadership studies have shown that, "Ministry flows out of beingness!" Beingness is a complex conglomerate of inner life factors including at least these three important ones: 1. The CORE OF BEINGESS which includes such factors as intimacy with God, conscience, character, personality; 2. FORCE OF BEINGNESS which includes giftedness; 3. RATIONALE OF BEINGNESS which includes such items as destiny, values drawn from experience, and gender influenced perspectives. This article focuses on the *conscience aspect of beingness.* To disregard one's conscience is to court disaster. See Ro 2:14,15 and surrounding context. God can change a conscience but until He does so, conscience is there as a governor of our behavior. We must heed it.

6. Conscience—Paul's Use of in 1,2 Ti

Introduction

Paul uses *conscience* (SRN 4893), some 21 times—four times in 1Ti, one time in 2Ti, one time in Tit and 15 times in his other epistles. His use of it in his closing letters at the end of his ministry is important. Here's why. He is connecting it to leadership issues. 1,2Tim and Tit are leadership books. And Paul is stressing to Timothy the importance of the inner life. Ministry flows out of being. Being is a complex diversity consisting of at least: intimacy with God, character, giftedness, gender, personality, destiny, learned values. Conscience, reflects the inner life governor of character. Leadership must have a moral foundation. And it is conscience which is the tail wagging the dog of character.

Definition   <u>Conscience</u> is the inner sense of right or wrong which is innate in a human being but which also is modified by values imbibed from a culture. This innate sense can also be modified by the Spirit of God.

    Integrity measures a leader's inner worth.

Definition   <u>Integrity</u> is by far the top leadership character quality. It is the consistency of inward beliefs and convictions with outward practice. It is an honesty and wholeness of personality in which one operates with a clear conscience in dealings with self and others.

Note how I connect integrity and conscience. If a leader lacks integrity you can be sure that leader also will have a shaky conscience.

    1,2Ti and Tit were the last letters Paul wrote. He was a leader finishing well. He was a leader passing on the leadership baton to his faithful co-worker Timothy. So when Paul, at the height of his mature leadership notes the importance of conscience, we should pay attention.

How Did Paul Use Conscience

Table 1,2 Ti 6-1, dealing with 1,2Ti and Tit, suggests a label for the use of conscience, lists the vs reference, gives the actual vs and gives a word of explanation.

Table 1,2 Ti 6-1. Paul's Use of Conscience—Relating it To Leadership Issues

Label	Vs	Scripture	Explanation
1. Ministry End Results	1Ti 1:5	Now the purpose for this strong command is to produce love that comes from a pure heart, and a clean conscience, and a genuine faith.	Paul points out that the end result of a pastoral or teaching ministry should be to produce mature believers who are characterized by love, purity, a *clean* conscience, and a genuine faith. Other words synonymous with *clean* in other versions include: *good, honorable, upright, pleasant, excellent, agreeable.*
2. Warning	1Ti 1:19	Keep faith and a clear conscience, which some having failed to listen to, have shipwrecked their faith.	Paul points out by example two leaders who did not heed their consciences with the result that they brought disaster on their lives and ministry. When a leader avoids the prompting of his/her conscience that leader is opening a door to Satanic control and eventual loss of ministry.
3. Aid to Understanding Truth	1Ti 3:9	One who has a clear understanding of the deep things of the faith with a clear conscience.	Put positively a leader can understand, especially moral truth, when he/she has a clear conscience about that truth personally in his/her own life. Conversely, when a leader has problems of conscience with some truth he/she can not teach that truth with power.
4. Seared Conscience	1Ti 4:2	These hypocritical leaders speak lies, having their conscience seared with a hot iron.	This reference to conscience shows it can become unreliable (seared = hardened to truth) if false teaching is accepted. Conscience alone is not a totally reliable guide, but a spirit-controlled conscience is. However, one should not violate conscience—a basic principle. Here Paul shows that a person's conscience can become dead to truth and hence can not function as a governor of the inner life. Leadership must have a moral edge to it. These teachers of heresy lacked this.
5. Assurance	2Ti 1:3	I thank God, whom I serve with a pure conscience just as my ancestors did.	Paul had a clear conscience that what he was doing, following Jesus, the Messiah, was true to the tradition of his Jewish ancestors. Messianic Jews today have this same conviction.
6. Judgmental Conscience	Tit 1:15	Unto the pure all things [are] pure: but unto them that are defiled and unbelieving [is] nothing pure; but even their mind and conscience is defiled.	Leaders with a tainted conscience will tend to suspect people as having that same problem. Leaders with a pure (clear conscience) will not be judgmental of others. Conscience is here identified also with thinking or cognition. It is not just a matter of the heart but of the head too.

Other Uses

Paul also uses conscience as the inner reflector of a universal moral law that God has created in humans to help them know right and wrong (Ro 2:15). The conscience can give underlying strength and conviction to strong beliefs. The conscience of others can affect our own actions (Ro 13:5). A person can model in such a way as to help another person defile his/her own conscience (1Co 8:7). Leaders should model lives and ministries that commend them to the consciences of others (2Co 4:2).

Conclusion

Once, Paul made a challenging statement about his life and ministry.

> **16 I make every effort to conduct my life and ministry so as to have a conscience pleasing to God and those around me.** Acts 24:16

A leader must have a clean conscience or suffer the inability to teach and preach on certain truth with power. A leader must have a clean conscience or recognize that tainted conscience issues offer hooks for Satan to use to demoralize the leader. A leader must have a clean conscience or face the possibility of destruction of his/her Christian life or ministry. A leader must have a clean conscience to teach truth with real conviction. A leader with judgmental tendencies may well have a tainted conscience in the judgmental area himself/herself. Conscience is the governor of character. Without character a leader can not lead.

Article 7

This article was originally written for use with Paul's mentoring ministry as reflected in the books of 1,2 Ti, Philippians, Philemon and Titus. Paul models in 1,2 Ti what it means to continue mentoring with a life long mentoree. Not all mentoring is life long. Most mentors will have a short time of development with a mentoree and release that mentoree after the empowerment. They may or may not have further mentoring with that same mentoree. But usually an accomplished mentor will have a core of mentorees to whom he/she feels obligated to provide mentoring over a whole lifetime. Paul demonstrates this life long mentoring relationship with two of his protégés, Timothy and Titus. He was an upward mentor for both and had a continued influence in their lives. See also **Article 47. Paul—Mentor For Many**. Our observations show that over a lifetime, a given leader needs several kinds of mentoring relationships: upward, downward, and lateral. This article describes these kinds of relationships. Paul received upward mentoring from Barnabas. Later this became a lateral mentoring relationship. His downward mentoring is seen throughout Acts and his epistles.

7. Constellation Model, Mentoring Relationships

Introduction

One of the major lessons[225] identified from a comparative study of many effective leaders is,

> **Effective Leaders See Relational Empowerment As Both A Means And A Goal Of Ministry.**

Both Jesus and Paul demonstrated this leadership principle in their ministries. In fact, both used mentoring as a means for applying this principle in their ministries. Jesus dominantly mentored in a small group context. Paul mentored both with individuals and in a small group context.

Definition   Mentoring is a relational experience in which one person, the mentor, empowers another person, the mentoree, by sharing God-given resources.[226]

Stanley researched leadership relationships for a number of years. From his observations on various kinds of mentoring relationships as well as his observations on leaders who finished well and who did not, he postulated a principle.[227]

---

[225] Seven such lessons have been identified: (1) Effective Leaders View Present Ministry in Terms Of A Life Time Perspective. (2) Effective Leaders Maintain A Learning Posture Throughout Life. (3) Effective Leaders Value Spiritual Authority As A Primary Power Base. (4) Effective Leaders Who Are Productive Over A Lifetime Have A Dynamic Ministry Philosophy. (5) Effective Leaders View Leadership Selection And Development As A Priority Function In Their Ministry. (6) Effective Leaders See Relational Empowerment As Both A Means And A Goal Of Ministry. (7) Effective Leaders Evince A Growing Awareness Of Their Sense Of Destiny.

[226] See the nine mentor roles: *mentor discipler, mentor spiritual guide, mentor coach, mentor counselor, mentor teacher, mentor sponsor, mentor contemporary model, mentor historical model, mentor divine contact,* **Glossary**. The apostle Paul demonstrated many of these roles in his relationships with team members and others in his ministry. See **Articles, 45. Paul—Developer Par Excellence; 47. Paul—Mentor For Many**. For further follow-up study, see Stanley and Clinton **Connecting** for a popular treatment of mentoring. See Clinton and Clinton **The Mentor Handbook** for a detailed treatment of mentoring.

[227] Paul Stanley, at this writing, is an International Vice President for the Navigators, a Christian organization heavily involved in developing laborers for the Kingdom. Mentoring is heavily used in

Stanley's Thesis
Over A Lifetime A Christian Leader Needs A Balanced Relational Network With other Christian Leaders Who Will Help Him/Her And Vice Versa.

What did he mean by a balanced relational network with Christian leaders? By it Stanley was saying that four kinds of relationships are needed over a lifetime:

<u>Upward Help:</u>
A Christian Leader needs to relate to Christian Leaders more experienced in the Christian life who will help them in their growth and give needed perspective as well as help them be accountable for growth.

<u>Lateral Help:</u>
A Christian Leader needs to relate to Christian Leaders who are peers in the Christian life who will share, care, and relate so as to encourage them to persevere.

<u>Downward Help:</u>
A Christian Leader needs to relate to younger emerging leaders who he/she can help to grow.

Stanley was talking about mentoring relationships. Both he and I have observed that over a lifetime, effective leaders who finished well experienced from five to 30 or more mentoring relationships for limited periods of time in their lives. Mentoring is one of the five major enhancement factors that accompany leaders who finish well. [228]

The Constellation Model

The popular name for the graphic representation of Stanley's thesis is *The Constellation Model*. Figure 1,2 Ti 7-1 shows this graphic representation.

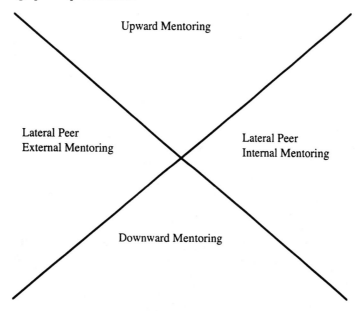

Figure 1,2 Ti 7-1. The Constellation Model

Navigator ministries. Stanley would never call this theorem by his name, but I have taken the liberty to do so, since he was the discoverer of it and taught it to me.
[228] See **Articles**, 15. *Finishing Well—Five Enhancement Factors; 16. Finishing Well—Six Characteristics.*

Upward mentors dominantly bring strategic accountability and perspective to a relationship.[229] When you have an *upward mentor* you are being mentored by someone else. *Lateral peer mentoring*, internal, means a mentoring relationship with someone in the same organization or someone coming from basically the same background as you. Such a mentor knows you and your organization fairly well. Confidential things can be shared. Accountability for each other is expected. An internal lateral mentor is roughly at the same stage of maturity as you. Lateral peer mentoring, external, means a relationship with some one from a very different background than you and a very different ministry experience. Such a person can bring objectivity to you and you to that person, since you will frequently ask the question, "Why do you do it that way?" Accountability and perspective are expected in such a relationship. Downward mentoring means that you are helping someone not as far along as you, at least in the area of the mentoring expertise. Such a relationship benefits both participants. The person being mentored of course receives the empowerment of the mentoring. The person doing the mentoring often experiences two things: (1) reality checks (mentorees frequently ask embarrassing questions about whether or not something is true for you); (2) a fresh injection of faith—often a by-product of being around a younger Christian is that they are not so cynical about things and trust God in ways that an older mentor used to do.

Each of the nine mentoring relationships can fit into any of the quadrants of *The Constellation Model.* Table 1,2 Ti 7-1 briefly lists the nine relationships.

Table 1,2 Ti 7-1. Nine Mentoring Relationships That May Happen in the Four Quadrants

Type	Definition
mentor discipler	A <u>mentor discipler</u> is one who spends much time, usually one-on-one, with an individual mentoree in order to build into that mentoree the basic habits of the Christian life. It is a relational experience in which a more experienced follower of Christ shares with a less experienced follower of Christ the commitment, understanding, and basic skills necessary to know and obey Jesus Christ as Lord.
mentor spiritual guide	A <u>spiritual guide</u> is a godly, mature follower of Christ who shares knowledge, skills, and basic philosophy on what it means to increasingly realize Christ-likeness in all areas of life. The primary contributions of a Spiritual guide include accountability, decisions, and insights concerning questions, commitments, and direction affecting spirituality (inner-life motivations) and maturity (integrating truth with life).
mentor coach	<u>Coaching</u> is a process of imparting encouragement and skills to succeed in a task via relational training.
mentor counselor	A <u>mentor counselor</u> is one who gives timely and wise advice as well as impartial perspective on the mentoree's view of self, others, circumstances, and ministry.
mentor teacher	A <u>mentor teacher</u> is one who imparts knowledge and understanding of a particular subject at a time when a mentoree needs it.
mentor sponsor	A <u>mentor sponsor</u> is one who helps promote the ministry (career) of another by using his/her resources, credibility, position, etc. to further the development and acceptance of the mentoree.
mentor model (contemporary)	A <u>mentor contemporary model</u> is a person who models values, methodologies, and other leadership characteristics in such a way as to inspire others to emulate them.
mentor model (historical)	A <u>mentor historical model</u> is a person whose life (autobiographical or biographical input) modeled values, methodologies, and other leadership characteristics in such a way as to inspire others to emulate them.
mentor divine contact	A <u>person whose timely intervention is</u> perceived of as from God to give special guidance at an important time in a life. This person may or may not be aware of the intervention and may or may not have any further mentoring connection to the mentoree.

---

[229] Many times an older person may get upward mentoring from a younger leader in terms of special skills the older leader wishes to gain. I myself have several upward mentors who are helping me with picking up additional computer skills (PowerPoint, film clips, updating computers, Skype, video capabilities, etc.).

Closing Observations

1. Mentoring relationships that fill the four quadrants are usually limited in time and are not permanent. They happen and meet a need and then terminate after the empowerment. The relationship may endure and be rekindled later for mentoring effectiveness.
2. A given leader will not necessarily have mentoring relationships in all the quadrants at once. But over a lifetime mentoring in each of the quadrants brings balance.
3. Internal lateral peer mentoring usually stresses relationship, accountability and perspective rather than specific mentoring relationships.
4. Upward mentors are harder to find as a leader matures and ages in life. This is because fewer and fewer leaders are upward to a mature leader.[230]
5. A leader with a strong learning posture will take proactive steps to find mentoring.

A closing exercise that is often used at mentoring workshops involves having leaders drawn a constellation diagram and have them fill in names of mentors and types of mentoring that they have experienced in the past, even if the mentoring was not deliberate or formal. I have them try to think through each of the four quadrants. Then I ask them to re-do the diagram and put in current mentoring relationships they are experiencing. Finally I ask them to draw a final diagram with the kind of profile they would like to have over the next year or two. These diagrams are called *Constellation Profiles*.

What does your *Constellation Profile* look like now?

---

[230] Except for in-and-out short-term special mentoring relationships such as coaching, teaching, and the like in order to upgrade one's skills in which case younger emerging leaders can help older leaders.

Relevance of the Article to 1,2 Timothy

This article was originally written for use with 1,2 Ti and 1,2 Co where Paul strongly asserts his apostolic authority. In those letters he needs that authority to bring correction. Paul's destiny is intimately tied to that apostolic calling. Paul exemplifies the threefold destiny pattern, explained in this article. The Ephesian ministry was part of that destiny. It is clear in Acts 20, from the warning to the Ephesian elders in his final address to them, that Paul was aware of his destiny and something of the future possibility of the Ephesian church. His final triumphant statement about completion of his destiny occurs in 2 Ti 4:6-8. Much can be learned from the study of Paul's life from a destiny perspective. In this article, Paul, along with Joseph and Moses, is used to show that destiny indeed is a relevant perspective to use in understanding a leader's life-time contribution. A later article treats destiny more specifically for Paul. This article basically validates the notion of sense of destiny and the three-fold pattern.

8. Destiny Pattern

Introduction

One of the major leadership lessons[231] that emerged from a comparative study of effective leaders concerned the concept, sense of destiny.

Effective leaders evince a growing sense of destiny over their lifetimes.[232]

A young emerging leader thinks of numerous questions when confronted with that major leadership lesson.

1. What is a sense of destiny? A Destiny pattern?
2. How does one get a sense of destiny?
3. Can emerging leaders be sensitized to destiny experiences?
4. Is this a biblical concept?
5. Can these young leaders be encouraged to seek and express these experiences and rely on them as their leadership unfolds?
6. Are there dangers in promoting a sense of destiny to young leaders?
7. Do all leaders have a sense of destiny?

Comparative studies of leaders—Biblical case studies, historical case studies, and contemporary studies—have suggested answers to these questions.

Some Basic Definitions and A Fundamental Destiny Pattern

What is a sense of destiny? How does one get a sense of destiny?

---

[231] Seven such lessons have been identified: (1) Effective Leaders View Present Ministry in Terms Of A Life Time Perspective. (2) Effective Leaders Maintain A Learning Posture Throughout Life. (3) Effective Leaders Value Spiritual Authority As A Primary Power Base. (4) Effective Leaders Who Are Productive Over A Lifetime Have A Dynamic Ministry Philosophy. (5) Effective Leaders View Leadership Selection And Development As A Priority Function In Their Ministry. (6) Effective Leaders See Relational Empowerment As Both A Means And A Goal Of Ministry. (7) Effective Leaders Evince A Growing Awareness Of Their Sense Of Destiny. It is this last one I am exploring in this article.

[232] This is a major key to an effective ministry. No Bible leader who had an effective ministry failed to have a sense of destiny. Paul is the exemplar in the N.T. Church Leadership Era. Over and over again in his epistles, Paul's makes statements that reflect on his understanding of his destiny with God.

Destiny experiences refer to those experiences which lead a person to sense and believe that God has intervened in a personal and special way in the leader's life. In a sense then, it is God's way of encouraging a leader toward embracing and accomplishing some purpose of God during that leader's lifetime.

Definition   A <u>sense of destiny</u> is an inner conviction arising from an experience or a series of experiences in which there is a growing sense of awareness that God has His hand on a leader in a special way for special purposes.

Definition   <u>Destiny processing</u> refers to the shaping activities of God in which a leader becomes increasingly aware of God's Hand on his/her life and the purposes for which God has intended for his/her leadership. This processing causes a sense of partnership with God toward God's purposes for the life and hence brings meaning to the life.

It is through God's shaping activities in the life of a leader that a leader gets a sense of destiny. Destiny experiences include preparation experiences, revelation experiences, and fulfillment experiences.

Sometimes the experience is awe inspiring and there is no doubt that God is in it and that the leader or emerging leader is going to be used by God. Such are the destiny revelation experiences of Moses in Ex 3 and Paul in Acts 9. But at other times it is not so clear to the individual. Over a period of time various experiences come to take on new light and an awareness of that sense of destiny dawns. For example, Moses' birth and deliverance into Pharaoh's palace was an indicator of God's hand on his life and in retrospect can be seen that way.

Bertelsen's study (1985) of sense of destiny in the scriptures pointed out that sense of destiny may be a process as much as a unique awe inspiring experience. A full blown destiny does not emerge all at once. It happens over time. The three-fold pattern describes how it happens. The idea of the destiny continuum came out of Bertelsen's[233] thinking. The destiny continuum graphically portrays the pattern Bertelsen discovered. Since Bertelsen's study, the notion of destiny processing and the destiny pattern have been confirmed many times with other case studies.

Definition   A <u>destiny pattern</u> is a leadership pattern. The development of a sense of destiny usually follows a three fold pattern of destiny preparation, destiny revelation, and destiny fulfillment. That is, over a period of time God shapes a leader with experiences which prepare, reveal, and finally brings about completion of destiny. The destiny continuum shown in Figure 1,2 Ti 8-1 graphically portrays the destiny pattern.

Destiny To Be Fulfilled		**Destiny Fulfilled**

time------------------>
emergence of leader unfolds-------------------->

Stage 1   **Stage 2**   **Stage 3**

preparation   **unfolding revelation,**
                                    increasing confirmation
                                                                              realization

Figure 1,2 Ti 8-1. The Destiny Continuum—A Pictorial Display of the Destiny
                    Pattern

---

[233] Walt Bertelsen studied with me in 1985. He did special studies throughout the scriptures, researching the concept of sense of destiny. His unpublished paper (1985) was helpful in identifying kinds of sense of destiny experiences and the notion of the destiny continuum.

Can emerging leaders be sensitized to destiny experiences? Yes. By knowing what a sense of destiny is and by recognizing the destiny pattern one can become sensitized to how God works and thus be able to hear and respond to God regarding one's destiny. Becoming sensitized to kinds of destiny experiences and seeing Biblical examples of them is an important next step in the process of becoming aware of a sense of destiny.

Four Categories of Destiny Experiences

Destiny processing can be categorized under four headings. Table 1,2 Ti 8-1 gives these categories with a brief explanation.

Table 1,2 Ti 8-1. Four Categories of Destiny Experiences

Category	Explanation
Type I destiny item	a destiny experience which is an awe-inspiring experience in which God is sensed directly as acting or speaking in the life. Example: Moses at the burning bush.
Type II destiny item	an indirect destiny experience in which some aspect of destiny is linked to some person other than the leader and is done indirectly for the leader who simply must receive its implications. Example: Hannah's promise to give Samuel to God.
Type III destiny item	the build-up of a sense of destiny in a life because of the accumulation of providential circumstances which indicate God's arrangement for the life. See Apostle Paul's birth and early life situation.
Type IV destiny item	the build-up of a sense of destiny in a life because of the sensed blessing of God on the life, repeatedly. Seen by others and recognized by them as the Hand of God on the life. See Joseph.

Are sense of destiny, the destiny pattern, and destiny processing biblical concepts? If you mean are there passages that say here is what a sense of destiny is or here is the destiny pattern or here are the four types of destiny experiences, then no. But if you mean are these concepts illustrated in the Scriptures? Do these concepts help us see things in the Scriptures? Then the answer is definitely yes. Consider the following three cases—Two O.T. and one N.T. You will see that, yes, these are certainly seen in the Bible.

Destiny To Be Fulfilled	**Destiny Fulfilled**

time----------------->
emergence of leader unfolds-------------------->

Stage 1   **Stage 2**   **Stage 3**

preparation   **unfolding revelation,**
                         increasing confirmation
                                              realization

(figure continued on next page)

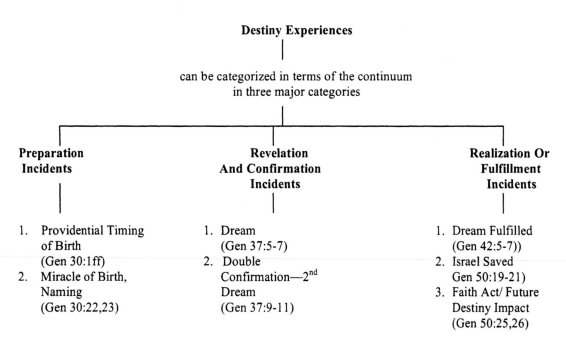

Figure 1,2 Ti 8-2. Joseph's Destiny Processing and Three Fold Destiny Pattern

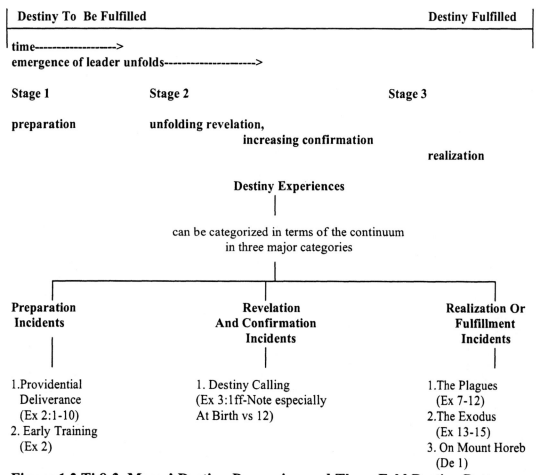

Figure 1,2 Ti 8-3. Moses' Destiny Processing and Three Fold Destiny Pattern

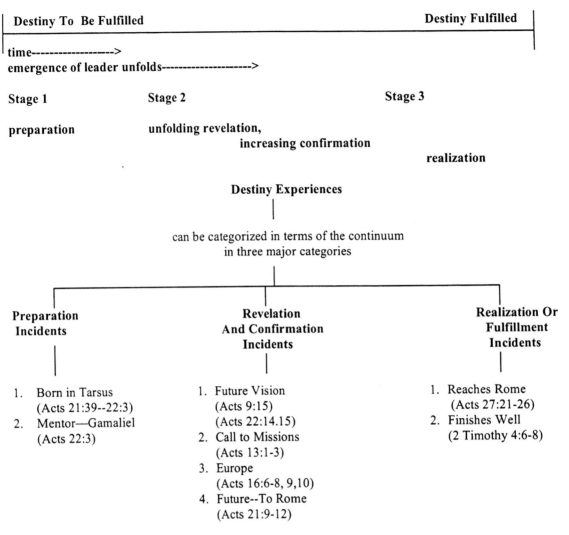

| Destiny To Be Fulfilled | | Destiny Fulfilled |

time------------------>
emergence of leader unfolds-------------------->

Stage 1   **Stage 2**   **Stage 3**

preparation   unfolding revelation,
                         increasing confirmation
                                            realization

Destiny Experiences

can be categorized in terms of the continuum
in three major categories

Preparation   **Revelation**   **Realization Or**
Incidents   **And Confirmation**   **Fulfillment**
                         Incidents   **Incidents**

1. Born in Tarsus   1. Future Vision   1. Reaches Rome
   (Acts 21:39--22:3)   (Acts 9:15)   (Acts 27:21-26)
2. Mentor—Gamaliel   (Acts 22:14.15)   2. Finishes Well
   (Acts 22:3)   2. Call to Missions   (2 Timothy 4:6-8)
                            (Acts 13:1-3)
                         3. Europe
                            (Acts 16:6-8, 9,10)
                         4. Future--To Rome
                            (Acts 21:9-12)

Figure 1,2 Ti 8-4. Paul's Destiny Processing and Three Fold Destiny Pattern

Final Questions

Can these young leaders be encouraged to seek and express these experiences and rely on them as their leadership unfolds? I noticed Joseph was young when God gave him his two dreams that foreshadowed his destiny. I have repeatedly encouraged young leaders in my classes (and older ones who have not experienced significant destiny processing) to be open to God's destiny processing. In fact, I have told them not only to be open, but I have told them to expect it. Reach out by faith and see God reveal their destiny to them. And God has done this.

Are there dangers in promoting a sense of destiny to young leaders? Yes, there are. Particularly is this true of young leaders who have strong egos and lots of ambition. They can easily impose their own desires on what they think might be their sense of destiny. But God has a way of bringing to earth those with high ambition and giving them a Holy Ambition. And I learned long ago that a leader can not afford to ignore some truth simply because others abuse it.

Do all leaders have a sense of destiny? All Biblical leaders who accomplished things for God did have a growing awareness of their sense of destiny. I think that leaders at higher levels of leadership responsibility will necessarily need a clearer sense of destiny since there leadership will influence so many more.

Conclusion

Remember, no leader in the Bible ever accomplished anything for God without a sense of destiny. Understanding how it develops is a good start on getting your sense of destiny.

See *life purpose,* **Glossary**. See **Articles,** *42. Paul—A Sense of Destiny; Life Purpose—Biblical Examples; Destiny Examples from Scripture.*

Relevance of the Article to 1,2 Timothy
This article was originally written for use with 1,2 Ti. It exposes several important ideas concerning giftedness. One, giftedness can be ignored by a leader with a result of less effective ministry. Two, giftedness can be imparted by Apostolic authority to an emerging leader. Three, a leader is responsible to steward his/her giftedness. Four, giftedness can be developed for more efficient use in ministry. Word Gifts must be developed. It also shows Paul's concern for his young mentoree to develop giftedness. Leaders moving into their late 30s and early 40s have a tendency to plateau, rather than continue developing their giftedness.

9. Developing Giftedness—Paul's Advice To Timothy

Introduction
Paul was concerned for Timothy's development. This concern flows throughout 1,2Ti. Table 1,2 Ti 9-1 lists passages and developmental implications. The central thrust of development—contained in 2Ti 2:15; 3:16,17—concerns developing his word gifts.[234]

Table 1,2 Ti 9-1. Paul's Advice To Timothy—Developmental Implications

Passage	Implications for Development
1Ti 4:6-10	• Foundational teaching in the Scriptures forms the basis for development. • **Spiritual disciplines promote growth and have implications for the here and now and eternity.** • Teaching foundational truth is a means of growth. A teacher learns far more than the learners.
1Ti 4:11-16	• Modeling growth and its end result—maturity provides a younger leader with the foundation for influencing others. • The public reading of Scriptures, appropriate for situations (with the study of them in private to see that they are appropriate) is a major means of development. • Development of public oratorical skills are necessary for a leader who applies Scripture with persuasive power. • **Development of one's spiritual gift is a responsibility of a leader.** • Development in a leader should be recognized by followers. • A leader is ultimately responsible for his/her own personal growth and for development of ministry. • **To ignore development is to open oneself to danger—plateauing at the least and being set aside from leadership at the most.**
1Ti 6:11-16	• Development implies growth in character as revealed by such things as integrity, holiness, faith, love, steadfastness, gentleness. • Development will involve appropriation of the resources of the Christian life so as to make them practical in life.

---

[234] *Word Gifts, Power Gifts, Love Gifts* describe corporate gifting. Primary *Word Gifts* include apostleship, prophecy, evangelism, pastoral, and exhortation. See **Glossary**. See **Articles**, 62. *Spiritual Gift Clusters; 63. Spiritual Gifts, Giftedness and Development.*

2Ti 1:3-10	• A foundational heritage pattern forms an advantageous basis for development. • **A leader must develop and use a spiritual gift or lose his/her influence via that gift.**
2Ti 2:14-19	• One goal of development of one's word gifts involves study and use of the Word of God with power. **The motivating factor for this is pleasing God in how the Word of God is used.**
2Ti 2:20-26	• Purity is a major character developmental goal. A leader with **purity** as a hallmark will be especially used by God. • **Gentleness** is a second major character developmental goal. A gentle leader wins opponents by persuasion.
2Ti 3:10-17	• Development in the Scriptures involves experiential demonstration of them in the life and breeds confidence in a leader. • The Foundational Heritage pattern should have as a major developmental goal the grounding of a young person in the Word. This grounding has great effect when the models themselves live out the Word. • **The Bible is the primary tool for developing a leader. It can develop a leader completely for leadership, that is, one who studies and uses it.**

Paul was a mentor (counselor, spiritual guide, teacher, model) who was concerned with development for Timothy—of particular concern was his grounding in the Scriptures.

See *Heritage Pattern*; **Glossary**. See **Article**, 5. *Bible Centered Leader*.

Relevance of the Article to 1,2 Timothy

This article was originally written to show how Paul committed to Timothy a sense of leadership responsibility—the notion of entrustment. The very existence of the two letters to the Corinthians illustrates Paul's own sense of responsibility for these two churches and by implications all the other church plants he had been involved in—indeed he stresses that in 2 Co 11:28 (Beside those things that are without, that which cometh upon me daily, the care of all the churches.). This was Paul's concern in his mid-fifties. Paul continued right up to the end to demonstrate this value of entrustment in his two letters to Timothy concerning the church at Ephesus. Paul has released this church to its own indigenous leadership (Acts 20). But he still feels the responsibility of it. And he not only models that entrustment, but also exhorts Timothy about it. Older leaders who recognize the importance of mentoring can impact mentorees with life changing effect by modeling what they teach. They back up their words with their own lives.

10. Entrustment—A Leadership Responsibility

In the midst of a trial Paul makes an astonishing statement.

> Yet I am completely confident. For I know whom I have believed, and am persuaded that he is able to keep that which was entrusted[235] to me until that day.   2Ti 1:12

What was entrusted to him?

> ...which is in harmony with the glorious gospel of the blessed God, which was entrusted to me. 1Ti 1:11

> And this is why I was established[236] as a preacher, and an apostle. I speak the truth in Christ, and lie not; a teacher of faith and truth to the Gentiles. 1Ti 2:7

> So I was divinely chosen[237] as a preacher, and an apostle, and a teacher. 12 For this reason I am suffering [in prison]. 2Ti 1:11

Paul viewed his call to ministry and its ensuing destiny as a special leadership task. He would take the Gospel to the Gentiles. This task was an entrustment.

---

[235] Paul viewed his leadership ministry as something entrusted to him—a leadership stewardship—that he was to use and fulfill. He also recognized that God would protect him in the carrying out of that trusteeship until it was finished. Finally, he knew he would have an accounting for it (That Day). One could not have this view nor the confidence about it without a strong sense of destiny—a major *leadership committal*, see **Glossary**.

[236] Again, an assertion of divine assignment from God. Established (SRN 5087) carries the sense of appointing or ordaining as was seen in putting in 1:12. See also 1:1 Apostle by the commandment of God and also the Pauline salutations: Ro 1:1; 1Co 1:1; 2Co 1:1; Gal 1:1; Eph 1:1; Col 1:1; 1Ti 1:1; 2Ti 1:1; Tit 1:1. These also strongly assert a divine calling. Leaders need a strong sense of God's calling for their lives if they are to persevere and be effective over a lifetime.

[237] The heart of a ministry that is effective begins here. This is a statement of a *leadership committal*, see **Glossary**—a response to God's call on a life for leadership. It is a *sense of destiny* experience, *a spiritual benchmark*, which a leader can always look back to and be bolstered in ministry. See **Article, 60. Spiritual Benchmarks.**

Definition   A <u>leadership entrustment</u> is the viewing of one's call to leadership and its ensuing ministry as a trust, something committed or entrusted to one to be used or cared for in the interest of God, who has given the trust. It is a leadership stewardship.

Paul ties his entrustment back to his destiny call. Further, he is certain that God will protect that entrustment. Four Pauline leadership values embedded in these forceful quotes include:

1. Paul believed that God had entrusted to him his leadership task to preach the Gospel to the Gentiles.
2. Paul believed that he was accountable to God for that entrustment.
3. Paul believed that he must guard that entrustment.
4. Paul believed that God would protect him until that entrustment was finished.

Further, Paul saw Timothy's ministry as an entrustment—an entrustment that he as an Apostolic leader had been involved in imparting.

This command I am entrusting to you, son Timothy. It is based on the prophecies which were given about you. These words should encourage you to fight on bravely. 1Ti 1:18

Don't keep on neglecting your spiritual gift, which was given to you by prophecy in conjunction with the laying on of the hands of the leaders. 1Ti 4:14

Dear Timothy, guard what has been entrusted to you. Avoid worldly and fruitless discussions and false tenets of "so called science." 1Ti 6:20

Guard carefully what was entrusted to you with the help of the Holy Spirit who lives within us. 2Ti 1:14

As leaders today, we should take away several lessons from this brief introduction of entrustment.

Lesson 1.   We should be sure of our call—the stronger is our call and our sense of divine establishment in our ministry, the better.
Lesson 2.   We should see our ministry as a leadership stewardship.
Lesson 3.   We should confidently trust God to preserve us in our ministry till He has done what He wants to do through us.
Lesson 4.   We may, with God's leading, responsibly pass on to others a leadership trust.

See **Articles**, 8. *Destiny Pattern; 60. Spiritual Benchmarks; 42. Paul—A Sense of Destiny; 3. Apostolic Functions—Comparison of Titus and Timothy.*

Relevance of the Article to 1,2 Timothy
This article was originally written to show the development of the Ephesian chuch over time and place 1,2 Ti into that time perspective. This article simply gives the time framework of the various happenings in this important church—especially as seen in Paul's ministry to it. Finally, we see in John's writing of the Revelation where the church was nearing the turn of the century. All in all, this tracing of the life of the Ephesian church over time should warn us that churches change over time—usually exhibiting the following: loss of vital life that develops inwardly and reaches out; increasing nominality; lack of solving its own church problems (all churches have them); deterioration of leadership—usually in character but often in abusive practices; heresy arises—either orthopraxic or orthodoxic practices creep in because of weakened leadership. John emphasizes that the church at Ephesus had responded somewhat to Paul's admonitions but had lost their initial passion for Christ and ministry (left their first love). The major implication of this article for churches today is that churches today should chart their development over time and be aware of the kinds of changes that may arise, so as to correct the negative emphases and maintain vibrancy in their ministry for God.

11. Ephesian Church—Its Time-Line

The Ephesian Church—Its Critical Times
It is important when studying 1,2Ti to recognize where the church was in terms of its history and development. Figure 1 below gives a time-line with approximate times when the Ephesian church is mentioned in Scripture. Table 11-1 gives a brief explanation of each marker event. From Paul's first encounter with the church at Ephesus till he wrote 1 and 2 Timothy was probably a minimum of 10 years and a maximum of 19 years—most likely about 15 years. When John wrote the church was 30-40 years old.

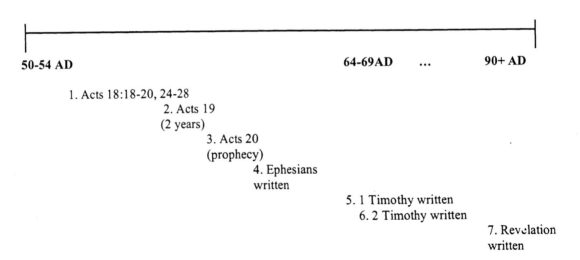

Figure 1,2 Ti 11-1. Time-Line of Church at Ephesus and Biblical Information

Table 1,2 Ti 11-1. Seven Marker Events in Ephesian Church

Marker Event	Brief Explanation
1. Acts 18:18-20 Acts 18:24-28	Paul travels to Ephesus with Priscilla and Aquila as part of his team. He leaves them behind and goes on to Jerusalem to keep his vow. In Paul's absence Priscilla and Aquila mentor Apollos. Apollos has a strong public gift and ministry at Ephesus.
2. Acts 19	Paul returns to Ephesus. He teaches on the Holy Spirit. Twelve men are baptized in the name of the Lord Jesus. Paul imparts the Holy Spirit to them by the laying on of hands. They speak in tongues and prophesy after receiving the Holy Spirit. Paul teaches there in the synagogue for three months. After opposition he moves to another location and teaches in the school of Tyrannus. This lasts for two years. So the Ephesian church should be one of the better taught churches. Spiritual warfare occurs with great power encounter, demons cast out, and the burning of demonic books and fetishes. Paul sends messengers into Macedonia in preparation for going there. The great controversy about the goddess Diana takes place. Demetrius, a silver smith, leads the opposition.
3. Acts 20:17-38	In one of the great leadership Passages Paul talks to the elders of the church of Ephesus. Note, this is now an indigenous church with its own leaders. Paul teaches on the responsibility of leadership. He exhorts to know and use the Word. He warns them with prophetic insight of heretical leaders who will come to the church from without and arising from within. He parts, knowing he will probably never see them again.
4. Ephesians written	At the time of the writing of the Ephesian letter the church is relatively stable. Paul does not single out heresies. He teaches on the nature and purpose of the church in God's plans. He talks about what it means to walk as Christians. He talks about unity in the church. He talks about various relationships. He has a brief passage on spiritual warfare. But on the whole the church here is fairly healthy.
5. 1 Timothy written	By this time a number of heresies have arisen just as Paul predicted in Acts 20. So Paul sends in Timothy from the outside to try to help straighten out the situation. Timothy is like an outside consultant coming into a church which has its own leadership. Paul mentors Timothy via this letter, particularly sponsoring him, counseling him, and giving spiritual advice about his life as well as teaching for the church situations.
6. 2 Timothy written	Paul sends his farewell letter. Again Paul mentors Timothy with particular emphasis on spirituality mentoring, counseling, and teaching for the church situation.
7. Revelation written	John writes. Apparently the church had taken hold and dealt with the heresies. But it was now an older church and was in need of renewal.

Remember, whenever you are studying one of the marker events given in Table 1,2 Ti 11-1, place the Ephesian church in its proper time perspective.

Relevance of the Article to 1,2 Timothy

Paul exhorts Timothy with the words of 1 Ti 6:12, "Struggle well in your Christian life as you *appropriate and realize the Christian life* you committed yourself to before many witnesses," In this admonition, Paul is touching on an attitude a young leader must have if that leader wants to continue well. This same attitude is captured by Paul's use of the *fear and trembling idiom*. This article explains that particular idiom and that important value—persevering in the Christian life, realizing who it is that enables that perseverance, God. This article also models how one captures an idiom. Usually an idiom is interpreted literally by one not in the culture. There are numerous idioms referred to in 1,2 Ti. This article should help assuage the reader's doubts about our careful references to these many idioms. Due diligence has been done.

12. Fear and Trembling—The Right Attitude

Paul the Apostle uses a strange phrase, *fear and trembling*, three times in his writings—Php 2:12, 2Co 7:15 and Eph 6:5. What is it? What does it mean? How is it used?

Fear and trembling is an idiom. An idiom is a group of words whose meaning is not given from the literal interpretation of the words making up the idiom. Some idioms follow patterns, like *the absolute for the relative*. Others do not, like *gnashing of teeth*. The idiom, fear and trembling, is not a pattern idiom. If an idiom has a pattern then you can then simply reverse the pattern whenever you see some manifestation of that idiom. Some idioms do not have a pattern. Speakers of a language know how to use the idiom or learn how by seeing it used in some context. But they don't always know exactly what it means but simply when and how to use it.

When someone doesn't know something is an idiom they try to interpret it literally. That is the case with most modern day Bible readers. And that is what most people do with *fear and trembling*. They somehow see a picture of someone in so much fear that their knees are shaking or physically trembling. But that is not what Paul is trying to convey with *fear and trembling*. There are at least three ways you can find out what an idiom is: 1. Ask a native speaker who knows; 2. If it is used in poetic sections of Scripture often the parallelism can help explain it; 3. Grasp the intended meaning from some explanation or shaping in the surrounding context. It is this third method that helps one see *fear and trembling*.

Definition   The fear and trembling idiom is the use of words to describe an attitude of appropriate respect for something. The something could be God, could a person, or could be a combination including some process.

Look at the 3 immediate verses in which the fear and trembling idiom occurs.

1. 2Co 7:15
15 And his affection abounds all the more toward you, as he remembers the obedience of you all, how you received him with *fear and trembling*.

2. Php 2:12, 13
12 So then, my beloved, just as you have always obeyed, not as in my presence only, but now much more in my absence, work out your salvation with *fear and trembling;*

3. Eph 6:5
5 Slaves, be obedient to those who are your masters according to the flesh, with *fear and trembling*, in the sincerity of your heart, as to Christ.

The 2Co passage gives information which helps define the idiom. The context makes it clear. Paul had sent Titus on a tough mission. He was to collect money from the Corinthians who had promised to send money a year before but had not followed through. Now Paul is in the midst of a conflict with them over his own spiritual authority with them. In the midst of this they could have refused to receive Titus. Instead, they received him with *fear and trembling*, that is, with the appropriate respect due him as a messenger of Paul. They listened to him, obeyed him, followed his advice. Here appropriate and proper respect is for a person. If you trace the idiom back to the other two passages with this idea in mind it is seen that appropriate respect can be for God and the salvation process He is working or the appropriate respect a slave should have for a slave owner.

The concept of capture has to do with reducing the idiom to regular language so a reader can understand it easily but giving it the emphasis intended. You have captured a figure or idiom when you can give its plain meaning yet emphasize it. Here is the capture of this idiom (boldfaced indicates the capturing language) in its three uses. For each of the three I give the surrounding contextual unit, not just the verse in which the idiom occurs.

The contextual unit for 7:15 is 7:13b-16. Here is the unit with the idiom captured (see bold print).

1. 2Co 7:15.
And besides our comfort, we rejoiced even much more for the joy of Titus, because his spirit has been refreshed by you all. 14 For if in anything I have boasted to him about you, I was not put to shame; but as we spoke all things to you in truth, so also our boasting before Titus proved to be [the] truth. 15 And his affection abounds all the more toward you, as he remembers the obedience of you all, how you received him **appropriately as if he were me and with respect due an apostle** (and followed his advice). 16 I rejoice that in everything I have confidence in you.

The entire context for the second passage is verses is 2:12-18. See bold print for capture.

2. Php 2:12,13.
12 So then, my beloved, just as you have always obeyed, not as in my presence only, but now much more in my absence, work out your **salvation always remembering who it is that is involved**; 13 for it is God who is at work in you, both to will (the wanting to do) and to work (and the doing of it) for [His] good pleasure. 14 Do all things without grumbling or disputing; 15 that you may prove yourselves to be blameless and innocent, children of God above reproach in the midst of a crooked and perverse generation, among whom you appear as lights in the world, 16 holding fast the word of life, so that in the day of Christ I may have cause to glory because I did not run in vain nor toil in vain. 17 But even if I am being poured out as a drink offering upon the sacrifice and service of your faith, I rejoice and share my joy with you all. 18 And you too, [I urge you,] rejoice in the same way and share your joy with me.

The entire context for the third passage is 6:5-9. See bold print for capture.

3. Eph 6:5.
5 Slaves, be obedient to those who are your masters according to the flesh, **with appropriate respect for them, that is, sincerity of your heart, just like you respect Christ**; 6 not by way of eyeservice, as men-pleasers, but as slaves of Christ, doing the will of God from the heart. 7 With good will render service, as to the Lord, and not to men, 8 knowing that whatever good thing each one does, this he will receive back from the Lord, whether slave or free. 9 And, masters, do the same things to them, and give up threatening, knowing that both their Master and yours is in heaven, and there is no partiality with Him.

So then *fear and trembling* is an idiom. It means *appropriate respect for*. It is used in Php 2:12 and Eph 6:5 to exhort hearers to have a proper respect. In Php 2:12, it presses for an awesome respect for growth in their lives because of who it is, God, who is working in and through them to accomplish this growth. In Eph 6:5, slaves are to have a proper respect for their masters, even though the slavery institution is not ideal. In 2 Cor 7:15 Paul uses the idiom to describe how well the Corinthians received Titus, for which is grateful. It is the Php 2:12 use which still applies today. Paul in the Php epistle is demonstrating in his own life what it means to have a Christ-centered life. And he is exhorting his hearers to the same life-style. Leaders everywhere, like Paul, want to see the people they are influencing having a clear understanding of the processes God uses to shape lives and bring growth. Further, they want them to have an awesome appropriate respect for God's working in their lives—such a respect as to call forth obedience and partnership with God in the process. The Php context makes it clear. That appropriate respect and obedient response will cause them to shine out like lights in darkness to the world in which they live. Such an attitude will impact those around who need the message of what it means to have a Christ-centered life.

See Also **Article** *13. Figures and Idioms in the Bible.* See **For Further Study, Bibliography,** Clinton **Interpreting the Scriptures: Figures and Idioms**. Altadena, Ca.: Barnabas Publisher

Relevance of the Article to 1,2 Timothy

Numerous idioms are referred to in 1,2 Ti. This article gives the underlying approach to the study of idioms along with the many idioms I have identified in my on-going study of the Bible.

13. Figures and Idioms in the Bible

Introduction to Figures

All language is governed by law—that is, it has normal patterns that are followed. But in order to increase the power of a word or the force of expression, these patterns are deliberately departed from, and words and sentences are thrown into and used in unusual forms or patterns which we call figures. A figure then is a use of language in a special way for the purpose of giving additional force, more life, intensified feeling and greater emphasis. A figure of speech is the author's way of underlining. He/She is saying, "Hey, take note! This is important enough for me to use a special form of language to emphasize it!" And when we remember the fact that the Holy Spirit has inspired this product we have—the Bible—we are not far wrong in saying figures are the Holy Spirit's own underlining in our Bibles. We certainly need to be sensitive to figurative language.

Definition   A <u>figure</u> is the unusual use of a word or words differing from the normal use in order to draw special attention to some point of interest.

For a figure, the unusual use itself follows a set pattern. The pattern can be identified and used to interpret the figure in normal language. Here are some examples from the Bible. I will make you fishers of people. Go tell that fox. Quench not the Holy Spirit. I came not to send peace but a sword. As students of the Bible we need to be sensitive to figures and know how to interpret and catch their emphatic meaning.

Definition   A figure or idiom is said to be <u>captured</u> when one can display the intended emphatic meaning in non-figurative simple words.

One of the most familiar figures in the Bible is Psalm 23:1. The Lord is my shepherd. I shall not lack. *Captured*: God personally provides for my every need.

E.W. Bullinger, an expert on figurative language, lists over 400 different kinds of figures. he lists over 8000 references in the Bible containing figures. In Romans alone, Bullinger lists 253 passages containing figurative language. However, w ɔ do not need to know all of those figures for the most commonly occurring figures number much less than 400. Figure 1,2 Ti 13-1 below list the 11 most common figures occurring in the Bible. If we know them we are well on our way to becoming better interpreters of the Scripture. In fact, you can group these 11 figures under three main sub-categories, which simplifies learning about them.

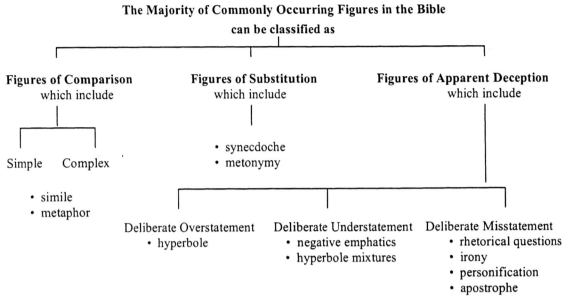

Figure 1,2 Ti 13-1.   11 Common Figures of Speech

Table 1,2 Ti 13-1 below gives these 11 figures of speech, a Scriptural reference containing the figure, and the basic definition of each of these figures.

Table 1,2 Ti 13-1: 11 Figures in the Bible Defined

Category/ Figure	Scriptural Example	Definition
Figures of Comparison: 1. Simile 2. Metaphor	simile—Isa 53:6 metaphor—Ps 23:1	A <u>simile</u> is a stated comparison of two unlike items (one called the real item and the other the picture item) in order to display one graphic point of comparison. A <u>metaphor</u> is an implied comparison in which two unlike items (a real item and a picture item) are equated to point out one point of resemblance.
Figures of Substitution 3. Metonymy 4. Synecdoche	metonymy—Ac 15:21 Moses for what he wrote synecdoche—Mt 8:8 roof for the whole house.	A <u>metonymy</u> is a figure of speech in which (usually) one word is substituted for another word to which it is closely related in order to emphasize something indicated by the relationship. A <u>synecdoche</u> is a special case of metonymy in which (again usually) one word is substituted for another to which it is related as, a part to a whole or a whole to a part.
Figures of Apparent Deception— Deliberate Overstatement: 5. Hyperbole 6. Hyperbolic mixtures	hyperbole—1Co 4:14-16 ten thousand instructors hyperbolic mixture—2 Sa 1:23 swifter than eagles, stronger than lions	A <u>hyperbole</u> is the use of conscious exaggeration (an overstatement of truth) in order to emphasize or strikingly excite interest in the truth. Hyperbole is sometimes combined with other figures such as comparison and substitution. When such is the case it is called a <u>hyperbolic mixture</u> figure.

Figures of Apparent Deception— Deliberate understatement: 7. Negative emphatics	negative emphatics—Mk 12:34 not far = very near	A figure of <u>negative emphasis</u> represents the deliberate use of words to diminish a concept and thus call attention to it or the negating of a concept to call attention to the opposite positive concept (I have deliberately merged two figures, litotes and tapenosis into one because of the basic sameness of negative emphasis).
Figures of Apparent Deception— Deliberate Misstatement: 8. Rhetorical questions 9. Irony 10. Personification 11. Apostrophe	rhetorical question—1Ti 3:5 irony—2Co 12:13 personification— Heb 4:12 apostrophe—1Co 15:55	A <u>rhetorical question</u> is a figure of speech in which a question is not used to obtain information but is used to indirectly communicate, (1) an affirmative or negative statement, or (2) the importance of some thought by focusing attention on it, or (3) one's own feeling or attitudes about something. <u>Irony</u> is the use of words by a speaker in which his/her intended meaning is the opposite of (or in disharmony with) the literal use of the words. <u>Personification</u> is the use of words to speak of animals, ideas, abstractions, and inanimate objects as if they had human form, character, or intelligence in order to vividly portray truth. <u>Apostrophe</u> is a special case of personification in which the speaker addresses the thing personified as if it were alive and listening.

I have developed in-depth explanations for all of the above figures. I have developed study sheets to aid one in analysis of them. Further I have actually identified many of these in the Scriptures and captured a number of them.[238]

Introduction to Idioms

Idioms are much more complicated than figures of speech.

Definition   An <u>idiom</u> is a group of words which have a corporate meaning that can not be deduced from a compilation of the meanings of the individual words making up the idiom.

What makes idioms difficult is that some of them follow patterns while others do not. For the patterned idioms, like figures, you basically reverse the pattern and capture the idiom. Table 13-2 lists the patterned idioms I have identified in the Bible.

Table 1,2 Ti 13-2.   13 Patterned Idioms

Idiom	Example	Definitive principle/ Description
Three Certainty Idioms: 1. Double certainty (pos/neg) 2. Fulfilled (promised/proposed) 3. Prophetic past	double certainty—1Ki 18:36 fulfilled—Ge 15:18 prophetic past—Jn 13:31	<u>double certainty</u>—a negative and positive statement (in either order) are often used to express or imply certainty. <u>fulfillment</u>—in the fulfillment idiom things are spoken of as given, done, or possessed, which are only promised or proposed. <u>prophetic past</u>—in the prophetic past idiom the past tense is used to describe or express the certainty of future action.
4. Superlative (repetitive superlative)	Ge 9:25 servant of servants Isa 26:3 peace, peace = perfect peace 2Ti 4:7	The <u>Hebrew superlative</u> is often shown by the repetition of the word. Paul uses a variation of this by often using the noun form and a verb form of the same word either back to back or in close proximity. (the good struggle I have struggled).

---

[238] See my self-study manual, **Interpreting the Scriptures**: **Figures and Idioms**.

5. Emphatic comparisons	1Pe 3:3,4	This takes three forms: absolute for relative: one thing (importance or focus item) is emphasized as being much more important in comparison with the other thing (the denial item). form not A but B really means A is less important than B. relative for absolute: One thing is positively compared to another when in effect it is meant to be taken absolutely and the other denied altogether. abbreviated emphatic comparisons: Half of the comparison is not given (either the focus item or denial items). Half of the statement is given. the half missing is an example of ellipsis and is to be supplied by the reader.
6. Climactic arrangement	Pr 6:16-19 Ro 3:10-18	To emphasize a particular item it is sometimes placed at the bottom of a list of other items and is thus stressed in the given context as being the most important item being considered.
7. Broadened kinship	Ge 29:5	Sometimes the terms son of, daughter of, mother of, father of, brother of, sister of, or begat, which in English imply a close relationship have a much wider connotation in the Bible. Brother and sister could include various male and female relatives such as cousins; mother and father could include relatives such as grandparents or great-great-grandparents, in the direct family line; begat may simply mean was directly in the family line of ancestors.
8. Imitator	Ge 6:2, 11:5	to indicate that people or things are governed by or are characterized by some quality, they are called children of or a son of. or daughter of that quality.
9. Linked noun	Lk 21:15	Occasionally two nouns are linked together with a conjunction in which the second noun is really to be used like an adjective modifying the first noun.
Indicator Idioms: 10. City indicator 11. List indicator 12. Strength Indicator	city indicator La 1:16, daughter of Zion list indicator Pr 6:16, these 6 yea 7 Strength indicator 1Sa 2:1,10	city indicator—idiomatic words, daughter of or virgin of or mother of. list indicator—2 consecutive numbers—designates an incomplete list of items of which the ones on the list are representative; other like items could be included. strength indicator—a horn denotes aggressive strength or power or authority.
13. Anthropomorphism	Lk 11:20	In order to convey concepts of God, human passions, or actions, or attributes are used to describe God.

In addition, to the patterned idioms there are a number of miscellaneous idioms which either occur infrequently or have no discernible pattern. I have labeled 32. Their meaning must be learned from context, from other original language sources, or from language experts' comments, etc.

Table 1,2 Ti 13-3:   15 Body Language Idioms

Name	Word, Phrase, Usually Seen	Example	Meaning or Concept Involved
1. Foot gesture	shake off the dust	Mt 10:14, Lk 9:5 et al	have nothing more to do with them
2. Mouth gesture	gnash on them with teeth; gnashing of teeth	Ps 35:16; 37:12 Ac 7:54 et al	indicates angry and cursing words given with deep emotion and feeling
3. Invitation	I have stretched forth my hand(s)	Ro 10:21; Pr 1:24; Is 49:22	indicates to invite, or to receive or welcome or call for mercy
4. New desire	enlighten my eyes, lighten my eyes	Ps 13:3; 19:8; 1Sa 14:29; Ezr 9:8	to give renewed desire to live; sometimes physical problem sometimes motivational inward attitude problem
5. Judgment	to stretch forth the hand; to put forth the hand	Ex 7:5; Ps 138:7; Job 1:11	to send judgment upon; to inflict with providential punishment
6. Fear	to shake the hand, to not find the hand, knees tremble	Is 19:16; Ps 76:8	to be afraid; to be paralyzed with fear and incapable of action.
7. Increase punishment	to make the hand heavy	Ps 32:4	to make the punishment more severe
8. Decreased punishment	to make the hands light	1SA 6:5	to make punishment less severe
9. Remove punishment	to withdraw the hands	Eze 20:22	to stop punishment
10. Repeat punishment	to turn the hand upon	Is 1:25	to repeat again some punishment which was not previously heeded
11. Generosity	to open the hand	Ps 104:28; 145:16	to generously give or bestow
12. Anger	to clap the hands together	Eze 21;17; 22:13	to show anger; to express derision
13. Oath	to lift up the hand	Ex 6:8; 17:16; De 32:40; Eze 20:5,6	to swear in a solemn; take an oath; an indicator of one's integrity to consider worthy to be accepted; to accept someone or be accepted by someone
14. Promise	to strike with the hands (with someone else)	Pr 6:1; Job 17:3	become a co-signer on a loan; to conclude a bargain
15. Accept	to lift up the face	Nu 6:26; Ezr 9:6; Job 22:26	to consider worthy to be accepted; to accept someone or be accepted by someone

Table 1,2 Ti 13-4:   14 Miscellaneous Idioms

Name	Word, Phrase, Usually Seen	Example	Meaning or Concept Involved
1. Success	tree of life	Pr 3:18; 11:30; 13:12; 15:4	idea of success, guarantee of success, source of motivation to successful life
2. Speech cue	answered and said	Mt 11:25; 13:2 and many others	indicates manner of speaking denoted by context; e.g. responded prayed, asked, addressed, etc.
3. Notice	verily, verily	Many times in Jn	I am revealing absolute and important truth; give close attention (this is a form of the superlative idiom)
4. Time	__ - days and ___ nights	Jn 1:17; Mt 12:40; 1Sa 30:11; Est 4:16	any portion of time of a day is indicated by or represented by the entire day
5. Lifetime	forever and ever	Ps 48;14 and many others	does not mean eternal life as we commonly use it but means all through my life; as long as I live
6. Separation	what have I to do with you	Jn 2:4; Jdg 11;12; 2Sa 16:10; 1Ki 17;18; 2Ki 3;13; Mt 8:29; Mk 5:7; Lk 8:28	an expression of indignation or contempt between two parties having a difference or more specifically not having something in common; usually infers that some action about to take place should not take place
7. Reaction	heap coals of fire	Ro 12:20; Pr 25:21	to incur God's favor by reacting positively to a situation in which revenge would be normal
8. Orate	open the mouth	Job 3:1	to speak at great length with great liberty or freedom
9. Claim	you say	Mt 26:25,63,64	means it is your opinion
10. Excellency	living, lively	Jn 4:10,11 Ac 7:38; Heb 10:20; 1Pe 2:4,5; Rev 1:17	used to express the excellency of perfection of that to which it refers
11. Abundance	riches	Ro 2:4; Eph 1:7; 3:8; Col 1:27; 2:2	used to describe abundance of or a great supply
12. Preeminence	firstborn	Ps 89:27; Ro 8:29; Col 1;15, 18; Heb 12:23	special place of preeminence; first place among many others
13. Freedom	enlarge my feet; enlarge	2Sa 22:37; Ps 4:1; 18:36	freed me; brought me into a situation that has taken the pressure off, taken on to bigger and better things
14. Reverential respect for	fear and trembling	Ps 55:5; Mk 5:33; Lk 8:47; 1Co 2:3; 2 Co 7:15; Eph 6:5, Php 2:12	describes an attitude of appropriate respect for something. The something could be God, could a person, or could be a combination including some process. Sometimes indicates confronting a difficult situation or thing with a strong awareness of it and possible consequences

Again I would recommend you refer to my manual **Figures and Idioms** to see the approach for capturing the patterned idioms.

Figures and Idioms should be appreciated, understood, and should be interpreted with emphasis.

Hardly any passage which is any one of the seven leadership genre will be without some figure or idiom.

Relevance of the Article to 1,2 Timothy
Here is a leadership value that Paul emphasizes strongly: *A Christian leader must handle finances with absolute integrity.* Financial integrity is a must for a leader. Paul has modeled that throughout his epistles. He is very careful in handling gifts, always being above board in his accountability for finances. In 1,2 Ti he deals, most openly, with the concept of leaders and finances. This article collects all of Paul's treatment of financial integrity, including the 1,2 Ti references.

14. Finances, Pauline Perspective On—A Barrier To Finishing Well

Introduction
One of the startling findings in our studies of leadership emergence theory[239] is a negative one. *Few leaders finish well.* Once this was seen, research shifted to find out why leaders don't finish well. Six barriers to finishing well were identified:
√   Barrier 1. Finances—their Use And Abuse
         Barrier 2. Power—its Abuse
         Barrier 3. Pride--which Leads To Downfall
         Barrier 4. Sex--illicit Relationships
         Barrier 5. FAMILY--Critical Issues
         Barrier 6. Plateauing.

This article is dealing with Barrier 1. Finances—their Use And Abuse .

Leaders, particularly those who have power positions and make important decisions concerning finances, tend to use practices which may encourage incorrect handling of finances and eventually wrong use. A character trait of greed often is rooted deep and eventually will cause impropriety with regard to finances. Numerous leaders have fallen due to some issue related to money. Some Biblical examples standout like Gideon's golden ephod in the Old Testament and Ananias and Sapphira's deceitful giving in the New Testament. Paul, the leader exemplar in the New Testament Leadership Era had a lot to say about leadership and finances.

Paul had a value,

Label   Value Statement
Financial Integrity.   A Christian leader must handle finances with absolute integrity.

This value stood him in good stead. Paul finished well. Paul was very careful about finances. This was not a barrier to trap him. He was cautious, maybe overly cautious with regard to leadership and finances. His careful attention to finances and their handling paid off. His general guidelines can help us today.

---

[239] Leadership emergence theory is a framework for viewing how God develops leaders over a lifetime. My research has involved the study of more than 3000 leaders, including Biblical leaders, historical leaders, and contemporary leaders.

Pauline Passages Dealing With Finances

Table 1,2 Ti 14-1 displays a number of passages. Paul talks either directly or indirectly about finances and leadership. Scan this list. Then I will print out the Biblical context of each of these and make some explanatory comments about them.

Table 1,2 Ti 14-1. Pauline Passages
On Finances and Leadership

From 1 Corinthians: 9:3-22, 16:1-4, 16:5-7, 16:10, 11, 15-18
From 2 Corinthians: 2:16b, 17, 8:16-24, 12:14, 15
From Galatians 6:6
From Philippians 4:14-20
From 1 Timothy 3:2b-5, 3:6, 5:9-16, 17-20, 6:6-10
From 2 Timothy 2:3-7
From Titus1:10, 11
From Titus 3:12-14

Paul's remarks are scattered throughout his letters. Only a couple of passages are large contexts: 2 Co 8 and 1 Co 9. These two were teaching that was concentrated teaching about special aspects of giving and financial support. The rest are incidental small ideas tucked away in the midst of other things. But a careful review of each can lead to some useful observations, guidelines, principles and values.

1 Co 9:3-22

3 When people criticize my leadership, here is how I respond. 4 Don't we have a right to be given food and drink because of our work? [We sure do] 5 Don't we have the right to take along a Christian wife, like the other apostles, the brothers of the Lord, and Peter? [Sure we have that right] 6 Or are Barnabas and I the only ones who have to work to support our own ministry? [No] 7 Who ever goes to war at his own expense? [No one] Who plants a vineyard and does not eat of its fruit? [No one] Or who tends a flock and does not drink of the milk of the flock? [No one]

8 Is this just human reasoning? [No] Doesn't the Old Testament law say the same also? [Yes, it does] 9 For it is written in the law of Moses,

"You shall not muzzle an ox
while it treads out the grain."

Is it just oxen God is concerned about? [No] 10 Wasn't He also speaking to us? [Yes] No doubt it is for our sakes, this is written. The person who plows and the person who reaps should do their work in anticipation of getting a share of the crop. 11 If we have sown spiritual seed among you, is it too much to expect to reap material benefits? [I don't think so] 12 If others have the right to expect benefits for ministering to you, don't we have an even greater right? [yes, we do; but here is my point!]

Nevertheless we have not used this right. We have had to put up with lots in order not to hinder the gospel of Christ. 13 Don't you know that those working in the temple have a share of the sacrifices brought to the altars? [for their meals] 14 In the same way, the Lord has commanded that those who preach the gospel should get their living from it. 15 But I have not used this right, nor do I now write these things in order to claim these rights. I would rather die first than impose these rights. 16 I have no right to boast because I preach the Gospel. I am compelled to do so due to my calling. What an awful thing it would be if I didn't preach the Gospel! 17 For if I did my ministry out of my own desire, I would deserve to be rewarded. But I do it because it has been given me as a trust. 18 Do I get any reward then? [You bet] I get satisfaction when I preach the Gospel without charging anyone. This certainly keeps me from abusing my authority and demanding my rights.

19 Since I am not under obligation to anyone I am free to minister; yet I have made myself a slave to all in order to win as many as possible. 20 With the Jews I live like a Jew to win them. When I am with those who strictly follow the law, I do too, even though I am free from the law. 21 In the same way, when I am with Gentiles who do not have the Jewish law, I identify with them as much as I can in order to win

them. I do not discard God's law but I do obey the law of Christ. 22 With those weak in the faith I become weak like them in order to win them. I can adapt to different situations that I might save some of them by any means.

Comment On 1 Co 9:3-22

Paul has used this large buildup of rhetorical questions[240] to show that he has a right to expect financial remuneration from these Corinthians to whom he has done a fundamental work in bringing the Gospel to them. Now he makes his point. "I gave up this right in order not to hinder the Gospel being received by you." He thus models the guideline of giving up a right for the better good that he has just taught on in chapter 8. He will come back to this support problem in chapter 16.

Paul is in this contextual flow dealing with two of the major barriers to a leader finishing well: (1) financial issues, (2) abuse of power. He is careful to avoid being trapped by either one.

There is an implication here. I am not paid by people; therefore they can't order me around. NLT captures this as, *This means I am not bound to obey people just because they pay me...*

Paul's flexibility in adapting to Jewish and non-Jewish situations implies: (1) He has a core (law of Christ) which he holds on to but he also has a lot of give and take in peripheral things; (2) More importantly, he can give up his rights with regards to these peripheral issues, like finances which to others may seem core. He does this in order to get the best hearing possible for the Gospel. When he speaks of being weak, he means on some disputed practice on which he, himself, has freedom. But he can give up that right[241]

1 Co 16:1-4

1 Now concerning the collection for the Church in Jerusalem— do what I told the churches in Galatia to do. 2 On the first day of every week each one of you should put some money aside, in proportion to what you have earned. That way there will be no need for special collections when I come. 3 And when I come, I will send the ones you approve, along with letters of recommendation, to take your liberal offerings to Jerusalem. 4 If appropriate, I may also accompany them.

Comments on 1 Co 16:1-4

Notice, Paul advocates proportionate giving, not a tithe. Note also the systematic giving.

Note the special care to maintain integrity with regard to finances; more than one person who these Corinthians know will be handling these finances. See also 2Co 8:18-21 for another reference to this integrity guideline. Paul is audacious—asking for money from this problem filled church. He expands on this quick teaching on giving in 2Co 8,9. Note he implies that the Galatian church is following his orders about giving—a motivating lever to challenge the Corinthians. In 2Co 8,9 he again uses this comparative motivational technique, there using the Philippian church.

1 Co 16:5-7

5 Now I will come to you after I have been to Macedonia—for I do intend to go through Macedonia. 6 And it could be that I will stay awhile, or maybe even spend the whole winter with you. And then you may *send* me on my journey, wherever I go. 7 For I do not wish to only have a short visit. I hope to spend a longer time with you, if the Lord permits.

---

[240] Rhetorical questions are figurative language. See **Article**, *Figures and Idioms in the Bible.*

[241] A <u>disputed</u> practice a practice for which a Christian has freedom to do, from a Biblical and conscience standpoint, but for which other Christians feel is wrong for whatever reasons, a matter of conscience for them. Essentially it deals with the notion of Christian liberty. Some would see the practice as legitimate for a Christian, others would not. Paul gives guidelines on how to approach disputed practices in 1Co 8-10 and Ro 14. See my major paper on this, *Disputed Practices,* included in the READER, BibleLeadership.pdf at my website.

Comments on 1 Co 16:5-7 1 Co 16:10, 11

When Paul uses *Send* (SRN 4311) he means to send him off and fit him out with the requisites for a journey—i.e. resources, money, whatever. See also verse 11 where Paul uses this same word to urge the Corinthians to financially back Timothy.

1 Co 16:10, 11

10 Now if Timothy comes, treat him with respect. He is doing the work of the Lord, just like me. 11 Don't look down on him. But send him on his journey in peace, so that he will come back to me. I am waiting for him with the brothers.

Comments on   1 Co 16:10, 11

Paul is here acting as a mentor sponsor for Timothy. Not only does he strongly ask for Timothy to be treated with respect, he also asks that they *send* (SRN 4311 propempo) him off—that is, give him financial backing. Young leaders in Asian and African setting often do not get respect for their leadership since the cultures respect age and tend to want older leaders.

1 Co 16: 15-18

15 You know that Stephanas and his family were the first Christians in Greece. They have dedicated themselves to serving Christians. 16 I urge you, fellow Christians that you respect their leadership, and others like them who also serve. 17 I am glad that Stephanas, Fortunatus, and Achaicus came. They have made up for your lack of help. 18 For they have encouraged me just like they did you. These men deserve to be honored.

Comments on 1 Co 16: 15-18

Again as with Timothy in 16:10,11, Paul acts as a mentor sponsor, this time for Stephanus. This time raising financial support.

Paul gives a slight admonition about lack of support for himself—a problem being repeatedly dealt with in these closing remarks.

2 Co 2:16b, 17

16b And who could claim sufficiency for such a task? 17 For I am not like many, using God's word to make money. I speak in utter sincerity as one sent by God, a minister accountable to God.

Comments on 2 Co 2:16b, 17

Using (SRN 2585) is a word which means peddle or sell something for profit (with negative connotations; putting something over on the buyer). Paul accuses several groups of doing this. See the heretical teachers in Ephesus and on Crete.

2 Co 8:16-24

16 I thank God for giving Titus the same enthusiasm for you that I have. 17 He not only responded to my challenge but he did it because he himself wanted to. 18 We are sending with him a brother, highly respected by all the churches for his work in proclaiming the Good News 19 He was appointed by the churches to travel with us as we take this gift to Jerusalem. This service of love brings the Lord glory and shows that we really want to help.

20 We vant to be very *careful in handling this gift* and *avoid any criticism.* 21 We want to do what is right, not only in the sight of the Lord but in the sight of everyone.

22 And we are sending along another brother who has been thoroughly tested on many occasions. He has always been eager to help. He is now even more eager to help because of his increased confidence in you. 23 Titus is my partner in my work with you. The other brothers going with him represent the churches and are honoring Christ. 24 So show them your love. Prove to all the churches that our boasting about you was justified.

Comments on 2 Co 8:16-24

Of the six barriers to leaders finishing well, improper handling of finances, whether deliberately or just carelessly done, is probably the number three barrier: 1. illicit sexual relationships, 2. abuse of power, and 3. money problems, in that order. Usually two and three go together. Financial issues often waylay a leader. Note the special care to maintain integrity with regards to finances that Paul suggests in 1 Co 16:3,4 and Ac 11:27-30.

2 Co 12:14, 15

14 I am ready to come to you, for the third time. And I am not going *to be a burden for you.* I don't want your money; I want you. For children shouldn't have to support parents. Parents should take care of their children. 15 I will very gladly spend all I have and all that I am in order to help you. Though it seems the more I love you, the less you love me.

Comments on 2 Co 12:14, 15

When Paul says be a *burden for you*, he means try to obtain money for my own needs. Paul was above board on any issues regarding his personal finances. Note how carefully he states over and over that he did not take finances from them. Obviously he had been accused of this by the false apostles. And probably just as obvious, he is accusing these apostles of doing that very thing. That is why he is so clear about his own finances.

Gal 6:6

But let the ones being taught in the Word share with their teachers.

Comments on Gal 6:6

Followers, who recognize spiritual authority in a leader and who have been helped by that leader's ministry in their lives will naturally be generous and help that leader with financial resources. They will need to do this voluntarily since a leader with spiritual authority will never exploit that authority for his/her personal benefit.

Php 4:14-20

14 However, I am glad you shared with me in my hardship. 15 Now you Philippians know also, that in the beginning of the gospel, when I departed from Macedonia, no church gave me gifts of money; but you did! 16 For even in Thessalonica you sent twice to meet my needs. 17 I say these things not because I desire a gift. But I desire fruit that may abound to your account.

18 But I have all, and abound. I am full, having received of Epaphroditus the things which were sent from you, an aroma of a sweet smell, a sacrifice acceptable, well pleasing to God. 19 But my God *shall supply all your need* according to his riches in glory by Christ Jesus. 20 Now unto God and our Father be glory for ever and ever. Amen.

Comments on Php 4:14-20

This is a passage on corporate giving. See also 1Co 9:1-19, Gal 6:6 and 2Co 8,9 for other Pauline teaching on giving. The first two references are dominantly referring to leaders; the third one gives principles for individuals giving in a corporate situation. Followers, who recognize spiritual authority in a leader, and who have been helped by that leader in their lives will naturally be generous and help that leader with financial resources. They will need to do this voluntarily since a leader with spiritual authority will never exploit that authority for his/her personal benefit. The Philippians were just such a sensitive church. They appreciated Paul's ministry.

This is a conditional promise.[242] Those who give sacrificially can claim it. The Philippians could claim this great promise, because they have fulfilled the conditions of it. Most people who want to claim this promise don't meet the conditions—those who have sacrificially given to others.

---

[242] See promise, **Glossary**. See **Article**, *Promises of God.*

1 Ti 3:2b-5

2b These things teach and urge strongly. 3 If anyone teaches differently, and doesn't agree with this solid teaching, true teaching right from our Lord Jesus Christ, which flows from godliness, 4 then that one is proud, knows nothing, and has an unhealthy focus on questions and argumentative things. This leads to envy, strife, slander, evil suspicions, 5 as well as useless occupation of people whose minds are corrupt. They are no longer concerned with truth but using religion to make money.

Comments on 1 Ti 3:2b-5

Here we are talking about using ministry as a means for making money and duping people.

In 1Ti 3:3 (money problems), 1Ti 3:6 (pride), and 1Ti 5:2 (illicit sexual relationships), I have noted three of the six barriers commonly seen as those which waylay leaders from finishing well. Timothy had his work cut out for him at Ephesus. Here money is mentioned again. Two others are hinted: family problems—the character traits for leaders states that positively leaders must rule their families well (3:4,5, 12)—and plateauing (4:14). The only barrier missing is abuse of power.

1 Ti 3:6

Other qualities include: one who is gentle, not hotheaded, not money-hungry...

Comments On 1 Ti 3:6

Paul is describing leadership traits that Timothy should use in selecting leaders for the church in Ephesus. A leader who is in ministry for money (that is, money-hungry) can easily be led into lack of financial integrity. Lack of integrity with finances, specifically, and money matters, in general, is identified as one of the six major barriers to finishing well.

1 Ti 5:9-16

9 Don't put a widow on the widow's list who is younger than sixty. Further she should having been a loyal wife— 10 A reputation for good works. She should have brought up her children well. She should have lodged strangers, and she should have washed the saints' feet. She should have assisted those in deep trouble. She should be a good worker.

11 But the younger widows refuse (to put on the list): for when they have strong desires to marry they turn away from Christ. 12 They are judged, because they have rejected their first faith. 13 Further they idle away their time, wandering about from house to house; and not only idle, but gossiping and minding others' business saying things which they ought not. 14 I would prefer that the younger women marry, bear children, manage their households, give no opportunity for opponents to speak reproachfully 15 For some are already turned aside after Satan. 16 If any Christian woman has relatives who are widows, she must take care of them, and keep the church from being burdened; It should take care of widows who are alone and needy.

Comments on 1 Ti 5:9-16

This is a social problem that the Ephesian church faced. While we as a church may not face this exact problem it is instructive to note how Paul advises solving it. Paul solves it contextually. His solution fit the Ephesian situation. It was concerned with the testimony of these widows in the Ephesians context. It is careful application.

1 Ti 5:17-20

17 Church leader. that are exercising good leadership should be *evaluated as worthy of double pay*— especially the ones who are working hard teaching the word. 18 For the scripture says, Don't muzzle the ox that is treading out the corn. And, The laborer is worthy of his reward. 19 Don't listen to an accusation against a leader unless it is backed by two or more witnesses. 20 Those leaders that are sinning rebuke before all, that others also may fear.

Comments On 1 Ti 5:17-20

Two implications are worth noting. (1) Leaders should be recompensed for their ministry. Those doing exceptional ministry, especially word oriented ministry should be amply rewarded. (2) There are differing functions of elders—ruling, teaching.

This is an important leadership principle. Accusations against leaders must be carefully examined. There should be strong confirmation where wrongdoing is involved. Note also in vs 20 that those found in the wrong should be publicly rebuked. This serves as part of the disciplinary action to restore the leader and to warn others. It also serves to guard the credibility of leadership. Today both of these guidelines are avoided. Frequently, accusations which are unfounded are given which destroy a leader even if later proved wrong. And very seldom is there public discipline of a leader found in the wrong.

Note that the principle concerning accusation occurs in a context dealing with money.

1 Ti 6:6-10

6 But a godly life with contentment is riches indeed. 7 For we brought nothing into this world, and it is certain we can carry nothing out. 8 So we should be content to have the food and clothing we need. 9 But those that set their hearts on becoming rich, can be easily trapped by foolish and harmful desires, which lead to ruin and destruction. 10 For the love of money is the root of all evil. Some have sought this and have strayed from the faith, and suffered deep grief because of it.

Comments on 1 Ti 6:6-10

Here Paul gives some solid teaching about money. Though useful, it can not rule our lives. *Contentment* (SRN 841) refers to an inner attitude satisfied with its lot, an inner sufficiency. *Riches* (SRN 4200) translates a word meaning source of gain, or a means to gain, or gain). *Indeed* (SRN 3173) simply means great or a lot. The idea being, there is an inner source of satisfaction that a godly person has which is far better than worldly riches.

Strayed from the faith is a repeated theme in 1 Ti (See also 1:6, 20; 5:11, 15; 6:10). This is a major problem that pastors and apostolic workers will face—especially in situations of radical conversions. The setting of ones heart on becoming rich can have disastrous result, even though reached. For the love of money is the root of all evil. Some have sought this and have strayed from the faith, and suffered deep grief because of it. This desire for money (or the power it can bring) can easily sidetrack a leader or a Christian follower.

2 Ti 2:3-7

3 So endure hardness, as a good soldier of Jesus Christ. 4 If you go on a military expedition you can't get enmeshed in civilian life or you won't please your commanding officer. 5 And if a person competes to win an athletic crown, that one follows the rules or else will not be crowned. 6 A hard working farmer ought to be the first to enjoy the harvest. 7 Consider these analogies and the Lord will help you understand them.

Comments on 2 Ti 2:3-7

I think these three analogies are applied directly to Timothy's situation. The *soldier illustration* is a warning for Timothy not to get sidetracked (this is repeatedly admonished in 1Ti also); the *athlete illustration* warns that it will take discipline to pull off the ministry. Timothy must maintain integrity (play by the rules) as he faces the Ephesian problems. The *farmer illustration* probably goes to the heart of the lack of financial support for Timothy. No leader likes to have to push his own situation where finances are concerned. 1Ti 5:17,18 also dealt with this. Timothy was not being supported. Paul says, "You need to be."

Tit 1:10, 11

10 The legalists, those especially advocating Jewish circumcision, are a rebellious bunch. Their talk is as cheap as it is deceitful. 11 They must be silenced. Their negative teaching is having a disastrous effect. Whole households are being affected by it. These teachers motives are questionable — they are in it dishonestly in order to make money.

Comments on Tit 1:10, 11

Paul has clean hands here. Throughout his ministry he has bent over backwards to avoid having a reputation for making money via ministry. See especially 2 Co where he rigorously defends himself on this issue and Philippians where he shows his personal view on ministry and finances.

Tit 3:12-14

12 As soon as I send Artemas or Tychicus to you, do your best to come to me at Nicopolis, because I have decided to winter there. 13 Do everything you can to help Zenas the lawyer and Apollos on their way and see that they have everything they need.[243] 14 Our people must learn to devote themselves to doing what is good, in order that they may provide for daily necessities and not live unproductive lives.[244]

Comments on Tit 3:12-14

Paul acts here as a mentor sponsor. He is attempting to raise financial support for Zenas and Apollos. He has done this previously for Timothy and Stephanus. He does this same function, supporting others, in the 2 Corinthian letters. This is an apostolic function, raising money to help support groundbreaking/ pioneering ministry.

Pauline Observations, Principles and Values About Finances

Finances can be a blessing and a curse. Having or not having wealth is not the issue. It is the stewardship of resources that is the major issue. What they are used for is what is significant. There are dangers of having financial resources—they can subtly turn away trust from God to trust in the resources. Paul admonishes to use resources well.

Leadership Principles/ Values Suggested by this concept:
- a. Money can not be trusted as a source of power or security.
- b. Money must be appreciated as coming from God.
- c. The use of money to bring enjoyment is valid.
- d. Money ought to be a strong power base useful to do good for people.
- e. Learning to use money wisely for God's kingdom work will allow a person to experience a reality in their Christian life.

Pauline Observations, Principles and Values About Fund Raising

Churches and parachurch organizations have financial needs just like any other organization in society. These needs must be met. How leaders influence followers with respect to meeting these needs is important. Paul demonstrates this delicate matter in 2Co 8,9. Paul also sponsors Christian workers (not himself, strangely enough), hoping, to link them up with financial resources to send them on their way in their itinerate ministries. He does not make a big issue of it but incidentally mentions the need of finances for various workers like Timothy, Stephanus, Zenas and Apollos.

Some observations concerning his raising money for various ministry things include the following.

Leadership Principles/ Values Suggested by this concept:
- a. A major motivational technique[245] relates the issue of giving to the issue of absolute surrender. True freedom to give flows from a life given to God.

---

[243] Paul acts here as a mentor sponsor. He is attempting to raise financial support for Zenas and Apollos. He does this same function, supporting others, in the 2 Corinthian letters. See *mentor sponsor*, **Glossary**. See **Articles**, 47. *Paul-- Mentor for Many; 14. Finances--A Barrier To Finishing Well; 3. Apostolic Functions--Comparison of Titus and Timothy.*

[244] Two positive benefits of leading productive Christian lives are: 1) Christians provide for the necessities of life in their own setting and are not a drain on society; 2) there is the availability of resources to support the advancement of Christian work elsewhere. Paul is certainly implying that here. Productive lives involves support of God work in the world.

[245] See **Article**, 41. *Motivating Principles: Pauline Influence.*

b. Another motivational technique involves competitive comparisons with others who are poorer and yet give beyond expectations.
c. Willingness to give, not the amount given, is the criterion for giving.
d. Resources in the wider body of Christ will include surplus and great need. Where there is surplus giving should shift resources to needs.
e. Integrity in the handling of money is essential.
f. Apostolic leaders should use their influence to help connect needy leaders with financial aid.
g. Apostolic leaders are not in ministry for money but they know its importance in getting Kingdom ministry done.

Pauline Observations, Principles and Values About Giving

Chapters 8 and 9 in 2 Co give us the most comprehensive treatment of N.T. Church giving. I am certain that Paul was deeply affected by his mentor, Barnabas, concerning giving. See Ac 4:36,37; 11:27-30. Paul advocates giving to help fellow churches in need. He also advocates giving to help Christian workers (see comments above on this in 1Co 9, 16 as well as Php 4:10-17). His strong exhortations on giving highlight a number of principles which I have identified below.

Leadership Principles/ Values Suggested by this concept:
a. Christians should be led of God to give (purpose in their hearts).
b. Christians should give proportionately as God has blessed them (as opposed to the O.T.'s various tithes given out of duty).
c. Christians should give as generously as they can.
d. Christians should give joyfully out of what they have, fully expecting God to bless it beyond its intrinsic worth.
e. Christians should give to those in need out of their extra that God has supplied; they can expect the same thing to happen when they have need.
f. Christians should expect God to give them more than their needs which they can then give generously.
g. Collections should be done systematically over time so they will be ready when needed.
h. God will receive honor and praise and thanksgiving from many who are helped.
i. Those helped will remember the givers in prayer with affection;
j. There should be integrity in the handling of money given for various needs. Multiple parties of trustworthy people should be involved in the handling, helps insure integrity.

Pauline Observations, Principles and Values About Receiving Money as a Minister

A leader's ministry is worthy of remuneration. This is not a big thing with Paul. But a leader who is effective should not be ashamed of reward for having done effective ministry. (2 Ti 2:6,7)

Leadership Principles/ Values Suggested by this concept:
a. Leaders deserve remuneration for effective ministry.
b. Leaders need not be ashamed of this fact but should assume it as a God-given resource.

Conclusion

Forewarned is forearmed. There are many other reasons why leaders don't finish well—usually all related to sin in some form. Money issues have trapped many leaders and taken them out of the race. Leaders who want to finish well, Take heed! The bottom line value from Paul's teaching and modeling on leadership and finances is,

Label   Value Statement
Financial Integrity.   A Christian leader must handle finances with absolute integrity.

Most cultures will have guidelines on what integrity with respect to finances is. Make sure you, like Paul, have *clean hands* with regards to money issues.

Relevance of the Article to 1,2 Timothy
Paul is the exemplar of a leader in the church era who finishes well. 1,2 Ti vividly demonstrate this great finish of this model church leader. He models all five of these enhancements.

15. Finishing Well—Five Factors That Enhance It

Introduction to Research on Finishing Well

In 1989 in an article entitled, *Listen Up Leaders! Forewarned is Forearmed!* I summarized my research on Biblical leaders with the following opening comments.

A repeated reading of the Bible with a focus on leadership reveals four crucial observations fraught with leadership implications:

Observation 1.   Few leaders finish well.
Observation 2.   Leadership is difficult.
Observation 3.   God's enabling presence is the essential ingredient of successful leadership.
Observation 4.   Spiritual leadership can make a difference.

And what is true of Biblical leaders is equally true of historical and contemporary leaders.[246] It is the first observation to which this article speaks. Identifying the fact that few leaders finish well was a breakthrough warning for me. This led to further study. Why do few leaders finish well? What stops them? What helps them?

Five Enhancements

Comparative study of effective leaders who finished well has identified five commonalities. Not all five always appear in leaders who finish well but at least several of them do. Frequently, effective leaders who finish well will have four or five of them seen in their lives. What are these enhancements?

Enhancement 1. Perspective.

We need to have a lifetime perspective on ministry. Effective leaders view present ministry in terms of a lifetime perspective.[247] We gain that perspective by studying lives of leaders as commanded in Hebrews 13:7,8. I have been doing intensive study of leaders' lives over the past 13 years. Leadership emergence

---

[246] At the time of this article I have studied nearly 1300 (now over 3000) cases with about 50 Bible leaders, perhaps 100 historical leaders and the rest contemporary leaders. The findings for enhancements and barriers generally hold true.

[247] This is one of seven major leadership lessons derived from comparative studies. See **Article**, 29. *Leadership Lessons—Seven Major Lessons Identified.*

theory is the result of that research. Its many concepts can help us understand more fully just how God does shape a leader over a lifetime.[248]

Enhancement 2. Renewal.[249]

Special moments of intimacy with God, challenges from God, new vision from God and affirmation from God both for personhood and ministry will occur repeatedly to a growing leader. These destiny experiences will be needed, appreciated, and will make the difference in persevering in a ministry. All leaders should expectantly look for these repeated times of renewal. Some can be initiated by the leader (usually extended times of spiritual disciples). But some come sovereignly from God. We can seek them, of course, and be ready for them.

Most leaders who have been effective over a lifetime have needed and welcomed renewal experiences from time to time in their lives. Some times are more crucial in terms of renewal than others. Apparently in western society the mid-thirty's and early forty's and mid-fifty's are crucial times in which renewal is frequently needed in a leader's life. Frequently during these critical periods discipline slacks, there is a tendency to plateau and rely on one's past experience and skills, and a sense of confusion concerning achievement and new direction prevail. Unusual renewal experiences with God can overcome these tendencies and redirect a leader. An openness for them, a willingness to take steps to receive them, and a knowledge of their importance for a whole life can be vital factors in profiting from **enhancement 2** for finishing well. Sometimes these renewal experiences are divinely originated by God and we must be sensitive to his invitation. At other times we must initiate the renewal efforts.

Enhancement 3. Disciplines.[250]

Leaders need discipline of all kinds. Especially is this true of spiritual disciplines. A strong surge toward spirituality now exists in Catholic and Protestant circles. This movement combined with an increasingly felt need due to the large number of failures is propelling leaders to hunger for intimacy. The spiritual disciplines are one mediating means for getting this intimacy. Such authors as Eugene Peterson, Dallas Willard, Richard Foster and Reggie McNeal (see bibliography) are making headway with Protestants concerning spirituality. Leaders without these leadership tools are prone to failure via sin as well as plateauing.

I concur with Paul's admonitions to discipline as a means of insuring perseverance in the ministry. When Paul was around 50 years of age he wrote to the Corinthian church what appears to be both an exhortation to the Corinthians and an explanation of a major leadership value in his own life. We need to keep in mind that he had been in ministry for about 21 years. He was still advocating strong discipline. I paraphrase it in my own words.

> **I am serious about finishing well in my Christian ministry. I discipline myself for fear that after challenging others into the Christian life I myself might become a casualty. 1Co 9:24-27**

Lack of physical discipline is often an indicator of laxity in the spiritual life as well. Toward the end of his life, Paul is probably between 65 and 70, he is still advocating discipline. This time he writes to Timothy, who is probably between 30 and 35 years old.

> **...Instead exercise your mind in godly things. 8 For physical exercise is advantageous somewhat but exercising in godliness has long term implications both for today and for that which will come. (1Ti 4:7b,8)**

---

[248] My findings are available in two books, **The Making of A Leader**, published by Nav Press in 1988 and a lengthy detailed self-study manual, **Leadership Emergence Theory**, that I privately publish for use in classes and workshops.

[249] See *Daniel—And Abraham: O.T. Exemplars for Renewal.*

[250] See also my section on spiritual guides and the appendix on the disciplines in **The Mentor Handbook**, available through Barnabas Publishers. See **Articles**, 61. *Spiritual Disciplines and On-Going Leadership*; *74. Word Disciplines and Bible Centered Leadership.*

Leaders should from time to time assess their state of discipline. I recommend in addition to standard word disciplines involving the devotional life and study of the Bible other disciplines such as solitude, silence, fasting, frugality, chastity, secrecy. My studies of Foster and Willard have helped me identify a number of disciplines which can habitually shape character and increase the probability of a good finish.

Enhancement 4. Learning Posture.[251]

The single most important antidote to plateauing is a well developed learning posture. Such a posture is also one of the major ways through which God gives vision. I will describe more about how to do this in the commentary which follows.

Another of the seven major leadership lessons is *Effective leaders maintain a learning posture all their lives.* It sounds simple enough but many leaders don't heed it. Two Biblical leaders who certainly were learners all their lives and exemplified this principle were Daniel and Paul. Note how Daniel observed this principle. In Da 9 when he is quite old we find that he was still studying his Bible and still learning new things from it. And he was alert to what God wanted to do through what he was learning. Consequently, Daniel was able to intercede for his people and become a recipient of one of the great messianic revelations. Paul's closing remarks to Timothy show he was still learning. "And when you come don't forget the books Timothy!" (2Ti 4:13).

There are many non-formal training events available such as workshops, seminars, and conferences covering a variety of learning skills. Take advantage of them. A good learning posture is insurance against plateauing and a helpful prod along the way to persevere in leadership. An inflexible spirit with regards to learning is almost a sure precursor to finishing so-so or poorly.

Enhancement 5. Mentoring.[252]

Comparative study of many leaders lives indicates the frequency with which other people were significant in challenging them into leadership and in giving timely advice and help so as to keep them there. Leaders who are effective and finish well will have from 10 to 15 significant people who came alongside at one time or another to help them. Mentoring is also a growing movement in Christian circles as well as secular.

The general notion of mentoring involves a relational empowerment process in which someone who knows something (the mentor) passes on something (wisdom, advice, information, emotional support, protection, linking to resources) to someone who needs it (the mentoree, protégé) at a sensitive time so that it impacts the person's development. The basic dynamics of mentoring include attraction, relationship, response, accountability and empowerment. My observations on mentoring suggest that most likely, any leader will need a mentor at all times over a lifetime of leadership. Mentoring is available if one looks for specific functions and people who can do them (rather than an ideal mentor who can do all). God will provide a mentor in a specific area of need for you if you trust Him for one and you are willing to submit and accept responsibility.

Simply stated a final suggestion for enabling a good finish is find a mentor who will hold you accountable in your spiritual life and ministry and who can warn and advise so as to enable you to avoid pitfalls and to grow throughout your lifetime of ministry.

Conclusion

A leader ought to want to finish well. I never give this warning, few leaders finish well, and this challenge, do you want to finish well?, without an overwhelming response. Yes, I do. Then heed these five factors. Proactively take steps to get these factors working in your life. Finish well!!!

See **Articles:** 16. *Finishing Well—Six Characteristics; 29. Leadership Lessons—Seven Major Lessons Identified.*

---

[251] See Daniel who highlights this trait. **Article**—*Daniel, Exemplar of a Learning Posture.*

[252] See **Articles,** *47. Paul—Mentor for Many; 38. Mentoring—An Informal Training Model.*

Relevance of the Article to 1,2 Timothy
Paul is the exemplar of a leader in the church era who finishes well. 1,2 Ti vividly demonstrate this great finish of this model church leader. He models all six of these characteristics of finishing well.

16. Finishing Well—Six Characteristics

Introduction to Research on Finishing Well

In 1989 in an article entitled, Listen Up Leaders! Forewarned is Forearmed! I summarized my research on Biblical leaders with the following opening comments.

A repeated reading of the Bible with a focus on leadership reveals four crucial observations fraught with leadership implications:

Observation 1. Few leaders finish well.[253]
Observation 2. Leadership is difficult.
Observation 3. God's enabling presence is the essential ingredient of successful leadership.
Observation 4. Spiritual leadership can make a difference.

And what is true of Biblical leaders is equally true of historical and contemporary leaders.[254] It is the first observation to which this article speaks. Identifying the fact that few leaders finish well was a breakthrough warning for me. This led to further study. Why do few leaders finish well? What stops them? What helps them? What does it mean to finish well? This article identifies six characteristics of those finishing well.

Six Characteristics

Comparative study of effective leaders who finished well has identified six characteristics. While there may be other characteristics that I have not seen, certainly these are important ones. Not all six always appear but at least several of them do in leaders who finish well. Frequently, effective leaders who finish well will have four or five of them seen in their lives. And some, like Daniel in the O.T. and Paul in the N.T. demonstrate all of them. What are these six characteristics of those finishing well.

Characteristic 1.
They maintain a personal vibrant relationship with God right up to the end.

Example: Daniel is the classic O.T. leader who exemplifies this. In the N.T., Peter, Paul and John all demonstrate this. See their last writings—the tone, the touch with God, the revelation from God, their trust in enabling grace for their lives.

---

[253] There are around 352 or so leaders named in the Bible. And some unnamed ones as well—less than 100. There are about 100 named ones who have data that alows you to interpret their leadership. About 50 of these have enough data for evaluation of their finish. About 1 in 3 finished well. Anecdotal evidence from today indicates that this ratio is probably generous. Probably less than 1 in 3 are finishing well today.

[254] At the time of this commentary article I have studied 3000+ cases with about 50 Bible leaders, perhaps 100 historical leaders and the rest contemporary leaders. The findings for enhancements and barriers generally hold true.

Characteristic 2.
They maintain a learning posture and can learn from various kinds of sources—life especially.

This characteristic is also one of the enhancement factors for finishing well.

Example: Daniel is the classic O.T. leader who exemplifies this. See Daniel chapter nine for a late in life illustration of one who continues to study and learn from the Scriptures. Paul and Peter are the classic N.T. leaders with a learning posture (see 2Pe 3:18 and 2Ti 4:13).

Characteristic 3.
They manifest Christ-likeness in character as evidenced by the fruit of the Spirit in their lives.

Example: Daniel is the classic O.T. leader who exemplifies godliness (See the summary references to him in Eze 14:14,20). In the N.T. note the evidence of character transformation in Paul's life (2Ti 2:24 and an illustration of it—the book of Phm). Paul was a man who over a lifetime moved from a strong personality with roughness in his leadership style to a strong personality with gentleness in his leadership styles. He is evidence that God can transform a life.

Characteristic 4.
Truth is lived out in their lives so that convictions and promises of God are seen to be real.

Example: Joshua's statement about God's promises never having failed him in his closing speech demonstrate this characteristic of someone believing God and staking his life on God's truth (Jos 23:14). Paul had deep convictions about core truth that must be held on to. See the many *aside truth statements* (noted in the commentary footnotes on a number of texts in 1,2 Ti: (1:15; 2:3,4,5,6; 3:1; 3:16; 4:9, 10; 6:15) that Paul weaves into his two letters to Timothy. See also his famous stirring convictions echoed in Ac 27:22-25.

Characteristic 5.
They leave behind one or more ultimate contributions.

In a study on legacies left behind by effective leaders who finished well I have identified the following categories:

Table 1,2 Ti 16-1. Categories of Lasting Legacies

Category	Explanation
saint	a model life that others want to emulate
stylistic practitioners	a ministry model that others want to emulate
Family	promote a God-fearing family, leaving behind children who walk with God carrying on that Godly-heritage.
mentors	extensive personal ministry; end product changed lives
public rhetoricians	extensive public ministry; end product changed lives
pioneers	start new works for God; end product is new churches, new movements, new works for God

crusaders	those who correct wrongs, end product, changed institutions, societies, etc. which reflect justice, fairness, etc.
artists	those who introduce creative ways of doing things; end products—whatever is created— as well as a model for how to do things differently
founder	a special category of pioneer who starts a new Christian organization; end product, the organization
stabilizers	those who can work in churches, movements, and other organizations to improve them and keep them alive and consistent; end product the organization revitalized and efficient
researchers	those who find out why things happen the way they do in Christian endeavor; end product an, understanding of the dynamics of things that can help others in Christian work
writers	those who can capture ideas in writing in order to help others in Christian work; end product, the writing produced
promoters	those who can motivate others and inspire them to use ideation, to join movements, etc.; end product people committing themselves to new ventures

Examples: Daniel's ultimate contributions include: saint, (mentor), writer, stabilizer. Paul's ultimate contributions include: saint, mentor, pioneer, crusader, writer, promoter.

Of course, in addition to these standard categories there are also unique legacies that leaders also leave behind. These have to be described individually for each leader.

Characteristic 6.
They walk with a growing awareness of a sense of destiny and see some or all of it fulfilled.

Definition   A <u>sense of destiny</u> is an inner conviction arising from an experience or a series of experiences in which there is a growing sense of awareness that God has His hand on a leader in a special way for special purposes.

Over a lifetime a leader is prepared by God for a destiny, receives guidance toward that destiny, and increasingly completes that destiny. No Biblical leader who accomplished much for God failed to have a sense of destiny, one that usually grew over his/her lifetime.

Examples: Joseph's dreams and his saving of the embryonic nation; Moses' saving of the nation; Paul's vision to take the Gospel to the Gentiles.

Conclusion

The classic example in the O.T. of a good finish is Daniel who manifests all six characteristics. The classic example in the N.T. other than Christ is Paul. There are gradations of finishing well. Some finish well but not quite having all six or lesser intensity on one or the other major characteristics. This list of characteristics is probably not complete. Others may not agree totally with them. In that case, they should at least provide an alternate list. But these are certainly evident in many leaders who have finished well.

See **Article,** 35. *Legacy-- Leaving One Behind.*

Relevance of the Article to 1,2 Timothy

Leadership emergence theory has identified six major barriers to leaders finishing well. Paul very carefully and deliberately avoids these barriers. In fact, in his epistles he warns leaders about these barriers. Several barriers receive attention in 1,2 Ti.

17. Finishing Well—Six Major Barriers Identified

Introduction to Research on Finishing Well

In 1989 in an article entitled, *Listen Up Leaders! Forewarned is Forearmed!* , I summarized my research on Biblical leaders with the following opening comments.

A repeated reading of the Bible with a focus on leadership reveals four crucial observations fraught with leadership implications:

Observation 1.   Few leaders finish well.
Observation 2.   Leadership is difficult.
Observation 3.   God's enabling presence is the essential ingredient of successful leadership.
Observation 4.   Spiritual leadership can make a difference.

And what is true of Biblical leaders is equally true of historical and contemporary leaders.[255] It is the first observation to which this article speaks. Identifying the fact that few leaders finish well was a breakthrough warning for me. This led to further study. Why do few leaders finish well? What stops them? What helps them?

Six Barriers To Finishing Well

Comparative study of effective leaders who finished well has identified six. barriers that hindered leaders from finishing well. It only takes one of them to torpedo a leader. But frequently a leader who fails in one area will also fail in others. What are these barriers? We can learn from those who didn't finish well. We can be alerted to these barriers. We can avoid them in our own lives. Pr 22:3 tells us that,

Sensible people will see trouble coming and avoid it, but an unthinking person will walk right into it and regret it later. Pr 22:3

Let me share with you six barriers to finishing well that I have identified. We need to look ahead in our lives and not walk right into these barriers. We need to avoid being entrapped by them.

Barrier 1. Finances—Their Use And Abuse

Leaders, particularly those who have power positions and make important decisions concerning finances, tend to use practices which may encourage incorrect handling of finances and eventually wrong

---

[255] At the time of this commentary article I have studied 3000+ cases with about 50 Bible leaders, perhaps 100 historical leaders and the rest contemporary leaders. The findings for enhancements and barriers generally hold true.

use. A character trait of greed often is rooted deep and eventually will cause impropriety with regard to finances. Numerous leaders have fallen due to some issue related to money.

Biblical Examples: O.T.: Gideon's golden ephod. N.T.: Ananias and Sapphira.

Barrier 2. Power—Its Abuse

Leaders who are effective in ministry must use various power bases in order to accomplish their ministry. With power so available and being used almost daily, there is a tendency to abuse it. Leaders who rise to the top in a hierarchical system tend to assume privileges with their perceived status. Frequently, these privileges include abuse of power. And they usually have no counter balancing accountability.

Biblical **Example**: Uzziah's usurping of priestly privilege.

Barrier 3. Pride--Which Leads To Downfall

Pride (inappropriate and self-centered) can lead to a downfall of a leader. As a leader there is a dynamic tension that must be maintained. We must have a healthy respect for our selves, and yet we must recognize that we have nothing that was not given us by God and He is the one who really enables ministry.

Biblical Example: David's numbering.

Barrier 4. Sex--Illicit Relationships

Illicit sexual relationships have been a major downfall both in the Bible and in western cultures.[256] Joseph's classic integrity check with respect to sexual sin is the ideal model that should be in leaders minds.

Biblical Example: David's sin with Bathsheba was a pivotal point from which his leadership never fully recovered. It was all downhill from there on.

Barrier 5. Family--Critical Issues

Problems between spouses or between parents and children or between siblings can destroy a leader's ministry. What is needed are Biblical values lived out with regard to husband-wife relationships, parent-children, and sibling relationships. Of growing importance in our day is the social base profiles for singles in ministry and for married couples.

Biblical Example: David's family. Ammon and Tamar. Absalom's revenge.

Barrier 6. Plateauing.

Leaders who are competent tend to plateau. Their very strength becomes a weakness. They can continue to minister at a level without there being a reality or Spirit empowered renewing effect. Most leaders will plateau several times in their life times of development. Some of the five enhancement factors for a good finish will counteract this tendency (perspective, learning posture, mentor, disciplines). There again is a dynamic tension that must be maintained between leveling off for good reasons, (consolidating one's growth and/or reaching the level of potential for which God has made you) and plateauing because of sinfulness or loss of vision.

Biblical Example: David in the latter part of his reign just before Absalom's revolt.

Forewarned is forearmed. There are many other reasons why leaders don't finish well—usually all related to sin in some form. But at least the six categories are major ones that have trapped many leaders and taken them out of the race. Leaders who want to finish well, Take heed! See **Articles**: *16. Finishing Well—Six Characteristics; 15. Finishing Well—Five Factors that Enhance It.*

---

[256] This is probably true in other cultures as well though I do not have a data base to prove this.

Article 18

Relevance of the Article to 1,2 Timothy
Paul is second only to Jesus as an exemplar in the New Testament of a leader who led a focused life. This article explains, in a broad brush, quick overview what a focused life is. Even before his Damascus Road experience Paul was a very focused individual. After that experience, his sense of destiny formed his life purpose and his activities.

18. Focused Life

Comparative study of effective leaders[257] who finished well led to the discovery of important strategic formation concepts.[258] The focused life was the all-embracing caption for these concepts.

Definition   A <u>focused life</u> is
- a life dedicated to exclusively carrying out God's unique purposes through it,
- by identifying the focal issues of life purpose, major role, effective methodology, or ultimate contribution, which allows
- an increasing prioritization of life's activities around the focal issues, and
- results in a satisfying life of being and doing.

The 4 focal issues—life purpose, major role, effective methodology, or ultimate contribution—are discovered over a lifetime. These are defined and explained in Table 1,2 Ti 18-1.

---

[257] The core study for this is contained in two Clinton works: 1. **Focused Lives** and 2. **Strategic Concepts—That Clarify a Focused Life. Focused Lives** analyzed the lives of 8 spiritual giants over a time span of mid-1700s to late 1980s: Charles Simeon (1759-1836)—A Strategic Mentor; A.J. Gordon (1836-1895)—A Missionary- Minded Pastor; Samuel Logan Brengle (1860-1936)—Public Saint; G. Campbell Morgan (1863-1945)—World class Bible Teacher; Robert Jaffray (1873-1945)—Missionary Pioneer; Robert C. McQuilkin (1886-1952)—Bible College Founder; Henrietta Mears—(1890-19.3)— Recruiter of Leaders; L.E. Maxwell (1895-1984)—Missionary Trainer.

[258] Developmental analysis over a lifetime of a leader can be categorized into three types of formational activity: spiritual formation, ministerial formation, and strategic formation. Spiritual formation is that shaping activity in a leader's life which is directed toward instilling godly character and developing inner life. Ministerial formation is that shaping activity in a leader's life which is directed toward instilling leadership skills, leadership experience and developing giftedness for ministry. Strategic formation is that shaping activity in a leader's life which is directed toward having that leader reach full potential and achieve a God-given destiny.

Table 1,2 Ti 18-1. Focal Issues Defined

Focal Issue	Definition	Explanation
Life Purpose	A life purpose is a burden-like calling, a task or driving force or achievement, which motivates a leader to fulfill something or to see something done.	Life purpose is usually closely related to destiny processing. God's intervening activity leading to a sense of destiny gradually leads to an explicit identification of life purpose. This usually happens as follows (though timing can vary with accelerated cases or delayed cases): During the 20s, committal, call, character, and life purpose intimations are the focus of God's shaping activity. During the 30s, basic life purpose forms up; this may be added to later or take on other major thrusts. During the 40s, One or more additional life purposes may be added or old ones clarified, modified and expanded but major role is the dominant focal issue in this period. During the 50s, & 60s, if health continues well, life purpose is very firm. Major role is clear. Unique methodologies are used with great power. This is a key time for a focused life. In the 60+ years, the major focus is on pressing on to the fulfillment of ultimate contributions. A further focus is on conserving the fruit of a lifetime.
Major Role	A major role is the official or unofficial position, or status/ platform, or leadership functions, or job description which basically describes what a leader does and which allows recognition by others and which uniquely fits who a leader is and lets that leader effectively accomplish life purpose(s).	A major role is made up of the **base component** and the **functional component** where, The **base component** provides: 1) the formal job description recognized by society and for which the leader gets paid; 2) status—positions with organizations either church or mission carry credibility which others recognize. This status is often needed in order to carry out functions. Traditional categories recognized include licensed, commissioned, ordained and various levels of official position (rector, bishop, archbishop; assistant pastor, associate pastor, senior pastor; intern, missionary, field superintendent, country leader, etc.); 3) logistics for ministry—home base out of which to operate; support—emotional, prayer, other resources; finances; 4) Tactical direction; the everyday basics. The **Functional Component**: 1) is the informal job actually done which has functions that the leader does to reflect giftedness and carry out life purpose achievements; some of these functions are described by the formal job description while others are informal and reflect giftedness and ministry beyond the described; 2) comprises the means for carrying out ministry insights and eventually effective methodologies; these are usually related tightly to giftedness and calling; preaching ministry, teaching ministry, personal work, administrative work, edification ministries, outreach ministries, etc.; 3) describes the scope or sphere of influence that is appropriate to the leader which may or may not be covered in the formal job description; 4) strategic direction; the long-term possibilities of the ministry. A major role usually forms up during the 40s. A leader will learn during the 20s and 30s those parts of role which enhance and block achievement of life purpose and reflect who the leader is. During the 40s one's role is adapted to try to build on enhancing things and diminish the blocking things.

Focal Issue	Definition	Explanation
Effective Methodology	An <u>effective methodology</u> is some ministry insight around which the leader can pass on to others the essentials of doing something or using something or being something, that is, a means of effectively delivering some important ministry of that leader which enhances life purpose or moves toward ultimate contribution.	The heart of an effective methodology is a ministry insight. A ministry insight is some breakthrough a leader gets concerning how to personally do ministry well. All leaders have ministry insights. These breakthroughs will come all during ministry. We may get them in any of the age brackets. But it is in the latter age brackets [40-50 and 50-60] that we really realize what we have and how powerful they can be if we focus on them. It is in the years 50-60 that we should reflect back and conserve those major breakthrough insights that we have gained in the past by converting them into **effective methodologies**, that is, repeated, effective use of good ministry insights. In other words, we should *use them to death* (to appl a good old southern idiom)—especially as we see their purpose in focusing our lives. In the 20s, the initial breakthroughs in how to do ministry usually involve use of giftedness with individuals or small groups. Frequently they have to do with how to present truth from God's word in an effective manner. In the mid to late 20s and early 30s, further breakthroughs usually come and have to do with the importance of relationships and organizational structures through which we work. Conflict processing usually forces us to learn quickly. In the late 20s and early 30s, all kinds of ministry insights come as we further explore different roles and discover more of our giftedness. In the 40s, we begin to use some of the accumulated ministry insights repeatedly. They become effective methodologies. In the 50s and 60s, we get maximum benefit from effective methodologies. We reflect back and remember some used in the past. We organize our ministry around them. We exploit them.
Ultimate Contribution	An <u>ultimate contribution</u> is a lasting legacy of a Christian worker for which he or she is remembered and which furthers the cause of Christianity by one or more of the following: • setting standards for life and ministry, • impacting lives by enfolding them in God's kingdom or developing them once in the kingdom, • serving as a stimulus for change which betters the world, • leaving behind	Leaders will leave behind unique contributions that flow out of who they are and what they do. But there are also some general categories of contributions that we have identified in research. <u>The ultimate contribution set</u> is the collection of ultimate contribution categories that a given leader will leave behind at the end of life. We have identified 13 types: *saint* (model life), *stylistic practitioner* (model ministry), *family* (godly heritage passed on), *mentor* (personal ministry), *public rhetorician* (public oratory ministry), *pioneer* (opens new types of ministry), *change person* (helps correct things), *artist* (creative breakthroughs in ministry), *founder* (begins an organization), stabilizer (improves an organization) , *researcher* (explores things for concepts underlying them), *writer* (produces literature about ideas researched), *promoter* (motivates people to use things and do things). <u>In the 20s</u>, some leaders happen upon an important need and as a result give their lives to meet that need. This is a *need-centered motivational pattern*. A person is drawn to a cause and gives his/her life to do something about that cause. The cause results in the discovery of an ultimate contribution that drives the leader. This is called the *discovery pattern* and is rare. Another pattern is the *destiny pattern*. This too may rarely occur in the 20s and more likely in the 30s. A leader has a mystical experience with God in which direction for all of life is given. That direction will naturally lead into what must be accomplished. This is a divine-centered pattern. Very few leaders get this early in or before leadership transition or in early provisional ministry. This is a rare pattern. A more normal pattern occurring throughout the 20s and 30s and early 40s is the *drift pattern*: A person is led in a step-by-step guidance fashion. There is

	an organization, institution, or movement that will further channel God's work, • the discovery of ideas, communication of them, or promotion of them so that they further God's work.	no purposeful deliberate attempt to have an ultimate contribution. The person simply follows what he/she thinks is God's guidance. Each major guidance decision will probably lead to some new accomplishment that will be the focus of efforts until God gives guidance for the next phase. This is the usual pattern for most leaders. In the late 40s and early 50s some leaders, as they grow, begin to understand more about themselves and those leaders begin to *deliberately move* toward training or roles that will enhance development and focus efforts. In the focusing of efforts, the ultimate contribution(s) become clear. This is called the *deliberate pattern*. It is an analytical, logical pattern centering on assessment of a person and a meaningful life that will contribute.

The end result of focused life study of an individual is a one to three page document called the Personal Life Mandate.

Definition   A <u>Personal Life Mandate</u> is a one to three page length description, made up of several paragraphs, which give in essence a person's life time goals in terms of what is known of the focal issues (life purpose, major role, effective methodology, and ultimate contribution) and using language which gives further intents toward these issues as well as describing being and doing achievements in harmony with these issues.

The first several paragraphs usually describe the life purpose. The next several describe the major role. Following the major role paragraphs come those describing the effective methodologies and how those can be exploited to achieve life purpose. Finally comes a description (often tentative for younger leaders) of ultimate contributions (legacies) that are part of the lasting ministry of the leader.

Below is a short personal life mandate of a Biblical leader in the Old Testament during the Post-Kingdom Leadership Era. It is of Ezra, the Bible teacher, and most focused leader in the Old Testament.

Personal Life Mandate—Ezra the Priest/Teacher

Life Purpose—My life purpose is to teach the truths of Moses to God's people in exile in such a way as to bring about renewal—that is, worship of God, an understanding of His requirements on our lives, and response so that God's people live out His truth in their lives and thus honor God.

Major Role—I see my major role as four-fold: 1. As a priest with a heritage all the way back to Aaron I expect to have spiritual authority, first of all from this role. 2. In addition, as a teacher who exposes the truths of Moses both publicly and in small groups and for training of other teachers I expect to see changed lives individually and seeds of a renewal movement—because my teaching will impact. My teaching itself, done competently, will generate spiritual authority 3. As a trainer I will train others as specialists in explaining God's truths from Moses. 4. Change Agent for Renewal: As a conservative ministering to a people who have gone far away from God's truth I am concerned about renewal.

Effective Methodology: I have disciplined myself to study the law of Moses and become an expert in it. I have also found that I must model it myself. This approach has given me insights in how to communicate the truth to those not familiar at all with God's law. By knowing the law very well and by modeling it I can explain clearly and simply truth in terms the common people can understand. Frequently, I use a team approach to do this. I read publicly and then break the large crowds into smaller groups. My team will explain in the common tongues what I have read. I then form administrative teams to apply the truth in individual situations.

Ultimate Contribution: I want to leave behind me a remnant in Jerusalem people who are purified and following God. I will come alongside the civil leaders and support them as they attempt to follow God's orders to rebuild. I want to leave behind a trained group of people who can read, study, and apply God's law and will train others in turn to keep the truth alive. We want to be a people prepared for God to use in the future. (Ultimate Contribution Set: Public Rhetorician, Mentor, Change Person, Stabilizer, Promoter).

The most focused leader in the New Testament church leadership era is Paul the Apostle. Below is given his personal life mandate.

Paul's Personal Life Mandate

My life **purpose** is to serve the risen Lord Jesus by witnessing to what he has shown me and will show me to Jews, Gentiles, and Kings. I know I am to be a part of expanding Jesus' work begun in Jerusalem. I will be the primary person who will contextualize truth into Gentile situations. I will take the Gospel to Gentiles, primarily where no one else has yet gone, and see them turn from the power of Satan, the Kingdom of Darkness, to the power of Christ, the Kingdom of Light, God's Kingdom. Occasionally, I will also speak truth into Jewish situations. I know I am destined to give my witness to Christ before high rulers.

I will primarily do this through the planting of churches and development of leaders to care for these churches. I recognize that my ministry is pioneer work and will become a model for many others. I will be an itinerant church planter and developer of leaders. From time-to-time I am prepared to be bi-vocational, providing some or all of my financial needs through my trade, tent making. I recognize that **my role** will include church planting via an apostolic/evangelistic ministry with power ministry to authenticate my work. I will also do leadership development work involving teaching and mentoring. Leadership training will be a dominant feature of my work.

I will use several **major methodologies** to break open a work. I will use a team-oriented approach to doing apostolic work. I will always try to have one or more people with me in ministry. I will also try to have prayer teams backing my pioneer work. Where possible I will do mentoring with them—always attempting to train them toward their potential so they can do what I do. I will move along networks where ever I can. This includes contacts via people who will help give an initial credibility. If there are no known contacts, no networking then I will use the local Jewish community (preferably a synagogue) to attempt to get a hearing. I will identify those non-Jewish people who are worshipping as God fearers, that is, Gentile proselytes to the Jewish religion. From those who are converted I will form small pre-church communities, give them Christian teaching and eventually identify local leadership and install it in place. I will always seek to model before the people I am developing those ideas I am teaching them. I have found that personal ministry, face-to-face with individuals or small groups is the place where I work most effectively. Where there is no natural networks via contacts or no Jewish community I will use open air debates and power breakthroughs, trusting God to give an occasion to demonstrate His power in some kind of power encounter. In every case, I will always seek to ground people in God's truth and to establish leadership who can stabilize the Christian community and bring growth.

When life is all over I want to know that I have led a meaningful life that fulfilled my life purpose. That includes seeing some or all of the following achievements reached in part or whole. I want to model a saintly life, that is one who has known intimately Jesus. I want to have touched many lives through my personal relationships (mentoring). I want to have pioneered breakthroughs in people coming to Christ and forming communities of witness in many different locales. I want to leave behind a body of writings which can help people understand their situations and bring growth both as individuals and churches. I want to have adapted Christian truth from its Jewish setting into the Gentile world. I want to leave behind many of my leadership values in a few good leaders who will pass them on. In short, I want my life to count. And I want it to continue to have impact after I have gone.

Conclusion

Focused Lives include some common elements such as,

- long term ministries in a major role crafted to fit the leader, or an expanding, changing role in a long term geographic locale, and/or use of an effective methodology to accomplish purposes which may include,
- a lifelong involvement of serving Christ to fulfill some specific destiny purpose, and/or
- a concentration on achieving certain important goals which leave behind legacies for the on-going work of Christ, and
- an importance on the Word of God for personal growth and ministry, and
- the shaping work of God to move these leaders toward their focus, all of which reflect insightful lessons and values helpful to present leaders.

In essence, we should remember two things as we think about focused lives and proactive decisions that lead to them.

1. The focused life is not so much a goal as it is the by-product of a goal. Our goal should be to obediently follow God and to seek to know and do His will. If that is our goal, we will see the focused life as a by-product.
2. We can learn from these leaders who have gone on before us. It is right and fitting that we do so. So what we have learned about the focused life can be applied to our lives. When we do that we are simply applying the leadership mandate. Glance through it.

Remember your former leaders. Think back on how they lived and ministered. Imitate those excellent qualities you see in their lives. For Jesus Christ is the same today, as He was in the past and as He will be in the future. What He did for them He will do for you to inspire and enable your leadership. Hebrews 13:7,8 (Personal Interpretive Paraphrase)

May you especially see the last concept of the focused life come true for you.

Definition   A focused life is
- a life dedicated to exclusively carrying out God's unique purposes through it,
- by identifying the focal issues, that is, life purpose, major role, effective methodology, or ultimate contribution, which allows
- an increasing prioritization of life's activities around the focal issues, and
- results in a satisfying life of being and doing.

See Also **For Further Study Bibliography,** Clinton's **Focused Lives** and **Strategic Concepts Which Clarify a Focused Life.**

Relevance of the Article to 1,2 Timothy

Leadership emergence theory has identified 23 patterns that leaders go through as God develops them. These patterns, once known and recognized, can help a leader anticipate next steps in response to God. Timothy illustrates one of the foundational patterns. This article describes the foundational patterns.

19. Foundational Patterns—Four Identified

Introduction

When Paul recalls to mind Timothy's heritage,

> 5 I recall your sincere faith, which your grandmother Lois had, and your mother Eunice
> had. I am persuaded that faith is still in you. 6 Because of this I am reminding you, fan
> the flame of your God-given spiritual gift, which you received when I laid hands on you,

he is pointing out something important to leaders who are concerned with leadership selection and development. He uses a motivational technique, applying Goodwin's expectation principle,[259] based on Timothy's background.

Timothy comes from a foundational heritage pattern.[260] This means, that growing up, he had background and teaching about God and his ways. He had modeled for him what it meant to follow God. His mother and grandmother were students of the O.T. which enabled them to embrace Christ as Messiah when Paul and his team came through there. Their modeling deeply impacted Timothy's early life. Modeling is one of the more important influence means. This heritage pattern will deeply influence Timothy's own growth processes. Paul's counts on this heritage pattern as he encourages Timothy's growth.

Effective leaders view leadership selection and development as a priority function.

Such leaders need to know as much as they can about how leaders develop. One challenge—such developmentally minded leaders should know the foundation from which a leader comes, especially one they are interested in helping develop. Four non-exclusive patterns have been identified. Each of the foundational patterns carries with it some inherent advantages and disadvantages. But each leader is unique

---

[259] Bennie Goodwin in a small booklet on leadership published by InterVarsity Press identified a social dynamic principle which is helpful in developing leaders. In my own words, *Emerging leaders tend to live up to the genuine expectations of leaders they respect.* The challenge embodied in the expectation must not be too much or the young leader will not be able to accomplish it and will be inoculated against further challenges. The challenge must not be too little or it will not attract. It must be a genuine expectation. Paul uses this with Timothy several times (see 1Ti 6:11 fn 95. See 2Ti 1:5 fn 8).

[260] The generalized time-line for a full time Christian worker consists of: Phase I. Sovereign Foundations; Phase II. Growth Ministry; Phase III. Focused Ministry; Phase IV. Convergent Ministry. The four patterns introduced in this article come from study of Phase I. Sovereign Foundations. See *time-line*, **Glossary**. See **Article, 68**. *Time-Lines: Defined for Biblical Leaders.*

and will reflect more or less the advantages or disadvantages of the pattern accordingly. It is helpful to recognize these patterns and implications of them in order to make decisions for training or concerning experiences which will build on the advantages and minimize disadvantages. Knowledge of these patterns and advantages and disadvantages can aid a leader concerned about leadership selection and development.

Heritage Foundational Pattern

The heritage foundational pattern is the most common pattern from which Christian leaders emerge.

Description   The heritage foundational pattern refers to the early development of a leader in the foundational development phase who comes from a Christian (or at least nominal Christian) background in which the leader is more or less processed into Christian values via the home or some church life.

Timothy is a biblical case of this pattern. Numerous contemporary cases of leaders abound from this background.

Usually there is not a radical conversion experience in this pattern unless the heritage was very nominal. Frequently, there may be a growing awareness of God. Family life helps shape characteristics in the leader which are based at least in part on Christian thinking. The educational pattern gives a prolonged time of development before adult responsibilities must be shouldered. This time of schooling allows for development of basic skills, such as experience in sports, clubs, or vocational efforts, competitiveness, perseverance, basic relational skills, organizational skills, entrepreneurial skills, or the like.

In a western setting, toward the end of the teen years or during early collegiate years there is usually some sort of more radical commitment[261] to God that resulted from previous conversion processing. Sometimes identified as conversion, or as a surrender to do God's will, this action frequently results in a desire to be a full time Christian worker. This can lead to learn-as-you-do-it training or an opting for formal training.

Advantages of this pattern include those normally associated with heritage such as:
1. belief in God, knowledge of Him, and Christian values which can be built upon,
2. inheriting promises from faithful ancestors who have prayed and claimed God's working upon progeny (frequently destiny preparation processing is involved here),
3. having exemplary models of Christianity which will have influenced toward basic ministry philosophy concepts,
4. having an experiential foundation for understanding giftedness (having seen leaders with different natural abilities, acquired skills, and spiritual gifts),
5. usually having support for Christian leadership aspirations (though more nominal backgrounds may actually oppose because of secular career ambitions for the potential leader).
6. usually having fewer lifestyle changes as the person moves into Christian leadership since the basic Christian ethic is already intact.

Disadvantages are few and may include the following:
1. Familiarity with Christian things which may dull the spiritual realities of them.
2. Enthusiastic committal to the accomplishing of God's work must be fostered by unusual experiences usually outside the routine of Christianity experienced while growing up.
3. The routine Christian experience may not provide stimulus for on-the-job experience which can be vital to early identification of leadership potential.
4. Ministry philosophy imbued via routine involvement in Christianity may not have challenged or apparently was irrelevant in terms of reaching out to a lost world or cross-cultural involvement.

The heritage foundational pattern usually correlates with the pre-service training pattern and hence the advantages and disadvantages of that training. Those mentors or divine contacts who have influence in the lives of potential leaders emerging from this foundational heritage pattern and who are sensitive to leadership emergence patterns do well to influence these young potential leaders toward apprenticeships or other significant ministry experiences which may break the standard training pre-service pattern.

---

[261] In some circles this radical decision is called a *Lordship committal.*

Radical Committal Foundational Pattern

Christian leaders who emerged from a non-Christian background fit this pattern. This pattern can offer great advantages or disadvantages or combinations of both upon which to emerge into leadership.

Description   The radical committal pattern refers to the early development of a leader, in the foundational development phase, who comes from a non-Christian background or at best a very nominal Christian background in which the leader is more or less processed into whatever values the environment supports (usually those of the secular society of the macro-context) and who makes a radical adult decision for Christ which involves a significant paradigm shift in terms of values and life-goals.

Titus would be a biblical example of this pattern.

Usually persons in this pattern were tracking along some secular career path when the adult conversion happened. The radical experience frequently changes this direction. The person imbibes the values of the family, whether good or bad, as he or she grows up. Usually there is little or no knowledge of vital Christianity.

Educational patterns of contemporary leaders coming from this pattern vary. In the west the educational pattern allows a prolonged time of development before adult responsibilities must be shouldered. This time of schooling allows for development of basic skills, such as experience in sports, clubs, vocational efforts, competitiveness, perseverance, basic relational skills, organizational skills, entrepreneurial skills, or the like. In non-western situations the educational patterns vary and may or may not allow prolonged time of development before adult responsibilities. If not, the person usually learns via traditional educational patterns the necessary basic and social skills for the society.

The turning point involves exposure to Christianity which provokes a radical decision to follow Christ. Usually coincidental with this decision is a whole hearted leadership committal to serve God. In the west, this radical experience can occur in high school, college, or during the normal vocation. But it is decisive whenever it occurs. Throughout life it will be looked back to as a major marker event.[262]

On-the-job training, which often starts with sharing of testimony about what has happened, usually follows the radical decision. The person is attracted to the means that brought about the radical change whether it be a person or an organization. Early on-the-job training usually follows that attraction. Ministry philosophy flows from this exposure.

Advantages of this pattern involve:
1. a decisive leadership committal process item which serves as foundational for all of later leadership activity. Attitudes of committal involve service to God right at the outset.
2. early gift identification (frequently the like-attracts-like gift pattern is a common occurrence).
3. destiny processing. Because of the radical nature of the committal frequently there is a destiny preparation or revelation experience which will set the tone for later development of focus in ministry philosophy.
4. a fresh perspective on Christianity. Since the person is usually unencumbered with a Christian tradition, frequently he or she is able to see new ideas and create new kinds of structures and roles that would not be thought of by a person of the heritage pattern.

Disadvantages include:
1. lack of Christian knowledge, especially about the Bible.
2. need for radical change of lifestyle. Frequently there must be extreme changes of lifestyle since the old is so incompatible with a Christian lifestyle. Old habits are hard to break and may result in early struggles regarding issues which are taken for granted by heritage pattern persons.

---

[262] This would be called a spiritual benchmark. Spiritual benchmarks are touchstones or watermarks for a lifetime of ministry. Spiritual benchmarks refer to something that happens in the life of the leader which serves as positive proof of God's activity in that life. It is something that a leader can look back upon and be encouraged to continue when confused or in a discouraging situation. Because it is foundational, sure and certain, and had the distinct imprint of God's Hand on the life. See also *destiny processing,* **Glossary.**

3. use of secular leadership patterns. Early leadership practices will follow the secular practices that have been experienced, whether good or bad.
4. instability. The emerging leader is often unstable and vacillates between the old way of life and the new.

If the people who were involved in the radical decision put stress on on-the-job training, then the transitional training pattern two, the in-service pattern, is followed. If they stress formal training then training pattern three, the modified in-service pattern, is often followed.

Accelerated Foundational Pattern

Each of the four foundational patterns or a modified version of them carries with it some inherent advantages and disadvantages. The accelerated foundational pattern has special advantages. It also carries a strong warning. It is a special case of the heritage pattern in which the heritage leads to early ministry involvement and rapid early development of ministry skills and basic character.

Description   The accelerated foundational pattern describes the early rapid developmental pattern of generational Christian leaders, that is, emerging leaders who have a family heritage of Christian leadership and respond positively very early in life to doing ministry (often co-ministering with parents).

The pattern is often seen also in some who do not come from a Christian heritage but are converted very early as in a *Child Evangelism* ministry, or in a junior high, or high school club and in which a pseudo-parent (mentor) helps encourage on-the-job training which launches one into ministry with a running start. The transitional testing patterns occur very early. Inner-life processing and ministry entry processing are compressed into the foundational phase so that the emerging leader is advanced even when beginning the ministry phase as compared to other emerging leaders moving along the generalized time-line. This rapid advancement means that by the time these accelerated leaders reach their thirties they are well into their ministry maturity phase.

Advantages This pattern includes all the normal advantages of the heritage pattern. But beyond that:
1. There is a committal that has been tested by experience.
2. Giftedness development occurs early.
3. A basic ministry philosophy formulates early.
4. The leader emerging from this pattern will move into unique ministry from five to ten years ahead of persons emerging via other patterns.

Disadvantages are few in this pattern. Two warnings should be given. One, there may be an over concern with ministry activity which may preclude mid-career formal training. Such training gives breadth and perspective that will later be needed as the leader moves into convergence. Without this perspective convergence may not be reached. Two, such an over concern for ministry can become a dysfunctionality that can lead to early burnout.

The in-service and modified in-service transitional training patterns usually correlate with the accelerated foundational pattern. Mentors should recognize the need for balance between cognitive and experiential learning. Over emphasis of ministry activity should be countered by suggesting appropriate training which will keep ministry momentum going yet balance it with needed perspectives that will improve it.

Delayed Foundational Pattern

The delayed foundational pattern is a special case of the heritage pattern in which the heritage leads to an early rejection by the potential leader of that heritage. This is later followed by a radical commitment (usually in late twenties) and then rapid development of ministry skills and basic character.

Description   The delayed foundational pattern describes the developmental pattern of generational Christian leaders (emerging leaders who have a family heritage of Christian leadership) who initially rebel against ministry very early in life but who eventually experience a deep leadership committal process item and enter the ministry phase late followed by rapid acceleration.

Numerous missionary kids and preachers kids have a tendency to rebel against the ministry because of perceived negative experiences during the foundational phase. This rebellion is turned around later (usually in the late twenties and early thirties) with a deep leadership committal experience. This late start, however, delays ministry entry. Rapid acceleration due to early foundational background often follows.

Advantages are few and include:
1. the person will usually have experienced some of the negative side of secular life. When recommittal comes they will experience a deliverance which allows them to identify with   non-Christians in their needs and know the power of God.
2. such a person who opts for formal training will usually learn more rapidly because of life experience upon which to relate input.
3. normal advantages of heritage belong to a person in this pattern but are not utilized until **late**.

Disadvantages often include:
1. the overcoming of guilt attitudes for having wasted so much of life and for missing early vital ministry experience.
2. less options for formal training. The person is usually too old for Bible School and may not meet requirements for entrance into seminary.

Usually a modified in-service transitional educational pattern is followed.

Conclusions

Leaders with *leadership selection and development eyes* will want to build on the advantages flowing from a leader's foundational pattern while minimizing the disadvantages.

These four patterns are not exclusive though one will usually dominate even in modified patterns. Paul was a modified pattern: *Heritage* and *Radical Committal*. But the *Radical Committal* dominated.

See *sense of destiny; destiny processing; giftedness set; spiritual gifts; paradigm, paradigm shift, spiritual benchmarks; testing patterns, positive and negative;* like-attracts-like gift pattern; **Glossary**. See **Articles**, *Training Modes—When They Fit; Paradigms and Paradigm Shifts—Biblical Examples*; 60. *Spiritual Benchmarks; Daniel—Four Positive Testing Patterns; 39. Ministry Entry Patterns;*

Relevance of the Article to 1,2 Timothy
The 1 Ti 2:13 passage is often referred to as prohibiting women from leading. In a much longer position paper, not included in this commentary, I have detailed my response to that passage and other so-called passages which prohibit women from leadership. In **LEADERSHIP TOPIC 6. LEADERSHIP GUIDELINES**, I touch on the gender issue. Gender and Leadership issues are treated in 1Ti. This is a male dominated culture. Paul honors that while at the same time leaving room for female leadership. The list idioms give both male and female leadership character traits that should be present in a leader. This article gives a quick overview of Paul's very forward thinking about women in leadership. He was ahead of his time and provided the springboard for our modern view of women in leadership.

20. Gender and Leadership

Introduction

I referred to a perspective, *the starting-point-plus-process model*, when I commented on slavery in Phm. In the article describing the *starting-point-plus-process model*, I mentioned that the model applied to women in leadership as well as to slavery and marriage, both institutions in which God moved from less-ideal held views to His ideals over long periods of time. It probably will apply as well to other issues, once they come into focus. For it describes how God works with people, graciously dealing with them to bring them to maturity. He begins where they are and moves them toward the ideal.

Basically the starting-point-plus-process model has four major assertions.

1. Assuming a valid faith-allegiance response,[263] God allows for a range of understanding of Himself and His will for people, for He starts *where people are* rather than demanding that they immediately conform to His ideals.
2. This range of understanding of God can assume a *variety of potential starting points* anywhere from sub-ideal toward ideal perception of God and His ways.
3. God then initiates a process which involves a *revelational progression* from a sub-ideal starting point toward the ideal. This on-going process often takes long time periods with small gains along the way.
4. This process of beginning with a range of sub-ideal starting points of perception and behavior and moving by revelational progression from the sub-ideal toward the ideal can be applied to any doctrine of Scripture and any Scriptural treatment of behavioral patterns.

Most of the cultures represented in the O.T. and N.T. have a sub-ideal starting point concerning leadership and the female gender. Most of these cultures were largely male-dominated cultures. This is an acceptable starting point, though sub-ideal.[264] People, who within these cultures accept God as their only God and His salvation, can be worked with to move toward the ideal. In this case of gender and leadership, that ideal is gifted leaders contributing to God's work, regardless of gender. Exceptions to the cultural norms as seen in the O.T. and N.T. which are blessed by God only serve to enforce what I am saying about movement toward an ideal.[265]

---

[263] That is, an acceptable starting place. By a faith-allegiance response I mean a valid decision to place God as top priority in a life—a trusting response for God's salvation and work in a life.

[264] I am assuming the ideal of a gift based leadership church in which the Holy Spirit gives gifts that are needed to people without gender bias. People with leadership gifts should lead. This is a theological argument based on the nature of the church and the ministry of the Holy Spirit in the church. I also am aware of the ideal described in Gal 3:28.

[265] Deborah is a case in point in the O.T. Priscilla, Phoebe, Syntyche, Euodias, Junia, Tryphena, and Tryphosa are fellow workers with Paul and are indications of movement toward the ideal.

Leadership and Giftedness—The Ideal

A leader is a person with God-given capacity and a God-given burden who is influencing specific groups of people towards God's purposes for them. Comparative studies of leaders identified the concept of leaders being word-gifted. Study of giftedness throughout the N.T. church era indicated that people receive word gifts without regard to gender. That is, the Holy Spirit gives leadership gifts to male and females who are part of the body of Christ. Because of the work of the Cross both males and females are accepted into . the body of Christ. Both are endowed with gifts from the Holy Spirit. The ideal is simply stated.

> **A gifted body operating interdependently allows the gifts of all its people to be used by God to mature the body and to expand it by bringing in new believers from the environment around it.**

Paul—Well Ahead of His Time

By the time of Paul's ministry, God had already begun strong movement toward the ideal. Jesus' ministry, in the Pre-Church Leadership Era inaugurated the movement toward the ideal by elevating the status of women in general.[266] Paul carried it further, co-ministering with women in local church situations, and sponsoring them elsewhere.[267]

When Paul describes selection of leaders to Timothy, even in a male dominated culture, he describes the characteristics for leaders not only in male terms but also in terms allowing for females.[268] For Paul the problem of female leaders is not so much theological (he is free here) but cultural (he recognizes that cultures may not be ready for it nor women in those cultures ready for it).

The so-called objections[269] to women in leadership in 1Co and 1Ti are not dealing with women as leaders, that is, giving a theological argument against women in leadership, but represent special cultural situations in which church behavior is not proper. Paul is correcting the church situations.

Conclusion

Both males and females, who are gifted with leadership gifts, bring advantages to leadership because of their genders. Both are needed to see a full range of effective leadership in churches. Should Christ's Second Coming be delayed, we will see further movement toward the ideal in these next years. Once God has moved His people to the ideal, looking back, they wonder how they could have ever held such sub-ideal positions as were held (think back on slavery and marriage). So it will be with gender and leadership.

See *giftedness; word gifts;* **Glossary.** See **Article,** *67. Starting-Point—Plus—Process Model..* **See For Further Study Bibliography**, Clinton positional paper entitled, *Gender and Leadership*, an extended treatment of this subject which also gives the author's journey and paradigm shifts which brought about this present understanding. It is available in the READER **BibleLeadership.pdf** at my web site.

---

[266] Luke's Gospel is particularly instructive along these lines. Jesus reaches out to gentiles and women upon numerous occasions in Luke's Gospel. See also, **Article,** *Jesus—Circles of Intimacy—A Developmental Technique.*

[267] See Ro 16:1,2 where Paul sponsors Phoebe as a minister of the Gospel.

[268] See Peterson's translation, in **The Message,** of 1Ti 3 where he recognizes female leadership in the contextual flow. I agree with his interpretation.

[269] I have studied all of these objections in depth. I have also read many present day authors who come down on both sides of the fence—those dead set against women as leaders and those who see women as leaders. I would expect that Paul would have written a very clear context placing men as leaders and showing that women cannot lead if that were the nature of the case. It is not. And Paul did not. His so called anti-women-in-leadership passages are really dealing with cultural church problems specific to those situations (Corinth, Ephesus). In my comments in the **Leadership Insights** in Eph, I even give a paraphrase of the 1Ti 2 passage which reflects this notion of a specific cultural problem.

Relevance of the Article to 1,2 Timothy

Paul, in an off-hand manner, points out an important Apostolic/Leadership function in 1 Ti 4:14. This same function ought to be used more today by Power Gifted leaders who are sending forth leaders to do church planting and other pioneer evangelistic work. Special spiritual gifts are needed in these pioneer efforts. Impartation of gifts by faith ought to be an important part of the sending process.

21. Impartation of Gifts—An Apostolic Function

Introduction

Paul alludes to a leadership concept not generally stressed except in some Pentecostal circles and in the new apostolic church movement. Note his words of admonition to his young mentoree, Timothy.

> Don't keep on neglecting your spiritual gift, which was given you by prophecy in conjunction with the laying on of the hands of the leaders. 1 Ti 4:14

He reemphasizes this admonition in a later epistle to Timothy.

> Because of this I am reminding you, fan the flame of your God-given spiritual gift, which you received when I laid hands on you. 2 Ti 1:6

Paul, in his apostolic role, apparently was led of God, when setting Timothy aside for ministry, to bless Timothy with a spiritual gift. We do not know exactly which one. He prophesied about this, that is, the gift and its use.

Laying on of hands, the means indicated by Paul in the above quotes, occurs in several passages. Table 1,2 Ti 21-1 groups the basic functions involved with laying on of hands and gives some representative passages.

Table 1,2 Ti 21-1. Passages—Laying On Of Hands

No.	Passage	Possible Implications
1	Ac 6:6, 13:3	Anointing leaders for service; public recognition, affirmation and backing.
2	Ac 8:17, Ac 9:17 et al	Impartation of Holy Spirit
3	Ac 9:12, 28:8	For healing
4	Heb 6:2	Unclear what the purpose is
5	1 Ti 5:22	Leadership selection and recognition of same publicly
6	1 Ti 1:14; 2 Ti 1:6	Impartation of Gifts

Four functions identified with laying on of hands include: anointing for service in a public way which affirms the emerging leader; imparting the Holy Spirit for service; for healing; for impartation of gifts. This last function should be more widely applied today.

Spiritual Gifts

In his teaching on spiritual gifts in 1Co, Paul indicates that it is the Holy Spirit who imparts gifts to believers. In Ro Paul implies that it is God, the Father, who imparts gifts. In Eph he indicates that gifts are imparted by Christ. So then the entire Trinity is involved in imparting spiritual gifts to believers.[270] But in the passages above Paul indicates that as an apostle, when prompted by the Holy Spirit (prophetic gift), he can impart a needed spiritual gift to a leader who is being set aside for ministry. These passages reveal the human side of impartation of spiritual gifts, at least one way that the Trinity imparts gifts.

Leaders today, particularly those with the gift of apostleship,[271] ought to be aware of the needed gifts for the ministry they are sending leaders into. So then, when selecting leaders and sending them into service Apostles ought to impart the needed gifts to them. This is not an abuse of power[272] but a responsibility of partnering with God in an endeavor. Speaking a word of faith about a gift for a leader ought to be the fruit of mature apostleship.

Conclusion

In any case a leader must remember Paul's final admonition to Timothy involving laying on of hands.

> Don't hastily lay hands on any person for leadership; neither be partaker of other's sins.
> 1Ti 5:22

Character in the emerging leader ought to be founded well before impartation of gifts. Nevertheless, it will take gifted power to break through in the post-modern world we face. Apostles should impart these needed break-through gifts to choice young leaders.

See *spiritual gifts, various definition of spiritual gifts*, **Glossary**. See **Article**, *9. Developing Giftedness...*

---

[270] In my opinion it is unclear, biblically speaking, when spiritual gifts are actually imparted. Possibilities include: at time of conversion and hence the initial receiving of the Holy Spirit; at an infilling of the Holy Spirit at some later time after conversion; when needed.

[271] The following gifts also would stimulate this impartation: faith, prophecy, word of knowledge.

[272] Motivation in this is a key. See Simon in Ac 8:18,19 who for his own use in an improper way wanted to get the power to lay hands on people and impart the Holy Spirit to them. I am talking about a mature apostleship gift which is being used in a discerning way with God's plans for the ministry involved.

Relevance of the Article to 1,2 Timothy

This article was originally included in the larger leadership commentary and first mentioned in conjunction with 2Co. There, Paul's spiritual authority was under fire. Wrong's typology helped explain how influence happens and how it relates to power and authority. Spiritual authority can be seen to be an amalgamation of several concepts on Wrong's scale. This article helps clarify these important issues.

22. Influence, Power and Authority Forms

Introduction

A major lesson concerning how a leader ought to influence states:

Effective leaders value spiritual authority as a primary power base.

To understand this important principle we need to define some terms. The terms that are used to describe leadership make a difference in how we see leadership. Three important terms are influence, power, and authority. Sometimes these important terms are used interchangeable in leadership literature. I use a simplified adaptation of Dennis Wrong's[273] basic schema for relating these concepts—though I have adapted it to fit my understanding of spiritual authority. Influence is the most embracing of the concepts. Power is intended use of influence. And authority is one kind of power usually associated with tight organizations.[274]

---

[273] See Dennis Wrong, **Power--Its Forms, Bases, and Uses**. San Francisco, CA: Harper and Row, 1979. This is a brilliant treatment involving definitions of power concepts as well as recognition of how these forms change over time. His analysis gave a complicated taxonomy which I have simplified and adapted.

[274] Christian organizations operate on a continuum from tight to loose. The more loose an organization is the more it is characterized by voluntary workers who are not paid to do some job but do it because they want to. Therefore leaders in loose organizations do not have as much authority as those in tight organizations which are characterized by paid workers, structures levels of leadership, and supervisory responsibility (that is, people have bosses who can fire them if they don't submit to authority).

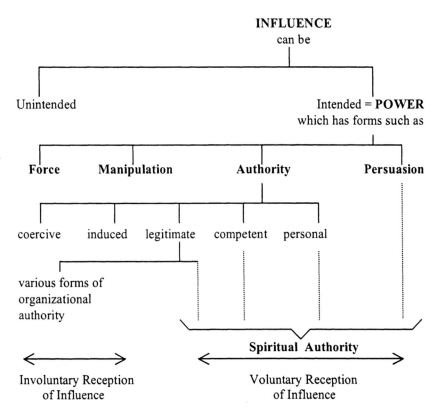

Figure 1,2 Ti 22-1. Leadership Influence Components—(Adapted from Wrong)

Explanation

Leaders are people with God-given capacities and God-given responsibilities who are influencing specific groups of people toward God's purposes for them. They are intentional in their use of means to influence, meaning using deliberate power forms. When we describe such leaders we are coming down the right side of the diagram in Figure 1. Leaders have a right to influence. The ability to influence comes through the control of power bases.

Definition   Power base refers to the source of credibility, power differential, or resources which enables a leader (*power holder*) to have authority to exercise influence on followers (*power subjects*).

Definition   Authority refers to the right to exercise leadership influence by a leader over followers with respect to some field of influence.

Power is manifested in power forms which bring about compliance. The four major power forms in our tree diagram include FORCE, MANIPULATION, AUTHORITY, AND PERSUASION. Authority is further sub-divided into coercive, induced, legitimate, competent, and personal. Spiritual authority is a hybrid combination of persuasion and legitimate, competent, and personal authority.

Power forms depend upon power bases. Bases come from power resources—those individual and collective assets such as organization, money, reputation, personal appeal, manipulative skills, interpersonal skills, kinds of knowledge, information, indwelling Holy Spirit, giftedness.

The central concept of authority is the right to exercise influence. That right is recognized both by leader and follower. It is based upon common assumptions about the *field of influence*. For a spiritual leader the *field of influence* has to do with God's purposes and His directions for accomplishing specific aims that He reveals. Morality, corporate guidance, and clarification of truth are three aspects within the *field of influence* which define the leader's range of use of authority.

Table 1,2 Ti 22-1 details a number of important concepts that help clarify how a leader influences.

Table 1,2 Ti 22-1. Influence, Power, Authority Concepts Defined

Influence, Power, Authority Concepts	Description
Power forms	Power forms refer to four general terms of influence means: force, manipulation, authority, and persuasion.
Force	A force power form refers to the use of physical and psychic influence means to gain compliance. This form is now rarely used by spiritual leaders though historically it has been used.
Manipulation	A manipulative power form refers to any influence means whereby a leader gains compliance of a follower where the follower does not have awareness of the leader's intents and therefore does not necessarily have freedom to exert moral responsibility in the situation.[275]
Authority	An authority power form refers to influence means such as: coercive authority, induced authority, legitimate authority, competent authority, personal authority and spiritual authority. See definitions which follow in this Table.
Persuasion	A persuasive power form refers to any influence means such as arguments, appeals or exhortations whereby the leader gains compliance of the follower yet protects the freedom of the follower to exercise moral responsibility.
Coercive Authority	Coercive authority is the form of power in which a leader obtains compliance by using influence means such as threat of force or of punishment.
Induced Authority	Induced authority is the form of power in which a leader obtains compliance by using influence means of promise of reward or some gain for the follower.
Legitimate Authority	Legitimate authority is the form of power in which a leader obtains compliance by using influence pressure consonant with common expectations of the role or positions held by the follower and leader.
Competent Authority	Competent authority is the form of power in which a leader obtains or can expect (but not demand) compliance by virtue of acknowledged expertise in some field of endeavor. The authority is limited to that field of endeavor.
Personal Authority	Personal authority is the form of power in which a leader obtains or expects compliance (but can not demand it) by virtue of the follower's recognition of the leader's personal characteristics.

Machiavelli[276] posited two real ultimate motivations: fear and love. For him, fear was the stronger of the two and hence a vital part of effective leadership. Jesus advocated love as the stronger. On the power continuum, those forms to the left of inducement all utilize the motivation of fear—they are categorized by the notion of involuntary reception of influence. Those from induced authority to the right all have in essence love as the primary motivation. They are categorized by the notion of voluntary reception of influence.

---

[275]Manipulation, in general. usually has only negative connotations in western societies since it usually implies influencing against one's wishes. While it is true that manipulation is usually bad, it does not have to be so. The definition above is neutral. It is the motivation behind and the ultimate purpose of the influence that is the key.

[276] His views were published in the classic, **The Prince**.

Hersey and Blanchard[277] give terms which help us understand further the *competent* authority form. They use the term *expert* to indicate a person who has expertise, skill and knowledge about something so as to command respect from followers. In addition, they define *information* to indicate the leader's possession of information that is valuable to followers. Competent power includes this as well. From a Christian standpoint, giftedness—a God-given capacity—fits under competent power.

Two terms from Hersey and Blanchard help us understand further the *personal* power sub-form. *Referent* power is a type of power based on the leader's personal traits. Such a leader is usually liked and admired by others because of personality, sincerity, or the like. *Modeling* describes the Christian equivalent of this form. Follower are influenced by leaders they admire. They want to emulate them. *Connection* power refers to a type of power that arises because a leader has connections to influential or powerful people. In leadership emergence theory this is called *networking power*.

Leaders will need the entire range of power forms and authority forms in order to lead followers. It is helpful to know this as well as the negative and positive aspects of these forms.[278]

Understanding Spiritual Authority Via Influence, Power, and Authority Concepts

Now we can examine that major trans-Biblical lesson I stated earlier.

Effective Leaders Value Spiritual Authority As A Primary Power Base.

While it will take a whole range of power forms to accomplish God's purposes to take immature followers to maturity, it should be the goal of spiritual leaders to move people toward the right on the power continuum so that these followers voluntarily accept leadership and follow for mature reasons.[279] So, leaders who are concerned with developing followers should be continually using spiritual authority whenever possible. From our diagram in Figure 1, spiritual authority is defined as a hybrid power form which includes influence via persuasion and authority, especially competent and personal. Legitimate authority frequently helps supplement spiritual authority but does not guarantee it. Notice the voluntary aspect of the spiritual authority definition.

Definition   Spiritual authority is the right to influence conferred upon a leader by followers because of their perception of spirituality in that leader.

An expanded clarification of this definition describes spiritual authority further as that characteristic of a God-anointed leader, which is developed upon an experiential power base that enables him/her to influence followers through:

1. Persuasion (a major power form),
2. Force of modeling (fits under the personal authority form) and
3. Moral expertise (fits under the competent authority form).

Spiritual authority comes to a leader in three major ways. As leaders go through deep experiences with God they experience the sufficiency of God to meet them in those situations. They come to know God. This *experiential knowledge of God and the deep experiences with God* are part of the experiential acquisition of spiritual authority. A second way that spiritual authority comes is through a life which *models godliness*. When the Spirit of God is transforming a life into the image of Christ, those characteristics of love, joy, peace, long suffering, gentleness, goodness, faith, meekness, temperance carry great weight in giving credibility that the leader is consistent inward and outward. Both of these sources of spiritual authority reflec themselves dominantly via the personal authority form. A third way that spiritual

---

[277] See Paul Hersey and Ken Blanchard, **Management of Organizational Behavior--Utilizing Human Resources.** Englewood Cliffs, N.J.: Prentice-Hall, 1977.

[278] See Dennis Wrong, **Power—Its Forms, Bases, and Uses.** New York: Harper and Row, 1979. He gives an excellent treatment of definitions as well as the dynamics of the forms. When certain forms are overused they tend to change to other types of forms.

[279] This is the model God uses with us as believers. He can force us to do things and sometimes does, but He always prefers for us to willingly obey.

authority comes is through *gifted power*. When a leader can demonstrates gifted power—that is, a clear testimony to divine intervention in the ministry—there will be spiritual authority. This source of spirituality buttresses the competent authority form. While all three of these ways of getting spiritual authority should be a part of a leader, it is frequently the case that one or more of the elements dominates.

Conclusion

Some closing observations on spiritual authority are worth noting:

1. Spiritual authority is the ideal form of influence that should be used by leaders.
2. Because of the responsibility of leaders, that is, they must influence—it will require more than just spiritual authority as a power base because of immature followers who cannot recognize spiritual authority.
3. Leaders must develop followers in maturity so that they can more sensitively see God's use of spiritual authority in a leader.
4. Leaders who do not develop followers in maturity will find they have to use the less ideal forms of power (coercive, inducive, legitimate) more often.
5. These forms tend to degenerate toward the left on the continuum becoming less effective over time. This in turn often drives a leader to abuse his/her authority because of the need to force influence.
6. Spiritual authority, like any of the authority forms, can be abused.
7. Mature leaders never abuse spiritual authority.
8. Spiritual authority is ideally used to build up followers and carry out God's purposes for them.
9. Leaders should treasure deep processing with God, knowing that God will use it to develop their spiritual authority.
10. Giftedness alone, even when backed by unusual power, is not a safe source of spiritual authority. Giftedness backed by godliness is the more balanced safe source of spiritual authority.

Jesus led almost totally by spiritual authority. Paul, having to deal frequently with immature believers, uses almost the whole range of authority forms. However, whenever Paul can, he uses spiritual authority. Both of these models set the pattern for Christian leaders.

An awareness of what spiritual authority is and how it relates to the basic ways a leader influences forms a solid foundation upon which to move toward spiritual authority.

Effective Leaders Value Spiritual Authority As A Primary Power Base.

Do you value spiritual authority? Are you using it to influence specific groups of God's people toward His purposes for them?

See **Articles,** *49. Pauline Leadership Styles, 59. Spiritual Authority— Six Characteristics.*

Relevance of the Article to 1,2 Timothy

Character is crucial. Paul underlines this both in 1Ti and Tit in his qualifications for leadership. At the heart of character is integrity. God shapes this important quality, early-on in the life of an emerging leader. Integrity will also be tested throughout the lifetime of a leader. Daniel certainly illustrates this. All of Paul's epistles either overtly or implicitly put forth integrity as a must in a leader. Leaders who fail to finish well can usually trace their failure to character issues, of which lack of integrity heads the list. Older leaders must model integrity throughout their entire lifetimes of leadership. And they must help younger emerging leaders to grasp the importance of integrity, as early as possible.

23. Integrity—A Top Leadership Quality

Introduction

I have been repeating a number of times in the leadership commentary, for a number of books, a major leadership principle.

Ministry flows out of being.

Being is a term describing a number of factors which refer to the inner life and essence of a person. It refers to at least the following, but is not limited to them: (1) intimacy with God; (2) character; (3) personality; (4) giftedness; (5) destiny; (6) values drawn from experience; (7) conscience, and (8) gender influenced perspectives. The axiom, ministry flows out of being means that one's ministry should be a vital outflow from these inner beingness factors.

It is integrity, the rudder that steers character, that I want to highlight in this discussion. Consider the following two words:

1. deception   noun 1.The use of deceit. 2.The fact or state of being deceived. 3. A ruse; a trick. [adapted from The American Heritage Dictionary of the English Language, Third Edition, 1992.] **Synonyms**: trickery, gulling, lying, juggling, craftiness. **Antonyms**: sincerity, frankness, honesty, openness, truthfulness, trustworthiness, genuineness, earnestness, innocence, candor, veracity, verity, probity, fidelity.

2. integrity   The uncompromising adherence to a code of moral, artistic or other values which reveals itself in utter sincerity, honesty, and candor and avoids deception or artificiality (Adapted from Webster). **Synonyms**: honesty, virtue, honor, morality, uprightness, righteousness. Antonyms: deception, dishonesty, corruption, infidelity.

The words are opposite.

Few leaders finish well.[280] Most major failures in ministry are dominantly rooted in spiritual formation issues (spirituality) rather than ministerial formation and strategic formation issues.[281] Most of these

---

[280] Of the Biblical leaders for whom there is evidence about finishing well, about one in three finish well. Probably it is even less for contemporary leaders if anecdotal evidence means anything. What do I mean by finish well? I have identified six characteristics of finishing well from a comparative study of leaders who finished well. A given leader will not necessarily demonstrate all six but at least several. These six characteristics include the following: (1) They maintain a personal vibrant relationship with God right up to the end. (2) They maintain a learning posture and can learn from various kinds of sources—life especially. (3) They manifest godliness (especially Christ-like attitudes and behavior) in character as evidenced by the

failures can ultimately be traced to basic failures of integrity.[282] Leaders who fail often do not have integrity but instead have some sort of deception about at least some of their leadership. On the other hand, leaders who finish well, across the board are leaders of integrity.

Let me remind you of the definition of a Christian leader: A Christian leader is a person with a God-given capacity and a God-given responsibility who is influencing a specific group of God's people toward God's purposes for the group. You cannot influence a group very effectively if they don't trust you. And if you are suspected of trickery, gulling, mendacity, juggling, craftiness—they won't trust you and you won't lead them.

At the heart of any assessment of biblical qualifications for leadership lies the concept of integrity—that uncompromising adherence to a code of moral, artistic or other values which reveals itself in utter sincerity, honesty, and candor and avoids deception or artificiality. So if we want to be leaders who finish well we want to be people of integrity. What is integrity? How do we get it?

Definition   Integrity, the top leadership character quality, is the consistency of inward beliefs and convictions with outward practice. It is an honesty and wholeness of personality in which one operates with a clear conscience in dealings with self and others.

God develops integrity in leaders. It is at the heart of character. A repeated observation on leaders whom God developed and used for his purposes resulted in the following helpful definition.

Definition   An integrity check refers to the special kind of shaping activity (a character test) which God uses to evaluate heart–intent, consistency between inner convictions and outward actions, and which God uses as a foundation from which to expand the leader's capacity to influence. The word check is used in the sense of test—meaning a check or check-up.

I'll come back to this notion of an integrity check and give detailed information on it. But first think with me about Biblical leaders and the notion of integrity.

Biblical Leaders of Integrity

If I were to ask you to name the top two O.T. leaders who demonstrated integrity, who would you suggest? If I were to ask you to name the top two N.T. leaders who demonstrate integrity, who would you suggest?

My top two O.T. leaders who demonstrated integrity are Joseph and Daniel. My top two N.T. leaders who demonstrated integrity are Jesus and Paul (Barnabas is a close second behind Paul).

Both Joseph and Daniel exemplify leaders who were tested by God as to their integrity and passed with flying colors. Joseph in Gen 39 refuses to have an affair with Potiphar's wife. He sees this as wrong. In fact, he states that to do so would be sin against God. God honors this stand and later elevates Joseph to the top administrative post in Egypt (under the Pharaoh). Daniel in Da 1 is tested as to integrity with regard to eating food unacceptable to a Jew. He stands on his convictions. He too is blessed by God and becomes a

---

fruit of the Spirit in their lives. (4) Truth is lived out in their lives so that convictions and promises of God are seen to be real. (5) They leave behind one or more ultimate contributions. (6) They walk with a growing awareness of a sense of destiny and see some or all of it fulfilled.

[281] Spiritual formation is the shaping activity in a leader's life which is directed toward instilling godly character and developing inner life (i.e. intimacy with God, character, values drawn from experience, conscience). Strategic formation is the shaping activity in a leader's life which is directed toward having that leader reach full potential and achieve a God-given destiny. Ministerial formation is the shaping activity in a leader's life which is directed toward instilling leadership skills, leadership experience, and developing giftedness for ministry.

[282] Studies of leaders who have failed to finish well has identified six major barriers to their finishing well. These include: finances—their use and abuse; power—its abuse; inordinate pride—which leads to a downfall; sex—illicit relationships; family—critical issues; plateauing. At the very heart of most of these major barriers lies an integrity issue.

high administrator under Nebuchadnezzar and eventually becomes the number one administrator under Darius. Jesus throughout his whole ministry demonstrates integrity, always showing unity between outward practice and inward conviction. (See especially the Satanic temptations in Mt 4.) Paul writes a whole epistle defending his integrity. He was being accused of all kinds of deception: lying, craftiness, dishonesty, trickery. The book of 2Co reveals Paul's answers to the accusations of deception. A major Pauline leadership value emerges in 2Co.

Label	Statement of Value
Integrity and Openness	*Leaders should not be deceptive in their dealings with followers but should instead be open, honest, forthright, and frank with them.*

Paul, throughout 2Co, refutes the accusations of deception in his leadership and lays out for us many principles underlying integrity in a leader.

Paul's instruction to Timothy in 1Ti about leadership qualifications should be noted here. His qualifications for leaders includes character and conscience. Paul's list of qualifications focuses on integrity and deals mainly with character not giftedness. See his three lists[283] in 1Ti 3:1-7; 8-10; 11-13. All three lists emphasize integrity. And this integrity should be seen by those outside the church as well as those within.

Integrity Check Revisited

God uses life situations to test and build up the inner character of a leader. Integrity is one of the main qualities God shapes in a leader. The *integrity check* is a major way this happens. From comparative study (e.g. Daniel in Da 1,5; Shadrach, Meshach, and Abednego in Da 3; Joseph in Gen 39; Abraham in Gen 24; Jephthah in Jdg 11; Paul in Ac 20:22,23 and many others), a list of kinds of integrity checks can be identified. And their use by God can be suggested. Table 1 gives the kinds of integrity checks. Table 2 lists their uses.

Table 1,2 Ti 23-1. Kinds of Integrity Check

Label	Explanation
temptation (conviction test)	An integrity check frequently is given to allow a leader to identify an inner conviction and to take a stand on it. Such a stand will deepen the conviction in the leader's life. Can a leader really take a stand on some conviction?
restitution (honesty testing)	Some integrity checks force a leader to make right things done wrong in the past, particularly those with on-going ramifications. This is particularly seen in money matters where in the past someone was defrauded. Will a leader be honest, especially about the past?
value check (ultimate value clarification)	Situations frequently force leaders to think through their beliefs about something so that they can identify explicitly a value(s). This value once identified can be evaluated. It can be used more strongly. It may be modified. It may be discarded as not really valid. Can a leader identify the underlying value in a situation?

---

[283] These three lists are apparently list idioms in which the initial item on the list is the main assertion and other items illustrate or clarify the primary item. If so, then the major leadership trait is integrity, a moral characteristic implying a consistency between inner and outer life. The items on the list would then illustrate in the Ephesian culture what moral character, integrity, looks like. So then these items in themselves are not necessarily universal characteristics for a leader but are indicative of what moral character and integrity look like in this culture. The obligatory item is inner integrity, moral character. Paul concludes this small section in vs 7 by returning to this important idea to reemphasize it. This is repeated in descriptions of the lesser leader lists described in vs 8-10, 11-13. Note especially vs 8 and 11. See *list idiom*, **Glossary**.

loyalty (allegiance testing)	God must be first in a life. Frequently, other things become first in a leader's life with perhaps it not even being known by the leader. God can bring to light those things which take His rightful place in our hearts and lives. Who is really first in our lives?
Guidance (alternative testing—a better offer after Holy Spirit led commitment to some course of action)	Frequently a leader is led by God to declare for a certain thing (a ministry, a choice, some option). It is clear that God has led the leader to that choice. After making the choice God may well bring an alternative which looks easier or better simply to test the follow-through on the original decision. Can a leader stick to God's former sure guidance when other challenging guidance comes along?
conflict against ministry vision (guidance/faith testing)	Frequently, a leader will be led into a situation and even have follower support in it. But down the line in the midst of the decision being worked out, particularly when negative ramifications arise, followers or others will oppose the situation. Conflict arises. Note that conflict is a mighty weapon in the hand of God. Usually this integrity check will enforce faith in the leader. Can a leader maintain guidance and believe God will under gird some ministry vision?
word conflict or obedience conflict (complexity testing usually in guidance)	Sometimes a leader will get a word from God or be challenged to obey God in some particular way. Usually this has to do with guidance. Conflict arises as in the previous description. Can a leader trust in his/her ability to hear from God? Or will a leader obey, even if conflict arises?

Table 1,2 Ti 23-2. The Ways that God Uses Integrity Checks

Identifying Label	Why It Is Used
Follow Through	to see follow-through on a promise or vow
Deepening Burden	to insure burden for a ministry or vision
Edification	to allow confirmation of inner-character strength
Faith Builder	to build faith
Value Clarifying	to establish inner values very important to later leadership which will follow
Lordship	to teach submission
Warnings	to warn others of the seriousness of obeying God

Often the integrity check happens completely unknown to people around the leader. That is because of its inward nature. The secondary causes may be events, people, etc. They may not even know that they are sources. The primary causal source is inward through the conscience. The Holy Spirit shapes the conscience.[284]

There is a three step pattern to an integrity check which is passed positively: (1) the challenge to consistency with inner convictions, (2) the response to the challenge, and (3) the resulting expansion. Sometimes the expansion may be delayed or take place over a period of time but it can definitely be seen to stem from the integrity check. Delayed expansion is seen in Joseph's classic test with Potiphar's wife. Immediate expansion is seen in Daniel's wine test.[285]

There is also a three part pattern to an integrity check which is failed: (1) the challenge to consistency with inner convictions, (2) the response to the challenge, and (3) the remedial testing. God will frequently repeat an integrity check until a leader gets it or will take more drastic action. Instead of remedial testing there may be discipline, or setting aside from ministry, or even death.

---

[284] Conscience refers to the inner sense of right or wrong which is innate in a human being but which also is modified by values imbibed from a culture. This innate sense can also be modified by the Spirit of God. See **Article**, 6. *Conscience, Paul's Use of.*

[285] See testing *patterns, positive and negative*, **Glossary**. See **Article**, *Daniel Four Positive Testing Patterns.*

Conclusion

Character is crucial to leadership. Integrity is the foundational trait of character in a leader. Let me summarize some observations, principles and values suggested by the importance of integrity in a leader.

a. Ministry flows out of being of which character is a major component and integrity the dominant necessary leadership trait within character.

b. Leaders without character cannot be trusted and will be followed only to the extent that they have coercive power to back up their leadership claims.

c. A leader must be conscious of what others think of him/her, character-wise. Integrity is universal and occurs in every culture as a notion. But it will take on cultural manifestations peculiar to a culture that demonstrates to those in the culture what integrity is.[286]

d. A leader must seek to have a testimony respected by others (within the bounds of God's ministry assignments).[287]

e. Even though the source of some character trial may be Satanic, a leader should use it to purge impure character traits and rest in God's overriding purposes through the testing.[288]

f. A leader should recognize that character integrity checks will be used by God as foundational training for increased usefulness.[289]

Do the people you influence see you as deceptive or a person of integrity? Do the people outside your ministry see you as deceptive or a person of integrity? Conscience is the inner governor of character—and especially integrity. Remember Paul's challenging statement.

Because I believe in an ultimate accounting before God, I make every effort always to keep my conscience clear before God and man. Ac 24:16

---

[286] For example, oath-keeping was a high value of integrity in the Hebrew O.T.

[287] Paul repeats this notion over and over in 1Ti when advising Timothy about his consulting ministry with the Ephesian church.

[288] Job shows us that behind the apparent things happening to us there may be an unseen spiritual source causing it (Satanic). But even where bad things happen, God can use them to shape character.

[289] A basic understanding of integrity checks can aid one in recognizing much earlier and giving a godly response to them. Forewarned is forearmed.

Relevance of the Article to 1,2 Timothy

Paul was experiencing isolation as he penned 1,2 Ti. Several times in his ministry Paul went through the deep processing experience of isolation. He learned many valuable lessons through this deep processing. And the end result of his isolation experiences was a deepened trust in God and the by-product of an increased spiritual authority. Our research has shown that 90% of leaders we have studied have experienced a Type I or Type II isolation experience. Forewarned is forearmed. This article gives perspective on isolation processing. All leaders need this kind of perspective. Otherwise isolation may blind side them and they may not make it in ministry.

24. Isolation Processing—Learning Deep Lessons From God

Introduction

Leaders get set aside from ministry. Isolation is the term used to describe this process. Sometimes the leader is directly set aside by God, sometimes by others, sometimes by self. Whatever the case, isolation results in deep processing in the life of a leader. More than 90% of leaders will face one or more important isolation times in their lives. Most do not negotiate these times very well. Knowing about them and what God can accomplish in them can be a great help to a leader who then faces isolation.

Defining and Describing Isolation

What is isolation?

Definition   Isolation processing refers to the setting aside of a leader from normal ministry or leadership involvement due to involuntary causes, partially self-caused or voluntary causes for a period of time sufficient enough to cause and/or allow serious evaluation of life and ministry.

Some notable Biblical examples include Job, Joseph, Moses, Jonah, Elijah, Habakkuk, Jesus, Paul. Usually this means the leader is away from his/her natural context usually for an extended time in order to experience God in a new or deeper way. Sometimes isolation can occur in the ministry context itself.

Isolation experiences can be short—like intensive time spent away in solitude to meet God. Or it can last up to several months and occasionally more than a year. Figure 1,2 Ti 24-1 describes isolation in terms of three major categories.

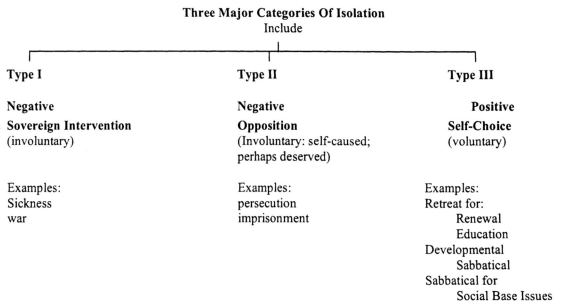

Figure 1,2 Ti 24-1. Three Types of Isolations

These isolation experiences can be viewed in terms of perceived intervention of God in them. Figure 24-2 gives a continuum correlating the isolation experiences to a leader's understanding of God's place in them.

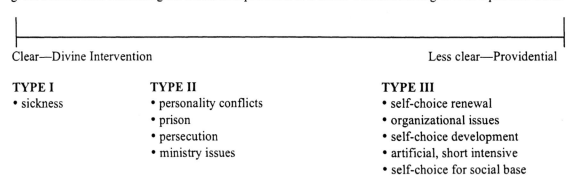

Figure 1,2 Ti 24-2. Isolation Sovereignty Continuum

Table 1,2 Ti 24-1 list some results that have been observed in comparative studies of leaders in isolation.

Table 1,2 Ti 24-1. Isolation Results

Isolation Type	Results or Uses of Isolation
I. Negative/ Sovereign Intervention	lessons of brokenness; learning about supernatural healing; lessons about prayer; deepening of inner life; an intensified sense of urgency to accomplish; developing of mental facilities; submission to God; dependence upon God.
II. Negative/ Opposition	lessons of brokenness; submission to spiritual authority; value of ot' ɛr perspectives; dependence upon God
III. Positive/ Self- choice	new perspective on self and ministry; rekindling of sense of destiny; guidance; oneself to change; upon wider body of Christ

Overlapping Features in Many Isolation Experiences

Table 1,2 Ti 24-2 lists some common things that happen to leaders in isolation.

Table 1,2 Ti 24-2. Common Happenings in Isolation

Isolation Type	Some Happenings
I or II	1. Sense of Rejection
I or II	2. Sense of stripping away--getting down to core issues
I, II or III	3. Eventually a deep need for God
I, II or III	4. Searching for God
I, II, or III	5. Submission to God
I, II, or III	6. Dependence upon God
I, II, or III	7. Rekindling of desire to serve God in a deeper way

Bible Characters and Isolation Lessons From Their Lives
Job, Moses, Elijah, and Paul provide some important isolation lessons. See the Tables which follow listing each of these Bible Characters and observations about isolation.

Job
Job faced sickness, loss of life, loss of wealth, loss of friends, and loss of status as an important person. Table 3 suggests some things that can be learned from Job's Type I isolation experience.

Table 1,2 Ti 24-3. Job and Type I Isolation

Step	Explanation
1.	**Begin With The End In Mind** (need a framework/ perspective). In isolation, deep-seated ideas are challenged in such a way as to capture our attention and force us to come to essential values. Maybe it is only in isolation that they could be challenged. But know that isolation will end and God will teach lessons even about deep-seated ideas.
2.	**Analyze From The Known To The Unknown.** Apart from unusual revelation, we can only search out answers in terms of what we know. That is, the first step in the isolation process—search out what is happening in terms of what you do know (e.g. paradigms).
3.	**Recognize That The Unknown Can Serve Two Functions.** When anomalies arise we must recognize that they may not really be anomalies and will be cleared up in the end (in which case it is a matter of faith and waiting), or they are real and will force us into new paradigms.
4.	**Expect God's Intervention.** God may give insight if a new paradigm is needed or may require a faith response.
5.	**Believe In God's On-Going Answer.** The book of Job shows us that God is in charge of our individual processing—no matter how or through whom it may come, even including Satanic origin. We do not have all the answers. He does. We must trust Him in them.

Moses
In Ex 2:11-15, there is an incident in which Moses kills an Egyptian and then flees (He 11:23-28 and Ac 7:23 give an interpretation of this). Then in Ex 3:7 and following, God calls Moses to a major task, the very one he had tried on his own and given up. There is a major difference in the Moses of Ex 2 and the Moses of Ex 3. Nu 12:3 describes it. Something happened. I want to suggest that it was a brokenness[290] experience. And that brokenness experience was part of isolation processing for Moses.

Moses experienced this Type II isolation processing. It included aspects of geographical and cultural isolation. Three characteristics of geographic and cultural isolation include: 1. It is more powerful in its

---

[290] See *brokenness*, **Glossary.**

early effects; wears off with time and as assimilation occurs. (This is seen also in the life of Daniel.) 2. In Geographic/ cultural isolation there is a loss of self-esteem. The things you were and value in the old culture are usually not so respected and valued in the new. 3. There is often a loss of momentum and vision.

Table 1,2 Ti 24-4. Moses and Type II Isolation

Lesson	Explanation/ Generalized
1	**Look for leadership committal processing as a means toward ending isolation.** Often isolation involves and may terminate with God's renewal of call. See *progressive calling; Glossary.*
2	**God has to sometimes take a vision away in order to later accomplish that vision in his way.** Keep an open hand to plans, visions, future work.
3	**Humility is often the fruit of isolation processing--an unhealthy egotism is broken.** God can unleash great power through a broken/ humble leader without fear of that leader abusing the power.

Elijah

Elijah had two impactful isolation experiences. The first was a Type I, clearly God directed. The second was a Type II. I do not think Elijah ever fully recovered from the second experience. Table 1,2 Ti 24-5 gives some observations about the Type I experience. Table 1,2 Ti 24-6 gives the Type II isolation experience which arose due to persecution.

Table 1,2 Ti 24-5. Elijah's Type I Isolation Experience, 1Ki 17:1-6—Some Observations

Observation	Explained
1	Isolation was God-directed (vs 2,3)
2	Success brings problems (vs 7 brook dries up--he prayed for no rain)
3	God will provide in isolation (vs 4, 9, 14)
4	God protects in isolation (I Kings 18:10).

Elijah's Type II isolation experience was the fallout from one of the most successful ministry events recorded in the O. T. He has just seen God move mightily in a power encounter[291] with the prophets of Baal on top of Mount Carmel—a true mountain top experience. When he flees from persecution he moves into an isolation experience—again a mountain top experience—this time, Mount Sinai. Note that again as with the first experience, success brings with it problems.

Table 1,2 Ti 24-6. Elijah's Type II Isolation Experience, 1Ki 19—Persecution— Running For His Life

Observation	Explained
1. The Situation	Vs4 Desert Isolation— 1. Hope gone; despair; take my life, (vs 4,5) 2. Angel touches him--provision (vs 5,7) 3. Horeb--Mountain of God--40 days/ 40 nights); cave What are you doing? God shows up.
2. Notice the Steps	Step 1. The feelings: I alone/ stood up for God/ persecution Step 2. Presence of God—the antidote to the feelings. Step 3. God answers--not you alone (vs11), 7000 who have not bowed the knee

---

[291] This is the classic power encounter which defines others. The steps of a *Power Encounter* include: 1. There is a confrontation between God and Evil. 2. The forces are recognized for that--the issues are who is more powerful and thus deserving of allegiance. 3. There is a public demonstration so that both forces can be seen by all as to who is more powerful. 4. God demonstrates publicly His power and defeats the evil forces so that there can be no doubt about to whom allegiance should be given. 5. Aftermath--God is glorified, evil forces are punished; there may be a response toward God. See *power encounter*, **Glossary**.

3. The Price To Pay	Power encounters can be costly—they drain away energy—After mountain-top experiences expect attacks from Satan, evil forces; you may well crash hard in the valley. Elijah never again has a major ministry success?
4. Rejection/ God's Affirmation	In isolation there is a sense of personal rejection and a need for divine affirmation. Notice how God does this. **Small Still Voice.** Not the spectacular like you might expect or hope for.
5. Leadership Selection	Elijah imparted power and authority to Elisha—one who was faithful, tenacious, wanted what Elijah had. He carried on Elijah's ministry with more power than Elijah. Elijah's isolation experiences brought spiritual authority. Emerging leaders are drawn to leaders with spiritual authority.

One of the most important things to see from Elijah's isolation experiences is that isolation is frequently accompanied by a sense of personal rejection. It is divine affirmation that we need. God will meet us—tmaybe not in the way we expect.

Paul

Paul had numerous isolation experiences. It is from his life that the concept of repeated isolation experiences occurring in a leader's life emerged. Five are worth noting—1) his short days in Damascus with Ananias, Ac 9; 2; 2) His 2 to 3 years in Arabia mentioned in Gal; 3) His short prison experience in Philippi seen in Ac 16:23; 4) His four years in Rome (during which Eph, Col, Phm, Php were written); 5) His short few months in Rome just before his death. Table 7 suggests nine observations drawn from a comparative study of Paul's isolation experiences.

Table 1,2 Ti 24-7. Nine Observations from Paul's Isolation Experiences

Isolation Experience	Description and Observations
Galatian Isolation 1. Reflection	**Paul's Galatian/Arabia--Pre-Ministry isolation was a Type III self-choice isolation.** It was a time of Reflection in which he worked out his Christology. Basic Principle: Reflection is a major goal and means of processing during isolation. Reflection will happen in isolation. Depending on the kind of isolation there will be questions. A seeking after something—time for thinking. (2Ti is especially filled with reflection; a looking back on a lifetime given to the Gospel.)
2. Prison Isolation; Response Attitude	A. In general, the following principle makes the difference in whether the isolation is profitable or not. **A sovereign mindset in processing makes the difference in immediate response and in long lasting results.** Attitude is everything. Notice Paul's attitude as reflected in: Eph 3:1; 4:1; Col 4:3,9,10; Phm 1; Php 1:12; 4:22. Paul saw a God-ordained purpose behind isolation. What does it mean to have a *sovereign mindset* in processing? It means to recognize that however the isolation may have come about—unjust determination, terrible circumstances, or whatever—you must recognize that God has an ultimate purposes in it: 1) to demonstrate the sufficiency of the supply of the Spirit of Christ, 2) to do specific things fitting the immediate situation, 3) to open up new thinking that could not have been possible, 4) to bring long-range productivity out of it (spiritual authority).
3. Intense Focus	**Critical issues come into focus during isolation processing.** Isolation forces one to focus usually first on why, causes of it, and then later on the purposes of it. And finally with a powerful concentration that allows for problem solving, new revelation to meet situations, and insights that could only come because of the situation.

4. Evaluation— Divine Perspective	**Divine evaluation of character, leadership commitment, and perspective is in focus in isolation processing.** Frequently, what happens is a recognition that God is allowing you to search your life and ministry and evaluate it in light of the situation and often with resulting paradigm shifts that will affect your ministry philosophy and the rest of your life.
5. Deepened Relationship	**A deepened relationship with god is always a major goal of isolation processing.** Philippians, the last of the first set of prison epistles and the most positive upbeat of all of Paul's letter culminates four years of isolation which have been filled with crises. It is filled with the importance of union with Christ. Its message points out what can happen in isolation processing—a grasping of the sufficiency of Christ for life.
6. Basis for Long Range Productivity	**Long lasting productivity is often rooted in isolation processing.** The prison epistles may never have been written had Paul been on the go. But set aside, reflection time produced thinking in regard to his own personal sanctification intimacy with Christians (Php), church problems (Col), the nature of the church (Eph), the solving of a problematic social institution (Phm). But not just products, attitudes and ideas are born in isolation which may come to fruition down road. 1. Specific things—people touched, saved, advise given, etc. 2. Modeling—an intangible product 3. written achievements—one product of isolation.
7. The importance of praise	**Praise is a major weapon in isolation processing.** In external isolation you probably feel less like praising than almost anything else, yet it is at that juncture that praise is probably the most important faith challenge. See Php jail experience, Ac 16, and the tone of praise in all the prison epistles--most of the opening prayers carry that note of praise. Praise will release power, new perspective in isolation.
8. Short Isolation	**Life changing and ministry changing revelation may come even in a short isolation experience.** Moses, 40 days of isolation by self-choice (divine drawing); Paul in two different times (Ac 9, Ananias, Ac 16 Philippian jail experience)
9. Intensified Prayer	**Isolation processing often presses a person into intensified prayer burdens and efforts.**

Let me summarize what we can see in Paul's isolation experiences. Such experiences will tell a leader whether or not that leader has a sovereign mindset. They will also force reflection and evaluation of one's self in relation to: God, truth, a ministry, the past, the future. Critical issues come into focus. Peripheral issues are seen for what they are. In normal times we worry about a lot of things--many peripheral and non-essential. But in isolation times we get down to basic issues: who we are, what we really know, where we are going, who God really is, what He wants from us, etc. A leader will deepen his/her relationship with God—because that is what really matters--more than our ministry, more than the problems around us. A leader may discover the importance of praise or see an intensified outpouring of prayer, or the roots for long range productivity in our lives.

Knowing these things, so what? How can observing these principles in the life of Paul help us as we life schedule or as we work through a present isolation experience? How can we be proactive? Here are some suggestions:

1. **Reflection**—If you are not a thinker or if you are a thinker but are confused in isolation, because you know that reflection is important, you should get with someone in the body of Christ who has either natural abilities of analytical skills, discernment, or spiritual gifts of exhortation, teaching, word of wisdom, word of knowledge and ask for help on getting an overall perspective on what the intent of God is in the isolation. In terms of mentor types, you need to get with a spiritual guide or mentor counselor.

2. **Response Attitude**—Acknowledge that God is in this isolation. By faith accept this and then move with a learning posture through it. I am going to learn great things from God. Others may be to blame but God is in it.

3. **Intense Focus**—Recognize that critical issues will be pointed out in the isolation processing.

4. Divine Perspective Evaluation—Do self-evaluation of your life and ministry. Some suggestions as to how to do this: Be alert to values. Expect new revelation. Know that paradigm shifts often occur in isolation.

5. Deepened Relationship—Spend time in intimacy disciplines with God; extended times of silence, solitude, prayer, Bible study, fasting.

Conclusion

Here are some final warnings and assurances about isolation.

1. **Expect it**. About 90% of leaders go through an isolation experience of Type I or II.
2. **Recognize that there will be a sense of rejection in it.** Because of this it is helpful to keep a log of your divine affirmation and ministry affirmation items. Review them alone with God and feel anew His acceptance.
3. **Determine beforehand to go deep with God**. He will take you into a place of more dependence, perhaps a place of intimacy that you could not have without this kind of processing.
4. **Know that God will indeed meet you in isolation** though at first He may appear remote. Do not try to move out of isolation on your own until God has met you. Otherwise, you may go through a repeated isolation experience.
5. **Know the uses of isolation** and seek to see and sense which of these God is working into your life.
6. For a Type III isolation experience **set goals** for personal growth that include dependence, intimacy, and a deeper walk with God.
7. **Talk to other Christians who have gone through deep processing**. They will give you perspective with a proper empathy.

As a leader you will face isolation. Will you meet God in it and see His purposes in it fulfilled? Remember, isolation processing comes to almost all leaders. Expect repeated isolation processing. It is needed throughout a lifetime. Don't forget, attitude is crucial. Perspective can make the difference—knowing what isolation does, that it does end, that it will accomplish many important things. If you sense you are plateauing then self-initiate an extended time of isolation—get help from mentor counselors and mentor spiritual guides.

Relevance of the Article to 1,2 Timothy

Paul illustrates all five philosophical models which under girded Jesus' ministry. If I were to prioritize the five with respect to Paul's long ministry I would put them in this order. Early ministry—Harvest and Steward seen fairly readily and dominant. Middle Ministry—Servant and Shepherd begin to emerge more prominently. Latter Ministry—all in focus. But note this final remark. Paul, more than any other N.T. church leader demonstrates the Intercessor Model throughout his whole ministry. It was foundational to all of the other philosophical models. See **Article** *46. Paul—Intercessor Leader.*

25. Jesus—Five Philosophical Leadership Models: Servant, Steward, Harvest, Shepherd, Intercessor

Introduction to the Five Models

Jesus' ministry, in the Pr*e-Church Leadership Era*, radically affected underlying notions of what leadership really was. The transition from the O.T. Leadership Eras to the N.T. Leadership Eras necessitated a new power base and new values underlying that base. No longer was leadership associated solely with national leadership as in the O.T. It was now concerned with spiritual leadership. And Jesus, while fully offering leadership to the Jewish national situation, was also introducing the bases for leadership to be expanded cross-culturally into all the world. This expansion would follow in *the Church Leadership Era.* What were the radical changes Jesus instilled? Consider the nine macro lessons identified with Jesus ministry given in Table 1,2 Ti 25-1 below. All were radically different from anything seen in O.T. leadership.

Table 1,2 Ti 25-1. Nine Radical Macro Lessons Seen in Jesus Ministry

Lesson Label	Statement of Lessons
28. Selection	The key to good leadership is the selection of good potential leaders which should be a priority of all leaders.
29. Training	Leaders should deliberately train potential leaders in their ministry by available and appropriate means.
30. Focus	Leaders should increasingly move toward a focus in their ministry which moves toward fulfillment of their calling and their ultimate contribution to God's purposes for them.
31. Spirituality	Leaders must develop interiority, spirit sensitivity, and fruitfulness in accord with their uniqueness since ministry flows out of being.
32. Servant	Leaders must maintain a dynamic tension as they lead by serving and serve by leading.
33. Steward	Leaders are endowed by God with natural abilities, acquired skills, spiritual gifts, opportunities, experiences, and privileges which must be developed and used for God.
34. Harvest	Leaders must seek to bring people into relationship with God.
35. Shepherd	Leaders must preserve, protect, and develop God's people.
36. Movement	Leaders recognize that movements are the way to penetrate society though they must be preserved via appropriate on-going institutions.

This article is concerned with the philosophical bases underlying the leadership models associated with macro lessons 32, 33, 34, and 35. In addition, another macro lesson originating in the O.T. is seen in minimum form in Jesus' ministry— *the Intercessor Model*. It becomes clearer that it was a significant part of Jesus' ministry philosophy with the writing of the epistle to the Hebrews—.

       8. Intercession   Leaders called to a ministry are called to intercede for that ministry.

For each of these radical macro lessons, Servant, Steward, Harvest, Shepherd and Intercessor I will describe a philosophical model. I define what I mean by ministry philosophy below. A model is simply an attempt to coherently interweave the definition, values, and implications associated with the idea.

Definition	<u>Ministry philosophy</u> refers to ideas, values, and principles, whether implicit or explicit, which a leader uses as guidelines for decision making, for exercising influence, and for evaluating his/her ministry.

These philosophical models are not exhaustively treated in one unified source in the N.T.. Much of the descriptive analysis comes as much from observations of practice of N.T. leaders as from explanatory passages. I will describe each of these models using the following format: introduction, definition, some supporting Biblical passages, basic values, and implications. I will also add explanatory comments. Finally, I will close by describing how the Holy Spirit applied these models into the Church.

The Servant Leader Model

introduction	Ministry philosophy refers to a related set of values that underlies a leader's perception and behavior in his/her ministry. The values may be ideas, principles, guidelines or the like. Each Christian leader will have a unique ministry philosophy that generally differs from others due to values God has taught experientially. But there will be some items in common with other leaders. The Servant Leader Model provides a set of values that should be common to the ministry philosophy of each Christian leader. Its central thrust says in essence that a leader's main focus is to use leadership to serve God by serving followers. A leader is great whose leadership capacities are used in service vertically to God and horizontally to followers.
Definition	The <u>servant leader model</u> is a philosophical model which is founded on the central thrust of Jesus' teaching on the major quality of great Kingdom leaders. That is, a leader uses leadership to serve followers. This is demonstrated in Jesus' own ministry.
passages	Mt 20:20-28, Mk 10:35-45.
secondary passages	Parable of the Waiting Servant—Mt 24:42-51, Lk 12:35-40, 41-48 Parable of the Unprofitable Servant—Lk 17:7-10. Isaiah's suffering Servant—Isa 52:13-53:12.

Basic Values
1. Leadership must be exercised primarily as service first of all to God and secondarily as service to God's people.
2. Service should require sacrifice on the leader's part.
3. Servant leadership ought to be dominated by an imitation modeling leadership style. That is, the dominant form of influence is modeling for the followers and setting expectancies for them to do the same.
4. Abuse of authority, Lording it over followers in order to demonstrate one's importance, cannot be compatible with servant leadership.
5. A major motivational issue for leadership must be anticipation of the Lord's return.
6. One ought to minister as a duty expected because of giftedness. Hence, there is no expectancy or demand or coercion for remuneration—no demanding one's due.

Implications
1. A servant leader does not demand rights or expect others to see him/her as one with special privileges and status.
2. A servant leader can expect God to give ministry affirmation and does not demand it from followers.
3. A servant leader expects to sacrifice. Personal desires, personal time, and personal financial security will frequently be overridden by needs of service in ministry.
4. The dominant leadership style to be cultivated is imitation modeling. While there is a place for other more authoritarian styles this style will dominate.
5. Spiritual authority, with its earned credibility, will be the dominant element of one's power-mix.
6. Leadership functions are performed always with a watchful spirit anticipating the Lord's return.
7. Finances will not dominate decision making with regard to acceptance of ministry.

comment   Balance is important, for the servant leader must lead and must serve. The servant leader must maintain a dynamic tension by recognizing Butt's (1975) assertion that a leader leads by serving and serves by leading.

comment   The Servant Model is a general leadership model applying to all leaders.

examples   Both Peter and Paul demonstrate the values of this leadership model.

The Stewardship Model   synonym: Accountability Model

introduction   Ministry philosophy refers to a related set of values that underlies a leader's perception and behavior in his/her ministry. The values may be ideas, principles, guidelines or the like which are implicit (not actually recognized but part of perceptive set of the leader) or explicit (recognized, identified, articulated). For any given leader a ministry philosophy is unique. It is dynamic and related to three major elements: Biblical dynamics, giftedness, and situation. Though a ministry philosophy is dynamic there are core issues which are stable and apply to all leaders. The stewardship model is one such set of stable Biblical values.

Definition   The <u>stewardship model</u> is a philosophical model which is founded on the central thrust of several accountability passages, that is, that a leader must give account of his/her ministry to God.

specific   Accountability parables: Mt 20 Laborers in the Vineyard, Mt 24 The Waiting
passages Servants, Mt 25 The Ten Virgins, Mt 25 The Ten Talents, Lk 16 The Worldly Wise Steward, Lk 19 The Pounds.

General   Ro 14:11,12; 1Co 3:5-9, 12-15; 2Co 5:10; Php 2:10,11; Heb 9:27. These passages indicate general judgment.

Special   Jas 3:1, Da 12:1-3, Heb 13:17. These are special leadership passages.

Other Passages   1Co 4:1-5; 2Co 4:1-6; Ac 20:17-38; 1Pe 5:1-4. These indicate accountability/ rewards.

Basic Values
1. Ministry challenges, tasks, and assignments ultimately must be seen as from God.
2. God holds a leader accountable for leadership influence and for growth and conduct of followers. A leader must recognize this accountability.
3. Leaders must recognize an ultimate accounting of a leader to God in eternity for one's performance in leadership.
4. Leaders should recognize that they will receive rewards for faithfulness to their ministry in terms of abilities, skills, gifts and opportunities. This is one motivating factor for leading.

5. Leaders ought to build upon abilities, skills, and gifts to maximize potential and use for God.
6. Leaders should recognize that they will be uniquely gifted both as to gifts and the degree to which the gift can be used effectively.
7. Leaders should know that they will receive rewards for their productivity and for zealously using abilities, skills, gifts, and opportunities for God.
8. Leaders ought to know that they frequently must hold to higher standards than followers due to . "the above reproach" and modeling impact they must have on followers.

Implications
1. Leaders must maintain a learning posture all of their lives—growing, expanding, developing.
2. Leaders must make certain of ministry tasks, challenges, and assignments in terms of God's guidance (calling) for them.
3. Leaders must perform in ministry as unto the Lord in all aspects of ministry.

comment   The Stewardship Model is the most general of the N.T. Philosophical models in that it applies to followers as well as leaders. Servant leadership applies only to leaders as does the Shepherd and Harvest Models. It is unclear about to whom the Intercessor Model applies—probably both to leaders and followers gifted with faith.

comment   Paul exemplifies this model.

Harvest Model

introduction   Ministry philosophy refers to a related set of values that underlies a leader's perception and behavior in his/her ministry. The values may be ideas, principles, guidelines or the like. Each Christian leader will have a unique ministry philosophy that generally differs from others due to values God has taught experientially. Leaders whose giftedness and calling line up with the central function of the Harvest Leader Model will find that its values are enmeshed in their own unique ministry philosophy. Leaders not so gifted may or may not have been shaped toward these particular ministry values. In any case the values are worth evaluation. Harvest leaders tend to have a leadership style bent which is fundamentally task oriented in nature.

Definition   The <u>harvest leader model</u> is a philosophical model founded on the central thrust of Jesus' teaching to expand the Kingdom by winning new members into it as demonstrated in the agricultural metaphors of growth in scripture.

central   Its central concern is with expansion of Kingdom so as to bring new members
thrust   into the Kingdom as forcefully commanded in the outward aspect of the Great Commission—Go ye into all the world and make disciples of all people groups.

primary   Mt 28:19,20: Great Commission—Outward Aspect. (See also Mk
passages   16:15, Lk 24:46,47, Jn 20:21, Ac 1:8). Kingdom Growth Parables:
                Mt 13:24-30 Tares.
                Mt 13:31,32 Mustard Seed; Mk 4:30-32 Mustard Seed.
                Mt 13:33-35 Leaven; Lk 13:33-35 Leaven.
                Mk 4:26-29 Mysterious Growth of Seed.
                Sending Passage: Lk 10:1-12 Sending of 70.

archetype   Paul is the archetype of a harvest leader in the N.T. Peter also in his early ministry.

Values
1. Harvest leaders must have a strong concern for those outside the kingdom and want to give them a choice to hear and enter the kingdom. (Great Commission Passages)

2. Harvest leaders should have a strong desire to motivate followers to take the kingdom message to others. (Lk 10:1-12)
3. Harvest leaders must have a strong concern for power in ministry—they know the value of power to gain a hearing for the gospel of the kingdom. (Mt 28:20, Mk 16:16,17, Lk 24:49, Ac 1:8)
4. Harvest leaders must concerned with the ultimate destiny of those outside the kingdom than the present state of those in the kingdom. (Mt 28:19 emphasis on outward not inward)
5. Harvest leaders should recognize that Kingdom expansion means will not always sift out the real from the unreal but know that ultimately there will be resolution. (Mt 13:24-30)
6. Harvest leaders by and large must exercise faith. They believe God will accomplish His expansion work and hence are not afraid of small beginnings. (Mt 13:31,32, Mk 4:30-32)
7. Harvest leaders should recognize the evangelistic mandate as taking priority over the cultural mandate since the cultural mandate will require large numbers before impact on a non-kingdom society can be made. (Mt 13:33-35, Lk 13:20-21)
8. Harvest leaders ought to value receptivity testing in order to discover movements of God. (Mk 4:26-29)

comment   Gift-mixes which correlate strongly with the Harvest Leader model include the various combinations of: the word gifts of apostle, faith, evangelist; the love gifts of mercy; the power gifts of healing, miracles, word of knowledge.

The Shepherd Leader Model

introduction   Each Christian leader will have a unique ministry philosophy that generally differs from others due to values God has taught experientially. Leaders whose giftedness and calling line up with the central function of the Shepherd Leader Model will find that its values are enmeshed in their own unique ministry philosophy. Leaders not so gifted may or may not have had shaping experiences imparting these particular ministry philosophy values. In any case the values are worth evaluation. Shepherd leaders tend to have a leadership style bent which is fundamentally relational in nature.

Definition   The <u>shepherd leader model</u> is a philosophical model which is founded on the central thrust of Jesus' own teaching and modeling concerning the responsibilities of leadership in caring for followers as seen in the various Shepherd/ Sheep metaphors in scripture.

central   Its central thrust is concern and care for the welfare of followers—that is, growth and
thrust   development in the Kingdom so that they know God's rule in their lives and hence bring God's righteousness in society. This model is concerned primarily with the inward aspects of the Great Commission—teach them to obey all that I have commanded.

primary   Mt 28:19,20, Great Commission, Inward Aspect. Mt 9:36,37 Shepherd Aspect
passages   of the Analogy. Mt 18:12 Parable of Lost Sheep, Lk 15:1-7 Parable of Lost Sheep. Jn 10:1-18 The Good Shepherd, Jn 21:15-17 Feed My Sheep. 1Pe 5:1-4 Peter's View, Shepherd Leadership. Ac 20:17-38 Paul's View, Watching for the Flock.

archetypes   Peter, in his latter ministry, and Barnabas are significant examples of shepherd leaders. Paul, occasionally as in his more lengthy stays in churches.

Values
1. Shepherd leaders value personal kingdom growth in each follower. That is, they have a strong desire to see realization of kingdom truth in followers that is, they have a drive to see followers increasingly experiencing the rule of God in their lives. (Mt 28:20, Jn 21, Ac 20)
2. Shepherd leaders should have a strong empathy with followers. They seek to assess where they are and to help meet their needs so as to develop them toward their potential for the kingdom. (Mt 9:36,37)
3. Shepherd leaders value each follower as important to the whole body and want to keep them incorporated in the body. (Ac 20:28 Lk 15:1-7, Mt 18:12,13)

4. Shepherd leaders value a personal relationship with followers. (Jn 10:3, 4, 14)
5. Shepherd leaders ought to give personal guidance to followers by setting examples—particularly in the area of kingdom values. They value imitation modeling as an influence means with followers. (Jn 10:4)
6. Shepherd leaders should protect followers from deviant teaching by giving positive truth that will aid them in assessing counterfeit teaching. (Jn 10:5, 10, 12 Ac 20:28)
7. Shepherd leaders value followers experiencing abundant life in Christ. (Jn 10:10)
8. Shepherd leaders ought to be willing to sacrifice and know that personal desires, personal time, and personal financial security will frequently be overridden by needs of service in ministry. (Jn 10:11)
9. Shepherd leaders should be willing to persevere through persecution or hard times in order to better the condition of followers. (Jn 10:11)
10. Shepherd leaders must transparently expose weaknesses, strengths and their heart with followers. (Jn 10:14)
11. Shepherd leaders value unity in body and wider body. (Jn 10:16)
12. Shepherd leaders ought to willingly take responsibility for followers. (1Pe 5:2)
13. Financial gain ought to be secondary to performing ministry in the values of a Shepherd leader. (1Pe 5:2)

comment | Gift-mixes of leaders correlating strongly with the Shepherd Leader model include the various combinations of: the word gifts of pastor, teaching; the love gifts of mercy, helps and governments; the power gifts of healing, word of wisdom. The word gifts of prophecy, exhortation and leadership can operate with both Shepherd and Harvest leader models.

The Intercessor Model   synonym: Accountability Model

introduction | Ministry philosophy refers to a related set of values that underlies a leader's perception and behavior in his/her ministry. The values may be ideas, principles, guidelines or the like which are implicit (not actually recognized but part of perceptive set of the leader) or explicit (recognized, identified, articulated). For any given leader a ministry philosophy is unique. It is dynamic and related to three major elements: Biblical dynamics, giftedness, and situation. The intercessor model flows out of the prayer macro lesson and shows the concern of a leader for God's intervention in ministry. It is not clear to who this model applies—all leaders or those leaders who have the gift of faith. It may also well apply to some who are not leaders but who have the gift of faith.

Definition | The intercessor model is a philosophical model which is founded on the central thrust of the prayer macro lesson (which applies to all leaders—as a role) and an additional responsibility for praying for a ministry, flowing out of the faith gift or some aspects of the prophetical gift.

general | Abraham and the macro lesson: Ge 18:16-33; Moses and the macro lesson: Ex 32:7-14; Samuel and the macro lesson: 1 Sa 12:1-25; Jesus and the macro lesson: some 44 different verses indicate Jesus praying throughout his ministry. One especially important prayer passage occurs in Jn 17.

Special | Matthew 9:36-38 links intercession with the raising up of emerging leaders. Heb 7:25 in the midst of an argument highlighting Jesus' eternal ministry as a priest, gives as an argument this phrase, "Wherefore he is able also to save them to the uttermost that come unto God by him, seeing he ever lives to make intercession for them."

Basic Values
1. A leader who is called to ministry must accept responsibility for prayer for that ministry.
2. A leader should show acceptance of responsibility for a ministry by interceding for that ministry and involving others to intercede.

3.   A leader must seek God's leading in prayer, the divine initiative, as to how and what to pray for.
4.   A leader should bathe major decision making in prayer.
5.   A leader ought to encourage the development of emerging leaders by praying for them and telling them of prayer for them.
6.   A leader should cultivate an attitude of prayer at all times and ought to break into prayer spontaneously.
7.   Crises should drive a leader deeper into intercessory ministry.
8.   Extended times alone in prayer should be used for intercession, for personal renewal and for revelation from God for guidance, breakthroughs in ministry, and for decision making.

Implications
1.   No ministry will long endure without intercessors behind it.
2.   Quantity (the number of and amount of time spent by) of intercessors is not as important as quality of intercession of the ones doing the interceding.
3.   Leaders with the gift of faith will do personal intercession with a zeal, passion and fruitfulness beyond that of leaders who do this as a role.
4.   Leaders should recruit faith gifted intercessors to help in the ministry.
5.   Power in ministry comes from giftedness and from prayer. Both are needed.

comment   The Intercessor Model is the most specific of the leadership models. It is the most gift related. Gifts of faith, apostleship, and in general, the revelatory gifts (word of knowledge, word of wisdom, prophecy, word of faith) will usually be associated with leaders operating strongly in this model. Now all leaders have the duty to intercede for their ministries. But those who are drawn to this model will be gifted to see its impact more than just that which results from praying in general. It is not clear to what extent each leader will be involved in this model. Jesus does exhort his followers to pray for emerging leaders.

comment   Paul exemplifies this model.

Applied To The Church Era Of Leadership
Four of these models, Servant, Steward, Harvest, and Shepherd, originated in Jesus' ministry in the *Pre-Church Leadership Era*. The fifth, Intercessor, is widespread across all leadership eras. It is clear with the emergence of the church and the spiritual leadership which accompanied it that the Holy Spirit applied all five of these models to the *Church Leadership Era*. Peter, John, and Paul, the leading models of church leaders strongly emphasize these models.

Table 1,2 Ti 25-2. The Three Archetype Church Leaders and Philosophical Models

Leader	Models Exemplified
Peter	Early on—Harvest Later Ministry—Shepherd Steward Servant
John	Shepherd Servant
Paul	Harvest Shepherd Steward Servant Intercessor

We have much more information on Paul than either of the other two. So it is easier to see examples of each of the models in his life. With more information it is likely that all five of the models would be seen in all three lives. Certainly John with his right brained approach and mysticism must have been involved in a intercessor model, though we do not see it in his writings, which are not autobiographical.

Conclusion

Our studies of leaders and giftedness indicate that leaders with apostleship, evangelism, and faith tend to be Harvest Model adherents. Leaders with pastoral, teaching, and governments tend to be Shepherd Model enthusiasts. Leaders with exhortation, prophecy, and leadership gifts can go in either direction— Harvest Model or Shepherd Model. However, most leaders tend to be one or the other and not both. All leaders are to be Servant Leaders (a model which does not naturally appear in most cultures). All leaders are to be Stewards. Some leaders will embrace fully the Intercessor Model personally (those faith gifted) while others will recruit people to utilize that model for them.

Leaders should be increasingly conscious of the values which under gird their ministries. Explicit understanding can increase proactive use. Value driven leaders are needed especially those who will embrace the models that Jesus instituted.

Related **Articles**: *36. Macro Lessons Defined; 37. Macro Lessons, List of 41 Across Six Leadership Eras; 26. Leadership Eras in the Bible—Six Identified; 71. Value Driven Leadership.*

Book Referred to: Howard Butt, **The Velvet Covered Brick: Christian Leadership in An Age of Rebellion**. 1973. New York: Harper and Row.

Relevance of the Article to 1,2 Timothy
Paul's ministry occurs in the sixth Biblical leadership era—the Church Era. Each of the eras contributes greatly to our understanding of leadership as it developed in the Biblical record. We must remember too, to analyze and judge leaders from a given leadership era in terms of what was known about leadership to that point in the Biblical record. A study of leadership across all six leadership eras allows for the identifying of macro lessons—those leadership observations, principle, guidelines and absolutes which appear to apply to all leadership.

26. Leadership Eras in the Bible—Six Identified

Introduction to the Six Leadership Eras

A <u>Bible Centered leader</u> refers to a leader whose leadership is informed by the Bible, who has been personally shaped by Biblical values, has grasped the intent of Scriptural books and their content in such a way as to apply them to current situations and who uses the Bible in ministry so as to impact followers. Notice that first concept again—

whose leadership is informed by the Bible.

Two of the most helpful perspectives for becoming a Bible centered leader **whose leadership is informed by the Bible** include:

(1) recognizing the differences in leadership demands on leaders throughout the Bible, i.e. seeing the different leadership eras, and
(2) Recognizing and knowing how to draw out insights from the seven genre of leadership sources in the Bible.

This article overviews the first of these helpful perspective—seeing the leadership eras in the Bible.

The Six Leadership Eras

Let me start by giving you one of the most helpful perspectives, a first step toward getting leadership eyes, for recognizing leadership findings in the Bible. That first helpful perspective involves breaking down the leadership that takes place in the Bible into leadership eras which on the whole share common leadership assumptions and expectations for the time period. These assumptions and expectations differ from one leadership era to the next, though there are commonalties that bridge across the eras.

Definition   A <u>leadership era</u> is a period of time, usually several hundred years long, in which the major focus of leadership, the influence means, basic leadership functions, and followership have much in common and which basically change with time periods before or after it.

An outline of the six eras I have identified follows.

I. **Patriarchal Era (Leadership Roots)—Family Base**

II. **Pre-Kingdom Leadership Era—Tribal Base**
    A.   The Desert Years
    B.   The War Years--Conquering the Land,
    C.   The Tribal Years/ Chaotic Years/ Decentralized Years--Conquered by the Land

III. **Kingdom Leadership Era—Nation Based**
    A.   The United Kingdom
    B.   The Divided Kingdom
    C.   The Single Kingdom--Southern Kingdom Only

IV. **Post-Kingdom Leadership Era—Individual/ Remnant Based**
    A.   Exile--Individual Leadership Out of the Land
    B.   Post Exilic--Leadership Back in the Land
    C.   Interim--Between Testaments

V. **New Testament Pre-Church Leadership—Spiritually Based in the Land**
    A.   Pre-Messianic
    B.   Messianic

VI. **New Testament Church Leadership—Decentralized Spiritually Based**
    A.   Jewish Era
    B.   Gentile Era

I have used the following tree diagram[292] to provide an overview of leadership. The three overarching components of leadership include: the leadership basal elements (leader, follower, situation which make up the What of leadership); leadership influence means (individual and corporate leadership styles which make up the How of leadership); and leadership Value bases (Biblical and cultural values which make up the Why of leadership).

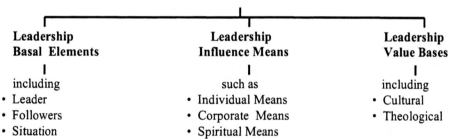

The Study Of Leadership
involves

Leadership Basal Elements	Leadership Influence Means	Leadership Value Bases
including	such as	including
• Leader	• Individual Means	• Cultural
• Followers	• Corporate Means	• Theological
• Situation	• Spiritual Means	

Figure 1,2 Ti 26-1. Tree Diagram Categorizing the Basics of Leadership

It was this taxonomy which suggested questions that helped me see for the first time the six leadership eras of the Bible. Table 1 below gives the basic questions/subjects/categories that helped me identify the different leadership eras. It is these categories that allows comparison of different leadership periods in the Bible.

---

[292] This was derived in a research project, the historical study of leadership in the United States from the mid 18th century to the present—for further study see **A Short History of Leadership Theory**, 1986, by Dr. J. Robert Clinton. Altadena, CA: Barnabas Publishers. See **Further Study Bibliography**.

Table 1,2 Ti 26-1. Basic Questions To Ask About Leadership Eras

1. **Major Focus**—Here we are looking at the overall purposes of leadership for the period in question. What was God doing or attempting to do through the leader? Sense of destiny? Leadership mandate?
2. **Influence means**—Here we are describing any of the power means available and used by the leaders in their leadership. We can use any of Wrong's categories or any of the leadership style categories I define. Note particularly in the Old Testament the use of force and manipulation as power means.
3. Basic **leadership functions**—We list here the various achievement/ responsibilities expected of the leaders: from God's standpoint, from the leader's own perception of leadership, from the followers. Usually they can all be categorized under the three major leadership functions of task, relational, and inspirational functions. But here we are after the specific functions.
4. **Followers**—Here we are after sphere of influence. Who are the followers? What are their relationship to leaders? Which of the 10 Commandments of followership are valid for these followers? What other things are helpful in describing followers?
5. **Local Leadership**—in the surrounding culture: Biblical leaders will be very much like the leaders in the cultures around them. Leadership styles will flow out of this cultural press. Here we are trying to identify leadership roles in the cultures in contact with our Biblical leaders.
6. **Other**—Miscellaneous catch all: such things as centralization or decentralization or hierarchical systems of leadership; joint (civil, political, military, religious) or separate roles.
    Thought Questions—Here try to synthesize the questions you would like answered about leaders and leadership if you could get those answers. We are dealing here with such things as the essence of a leader (being or doing), leadership itself, leadership selection and training, authority (centralized or decentralized), etc.

Using these leadership characteristics I studied leadership across the Bible and inductively generated the Six Leadership Eras as given above.[293] Table 1,2 Ti 26-2 adds some descriptive elements of the eras.

Table 1,2 Ti 26-2. Six Leadership Eras in the Bible—Brief Characterizations

Leadership Era	Example(s) of Leader	Definitive Characteristics
1. Foundational (also called patriarchal)	Abraham, Joseph	Family Leadership/ formally male dominated/ expanding into tribes and clans as families grew/ moves along kin ship lines
2. Pre-Kingdom	Moses, Joshua, Judges	Tribal Leadership/ Moving to National/ Military/ Spiritual Authority/ outside the land moving toward a centralized national leadership
3. Kingdom	David, Hezekiah	National Leadership/ Kingdom Structure/ Civil, Military/ Spiritual/ a national leadership—Prophetic call for renewal/ inside the land/ breakup of nation
4. Post-Kingdom	Ezekiel, Daniel, Ezra	Individual leadership/ Modeling/ Spiritual Authority
5. Pre-Church	Jesus/ Disciples	Selection/ Training/ spiritual leadership/ preparation for decentralization of Spiritual Authority/ initiation of a movement/

---

[293] I have a short form of answers to each of these questions for each of the six leadership eras. See **Biblical Leadership Eras** in the collection of articles given in the **Biblical Leadership Encyclopedia** series.

6. Church	Peter/ Paul/ John	decentralized leadership/ cross-cultural structures led by leaders with spiritual authority which institutionalize the movement and spread it around the world

When we study a leader or a particular leadership issue in the Scriptures we must always do so in light of the leadership context in which it was taking place. We cannot judge past leadership by our present leadership standards. Conversely, we will find that major leadership lessons learned by these leaders will usually have broad implications for our leadership.

See **Articles**: *28. Leadership Genre—Seven Types; 36. Macro Lessons Defined; 37. Macro Lessons —List of 41 Across Six Leadership Eras.* See **Leadership Eras Section** for a detailed overview.

Relevance of the Article to 1,2 Timothy

Paul was a Type E leader (international sphere of influence—that is, influence in many countries and cultural settings. See **Article** *30. Leadership Levels—Looking At a Leadership Continuum.* Paul was dominantly a task-oriented leader (the first of the 3 high level leadership priorities) who was also a powerful inspirational leader (the third of the 3 high level leadership priorities). He learned somewhat to operate as a relational leader (the second of the high level leadership priorities). This third function is seen best in his mentor/training with individuals or small groups. He went through a number of conflicts, which softened his task orientation and taught him the need for the relational function. So as you read this article, think to yourself, which of these functions are evident in the Corinthian ministry? How are they seen?

27. Leadership Functions—Three High Level Generic Priorities

Introduction

High level Christian leaders[294] perform many leadership functions. In addition to direct ministry functions based on giftedness there are those additional functions that characterize leaders simply because they are people responsible for others.

description <u>Leadership functions</u> describe general activities that leaders must do and/or be responsible for in their influence responsibilities with followers.

Leadership studies in the mid-50s[295] analyzed the kinds of things leaders did in secular organizations. From a list of over a thousand they reduced them by factor analysis to two major categories. These two categories are roughly equivalent to what we would call today task-oriented leadership and relational-oriented leadership. In the early 80s and 90s leadership research began to identify another high level function, which I call inspirational leadership.[296]

Figure 1,2 Ti 27-1 below groups leadership functions into three generic categories: task oriented leadership, relational oriented leadership, and inspirational leadership.

Three High Level Leadership Functions
include

Task-Oriented Leadership Relational-Oriented Leadership Inspirational Leadership

Figure 1,2 Ti 27-1. Three High Level Leadership Functions

---

[294] I use a five-fold leadership typology adapted from McGavran: Type A—local internal influence in the church or Christian organization; Type B—local external influence in the church or Christian organization; Type C—local/regional influence; Type D—national influence; Type E—international influence. I am speaking mostly about Type C, D, and E leaders when I talk about generic leadership functions for high level leaders. See **Article, Leadership Levels—Looking At A Leadership Continuum**.

[295] The Ohio State Leadership Research (1948-1967) reduced the many observed functions of secular leadership by factor analysis to two major generic categories: consideration and initiation of structure.

[296] McGregor and others were doing research on motivation. There was also a growing interest in values underlying why leaders did things.

Task Oriented Leadership

Task oriented leadership (technically called *Initiation of structure* in the Ohio State Research) groups all of those activities which a leader does to accomplish the task or vision for which the structure exists. Task behaviors involve clarifying goals, setting up structures to help reach them, holding people accountable, disciplining where necessary and in short, to act responsibly to accomplish goals. Table 27-1 displays a list of typical task oriented leadership functions.

Table 1,2 Ti 27-1. Typical Task-Oriented Leadership Functions

Christian leaders:
1. must provide structures which facilitate accomplishment of vision;
2. will be involved in crisis resolution related to structural issues;
3. must make decisions involving structures;
4. will do routine problem solving concerning structural issues;
5. will adjust structures where necessary to facilitate leadership transitions;
6. must do direct ministry relating to maintaining and changing structures (extent depends on giftedness).

Relational-Oriented Leadership

Relational-oriented leadership (technically called *Consideration* in the Ohio State research) groups all of those activities which a leader does to affirm followers, to provide an atmosphere congenial to accomplishing work, to give emotional and spiritual support for followers so that they can mature. In short, it is to act relationally with followers in order to enable them to develop and be effective in their contribution to the organization. Table 1,2 Ti 27-2 lists some typical relational oriented leadership functions.

Table 1,2 Ti 27-2. Typical Relational-Oriented Leadership Functions

Christian leaders:
1. must be involved in selection, development and release of emerging leaders;
2. are called upon to solve crises involving relationships between people;
3. will be called upon for decision-making focusing on people;
4. must do routine problem solving related to people issues;
5. will coordinate with subordinates, peers, and superiors;
6. must facilitate leadership transition—their own and others;
7. must do direct ministry relating to people (extent depends on giftedness).

Inspirational Leadership

Christian leadership is *externally directed.* That is, goals result from vision from God. Such leadership must move followers toward recognition of, acceptance of and participation in bringing about that God-given vision. Leaders will answer to God for their leadership.[297] Inspirational leadership is needed for this. Some typical inspirational functions are shown in Table 1,2 Ti 27-3.

Table 1,2 Ti 27-3. Typical Inspirational Leadership Functions

Christian leaders:
1. must motivate followers toward vision.
2. must encourage perseverance and faith of followers.
3. are responsible for the corporate integrity of the structures and organizations of which they are a part.
4. are responsible for developing and maintaining the welfare of the corporate culture of the organization.
5. are responsible for promoting the public image of the organization.

---

[297] See **Article**, *1. Accountability—Standing Before God as a Leader.*

6.   are responsible for the financial welfare of the organization.
7.   are responsible for direct ministry along lines of giftedness which relate to inspirational functions.
8.   must model (knowing, being, and doing) so as to inspire followers toward the reality of God's intervention in lives.
9.   have corporate accountability to God for the organizations or structures in which they operate.

Summarizing Leadership Functions

There are common activities and unique activities for the three categories of leadership functions. A single list helps pinpoint the essential activities of Christian leaders.

1.   Utilize giftedness for direct ministry to those in their sphere of influence.
2.   Solve crises.
3.   Make decisions.
4.   Do routine problem solving.
5.   Coordinate people, goals, and structures.
6.   Select and develop leaders.
7.   Facilitate leadership transition at all levels.
8.   Facilitate structures to accomplish vision.
9.   Motivate followers toward vision. This usually involves changing what is, and providing/ promoting a sense of progress.
10.   Must encourage perseverance and faith of followers. This usually involves maintaining what is and creating a sense of stability. This is usually in dynamic tension with activity 9.
11.   Accept responsibility for corporate functions of integrity, culture, finances, and accountability.
12.   Must model so as to inspire followers toward the reality of God's intervention in lives and history.

Conclusion

These three functions must be carefully tended to if an organization is to go on.[298] Yet, a given leader usually has a predilection toward either task-oriented leadership or relational-oriented leadership. It is a rare leader who can do both well. But either a task-oriented leader or a relational-oriented leader can do inspirational leadership. That is, motivational functions can be done by either a task-oriented leader or relational-oriented leader. What ever the case, it is up to a high-level leader to make sure the functions are done despite his/her own particular bent. To do this a high-level leader must be willing to delegate, to depend on and release to others functions that are not his/her own strength. And a leader should realize that the higher the level of leadership the more important it is that the leader demonstrates the inspirational function, himself or herself, and repeatedly so that the whole organization is motivated.

See **Article**, *30. Leadership Levels.*

---

[298] Most task oriented Christian organizations simply assume that these are happening.

Relevance of the Article to 1,2 Timothy

Six of the seven leadership genre are illustrated in 1,2 Ti. The (1) biographical genre is especially informative as God's shaping activity in Paul's life comes to a close. (2) The leadership qualification passage in 1 Ti 3 is a direct leadership passages. (3) The two books, 1, 2 Ti taken as a whole, illustrate in great detail a leadership act. (4) Only the parabolic leadership genre is missing. (5) This whole commentary is demonstrating the notion of book as a whole. (6) Indirect passages and (7) Macro lessons are also present. In fact, one could teach on these genre and illustrate them well by using 1,2 Ti.

28. Leadership Genre—Seven Types

Introduction to the Seven Leadership Genre

A Bible Centered leader refers to a leader whose leadership is informed by the Bible, who has been personally shaped by Biblical values, has grasped the intent of Scriptural books and their content in such a way as to apply them to current situations and who uses the Bible in ministry so as to impact followers. Notice that first concept again—

whose leadership is informed by the Bible.

Two of the most helpful perspectives for becoming a Bible centered **leader whose leadership is informed by the Bible** include:

(1) recognizing the differences in leadership demands on leaders throughout the Bible, i.e. seeing the different leadership eras, and

(2) Recognizing and knowing how to draw out insights from the seven genre of leadership sources in the Bible.

This article overviews the second of these helpful perspectives—the seven leadership genres and how to get leadership information from them.

The Seven Genre—Derived From Study Across Six Leadership Eras

In a related treatment (see *Overview of Six Leadership Eras in the Bible* in **Section III**) I identified six periods of time, each of which characterized a major leadership era in the Bible. See Table 1,2 Ti 28-1 below.

Table 1,2 Ti 28-1. Six Leadership Eras in the Bible

Era	Name	Central Feature
I.	O.T. Patriarchal Era (Leadership Roots)	Family Base
II.	O.T. Pre-Kingdom Leadership Era	Tribal Base
III.	O.T. Kingdom Leadership Era	Nation Based
IV.	O.T. Post-Kingdom Leadership Era	Individual/ Remnant Based
V.	N.T. Pre-Church Leadership	Spiritually Based in the Land
VI.	N.T. Church Leadership	Decentralized Spiritually Based

Further study of each of these leadership eras resulted in the identification of seven leadership genre which served as sources for leadership findings. I then worked out in detail approaches for studying each of these genre.[299] These seven leadership genre are shown in Table 1,2 Ti 28-2.

---

[299] These detailed approaches are given in my manual, **Leadership Perspectives—How To Study The Bible for Leadership Insights.**

Table 1,2 Ti 28-2. Seven Leadership Genre—Sources for Leadership Findings

Type	General Description/ Example	Approach
1. Biographical	Information about leaders; this is the single largest genre giving leadership information in the Bible/ Joseph.	Use biographical analysis based on leadership emergence theory concepts. See **Article**, *Biographical Studies in the Bible— How To Do.*
2. Direct Leadership Contexts	Blocks of Scripture which are giving information directly applicable to leaders/ leadership; relatively few of these in Scripture/ 1 Peter 5:1-4.	Use standard exegetical techniques. Note the passages in 1, 2Ti and Tit which deal with leadership. These three books have more direct contexts dealing with leadership than any other books in the Bible. See my running commentary, overviews and leadership insights sections for these books.
3. Leadership Acts	Mostly narrative vignettes describing a leader influencing followers usually in some crisis situation; quite a few of these in the Bible/Acts 15 Jerusalem Council	Use three fold leadership tree diagram as basic source for suggesting what areas of leadership to look for. See Figure 1 in **Article**, *Leadership Tree Diagram* for categories helpful for analyzing.
4. Parabolic Passages	Parables focusing on leadership perspectives: e.g. stewardship parables, futuristic parables; quite a few of these in Matthew and Luke./ Luke 19 The Pounds	Use standard parable exegetical techniques but then use leadership perspectives to draw out applicational findings; especially recognize the leadership intent of Jesus in giving these. Most such parables were given with a view to training disciples.
5. Books as a Whole	Each book in the Bible; end result of this is a list of leadership observations or lessons or implications for leadership/ Deuteronomy	Consider each of the Bible books in terms of the leadership era in which they occur and for what they contribute to leadership findings; will have to use whatever other leadership genre source occurs in a given book; also use overall synthesis thinking. I have done this in the Leadership Bible Commentary in the Leadership Insights Section for each of the 14 leadership commentaries I have done. I also have done this for each book of the Bible in another manual, **The Bible and Leadership Values**.
6. Indirect Passages	Passages in the Scripture dealing with Biblical values applicable to all; more so to leaders who must model Biblical values/ Proverbs; Sermon on the Mount	Use standard exegetical procedures for the type of Scripture containing the applicable Biblical ethical findings or values
7. Macro Lessons	Generalized high level leadership observations seen in an era and which have potential for leadership absolutes/ Presence Macro	Use synthesis techniques utilizing various leadership perspectives to stimulate observations. I have made a start on this. See **Articles**, *36. Macro Lessons Defined;37. Macro Lessons, List of 41...*

A major step in becoming informed about leadership in the Bible is to recognize the various kinds of leadership information sources the seven genre described above. But the more important step is to start studying these sources for leadership observations, principles, guidelines, macro lessons, and absolutes.

See **Articles**, 36. *Macro Lessons Defined; 37. Macro Lessons, List of 41 Across Six Leadership Eras; 5. Bible Centered Leader.*

Relevance of the Article to 1,2 Timothy

Other than Jesus, Paul is the strongest leader in the N.T. in terms of these 7 lessons. And for the most part he was deliberate in using these leadership principles in his life. Many times in my comparative study of leaders it is evident that some of the lessons were known and used deliberately while others are seen but not necessarily explicitly known by the leader. However, in Paul's case it can be shown that he proactively operated with these leadership principles in mind. He models these lessons well. In 1,2 Ti all seven lessons are seen to be part of the fabric of who Paul is. As Christian leaders today, we do well to explicitly recognize these seven major leadership lessons and proactively demonstrate the ones which are part of who we are.

29. Leadership Lessons—Seven Major Lessons Identified

Introduction

From comparative study of over 3000 leader case studies, seven major leadership lessons have emerged. These leadership lessons are listed below with a brief explanation, a value suggested which flows from the lesson, reasons why important, a Biblical and a contemporary example and some suggestions for follow-up.

1. Lifetime Perspective

Effective Leaders View Present Ministry in Terms Of A Lifetime Perspective.

Explanation: Leaders who recognize the big picture for their lives have a jump start on surviving present circumstances which may be both negative and overwhelming. A leader needs to recognize the notion of developmental phases over a lifetime and boundaries transitioning between them. He/she needs to understand the shaping activity of God over a lifetime. If such a leader also knows the basic goal toward which God is moving, he/she can respond to present day shaping for maximum benefit. In general, a leader knowing what it means to finish well, determines to have that for his/her life. That leader recognizes the barriers to finishing well: 1. lack of financial integrity, 2. sexual impropriety, 3. abuse of power, 4. family related problems, 5. problems with pride, 6. plateauing. That leader recognizes the factors that will promote a good finish: 1. a learning posture, 2. mentoring help, 3. renewal experiences, 4. disciplines, 5. a lifelong perspective. A leader thus armed can perceive what is happening today from a sovereign mindset. In short, it allows the leader to go through present happenings because of the hope of the future and knowledge that God is in them.

Value Suggested: A leader ought to gain perspective on what is happening today in his/her life by interpreting it in the light of his/her whole lifetime and God's overall purposes in it.

Why Important: 1) Few leaders finish well. Perspective is one of the enhancements that can help a greater number of leaders finish well. 2) Making it through tough times in leadership may well depend on gaining perspective. Without perspective, a longer range viewpoint on what is happening, few leaders will persevere through hard times. 3) A critical difference between leaders and followers is perspective. The difference between leaders and more effective leaders is better perspective. Effective leaders will be broadening their perspective.

Biblical Examples: Jesus, Paul

Contemporary Example: Billy Graham

Suggestions for Follow-Up:　Read Clinton's **The Making of a Leader** for a popular treatment of a lifetime perspective on a leader's development. See also the *Article 68. Time-Lines—Defined for Biblical Leaders*. See Graham's autobiography, **Just As I Am.**

2. Learning Posture

Effective Leaders Maintain A Learning Posture Throughout Life.

Explanation: The ability to learn from the Bible, current events, people, reading, ministry experience, and other sources in such a way as to affect one's leadership is fundamental to being an effective leader. Flexible leaders usually do have a good learning posture (has to do with an attitude, a mental stance toward learning). Inflexible leaders are not usually active learners. God will bring into a leader's life necessary information and wisdom to meet leadership situations if that leader is open to learning. Leadership is dynamic. Changing situations demand that a leader be constantly learning. One of the five major factors identified with leaders who finish well is a good learning posture.
Value Suggested: A leader ought to be continually learning from a wide variety of sources in order to cope effectively with life and ministry.

Why Important: A good learning posture is one of the enhancements toward a good finish. It is also the key to ministry insights, paradigm shifts, and other leadership lessons that can make the difference in effective on-going leadership.

Biblical Examples: Daniel, the classic Old Testament leader, models an exemplary learning posture. The Apostle Paul does the same in the New Testament.

Contemporary Examples: Watchman Nee (Chinese church/para church leader who died in prison in the early 70s); A. J. Gordon, Baptist pastor in Boston area and developer of one of the first flagship churches in the U.S. (1836-1895). Examples from today include Phil Yancey, Hans Finzel and Robertson McQuilkin.

Suggestions for Follow-Up:　See Kinnear's book on Nee, **Against The Tide**. See **For Further Study Bibliography**, Clinton's chapter 3 on A.J. Gordon in **Focused Lives**.

3. Spiritual Authority

Effective Leaders Value Spiritual Authority As A Primary Power Base.

Explanation: Spiritual authority is the right to influence conferred by followers because of their perception of spirituality in a leader. It is that characteristic of a God-anointed leader which is developed upon an experiential power base that enables him/her to influence followers through: 1) Persuasion, 2) Force of modeling, and 3) Moral expertise. Spiritual authority comes to a leader in three major ways. First as leaders go through deep experiences with God they experience the sufficiency of God to meet them in those situations. They come to know God more intimately by experiencing Him. This experiential knowledge of God and the deep experiences with God are part of the experiential acquisition of spiritual authority. A second way that spiritual authority comes is through a life which models godliness. When the Spirit of God is transforming a life into the image of Christ, those characteristics of love, joy, peace, long suffering, gentleness, goodness, faith, meekness, temperance carry great weight in giving credibility. They show that the leader is consistent inwardly and outwardly. A third way that spiritual authority comes is through gifted power. When a leader demonstrates gifted power in ministry —that is, a clear testimony to divine intervention in the ministry—there will be spiritual authority. While all three of these means of developing spiritual authority should be a part of a leader, it is frequently the case that one or more of the elements dominates. Ideally spiritual authority is the major influence means used with mature followers. Other power bases such as coercion, inducement, positional, and competence may have to be used as well as spiritual authority because of lack of maturity in followers. Mature followers will recognize spiritual authority. Leaders who command and demand compliance are not using spiritual authority.

Values Suggested: 1) Leaders should respond to God's processing in their life so as to let spiritual authority develop as a by-product of the processing. 2) Leaders ought to recognize and use spiritual authority whenever they can in their ministry.

Why Important: Leaders who rely on privilege and power associated with a position tend to abuse power in their ministry. Spiritual authority counters the abuse of power. Spiritual authority honors God's maturity processes in followers.

Biblical Examples: Moses, Jesus, Paul

Contemporary Examples: Henrietta Mears, Bible teacher/ entrepreneur (1890-1963); Watchman Nee (Chinese church/para church leader who died in prison in the early 70s). John Wimber was a leader who especially had spiritual authority because of gifted power.

Suggestions for Follow-Up: See **For Further Study Bibliography**, Clinton's chapter 8 on Mears in **Focused Lives** and teaching by Nee on this subject, **Spiritual Authority**.

4. Dynamic Ministry Philosophy

> **Effective Leaders Who Are Productive Over A Lifetime Have A Dynamic Ministry Philosophy.**

Explanation: An unchanging set of core values and a changing set of peripheral values comprise a dynamic ministry philosophy. Such a ministry philosophy expands due to a growing discovery of giftedness, changing leadership situations, and greater understanding of the Scriptures. A leader's discovery of his/her giftedness and development of the same takes place over 10 to 15 years of ministry. Continued discovery will bring about issues of ministry philosophy not previously seen or anticipated. The same is true of the Scriptures. A leader will continue to master the Word over a lifetime. New input will lead to new philosophical values which will add to, clarify, or even replace earlier philosophical values which now become less important. Finally, leaders will usually move through three or four very different ministry situations over a lifetime. Each new situation will demand discovery of new leadership values. But a leader will also have some core values which continue throughout all phases. This core will also expand as new critical leadership values are added. But that leader will also have numerous periphery leadership values which will change, come and go, over a lifetime.

Value Suggested: A leader ought to identify core and peripheral leadership values under girding his/her leadership philosophy and be ready to adapt and changes these over a lifetime.

Why Important: Ministry essentially flows out of being. A conglomerate of factors make up one's being including (but not limited to): intimacy with God, personality, gender, giftedness, character, and values (convictions) learned via ministry experience. One's ministry philosophy emerges from those values. Hence, if we are to operate in terms of who God has made us to be, we must increasingly become explicitly aware of the values that under gird our leadership.

Biblical Examples: Joseph, Habakkuk (generally prophetic ministry demands a ministry that is value based), Paul.

Contemporary Examples: G. Campbell Morgan, British pastor and international Bible teacher (1863-1945), Warren Wiersbe, Billy Graham.

Suggestions for Follow-Up: See **Article**, *71. Value Driven Leadership*. See also **For Further Study Bibliography**, Clinton's chapter 5 on Morgan in **Focused Lives**.

5. Leadership Selection And Development

Effective Leaders View Leadership Selection And Development As A Priority Function In Their Ministry.

Explanation: God raises up future leaders in present ministries. A major responsibility of Christian leaders is to partner with God in the on-going selection and development of leaders. The processes of identifying and developing leaders is both a means and an end. It is an end in itself by producing new leaders. But it is also a means for stimulating life in the ministry that is doing it. Emerging leaders also bring new life to a ministry. Strong leaders usually attract emerging leaders to themselves who are potentially like-gifted. Leaders should recognize this pattern and proactively respond to it by developing those potential leaders so attracted. Leaders who fail to recognize, select, and develop emerging leaders in their ministry miss out on personal growth that comes through this experience. They may almost be guaranteeing a weak future ministry that is overly dependent upon themselves.

Value Suggested: Leaders ought to be involved in the selection and development of emerging leaders.

Why Important: No work of God can last long that is not producing new leaders. Any work of God is only one generation away from nominality and mediocrity. New leadership emerging offsets nominality and plateauing ministry.

Biblical Examples: See Jesus ministry in the Gospels. See Paul's ministry. Both of these leaders selected and developed leaders.

Contemporary Examples: Robert Jaffray (1873-1945), Christian Missionary and Alliance missionary to Indo-China and Indonesia. Howard Hendricks. Paul Stanley. Alan Andrews.

Suggestions for Follow-Up: See **For Further Study Bibliography**, Clinton's chapter 6 on Jaffray in **Focused Lives**.

6. Relational Empowerment

Effective Leaders See Relational Empowerment As Both A Means And A Goal Of Ministry.

Explanation: Personal relationships between a leader and followers allow for interdependence in the body. Leaders need the feedback that comes through personal relationships with their followers. Leaders should developing body life (reciprocal living—the one-another commands) as a major goal. This kind of behavior in a group provides a base from which all kinds of development can occur. For example, personal relationships will develop which will lead to mentoring. Mentoring is probably the best informal means for developing followers and especially emerging leaders. It is in the context of close, accountable, personal relationships that younger leaders can be encouraged and truly empowered.

Value Suggested: A leader ought to view personal relationships as a Biblical and critical priority in ministry both for developing ambiance for growth and for empowering others via mentoring methods.

Why Important: Mentoring is one of the most appropriate means of developing followers and challenging emerging leaders. Modeling, one form of mentoring, is one of the most important influence means. Personal relationships form the seedbed for both mentoring and modeling.

Biblical Examples: Jesus, Paul

Contemporary Examples: Henrietta Mears (1890-1963); Dawson Trotman (1906-1956), founder of the Navigators, Howard G. Hendricks, Paul Stanley, Bill Hull.

Suggestions for Follow-Up: See **Articles** *Reciprocal Living—The One-Another Commands; 47. Paul—Mentor for Many; 38. Mentoring—An Informal Training Model; 48. Paul—Modeling As An Influence Means*. See **For Further Study Bibliography**, Clinton's chapter 8 on Mears in **Focused Lives**. See Skinner's book, **Daws—The Story of Dawson Trotman, Founder of the Navigators**. See Clinton and Clinton, **The Mentor Handbook**. See Stanley and Clinton, **Connecting**.

7. Sense Of Destiny

Effective Leaders Evince A Growing Awareness Of Their Sense Of Destiny.

Explanation: A sense of destiny is an inner conviction arising from an experience (or a series of experiences) in which there is a growing awareness that God has His hand on a leader in a special way for special purposes. This typically happens along a three-fold destiny pattern: destiny preparation, destiny revelation, and destiny fulfillment. That is, a leader is usually unaware of preparation items as they happen, but in retrospect can reflect and see how God was preparing for a destiny. The sense of destiny deepens as God begins to unfold more clearly life purpose, role, and strategic guidance. And finally some or all of the destiny is fulfilled. Leaders become gradually aware of a destiny with God as He continues to shape them over a lifetime.

Value Suggested: A leader ought to be sensitive to destiny shaping activities in his/her past and present, and be anticipating their future implications. This awareness informs decision making reflecting partnership with God toward fulfilling that destiny.

Why Important: No Biblical leader greatly used by God failed to have a strong sense of destiny. A strong sense of destiny will buttress a leader to persevere toward a strong finish.

Biblical Examples: Abraham, Joseph, Moses, Jesus, Paul. Joseph, Moses, and Paul vividly demonstrate the threefold pattern of destiny preparation, destiny revelation and destiny fulfillment.
Contemporary Examples: Samuel Logan Brengle (1860-1936), Salvation Army Stalwart, Bill Bright.

Suggestions for Follow-Up: See **Article** *8. Destiny Pattern*. See **Glossary** for *destiny pattern; destiny processing; sense of destiny*. See also these same concepts in **Clinton's Leadership Emergence Theory Manual**. See Clarence Hall's work, **Samuel Logan Brengle, Portrait of a Prophet**. See **For Further Study Bibliography**, Clinton's chapter 4 on Brengle in **Focused Lives**.

Conclusion

Not all these lessons appear in a specific example of an effective leader. Some leaders exemplify three or four of them, others five or six and in a few cases all seven. But they are certainly goals for which to strive. It is not clear whether these lessons are by-products of effective leaders or causes of them being effective. Hopefully they are some of both so that if we deliberately try to put these in our lives they will improve our effectiveness.

Note: Not all articles listed in the Suggestions for Follow-Up section are contained in this commentary. See the **For Further Study Bibliography** for full citations of books or manuals.

Relevance of the Article to 1,2 Timothy

Even before Paul's conversion it was clear that he would have wide spread influence. He was operating in several different culture/countries as he pursued the persecution of Christians. At *the critical incident*—the *On the Road To Damascus revelatory Type I Awe Inspiring destiny* incident—it was clear that Paul would eventually have a Type E level influence. And Paul did. He also illustrates Types C and D and some Type A leadership in the church planting situations in which he established a longer residential ministry. In 1,2 Ti Paul is near the end and it has clear that he has fulfilled his destiny and become a Type E leader. His epistles alone, a major legacy of his ministry, continue to exert, even today, world-wide influence on Christian leaders. Paul is a good study to see how a leader progresses all the way along the levels of influence continuum. He personally experience the effects of all three major barriers to moving along the continuum: 1. The Experience Gap; 2. The Logistics Barrier, and 3. The Strategic Barrier. In Paul's own ministry and his leadership selection and development of many others it is clear that levels of leadership are distinguished to imply two things: 1. not to stress that bigger is better but to indicate that problems will be faced as leaders develop to higher levels of leadership; 2. the responsibilities of those levels. Bigger is not better—appropriate levels in terms of God-given potential is the standard.

30. Leadership Levels
Looking At A Leadership Continuum: Five Types Of Leaders

Introduction

It is helpful to differentiate leaders in terms of some criteria. Several can be constructed. One typical example looks at Christian leadership in a church or denomination or parachurch organization. The primary criterion involves sphere of influence.[300] This typology of leaders along the continuum helps us pinpoint three major problems leaders face as they emerge from low level influence to high levels. These problems will repeatedly be faced around the world as the church emerges.

1. The Experience Gap,
2. The Financial (Logistics) Barrier,
3. The Strategic (Psychological) Barrier

Five Types of Leaders Along An Influence Continuum

Examine Figure 1,2 Ti 30-1 below which presents a continuum of leaders based on sphere of influence and shows some potential problems along the way.

---

[300] Sphere of influence refers to the totality of people being influenced and for whom a leader will give an account to God. The totally of people influenced subdivides into three domains called direct influence, indirect influence, and organizational influence. Three measures rate sphere of influence: 1. Extensiveness—which refers to quantity; 2. Comprehensiveness—which refers to the scope of things being influenced in the followers' lives; 3. Intensiveness—the depth to which influence extends to each item within the comprehensive influences. Extensiveness is the easiest to measure and hence is most often used or implied when talking about a leader's sphere of influence.

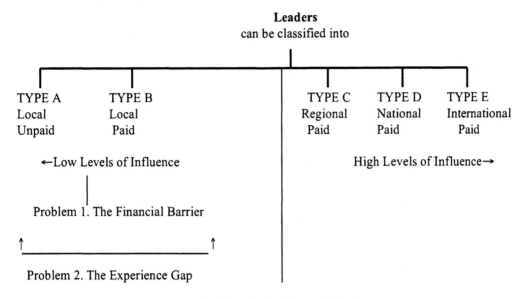

Figure 1,2 Ti 30-1. Five Types of Leaders—Expanding Sphere of Influence/ Three Problems

Table 1,2 Ti 30-1 further identifies each of the types of leaders.

Table 1,2 Ti 30-1. Five Types of Leaders Described

Type	Description
A	These are volunteer workers who help local churches get their business done. Low level workers in a Christian organization, who do clerical work or other detailed staff administration work, fit this level of influence also.
B	Paid workers in small churches like pastors of small congregations or pastors of multi-congregations fit here. Sometimes these are bi-vocational workers having to supplement their salaries with outside employment. Associate pastors on staff in a larger church also have this same level of influence. Paid workers doing administrative work in Christian organizations have the equivalent level of influence from an organizational standpoint.
C	This level of influence includes senior pastors of large churches who influence other churches in a large geographic area (e.g. via Radio/TV ministry, Pastor Conferences, separate organization promoting the pastor's publications, workshops, etc.). It also includes leaders in Christian organizations or denominations who are responsible for workers in a large geographic region.
D	These include senior pastors of large churches who have national influence usually via organizations created by them to promote their ministry. Denominational heads of a country would fit here too. Professors in prestigious seminaries which train high level leaders and are writing the texts which others use would fit here too. Some influential Christian writers might fit here.
E	Heads of international organizations with churches in various countries and or missionaries in many countries fit here. Some influential Christian writers might fit here. Leaders at this level dominantly do strategic thinking. Often Type E leaders will control large resources of people, finances, and facilities. They will have very broad personal networks with other international leaders and national leaders. They will often be on boards of very influential organizations.

It should be explicitly stated here that there is no inherent value attached to any of the types. That is, a Type E leader is not better than a Type A leader. All of the various types are needed in the church and mission organizations. More types A and B are needed than Type E leaders. The type of leader we become depends on capacity that God has given and God's development of us toward roles which use that capacity. To be gifted for Type B leadership and to aspire for Type D is a mismanagement of stewardship. So too, to be gifted for Type E and yet remain at Type C. None of the types are better than any other. All are needed. We need to operate along the continuum so as to responsibly exercise stewardship of our giftedness and God's development of our leadership. Bigger is not better. Appropriate is best.

Problem 1. The Financial Barrier

Problem 1, also called the *Logistics Barrier* or the *Lay/Clergy Dilemma*, deals with finances.[301] In most situations where a church is emerging, a need for workers who can devote their full time and giftedness to accomplish ministry goals will arise. In the Christian enterprise there are non-professional workers, people doing necessary work in churches. There are para-professional workers, those who give their most energy to church work and have some developed giftedness but who support themselves financially with some sort of secular job. And finally there are semi-professional workers. Some leaders get partial pay for their Christian work. When a worker moves from non-professional, para-professional, or semi-professional status to full time paid Christian worker, that is, workers move from Type A to Type B, he/she will face the financial barrier. How can such workers be financed? [302]Many potential leader stumbles over this barrier and never makes it in to full time ministry (and perhaps because of discouragement, drops out of ministry altogether). Paul was dealing with this problem in 1Co 16 when he exhorts the Corinthians about finances for Christian workers—his own self (subtlety given), Timothy, and Stephanus.

Additional Problems with Problem 1 Moving Across the Financial Barrier

There is a tendency, which I call, *The Projection Tendency,* to seek to pressure effective Type A leaders to *go full time.* The idea involves the subtle implication that full time Christian leaders are more dedicated to God than lay leaders.

There is another minor problem involved in moving from Type A to Type B leadership. I call it *The Expectation Problem.* When leaders cross the logistics barrier, it involves a major status change for leaders. Laity perceive full time Christian workers differently than lay leaders. Movement from Type A to Type B leadership means that people will view them differently (perhaps have higher expectations of them) even though their roles may not change.

Problem 2. The Experience Gap

Problem 2, also called the pre-service training problem, basically deals with a modern problem. Where churches have spread in a given geographical area, training institutions like seminaries and Bible colleges have also emerged. Normally, as a church is emerging, leaders are trained on-the-job and take on more responsibility as they are ready for it. But once there is a large number of churches and larger individual churches, people who are untrained on the job and with little or no leadership experience go to these training institutions and in a short period of time are academically trained (sort of) for ministry. They then attempt to enter ministry at Type B or higher level if they can. They don't have the experience for it. So we have people leading at levels they are not experienced to lead. A similar but not identical problem is being dealt with in 1Ti where Paul is seeking to give Timothy, a younger worker, to be accepted by older leaders, the Ephesian elders. The problem is not exactly the same, since Timothy did have experience—but the culture did not respect younger leaders. *The Experience Gap* is a double problem in some cultures since they respect age and experience, and training institutions turn out potential leaders who fit neither requirement.

---

[301] Leaders who hold to the major leadership lesson on selection and development, as a value, will face this problem repeatedly as they seek to find ways to move leaders along in development. That lesson (Effective leaders view leadership selection and development as a priority function) carries with it some heavy responsibility.

[302] This is a major problem that will be faced around the world as the model which arose in the 19th and 20th centuries in countries with financial resources, that is, at least one full time paid pastor per congregation, go by the by. Bi-vocational workers will most likely dominate in the early part of the next century.

Problem 3. The Strategic Barrier—Its Two Problems

Problem 3, also called the *ministry focus problem*, deals with a giftedness/ responsibility problem seen in leaders who move from Type C ministry to Type D or E ministry. That is, they become leaders who do less direct ministry and more indirect ministry. Heads of organizations with a big sphere of influence face this problem. Direct ministry means dominantly using word gifts to influence people directly. Indirect ministry means leaders who are now helping or directing other leaders in direct ministry but are themselves not primarily doing direct ministry. Usually leaders who rise to these levels do so because they were successful in direct ministry at lower levels of influence. Simply because they were effective at that lower level doing direct ministry depending on their word gifts does not insure that they will be successful at a higher level not dominantly using their word gifts. In short, they are not trained for the functions at the higher level. And what is more startling, little or no formal training exists to develop leaders to do these higher level leadership functions.

A second problem arises. It is a psychological one. It has to do with satisfaction in ministry. When one is doing direct ministry and dominantly using word gifts, there is a constant feedback of things happening in lives which gives affirmation and satisfaction. At higher levels most leaders are doing leadership functions like problem solving, crises resolution, structural planning, and strategizing. These functions do not reward one in the same way as direct ministry. They do not receive the same satisfaction in doing these things and getting little affirmation as they did when they effectively did direct ministry.

Two things can help overcome these two problems. One, leaders should be trained for the higher level functions, dominantly by mentoring from leaders who are doing them well, and then transitioned into them. Two, the psychological loss perceived by leaders crossing the strategic barrier can also be addressed in at least the following two ways that I have observed in leaders at high level. One, they can from time to time do forays back into direct ministry which bring satisfaction that was experienced previously. Two, they can learn to see that what is being accomplished has broader potential and more far reaching results than their former direct ministry which had to be sacrificed in accepting the higher level of leadership. This requires strategic thinking and an application of the servant leadership model at a higher capacity level. Paul's later ministry dealt with this strategic barrier problem. Most of his latter ministry was indirect. Note his epistles are largely indirect ministry. He is helping other leaders deal with their issues—problem solving, dealing with crises, etc. He is not out there teaching and preaching directly. Note he got strategic eyes—see 2Co 11:28,Then besides all this, daily, I am burdened with my responsibility for the churches.

Conclusion

Types of leaders, that is, levels of leadership, are distinguished not to imply that bigger is better but to indicate that problems will be faced as leaders develop to higher levels of leadership. Further, leadership issues will vary noticeably with the different types. Types D and E are much more concerned with leadership means/resources, items of organizational structure, culture, dynamics, and power. They are multi-style leaders. They are more concerned with leadership philosophy and with strategic thinking. They know they will have heavy accountability to God in these areas. They are concerned with macro-contextual factors. Because leadership functions vary greatly along the continuum, different training is needed for each type. Informal/non-formal training focusing on skills for direct ministry is needed for Types A/B and should usually be in-service. All three modes (informal, non-formal, and formal) are needed to provide skills and perspectives for Types C, D, and E. In-service and interrupted in-service should dominate for Types C, D, and E.

See *sphere of influence, pre-service training, in-service training, word gifts, mentoring definitions, leadership styles, formal training, non-formal training, informal training,* **Glossary**. See **Articles**, *49. Pauline Leadership Styles; Training Modes—When They Fit.*

Relevance of the Article to 1,2 Timothy

Paul shines here. Read *Article 43. Paul and His Companions* to get a view of his fishing pool. Paul had a great number of personal relationships from which to ascertain potential leaders and select them for further training. See also **Articles** *45. Paul—Developer Par Excellence, 47. Paul—Mentor For Many, 48. Paul—Modeling as An Influence Means and 38. Mentoring—An Informal Training Model*. In all these articles as well as the concepts seen below in this article, you will see that Paul is an exemplar in Leadership Selection and Development. His three-year training time in the Bible School at Ephesus probably is the highlight of his leadership development. His deliberate selection of the six future apostolic leaders, (from different geographical situations) stands out. He deliberately invited Timothy, Titus, Aristarcus, Segundus, Gaius, Sopater to his on-the-job training institute in Ephesus. Later Trophimus, Tychicus, and Epaphras also came and spent residential time there. This training at Ephesus really is the highpoint of Paul's leadership selection and development. It is clear he was aware of a limited time left him. He wanted to train those who could carry on his legacy. Major Leadership Lessons, 5. Leadership Selection And Development (Effective Leaders View Leadership Selection And Development As A Priority Function In Their Ministry) and 6. Relational Empowerment (Effective Leaders See Relational Empowerment As Both A Means And A Goal Of Ministry), standout out in Paul's ministry. This article highlights the selection perspectives that are needed to emulate Paul's leadership and selection accomplishments.

31. Leadership Selection

Introduction

A major lesson identified from a comparative study of leaders[303] challenges to the core,

Effective Leaders View Leadership Selection and Development as a priority function.

This value dominated Christ's ministry. To instill an on-going movement Christ had to inculcate his values in a band of leaders who would continue to propagate his movement. And he had to train them well in order for them to carry on. This he did. *Selection and Development* are stressed in Christ's Ministry.[304] Paul held to this value very strongly in his ministry.[305] What should we know about leadership selection and development if we want to have this important value in our lives? Two things will help us: (1) terminology that describes what happens and (2) an overall time perspective integrating the things that happen. [306]

---

[303] Seven such lessons have been identified: (1) Effective Leaders View Present Ministry in Terms Of A Life Time Perspective. (2) Effective Leaders Maintain A Learning Posture Throughout Life. (3) Effective Leaders Value Spiritual Authority As A Primary Power Base. (4) Effective Leaders Who Are Productive Over A Lifetime Have A Dynamic Ministry Philosophy. (5) Effective Leaders View Leadership Selection And Development As A Priority Function In Their Ministry. (6) Effective Leaders See Relational Empowerment As Both A Means And A Goal Of Ministry. (7) Effective Leaders Evince A Growing Awareness Of Their Sense Of Destiny. It is the fifth one I am exploring in this article.

[304] See Bruce's, **The Training of the Twelve**, a famous treatise dealing with Jesus' approach to leadership selection and development. See also, **Articles**, *Jesus—Circles of Intimacy, A Developmental Technique; Jesus—Recruiting Techniques.*

[305] Whereas both selection and development are seen equally well in Jesus' ministry, development dominates Paul's ministry. See **Articles**, 43. *Paul—And His Companions; 47. Paul—Mentor for Many; 48. Paul—Modeling as An Influence Means.*

[306] To really appreciate leadership selection over a lifetime one needs to have a thorough grasp of leadership emergence theory.

Leadership Selection—The Basic Concept Defined

When God touches a life for leadership, there will be indications that can be recognized by observant Christian leaders. Mature leaders who know the importance of leadership selection and development are constantly on the lookout for just such recognition features. They want to partner with God in what He is doing to raise up emerging leadership. The process of God's selection, the recognition and affirmation by human leadership, and the subsequent development comprise what leadership selection is all about.

Definition	<u>Leadership selection</u> is the life-long process of divine initiative and human recognition whereby a leader[307] emerges.

Leadership selection describes a life-long recognition process which is punctuated with critical incidents, as viewed from a two-fold intermeshing perspective—the divine and the human. The process starts from earliest symptomatic indications of a leader emerging. It continues right on up to maturity. God will continue to select a leader throughout his/her lifetime. Mature selection involves God strategically guiding the leader on to a focused life. But note this is a threefold interactive process: (1) God is involved; (2) the leader is involved; and (3) other human leadership is involved. God gives confirmation to the selection of a leader via others leaders as well as directly to that leader.

The Ministry time-line is shown below in Figure 1 highlights the threefold interactive process. The Divine perspective involvement occurs above the time-line. The entries below the line portray some of the human interactions—both the individual leader's processing and what other human leaders see and confirm.

---

[307] The definition of leader used in this commentary pre-supposes the divine element of leadership selection. A leader is a person with God-given capacity and God-given responsibility who is influencing a specific group of God's people toward God's purposes.

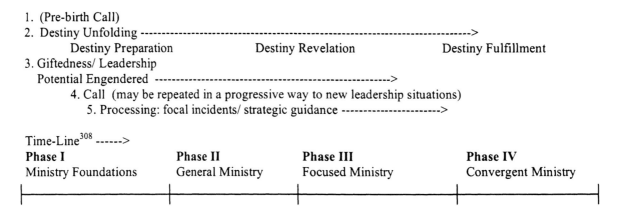

<u>Divine Initiative/ Perspective</u>

1. (Pre-birth Call)
2. Destiny Unfolding -->
           Destiny Preparation   Destiny Revelation   Destiny Fulfillment
3. Giftedness/ Leadership
     Potential Engendered -->
           4. Call (may be repeated in a progressive way to new leadership situations)
             5. Processing: focal incidents/ strategic guidance ---------------------->

Time-Line[308] ------>

| **Phase I** | **Phase II** | **Phase III** | **Phase IV** |
| Ministry Foundations | General Ministry | Focused Ministry | Convergent Ministry |

<u>Human Recognition Vantage Point</u>

1. Response to God
   2. Potential Seen
     3. Emerging Leader Symptoms, Word Gifts/ Obedience Attitude
       4. Challenge Toward Expectations
         5. Foundational Patterns
         6. Foundational Ministry Pattern
         7. Like--Attracts-Like Gift Pattern
         8. Ministry Entry Patterns
         9. Give Affirmation
             10. Transitional Training Patterns
             11. Mentoring
             12. Giftedness Development Pattern

Figure 1,2 Ti 31-1. The Leadership Selection Process Viewed Pictorially Over a Time-line

Illustrations from Jesus' and Paul's Ministry

Table 1,2 Ti 31-1 illustrates important leadership selection concepts in Jesus own life, Paul's own life and in their ministry.

Table 1,2 Ti 31-1. Leadership Selection Concepts Illustrated

Concept	Illustration
Divine 1. (Pre-birth Call)	See Gal 1:15—indication in Paul's life; See also Samuel; Samson; John the Baptist.
Divine 2. Destiny Unfolding	See **Article**, *8. Destiny Pattern*, for Paul's destiny unfolding.
Divine 3. Giftedness/ Leadership Potential Engendered	Php 3:4-6 Paul's advancement before conversion—indications of great potential. Apollos—Ac 18:24-26;

---

[308] See **Article**, *68. Time-Line, Defined for Biblical Leaders*. The time-line shown here is a generic time-line used to assess where a leader is in development over a life time. The four phases represent segments correlating to development in a life. Each phase to the right represents a more mature stage. General ministry is a time of learning for the leader. God is doing more in the leader's life than through him/her. Focused ministry is a time of efficient ministry. The leader knows his/her own giftedness and uses it well—a time of tactical ministry. Convergent ministry represents a time of strategic ministry. If Focused Ministry can be described as doing things right then Convergent Ministry means doing the right things right. It is a time of strategic accomplishment.

Divine 4. Call	Jesus ministry: See Jn 1 for call of John, Andrew, Simon Peter, James, Philip, Nathanael. For (repeated) call trace the phrase, *follow me*: see Mt 4:19; 8:22; 9:9; 16:24; 19:21; Mk 2:14; 8:34; 10:21; Lk 5:27; 9:23; 9:59; 18:22; Jn 1:43;12:26.
Divine 5. Processing: focal incidents/ strategic guidance	See Section, **Biblical Leaders Time-Lines** where critical incidents are shown along time-lines. See Paul's Time-Line; See Jesus' Time-Line. See *critical incident*, **Glossary**.
Human 1. Response to God	See Paul, Ac 9, 22, 26—conversion story; Ac 13 further ministry call; Ac 16 further call to Europe. All show Paul's response well.
Human 2. Potential Seen	See Timothy Ac 16:2.
Human 3. Emerging Leader Symptoms, Word Gifts/Obedience/Attitude	Obedience and Attitudes seen in lives of Paul's companions. But symptoms of Word Gifts not seen in a detailed way in Biblical examples. This selection observation arises from many contemporary case studies.
Human 4. Challenge Toward Expectations	See Paul's writings to Timothy for numerous illustrations of this. See especially the concept of Goodwin's Expectation principle, 2Ti 1:5;
Human 5. Foundational Patterns	See Timothy for Heritage pattern; see Titus for Radical Conversion;
Human 6. Foundational Ministry Pattern	See Lk 16:10 for Jesus teaching on this. Faithfulness in ministry leads to other ministry. Illustrated in ministry assignments given Timothy and Titus.
Human 7. Like--Attracts-Like Gift Pattern	Difficult to see in Biblical characters because of lack of details but seen repeatedly in contemporary case studies.
Human 8. Ministry Entry Patterns	The most important ministry entry pattern *self-initiated creation of new ministry structures* is seen repeatedly in Paul's life.
Human 9. Give Affirmation	This is demonstrated repeatedly in Paul's life and ministry.
Human 10. Transitional Training Patterns	The transitional training in-service pattern is seen repeatedly in both Jesus' and Paul's training of emerging leaders.
Human 11. Mentoring	Jesus mentors in a group context with occasional personal mentoring with Peter, James and John. Paul demonstrates mentoring at group level and many illustrations of individual mentoring. Both Jesus and Paul move along into partnering with God in developing leaders via deliberate proactive intervention in lives via mentoring.
Human 12. Giftedness Development Pattern	Not seen in Biblical examples because of lack of details. But seen in numerous contemporary case studies.

Observations on Leadership Selection

Observations flowing from this leadership selection model include:

1. The on-going operation of a movement, organization, or church require leadership selection and development. To ignore selection is to cut off the next generation of leaders. To ignore development is to provide a big back door whereby your recruited leaders leave and are developed by others.

2. To partner with God in leadership selection and development effectively, a leader needs to be very familiar with developmental theory—that is, how a leader develops over a lifetime.[309] Or to say it another way, the more familiar you are with how God develops a leader the more you will be sensitive to when you can intervene in a godly way to help develop that leader.

3. Rarely will all 17 selection elements be seen in a given individual. Some are missing altogether. Others are more prominent. The list was synthesized from comparative study of many leaders.

4. The prime responsibility for leadership selection and development is God's. But an important secondary responsibility involves God's use of other human leaders to select and develop leaders. Without human affirmation of God's call in a life, a potential leader is subject to only internal subjective discernment of God's working. Self-deception can run rampant. External human recognition and affirmation is desperately needed to protect both an individual leader and those he/she will influence.

5. Progressive calls over a lifetime (see Jesus ministry with his own and God's dealing with Paul) highlight the concept of selection taking place over a lifetime.

Conclusion

No strategic thinking leader will overlook this important leadership value,

> **Effective Leaders View Leadership Selection and Development as a priority function.**

No effective leader can carry out all the functions that need to be done to select and develop. But every leader can look for and join with other leaders who can help carry out this important function. Needed are recruiter specialists, early developer specialists, strategic developers. Recruiters hook potential leaders. Early developer specialists develop efficiency in a maturing leader. Strategic developers develop effectiveness in mature leaders.

See *progressive calling*, **Glossary**. See **Articles**, 9. *Developing Giftedness; 8. Destiny Pattern; Divine Affirmation in the Life of Jesus; 10. Entrustment—A Leadership Responsibility; 18. Focused Life; 19. Foundational Patterns; God's Shaping Processes With Leaders; 21. Impartation of Gifts; 23. Integrity—A Top Leadership Quality; 24. Isolation Processing—Learning Deep Lessons from God; Jesus—Circles of Intimacy—A Developmental Technique; 29. Leadership Lessons—Seven Identified; Leadership Continuum—Five Types of Leaders; 39. Ministry Entry Patterns; 42. Paul—Sense of Destiny; 43. Paul—And His Companions; 44. Paul—Deep Processing; 45. Paul—Developer; 47. Paul—Mentor; 60. Spiritual Benchmarks;63. Spiritual Gifts, Giftedness and Development; Training Models—When They Fit.*

---

[309] My leadership emergence theory has developed over the past 25 years. It views how God develops a leader over a lifetime. All of the concepts alluded to in the leadership selection model of this article are defined or described in leadership emergence theory. See **For Further Study, Bibliography**, the manual, **Leadership Emergence Theory.**

Relevance of the Article to 1,2 Timothy

Leadership transitions in the Scripture have only a few shining examples. Most are poorly done. Seven come to mind as having some good information. You may wish to study them— Moses to Joshua, Samuel to Saul (though Saul later fails), Elijah to Elisha, Jesus to the Disciples, Barnabas to Paul, Paul to the Ephesian elders, and finally, Paul to Titus and Timothy. Paul's missionary band gave him ample opportunity to transition various pieces of his ministry to those he was training. His use of ministry tasks provided a means to gradually transition those on his traveling team into competent roles and ministry. His authoritative backing given to Titus in his ministry at Crete and Timothy in his ministry at Ephesus are his final swansongs and show a mature transition of Titus and Timothy into Apostolic ministry on their own merits. Paul did a fine job of sponsoring them so that their future ministry would be powerful. Notice the sub-title to this 1,2 Timothy commentary— Apostolic Leadership Picking Up the Mantle. Paul dropped the mantle squarely on Timothy's shoulders. 2 Ti 4 highlights the leadership transition from Paul to Timothy.

32. Leadership Transitions

Background/ Definitions

An important macro lesson discovered in the Pre-Kingdom Leadership Era is stated as:

15. [310]Transition   **Leaders must transition other leaders into their work in order to maintain continuity and effectiveness.**

This lesson was discovered during Moses' leadership. His transition of Joshua into leadership over a long period of time stands out as the classical model for transitioning a leader into an important leadership role.

Transition times in movements, organizations and churches are hard, complex times. How leaders transition new leaders into leadership can make or break the on-going ministry. It is a special time of problems and opportunities. The process is best understood when viewed along a continuum.

Definition   Leadership transition is the process whereby existing leaders prepare and release emerging leaders into the responsibility and practice of leadership positions, functions, roles, and tasks.

Leadership Transition Continuum

←REPLACEMENT OF LEADERSHIP (What the leader does; Tasks, Roles, Functions)				REPLACEMENT OF LEADER→ (The person himself/herself)	
simple task	more or complicated task(s)	role with many tasks	pick up some functions	major responsibility for functions	the leader's role

Practicing Leader increasingly RELEASES-->
Emerging Leader increasingly accepts RESPONSIBILITY----------------------->

Figure 1,2 Ti 32-1 Leadership Transition Continuum

---

[310] This is number 15 of 41 macro lessons listed over the six leadership eras. See **Article**, *37*. Macro Lessons, List of 41.

Continuum Definitions

Definition	A <u>task</u> is an observable assignment of usually short duration.
Definition	A <u>role</u> is a recognizable position which does a major portion of the ministry. It probably has several ongoing tasks associated with it.
Definition	<u>Leadership functions</u> is a technical term which refers to the three major categories of formal leadership responsibility: task behavior (defining structure and goals), relationship behavior (providing the emotional support and ambiance), and inspirational behavior (providing motivational effort).
Comment	Each of these major leadership functions has several specific sub-functions.
Definition	<u>Leadership release</u> is the process whereby an existing leader deliberately encourages and allows an emerging leader to accept responsibility for and control of leadership positions, functions, roles, and tasks.
Definition	<u>Overlap</u> is that unique time in a leadership transition when the emerging leader and existing leader share responsibility and accountability for tasks, roles, and functions.
Definition	<u>Tandem training</u> describes the training technique during overlap used by an existing leader with an emerging leader.

Let me comment on the two extremes on the continuum. On the right of the continuum is the maximum limit of leadership transition, that is, the leader himself/ herself is replaced totally from the leadership situation. The emerging leader thus becomes the new leader and is totally responsible for the leadership situation. On the left is the minimum, the present leader turns over some small piece of leadership, e.g. a simple task. In between the two extremes, various levels of transition are experienced

The process across the continuum is simply described. As one moves across the continuum faithful performance of simple tasks leads to increasing responsibility such as a role. Faithful or successful accomplishment of a role will lead to greater responsibility—usually wider roles and responsibility for important functions of the ministry as a whole.

Two tendencies have been observed as the transition process goes on. As you move from left to right on the continuum, the present leader is increasingly releasing more tasks, functions and finally major responsibility for the ministry. This is signified by the arrow moving toward the right. The function of release is a difficult one for most leaders. The tendency is to either *over-control* on the one hand (*authoritarian defensive posture*), or to *give too much responsibility without adequate supervision* or transitional training on the other (*the quick release posture*). The first tendency suffocates emerging leaders and frustrates them in their attempt to grow and assume leadership. Such a posture usually drives them out of the organization to another ministry where they can be released. The second tendency overwhelms them and usually insures failure in their first attempt at leadership. This can be discouraging and cause some to decide not to move into leadership in ministry.

The rate at which the release should occur ought to depend on the ability of the emerging leader to pick up responsibility for it and not an authoritarian posture or a quick release posture. The arrow moving to the right demonstrates that the emerging leader should be picking up responsibility for the tasks, roles, or functions. As this is done, the leader should be releasing.

Overlap is the time in which both the leader and emerging leader are working together in an increasing way to release and accept responsibility. Overlap can occur anywhere along the continuum.

Tandem training allows the younger leader to share the learning experiences of the older leader via modeling, mentoring, apprenticeship, or internships so as to leapfrog the younger leader's development.

Leadership Transitions in the Bible

There are numerous instances in Scripture of leadership transitions. Most are not ideal as suggested by the transitional continuum. The Moses/Joshua transition which took place over an extended time does follow the description given above of the transitional continuum. It is one of the positive models of leadership transition in the Scriptures. Another positive model occurs in the New Testament —that of Barnabas and Saul. Other leadership situations in Scripture are worthy of study, mostly for the negative lessons and identification of the items on the transitional continuum that are missing. Table 1 lists some of the instances of Scripture that provide data for observing the positive and negative effects of leadership transitions -- be they good or bad.

Table 1,2 Ti 32-1. Examples of Leadership Transitions in Scripture Providing Insights

Joseph (sovereign transition)

Moses (sovereign transition)

Moses/Joshua (tandem transition)

Joshua/? (none)

Jephthah (other judges—negative)

Eli/sons (negative)

Samuel (sovereign transition)

Samuel/Saul (modified negative)

Saul/David (negative)

David/Absalom (aborted)

David/Solomon (negative)

Elijah/Elisha (minimum)

Daniel (sovereign)

Jesus/disciples

Apostles/deacons (Acts 6)

Barnabas/ Paul (leader switch)

Acts 20 Paul/Ephesian elders

Paul/ Timothy (2Ti)

Probably the best leadership transition to observe in which the continuum concepts are more readily seen involves Moses' transition of Joshua into leadership.

10 Steps In Moses/Joshua Transition

In the Moses/Joshua transition several steps, stages, or discernible events can be ordered. These give insights into why the transition was successful and led to a great leader being raised up to follow a great leader. Table 1,2 Ti 32-2 lists observations which suggest why the transition was successful.

Table 1,2 Ti 32-2. Observations on the Moses/ Joshua Leadership Transition

Step	Label	Description
1	Definite Leadership Selection	There was deliberate and definite leadership selection. Moses chose Joshua. Joshua came from a leading family with leadership heritage (note the march order in Exodus -- his grandfather prominent). Notice Moses Nepotism, see comment which follows these steps.
2	Ministry Task	Moses gave him ministry tasks with significant responsibility: a. First, select recruits and lead battle among the Amalekites who were harassing the flanks of the exodus march. b. Second, spy out the land (probably one of the younger ones to be chosen). Moses checked Joshua's: (1) faith, (2) faithfulness, (3) giftedness (charismatic ability to lead) with these increasing responsibilities.
3	Spirituality/ Tandem Training	Moses included Joshua in his own spiritual experiences with God. Joshua had firsthand access to Moses' vital experiences with God. Moses took him into the holy of holies, frequently into the tabernacle into the presence of God and up on the mountain when he was in solitude alone with God. This was tandem training in spirituality using mentoring as the means of training.

4	Leadership span	Moses recognized the complexity of the leadership situation toward the end of his life. He knew Joshua could not do it all. When transitioning him into leadership he saw that Joshua was a charismatic militaristic leader who needed a supportive spiritual leader. He set Eleazar up as the spiritual leader. He publicly did this—bolstered Eleazar in the eyes of the people, recognized Joshua's strengths and weaknesses. Moses knew that any leader coming into his position would have trouble—most likely could not fill his shoes; he would need help. Actually Joshua developed real spiritual authority and became a spiritual leader in terms of inspirational leadership.
5	Public Recognition .	Moses recognized the importance of followers knowing whom he had appointed to be the next leader. No ambiguity. No scramble of leaders for that position after Moses' death. He settled it ahead of time and gave a public ceremony stipulating his backing of Joshua.
6	New Challenge	The new leader following an old leader must not look back and compare. One way of overcoming this tendency is to have a big challenge, a new task not done by the old leader. There was a big task to do. It would be his own contribution—possess the land.
7	Divine Affirmation	The new leader needed to know not only that Moses had appointed him as leader but that God had confirmed this appointment. Dt 31:14-18 and Joshua 1 point out Joshua's experiences personally with God concerning the appointment.
8	Public Ceremony	Not only must there be personal assurance that God has appointmed him/herbut there must be public recognition of this. God gives this in Joshua 3 (note Joshua 3:7: "What I do today will make all the people of Israel begin to honor you as a great man, and they will realize that I am with you as I was with Moses." See also Joshua 4:14: "What the Lord did that day made the people of Israel consider Joshua a great man. They honored him all his life, just as they had honored Moses.")
9	Initial Success	A leader moving into full responsibility needs an initial success that can bolster spiritual authority and demonstrate that the leader can get vision from God in his/her own right. Joshua's experience with the Captain of the Lord's Army was a pivotal point that did this. It gave him vision -- tactical plan with strategic implications. Its success came early on and stimulated followers. With it there was assurance that brought closure to the whole transition experience.
10	Initial Failure	A final thing that ensured a successful transition was the early failure at Ai. Leaders must know they are not infallible. They must trust God in their leadership. An early failure after initial success was a major deterrent to pride, showed the moral implications of godly leadership, and the notion that leaders must always move followers along toward God's purposes for them in God's way.

Commentary On Moses/Joshua Transition

Is this model transferable? Peculiar dynamics occur in this model. Its uniqueness may preclude its application in other situations. There was a long period of overlap due to the disciplining of the people in the wilderness. Joshua essentially led the next generation—not his own. A mighty expectation existed for the new task that challenged everyone. Joshua was a home-grown leader from a leadership heritage who had proved himself in many ways. He was a charismatic/military leader with a good spiritual track record of sensing and obeying God. Certain of the underlying ideas of these observations will probably be applicable even if the overall dynamics are not identical.

Notice that Moses avoids the problem of nepotism.[311] Joshua was hand-picked early for leadership. Yet when the final transition time arrived, Moses did not just assume that Joshua was the Lord's choice but

---

[311] It is not clear but it appears from hints given that Moses really had family problems and probably was separated from his family for extended times during his desert leadership. His sons are never prominently

sought the Lord's confirmation. And when it came *he did all he could to give Joshua the best chance of success*. This leadership transition is the most successful in Scripture. Moses was well aware that if his ministry was to be established beyond his lifetime as he wished (Psalm 90:17), providing leadership for it was necessary. He certainly exemplifies the *continuity* or *transition* macro-lesson.

Transition   **Leaders must transition other leaders into their work in order to maintain continuity and effectiveness.**

Four implications about leadership transition should be noted.

1. *Continuity.* No ministry can be expected to continue well without deliberate transition efforts.
2. *Nepotism.* Rarely can a leader replace his/her father/ mother with the same leadership effectiveness. The appropriate leader, gifted for the job, is the proper selection.
3. *Best Start.* Whenever leaving a ministry, insure that the next leader has the best possible chance of success.
4. *Models.* Study negative and positive Biblical models for guidelines. The positive models include Moses/ Joshua, Elijah/ Elisha, Jesus/ Disciples, Barnabas/ Paul, Paul/Timothy. A particularly negative one to see is Solomon/ Rehoboam.

See *leadership transition, leadership functions, leadership release, overlap, tandem training*, **Glossary**.
See **Article**, *Regime Turnover*.

---

mentioned anywhere. His wife and children visit him when Jethro comes. So perhaps he was never tempted to try to place them in leadership as many charismatic leaders do today.

Relevance of the Article to 1,2 Timothy

Any ministry is just one generation away from obsolescence if something is not done to maintain continuity. Paul, probably more than any other leader, except Jesus, knew this and sought to exemplify the leadership macro lesson, **15. Leaders must transition other leaders into their work in order to maintain continuity and effectiveness.** 1,2 Ti and Tit are Paul's final attempt to maintain continuity by transitioning in his two most trusted and trained followers, Timothy and Titus. Increasing ministry tasks across the *Leadership Transition Continuum* are shown to be the major means whereby Paul transitioned Titus and Timothy into Apostolic Roles, replacing his own ministry. We, as present day leaders do well, to learn about ministry tasks and use them well as we replace ourselves and give credibility to leaders who will continue ministry with many of our same leadership values.

33. Leadership Transitions—Timothy and Titus

Introduction

On the whole, leadership transitions in the Bible have not been done very well. An important macro lesson discovered in the Pre-Kingdom Leadership Era is stated as:

15. Transition[312]   **Leaders must transition other leaders into their work in order to maintain continuity and effectiveness.**

This lesson was discovered during Moses' leadership.[313] His transition of Joshua into leadership over a long period of time stands out as the classical model for transitioning a leader into an important leadership role. Imagine trying to step into Moses' shoes, arguably the greatest Old Testament leader. That was a tough job, yet, Joshua did it and made his own unique contribution to the redemptive drama. Well imagine again, stepping into Paul's shoes.[314] Again, who could do this. Well, I am going to suggest that two men did, Timothy and Titus. And again, like Moses' work, the transition process was extended over a long time and involved lots of hands-on co-ministry with Paul.

Transition times in movements, organizations and churches are hard, complex times. Such was the case with Moses and Joshua. And such was the case with Paul and his two close mentorees, Timothy and Titus.

How leaders transition new leaders into leadership can make or break the on-going ministry. It is a special time of problems and opportunities. The process is best understood when viewed along a continuum.

Definition   <u>Leadership transition</u> is the process whereby existing leaders prepare and release emerging leaders into the responsibility and practice of leadership positions, functions, roles, and tasks.

This article will offer some observations of Paul's transition of two leaders, Timothy and Titus, into ministry. The leadership transition continuum will be used to assess Timothy's and Titus' transitions.

---

[312] This is number 15 of 41 macro lessons listed over the six leadership eras. See **Article**, *37. Macro Lessons, List of 41...*

[313] See **Article**, *32. Leadership Transitions*, for a detailed explanation of the Moses/Joshua transition model.

[314] Arguably this is an even tougher task since the Church Leadership Era is so complex with dispersed leadership all over the globe and no one structure permeating all followers.

Leadership Transition Continuum

←REPLACEMENT OF LEADERSHIP	REPLACEMENT OF LEADER→
(What the leader does; Tasks, Roles, Functions)	(The person himself/herself)

simple task	more or complicated task(s)	role with many tasks	pick up some functions	major responsibility for functions	the leader's role

Practicing Leader increasingly RELEASES--->
Emerging Leader increasingly accepts RESPONSIBILITY----------------------->

Figure 1,2 Ti 33-1. The Leadership Transition Continuum

In order to understand the continuum, several concepts must be defined.

Definition   A task is an observable assignment of usually short duration.

Definition   A role is a recognizable position which does a major portion of the ministry. It probably has several ongoing tasks associated with it.

Definition   Leadership functions is a technical term which refers to the three major categories of formal leadership responsibility: task behavior (defining structure and goals), relationship behavior (providing the emotional support and ambiance), and inspirational behavior (providing motivational effort).

Comment   Each of these major leadership functions has several specific sub-functions.

Definition   Leadership release is the process whereby an existing leader deliberately encourages and allows an emerging leader to accept responsibility for and control of leadership positions, functions, roles, and tasks.

Definition   Overlap is that unique time in a leadership transition when the emerging leader and existing leader share responsibility and accountability for tasks, roles, and functions.

Definition   Tandem training describes the training technique during overlap used by an existing leader with an emerging leader.

Let me comment on the two extremes on the continuum. On the right of the continuum is the maximum limit of leadership transition, that is, the leader himself/ herself is replaced totally from the leadership situation. The emerging leader thus becomes the new leader and is totally responsible for the leadership situation. On the left is the minimum, the present leader turns over some small piece of leadership, e.g. a simple task. In between the two extremes, various levels of transition are experienced.

As one moves across the continuum, faithful performance of simple tasks leads to increasing responsibility, such as a role. Faithful or successful accomplishment of a role will lead to greater responsibility— usually wider roles and responsibility for important functions of the ministry as a whole.

Two tendencies have been observed as the transition process goes on. As you move from left to right on the continuum, the present leader is increasingly releasing more tasks, functions and finally major responsibility for the ministry. This is signified by the arrow moving toward the right. The function of release is a difficult one for most leaders. The tendency is to either *over-control* on the one hand *(authoritarian defensive posture)*, or to *give too much responsibility without adequate supervision* or transitional training on the other *(the quick release posture)*. The first tendency suffocates emerging leaders and frustrates them in their attempt to grow and assume leadership. Such a posture usually drives them out of the organization to another ministry where they can be released. The second tendency overwhelms them and usually insures failure in their first attempt at leadership. This can be discouraging and cause some to decide not to move into leadership in ministry.

The rate at which the release should occur ought to depend on the ability of the emerging leader to pick up responsibility for it and not an authoritarian posture or a quick release posture. The arrow moving to the right demonstrates that the emerging leader should be picking up responsibility for the tasks, roles, or functions. As this is done, the leader should be releasing.

Overlap is the time in which both the leader and emerging leader are working together in an increasing way to release and accept responsibility. Overlap can occur anywhere along the continuum. Tandem training allows the younger leader to share the learning experiences of the older leader via modeling, mentoring, apprenticeship, or internships so as to leapfrog the younger leader's development.

Paul's Leadership Transitions Efforts with Timothy and Titus

Figure 1,2 Ti 33-2 shows the leadership transition continuum. On it I have placed Timothy and Titus beside each item on which I have indications or implications that Paul worked on transition items with them.

Leadership Transition Continuum

←REPLACEMENT OF LEADERSHIP (What the leader does; Tasks, Roles, Functions)				REPLACEMENT OF LEADER→ (The person himself/herself)	
simple task	more or complicated task(s)	role with many tasks	pick up some functions	major responsibility for functions	the leader's role
Titus (1)	Titus (2)	Titus (3)	Titus (4)	Titus (5)	Titus(6?)
Timothy (1)	Timothy (2)	Timothy (3a)	Timothy (3b)	Timothy (4a)	Timothy (4b)

Practicing Leader increasingly RELEASES--->
Emerging Leader increasingly accepts RESPONSIBILITY----------------------->

Legend (continued on next page)
Titus (1) Titus goes with Paul to Galatia. This was a critical contextualization issue (see Galatians 2:1,3). Later Titus would have to do contextualization work with the believers on Crete.
Titus (2) Ministry Task 1.[315] Titus initiates giving for Jerusalem project in Corinthian church. .
Titus (3) Ministry Task 2. Titus was sent to Corinth to ascertain accountability; He was to take disciplinary measures depending on how they were responding. This was part of Paul's dealing with the crises in his ministry stemming from the attempts within the Corinthian church to reject his apostolic leadership.
Titus (4) Ministry Task 3. Titus is resent to Corinth to 1. complete the Jerusalem project, 2. test loyalty to Pauline authori *y*, and 3. follow-up on discipline. The results of this are not known. However, the inclusion of 2 Corinthians in the canon is probably indicative of a successful completion of this task.
Titus (5) Ministry Task 5. Titus is sent to Crete. Titus transitions into apostolic Leadership with his major ministry task at Crete. It involved: 1. the appointment of leaders, 2. the grounding in teaching of the

---

[315] A ministry task is an assignment from God which primarily tests a person's faithfulness and obedience but often also allows use of ministry gifts in the context of a task which has closure, accountability, and evaluation. It is one of 51 shaping activities, called process items, describing how God develops a leader. Titus had 5 of these that we can identify. See **Article**, *Titus and Ministry Tasks*.

believers in this regional church, 3. the modeling of a Christian lifestyle and the 4. establishing of mission giving. Here the thrust is on appointing leadership which will model a Christian lifestyle in the Cretan context. The exact outcome is not known but tradition indicates it was successful. See Titus 3:15 footnote in which Titus is implied as having an important role in Crete. It is clear from the letter that Titus is released to operate in full apostolic ministry in Crete.

Timothy (1) Philippian Ministry Task

Timothy (2) Stayed behind in Berea with Silas (stabilizing believers probably); Goes with Erastus on an Errand into Macedonia for Paul (not clear exactly what they did); Goes to Troas (with team) probably to set up things for Paul's coming there. Sent to Thessalonica with multiple tasks involving building up the group.

Timothy (3a) Lots of overlap time with Paul in Corinth (would receive most of Paul's Teaching); Paul mentions Timothy in Ro 16 showing he was fully versed with a theology of redemption, etc.

Timothy (3b) Sent to Corinth. Co-ministry with Paul in writing Corinthian letters. Sent to clarify Paul's teaching. Co-writes letter to Colossians.

Timothy (4a) Ephesus Timothy sent to Ephesus. Full orbed ministry there, apostolic. Appoints leaders, etc.

Timothy (4b) Ephesus In 2nd Timothy, it is clear Paul is handing the baton over to Timothy. Did Timothy pick it up--see Heb 13:23

Figure 1,2 Ti 33-2. Timothy and Titus--Transition Functions Done

Some Comparisons--Moses and Paul, Leadership Transition

Both Moses and Paul were at least relatively successful in transitioning in leaders to carry on their ministries. Remember the basic goal in leadership transition is have leaders who will carry on ministry so as to maintain *continuity* and *effectiveness*. Remember the transition macro lesson.

Transition   **Leaders must transition other leaders into their work in order to maintain continuity and effectiveness.**

Moses and Paul did this. What were the common things they did?

1. They spent lots of personal time with their mentorees.
2. They co-ministered so that others saw they were associated in leadership.
3. They sponsored their mentorees so that it was known that they backed them and that these mentorees represented them.
4. They publicly named these mentorees as successors.

What were the differences in their transition processes?

Moses ministered to the same followers over a long period of time, facing the same obstacles in the same geographical locale. Continuity was easier since all the followers knew Joshua and observed the many tasks and responsibilities he did over the years. Joshua, the leader being transitioned in, was of the same language and culture as the followers. It was clear that Joshua and Moses basically had the same values about leadership. And Moses was able to have an official public ceremony inaugurating Joshua's forthcoming leadership with the important followers present. Continuity was assured since it was clear that there was a top position, a role, and Joshua was to fill it.[316]

Paul, on the other hand, had an itinerant non-on-going leadership/ relationship with lots of different groups of followers in different cultures and geographical locales. In addition, he did not have a formal position as a leader over any of these groups. His leadership was basically determined by spiritual authority

---

[316] Moses' situation is closer to an organizational situation than was Paul's. In today's ministries, organization transition has its dangers. See **Article**, *Regime Turnover*.

alone. So to transition new leaders in, he had to make sure these new leaders had spiritual authority with the followers. Paul did this in four major ways:

1. He *embedded his leadership values* in these mentorees so that he could rest assured that what ever ministry they faced in the future, they would carry on ministry similar to the way he did it. He used mentoring, particularly that of discipler, spiritual guide, coach, teacher and contemporary model to insure the embedding of values. He had strong personal relationships with his mentorees. He was transparent with them. He was vulnerable with them. He made sure they knew how he thought and lived. While we don't have as much evidence of this with Titus as with Timothy we can assume it, knowing that Titus was traveling a lot with Paul.

Notice this excerpt in his final letter to Timothy which shows this personal relationship and its impact for embedding values.

> 2 Timothy 3
> 10 But you fully know my teaching, my lifestyle, my purpose in life, my faith, my steadfastness, my love, my endurance.[317] 11 I was persecuted at Antioch, at Iconium, at Lystra; I endured those persecutions. Yet the Lord delivered me out of them. 12 And indeed all who will live godly lives—in union with Christ Jesus— will suffer persecution. 13 But evil people and impostors will go from bad to worse. They will deceive others, and they will be deceived themselves.[318] 14 But, as for you, stay with that which you have experientially learned. You are confident of it because you know who you have learned it from.[319] 15 From early childhood[320] you have known the holy scriptures.[321] They have given you the wisdom to accept salvation through faith which is in Christ Jesus. 16 Every scripture inspired by God is profitable for teaching, for reprimand, for correction, for leading one to righteous living.[322] 17 That a person of God may be equipped, completely ready[323] to do well.[324]

---

[317] This, vs 3:10-17, is one of the great passages on a mentoring relationship. Here you have the mentor, Paul, describing a very personal, open, transparent, vulnerability in his mentoring with Timothy. The mentoring types of teacher, counselor, and contemporary model are reflected in this intense passage, appealing to Timothy. See *mentor, mentor teacher, mentor counselor, mentor model,* **Glossary**. See **Articles**, 38. *Mentoring—An Informal Training Model; 45. Paul the Developer.*

[318] Any leader can be blindsided by self-deception. One of Paul's antidotes is to recognize good models who have experientially confirmed truth for you (verse 14). When you differ from them you are in danger of self-deception. See *modeling, contemporary models,* **Glossary**.

[319] Trustworthy models are needed early on in the life of a developing leader. This is particularly true when transitioning into ministry and/or when facing a new situation. But it is also true that leaders will need various kinds of mentoring all of their lives. comparative case studies have shown that effective leaders will have from 10-25 important mentoring experiences throughout their lifetime. See *mentor,* **Glossary**.

[320] The foundational heritage pattern is referred to here, highlighting one of its advantages (vs 15). Also one who is familiar with the Scriptures, even just the facts of them, has a jump start on learning the Scriptures for use in ministry once the call of God on a life is received. See *heritage pattern,* **Glossary**.

[321] Paul is here referring to the O.T. Scriptures which can be expanded today to include the N.T. Scriptures as well. See *Bible centered leader,* **Glossary**. See **Article**, 72. *Vanishing Breed.*

[322] This verse has as its intent, not the doctrine of the inspiration of Scripture, but that every inspired (God breathed) Scripture has usefulness for equipping Timothy for his leadership (and by extension other leaders). See *Bible ce .tered leader,* **Glossary**. See **Article**, 72. *Vanishing Breed.*

[323] This is an instance of the superlative (i.e. repetitive idiom) being used. *Completely ready* (SRN 1822) is a combination of two words, one an intensifying preposition and a root word which is a derivative of *equipped,* (SRN 739). So what we have here is equipped, thoroughly equipped, that is, really really equipped. I captured it using *equipped, really ready.* My concepts 1 and 2 of the Bible centered leader flow from this verse: (1) whose leadership is being informed by the Bible and (2) who personally has been shaped by Biblical values. See *superlative idiom, capture, Bible centered leader,* **Glossary**,

[324] Seeing that this admonition is given to a leader in a leadership situation, I don't think I am far wrong to paraphrase this passage as follows. *Every Scripture inspired of God is profitable for (1) leadership insights*

Did Paul embed his important values? One incidental comment in the Philippian letter indicates that Paul was very confident that his values had taken with Timothy.

> Philippians 2
> 19 But I trust the Lord Jesus will let me send Timothy shortly,[325] that I also may be encouraged when I know what is happening to you. 20 For I have no one like-minded,[326] who will naturally care for what is happening to you. 21 For all seek their own, not the things which are Jesus Christ's. 22 But you know his proven character,[327] that, as a son with the father,[328] he has served with me in the gospel. 23 So I hope to send him shortly, as soon as I shall see how it will go with me.

Those words *like-minded and who will naturally care for what is happening to you*, say it all. Paul knew Timothy had those basic leadership values that he himself had.

2.   He co-ministered with his mentorees in a *team setting* as well as *individually* over long periods of time. He made sure others knew of this co-ministering.

3.   Paul was very *deliberate in his training efforts*. His word to Timothy (2 Ti 2:2) was indicative of a value he himself possessed. His mentor teaching, contemporary modeling and in particular, use of ministry tasks were three powerful ways that he trained his team members

4.   *Functional Equivalent of Moses' public ceremony.* Moses was able to have an official public ceremony in which Joshua was ordained to lead in Moses stead. Paul did not have that luxury. But he did the functional equivalent. The second letter to Timothy and the letter to Titus on Crete were the functional equivalents of Moses' public ceremony with Joshua. They were written proof to these dispersed followers that Paul was tapping Timothy for leadership in Ephesus and Titus in Crete.

If you want your ministry to live on beyond you, then embed your values in leaders who can carry them on. Co-minister with them so that others perceive your high view of them. Train them, with much on-the-job practice. Mentor them. Find ways to let it be known that they represent you.

(doctrine), *(2) pointing out of leadership errors* (reproof), *(3) suggesting what to do about leadership errors* (correction), *(4) for highlighting how to model a righteous life* (instruction in righteousness) *in order that God's leader* (Timothy) *may be well equipped to lead God's people* (the special good work given to the young leader Timothy). (Clinton paraphrase—slanted toward Timothy's leadership situation).

[325] Timothy and Titus and others were often sent on ministry trips. These trips served a twofold function— training of those sent and accomplishment of the given mission. See *ministry task*, **Glossary**. See **Articles**, 43. *Paul—and His Companions; 69. Timothy—A Beloved Son in the Faith.*

[326] This word, *like-minded* (SRN 2473) is a strong relational word. Paul's leadership value of personal relationships in ministry reach their high point in his relationship with Timothy. See also verse 22, the phrase, *as a son with the father*. Paul felt ministry ought to be very personal. Stated more generally for all leaders, *Leaders should view personal relationships as an important part of ministry, both as a means for ministry and as an end in itself of ministry.* Leaders best pass on values when they have a strong relationship like this one. See 2Ti 3:10-17, fn 3:10. See *leadership value*, **Glossary**. See **Article**, 69. *Timothy—A Beloved Son in the Faith.*

[327] This Greek word for proven *character* (SRN 1382) highlights the foundation of a leader. Integrity and proven character are the essential traits of a leader. See fn 1Ti 3:2. See *integrity*, **Glossary**. See **Article**, 23. *Integrity—A Top Leadership Quality.*

[328] Here we see again Paul's strong leadership value of personal relationships as part of the ministry. Of all the people he lists in his letters, nearly 80, only three does he call sons in the faith—Timothy, Titus, Onesimus. Timothy was closest. See **Article**, 69. *Timothy, A Beloved Son in the Faith.*

Conclusion

Glance again at the transition macro lesson.

15. Transition   **Leaders must transition other leaders into their work in order to maintain continuity and effectiveness.**

Any ministry is just one generation away from obsolescence if something is not done to maintain continuity. No ministry can be expected to continue well without deliberate transition efforts. Work on leadership transition and practice it at every level of ministry you are involved it. See it as a process that you are working at all the time. And when you are bringing closure to a given leadership transition effort, insure that the next leader has the best possible chance for success. Do what you can to sponsor that transitioning leader into your vacated role.

We need some good contemporary leadership transitions. Let yours be one of these needed case studies.

Relevance of the Article to 1,2 Timothy

The following taxonomy was derived from a tracing of leadership in a western context. However, it became clear that the taxonomy applied to every Biblical leadership era—the four in the O.T. and the two in the N.T. And it became clearer in the School of Intercultural Studies of Fuller Theological Seminary that this taxonomy applied across cultures. It is a handy taxonomy for studying leadership issues anywhere. You can study Paul's *Ephesus Intervention,* as revealed in 1,2 Ti, using this taxonomy. See the Preface section, p XVff where this tree diagram framework is applied to the 1,2 Ti Commentary.

34. Leadership Tree Diagram

Introduction

The leadership tree diagram was developed from a survey of leadership history from the mid 1800s to the present. From the five leadership eras,[329] basic concepts of this tree diagram were integrated into an overall framework for evaluating leadership in any culture, including the various cultures in the Bible. Figure 1 below gives the tree diagram. Table 1 shows when each component was identified in terms of leadership history. Then Table 2 gives a brief description of each of the components of this tree diagram. This diagram proved especially helpful when analyzing the six Biblical leadership eras.[330] It continues to prove fruitful when analyzing leadership acts and other leadership genre in the Bible.

The Three Categories Of A High Level Leadership Framework

Three categories are involved in a high level leadership framework. The first, The *Leadership Basal Elements*, deals primarily with the *What of Leadership.* The second, The *Leadership Influence Means* categorizes the *How of Leadership.* The final element, *Leadership Value Bases*, pinpoints the *Why of Leadership.* These three cross-cultural leadership components can be used to comparatively describe leadership anywhere in the world.

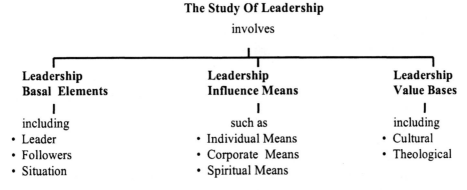

The Study Of Leadership

involves

Leadership Basal Elements	Leadership Influence Means	Leadership Value Bases
including	such as	including
• Leader	• Individual Means	• Cultural
• Followers	• Corporate Means	• Theological
• Situation	• Spiritual Means	

Figure 1,2 Ti 34-1. Graphic Display of Three High Level Generic Leadership Components

---

[329] Five periods are identified: Phase I. Great Man Era—1841–1904; Phase II. Trait Era—1904–1948;; Phase IV. Contingency Era—1967–1980; Phase V. Complexity Era—1980–present. Each of these eras contributed to the basic elements seen in the tree diagram framework.

[330] The six Biblical leadership eras include: I. The Patriarchal Era; II. The Pre-Kingdom Era; III. The Kingdom Era; IV. The Post-Kingdom Era; V. The Pre-Church Era; VI. The Church Era.

Table 1,2 Ti 34-1. When Each Component Was In Focus in Leadership Eras

Era	Element in Focus	Explanation
Phase I. Great Man Era—1841–1904	Leaders	Great Man Theory dominated. Great leaders were studied to see what could be learned about leadership. Was leadership innately a genetic thing (leaders are born)? Do they make things happen? Or do the opportunities allow one to rise to the occasion (leaders are made)?
Phase II. Trait Era—1904–1948	Leaders/ Followers	Trait Theory Dominated. Could traits of great leaders be identified at the beginning stages of development of potential leaders.
Phase III. Behavior Era—1948–1967	Individual Influence Means/	Trait theory having been debunked, theorist went on to study what leaders did and how they influenced followers. Leadership style theory emerged.
Phase IV. Contingency Era—1967–1980	Corporate means	Organizational systems begin to be studied and their impact on influence. Cross-cultural studies recognized that in other cultures corporate groups influence as much or more than individuals.
Phase V. Complexity Era—1980–present	Spiritual influence means/ cultural values/ theological values/	No one leadership theory dominates because leadership is now recognized as a very complex thing. There are numerous complex theories being studied. Motivational theory emerged. How do people influence? Christian studies looked at spiritual authority. What are the underlying theological frameworks, or cultural frameworks influence why leaders lead like they lead? Value theory began to emerge. What are the underlying concepts of one's leadership?

Table 1,2 Ti 34-2. Elements of the Tree Diagram Described

Element	Description
Leadership Basal Elements	The fundamental elements of leadership anywhere are leaders, followers, situations. What leaders, followers, and situations are in different cultures will vary. Expectations will determine much. Situations will determine much. But whatever the manifestation, these three elements can be studied in any cultures.
a. leaders	All cultures recognize the right/authority of some to dominantly influence others. How they recognize, why they recognize, and how they influence others differs markedly but all cultures have leaders. They can be studied and their development analyzed.
b. followers	All cultures recognize that most people will be influenced by leaders. Those being influenced are followers. Various factors determine who followers are. Followers can be studied and the dynamics between followers and leaders can be studied. These will vary markedly in different cultures, but all cultures have dynamics underlying interplay between followers and leaders.
c. situations	Situations affect leaders, followers and the dynamics between them. The major reason trait theory was debunked was that traits of leaders varied with situations. Situations are fluid and dynamic and can even force changes in expectations on leaders and followers.
Leadership Influence Means	In every culture groups are influenced by others. Some cultures are more individualized than others and so individual influence means takes on importance. Some cultures require more conformity to group thinking. Corporate influence means carries more weight in such cultures. Spiritual influencers occur in all cultures. How they influence differs but they exist.
a. individual influence means	Individuals use leadership styles to influence followers. Leadership styles vary greatly between cultures. These can be studied.
b. corporate influence means	How groups influence, whether in formal organizations, or in cultures, can be studied. Coming to the front now is systemic theory which sees interplay between all kinds of organizational elements which exert sometimes hidden influence.

c. spiritual influence means	Spiritual leaders can influence by manipulating the spirit world power. Spiritual leaders can exert great influence because of perceived moral standards or competency or giftedness.
Leadership Value Bases	All cultures have underlying values which undergird their practices. Some are explicit. Others are highly implicit.
a. cultural value bases	Most leaders dominantly are influence by cultural values of what leaders are to be and do and how they do it.
b. theological value bases	There is a growing concern, especially among Christian leaders, that biblical leadership values ought to inform and influence Christian leaders and leadership.

Conclusion

The strength of this framework for identifying, studying, and assessing leadership is fourfold:

1. It is a framework that developed from synthesizing the best of leadership theoretical studies for the past 150 years. There is a **long-term perspective** involved.
2. It is an integrated framework manifesting the **what, how,** and **why** of leadership.
3. Its categories are generically broad enough to **guide analysis** in any culture **but allow for major differences** in what the manifestations may be.
4. Any theoretical leadership studies done today can be properly evaluated in terms of what they focus on and what they leave out.

Its basic weakness is that it is a static framework. In real life all of these elements are interacting with each other and modifying each other constantly. There is feedback and feedforward between these elements. The framework is changing constantly in terms of what is in focus and what is being defined.

However, the tree diagram depicts leadership issues that must be considered when studying leadership or training leaders.

Relevance of the Article to 1,2 Timothy

1,2 Ti describes the finish of a leader whose life really counted. Paul left behind an invaluable legacy. All leaders leave behind results of their life work. Most do not do so deliberately. It just happens. Sometimes they miss doing or being something that they should have. Perhaps with more proactive deliberate decisions they could have left behind God-intended legacies had they been more aware. Paul's legacy in terms of ultimate contribution theory includes: saint, stylistic practitioner, mentor, pioneer, promoter, writer. Paul sets a real model for leaders who operate in the Church Leadership Era, namely us. His life counted. He left behind a legacy. Will you?

35. Legacy—Leaving One Behind

Introduction

Paul closed his life triumphantly. Listen to his challenging words.

> 6 As for me, I am ready to be sacrificed. The time for me to depart this life is near. 7 I have run a good race. I have fulfilled my God-given destiny. I still have my faith intact. 8 And now for my prize, a crown of righteousness. The Lord, the righteous judge, will award it to me at that day. And not to me only, but unto all those who eagerly await his return. 2Ti 4:6-8

Paul led a focused life. He left behind a legacy. The concept, ultimate contribution, describes one of the four focal elements of a focused life. Briefly, *ultimate contribution* refers to the long-term results of a life effort, that is, the legacy a person will look back on and enjoy in eternity.[331]

Defining Ultimate Contribution More Fully

Definition | An <u>ultimate contribution</u> is the lasting legacy of a Christian for which he/she is remembered and which furthers the cause of Christianity by one or more of the following:

1. setting standards for life and ministry,
2. impacting lives by enfolding them in God's Kingdom or developing them once in the Kingdom,
3. serving as a stimulus for change which betters the world,
4. leaving behind an organization, institution, or movement that can serve as a channel for God to work through, or
5. the discovery of ideas, communication of them, or promotion of them so that they further God's work.

---

[331] A <u>focused life</u> is a life dedicated to exclusively carrying out God's unique purposes through it, by identifying the focal issues (that is, the l e purpose, effective methodology, major role, or ultimate contribution), which allows an increasing prioritization of life's activities around the focal issues, and results in a satisfying life of being and doing. The four focal issues are described succinctly as: *life purpose*— the integrating force for my life which moves me forward toward that for which I was created (synonym: my passion in life); *major role*— the job description which I will have to create in order to effectively do my life purpose (synonym: the platform for my ministry); *effective methodology*— one or more effective means I have for accomplishing ministry objectives that flow out of my life purpose and contribute toward it (synonym: what I love to do when I minister with power); *Ultimate contribution*—the long term results of my life effort (synonym: legacies I will look back on and enjoy in eternity).

Table 1 lists 13 prime types of more common ultimate contribution types that have been discovered from comparative studies of leaders who led focused lives.[332] These 13 prime types are grouped under five major kinds: Character, Ministry, Catalytic, Organizational, Ideation.

Table 1,2 Ti 35-1. Ultimate Contribution Types

Type	Basic Notion
CHARACTER:	
Saint	A model life, not a perfect one, but a life others want to emulate.
Stylistic Practitioner	A model ministry style which sets the pace for others and which other ministries seek to emulate.
Family	Promote a God-fearing family, leaving behind children who walk with God carrying on that Godly-heritage.
MINISTRY:	
Mentor	A productive ministry with individuals, small groups, etc.
Public Rhetorician	A productive public ministry with large groups.
CATALYTIC:	
Pioneer	A person who starts apostolic ministries.
Change Person	A person who rights wrongs and injustices in society and in church and mission organizations.
Artist	A person who has creative breakthroughs in life and ministry and introduces innovation.
ORGANIZATIONAL:	
Founder	A person who starts a new organization to meet a need or capture the essence of some movement or the like.
Stabilizer	A person who can help a fledgling organization develop or can help an older organization move toward efficiency and effectiveness. In other words, help solidify an organization.
IDEATION:	
Researcher	Develops new ideation by studying various things.
Writer	Captures ideas and reproduces them in written format to help and inform others.
Promoter	Effectively distributes new ideas and/or other ministry related things.

Paul's Legacy

Paul left behind significant ultimate contributions. His ultimate contribution set includes: saint, stylistic practitioner, mentor, pioneer, promoter, writer. The following table comments on these.

---

[332] In 1988 I did preliminary research on legacy articles in order to confirm concepts dealing with leadership emergence theory. This led me to identify some early concepts and to form a tentative typology of ultimate contributions. In 1989 I supervised a research project by M. Whitworth. She did a comparative study of 42 biographical/legacy articles on prominent missionaries and pastors in order to verify or alter the tentative typology and to illustrate in the lives of these legacy people. Her research forms the basis for findings on ultimate contribution theory. For Further Study, See paper—*Ultimate Contribution* contained in my FocLivesReader.pdf at my web site.

Table 1,2 Ti 35-2. Paul's Ultimate Contribution Set

Type	Explanation
saint	Paul's life was transformed during his 30+ years of ministry. The gentle leader seen in 2Ti differs markedly from the abrupt brusque leader who was let down outside the town wall in a basket. What he talked about in Ro 6-8 about union life and life (victory) in the Spirit and described in Gal 5:22,23 (the fruit of the Spirit) was true for him. He was not a perfect person, but certainly a model of what God can do to transform a life. He finished well. Today more than ever we need models who are finishing well. Paul showed us that it could be done.
stylistic practitioner	He was a full time missionary who broke open new fields for the Gospel. His use of team ministry, breakthrough methods for the Gospel—power ministry, networking, redemptive analogies—and development of leaders—mostly through mentoring—as well as his analyzing and solving church problems all contribute to us an important ministry model. Those engaged in taking the Gospel to areas yet unreached by the Gospel all will do well to emulate much of Paul's ministry in their own lives.
mentor	Paul is the premiere model for mentoring in the N.T. He developed people through on-the-job experience and using personal relationships. He left behind a large cadre of mentorees who passed on his leadership values.
pioneer	Paul broke open new ground for the Gospel. This involved new methodologies, new structures, and new contextualized theology. He essentially defined what church leadership is all about in the Church Leadership Era.
promoter	If ever there was a proponent for foreign missions, Paul was it. He did it. He believed in it. He recruited for it. He raised money for it. He established foreign missions as a legitimate enterprise in God's Kingdom. Paul also promoted union life—that is, a Spirit led victorious life—as the norm for all Christians.
writer	This missionary theologian combined an experiential exposure to cultures with a keen analytical mind. And out of this came forth treatises dealing with real live leadership problems. Paul's 13 epistles: Ro, 1Co, 2Co, Gal, Eph, Php, Col, 1Th, 2Th, 1Ti, 2Ti, Tit, Phm are probably one of the most important legacies any Christian leader has left behind.

Please carefully note. Paul did not have these as life goals. His goal was to serve the resurrected Christ and carry out his life purpose. But in doing that, these were the by-products of his life purpose. But the two are not exclusive. An understanding of life purpose allows for decisions to be made which will move one toward ultimate contributions.

Conclusion

All leaders leave behind results of their life work. Most do not do so deliberately. It just happens. Sometimes they miss doing or being something that they should have. Perhaps with more proactive deliberate decisions they could have left behind God-intended legacies had they been more aware. This article exposes you to categories of lasting legacies that have been derived from comparative study of effective leaders. Most present day leaders can identify readily with these lasting legacies. Intuitively they can identify a set of two to five of these legacies that both appeal to them and seem to be items that can be achieved. Once these are recognized there can be proactive decision making in terms of how major role and unique methodologies can be focused toward end of life results.

But be cautioned. Your main responsibility in life is not aiming for an ultimate contribution set—your major responsibility in life is simply to obey God. If you are hearing from God and obeying Him, He will help you see and make decisions that will lead to your ultimate contribution that fits His focus for you.

So don't be too hasty to leave behind legacies. On the other hand, learn all you can about who you are and the legacies you desire to leave behind You are responsible for who you are and who God is making you to be and do. You are responsible for b ing a good steward of what you have and what you ought to achieve. Wise decision making which moves toward lasting legacies appropriate to your focus is certainly compatible with following God. For He has uniquely made you and is shaping you for His purposes. Ministry flows out of being. And you were created with God's purposes in mind.

Paul sets a real model for leaders who operate in the Church Leadership Era, namely us. His life counted. He left behind a legacy. Will you?

See **Article**, *18. Focused Life*

Relevance of the Article to 1,2 Timothy

Macro lessons, that is, major leadership observations across the various leadership eras of the Bible, provide some important guidelines for leaders today. This article defines the concept of macro lessons. The next article, 37, lists them. Paul demonstrates a number of these macro lessons in his leadership influence as seen in his epistles, some of which occur in the letters to Timothy.

36. Macro Lessons—Defined

Macro Lessons inform our leadership with potential leadership values that move toward the absolute. We live in a time when most do not believe there are absolutes. In my study of leadership in the Bible, I have defined a leadership truth continuum which recognizes the difficulty in deriving absolutes but does allow for them.[333] Figure 1,2 Ti 36-1 depicts this.

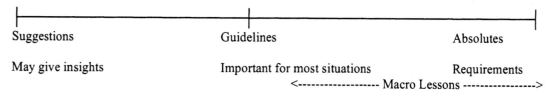

Suggestions	Guidelines	Absolutes
May give insights	Important for most situations	Requirements

<------------------ Macro Lessons ----------------->

Figure 1,2 Ti 36-1. Leadership Truth Continuum/ Where Macro Lessons Occur

Introduction to Macro lessons

In the *Complexity Era* in which we now live,[334] the thrust of leadership theory has moved, toward the importance of leadership values. The questions being asked today are not as much what is leadership (the leadership basal elements—leader, followers, and situations) and how does it operate (leadership influence means—corporate and individual) as it is why do we do what we do (leadership value bases). The first three eras (Great Man, Trait, and Ohio State) answered the question, "What is leadership?" The Contingency and early part of the Complexity Era answered the question, "How do we do it?" Now we are grappling with, "Why do we lead? or What ought we to do?" We are looking for leadership values. A leadership value is an underlying assumption which affects how a leader behaves in or perceives leadership situations. They are usually statements that have *ought* or *must* or *should* in them. Macro-Lessons are statements of truth about leadership which have the potential for becoming leadership values. These macro-lessons are observations seen in the various leadership eras in the Bible. Many of these became values for

---

[333] See Clinton, **Leadership Perspectives** for a more detailed explanation of the continuum and for my approach to deriving principles from the scriptures. See **Article**, 54. *Principles of Truth.*

[334] A study of leadership history in the United States from 1850 to the present uncovered 6 Eras (an era being a period of time in which some major leadership theory held sway): 1. Great Man Era (1840s to 1904); 2. Trait Theory (1904-1948); 3. Ohio State Era (1948-1967); Contingency Era (1967-1980); Complexity Era (1980-present). See Clinton, **A Short History of Leadership Theory.** Altadena, Ca.: Barnabas Publishers.

numerous Bible leaders. These macro-lessons move toward the right (requirement, value) of the leadership truth continuum.

What is a macro lesson?

Definition   A <u>macro-lesson</u> is a high level generalization
- of a leadership observation (suggestion, guideline, requirement), stated as a lesson,
- which repeatedly occurs throughout different leadership eras,
- and thus has potential as a leadership absolute.

Macro lessons even at their weakest provide strong guidelines describing leadership insights. At their strongest they are requirements, or absolutes, that leaders should follow. Leaders ignore them to their detriment.

examples   **Prayer Lesson**: If God has called you to a ministry then He has called you to pray for that ministry.
Accountability: Christian leaders minister ought always with a conscious view to ultimate accountability to God for their ministry.
Bible Centered: An effective leader who finishes well must have a Bible centered ministry.

Macro Lessons are derived from a comparative study of leadership in the Six Leadership Eras. These Six Leadership Eras and number of macro lessons identified are shown in Table 1,2 Ti 36-1.

Table 1,2 Ti 36-1. Leadership Eras and Number of Macro Lessons

Leadership Era	Number of Macro Lessons
1. Patriarchal Era	7
2. Pre-Kingdom Era	10
3. Kingdom Era	5
4. Post-Kingdom Era	5
5. Pre-Church Era	9
6. Church Era	5

I have identified 41 macro lessons, roughly 5 to 10 per leadership era. When a macro-lesson is seen to occur in varied situations and times and cultural settings and in several leadership eras it becomes a candidate for an absolute leadership lesson. When that same generalization becomes personal and is embraced by a leader as a driving force for how that leader sees or operates in ministry, it becomes a leadership value.

The top three Macro Lessons for the four O.T. Leadership Eras are listed in Table 1,2 Ti 36-2.

Table 1,2 Ti 36-2. Top Three Macro Lessons in O.T. Leadership Eras

Priority	Leadership Era	Label	Statement
1	Pre-Kingdom	Presence	The essential ingredient of leadership is the powerful presence of God in the leader's life and ministry. (*Therefore a leader must not minister without the powerful presence of God in his/her life.*)
2	Patriarchal	Character	Integrity is the essential character trait of a spiritual leader. (*Therefore, a leader must maintain integrity and respond to God's shaping of it.*)
3	Pre-Kingdom	Intimacy	Leaders develop intimacy with God which in turn overflows into all their ministry since ministry flows out of being. (*Therefore a leader must seek to develop intimacy with God.*)

The top three Macro Lessons for the two N.T. Leadership Eras are listed in Table 1,2 Ti 36-3:

Table 1,2 Ti 36-3. Top Three Macro Lessons in N.T. Leadership Eras

Priority	Leadership Era	Label	Statement
1	Church Centered	Word	*God's Word must be the primary source for equipping leaders and must be a vital part of any leader's ministry.*
2	Pre-Church	Harvest	*Leaders must seek to bring people into relationship with God.*
3	Pre-Church	Shepherd	*Leaders must preserve, protect, and develop those who belong to God's people.*

You will notice that some of these macro lessons are already described in value language (should, must, ought) while others are simply statements of observations. I have put in italics my attempt to give the value associated with the observation.

Comparative study across the six leadership eras for macro lessons makes up one of the seven leadership genres, i.e. sources for leadership findings from the Bible.

See **Articles,** *37. Macro Lessons, List of 41...; 28. Leadership Genre—Seven Types (Macro Lessons, Biographical Material, Books as A Whole, Direct Context, Indirect Context, Leadership Acts, Parabolic).* See Clinton, **A Short History of Leadership Theory**. Altadena, Ca.: Barnabas Publishers. See also Clinton, **Leadership Perspectives**. Altadena, Ca.: Barnabas Publishers.

Relevance of the Article to 1,2 Timothy

It would be easier to mark the macro lessons not as prominent in Paul's ministry as to mark the ones that are prominent. Many of the macro lessons from the O.T. leadership era show up in Paul's ministry. All of the pre-church and church leadership era macro lessons are very evident in Paul's life. It is clear that the church macro lessons were drawn from a study of Paul's missionary career. A quick glance at each of these will readily bring to mind incidents in Paul's missionary trips in the Acts or the purposes of specific epistles he wrote. Note those church leadership era macros: 37. STRUCTURE—CHURCH LEADERS MUST VARY STRUCTURES TO FIT THE NEEDS OF THE TIMES IF THEY ARE TO CONSERVE GAINS AND CONTINUE WITH RENEWED EFFORT. Paul progressively did this as the church was carried from one Gentile situation to another. 38. UNIVERSAL—THE CHURCH STRUCTURE IS INHERENTLY UNIVERSAL AND CAN BE MADE TO FIT VARIOUS CULTURAL SITUATIONS IF FUNCTIONS AND NOT FORMS ARE IN VIEW. Paul showed that the church structure could be contextualized in the various cultures he worked with. Note especially his work with Titus on Crete in this regard. 39. GIFTEDNESS— LEADERS ARE RESPONSIBLE TO HELP GOD'S PEOPLE IDENTIFY, DEVELOP, AND USE THEIR RESOURCES FOR GOD. Paul did this. Note in 1 Co, Eph, and Ro his teaching on this and in 1,2 Ti his application in Timothy's life. 40. WORD CENTERED —GOD'S WORD IS THE PRIMARY SOURCE FOR EQUIPPING LEADERS AND MUST BE A VITAL PART OF ANY LEADER'S MINISTRY. In 2 Ti he lays this principle out for Timothy—and us. 41. COMPLEXITY— LEADERSHIP IS COMPLEX, PROBLEMATIC, DIFFICULT AND FRAUGHT WITH RISK—WHICH IS WHY LEADERSHIP IS NEEDED. The Epistles, each written to deal with some areas of church problems certainly endorse this macro. However, please note that Macro lessons 40 and 41 dominate Paul's ministry. And macro lesson 40 is foundational to leaders today.

37. Macro Lessons—List of 41 Across Six Leadership Eras

Macro Lessons inform our leadership with potential leadership values that move toward the absolute. The following are the 41 lessons I have identified as I comparatively studied the six different leadership eras for leadership observations.

No.	Label	Leadership Era	Statement of Macro Lesson
1.	Blessing	Patriarchal	God mediates His blessing to His followers through leaders.
2.	Shaping	Patriarchal	God shapes leader's lives and ministry through critical incidents.
3.	Timing	Patriarchal	God's timing is crucial to accomplishment of God's purposes.
4.	Destiny	Patriarchal	Leaders must have a sense of destiny.
5.	Character	Patriarchal	Integrity is the essential character trait of a spiritual leader.
6.	Faith	Patriarchal	Biblical Leaders must learn to trust in the unseen God, sense His presence, sense His revelation, and follow Him by faith.
7.	Purity	Patriarchal	Leaders must personally learn of and respond to the holiness of God in order to have effective ministry.
8.	Intercession	Pre-Kingdom	Leaders called to a ministry are called to intercede for that ministry.
9.	Presence	Pre-Kingdom	The essential ingredient of leadership is the powerful presence of God in the leader's life and ministry.
10.	Intimacy	Pre-Kingdom	Leaders develop intimacy with God which in turn overflows into all their ministry since ministry flows out of being.
11.	Burden	Pre-Kingdom	Leaders feel a responsibility to God for their ministry.
12.	Hope	Pre-Kingdom	A primary function of all leadership is to inspire followers with hope in God and in what God is doing.

13.	Challenge	Pre-Kingdom	Leaders receive vision from God which sets before them challenges that inspire their leadership.
14.	Spiritual Authority	Pre-Kingdom	Spiritual authority is the dominant power base of a spiritual leader and comes through experiences with God, knowledge of God, godly character and gifted power.
15.	Transition	Pre-Kingdom	Leaders must transition other leaders into their work in order to maintain continuity and effectiveness.
16.	Weakness	Pre-Kingdom	God can work through weak spiritual leaders if they are available to Him.
17.	Continuity	Pre-Kingdom	Leaders must provide for continuity to new leadership in order to preserve their leadership legacy.
18.	Unity	Kingdom	Unity of the people of God is a value that leaders must preserve.
19.	Stability	Kingdom	Preserving a ministry of God with life and vigor over time is as much if not more of a challenge to leadership than creating one.
20.	Spiritual Leadership	Kingdom	Spiritual leadership can make a difference even in the midst of difficult times.
21.	Recrudescence	Kingdom	God will attempt to bring renewal to His people until they no longer respond to Him.
22.	By-pass	Kingdom	God will by-pass leadership and structures that do not respond to Him and will institute new leadership and structures.
23.	Future Perfect	Post-Kingdom	A primary function of all leadership is to walk by faith with a future perfect paradigm so as to inspire followers with certainty of God's accomplishment of ultimate purposes.
24.	Perspective	Post-Kingdom	Leaders must know the value of perspective and interpret present happenings in terms of God's broader purposes.
25.	Modeling	Post-Kingdom	Leaders can most powerfully influence by modeling godly lives, the sufficiency and sovereignty of God at all times, and gifted power.
26.	Ultimate	Post-Kingdom	Leaders must remember that the ultimate goal of their lives and ministry is to manifest the glory of God.
27.	Perseverance	Post-Kingdom	Once known, leaders must persevere with the vision God has given.
28.	Selection	Pre-Church	The key to good leadership is the selection of good potential leaders which should be a priority of all leaders.
29.	Training	Pre-Church	Leaders should deliberately train potential leaders in their ministry by available and appropriate means.
30.	Focus	Pre-Church	Leaders should increasingly move toward a focus in their ministry which moves toward fulfillment of their calling and their ultimate contribution to God's purposes for them.
31.	Spirituality	Pre-Church	Leaders must develop interiority, spirit sensitivity, and fruitfulness in accord with their uniqueness since ministry flows out of being.
32.	Servant	Pre-Church	Leaders must maintain a dynamic tension as they lead by serving and serve by leading.
33.	Steward	Pre-Church	Leaders are endowed by God with natural abilities, acquired skills, spiritual gifts, opportunities, experiences, and privileges which must be developed and used for God.
34.	Harvest	Pre-Church	Leaders must seek to bring people into relationship with God.
35.	Shepherd	Pre-Church	Leaders must preserve, protect, and develop God's people.
36.	Movement	Pre-Church	Leaders recognize that movements are the way to penetrate society though they must be preserved via appropriate ongoing institutions.

37.	Structure	Church	Leaders must vary structures to fit the needs of the times if they are to conserve gains and continue with renewed effort.
38.	Universal	Church	The church structure is inherently universal and can be made to fit various cultural situations if functions and not forms are in view.
39.	Giftedness	Church	Leaders are responsible to help God's people identify, develop, and use their resources for God.
40.	Word Centered	Church	God's Word is the primary source for equipping leaders and must be a vital part of any leaders ministry.
41.	Complexity	All eras	Leadership is complex, problematic, difficult and fraught with risk—which is why leadership is needed.

See Also **Article** *36. Macro Lessons—Defined.*

Relevance of the Article to 1,2 Timothy

I personally have done much study concerning Paul's mentoring. See **Article** *45. Paul—Developer Par Excellence,* which shows Paul as a trainer—using formal, non-formal and informal means of training but with the informal methodology of mentoring dominating. Note also **Article** *47. Paul—Mentor for Many,* which specifically looks at Paul's mentor-mix—that is, the types of mentoring he did with some of his prominent leaders—like Timothy and Titus. This article describes the results of empirical research in contemporary leaders. It gives the framework for looking at mentoring in general. These categories certainly are useful in analyzing Paul's mentoring ministry. 1,2 Ti show Paul at his very best mentoring with a life-long mentoree, Timothy. In 1,2 Ti, Paul demonstrates five (Teacher, Contemporary Model, Sponsor, Spiritual Guide, and Counselor) of the nine mentor functions with Timothy. In this article, note the central thrust of those five mentoring functions specifically and immediately passages from 1,2 Ti will jump to mind showing Paul doing those thrusts. Note also the five mentoring dynamics—all were present in Paul's mentoring of Timothy in 1,2 Ti.

38. Mentoring—An Informal Training Model

Training Modes

Today's training can be categorized under three modes as shown in Figure 1,2 Ti 38-1.

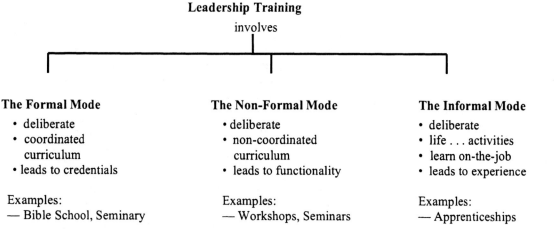

Leadership Training
involves

The Formal Mode
- deliberate
- coordinated
  curriculum
- leads to credentials

Examples:
— Bible School, Seminary

The Non-Formal Mode
- deliberate
- non-coordinated
  curriculum
- leads to functionality

Examples:
— Workshops, Seminars

The Informal Mode
- deliberate
- life . . . activities
- learn on-the-job
- leads to experience

Examples:
— Apprenticeships

Figure 1,2 Ti 38-1. Three Training Modes

Mentoring as a training means, while definitely informal in its essence, can be applied to any of the three modes.

Jesus and Paul used the informal training mode as their major training methodology. On-the-job training, modeling, cultural forms of apprenticeships and internships were used. But dominantly it was mentoring which was the primary informal means of training.

Mentoring Defined

Definition   <u>Mentoring</u> is a relational experience in which one person, the mentor, empowers another person, the mentoree, by a transfer of resources.

Empowerment can include such things as new habits, knowledge, skills, desires, values, connections to resources for growth and development of potential. We[335] have identified a number of mentoring functions. Table 1,2 Ti 38-1 identifies nine mentoring functions we have categorized.

Table 1,2 Ti 38-1. Nine Mentor Functions

Type	Central Thrust
1. Discipler	Basic habits of the Christian life dealing with hearing from God and talking with God; operating in a fellowship of Christians; learning to minister in terms of giftedness; learning to get input from God.
2. Spiritual Guide	Evaluation of spiritual depth and maturity in a life and help in growth in this.
3. Coach	Skills of all kind depending on the expertise of the coach
4. Counselor	Timely and good advice which sheds perspective on issues and problems and other needs.
5. Teacher	Relevant knowledge that can be used for personal growth or ministry or other such need.
6. Sponsor	Protective guidance and linking to resources so that a leader reaches potential.
7. Contemporary Model	Values impactfully demonstrated in a life that can be transferred and used in one's own life.
8. Historical Model	Values demonstrated in a life and inspiration drawn from that life so as to encourage ongoing development in ones own life and a pressing on to finish well.
9. Divine Contact	Timely Guidance from God via some human source.

Mentoring is a relational experience. Five dynamics are involved: attraction, relationship, responsiveness, accountability, empowerment. The more each of these dynamics are in place the more impactful is the empowerment. Table 1,2 Ti 38-2 gives the essence of each of the dynamics.

Table 1,2 Ti 38-2. Five Mentoring Dynamics

Dynamic	Responsibility of	Explanation
attraction	both mentor and mentoree	A mentoree must be attracted to a mentor—that is, see something in the mentor that is desired in his/her own life; A mentor must be attracted to a mentoree and see potential value in working with the mentoree—that is, development of potential for the mentoree is a worth while investment of time and energy.
relationship	both mentor and mentoree	A mentor must build the relationship with a mentoree and vice versa. The stronger the relationship the more likely that the responsiveness and the accountability functions will take place naturally instead of forced.
responsiveness	mentoree	The mentoree must respond to the mentor's suggestions and growth projects. Faithfulness in carrying out assignments is a major trait of responsiveness. The mentor is responsible to help the mentoree grow. The mentoree is responsible to respond/submit to the mentor's plan and methodology for growth.
accountability	mentor	The mentor is responsible to evaluate how the mentoree is doing and to hold the mentoree accountable for following suggestions for growth, for doing what is asked, etc
empowerment	mentor dominantly; mentoree secondarily	Both mentor and mentoree should evaluate and recognize empowerment out of the relationship. The mentor knows and has the best perspective to evaluate empowerment. But the mentoree also should recognize growth in his/her life.

---

[335] My son Dr. Richard W. Clinton, my colleague Paul Stanley and I have all been busily researching and using mentoring in our own personal ministries. See **Connecting** by Stanley and Clinton. See The **Mentor Handbook** by Clinton and Clinton.

All of these dynamics do not always appear in fullness in the different relationships. They are necessary for the intensive mentoring functions (heavy face-to-face time commitments are usually involved): discipling, spiritual guide, coaching. All do not have to be present in the occasional mentoring functions: counseling, teaching, sponsoring. Empowerment can happen even when all the dynamics are not present. However, the stronger the five dynamics, even in occasional mentoring, the more impactful will be the resulting empowerment. In the passive mentoring functions—contemporary modeling, historical modeling, and divine contact—attraction is present, responsiveness is present and empowerment takes place. But relationship and accountability are essentially missing.

Both Jesus and Paul used mentoring. They had individual relationships with trainees. But they also combined individual mentoring relationships with training of groups.

Mentoring relates directly to two of the seven major lessons observed in comparative study of effective leaders.

> **Effective leaders view leadership selection and development as a priority function in their ministry.**

> **Effective leaders see relational empowerment as both a means and a goal of ministry.**

Mentoring will be one of the dominant forces in the training of emerging leaders in the years to come.

See **Articles**: *29. Leadership Lessons— Seven Major Identified*; *47. Paul—Mentor for Many*. See **For Further Study Bibliography**: J. Robert Clinton and Paul D. Stanley, **Connecting—The Mentoring Relationships You Need to Succeed in Life**; J. Robert Clinton and Richard W. Clinton, **The Mentor Handbook—Detailed Guidelines and Helps for Christian Mentors and Mentorees.**

Relevance of the Article to 1,2 Timothy

This article was done from observations of contemporary leaders and more aptly fits present ministry situations. However, you can observe in Paul's ministry that he was aware of some of the barriers involved in seeing adequate church leadership in place as well as the problems involved in his strategic leadership via his missionary band. He certainly deals with the financial problem in several different ways. His major effort with his rising apostolic mentorees was sponsoring them for higher-level leadership. His use of ministry tasks with Tychicus, Titus, Timothy and others helped bridge the entry of these men into ministry. In 1,2 Ti Paul is asking Timothy to do leadership selection. One of the major problems in the church at Ephesus dealt with removing some inadequate leaders and replacing them with upcoming leaders. Ministry Entry was a subject that Timothy had to apply immediately to this local church situation.

39. Ministry Entry Patterns

Introduction

Ministry entry can refer to the initial ministry an emerging leader takes part in (all types[336] of leaders). Or it can refer to any new ministry task, assignments, or challenges that a growing leader assumes (all types of leaders). Further, it also usually refers to the first full time ministry of a Type C, D or E leader. Ministry entry patterns give perspective to any leader who is aware of and wants to put into practice two major leadership lessons:[337]

Leadership Selection	Effective leaders view leadership selection and development as a priority function.
Perspective	Effective leaders view present ministry in terms of a lifetime perspective.[338]

What can we learn from comparative study of contemporary leaders about ministry entry? Perhaps some things that will renew us to challenge people into ministry.

The Three Basic Types of Ministry Entry

Each of the three types—first attempts, new ministry, or initial entry into full time ministry—yield observations helpful to emerging leaders and those concerned with emerging leaders—leaders with a developmental perspective.

---

[336] See **Article**, *30. Leadership Levels*. Briefly the types of leaders are: Type A—local, unpaid, small influence; Type B—local, paid, more influence; Type C—regional, paid, broader influence; Type D—national, paid, wide influence, indirect ministry; Type E—international, paid, widest influence, indirect ministry or direct ministry with unusual expertise.

[337] Seven such lessons have been identified: (1) Effective Leaders View Present Ministry in Terms Of A Life Time Perspective. (2) Effective Leaders Maintain A Learning Posture Throughout Life. (3) Effective Leaders Value Spiritual Authority As A Primary Power Base. (4) Effective Leaders Who Are Productive Over A Lifetime Have A Dynamic Ministry Philosophy. (5) Effective Leaders View Leadership Selection And Development As A Priority Function In Their Ministry. (6) Effective Leaders See Relational Empowerment As Both A Means And A Goal Of Ministry. (7) Effective Leaders Evince A Growing Awareness Of Their Sense Of Destiny. It is this last one I am exploring in this article.

[338] In this case, Effective leaders view present ministry in terms of a lifetime perspective—both their own ministry and other leaders' ministries.

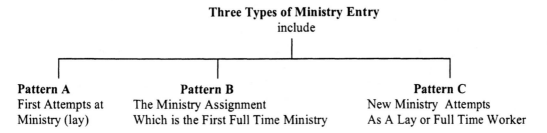

Figure 1,2 Ti 39-1. Three Types of Ministry Entry

description   The <u>ministry entry patterns</u> describe the ways that challenges come to leaders and potential leaders as they accept various ministry tasks and assignments during early, middle and latter ministry. These patterns relate three factors:
1. how the challenge comes—motivated externally or internally,
2. the structures or roles that relate to the challenge—existing structures/roles, modification of structures or role, or creation of new structures or roles,
3. the frequency of occurrence.

Tables 1,2 Ti 39-1, 39-2, and 39-3 below show typical ministry challenges for the three ministry entry patterns.

Table 1,2 Ti 39-1. Pattern A—Early Ministry Entry

Challenge	How The Challenge Comes	Structure or Roles It Relates To	Frequency of Occurrence
A1. Help our ministry; we need workers.	External/ existing leaders point out needs and ask for help	Work in existing ministry structures/roles	Most common
A2. I see a need in this ministry; they need …Maybe I can help.	Internal—self-initiated; maybe I can help this ministry	Work in existing ministry structures/roles	Next most common
A3. We have some needs which in our ministry are unmet; need to establish a new thing to meet these needs.	External/ existing leaders point out needs for new kind of ministry; who can do it?	Create new ministry role or structures	Rarer
A4. I see some unmet needs in this ministry; I wonder if I could do … to meet them.	Internal—self initiated; Maybe I can start something new to solve these ministry needs.	Create new ministry roles or structures	Rarest

Most leaders entering into first ministry do so as the result of challenges by leaders in ministry who need help to fill ministry slots already existing (A1). Potential leaders usually do not see needs on their own and hence volunteer for ministry (A2). Most recruiters also do not see the need for new roles or structures. (A3) They are harassed enough just to fill existing needs. Emerging leaders who create new roles or ministry structures on their own (A4) are usually: 1) brash people; 2) threaten the system; 3) won't work in the old ways which are not meeting the new felt needs. This is the rarest of pattern A. It is also an symptom of a leader who will rise to higher levels of leadership influence. The challenge to existing leaders is how to work with such potential leaders to incorporate their ideas and keep them in the system.

Table 1,2 Ti 39-2. Pattern B—
Ministry Assignment which is the First Full Time Ministry

Challenge	How The Challenge Comes	Structure or Roles It Relates To	Frequency of Occurrence
B1. Come over and help us—fulltime?	External/ existing leaders point out needs and ask for help; we need a full time worker; who will go?	Work in existing ministry structures/roles; a slot is open for a full time worker	Most common
B2. I know God's call is on my life; I need to do…with…	Internal—I would like to do this; I wonder if they would take me.	Work in existing ministry but change structures/roles to fit the one being recruited	Very common
B3. Here is a need; I could meet it if they would…	Internal/ self initiated; this ought to be changed; if so, I would want to do this full time.	Change existing ministry structures/ roles	Very common
B4. We have a need; can you help us figure out how to change what we have to meet it?	External/ existing leaders point out needs for new kind of ministry; who can do it?	Change existing ministry structures/ roles	Not so common
B5. We have a need; can you help us start something new to meet it?	External/ We need to do some new things; can you help us innovate?	Create new ministry roles or structures	Occasional
B6. Here is a bright idea on how we could start something new. What do you think?	Internal/ They need something new; I can help them do it. Will they let me?	Create new ministry roles or structures	Rare

Successful initial ministry entry for full time Christian workers depends upon several factors: 1. previous experience as Type A leader; 2. type of transitional training pattern; 3. degree of balanced learning in the training (cognitive, affective, volitional, experiential); 4. time/ ministry context perspectives (A-service, pre-service, in-service); 5. how to finance.

Leaders with on-the-job experience who have learned and who have had some successful ministry move more easily into a full time ministry based on what they have been doing than otherwise. This would describe the transitional training pattern, in-service. Emerging leaders from the pre-service pattern, that is, who by-passed Type A experience, will find initial ministry entry more difficult. They face a high probability of experiencing the abbreviated entry pattern (drop out). This is especially true if the pre-service training is unbalanced toward the cognitive side rather than experiential side.

How to finance is a question that depends on whether the emerging leader is going to existing works (primary responsibility for finances with the leaders of that work—denominational work or going on a staff of a large church or pastoral responsibility in an existing church); existing works (but primary responsibility for finances is on the new leader joining the work—most faith missions); starting a new work (primary responsibility on the emerging leader to finance the new work somehow).

Table 1,2 Ti 39-3. Pattern C—New Ministry Attempts

Challenge	How The Challenge Comes	Structure or Roles It Relates To	Frequency of Occurrence
C1. Change to new job; learn some new skills; build on what you have.	Internal/ I see something in our group I would like to do ,different from what I am doing now	Work in existing ministry structures/roles	Very common
C2. I would like to change the job I have to better fit me.	Internal—self-initiated; maybe I could do better if we could just alter what I am doing.	Change existing ministry structures/roles	Very common
C3. You don't fit here. But if you can change to this we can use you.	External/ existing leaders point out needs for changing.	Create new ministry role or structures in the group.	Not so common
C4. More can be done here than I am doing. How can I change what is being done and me to meet these needs.	Internal—self initiated; Maybe I can start something new to challenge me to grow and to meet needs unmet now.	Create new ministry roles or structures in the group.	Rare
C5. God's call on me is to leave this ministry and start a new one.	Internal—self initiated; I have to leave to get done what needs to be done. This group is not going to do it.	Create new ministry roles or structures outside the group; in another organization; or begin one.	Rare

Ministry challenge is the shaping activity which describes the means whereby a leader or potential leader is prompted to accept a new ministry assignment and sense the guidance of God into service. The most common pattern of entry into a ministry assignment is an external challenge to work in some existing role in a ministry situation. The rarest entry patterns involve self-initiated challenges to create new ministry roles and structures. Frequently new challenges come via a paradigm shift (see some breakthrough ministry insight that needs to be done), a renewal experience (God challenges afresh to commit to something He wants done, or a deliberate movement toward fulfilling one's destiny (recognizing one's focused life components—life purpose; major role; effective methodologies; ultimate contributions).

An important entry pattern in all three ministry entry patterns involves usually internal (self-initiated) challenges to adapt present roles or ministry structures or create new ones. This signals potential for high level leadership. Self-initiative type people rise to challenges and create new opportunities for ministry. They become leaders of influence.

Conclusions

Three implications come to mind. The first two are leadership selection insights and are for leaders selecting other leaders. The third is for any leader to consider for self-evaluation.

1. The majority of leaders will follow common entry patterns.
2. It is the self-initiation instinct which indicates strong potential for upper level leadership.
3. Plateauing is indicated by a lessening frequency of interest in ministry challenges and ministry assignments.

Application of implication 1 is straightforward. A major function of all leadership is the selection and development of potential leaders. Thus, present leaders should openly and deliberately challenge potential leaders in terms of specific roles and the needs of existing ministries. Over the years the enthusiasm of ministry often wanes as leaders move toward latter ministry processing. As a result there is a corresponding lack of challenging and recruiting. This insight should help people in ministry, whether in early, middle or latter processing to see the value of continuing to enthusiastically challenge others for ministry.

Self-initiated ministry tasks or assignments carry with them the seeds of higher level leadership. Leaders should recognize that this quality is important and be on the alert for those who are constantly doing this kind of thing. One problem does exist. Often those who self-initiate ministry tasks and assignments are challenging the status quo and threatening leaders over them. Often when defensiveness arises in the midst of threatening situations, the sparkling quality of self-initiative is quickly by-passed and set aside for re-enforcing the status quo. Thus, implication 2 is very important. Later, in guidance processing, the mentor process item will be stressed. Mentors tend to be alert to this predictive quality and can patiently work to see it developed.

Most initial ministry entry activities come while the emerging leader is a lay person and is usually the result of some sort of challenge. So, as an existing leader, identify the ministry opportunities in your group and challenge lay people with them. Then watch the ones who respond to God and work with them.

See *ministry task; ministry assignment; ministry challenge; mentor definitions;* **Glossary**. See **Articles**, *Jesus Recruiting Techniques; Training Modes—When They Fit; 18. Focused Life.*

Relevance of the Article to 1,2 Timothy

Paul was a motivated leader. To motivate people a leader must first be motivated himself/herself. This article delves into what motivated Paul to ministry. In 1,2 Ti six of the of the nine motivating factors are emphatically stressed (1. Finishing Well; 2. Return of Christ; 3. Giftedness; 7. Handling God's Word Appropriately; 8. Eternal Realities; 9. Love). No doubt Timothy was motivated by Paul to face up to the tough situation in Ephesian in his Phase III Corrective Work. See **Article** *3. Apostolic Functions Comparison of Titus and Timothy.*

40. Motivating Factors For Ministry

Introduction

What motivated Paul to be and do—to be what God intended him to be and to accomplish what God intended him to accomplish? Some factors which motivated Paul, who is our major model for leadership in the **Church Leadership Era**, are given below. Many of these same factors should motivate leaders today.

Factors That Motivated Paul

Table 1,2 Ti 40-1 lists motivating factors observed in the Pauline epistles (for which I have already done commentary work on[339]).

Table 1,2 Ti 40-1. Motivational Factors for Paul's Ministry

Factor	Where Observed	Explanation
1. Finishing Well; (Achieving/ Becoming/ Fulfilling Life Purpose)	2Ti 4:7,8; 1Co 9:24-27; 1Ti 6:11,12; 2Ti 4:6; Php 3:14.	Paul is the classic N.T. case of a leader finishing well. Christ is still Lord of His life. He is ministering looking for the return of Christ. All six characteristics of a good finish are indicated. (a) His relationship with God via Christ is still warm and personal. (1Ti 4:17). (b) He evinces a learning posture (1Ti 4:13). (c) He has been shaped by the Holy Spirit over his lifetime into the image of Christ. That is, he demonstrates Christ-likeness (1Ti 4:16). (d) He lives by Biblical convictions, his faith intact (2Ti 4:7). (e) He is leaving behind a legacy. His ultimate contributions include those associated with saint, stylistic practitioner, mentor, pioneer, writer, promoter. To finish well, go the full distance, to finish his course all were drives under lying Paul's motivation for ministry. Principles: a. Present ministry should always be seen in the light of a whole life of ministry and particularly the end of ministry a good finish. A good thought question, "In what way is my present shaping circumstances going to affect my finish?" b. One's sense of destiny guides toward and highlights a good finish. c. An anticipation of the Lord's return is a major motivating factor for a leader to minister well and finish well.

---

[339] Missing would be Ro, Gal, Eph, Col, 1,2Th. Probably some new factors might emerge but the major ones will have been identified from the epistles I have already done commentary work on.

2. Return of Christ (and the Ultimate Accountability associated with it)	2Ti 4:7,8 (see also Tit 2:11-13). Php 1:6,10; 2:16; 4:1; 2Th 2:2; 2Co 1:14; 5:10.,11; 11:30; 1T 6:14; 2Ti 4:8; many others	Paul always ministered with a conscious view to ultimate accountability to God for their ministry. Paul was conscious of a future day in which God would hold him and others accountable for their actions (see 1:16, 4:8, 4:14). This is more fully developed in 2Co and 1, 2Th but is affirmed in many epistles. (See especially He 13:17). Principles: a. Leaders will be held accountable for their ministry efforts. b. Leaders will be rewarded for their positive achievements in ministry. c. A final accountability is one motivating factor for a leader.
3. Giftedness (especially the Apostolic Functions with it)	1Co; 1Ti; 2Co 11:4	Paul exemplifies all of the apostolic functions. For example, a number of his epistles were written in part to correct heresy. His word giftedness dominated all that he did: apostleship, teaching, evangelism, and sometimes pastoring. His giftedness was a major factor in motivating and directing/ guiding him into ministry.
4. Confidence in the Gospel	2Co 3:12; (see also Ro 1:16); 1 Co 6:11.	Confidence in the power of the Good News about Christ is a strong motivating factor leading to bold ministry. Paul spoke boldly because he had experienced the power of the Gospel in lives. He saw people delivered from sins and from addictive sin.
5. Burden for Ministry	2Co 2:4; 2Co 11:28;	Paul, like Moses, had a heavy calling on his life. This calling gave him a burden which drove him to reach Gentiles and to do the apostolic functions he did with them. His strong concerns for those he influenced are interwoven throughout all he does. He exemplifies the double thrust of burden—downward toward ministry with those he was influencing and upward, answering to God for them.
6. Resurrection	1Co 15; 2Co 4:14; Php 3:10;	Paul was driven to know that there was a life after death. His conversion experience convinced him that it was real. From then on, he was obsessed with realizing this for his own life; particularly he wanted to experience resurrection power in his ministry.
7. Handling God's Word Appropriately	2Ti 2:15; 2Co 4:2; 2Ti 3:16,17	Paul used the Word of God with great impact. He maintained integrity in how he handled the Word. Knowing the Word of God and used it properly with impact in ministry was a motivating guideline for Paul.
8. Eternal Realities	2Co 4:18; 2 Ti 4	Paul viewed present problems, pressures, physical problems as being bearable in the light of eternity. He always ministered looking forward to resurrection life. He saw these kinds of things *as negative preparation* making him ready and longing for heaven and eternal reality.
9. Love	1Co 12:29; 13; 2Co 5:14; 1Ti 4:11; 6:11; 2Ti 1:3-7; 3:10-17	Paul believed that love should be a major underlying motivating and driving force for using giftedness and for ministry in general. His love for Christ compelled him in ministry.

Conclusion

What motivates you in ministry? Strangely absent from Paul's motivation was a drive for prestige, power, or money—factors driving numerous present day leaders.

See *negative preparation*, **Glossary**.

Relevance of the Article to 1,2 Timothy

Paul, like Haggai, Ezra and Nehemiah, stands out as an inspirational leader who motivated people. In the last article I examined the motivating factors, which inspired Paul to ministry. In this article I examine how these factors were worked out in his ministry as he influenced others. Leaders need to identify their own principles for motivating others. This allows more deliberate inspirational leadership to be accomplished. A study of Paul's motivating principles is a first step, perhaps, in identifying one's own motivational leadership. Notice that the first five principles are illustrated in 1,2 Ti.

41. Motivating Principles—Pauline Influence

Introduction

Paul was a powerful leader who influenced numerous people and churches in *the Church Leadership Era*. What principles or techniques did he use? Following are given some observations (some are statements of principles; others are techniques) which Paul used to motivate individuals and churches. Many of these same principles/techniques can be used by leaders today. Paul, the major model for leadership in the **Church Leadership Era**

Paul's Motivational Principles and Techniques

Table 1,2 Ti 41-1 list some principles/ techniques observed in the Pauline epistles on how Paul motivated followers. Not all the Pauline epistles were considered; just those on which I have done extensive commentary work.[340]

Table 1,2 Ti 41-1. Paul's Motivational Principles and Techniques

Principle/ Technique	Where Observed	Explanation
Goodwin's Expectation Principle	1Ti 6:11; 2Ti 1:5 et al	Principle: Paul uses the dynamic under lying Goodwin's expectation principle—emerging leaders tend to live up to the genuine expectations of leaders they admire.
Teach For Results	1Ti 1:5	Principle: True teaching ought to result in people who have love, a pure heart and a genuine faith. Paul contrasts this result with the heretical teachers who are producing argumentative people.
Prophecy	1Ti 1:18; 4:14	Principle: Paul recalled a prophecy about a spiritual gift made over Timothy in order to motivate Timothy to use that gift with impact. He recalled a prophecy about Timothy living the Christian life.
Touchstone	1Ti 6:11,12	Principle: Use public committals as a motivating factor for continuing on in the Christian life. Public committals on major decisions form a touchstone.
Heritage	2Ti 1:5	Principle: Paul affirmed a foundational heritage for Timothy in order to exhort him to move on in faith (like his mother and grandmother).
Get It On the Agenda	1Co 1:1, 4, 5;	Principle: Paul often subtly introduced subjects he would later deal with in depth. Later when he began to deal with the subject the hearers were already somewhat primed for it.
Future/ Hope	1Co 1:4-9;	Principle: Inspirational leaders point toward the future and what God will do in order to give followers hope.
Competition	1Co 16:1, 4;	Principle: Paul compares churches with churches always pointing

---

[340] Missing would be Ro, Gal, Eph, Col, 1,2Th. Probably some new factors might emerge but the major ones will have been identified from the epistles on which I have done extensive commentary work.

	2Co 8:1-5, 24; 9:1,2;	out the strengths of churches in order to motivate the other churches to attain that level.
Absolute Surrender	2Co 8:5	Principle: Paul challenged believers to commit themselves totally to God. From that standpoint, then he could motivate them to give freely of all kinds of their resources. Without it, at best he would get some grudging help.
Openness	2Co 8:8	Principle: Paul was open and above board even about using motivational techniques. He would sometimes explain his motivational technique.
Modeling/ Jesus	2Co 8:9; Php 2:1-11.	Principle: Paul appealed to Jesus as a model to motivate followers of Jesus to emulate that modeling.
Spiritual Authority	2Co 12:19;	Principle: Paul used strong authoritative techniques but always in line with spiritual authority which seeks the best for the ones being helped.
Foreshadowing	2Co 12:21.	Principle: Paul lays out for them a future scenario that could happen should they not follow his advice. And he promises to back this scenario up with power.
Modeling/ Jesus	See Php	Principle: One of Paul's strongest motivating means is the modeling in his own life. Over and over this is stressed throughout all his epistles. Paul knows it is a motivating force.
Accountability	Php 2:16; 3:17.	Principle: Paul uses his own ultimate accountability to motivate followers.

Conclusion

Paul demonstrates several techniques for motivating followers, especially the Corinthians. Leaders are people with God-given capacities and a God-given burden who are influencing a specific group of people toward God's purposes for them. Influence is the key word. And motivational techniques are means of exerting that influence. Motivation in this case is even more difficult since Paul is confronting a problem church in which a minority are not responding to him. Paul uses several means of motivating which I have given in the table above. However, let me summarize the more important ones. Motivational Leadership Principles/ Observations include:

    a. Goodwin's Expectation Principle, a social dynamic usually dealing with individuals, which recognizes that emerging leaders will usually rise to the level of expectancy of someone they respect, is applied by Paul to a group situation of followers. Paul states his personal positive outcome expectancies for the churches (see especially the Corinthians, both concerning their giving and their following of his exhortations).

    b. Paul uses the gift of exhortation throughout all his books, deliberately, openly, and with clear application to situations. See footnotes identifying the gift of exhortation in use.

    c. Paul uses a form of comparative competition. He describes what other churches have done with respect to giving (in a rather positive ideal description) in order to set expectancies for giving from the churches (both Philippians and Corinthians).

    d. Paul tells churches that he has said great things about their giving to other churches. Their failure to give would make them lose face in the eyes of these other churches.

    e. In the Corinthian case, Paul commissions a delegate from one of the churches which has given and been used as a model to go to Corinth to be part of the group that will administer the gift.

    f. Paul uses Jesus as a model of giving and as a model for humility and putting others first.

    g. Paul uses coercive authority (threatens to exercise spiritual power to correct situations if people do not respond voluntary) backed by a personal visit to motivate.

    h. Paul uses well reasoned out logic in giving solutions to issues and defending his own character.

    i. In the Corinthian case, Paul uses irony (sometimes bordering on sarcasm), often, in order to force the Corinthians to see their positions on things and to challenge them to respond.

Paul motivated people—even in very complex and problematic situations. An awareness of some of his techniques might prove helpful to leaders today who must motivate followers in equally if not more complex and problematic situations.

Relevance of the Article to 1,2 Timothy

Paul is a prototype of a leader who explicitly understood and followed the major destiny leadership lesson identified earlier in **Article** 29. *Leadership Lessons—Seven Major Lessons Identified*. That major lesson— *Effective leaders evince a growing sense of destiny over their lifetimes*—is foundational to one's persevering and finishing well. This article describes Paul's sense of destiny. Note, his sense of destiny was tied to his apostolic calling and authority for his ministry—a fact, which he underscored when dealing with church problems such as the Ephesian situation. He uses that authority when backing Timothy as in 1,2Ti. Paul mentions in 2Ti 4:7,8 the completion of his destiny in a beautiful triumphant statement.

42. Paul—A Sense of Destiny

Introduction

The Apostle Paul had a strong sense of destiny. You see it all over the pages of his epistles. One of the major leadership lessons[341] that emerged from a comparative study of effective leaders concerned the concept, sense of destiny.

Effective leaders evince a growing sense of destiny over their lifetimes.[342]

You will notice reminders of Paul's sense of destiny sprinkled throughout my leadership commentary notes on the Pauline Epistles. He exemplifies in the N.T. Church Leadership Era the importance of a sense of destiny. Such an awareness stabilizes a leader, encourages perseverance, and becomes a Pole Star to shed directive light in major decisions about guidance.

Definition   A <u>sense of destiny</u> is an inner conviction arising from an experience or a series of experiences in which there is a growing sense of awareness that God has His hand on a leader in a special way for special purposes.

Definition   <u>Destiny processing</u> refers to the shaping incidents or means God uses to instill this growing sense of awareness of a destiny is called **destiny processing**.

It is through these shaping activities of God that a leader becomes increasingly aware of God's Hand on his/her life and the purposes for which God has intended for his/her leadership. This processing causes a sense of partnership with God toward God's purposes for the life and hence brings meaning to the life.

A sense of destiny and accompanying destiny processing form the seedbed for life purpose—not only the driving force behind our lives but the defining essence of it. When a leader surrenders to God, in terms of an all out commitment to be the leader God wants, a whole process begins in which that leader begins to

---

[341] Seven such lessons have been identified: (1) Effective Leaders View Present Ministry in Terms Of A Life Time Perspective. (2) Effective Leaders Maintain A Learning Posture Throughout Life. (3) Effective Leaders Value Spiritual Authority As A Primary Power Base. (4) Effective Leaders Who Are Productive Over A Lifetime Have A Dynamic Ministry Philosophy. (5) Effective Leaders View Leadership Selection And Development As A Priority Function In Their Ministry. (6) Effective Leaders See Relational Empowerment As Both A Means And A Goal Of Ministry. (7) Effective Leaders Evince A Growing Awareness Of Their Sense Of Destiny. It is this last one I am exploring in this article.

[342] This is a major key to an effective ministry. No Bible leader who had an effective ministry failed to have a sense of destiny. Paul is the exemplar in the N.T. Church Leadership Era. Over and over again in his epistles, Paul's makes statements that reflect on his understanding of his destiny with God.

discover for what purposes he/she was uniquely created. **Life purpose** represents the descriptive label that characterizes the underlying motivational thrust(s) that energizes a given leader to be and do and around which life begins to center. It becomes that overall centralizing ideal or accomplishment or task to which all of a leader's life is committed. **Life purpose** is the most important of four focal issues which define the focused life.[343]

Definition   A <u>life purpose</u> is a burden-like calling, a task or driving force or achievement,
                   which motivates a leader to fulfill something or to see something done.

Paul and The Destiny Pattern
Paul exemplifies the N.T. church leadership prototype for the destiny pattern.

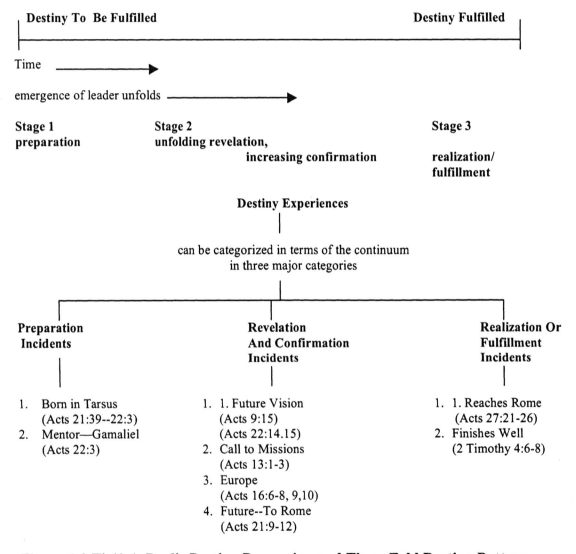

Figure 1,2 Ti 42-1. Paul's Destiny Processing and Three Fold Destiny Pattern

---

[343] A <u>focused life</u> is a life dedicated to exclusively carrying out God's unique purposes through it, by identifying the focal issues, that is, life purpose, major role, effective methodology, or ultimate contribution, which allows an increasing prioritization of life's activities around the focal issues, and results in a satisfying life of being and doing. The 4 focal issues—life purpose, major role, effective methodology, or ultimate contribution—are discovered over a lifetime.

Paul's Destiny And Ensuing Life Purpose—Progressively Seen

Paul progressively grasped his sense of destiny. God used a number of special events over time to build into Paul a more detailed awareness of his sense of destiny.

Definition   A **prime critical incident** is a special intervention (could be a series over time) in which God gives a *major value* that will flow through the life or will give *strategic direction* to narrow the leader's life work.

1. Some produce a dominant value which pervades the leader's ministry philosophy.
2. Some pinpoint a key strategic directional factor.
3. Some do both.

Table 1,2 Ti 42-1 gives seven prime critical incidents in the life of Paul. I synthesize how each of these progressively fed into Paul's life purpose.

Table 1,2 Ti 42-1. Paul's Life Purpose Unfolding

Incident	Label/ Scripture	Life Purpose
C_1	Damascus Road	My life purpose is to serve the risen Lord Jesus by witnessing to what he has shown me and will show me to Jews, Gentiles, and Kings.
C_2	Barnabas Sponsors Acts 9	My life purpose is to serve the risen Lord Jesus by witnessing to what he has shown me and will show me to Jews, Gentiles, and Kings. **I know I am to be a part of expanding Jesus' work begun in Jerusalem.**
C_3	Barnabas sponsors in Antioch Acts 11	My life purpose is to serve the risen Lord Jesus by witnessing to what he has shown me and will show me to Jews, Gentiles, and Kings. I know I am to be a part of expanding Jesus' work begun in Jerusalem. **It will involve working with a team and development of local groups of Christians.**
C_4	Apostolic Call/ Acts 13	My life purpose is to serve the risen Lord Jesus by witnessing to what he has shown me and will show me to Jews, Gentiles, and Kings. I know I am to be a part of expanding Jesus' work begun in Jerusalem. It will involve working with a team and development of local groups of Christians. **Further, I know that I will be in an itinerant ministry, having been sent by the Holy Spirit, confirmed by other leaders, to witness to Gentiles on Cyprus.**
C_5	Conflict and the Jerusalem Council/ Gospel Clarified Acts 15	My life purpose is to serve the risen Lord Jesus by witnessing to what he has shown me and will show me to Jews, Gentiles, and Kings. I know I am to be a part of expanding Jesus' work begun in Jerusalem. It will involve working with a team and development of local groups of Christians. Further, I know that I will be in an itinerant ministry, having been sent by the Holy Spirit, confirmed by other leaders, to witness to Gentiles on Cyprus. **I will be the primary person who will contextualize truth into Gentile situations. Occasionally, I will also speak truth into Jewish situations.**

C$_6$	European/ Western Gentiles Acts 16	My life purpose is to serve the risen Lord Jesus by witnessing to what he has shown me and will show me to Jews, Gentiles, and Kings. I know I am to be a part of expanding Jesus' work begun in Jerusalem. It will involve working with a team and development of local groups of Christians. Further, I know that I will be in an itinerant ministry, having been sent by the Holy Spirit, confirmed by other leaders, to witness to Gentiles on Cyprus, **Asia Minor and Europe. My ministry will thus be widespread, an itinerant ministry among Gentiles. I** will be the primary person who will contextualize truth into Gentile situations. **I know that my ministry will be pioneering, breaking open new situations to western Gentiles as well as others.** Occasionally, I will also speak truth into Jewish situations.
C$_7$	Destiny in Rome Via Jerusalem Persecution Acts 21	My life purpose is to serve the risen Lord Jesus by witnessing to what he has shown me and will show me to Jews, Gentiles, and Kings. I know I am to be a part of expanding Jesus' work begun in Jerusalem. It will involve working with a team and development of local groups of Christians. Further, I know that I will be in an itinerant ministry, having been sent by the Holy Spirit, confirmed by other leaders, to witness to Gentiles on Cyprus, Asia Minor and Europe. My ministry will thus be widespread, an itinerant ministry among Gentiles. I will be the primary person who will contextualize truth into Gentile situations. I know that my ministry will be pioneering, breaking open new situations to western Gentiles as well as others. Occasionally, I will also speak truth into Jewish situations. **I know I am destined to give my witness to Christ before high rulers.**

Conclusion

Paul finished well. One reason, he led a focused life. At the heart of that focus was the sense of destiny that drove him on to serve God. He struggled a good struggle. He finished his course. He fulfilled his life purpose. He stands as a model for us.

> 6 As for me, I am ready to be sacrificed. The time for me to depart this life is near. 7 I have run a good race.[344] I have fulfilled my God-given destiny.[345] I still have my faith intact. 8 And now for my prize, a crown of righteousness. The Lord, the righteous judge, will award it to me at that day. And not to me only, but unto all those who eagerly await his return.[346]

---

[344] Literally, this is *the good struggle I have struggled*, a use of the superlative repetitive idiom. The two words for struggle are the noun form and verb form from which we derive our words agony and agonize and refer to an Olympic athlete who is disciplining himself for a marathon or other event.

[345] Fulfilled my destiny, literally I have finished or completed (SRN 5758) a perfect action, i.e. already done it with on going results, my course (SRN 1408). Course, used three times in the N.T., refers to life's destiny, the pathway set before one to do. The destiny pattern usually follows a threefold pattern: destiny preparation, destiny revelation, and destiny fulfillment. This idea of already completing it is the use of a certainty idiom, the prophetic past. It is so certain that he speaks of it in the past tense as if it had already happened. See Ac 20:24 where Paul states his desire to finish his course. See also, Ac 13:25 where the same word refers to John the Baptist's having finished his course. See *certainty idiom, prophetic past, sense of destiny, destiny preparation, destiny revelation, destiny fulfillment,* **Glossary**. See **Article,** *8. Destiny Pattern.*

[346] Vs 4:6-8 show that Paul finished well. He is the classic case of a N.T. church leader finishing well. All six characteristics of a good finish are seen: (1) vibrant personal relationship with God; (2) have a learning posture; (3) Christ-likeness in character; (4) live by Biblical convictions; (5) leave behind ultimate contributions; (6) fulfill a sense of destiny. One of the major leadership contributions of 2Ti is this challenge to finish well, which Paul models. See *modeling,* **Glossary**. **Article,** *16. Finishing Well—Six Characteristics.*

Relevance of the Article to 1,2 Timothy

Paul had a great fishing pool from which to identify and select and develop leaders. Paul, more than any other leader in Scripture identifies by name people he influenced. This article lists those people named in scripture who Paul identified with in some way or other. Seventeen of these folks are actually listed in the Ephesians epistle and in 1,2Ti. Paul exemplifies two of the seven major leadership lessons as can be clearly seen by a study of these people associated with Paul. Lesson 5—*Effective Leaders View Leadership Selection And Development As A Priority Function In Their Ministry* and Lesson 6— *Effective Leaders See Relational Empowerment As Both A Means And A Goal Of Ministry*, certainly are evident when one sees the number of people Paul related to and how he used these relationships to move many of these folks into ministry.

43. Paul—And His Companions

Introduction

Paul developed leaders. He did this through teaching, modeling, and on-the-job training. A comparative study of his relationships with numerous leaders reveals that he exemplifies a number of mentoring roles: discipler, spiritual guide, coach, teacher, contemporary model, sponsor. He operated as a mentor with individuals. He also mentored in a team context.

Several Pauline leadership values[347] under girded this drive to develop leaders.

Leaders Must Be Concerned About Leadership Selection And Development.

Leaders Should View Personal Relationships As An Important Part Of Ministry.

A Christian Leader Ought To Have Several Life Long Mentorees Who He/She Will Help Over A Lifetime To Reach Their Potential In Leadership.

And the following two major lessons are the foundation for the above three.

Effective Leaders View Leadership Selection And Development As A Priority In Ministry.

Effective Leaders View Relational Empowerment As Both A Means And A Goal In Ministry.

This article simply points out that Paul had a personal ministry. Paul developed many leaders, his companions in ministry. It also seeks to exhort us by example.

Paul's Companions

Luke's *we sections* in Ac points out that Paul frequently had a team with him. A number of the people listed below actually traveled on teams with Paul. Others were in ministry with him in various locales. Still other were acquaintances he thought highly of. But all of them had some person.l relationship with Paul. Table 1,2 Ti 43-1 lists the many folks Paul related to personally. Many of them were leaders.

---

[347] A leadership value is an underlying assumption which affects how a leader perceives leadership and practices it. Leadership values contain strong language like should, ought, or must. Must statements are the strongest.

Table 43-1. Paul's Companions—Reflected in His Epistles

Who	Vs	Comments
Achaicus	1Co 16:17, 24	One of three men who brought Paul financial support when he was in Philippi, from the Corinthian church. Also one of three men who were present when the first letter to the church at Corinth was penned. So, he along with the other two probably supplied Paul with lots of information about the church at Corinth.
Ampliatus	Ro 16:8	A close friend in the church at Rome.
Andronicus	Ro 16:7	An apostle and Christian before Paul. Was in prison probably with Paul. Paul calls him a kinsman but whether this is a brother in Christ or physically is not certain.
Apelles	Ro 16:10	A Christian friend well thought of by Paul in the church at Rome. In his greeting he gives affirmation for this person.
Apollos	Seen 10 times in Ac, 1Co, Tit	A strong Christian worker and well known as a public rhetorician, mighty in the Scriptures. Was mentored by Priscilla and Acquilla. Associated with the church at Corinth. Late in Paul's ministry, when Titus was in Crete, Paul asked Titus to raise funds in Crete to support Apollos.
Apphia	Phm 2	A female Christian, probably the wife of Philemon. Paul loved her dearly and thought highly of her in his greeting in the Phm letter.
Aquila	Ac 18:2, 18, 26; Ro 16:3, 1Co 16:19; 2Ti 4:19.	A Jewish believer married to Priscilla. They were persecuted under Claudius and driven out of Rome. A tentmaker by trade he and his wife associated with Paul (bi-vocational; financial support) and were taught by him in the Christian faith. They were teammates with Paul and made a ministry trip with him. Paul affirmed them to the church at Rome as co-ministers with him and as those who had saved his life—putting their own lives on the line. Priscilla and Aquila apparently had house churches where ever they went. They were in Ephesus when Timothy went there to do apostolic consulting work.
Archippus	Col 4:17; Phm 1,2	A Christian worker well thought of by Paul. He ministered in the church at Colossee and in the church in Philemon's home. Paul calls him a fellow soldier—a beautiful compliment.
Aristarchus	Ac 19:29; 20:4; 27:2	A fellow preacher with Paul. He was persecuted in Ephesus. He traveled on one of Paul's teams from Ephesus to Turkey. Also accompanied Paul to Rome. Suffered in prison with Paul. Mentioned in Phm as a fellow worker.
Aristobulus	Ro 16:10	A Christian friend well thought of by Paul in the church at Rome. In his greeting he gives affirmation for this person.
Artemas	Tit 3:12	On Paul's team when he wintered in Nicopolis, late in Paul's ministry. Probably sent as a messenger to Titus on Crete.
Asyncritus	Ro 16:14	One of several Christians at Rome that Paul greeted warmly. Most likely a small group leader since he greets not only him but the Christians with him. See Ro 16:14 Salute **Asyncritus**, Phlegon, Hermas, Patrobas, Hermes, and the brethren which are with them.
Barnabas	Mentioned 33 times; Many times in Ac; 1Co 9:6, Ga 2:1,9, 13 ; Col 4:10	A mentor sponsor of Paul who brought Paul into the work at Antioch. He led the first missionary team (Paul and his nephew John Mark). Paul became the leader of that team when it moved from Cyprus to Asia minor. Barnabas continued to sponsor Paul with the Jerusalem church. His generosity and giving values impacted Paul. He and Paul had a falling out and split before Paul · second missionary journey. Paul still thought highly of him as seen by his mentioning him in 1Co.

Cephas	1Co 1:12; 3:22; 9:5; 15:5; Gal 1:18; 2:9, 11, 14.	Paul uses this name for Peter several times. Paul recognized and respected Peter as the leader of the Jewish Christian movement. He also clashed with Peter concerning contextualizing the Gospel. Peter respected Paul and recognized that God had revealed truth through him—Scriptural truth.
Claudia	2Ti 4:21	A Christian at Rome. Paul mentions her in his last words to Timothy in 2Ti. She is probably a local house church leader or small group leader since Paul singles our her name and then says also all the Christians. Probably among those Christians giving support to Paul in Rome.
Clement	Php 4:3	A fellow Christian worker with Paul in Phillipi. Paul ask the unnamed pastoral leader at Philippi to aid Clement.
Crescens	2Ti 4:10	Crescens was part of a team around Paul in his second Roman imprisonment. He is mentioned as having left Paul. The context is not clear whether he was on some mission or left for some other reason.
Crispus	Ac 18:8; 1Co 1:14	He was the chief ruler of the Jewish synagogue at Ephesus. Paul led him to Christ. And Paul baptised him. Crispus led his family to the Lord, always a difficult thing with Jewish people.
Demas	Col 4:10; Phm 24; 2Ti 4:10	Demas was part of a team around Paul in his second Roman imprisonment along with Luke and Titus. He is mentioned as having deserted Paul to go to Thessalonica. The context indicates this was not pleasing to Paul. He loved this present world (does that mean he didn't want to be martyred with Paul or that he loved worldliness?)
Epaphroditus	Php 2:25; 4:18	Took a gift from the Php church to Paul while Paul was in prison. He helped Paul while Paul was imprisoned. Nearly died of some sickness. He was a fellow Christian worker with Paul. Paul sponsored him to the Philippians.
Epaphras	Col 1:7; 4:12; Phm 23.	A fellow minister of the Gospel, from the church in Colosse and probably sent out by them. Paul speaks very highly of him calling him a faithful servant of Christ, an intercessor praying for the maturity of the church at Colosse. He was also a fellow prisoner with Paul.
Epenetus	Ro 16:5	Paul speaks highly of this Christian calling him beloved and identifying him as the first Christian in the Achaia (region surrounding Corinth). Probably was in Rome at the time of Paul's writing the Roman epistle.
Erastus	Ac 19:22; Ro 16:23; 2Ti 4:20	He was a missionary with Paul, on one of his traveling teams on his third missionary journey. He was a city treasurer at Corinth so a man of influence. He is mentioned as staying in Corinth when Paul was in prison the second time in Rome. He was one of several people, probably a support team for Paul, who heard Paul dictate the letter to the Romans. One of the team took the dictation.
Eubulus	2Ti 4:21	A Christian at Rome. Paul mentions him in his last words to Timothy in 2Ti. He is probably a local house church leader or small group leader since Paul singles our his name and then says also all the Christians. Probably among those Christians giving support to Paul in Rome.
Eunice	2Ti 1:5	Timothy's mother. A woman of real faith whom Paul highly respected. She gave Timothy a foundation in the O.T. Scriptures and modeled a life of faith and piety for him.
Euodias	Ph 4:2,3	A woman who co-labored in the Lord with Paul at Philippi. She was having problems with another woman, Syntyche, in the church at the time Paul wrote the Php epistle. He spoke highly of her as he entreated her to make up her differences with Syntyche.

Fortunatus	1Co 16:17,24	One of three men who brought Paul financial support when he was in Philippi, from the Corinthian church. Also one of three men who were present when the first letter to the church at Corinth was penned. So, he along with the other two probably supplied Paul with lots of information about the church at Corinth.
Gaius	Ro 16:23; 1Co 1:14	Gaius was led to Christ and baptized by Paul in the city of Corinth. Later Paul stayed in his home, at the time of the writing of the epistle to the Romans. Gaius was part of a small group of people that heard Paul dictate the letter to the Romans.
Hermas	Ro 16:14	A Christian at Rome that Paul greeted warmly. Most likely a small group leader since he greets not only him but the Christians with him.
Hermes	Ro 16:14	A Christian at Rome that Paul greeted warmly. Most likely a small group leader since he greets not only him but the Christians with him.
Hermogenes	2Ti 1:15	He is described as one who has turned away from Paul.
Herodion	Ro 16:11	A Christian at Rome that Paul greeted warmly. Paul identified him as a kinsman (spiritual or other, it is not clear).
Jason	Ro 16:21	Maybe a relation of Paul. One of a privileged group who heard Paul dictate the letter to the church in Rome (Timothy, Lucius, Jason, Sosipater, Tertius, Gaius, Erastus and Quartus).
John Mark (Marcus)	Ac 12: 25; 13:5, 13; 15:37, 39; Col 4:10; Phm 24; 2Ti 4:11; 1Pe 5:13	Also called Mark or John. John Mark was a relative of Barnabas (most likely a cousin or nephew). He was on Barnabas and Paul's missionary team which went to Cyprus. He quit the team when it went on to Asia minor. Paul would not have him on his second missionary journey. Paul and Barnabas split over this. Later he went with Barnabas back to Cyprus and Paul took Silas with him on his 2nd missionary journey. Later Paul received him back and sponsored him. Mark also served with Peter and is the author of the Gospel of Mark.
Julia	Ro 16:15	A Christian woman at Rome greeted warmly by Paul. Probably a local church leader since Paul also mentions the saints that are with her.
Junia	Ro 16:7	A female apostle and Christian before Paul. Was in prison probably with Paul. Paul calls her a kinsperson but whether this is a sister in Christ or physically is not certain.
Linus	2Ti 4:21	A Christian at Rome. Paul mentions him in his last words to Timothy in 2Ti. He is probably a local house church leader or small group leader since Paul singles our his name and then says also all the Christians. Probably among those Christians giving support to Paul in Rome.
Lois	2Ti 1:5	Timothy's grand mother. A woman of real faith whom Paul highly respected. She along with Timothy's mother Eunice gave Timothy a foundation in the O.T. Scriptures and modeled a life of faith and piety for him.
Lucius	Ro 16:21	One of a privileged group who heard Paul dictate the letter to the church in Rome (Timothy, Lucius, Jason, Sosipater, Tertius, Gaius, Erastus and Quartus). He could possibly be the prophet who was at Antioch in Ac 13:1 when Paul and Barnabas received their great sense of destiny call to missions.
Luke	2Co 13:14; Col 4:14; 2Ti 4:11; Phm 24	Luke was called the beloved physician. He was on one of Paul's traveling teams, the second missionary journey. He went to Rome with Paul (including the shipwreck). He ministered faithfully to Paul in his imprisonments. He authored the Gospel of Luke and the book of Acts. Both these writings reflect the deep impact that Paul made on Luke.
Mary	Ro 16:6	A Christian at Rome who was noted for her ministry of helps to Paul.
Narcissus	Ro 16:11	A Christian at Rome who Paul greeted warmly. Probably a small group leader or house church leader as Paul also mentions his household (could be only his kin or a housechurch set up).
Nereus	Ro 16:15	A Christian at Rome that Paul greeted warmly. Probably a local church leader since Paul also mentions the saints that are with him.
Nymphas	Col 4:15	Said to have been a wealthy and zealous Christian in Laodicea. Hosted a house church and was probably a small group leader.

Olympas	Ro 16:15	A Christian at Rome that Paul greeted warmly. Probably a local church leader since Paul also mentions the saints that are with them.
Onesimus	Col 4:9, 18; Phm 10, 11;	A runaway slave whom Paul led to the Lord while he was in prison in Rome. After some mentor discipling, Paul sent him back to his master, Philemon, a Christian who had a church in his home. This was a challenge both to Onesimus and Philemon, showing the power of the Gospel to break up a major social institution, slavery. Tradition had it that Onesimus became a very influential church leader in the region.
Onesiph-orus	2Ti 1:16; 4:19	This man ministered unashamedly to Paul during his second imprisonment. He was probably a small group leader or elder in the work at Ephesus.
Patrobas	Ro 16:14	A Christian at Rome that Paul greeted warmly. Most likely a small group leader since he greets not only him but the Christians with him.
Persis	Ro 16:12	A Christian woman at Rome. Paul uses the word beloved in describing her and that she labored much in the Lord's work.
Philemon	Phm 1. See whole book.	A wealthy landowner in the Colosse region. He became a Christian under Paul's two year teaching ministry at Ephesus. Philemon hosted a house church. Paul asked him a special favor—to take back a runaway slave named Onesimus. He gave strong affirmation to Philemon for his Christian testimony.
Philologus	Ro 16:15	A Christian at Rome that Paul greeted warmly. Probably a local church leader since Paul also mentions the saints that are with him.
Phlegon	Ro 16:14	A Christian at Rome that Paul greeted warmly. Most likely a small group leader since he greets not only him but the Christians with him.
Phoebe	Ro 16:1	A fellow leader, female, in the church at Corinth. Paul sponsored her to the church in Rome.
Phygellus	2Ti 1:15	He is described as one who turned away from Paul.
Priscilla	Ac 18:2, 18, 26; Ro 16:3, 1Co 16:19; 2Ti 4:19.	A Jewish woman, a believer married to Acquila. They were persecuted under Claudius and driven out of Rome. A tentmaker by trade he and his wife associated with Paul and were taught by him in the Christian faith. They were teammates with Paul and made a ministry trip with him. Paul affirmed them to the church at Rome as co-ministers with him and as those who had saved his life—putting their own lives on the line. Priscilla and Aquila apparently had house churches where ever they went. Their final ministry was in Ephesus. They were in that church when Timothy went there to do apostolic consulting work. Priscilla was apparently the word gifted person of the pair.
Pudens	2Ti 4:21	A Christian at Rome. Paul mentions him in his last words to Timothy in 2Ti. He is probably a local house church leader or small group leader since Paul singles our his name and then says also all the Christians. Probably among those Christians giving support to Paul in Rome.
Quartus	Ro 16:23	One of a privileged group who heard Paul dictate the letter to the church in Rome (Timothy, Lucius, Jason, Sosipater, Tertius, Gaius, Erastus and Quartus).
Rufus	Ro 16:13	A Christian at Rome. Paul makes a strong destiny statement about him. He also praises Rufus' mother whom he addresses as his own mother—so close was the relationship.
Sosipater	Ro 16:21	One of a privileged group who heard Paul dictate the letter to the church in Rome (Timothy, Lucius, Jason, Sosipater, Tertius, Gaius, Erastus and Quartus).
Sosthenes	1Co 1:1	Co-authored 1Co with Paul. A respected leader in Corinth. He most likely filled Paul in on many issues of the church situation at Corinth.
Stachys	Ro 16:9	A Christian in Rome greatly loved by Paul.

Stephanas	1Co 16: 15, 17,24	One of three men who **brought** Paul financial support when he was in Philippi, from the Corinthian church. Also one of three men who were present when the first letter to the church at Corinth was penned. So, he along with the other two probably supplied Paul with lots of information about the church at Corinth. Paul asks the Corinthian church to support this man who has gone into full time ministry.
Silvanus	2Co 1:19; 1Th 1:1; 2Th 1:1	A Roman citizen and fellow missionary. A part of Paul's traveling team. Co-authored two books, 1,2Th. A respected leader by Paul.
Syntyche	Php 4:2,3	A woman who co-labored in the Lord with Paul at Philippi. She was having problems with another woman, Euodias, in the church at the time Paul wrote the Php epistle. He spoke highly of her as he entreated her to make up her differences with Euodias.
Tertius	Ro 16:22	One of a privileged group who heard Paul dictate the Roman epistle (Timothy, Lucius, Jason, Sosipater, Tertius, Gaius, Erastus and Quartus).
Timothy	Occurs 31 times	The most intimate follower of Paul. Traveled with him on many missionary trips. Was sent on ministry trips for Paul. Best known for his apostolic consultation ministry at Ephesus. One of a privileged group who heard Paul dictate the letter to the church in Rome (Timothy, Lucius, Jason, Sosipater, Tertius, Gaius, Erastus and Quartus). Received two special letters while at Ephesus which reveals the mentoring relationship between Paul and Timothy. These two letters are the top two leadership books in the N.T. Church Leadership Era. In 2Ti Paul passes the baton of leadership over to Timothy.
Titus	Occurs 15 times	Next to Timothy, Paul's closest worker. He was given some of the toughest ministry assignments including one at Corinth dealing with finances and authority problems. He also was given an apolstolic assignment in Crete. The book of Tit written to sponsor him is the third most important book on leadership in the N.T. Church Leadership Era.
Trophimus	2Ti 4:20	He was one of a small group of people close to Paul during Paul's second imprisonment. He became sick and was left at Miletum.
Tryphena	Ro 16:12	A Christian woman in Rome who was described as a worker for the Lord.
Tryphosa	Ro 16:12	A Christian woman in Rome who was described as a worker for the Lord
Tychicus	Eph 6:21, 24; Col 4:7, 18; 2Ti 4:12; Tit 3:12	A Christian worker, part of Paul's support team during his second imprisonment. He also was involved in transcribing and carrying the Ephesian and Colossian letters and traveled with Onesimus as he carried the Philemon letter. Tychicus was well thought of by Paul—described as a beloved brother. He was sent on a mission to Ephesus during the time of the writing of 2Ti.
Urbanus	Ro 16:9	A Christian worker in Rome who had helped Paul in the past (financially or ministry wise—unclear).
Zenas	Tit 3:13	A lawyer whom Titus was to bring to Paul.

Some Observations

Several important observations from Paul's co-ministry and relationship with others should be noted.

1. Paul believe in affirmation both public and private. Affirmation is one of the strongest means a leader has in encouraging emerging workers. Frequently, affirmation involves use of Goodwin's Expectation Principle: *Emerging leaders tend to live up to the genuine expectations of leaders they respect.* Paul not only affirms but challenges through the affirmation.

2. Paul personally related to leaders all up and down the levels of leadership: local church members, lay leaders in general, bi-vocational leaders at small group level, local church elders, fellow bi-vocational workers, full time workers of regional influence, leaders of Christian movement in Jerusalem, etc. He was at home with kings, ambassadors, and with common folk.

3. Paul used networking power as a means of strong influence in numerous leadership ways. He could not have accomplished all that he did with out all kind of help from people whom God had given to him in relationships.
4. Most of Paul's companions, whom he knew at one time or another and supported him, stayed faithful to him. Only a very small few are said to have fallen away from him.
5. A number of Paul's companions were women who ministered in local church situations. Paul did not have a problem with women in ministry (at least from a giftedness or theological standpoint; yes, there were cultural problems).

Conclusion

Paul certainly sets a standard for those who would invest personally in the lives of others. He exemplifies one who held this important value.

Leaders Should View Personal Relationships As An Important Part Of Ministry.

Leaders today with their thoughts on bigness and success may well miss this most important aspect of ministry.

See *mentor; mentoree; mentoring; mentor discipler; mentor spiritual guide; mentor coach; mentor teacher; mentor contemporary model; mentor sponsor;* **Glossary**. See **Articles**, *47. Paul—Mentor For Many; 45. Paul—Developer Par Excellence; 69. Timothy—A Beloved Son in the Faith.*

Relevance of the Article to 1,2 Timothy

Paul's life is about to end (2 Ti 4:6). He has just gone through several years of deep processing via imprisonment and various trials. He has been set aside from direct ministry (except in the various prison settings). This has forced him to write the prison epistles, which have greatly blessed us today. Deep processing can be very fruitful even though painful. The 1,2Ti epistles have blessed apostolic and pastoral workers down through church history. Paul knew first hand about deep processing and God's use of it to shape a leader.

44. Paul—Deep Processing

Introduction

Do you know someone who has quit the full time ministry? Have you ever felt like quitting the full time ministry? Did you know that there is a large dropout from full time ministry? Well if ever a Christian worker had reasons to quit, it was Paul at the time he wrote 2Co. He was in his mid-fifties and had over 20 years of tough ministry experience behind him.

Here is what he faced. Paul's first letter to Corinth was probably written at Ephesus.[348] Shortly after writing it, he was forced to flee because of the hubbub caused by the shrine makers honoring the goddess Diana.[349] Paul went on to Troas to revisit churches in Macedonia. He intended to travel south to Corinth and visit churches in Achaia.[350] He did eventually get there and stayed about three months.[351] It was in the interval between leaving Ephesus and reaching Corinth that he wrote again to the Corinthians. At the time he was going through deep processing. What he was going through was enough to make any Christian worker give up?

What was he facing? No news from Titus.[352] He had sent Titus to Corinth to deal with some of the problems there. He was anxious about what was happening there. He describes this time in Macedonia as a time when he had *no rest within and deeply troubled from without* as well. The church at Corinth appeared to be in revolt against his leadership. The churches in Galatia were falling away to another Gospel. He had narrowly escaped with his life from the uproar in Ephesus. In addition to disappointment and apprehensiveness, Paul had a physical illness which was almost fatal. Paul described it in his own words,

> 8 I want you to know, dear Christian friends, of the very trying experiences[353] which we faced in the province of Asia. I was overwhelmed,[354] beyond my ability[355] to cope with it. I thought[356] I was going to die. 9 I concluded[357] that I would die. 2Co 1:8,9.

---

[348] See 1Co 16:8.

[349] See Ac 19 for the vignette.

[350] See Ac 20:1,2.

[351] See Ac 20:3.

[352] See 2Co 2:13.

[353]*Trying experiences* (SRN 2347) represents the same Greek word used several times in 2Co 1:3,4 and often translated as tribulation or affliction.

[354]*Overwhelmed* (SRN 5236) is a translation of a word meaning excessively so (**KJV** beyond measure).

[355]*Ability* (SRN 1411) is a translation of the Greek word, power.

[356]*Thought* (SRN 1820) is a very strong word meaning despaired or to be destitute. It probably would not be too strong to say Paul was depressed.

But look at what he learned.

> But as a result I learned not to trust myself but to rely on God, who can raise the dead. 10 He delivered me from that tremendous near death experience. He continues to deliver. He will do so in the future too! 11 You play a part in this by praying for us. As a result, because many prayed, many will give thanks to God for his answered prayer—our safety.[358]

This experiential acknowledging of total dependence on God in a deep processing situation is usually a turning point in this shaping activity by God. Paul was at death's door. To all outward appearances his life and work were coming to an end—and not on a good note. His life, his work, and the fate of the potential of the worldwide movement of Christianity in the Gentile world all hung in the balance. Probably never before had he felt himself so helpless, so beaten down and disconcerted, as he was on that journey from Ephesus to Macedonia. He was laid up sick, unto death, and awaited Titus, not even sure he would last long enough to see Titus. And Titus came. And the news was not all good. For whatever Titus shared prompted a further letter to Corinth. Paul's apostolic authority was in question and with it the whole of the future ministry to the Gentiles. So I do not overstate it when I say Paul knew about deep processing.

If Paul ever felt like quitting, and I am sure he did, this Corinthian thing was top of the list for quitting time. If he wasn't gray headed before I am sure he had gray hairs after this thing. Now listen carefully. This was Paul's finest hour. Two other times run a close second: the Philippian epistle—he is isolated and in jail. 2 Timothy—he is in jail and awaiting death, near the end of his life. But this is his finest hour. What you are in deep processing is what you really are!

Definition | Deep processing refers to a collection of process items which intensely work on deepening the maturity of a leader. The set includes the following process items: conflict, ministry conflict, crisis, life crisis, leadership backlash and isolation.

Paul knew what deep processing was. He also knew the benefits of it.

Deep Processing—Some Shaping Activities

While God may use a number of things to take a leader deep with himself, several occur so often with leaders that they can be labeled and described. Six common deep processing items are given.

Definition | The conflict process item refers to those instances in a leader's life-history in which God uses conflict, whether personal or ministry related to develop the leader in dependence upon God, faith, and inner-life.

Definition | The ministry conflict process item refers to those instances in a ministry situation, in which a leader learns lessons via the positive and negative aspects of conflict with regards to: 1. the nature of conflict, 2. possible ways to resolve conflict, 3. possible ways to avoid conflict, 4. ways to creatively use conflict, and 5. perception of God's personal shaping through the conflict.

---

[357]*Concluded* (SRN 610) represents the noun word usually translated as *sentence* or *judgment*. Hamel comments: 2Co. 1:9 ... the meaning is "on asking myself whether I should come out safe from mortal peril, I answered, I must Die." Paul was in deep trouble.

[358] Paul recognizes an important dynamic. *Transparency and vulnerability, in sharing by a leader, allows others to identify with and pray more fervently and with understanding for God's answers.* By this sharing then, God receives much more praise and honor because many are partnering with Him. Prayer backers make a big difference in the life of a leader who can share openly with them. Many leaders fear sharing vulnerably and openly. They miss out on one of God's resources for them. Paul models here the kind of open sharing that leaders need to do. See **Article**, *Daniel—Leaders and Prayer Backing.*

Definition   <u>Crisis process items</u> refer to those special intense situations of pressure in human situations which are used by God to test and teach dependence

Definition   A <u>life crisis process item</u> refers to a crisis situation characterized by life threatening intense pressure in human affairs in which the meaning and purpose of life are searched out with a result that the leader has experienced God in a new way as the source, sustainer, and focus of life

Definition   <u>Isolation processing</u> refers to the setting aside of a leader from normal ministry involvement in its natural context usually for an extended time in order to experience God in a new or deeper way.

Definition   The <u>leadership backlash process</u> item refers to the reactions of followers, other leaders within a group, and/or Christians outside the group, to a course of action taken by a leader because of various ramifications that arise due to the action taken. The situation is used in he leader's life to test perseverance, clarity of vision, and faith.

Paul and Deep Processing

Paul faced all of these kinds of deep processing—these shaping activities of God which make a person of God. How did Paul face these kinds of shaping activities and not give up? Let me suggest several under girding values that made the difference. They are contained in the following verses.

1. 2Co 4:1
    1 Because God in His mercy has given me this ministry, I am not going to become discouraged and give up.

Let me paraphrase it emphatically.

   Therefore since God put me in this ministry I am not going to quit!

2. 1Co 9:24-27
    24 Don't you know that those in a race all run, but only one wins the prize? Run in such a way that you will receive the prize. 25 And everyone who competes[359] for the prize exercises real discipline[360] in order to be ready. Now they do it to win a fleeting prize.[361] We do it for an eternal prize. 26 Therefore I, personally, run my course with definite purpose, to win—to finish well. Thus I box making my punches count. 27 So I discipline myself and exercise strict control, lest after preaching to others, I myself should become a loser.[362]

3. 2 Co 12:9
    9 His answer was, "My enabling presence is all you need. My power shows forth much stronger in your weakness." So you can see then, why I boast about my weaknesses.

---

[359] The word translated as *competes* (SRN 75) is the word from which we get our word agonize. It means really struggles (to get ready and participate). Present day marathon runners do train this rigorously.

[360] The word translated as *Exercises real discipline* (SRN 1467) means to practice self-control. It described athletes who were preparing for the Olympic Games. Suc, an athlete abstained from unwholesome food, wine, and sexual indulgence.

[361] *Prize* (SRN 4735) the wreath or garland which was given as a prize to victors in public games.

[362] This whole context, 9:24-27, is promoting one of the important enhancements that helps leaders finish well. Discipline in the life, is one of five enhancement factors that have been identified with effective leaders who have finished well. All kinds of disciplines, especially spiritual disciplines, will be needed and used with purpose in order to continue toward the finish. Paul is in his 50s here, a time when leaders tend to plateau. Disciplines are needed. See **Articles**, *15. Finishing Well—5 Factors Enhancing; 61. Spiritual Disciplines.*

Christ's power will work through me. Therefore I will boast all the more gladly about my weaknesses, so that Christ's power may rest on me.

4.   Acts 26:15-20
   "Then I asked, `Who are you, Lord?' "`I am Jesus, whom you are persecuting,' the Lord replied.   16 `Now get up and stand on your feet. I have appeared to you to appoint you as a servant and as a witness of what you have seen of me and what I will show you.   17 I will rescue you from your own people and from the Gentiles. I am sending you to them 18 to open their eyes and turn them from darkness to light, and from the power of Satan to God, so that they may receive forgiveness of sins and a place among those who are sanctified by faith in me.'   19 "So then, King Agrippa, **I was faithfully obedient to this heavenly mandate.** 20 First to those in Damascus, then to those in Jerusalem and in all Judea, and to the Gentiles also, I preached that they should repent and turn to God and prove their repentance by their deeds."

Let me suggest four reasons why Paul persevered in ministry. The first two are from the human side. Paul took responsibility. The last two are from the divine side. Paul counted on God taking responsibility too.

1. He had a sense of responsibility.

1 Because God in His mercy has given me this ministry, I am not going to become discouraged and give up.[363] 2Co 4:1

2. He was Disciplined With A Purpose. He wanted to finish well.
Listen to my paraphrase of 1Co 9:24-27. It was the motivational secret underlying one great leader's sustaining his life and ministry.

I am serious about finishing well in my Christian ministry. I discipline myself for fear that after challenging others into the Christian life I myself might become a casualty. 1Co 9:24-27.

Paul was aware that many did not make it. He was in his 50s; a time when Christian leaders tend to plateau. He didn't want that. So he did something about it. Did it work? More on this later.

3. He counted on Experiencing The Grace Of God.
There are three great leaders during the Church Era of leadership: Peter, John, Paul. All three knew this under girding principle. Their final words confirm it.

But grow in the **grace** and knowledge of our Lord and Savior Jesus Christ. To him be glory both now and forever! Amen. 2Pe 3:18

The **grace** of the Lord Jesus be with God's people. Amen. Rev 22:21

The Lord be with your spirit. **Grace** be with you. 2Ti 4:22

It is interesting how each of them came to the same inescapable conclusion. You will not make it in the Christian life without grace. Now grace as described here is not unmerited favor—not referring to our standing before God. It is referring to an enabling energy of God.

Definition   **Grace** is the inspirational, enabling presence of God in a life which encourages one to persevere in Victory throughout life's circumstances.

---

[363] This is one of Paul's stronger expressions of his personally embracing the stewardship model. His call from God, his anointing by God and his sense of destiny are behind these words. *See Stewardship Model,* **Glossary**. See **Articles**, *10. Entrustment—A Leadership Responsibility, 25. Jesus' Five Leadership Models: Shepherd, Harvest, Steward, Servant, Intercessor.*

So Paul was not just talking lightly when he said in 2Co 12:9,

> 9 His answer was, "My enabling presence is all you need. My power shows forth much stronger in your weakness." So you can see then, why I boast about my weaknesses. Christ's power will work through me. Therefore I will boast all the more gladly about my weaknesses, so that Christ's power may rest on me. 2Co 12:9.

You will not make it apart from knowing and counting upon this grace. The second reason Paul profited from deep processing and made it through it was that he knew how to experience the grace of God, that enabling presence of God.

4. He had a strong Sense Of Destiny Integrated Into A Life Purpose.

So then, King Agrippa, I was faithfully obedient to this heavenly mandate. Ac 26:19.

But the most important reason for not giving up, not dropping out of ministry, not quitting: a strong sense of destiny that imparted a **life purpose**.[364] His life was tightly integrated, that is, extremely focused around a solid life purpose. In a nutshell, Paul had a sense of destiny. And that destiny focused his life and enabled him to make it through deep processing. Notice his triumphant finish.

> 6 As for me, I am ready to be sacrificed. The time for me to depart this life is near. 7 I have run a good race. I have fulfilled my God-given destiny.[365] I still have my faith intact. 8 And now for my prize, a crown of righteousness. The Lord, the righteous judge, will award it to me at that day. And not to me only, but unto all those who eagerly await his return.[366] 2Ti 4:6-8.

A Major Insight—Paul's Inner-Life Attitude

Paul had a particular attitude about deep processing which made all the difference in his life and ministry. I have labeled it a *Sovereign Mindset*.

---

[364] A <u>life purpose</u> is a burden-like calling, a task or driving force or achievement, which motivates a leader to fulfill something or to see something done. This is the core focal issue and around which a life is integrated over a lifetime. See **Articles**, *Life Purpose, Biblical Examples; 42. Paul—A Sense of Destiny; 8. Destiny Pattern.*

[365] Fulfilled my destiny, literally I have finished or completed (SRN 5758) a perfect action, i.e. already done it with on going results, my course (SRN 1408). Course, used three times in the N.T., refers to life's destiny, the pathway set before one to do. The destiny pattern usually follows a threefold pattern: destiny preparation, destiny revelation, and destiny fulfillment. This idea of already completing it is the use of a certainty idiom, the prophetic past. It is so certain that he speaks of it in the past tense as if it had already happened. See Ac 20:24 where Paul states his desire to finish his course. See also, Ac 13:25 where the same word refers to John the Baptist's having finished his cou se. See *certainty idiom, prophetic past, sense of destiny, destiny preparation, destiny revelation, destiny fulfillment,* **Glossary**. See **Articles**, *8. The Destiny Pattern; 42. Paul—A Sense of Destiny.*

[366] Vs 4:6-8 show that Paul finished well. He is the classic case of a N.T. church leader finishing well. All six characteristics of a good finish are seen: (1) vibrant personal relationship with God; (2) have a learning posture; (3) Christ-likeness in character; (4) live by Biblical convictions; (5) leave behind ultimate contributions; (6) fulfill a sense of destiny. One of the major leadership contributions of 2Ti is this challenge to finish well, which Paul models. See *modeling,* **Glossary**. Article, *16. Finishing Well—Six Characteristics.*

Definition   A <u>sovereign mindset</u>[367] is an attitude demonstrated by the Apostle Paul in which he
tended to see God's working in the events and activities that shaped his life, whether or
not they were positive and good or negative and bad. He tended to see God's purposes in
these shaping activities and to make the best of them.

There were four keys to Paul's getting and maintaining a sovereign mindset:
1. Paul recognized God's hand in life happenings—no matter who or what the immediate cause.
2. Paul submitted to God's deeper purposes in life happenings.
3. Paul learned and used the lessons derived from these life happenings.
4. Paul shared those lessons (and God's provision in them) with others.

Conclusion

Some one has said, "All great leaders walk with a limp!" The allusion is to Jacob's deep experience
with God, wrestling with the Angel of God, and thereafter always walking with a limp due to the injury
sustained. Now this of course is a hyperbolic description of something important. Stated in less colorful
language,

> **God matures leaders He uses via shaping activities that deepen their walk with
> God and increase their effectiveness for God.**

These activities for the most part are not pleasant. They may involve physical suffering, or persecution, or
crises in the life. In short they will force the leader to go deep with God in order to survive in ministry. Or
to say it another way, all leaders will go through some deep processing as they serve the Lord. Some
leaders will be repeatedly shaped with deep processing. A very few leaders will experience it to an extent
not seen in ordinary leaders. Such a leader was Paul. He was greatly used by God. He was greatly shaped
by deep processing.

Two common reactions by leaders in deep processing include:

1. **Turn away from God** (Well, if this is the way God is I don't need or want God!).
2. **Turn toward God. Go deep with God** (God will meet me and take me into more intimacy in this
processing and I will walk away from it with God's lessons in my life. I will benefit from this!).

Don't wait till you are in deep processing to make up your mind which of these you will do. In deep
processing you most likely will not be able to think clearly. Decide now, as an act of the will, that when
deep processing comes, you will go deep with God. And don't forget the basic lessons Paul gives in 2Co
1:3-7, a foundational passage for deep processing.

1. God will meet you in deep processing.
2. You are helped in order to help.
3. Deep processing tests your own belief in the sufficiency of Christ.
4. Your own development through deep processing gives hope that your followers can also know the
sufficiency of Christ in their deep processing.

You are modeling and never with more impact than when you are in deep processing.

---

[367] Sovereign Mindset is a Pauline leadership value seen all through 2Co. *Leaders ought to see God's hand
in their circumstances as part of His plan for developing them as leaders.* See **Article**, *58. Sovereign
Mindset.*

Relevance of the Article to 1,2 Timothy

The Ephesian situation illustrates how Paul used ministry situations to develop leaders. Timothy was sent on several missions. This important mission to the Ephesian church was his final mission before being released into his own Apostolic ministry. Paul is helpful to give Timothy advice and to sponsor him in the eyes of the Ephesian leaders. Paul believed in on-the-job training. He also took risks in doing this. Timothy could have failed. I don't think he did. I believe he lived up to the expectations Paul had of him as a leader. Paul developed people. Timothy was a case in point. This article examines some of Paul's approaches to developing leaders. Mentoring was certainly involved. Training in a team context was also.

45. Paul—Developer Par Excellence

Introduction

Paul selected and trained leaders. No matter where he was or what actual ministry he was actively pursuing he was always developing those around him. He demonstrates, forcefully, two of the major leadership lessons observed from comparative studies of effective leaders.[368]

> **Effective leaders view leadership selection and development as a priority in their ministry.**

> **Effective leaders see relational empowerment as both a means and a goal of ministry.**

Paul was a developer of leaders.

Two Pauline leadership values explain this bent for Paul. A leadership value is an underlying assumption which affects how a leader perceives leadership and practices it. Let me state them first as Pauline leadership values and then generalize them for possible application in other leader's lives.

Value 1 Leadership Development

Statement of Value	Paul felt he must identify potential leadership and develop it for ministry in the church.
Generalized	Leaders must be concerned about leadership selection and development.

Value 2 Personal Ministry

Statement of Value	Paul saw that in his own life he should use personal relationships as a strong means for doing ministry.
Generalized	Leaders should view personal relationships as an important part of ministry.

---

[368] I have identified seven which repeatedly occur in effective leaders: 1. Life Time Perspective—Effective Leaders View Present Ministry In Terms Of A Life Time Perspective. 2. Learning Posture—Effective Leaders Maintain A Learning Posture Throughout Life. 3. Spiritual Authority—Effective Leaders Value Spiritual Authority As A Primary Power Base. 4. Dynamic Ministry Philosophy—Effective Leaders Who Are Productive Over A Lifetime Have A Dynamic Ministry Philosophy Which Is Made Up Of An Unchanging Core And A Changing Periphery Which Expands Due To A Growing Discovery Of Giftedness, Changing Leadership Situations, And Greater Understanding Of The Scriptures. 5. Leadership Selection And Development—Effective Leaders View Leadership Selection And Development As A Priority Function In Their Ministry. 6. Relational Empowerment—Effective Leaders See Relational Empowerment As Both A Means And A Goal Of Ministry. 7. Sense Of Destiny—Effective Leaders Evince A Growing Awareness Of Their Sense Of Destiny. See the **Article,** *29. Leadership Lessons—Seven Major Identified.*

These two values are at the heart of being a developer.

Defining a Developer

What is a developer? Let me define it.

Definition   A <u>developer</u> is a person with a mentoring bent who readily sees potential in an emerging leader and finds ways to help move that emerging leader on to becoming an effective leader.

Developers are mentors who have a variety of mentoring methods. Mentoring is a relational experience in which one person, the mentor, empowers another person, the mentoree, by a transfer of resources. The resources which empower can be habits, skills, perspectives, specific advice, training, connection to other resources, etc..

What does it take to be a developer? It takes the ability to do several key mentoring functions. A developer is a mentor who usually uses three or more of the following mentoring functions effectively in developing people:

Mentor Function	Basic Empowerment
Discipler	basic habits of Christian living
Spiritual Guide	perspective on spiritual growth
Coach	basic skills usually related to doing ministry
Counselor	perspective and advice to meet situational and growth needs
Teacher	basic information that applies to the emerging leader's situation
Model	demonstrates values and skills for possible emulation
Sponsor	watches over the mentorees development and makes sure doors are open for development to potential

Paul operated in all the above mentor functions. This is best seen in his developing ministry with Timothy. Frequently, his development involved a traveling team ministry using on-the-job experience. Leaders whom he worked with and developed include: Priscilla, Acquila, Timothy, Titus, Luke, Silas, Epaphras, Archippus, John Mark, Aristarchus, Philemon, Onesimus and many others.

Developers are concerned about the future of ministry. Paul was. Paul represents the most prominent leader in the Church leadership Period. He is an important model. We need to learn from his life. Paul The Developer sets the pace for us, concerning leading with a developmental bias.

No organization or church will last long with effectiveness if it is not developing people. Churches and Christian organizations, without exception, need developers. What should they do? They should identify developers, reward developers, help the developers develop themselves, and help promote mentoring relationships so that these developers not only have access to emerging leaders but are encouraged in behalf of the organization or church to develop people. And keep it simple. No programs. Just relationships.[369]

See Also **Articles,** *29. Leadership Lessons—Seven Major Lessons Identified; 51. Pauline Leadership Values; 38. Mentoring—An Informal Training Model; 69. Timothy A Beloved Son of the Faith; 43. Paul— and His Companions; Leading With A Developmental Bias.*

---

[369] Most developers need the freedom to move a mentoring relationship along the most natural lines for developing it. They can work within programs of development which are broad enough to let them freely identify mentoring needs and pursue them.

Relevance of the Article to 1,2 Timothy

Paul exemplifies the prayer macro lesson—IF A LEADER IS CALLED TO A MINISTRY THEN HE/SHE IS CALLED TO INTERCEDE FOR THAT MINISTRY. Paul prayed for the Ephesian church as well he did for all the churches he was involved with. Paul, then, relates well to the philosophical leadership model introduced by Jesus—The Intercessor Model. See **Article 25**. *Jesus—5 Leadership models; Shepherd, Harvest, Steward, Servant, Intercessor.* See especially in his epistle to the Ephesians the beautiful prayers that Paul prayed for this church.

46. Paul—Intercessor Leader

Introduction

A prayer macro lesson identified in every leadership era, and specifically highlighted in Moses, Samuel, Jesus, and Paul's ministries states,

Intercession Leaders Called To A Ministry Are Called To Intercede For That Ministry.

Paul interweaves this throughout his ministry. Paul mentions praying in every single Church epistle except one.[370]

The Leader Intercessor Model

Ministry philosophy refers to a related set of values that underlies a leader's perception and behavior in his/her ministry. The values may be ideas, principles, guidelines or the like which are implicit (not actually recognized but part of the perceptive set of the leader) or explicit (recognized, identified, articulated). For any given leader a ministry philosophy is unique. It is dynamic and related to three major elements: Biblical dynamics, giftedness, and situation. The intercessor model flows out of the prayer macro lesson and shows the concern of a leader for God's intervention in ministry. It is not clear to who this model applies—all leaders or those leaders who have the gift of faith. It may also well apply to some who are not leaders but who have the gift of faith.

definition The <u>intercessor model</u> is a philosophical model which is founded on the central thrust of the prayer macro lesson (which applies to all leaders—as a role) and an additional responsibility for praying for a ministry, which flows out of the faith gift or some aspects of the prophetical gift.

Biblical examples reflecting the prayer macro lesson and intercession occur in every leadership era.[371] Abraham and the macro lesson: Ge 18:16-33; Moses and the macro lesson: Ex 32:7-14; Samuel and the macro lesson: 1 Sa 12:1-25; Daniel and the macros lesson: Dan 9; Jesus and the macro lesson: some 44 different verses indicate Jesus praying throughout his ministry. One especially important prayer passage occurs in Jn 17. Paul and the macro lesson: see this article.

---

[370] He mentions pray, prayer, praying, etc. 60 times in his epistles. Only Gal of his epistles to churches has prayer references left out. Paul hits the ground running in Gal to correct a fundamental heresy. Apart from a possible veiled allusion to prayer in Gal 4:19 (travail SRN 5605) Paul does not speak of praying. He is angry with the Galatians and bent on correcting a fundamental heresy. Paul also omits prayer references in his personal letter to Titus.

[371] There are six leadership eras in the Bible: 1. Patriarchal; 2. Pre-Kingdom; 3. Kingdom; 4. Post-Kingdom; 5. Pre-Church; 6. Church.

Basic Values Underlying the Intercessor Model
1. A leader who is called to ministry must accept responsibility for prayer for that ministry.
2. A leader should show acceptance of responsibility for a ministry by interceding for that ministry and involving others to intercede.
3. A leader must seek God's leading in prayer, the divine initiative, as to how and what to pray for.
4. A leader should bathe major decision making in prayer.
5. A leader ought to encourage the development of emerging leaders by praying for them and telling them of prayer for them.
6. A leader should cultivate an attitude of prayer at all times and ought to break into prayer when prompted to do so.
7. Crises should drive a leader deeper into intercessory ministry.
8. Extended times alone in prayer should be used for intercession, for personal renewal and for revelation from God for guidance, breakthroughs in ministry, and for decision making.

Some Implications Flowing From the Model
1. No ministry will long endure without intercessors behind it.
2. Quantity (the number of and amount of time spent by) of intercessors is not as important as quality of intercession of the ones doing the interceding.
3. Leaders with the gift of faith will do personal intercession with a zeal, passion and fruitfulness beyond that of leaders who do this as a role.
4. Leaders should cultivate relationships with faith gifted intercessors and recruit them to help in the ministry.
5. Power in ministry comes from giftedness and from prayer. Both are needed.

The Intercessor Model is the most specific of the leadership models. It is the most gift related. Gifts of faith, apostleship, and in general, the revelatory gifts (word of knowledge, word of wisdom, prophecy, word of faith) will usually be associated with leaders operating strongly in this model. Now, all leaders have the duty to intercede for their ministries. But those who are drawn to this model will be gifted to see its impact more than just that which results from praying in general. It is not clear to what extent each leader will be involved in this model. Paul exemplifies this model.

Prayer Concerns of Paul for the Churches
Paul had a burden for the churches that he had founded and was associated with.

> Beside outward circumstances pressing me, there is the inward burden, i.e. the anxiety and care, I feel daily for all the churches. 2Co 11:28

He expresses this burden so beautifully in his prayers for the churches. Table 1,2 Ti 46-1 lists just a few of his references to prayer for the various churches. Notice the thrust of his burden for the churches.

Table 1,2 Ti 46-1. Paul's Prayer Concerns for the Churches

Church	Passage	Prayer Thrust
At Rome	Ro 1:8-10 12:12	(1) Thankfulness for this church's strong testimony of faith toward God—its worldwide impact. (2) That God would take him to this church for ministry there.
At Corinth	1Co 1:4	That the Corinthian church respond to his admonitions so that he would not have to come and discipline them in person.

At Ephesus	Eph 1:15-20; 3:1, 14-21	(1) Continuously gives thanks for them. (2) Holy Spirit imparted wisdom. (3) Intimacy with God. (4) Perspective, especially promises, which will give hope. (5) Recognize and appropriate the resurrection-like power available in them. (6) Gentile acceptance into God's kingdom. (7) Inward strength via the Holy Spirit. (8) Realization of the indwelling Christ in their inner selves. (9) Know more fully the love of God.
At Philippi	Php 1:3	(1) Thankfulness for this church—the joy it brings and for its support of Paul and for its co-ministry with him. (2) God's continued work in their midst.
At Colosse	Col 1:3 1:9-14; 2:1	(1) Thankfulness for faith toward God and love for God's people. (2) Fruit of the Spirit, love. (3) Knowledge of God's will. (4) Spirit given wisdom. (5) Lead lives pleasing to the Lord. (6) Enabled by God's power to endure. (6) That these believers would be thankful to God.
At Thessalonica	1Th 1:3, 2:13; 5:23; 2Th 1:3,11-13; 2:13	(1) Thankfulness to God for them. (2) Put their faith into practice. (3) Thankfulness for response to Gospel. (4) Thankfulness for a growing faith. (5) Thankfulness for greater expression of love. (6) Thankfulness for the way they are bearing up in persecution. (7) That their lives may express God's work. (8) Entire final and full sanctification. (9) That they might be enabled by God's power to complete their walk and honor Jesus. (10) Thankfulness for them in that they responded first to the Gospel.
In Philemon's home	Phm 4-6	(1) Thankfulness for Philemon's love and faith. (2) Realization of union with Christ in everyday life. (3) Thankfulness for joy resulting from Philemon's testimony.

What Can We Learn From Paul's Prayers And His Teaching on Prayer?

Here are a few observations that may help us see more of what an intercessor leader is all about.

1. Paul shows how important thankfulness is in praying. Over and over again he is thankful to God for individuals and for churches (see references in table above).
2. Paul operates daily with a spirit of prayer which bursts into praying. He openly states that he prays continually for people and churches (see 1Th 5:17; see Ro 12:12 and many others).
3. Paul prays specific requests for individuals and tells them what he is praying (2Ti 1:3 et al, see *prayer encouragement principle*, **Glossary**).
4. Paul prays for churches almost always giving thanks for them and almost always praying for their growth and appropriation of resources they have in Christ.
5. Intercessory prayer is hard agonizing work (see Ro 15:30, Col 2:1; 4:12. Note especially SRN 4865 used both in Ro 15:30 and Col 2:1, a word meaning agonize, strive at).
6. Paul shares vulnerably concerning his own situation so that people can pray knowingly and with empathy for him (Ro 15:30,31; 2Co 1:11 and many others).
7. Paul prays for believers to know God's power; that the Holy Spirit might enable them to live strong Christian lives.
8. Paul admonished that believers lift holy hands (that is, come to God with clean consciences and an awareness of what the Gospel has done for them) as they pray.
9. Paul admonishes believers to pray for governmental leaders (1Ti 1:1,2).
10. Paul exhorts believers to pray in the Spirit—meaning led of the Spirit in what and how to pray (Eph 6:18; see also Jude 20). He also speaks of praying in the Spirit meaning praying in tongues (and singing in tongues). Both are talked about. Paul also recognizes a praying in which the Spirit prays through us (Ro 8:26) in utterances that express what we should pray for even when we may not know what it is about or what we ought to pray.
11. Paul, not only prays for his own ministry, but prays for others' ministry (i.e. the Jews, see Ro 10:1).
12. Paul recognizes that believers will need to exercise disciplines involving fasting and praying—though he never commands believers to do this (1Co 7:5).
13. Paul suggests that believers should pray for needed giftedness (1Co 14:1, 13).

14.   Paul prays for financial resources for needy churches, for individual Christian workers, and for his own self (2Co 8:14; 9:14 et al).
15.   Paul asks prayer for himself for God-given opportunities for ministry and for effective impactful ministry (Col 4:3,4; 2Th 3:1).

Paul was an intercessor leader.

Conclusion

Apostolic leaders (especially Harvest leaders) need intercession for their ministries. Pastors (especially Shepherd leaders) need intercession for their ministries. God can gift them for this and/or provide others in their sphere of influence to carry this out. The prayer macro is still valid today.

Intercession   Leaders Called To A Ministry Are Called To Intercede For That Ministry.

See *modeling*, **Glossary**. See **Articles**, *Vulnerability and Prayer Power*; *25. Jesus—Five Leadership Models: Shepherd, Harvest, Steward, Servant, Intercessor.*

Relevance of the Article to 1,2 Timothy

Paul developed leaders in ministry. He had a very personal ministry with many folks. One prominent way he did that was by mentoring. This article identifies his mentor-mix and gives some observations about his mentoring work. The two epistles to Timothy show Paul operating as a multi-faceted mentor (Teacher, Contemporary Model, Sponsor, Spiritual Guide, and Counselor), i.e at least five of the nine mentor functions. Timothy was a life-long mentoree of Paul's. All five of the mentoring dynamics were present in Paul's mentoring of Timothy in 1,2 Ti.

47. Paul—Mentor for Many

Paul was an outstanding mentor. He used mentoring as a major means of developing leaders. Mentoring is a relational experience in which one person, called the mentor, empowers another person, called the mentoree, by a transfer of resources. Empowerment can include such things as new habits, knowledge, skills, desires, values, connections to resources for growth and development of potential. We[372] have identified a number of mentoring functions. Usually any given leader will not be an ideal mentor and perform all of the mentoring functions. Instead a given leader will usually be proficient in three or four of the mentor functions. The set of mentoring functions that a leader uses in ministry is called his/her mentor-mix. It is easiest to demonstrate that Paul was an outstanding mentor by illustrating his mentoring relationship with Timothy.

Table 1,2 Ti 47-1 identifies the nine mentoring functions:

Table 1,2 Ti 47-1. Nine Mentor Functions

Type	Central Thrust
1. Discipler	Basic Habits of the Christian Life dealing with hearing from God and talking with God; operating in a fellowship of Christians; learning to minister in terms of giftedness; learning to get input from God.
2. Spiritual Guide	Evaluation of spiritual depth and maturity in a life and help in growth in this.
3. Coach	Skills of all kind depending on the expertise of the coach.
4. Counselor	Timely and good advice which sheds perspective on issues and problems and other needs.
5. Teacher	Relevant knowledge that can be used for personal growth or ministry or other such need.
6. Sponsor	Protective guidance and linking to resources so that a leader reaches potential.
7. Contemporary Model	Values impactfully demonstrated in a life that can be transferred and used in one's own life.
8. Historical Model	Values demonstrated in a life and inspiration drawn from that life so as to encourage on-going development in ones own life and a pressing on to finish well.
9. Divine Contact	Timely Guidance from God via some human source.

Paul over the course of his 30+ years in ministry demonstrated almost all of the nine functions. With Timothy, as seen in the Acts and the two epistles to Timothy, several of the mentoring functions can be

---

[372] My son Dr. Richard W. Clinton, my colleague Paul Stanley and I have all been busily researching and using mentoring in our own personal ministries.

seen. Figure 1,2 Ti 47-1 gives Paul's Mentor-Mix[373] in a pictorial format. This is called a Venn diagram. Each separate oval represents a mentor function. The larger the size of a symbol the more important it is. Overlap of symbols indicates some of both functions taking place. Non-overlap of a symbol with other symbols indicates exclusive manifestation of the symbol. Table 47-2 takes these mentor functions and indicates where the mentoring function is indicated in the Scriptures and perhaps some empowerment.

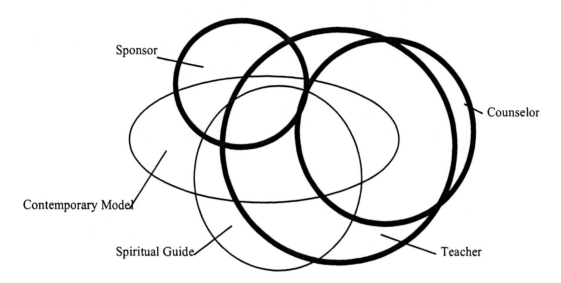

Figure 1,2 Ti 47-1. Paul's Mentor-Mix with Timothy

From the Venn diagram in Figure 1 it can be seen that the three most important mentor functions (indicated by the heavier lines) that Paul did with Timothy were teacher, Counselor, and sponsor. He also models and gives spiritual advice for Timothy's own growth.

Table 1,2 Ti 47-2. Mentor Functions of Paul With Timothy

Kind	Where Seen	Empowerment
Teacher	Ac 16, 17, 18, 19, 20; 2Ti 3:10 Ro 16:21; 1Co 4:17; 2Co 1:19	Timothy was familiar with all of Paul's teaching from the Scriptures. For example, he heard the teaching on the material that was later incorporated as Romans given at Corinth; he was present for the dictation of the book of Romans. He spent hours on the road with Paul and chatted with him.
Counselor	1,2Ti are laced with words of advice	1Ti ch 1,2 Paul's advice on major problems in the church, 1Ti ch 3 Paul's advice on local leadership selection, 1Ti ch 5 Paul's advice on the problem of widows and discipline of leaders.
Sponsor	1,2Ti	He is listed by Paul as co-author (a sponsoring function) of six epistles (See 2Co 1:1; Php 1:1; Col 1:1; 1Th 1:1; 2Th 1:1, Phm 1:1). The material in 1,2Ti is dominantly written with a view to the church there reading it and knowing that Paul was giving Timothy instructions for that church.
Model	2Ti 3:10-17; Php	Philippians gives Paul's comprehensive treatment of his use of modeling.
Spiritual Guide	1,2Ti	See especially 1Ti 4 Paul's personal advice to Timothy on How to Handle Himself.—especially maintaining the balance of developing self and developing ministry.. See also 2Ti 1;3-10 on developing giftedness.

---

[373] Mentor-mix refers to the set of mentoring functions that a leader demonstrates in his/her ministry over time—not necessarily seen at any one given time but over a lifetime.

Five Features of Paul's Mentoring

Table 1,2 Ti 47-3 below lists five features noticeable in Paul's mentoring.

Table 1,2 Ti 47-3. Five Features About Paul's Mentoring

Feature	Explanation
Personal Value	Paul often talked straight from the heart to those he ministered to. He illustrates one of his strongest leadership values when he does that. And this is even more true in his mentoring relationships. A <u>leadership value</u> is an underlying assumption which affects how a leader behaves in or perceives leadership situations. Paul felt ministry ought to be very personal. Stated more generally for all leaders, *Leaders should view personal relationships as an important part of ministry both as a means for ministry and as an end in itself of ministry.* In his epistles Paul names almost 80 people by name—most of whom he ministered with or to or in some way they ministered to him. Of the five dynamics of mentoring (attraction, relationship, responsiveness, accountability, empowerment) relationship was Paul's strong suit. And with Timothy relationship is seen more clearly than any of Paul's companions. See **Article**, *69. Timothy, A Beloved Son in the Faith.* Principle: *The development of a personal relationship between a mentor and mentoree will increase the effectiveness of the mentoring.*
Took People With Him; On-the-Job training.	Whenever possible, Paul never went into ministry alone. He almost always took someone with him—frequently, one he had a mentoring relationship with, one who he was developing as a leader. Principle: *Modeling as a major means of influencing or developing emerging leaders best happens in on-the-job training.*
Teams	Whenever possible, Paul took more than one person with him. He used teams of people. And he would send various team members on important errands. See **Article**, *43. Paul and His Companions.* Note especially the *we sections* in Acts 16 etc.. See also the number of folks around in Romans 16:20-22 (Timothy, Lucius, Sosipater, Tertius, Gaius, Erastus, Quartus) when he dictated the letter.
Little/Big; Ministry Tasks	Paul used the basic principle of the Luke 16:10 little/ big: *The one faithful in little things will be faithful in bigger things.* Give people little things to do and if they are faithful in them, give them bigger things to do. This was especially true of the ministry tasks given Titus and Timothy. A <u>ministry task</u> is an assignment from God which primarily tests a person's faithfulness and obedience but often also allows use of ministry gifts in the context of a task which has closure, accountability, and evaluation. See Titus' five ministry tasks (3 in Corinth 1 in Crete and 1 in Dalmatia). As the person grows the ministry task moves more from the testing of the person's faithfulness toward the accomplishment of the task.
Goodwin's Expectation Principle	Goodwin's expectation principle states, *Emerging leaders tend to live up to the genuine expectations of leaders they respect.* A well respected leader can use this dynamic to challenge younger leaders to grow. The challenge embodied in the expectation must not be too much or the young leader will not be able to accomplish it and will be inoculated against further challenges. The challenge must not be too little or it will not attract. It must be a genuine expectation. Paul uses this with Timothy, Philemon, and Titus several times (see fn 1Ti 6:11. See fn 2Ti 1:5).

The end result of mentoring is the empowerment of the mentorees. Luke, Titus, Timothy, Philemon, Onesimus, Archippus, Priscilla, Phoebe and many others attest to the power of Paul's mentoring. And of all of Paul's mentoring functions, probably the most effective was the modeling. Note in his mentor-mix how modeling subtly interweaves itself throughout every other mentoring function. Paul personally related to numerous leaders to develop them. He left behind a heritage—men and women who could continue to lead and carry out his life purpose and use his values in their lives and ministry.

See **Articles**: *45. Paul the Developer; 43. Paul and His Companions.* For more detailed study see **Bibliography for Further Study**, Stanley and Clinton 1992, **Connecting.** Clinton and Clinton 1993, **The Mentor Handbook.**

Relevance of the Article to 1,2 Timothy

Paul developed people. In his mentoring relationships with many, one dominant feature was contemporary modeling. He knew that his example would inspire his mentorees. But in addition, his life was a model for others as well. He was what he taught. And he was relatively transparent in his epistles about who he was and what he did and why he did it. This modeling was a powerful means of influence. This article describes the essentials of modeling as a means of influence. Jesus is the prime example of a leader who deliberately used modeling to influence others (see especially Jn 13). Daniel is the exemplary modeler in the O.T. Paul is the exemplary modeler in the Church Era. This article describes Paul's use of modeling.

48. Paul—Modeling As An Influence Means

A discovery of an important macro lesson emerged from the Post-Kingdom Leadership Era.[374] In that leadership era, leaders had little or no structure through which to influence other followers of God. They were shut up by sovereign circumstances to influence dominantly with their lives. Their convictions and beliefs must be seen in how they lived and acted and talked. Respected leaders, like Daniel, set examples for other to follow. Because they were respected and had integrity in their lives, others wanted to emulate them. Out of this kind of situation, particularly demonstrated by Daniel, the modeling macro lesson emerged.

Modeling—A Post-Kingdom Macro Lesson

> **Leaders can most powerfully influence by modeling godly lives, the sufficiency and sovereignty of God at all times, and gifted power.**

Remember, a leader is a person who has God-given capacity, and God-given responsibility to INFLUENCE specific groups of people toward God's purposes for them. Modeling is a powerful way of influencing.

Modeling

Definition   Modeling is the use of various life situations to impress upon followers godly behavioral responses, values, convictions, paradigms, and leadership lessons in order to impact their lives with these same items.

Effective leaders recognize that followers who respect their leadership are deeply impacted by their life examples, their beliefs, their behavior, and their desires or expectations. These followers will have a tendency to emulate what they see in these leaders—even if it is not recognized explicitly.

Paul, Philippians and Modeling.

Probably more than any other of Paul's writings the book of Philippians deliberately invokes modeling as a major means of influence both by deliberate example and by teaching it plainly (3:15-17, 4:8,9). Modeling is a technique whereby a leader is transparent with followers concerning life and ministry with a view toward influencing them to imitate him/her. In fact, followers do imitate leaders whether the leaders want them to or not. Leaders should take advantage of this and deliberately strive to model in such a way as to demonstrate what Christian living is all about. A contemporary model is a mentor who uses modeling

---

[374] See **Article,** *26. Leadership Eras in the Bible—Six Identified.*

in order to set ministry examples for emerging leaders. Listen to Paul's admonition and the promise attached to it. There is no doubt, he knew he was a contemporary model.

> Those things that you have both learned and received and heard and seen in me do. And the God of Peace shall be with you. Php 4:9

A secret to having the God of Peace with you is a simple one. Find some good models to imitate. Get some mentor models for your life. Put their values into your life. And Paul says, the God of Peace shall be with you. That is a blessing Paul promises. I believe any good contemporary model can echo that blessing.

Our studies have shown that one of the enhancements for finishing well is to have some good mentors. My advice is for you to get some good mentors and imitate those God-honoring qualities in their lives. You will be disappointed some times in them. But on the whole if you put those God-honoring qualities in your life you can count on the God who gives peace being with you.

The Apostle Paul knew the power of modeling as an influence means. No where is this seen more clearly than in the life of his closest associate Timothy. Consider the story of their meeting and Paul's modeling influence in his life. Notice how Paul knew that the impact of modeling increased with an increase in relationship. That is, the deeper the relationship between a mentor and mentoree the more likely it is that modeling will impact profoundly.

The Story-Reflecting Back on A Relationship

There were tears in his eyes as he said good-bye. Paul knew that hardships, conflict, and troublesome people awaited him. Yet Paul knew God would use those in Timothy's life. Paul was proud of Timothy. Today he was sending him off to the toughest assignment he had ever given him. He was going to Ephesus—a church having subtle heresies and power issues; a church needing the Word of God in a fresh way; a church with social problems, leadership problems, financial problems. But Paul was confident. Timothy would do just fine. Paul knew that because Paul knew his heart. He knew how he had been trained on the job. He knew how Timothy had seen God work on behalf of the team—over and over. Paul's mind wandered back. He saw himself along the road leading to Derbe. And the past events, the selection of Timothy, his training—they all flashed before his eyes. He remembered …

The First Visit

They had trudged along all day and finally arrived in Derbe. Paul had had much time to think over his split with Barnabas. He and Silas had decided to return and follow-up on the converts in Asia minor. He wondered how Barnabas and Mark were doing in Cyprus. Paul knew that personality conflicts and disagreements were sometimes an on-going thing with Jewish people. But somehow he did not feel right about the whole Barnabas and Mark controversy. After all Barnabas had been the sponsor who promoted him in Antioch and then stood up and defended his work at the Jerusalem council. He dearly loved Silas and was glad for the opportunity to minister with him. But he wished that his dispute with Barnabas had not been so final.

After an overnight stay the next morning they went on Lystra. As he neared Lystra Paul remembered how just a few short years ago he and Barnabas had in desperation fled from Iconium–just in front of a mob bent on stoning them. They had some success there including authentication of their ministry by God's miraculous working. But still a number of Jews had forced them out. It was on that journey, that frightening race away from persecution, that they had been led to Derbe and Lystra just a few short years ago. And as was often the case after a frightening experience, God had affirmed them.

It was at Lystra that Paul had seen God accomplish an amazing healing. Paul remembered it as if it were only yesterday. The man was crippled and sat listening to Paul as he explained the Way and talked about the person Jesus. Paul, as he looked at the man, suddenly knew within that this man could be healed—there was healing faith there. On the spot, Paul looked him directly in the eye and commanded him to stand up on his own two feet. This man, in a moment of time, leaped to his feet. He was healed. All who knew him were instantly amazed. Paul remembered that this man's healing led everyone immediately to believe that Paul and Barnabas were divine beings—incarnate beings representing Hermes and Zeus. Paul had immediately stopped that. A good ministry then followed.

But after some time the Jews from Antioch and Iconium who had opposed Paul's ministry earlier came to Lystra to stir up folks against Paul and Silas. And they did. Paul and Silas left for Derbe to escape the persecution. Not again, Paul had thought. Will it always be this way?

However, Paul thought back to the fruit in that town. During their stay Paul was impressed with a number of Jewish people who both demonstrated faith in the living God but also knew their Old Testament Scriptures. He wondered why it was so often the case that women were the more spiritual. Women responded to the Gospel eagerly, frequently sooner than Jewish men. Eunice and Lois were just such women. These Lystran women knew the Scriptures very well. When Paul began to teach Christ from the Old Testament Scriptures, their background allowed them to enter in quickly to Paul's explanation. They had opted to become followers of the Way. Paul was looking forward to seeing Eunice and Lois and others who had responded to the Gospel.

Much had happened since their last visit. There was the great Jerusalem council dealing with the essence of the Gospel. There was the controversy with Barnabas which centered on the young disciple, John Mark. That had led to the split. Time had gone by. Paul was anxious to see the growth in the believers at Lystra. He was particularly interested in Lois' son, Timothy. For he had heard good things about him.

The Return Visit To Lystra

Paul knew that to get the Gospel out he would need help. He constantly had his eyes open for potential leaders. At Iconium the assembly there had spoken about Timothy—the son of Lois. High on their list were two things: his character, he was a person of integrity and sincerity, and his love for the Scriptures. His own mother and grand mother, so alive to the Word, had been teaching Timothy since he was a small lad. Paul would assess Timothy himself. But if all went well Paul was going to ask Timothy to come along with the team. And right now that was just Silas.

And so it happened. Paul met Timothy. He invited him to come along. Because he was the son of a Greek father and a Jewish mother Paul had him circumcised. For there was much Jewish opposition in the area. And so a relationship began—Paul and Timothy.

A mentoring relationship—what does it take? time and sharing of experiences. A growing respect for one another. Paul made sure these happened with Timothy.

A Close Relationship

How close was their relationship?

> 19 But I trust in the Lord Jesus to send Timothy shortly unto you, that I also may be encouraged when I know what is happening to you. 20 For I have no one like-minded, who will naturally care for what is happening to you. 21 For all seek their own, not the things which are Jesus Christ's. 22 But you know his proven character, that, as a son with the father, he has served with me in the gospel. 23 So I hope to send him shortly, as soon as I shall see how it will go with me. 24 But I trust in the Lord that I myself shall also come shortly. Php 2:19-24

> 2 To Timothy my true son in the faith: Grace, mercy and peace from God the Father and Christ Jesus our Lord. 1Ti 1:2

Their Experiences Together

> 10 But you have fully known my teaching, manner of life, purpose, faith, longsuffering, love, patience, 11 Persecutions, afflictions, which happened in Antioch, in Iconium, in Lystra; what persecutions I endured: but out of them all, the Lord delivered me. 12 You can be sure that all that will live godly in Christ Jesus will also suffer persecution. 13 But evil men and seducers shall grow worse and worse, deceiving, and being deceived. 14 But you continue in the things which you have learned and have been assured of, knowing of whom you have learned them; 15 I know that from a child you have known the holy scriptures, which are able to make you wise unto salvation through faith which is in Christ Jesus. 16 Every scripture given by inspiration of God is profitable for teaching, for reproof, for correction, for instruction in righteousness: 17 That the man of God may be mature, thoroughly equipped for all good works. 2Ti 3:10-17

The Training

Follow along with me as I relate some of the things Timothy experienced. Remember Timothy experienced first hand these things and watched Paul in these situations:

- The Macedonian happenings,
- The evangelization efforts at Thessalonica,
- The particularly word oriented efforts at Berea,
- The tumultuous exits from both those places caused by the opposition and persecution.
- The ministry with Priscilla and Aquila in Corinth, including the Bible school ministry and all of the tremendous teaching that Paul gave,

I could go on and on. There is nothing like on-the-job training with a person with a mentoring heart.

The Main Mentor Functions Seen Here

Overwhelmingly the dominant mentoring function seen here was contemporary modeling. A strong secondary mentoring function especially at Corinth was teacher. I will say a word about the teaching mentoring function even though this article is concentrating on modeling.

> 10 But you have fully known my **teaching**, manner of life, purpose, faith, longsuffering, love, patience, 11 Persecutions, afflictions, which happened in Antioch, in Iconium, in Lystra; what persecutions I endured: but out of them all, the Lord delivered me. 2Ti 3:10,11

> 8 And he went into the synagogue, and spoke boldly for three months, disputing and persuading the things concerning the kingdom of God. 9 But when different ones were hardened, and believed not, but spoke evil of *The Way* before the multitude, he departed from them, and separated out the disciples, disputing daily in the school of one Tyrannus.10 And this continued by the space of two years; so that all they which dwelt in Asia heard the word of the Lord Jesus, both Jews and Greeks. Ac 19:8-10

Let me suggest that Paul's teaching was not confined to his public lectures. I am sure that in his tentmaking time with Priscilla and Acquilla, there was lots of time to talk as you cut the cloth and sew. And on the road—lots of time when walking from place to place. And I guarantee you that Paul would be sharing. He would be explaining about Christ, his updating of his own theology, his understanding of God's great plan of salvation. And even in this teaching he was modeling and important methodology—you teach in the context of every day life as well as in public situations.

The Contemporary Mentor Modeling, Was It Deliberate?

Was this modeling deliberate? Was this modeling intentional? Probably not at first. But it became increasingly clear to Paul as he traveled with his team, spent much time with them, demonstrated the effectiveness of the Gospel in the lives of others and himself that his modeling was an important part of his training methodology.

In general, this is a biblical concept.

> Remember your leaders, who spoke the word of God to you. Consider the outcome of their way of life and imitate their faith. Heb 13:7

> We do not want you to become lazy, but to imitate those who through faith and patience inherit what has been promised. Heb 6:12

But does that mean that we as leaders can deliberately use this to impact and influence. Yes! For Jesus himself deliberately modeled as a means of influence. The two top New Testament leaders, Jesus and Paul demonstrated the importance of modeling as a means of influence.

Jesus Ministry—The Prime Example

John 13 is the pre-eminent example of deliberate intentional modeling to impact.

3 Jesus knowing that the Father had given all things into his hands, and that he was come from God, and went to God; 4 rose from supper, and laid aside his garments; and took a towel, and girded himself.12 So after he had washed their feet, and had taken his garments, and was set down again, he said unto them, Do you Know what I have just done to you?...14 If I then, your Lord and Master, have washed your feet; you also ought to wash one another's feet. 15 For I have given you an example, that you should do as I have done to you. Jn 13:3-15

Paul's Deliberate Modeling—Almost From the Very Beginning

I think that fairly early on in his ministry Paul became aware of this dynamic.

6 And you became imitators of us, and of the Lord, having received the word under much affliction, yet having the joy of the Holy Spirit: 7 So that you yourselves were models to all that believe in Macedonia and Achaia. 1Th 1:6,7

7 For you know how you ought to imitate us: for we did not behave ourselves disorderly among you; 8 Neither did we eat any man's bread for nothing; but worked hard night and day, that we might not be chargeable to any of you: 9 Not because we have not power, but to make ourselves as models so you could follow us. 2Th 3:7-9

For this reason I strongly invite you, use me as a model. 1Co 4:16

Use me as a model, just as I also follow Christ as my model. 1Co 11:1

Christian followers, join in following my example and observe those who walk according to the pattern you have seen in us. Php 3:17

The things you have learned and received and heard and seen in me, practice these things; and the God of peace shall be with you. Php 4:9

Yes, Paul deliberately used modeling as a strong means of influencing followers. The essential empowerment of modeling, this indirect mentoring relationship, is the embodiment of values in such a way as to challenge the observing mentoree into emulation of these values.

Closure—What About You and Modeling

Let me go back to where I began this article. A discovery of an important macro lesson occurred in the Post-Kingdom Leadership Era.

Leaders can most powerfully influence by modeling godly lives, the sufficiency and sovereignty of God at all times, and gifted power.

Some questions for you:

Have you discovered modeling as a powerful means of influencing?

Are you conscious that in situations you are modeling?

Who is imitating you?

As you consider who you are and what you do, what are the things you really want people to imitate? Remember, if you are a leader, you are modeling. People are going to imitate you. Why not take advantage of this! Model for them in you various life situations so as to impress upon followers godly behavioral responses, values, convictions, paradigms, and leadership lessons. And pray that God would use this in order to impact their lives with these same items.

See also **Articles** *37. Macro Lessons, List of... 49. Pauline Leadership Styles; 26. Leadership Eras in the Bible—Six Identified.*

Relevance of the Article to 1,2 Timothy

Paul was seeking to influence the Ephesian church through Timothy's ministry. The letters to Timothy were meant not only to influence Timothy but the church also. Paul knew they would be reading the letters too. In fact, he was desperate to influence them to concerning the four heresies he saw there in their midst. How a leader influences followers involves what is known as leadership styles. Most leadership styles are imbibed from one's observations of leaders around him/her during one's foundational years—up to age 20 or so. Cultural leadership styles will dominate a church leader. Various leadership styles are needed as a leader faces unique situations. This article defines leadership styles, identifies a leadership style continuum to help identify some of the factors in exercising a leadership style and finally looks at leadership styles Paul used as he influenced followers. In the Ephesian intervention, Paul was multi-styled, a fact Helen Doohan aptly demonstrates in her book, **Leadership in Paul.**

49. Pauline Leadership Styles

Introduction

Consider the fundamental definition for leader that permeates this Handbook.

Definition   A <u>leader</u> is a person with God-given capacity and God-given responsibility who is influencing a specific group of people toward God's purposes.

How does one influence? Leadership style is one measure of how a leader influences. Paul again sets an example for leaders in the N.T. Church Leadership Era.

In Php, I point out that Paul uses the maturity appeal (opening salutation) and imitation modeling leadership styles (throughout the book, see especially Php 4:9). In Phm, I show how Paul uses several leadership styles: father-initiator (Phm 19), maturity appeal (Phm 9), and obligation persuasion (Phm 8-21). In 1Co and 2Co I repeatedly make comments on Paul's leadership styles. In 1Co I point out his Father-initiator style (4:14,15), his Apostolic leadership style (9:1,2), his confrontation style (1Co 5:1-5), his indirect conflict leadership style (1Co 5:1-4) and his imitator leadership style (1Co 4:16). In 2Co I point out maturity appeal (6:9,10), obligation persuasion (8:8), Father-initiator (2Co 10:14). Paul is a multi-style leader—a very modern concept in leadership style theory. What is a multi-style leader? Some definitions are needed in order to understand leadership style. Then I will move on to examine Pauline leadership styles.

Definition: The <u>dominant leadership style</u> of a leader is that,
1. highly directive or
2. directive or
3. non-directive or
4. highly non-directive
consistent behavior pattern that underlies specific overt behavior acts of influence pervading the majority of leadership functions in which that leader exerts influence.

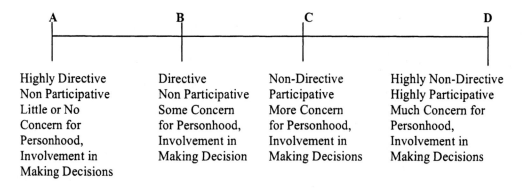

Figure 1,2 Ti 49-1. Influence Behavior Along a Continuum

Leadership style, deals with the individual behavioral expression a leader utilizes in influencing followers. This individual expression includes methodology for handling crises, methodology for problem solving, methodology for decision making, methodology for coordinating with superiors, peers and subordinates, methodology for handling leadership development. The individual methodology for a specific leadership act or series of acts can often be labeled as well as identified on the Directive—Non-Directive continuum.

My study of Paul's influence identified ten styles. These were given specific labels. Paul was multi-styled[375] in his approach to influencing followers. The styles are not defined exclusively. That is, there is some overlap of concepts between different styles. Let me describe the ten styles I labeled.

Ten Pauline Styles Observed

1. Apostolic Style

Where a person demonstrates with self-authenticating evidence that he/she has delegated authority from God—that is, there is a sense of spiritual authority about the leadership—then that person can use the apostolic leadership style.

Definition: The <u>apostolic leadership style</u> is a method of influence in which the leader

- assumes the role of delegated authority over those for whom he/she is responsible,
- receives revelation from God concerning decisions, and
- commands obedience based on role of delegated authority and revelation concerning God's will.

A synonym for this style is the command/demand style. This style is implied in 1Th 5:12, 13. "And I want you, fellow Christians, to personally know the leaders who work among you, and are over you in the Lord, and warm you. Lovingly honor them for their work's sake." It is implied in 1Ti 5:17: "Church leaders that are exercising good leadership should be evaluated as worthy of double pay—especially the ones who are working hard teaching the word." Another example implying this style is seen in Heb 13:17: "Obey those leaders who are set over you. Submit to their leadership. For they watch for your souls, as those who must give account. And they want to do so with joy and not with grief. Make it worth their while." This style is also seen in 1Th 2:6; even though P ul chooses not to command obedience, he asserts that he could have done so as was his apostolic right. The essence of the apostolic style is the legitimate right from God to make decisions for others and to command or demand their compliance with those decisions.

---

[375] Doohan, a noted author on Pauline leadership also concludes that Paul is multi-styled. See Helen Doohan, **Leadership in Paul**. Wilmington, Del.: Michael Glazier, Inc., 1984.

This style with its top-down command/demand approach is considered the most highly directive leadership style.

2. Confrontation Style

Many leaders try to avoid problems, particularly those involving troublesome people and those carrying heavy emotional ramifications. The basic rationale seems to be, "this is a tough problem; if I try to do anything about it I'm going to incur wrath, maybe have my character maligned, lose some friends and be drained emotionally. Perhaps if I just ignore it, it will go away by itself." For some problems, perhaps this is a good philosophy; time does give opportunity for a clearer perspective, for healing, and for indirect conflict to occur. But for most problems, leaders must confront the problem and parties involved directly. At least this seems to be the approaches exemplified in Jude, John, Peter, and Paul in their Scriptural writings.

Definition: The confrontation leadership style is an approach to problem solving

- which brings the problem out in the open with all parties concerned,
- which analyzes the problem in light of revelational truth,
- and which brings force to bear upon the parties to accept recommended solutions.

This style is usually seen in combination with other styles. Seemingly, the majority of cases emphasize *obligation-persuasion* as the force for accepting the solution, but *apostolic* force is also seen in the Scriptures. The book of Jude is an example. Several of the leadership acts in the book of 1Co utilize this style. Paul also uses this style in the Philippian church. See the problem between Euodia and Synteche. This style, like the apostolic style, is highly directive since the solutions to the problems are often the leader's solutions.

3. Father-Initiator Style

Paul resorts to this leadership style when exerting his influence upon the Corinthian church. He is establishing his authority in order to suggest solutions to some deep problems in the church.

Definition: The father-initiator leadership style is related to the apostolic style which uses the fact of the leader having founded the work as a lever for getting acceptance of influence by the leader.

In 1Co 4:14, 15 Paul writes, "14 I do not write these things to shame you, but as my beloved children I warn you. 15 For though you might have ten thousand Christian teachers, you only have one father in the faith. For I became your spiritual father when I preached the Gospel to you." Paul uses the father-initiator style in this case. Note in this example the force of the two powerful figures: the absolute for the relative in verse 14 and the hyperbole in verse 15.

The father-initiator style is closely related to the obligation-persuasion style, in that obligation (debt owed due to founding the work) is used as a power base. However it differs from obligation-persuasion in that more than persuasion is used. The decision to obey is not left to the follower. It is related to the apostolic style in that it is apostolic in its force of persuasion.

This style is highly directive/directive style.

4. Obligation-Persuasion Style

One method of influencing followers over which you have no direct organizational control involves persuasion. The leader persuades but leaves the final decision to the follower. A particularly powerful technique of persuasion is obligation-persuasion in which normal appeal techniques are coupled with a sense of obligation on the part of the follower due to past relationship/experience with the leader. Such a leadership style is seen with Paul's treatment of the Onesimus/Philemon problem.

Definition: An <u>obligation-persuasion leadership style</u> refers to an appeal to followers to follow some recommended directives which

- persuades, not commands followers to heed some advice;
- leaves the decision to do so in the hands of the followers, but
- forces the followers to recognize their obligation to the leader due to past service by the leader to the follower;
- strongly implies that the follower owes the leader some debt and should follow the recommended advice as part of paying back the obligation; and finally
- reflects the leader's strong expectation that the follower will conform to the persuasive advice.

The classic example of this is illustrated in the book of Philemon. Paul uses this style in combination with other styles in 1,2Co also.

This is a directive style. The expectation is high, though the actual decision to do so passes to the follower.

5. Father-Guardian Style

This style, much like the nurse style, elicits an empathetic concern of the leader toward protection and care for followers.

Definition: The <u>father-guardian style</u> is a style which is similar to a parent-child relationship and has as its major concern protection and encouragement for followers.

Usually this style is seen when a very mature Christian relates to very immature followers. 1Th 2:10, 11 illustrates this style. "You know it to be true, and so does God, that our behavior toward you believers was pure, right, and without fault. You know that we treated each one of you just as a father treats his own children. We encouraged you, we comforted you, and we kept urging you to live the kind of life that pleases God, who calls you to share in his own Kingdom and glory."

Usually this style is directive, but because of the caring relationship between leader and follower and the follower maturity level it does not seem directive, since influence behavior always seem to have the follower's best interest at heart.

6. Maturity Appeal Style

The book of Proverbs indicates that all of life is an experience that can be used by God to give wisdom. And those who have learned wisdom should be listened to by those needing yet to learn. Maturity in the Christian life comes through time and experience and through God-given lessons as well as giftedness (see *word of wisdom gift*, **Glossary**). Leaders often influence and persuade followers by citing their *track record* (learned wisdom) with God.

Definition: A <u>maturity appeal leadership style</u> is a form of leadership influence which counts upon

- Godly experience, usually gained over a long period of time,
- an empathetic identification based on a common sharing of experience, and
- a recognition of the force of imitation modeling in influencing people in order to convince people toward a favorable acceptance of the leader's ideas.

Heb 13:7 carries this implication: "Remember your former leaders who spoke God's message to you. Think back on how they lived and died and imitate their faith."

See also 1Pe 5:1–4, 5–7 where Peter demonstrates maturity appeal. "I, an elder myself, appeal to the church elders among you. I saw firsthand Christ's sufferings. I will share in the glory that will be revealed. I appeal to you to be shepherds of the flock that God gave you. Take care of it willingly, as God wants you to, and not unwillingly. Do your work, not for mere pay, but from a real desire to serve. Do not try to rule over those who have been put in your care, but be an example to the flock. And when the chief Shepherd appears, you will receive the glorious crown which will last."

Paul's description of his sufferings as an Apostle (2Co 11:16–33) and experience in receiving revelation (2Co 12:1–10) are exemplary of the maturity appeal style leadership.

This style moves between the categories of directive to non-directive depending on how forcefully the desired result is pushed for.

7. Nurse Style

In 1Th 2:7, Paul uses a figure to describe a leadership style he used among the Thessalonian Christians. The figure is that of a nurse. It is the only use of this particular word in the N.T., though related cognates do occur. The essential idea of the figure is the gentle cherishing attitude of Paul toward the new Christians in Thessalonica with a particular emphasis on Paul's focus on serving in order to help them grow.

Definition: The nurse leadership style is a behavior style characterized by gentleness and
               sacrificial service and loving care which indicates that a leader has given up
               "rights" in order not to impede the nurture of those following him/her.

The primary example is given in 1Th 2:7, "But we were gentle among you, even as a nurse cherishes her children." Paul commands an attitude of gentleness to Timothy in 2Ti 2:24–25. "24 The Lord's servant must not quarrel; instead be gentle unto all, skillfully teaching and being patient, 25 gently instructing those opponents. Perhaps God will give them opportunity to repent and see the truth."

The nurse style is similar to the father-guardian style in that both have a strong empathetic care for the followers. It differs in that the father-guardian style assumes a protective role of a parent to child. The nurse role assumes a nurturing focus which will sacrifice in order to see nurture accomplished.

The nurse style is non-directive.

8. Imitator Style

Paul seemed continually to sense that what he was and what he did served as a powerful model for those he influenced. He expected his followers to become like him in attitudes and actions. It is this personal model of *being* and *doing* as a way to influence followers that forms part of the foundational basis for spiritual authority.

Definition: The *imitator style* refers to a conscious use of imitation modeling as a means for
               influencing followers. It reflects a leader's sense of responsibility for what he/she
               is as a person of God and for what he/she does in ministry with an expectant view
               that followers must and will and should be encouraged to follow his/her example.

Paul emphasizes this in Php 4:9 which illustrates this leadership style. "9 Those things, which you have both learned, and received, and heard, and seen in me, do—and the God of peace shall be with you. A second Pauline illustration is seen in 2Ti 3:10,11. 10 "But you fully know my teaching, my lifestyle, my purpose in life, my faith, my steadfastness, my love, my endurance. 11 I was persecuted at Antioch, at Iconium, at Lystra; I endured those persecutions. Yet the Lord delivered me out of them." Paul goes on to give the response he expects of Timothy based on this imitation modeling and maturity appeal.

The whole book of Php emphasizes t is influential methodology as being one of the most powerful tools a leader can use to influence followers. This style is highly non-directive.

9. Consensus Style

Decisions which affect people's lives and for which leaders must give account require careful spirit-led consideration. One leadership style approach to decision making involves consensus decision making. This style is often used in coordination situations where ownership is desired. Cultures which stress group solidarity, such as many of the tribes in Papua New Guinea, see this style used frequently by leaders.

Definition: <u>Consensus leadership style</u> refers to the approach to leadership influence which involves the group itself actively participating in decision making and coming to solutions acceptable to the whole group. The leader must be skilled in bringing diverse thoughts together in such a way as to meet the whole group's needs.

In a consensus style there is much give and take in arriving at decision. Unless there is a *check in the spirit* which prohibits an agreement, the final decision carries the weight of the entire group and thus will *demand* all to follow through on implications and ramifications which follow. James apparently gives a consensus decision reflecting the entire group's corporate will in the Ac 15 decision. Note this decision was identified as Spirit-led. The Ac 6 decision concerning distribution of good to widows is an example of both of consensus (within the plurality of Apostles) and apostolic (commanded to the followers) leadership styles.

This style is highly non-directive.

10. Indirect Conflict Style

A powerful style for dealing with crises and problem solving involves the concept of dealing with *first causes*, that is, the primary motivating factors behind the problem rather than the problem itself. This style recognizes that spiritual conflict is behind the situation and must be dealt with before any solution will take hold. The parties directly involved may not be aware that the leader is even doing problem solving. A leader who uses this approach must be skilled in prayer, understand spiritual warfare and either have the gift of discerning spirits or access to a person with that gift.

Definition   The <u>indirect conflict leadership style</u> is an approach to problem solving which requires discernment of spiritual motivation factors behind the problem, usually results in spiritual warfare without direct confrontation with the parties of the problem Spiritual warfare is sensed as a necessary first step before any problem solving can take place.

See the context of Mt 16:21–23 especially verse 23: "Get away from me Satan. You are an obstacle in my way, because these thoughts of yours don't come from God, but from man." This is an example of indirect conflict leadership style. Mk 3:20–30 gives the underlying idea behind this style. See especially verse 27: "No one can break into a strong man's house and take away his belongings unless he first ties up the strong man; then he can plunder his house." See also Eph 6:10–20, especially verse 12: "For we are not fighting against human beings but against the wicked spiritual forces in the heavenly world, the rulers, authorities, and cosmic powers of this dark age."

Conclusions

I think the following are worth noting because they point out what I have been attempting to do in this section dealing with biblical styles, most of which come from Pauline material.

1.   I have demonstrated how to use the generic (directive/non-directive continuum) as the overarching umbrella on which to pinpoint specific leadership-style behaviors.
2.   I have identified 10 different Pauline leadership styles.
3.   These 10 models of specific styles are transferable to many situations, which we as leaders face today.
4.   I have indicated that Paul's leadership style was multi-styled.
5.   I have pointed out that Paul was a flexible leader who matured in his leadership as he grew older and was able to change to meet change to meet changing situations.

Current leadership style theories differ on whether or not a leader can actually change his/her leadership style. My own observations recognize that some leaders are flexible and can change. Others are not. Perhaps the ideal is a flexible leader who can change. But where this is not possible, then a leader who dominantly uses a certain leadership style should be placed in a situation where that style fits. Directive styles fit best with immature followers who need that direction. As followers mature the leadership styles should move to the right on the directive-non-directive continuum. This allows for follower maturity and for emerging leaders to arise.

Relevance of the Article to 1,2 Timothy

Paul demonstrated both macro lesson 37. STRUCTURE—LEADERS MUST VARY STRUCTURES TO FIT THE NEEDS OF THE TIMES IF THEY ARE TO CONSERVE GAINS AND CONTINUE WITH RENEWED EFFORT and macro lesson 38. UNIVERSAL—THE CHURCH STRUCTURE IS INHERENTLY UNIVERSAL AND CAN BE MADE TO FIT VARIOUS CULTURAL SITUATIONS IF FUNCTIONS AND NOT FORMS ARE IN VIEW. In accordance with the ideas behind these two macros, as his ministry expanded into more and more Gentile cultures, he continually identified and met varying leadership needs. As a result leadership terms were added as needed. The following article seeks to identify the leadership terms seen in Paul's epistles and define them in terms of the time in which they were used. Leadership in the Ephesian church was one of the major problems Paul was addressing in his two letters to Timothy.

50. Pauline Leadership Terms

One of the interesting questions that I ask of my leadership classes in seminary is what terms do you have for leaders and leadership in your cultures. Since students in the School of Intercultural Studies come from 60 or more countries, in a given leadership class 10-20 different cultures will be represented. And the answers tell a lot about a culture's views of leaders. This article looks at the terms that Paul uses for leaders with a view toward:

1. identifying the different terms for leaders and implications of them,
2. understanding levels of leadership and the responsibility of leadership,
3. suggesting implications concerning leaders and giftedness.

1. Different Leader Terms in the Bible

Paul uses the following terms when talking about leaders.

Table 1,2 Ti 50-1. Pauline Terms for Leaders

Term	Scripture	Referring To	Description/ Definition
apostle	Eph 4:11 et al	A leader given to the church; unclear if local, regional, or international church.	An apostle (SRN 652) is a leader who has capacity to move with authority from God to found works of God to meet needs and to develop and appoint leadership in these structures as well as preserve doctrinal purity.
bishop	1Ti 3:1, 2Tit 3:2	A local church leader; in the New Testament it is synonymous with elder.	A leadership term (SRN 1985) used in Php 1:1, 1Ti 3:2, Tit 1:7 and 1Pe 2:25. Occurs as the word overseer in Ac 20:28 and which probably best describes its function. As used in Paul's life time, a person responsible for the spiritual welfare of others in a local church situation. Also used simultaneously with shepherd (pastor).

258

deacon	1Ti 3:8,12; Php 1:1	A local church leader probably under an overseer or elder.	A leadership term (SRN 1249) translated: as deacon three times—Php 1:1, 1Ti 3:8, 3:12; as minister 20 times; as servant 8 times. Paul uses this to describe his own self and Phoebe. It is not clear how this role relates to that of bishop or elder. It is distinguished as a separate leadership role from bishop in 1Ti 3 and probably of less influence.
elder	15 times in Ac, 1Ti, Tit	1. Jewish leaders along with Scribes and Pharisees; 2. Elderly people in the church (male and female); 3. Local church leaders.	A leadership term (SRN 4245) used by Paul and Luke 14 times in Scripture to refer to local church leadership in Ephesus. It is unclear as to how this leadership role, elder, differs from bishop. In the book of Tit the word bishop and elder is used synonymously. They are also used simultaneously in Ac 20. In 1Ti elders are described as ruling and teaching in the local congregation. Also used once to describe elderly women in a local church and one time to possibly describe elderly men in the congregation (could be speaking of a local church leader).
evangelist	Eph 4:11, Ac 21:8; 2Ti 4:5	1. A leader who proclaims the Gospel—probably an itinerant leader; 2. Timothy's role to play out in Ephesians church; 3. Philip.	A leadership term (SRN 2099) used to describe Phillip the Evangelist, to leaders given to the church to help build it up, and to the role Timothy must do in Ephesus as part of his ministry straightening out that church. The emphasis in the Eph 4:11ff passage is the building up (making mature) of the body. This is a gift given to the church.
minister	many	A general term applied to various leaders local or otherwise— the thrust of it is not on positional leadership or role but on the service involved in leading.	Three different Greek words are translated as minister: 1. A leadership term (SRN 1249) translated: as minister 20 times; as servant 8 times and as deacon three times—Php 1:1, 1Ti 3:8, 3:12. Paul uses this to describe his own self and Phoebe. It is not clear how this role relates to that of bishop and elder. It is distinguished as a separate leadership role and probably of less influence than bishop in 1Ti 3 and possibly less influence in Php 1:1. 2. A leadership term (SRN 5257) used to describe Paul, Apollos, the Roman emperor, and other church leaders—its emphasis is responsible service as a leader. 3. A leadership term (SRN 5257) literally an under rower, that is, someone who a leader under the authority of someone else. Ananias describes Paul with this term.

overseer	Ac 20:28	A local church leader; used as such in Ephesus church and Philippian church.	A leadership term (SRN1985) Occurs as the word overseer in Ac 20:28 and which probably best describes its function. As used in Paul's life time a person responsible for the spiritual welfare of others in a local church situation. Probably synonymous with the term elder. Also used in Php 1:1, 1Ti 3:2, Tit 1:7 and 1Pe 2:25 where it is translated by bishop.
pastor	Eph 4:11	Unclear, could be a local church leader as in 1Pe 5:1-4 or Ac 20:28 but also a regional or national or international itinerant leader as in Eph 4:11.	A leadership term (SRN 4166) occurs as other English word shepherd or tend referring metaphorically to a leader who tends a flock (Christian followers); used simultaneously with bishop and elder in Ac 20.
prophet	Eph 4:11	A leader given to the church; unclear if this means local church, regional church, international church to bring corrective truth to situations; probably itinerant.	A leadership term (SRN 4396) describing strong spokespersons in the Old Testament and New Testament. In the New Testament Silas and Agabus illustrate this kind of leadership. Agabus worked in a local situation but also traveled about in his prophetic ministry. Silas traveled also as a missionary.
rule, ruler	1Ti 3:4, 5,12; 5:12; 5:17; Ro 12:5-9	One who functions over others; most likely a local church leader.	Several Greek words underlie this leadership descriptive word. 1. A leadership term (SRN 4291) describing one who is placed over another. Used in 1Ti 3:4,5 to describe a characteristic of a bishop; Used in 1 Th 5:12 to describe a leader who is over others; used in 1Ti 3:12 describing a characteristic of a deacon; used in 1Ti 5:17 to describe the function of an elder. 2. A leadership term (SRN 2233) meaning to rule, command, have authority over. Also used in the Ro 12:5-9 gifts passage to describe a gift.

Servant (bond slave)	Php 1:1	Specially committed leaders to the cause of Christ.	A special leadership term which Paul uses to describe himself and Timothy (SRN 1401). It is used of one who gives himself up to another's will, those whose service is used by Christ in extending and advancing his cause among people. It emphasizes leadership wise the vertical aspect of servant leadership. A leader first of all serves Christ. Secondly, he/she serves those being influenced or led. Peter uses this term to describe himself. Paul uses it several times when speaking of leaders in a church setting. Also used of Jesus (Php 2).
shepherd	Ac 20:28 1Pe 5:1	A local church leader caring for those under his/her influence.	A leadership term (SRN 4165) relating to a leader who cares for and protects a group of followers; used simultaneously with bishop and elder in the Ac 20 and simultaneously with bishop in 1Pe 2:25. Occurs both in noun and verb form.
teacher	Eph 4:11	A leader given to the church; unclear if this means local church, regional church, international church to bring corrective truth to situations; probably itinerant.	A leadership term (SRN 1320) describing a major function needed in a local church, that of teaching or explaining truth about God and His ways and His will for followers.

2. Understanding Levels of Leadership/ Accountability

A leader is a person with a God-given capacity and a God-given burden (responsibility) who is influencing a specific group of people toward God's purposes for the group. Now all members of the body influence each other when ever they use their gifts. But a leader is one who not only influences but has a responsibility from God to do so and who will answer to God for it. So then there is a distinction between leaders, in this sense, and followers. These leaders are set over (i.e. get a burden for and have responsibility for) the followers (in the sense of Heb 13:7, 17 and the use of rule in 1Th 5:12 and 1Ti 5:17). Further, these leaders will give an account for them (see **Accountability** in **Php Leadership Insights Section**). So then there is a major distinction between followers and leaders.

Within the category of leaders in a local church there is a distinction between elders, bishops, pastors (basically used synonymously) and deacons (see 1Ti 3 where characteristics of these two different leaders are distinguished). The Ephesians 2 passage seems to indicate that apostles and prophets at least in the early church are foundational and a cut above other leaders because of their inaugural work in getting the church going.

The gifts passage in 1Co 12:27-31 apparently lists the spiritual gifts given there in a priority order: apostles, prophets, teachers which are described higher than other gifts.

The Ephesians giftedness passage (also leadership passage) also distinguishes a group of leaders from followers: apostles, prophets, evangelists, pastors, teachers. These leaders are obviously different in their responsibility from the other members of the body.

The most important thing to recognize from this section is simply that leaders are distinguished from followers and will give an account for their leadership. Thus passages like Php 2:16 (that my ministry efforts have been worth while, not wasted effort) and 4:1 (my joy and crown), Heb 13:17 (must give an account for you).

A second thing to recognize is that the terms bishop, pastor, elder, shepherd as seen in the N.T. are essentially used synonymously. They do not carry the connotations that have emerged over history of hierarchical positions. The present day use of the Pauline terms bishop, elder, and pastor have taken on traditional and historical meaning that was not true of them in New Testament times.

3. Leadership and Giftedness

From the Scriptures it seems clear that at least apostleship, prophecy, evangelism, pastoring, and teaching are leadership gifts. From my own empirical study of over 1200 contemporary case studies of leaders I have deduced the following leadership observation.

> **All leaders have at least one word gift and most have more than one in their gift-mix.**

I define word gifts as a category of spiritual gifts used to clarify and explain about God. These gifts when used in the body highly influence those receiving the ministry. And leaders are those who influence. These word gifts help us understand about God including His nature, His purposes and how we can relate to Him and be a part of His purposes. Word gifts include: teaching, exhortation, pastoring, evangelism, apostleship, prophecy, ruling, and sometimes word of wisdom, word of knowledge, and faith (a word of). All leaders have at least one of these and often several of these.

Let me define these gifts:

apostleship	one of the 19 spiritual gifts. The <u>gift of apostleship</u> refers to a special leadership capacity to move with authority from God to create new ministry structures (churches and para-church) to meet needs and to develop and appoint leadership in these structures. **Its central thrust is Creating New Ministry.**
teaching	one of the 19 spiritual gifts. It belongs to the Word Cluster. A person who has the <u>gift of teaching</u> is one who has the ability to instruct, explain, or expose Biblical truth in such a way as to cause believers to understand the Biblical truth. **Its central thrust is To Clarify Truth.**
ruling	one of the 19 spiritual gifts. It is in the word cluster. A person operating with a <u>ruling gift</u> demonstrates the capacity to exercise influence over a group so as to lead it toward a goal or purpose with a particular emphasis on the capacity to make decisions and keep the group operating together. **Its central thrust is Influencing Others Toward Vision.**
prophecy	one of the 19 spiritual gifts. It is in the word cluster and power cluster. A person operating with the <u>gift of prophecy</u> has the capacity to deliver truth (in a public way) either of a predictive nature or as a situational word from God in order to correct by exhorting, edifying or consoling believers and to convince non-believers of God's truth. **Its central thrust is To Provide Correction Or Perspective On A Situation.**
pastoring	one of the 19 spiritual gifts. It belongs to the Word Cluster and the Love Cluster. The <u>pastoral gift</u> is the capacity to exercise concern and care for members of a group so as to encourage them in their growth in Christ which involves modeling maturity, protecting them from error and disseminating truth. **Its central thrust is Caring For The Growth Of Followers.**
governments	one of 19 spiritual gifts occurring primarily in the Love Cluster. The <u>gifts of governments</u> involves a capacity to manage details of service functions so as to support and free other leaders to prioritize their efforts. **Its Central Thrust Is Supportive Organizational Abilities.**
exhortation	one of the 19 spiritual gifts. It is a spiritual gift belonging to the word cluster. The <u>gift of Exhortation</u> is the capacity to urge people to action in terms of

applying Biblical truths, or to encourage people generally with Biblical truths, or to comfort people through the application of Biblical truth to their needs. **Its central thrust is To Apply Biblical Truth.**

Closure

Some implications of this study include the following:

1. The large range of terms show us that leadership in terms of the many functions needed is complex. We as leaders can not perform all these functions. And our giftedness will direct us to those that are ours to perform. Thus, we need the interdependent help of others.
2. Leaders are those who see themselves as serving God (bondslave) first of all and ministering (servant) to others secondly.
3. Leaders do have responsibility to influence others with authority.
4. Leaders must care for those being led.
5. Leaders will give an account for their leadership.
6. Leaders are gifted to lead.
7. The functions of leadership are much more important than the status, privilege, or position of leaders.
8. The higher level leadership functions (apostle, prophet, evangelist, pastor, teacher) are given to equip the body. The implication being that each of these level gifted leaders are raising up others to do these functions in the body.

Remember, in closing, three important verses:

> **Listen, this is an important fact, "If a person is eager to be a Church leader, that is a good thing." 1Ti 3:1**

It is a good thing to desire leadership. This desire should be backed up by calling and giftedness and should be recognized by others in the body.

> **Remember your former leaders. Imitate those qualities and achievements that were God-Honoring, for their source of leadership still lives -- Jesus! He, too, can inspire and enable your own leadership today.** Heb 13:7,8

As a leader you will be modeling for others. And you will be following those leaders who have gone before you. And you have the same source of leadership as they—Jesus Christ.

> **Obey them that have the rule over you, and submit yourselves: for they watch for your souls, as they that must give account, that they may do it with joy, and not with grief: for that [is] unprofitable for you.** Heb 13:17

You will give an account for your leadership. You will be rewarded for those things in your leadership which were good. You will also account for those things not so good.

See *accountability*, **Glossary**. See **Articles**, *1. Accountability—Standing Before God As A Leader. 2. Apostolic Functions.*

Article 51

Relevance of the Article to 1,2 Timothy

Because Paul had no formal leadership role at Ephesus (remember in Ac he had released the church leadership to the elders) he had to rely on his spiritual authority. He used it to sponsor Timothy as his representative. My original work on Pauline leadership values was done in 1,2 Co where Paul defended his actions by exposing the values underlying them. I identified 19 leadership values in that original study. This article extends that study into other Pauline epistles. Note that in 1,2 Ti I identify another 19 values. Paul demonstrates that he is a value-based leader. 1,2Ti corroborate that accolade. See **Article** *71. Value Driven Leadership.* Paul was a person of integrity. His inner thinking was reflected in his outward behavior. And his inner thinking was deeply influenced by Biblical precepts.

51. Pauline Leadership Values

Introduction

One of the six characteristics[376] of a leader who finishes well is described as,

> **Truth is lived out in their lives so that convictions and promises of God are seen to be real.**

A leader who has values and lives by them will exemplify this characteristic. Paul did. All during the leadership commentary for Paul's epistles, I have indicated Pauline values. Some of these value are unique to Paul and are at best only suggestive for other leaders. And some are guidelines that can help leaders today. But many are possibly absolutes that must be considered carefully as required of leaders today.[377]

Definition   A <u>leadership value</u> is an underlying assumption which affects how a leader perceives leadership and practices it.

Leadership values contain strong language like should, ought, or must. Must statements are the strongest.

Definition   A leader's ministry is said to be <u>value driven</u> if that leader consciously attempts to identify, make explicit, and explain leadership values that under gird his/her ministry and deliberately operates his/her ministry based on these values.

Paul was a value driven leader. 2Co is the pre-eminent book demonstrating this. Because Paul had to defend his ministry and his apostolic authority, he gave the underlying reasons why he operated the way he did. This article simply summarizes in one place statements which attempt to describe the Pauline leadership values I have identified all through his epistles. There is no attempt made here to evaluate the certainty with which these values should be applied along the principle of truth continuum. I will list the 2Co values first since that book is basal for understanding leadership values. I will number the values for later reference purposes only. These numbers do not indicate any kind of priority. Repeated listing of a value occurs just for emphasis.

---

[376] The six characteristics include: 1. They maintain a personal vibrant relationship with God right up to the end. 2. They maintain a learning posture and can learn from various kinds of sources—life especially. 3. They manifest Christ-likeness in character as evidenced by the fruit of the Spirit in their lives. 4. Truth is lived out in their lives so that convictions and promises of God are seen to be real. 5. They leave behind one or more ultimate contributions. 6. They walk with a growing awareness of a sense of destiny and see some or all of it fulfilled.

[377] See **Article**, *54. Principles of Truth*, which define principles along a continuum of suggestions, guidelines, requirements (absolutes).

Table 1,2 Ti 51-1. Pauline Leadership Values Summarized—2 Corinthians

Value
1. **Divine Appointment.** Leaders ought to be sure that God appointed them to ministry situations.
2. **Training Methodology.** Leaders must be concerned about leadership selection and development.
3. **Personal Ministry.** Leaders should view personal relationships as an important part of ministry.
4. **Sovereign Mindset.** Leaders ought to see God's hand in their circumstances as part of His plan for developing them as leaders. See *sovereign mindset*, **Glossary**. See **Article**, *58. Sovereign Mindset*.
5. **Integrity and Openness.** Leaders should not be deceptive in their dealings with followers but should instead be open, honest, forthright, and frank with them. See **Article**, *23. Integrity—A Top Leadership Quality*.
6. **Ultimate accountability.** Leaders' actions must be restrained by the fact that they will ultimately give an account to God for their leadership actions. See **Articles**, *Day of Christ—Implications for Leaders; 40. Motivating Factors for Ministry*.
7. **Spiritual Authority—Its ends.** Spiritual authority ought to be used to mature followers. See **Articles**, *59. Spiritual Authority Defined—Six Characteristics; Followership—Ten Commandments*.
8. **Loyalty Testing.** Leaders must know the level of followership loyalty in order to wisely exercise leadership influence. See **Article**, *Followership—Ten Commandments*.
9. **True Credentials** (competency and results). A leader should be able to point to results from ministry as a recommendation of God's authority in him/her.
10. **True Competence** (its ultimate source). A leader's ultimate confidence for ministry must not rest in his/her competence but in God the author of that competence.
11. **Transforming Ministry.** Followers, increasingly being set free by the Holy Spirit and being transformed into Christ's image ought to be the hope and expectation of a Christian leader.
12. **Prominence of Christ in Ministry.** A leader must not seek to bring attention to himself/herself through ministry but must seek to exalt Christ as Lord.
13. **Servant Leadership.** A leader ought to see leadership as focused on serving followers in Jesus' behalf. See **Article**, *25. Jesus—Five Leadership Models*.
14. **Death/Life Paradox.** The firstfruits of Jesus resurrection life ought to be experienced in the death producing circumstances of life and ought to serve as a hallmark of spiritual life for followers. In other words, Christianity ought to work in thick or thin.
15. **Motivational Force.** Leaders should use obligation to Christ (in light of his death for believers) to motivate believers to service for Christ.
16. **True Judgment Criterion.** Leaders should value people in terms of their relationship to God in Christ and not according to their outward success in the world (even in the religious world).
17. **Unequally Yoked.** Christian leadership must not be dominated by relationships with unbelievers so that non-Christian values hold sway.
18. **Financial Equality Principle.** Christian leadership must teach that Christian giving is a reciprocal balancing between needs and surplus.
19. **Financial Integrity.** A Christian leader must handle finances with absolute integrity

Table 1,2 Ti 51-2. Pauline Leadership Values Summarized—1 Timothy

20. A Christian leader ought to have several life long mentorees who he/she will help over a lifetime to reach their potential in leadership.
21. Giftedness must be developed.
22. Giftedness should receive less stress in leadership selection and development than character building. Leadership selection must be based primarily on character.
23. Leaders should avoid prejudging a problematic situation without careful investigation.
24. Leaders should be disciplined with a view toward recovery.

25. Leaders must expect heresy both as to belief (orthodoxy) and practice (orthopraxy) to arise both from within the church and without it.
26. Integrity, as reflected in a purse conscience, should be the goal of every leader for himself or herself personally (Ac 24:16).
27. Money ought to be a strong power base useful to do good for people.
28. Every leader ought to know about and be able to deal with spiritual warfare problems in the church.

Table 1,2 Ti 51-3. Pauline Leadership Values Summarized—2 Timothy

29. Present ministry should always be seen in the light of a whole life of ministry and particularly the end of ministry—a good finish.
30. One's sense of destiny ought to guide a leader toward a good finish.
31. An anticipation of the Lord's return should be a major motivating factor for a leader to minister well and finish well.
32. Recognition of giving a final accountability for one's leadership ought to be a strong motivating factor for a leader to minister well and finish well.
33. Leaders should be responsible for prayer for their ministries. A leader should pray personally for those in his or her ministry. A leader should seek God for specific prayers for those in his/her ministry. A leader should tell those in his/her ministry about those prayers and thus encourage them to believe also that God will answer those prayers.
34. Leadership selection and development should be a responsibility of a leader.
35. Emerging leaders should be taught how to handle correctly God's written word.
36. Gentleness ought to be a primary trait of a leader who wants to persuade (as opposed to one who wants to prove he/she is right).
37. A leaders should proactively use modeling to influence followers.
38. A leader ought to have a strong learning posture all of life.

Table 1,2 Ti 51-4. Pauline Leadership Values Summarized—1 Corinthians

39. Gifts, operating harmoniously together, each contributing its function, should have as its purpose the edification of the church as a whole.
40. The proper attitude behind exercising gifts ought to be that of love. This attitude is essentially more important than the exercise of the gifts or results coming from those gifts.
41. Orderliness in public worship, which is consistent with the way God does things, ought to be the norm for churches.
42. A leader ought to see his/her leaders as a responsibility entrusted by God.
43. Leaders should vary their leadership styles according to the situation, personal ability, and follower maturity.
44. Leadership must be exercised primarily as service foist of all to God and secondarily as service to God's people.
45. Leaders who want to finish well must maintain disciplines during the stressful middle stages of leadership in order to continue well.
46. Bible study and prayer are major disciplines that a leaders should maintain, especially during the plateauing years (40-60).

Table 1,2 Ti 51-5. Pauline Leadership Values Summarized—Philippians

47. A leader must recognize God's sovereignty in deep processing.
48. A leader should seek, in deep processing, to ask what the Lord is doing in it both in a personal way and in the ministry, with a view toward the whole of life, not just the specific time it is happening.
49. A leader in deep processing must be transparent and vulnerable enough to share with others in his/her community so as to garner support and prayer backing.
50. A leader must be aware of the fact that his/her response to deep processing will be a model for those being influenced.
51. A leader must, in deep processing, reevaluate life purpose and affirm it, modify it, or add to it, recognizing that God will often use deep processing to expand one's horizons as to life purpose.

52. A leader should proactively use modeling to influence followers.
53. A leader who models must be transparent and vulnerable to share God's working in the life both in the positive and negative shaping activities of life. It is God's working in the negative shaping activities of life that often has more impact than even the positive.
54. Effective leaders view relational empowerment as both a means and a goal in ministry.
55. An effective leader must learn to vary his/her leadership style to fit the situation and people being influenced.
56. An effective leader should view spiritual authority as a primary power base but recognize that other bases will be needed to influence.
57. A leader should have a life purpose which serves as a guidance check for decisions about ministry and for doing ministry. Does what I am doing enhance my life purpose?
58. A leader ought to demonstrate union life for followers to see what a Christ-centered life looks like.

Table 1,2 Ti 51-6. Pauline Leadership Values Summarized—Philemon

59. Obligation-persuasion is a leadership style in harmony with spiritual authority and should be used with mature followers with whom a leader has a good relationship.
60. An effective leader must learn to vary his/her leadership style to fit the situation and people being influenced.
61. An effective leader should view spiritual authority as a primary power base but recognize that other bases will be needed to influence.
62. Sensitivity to God's shaping processes must be cultivated in a leader.

Conclusions

These Pauline leadership values are not posited as final statements. They are first attempts at getting at the driving ideas behind Paul's ministry. These are given to stimulate thought. They should be assessed and then modified, reworded, or even discarded depending on the assessment.

See **Article**, *71. Value Driven Leadership.*

Relevance of the Article to 1,2 Timothy

Paul, more than any other N.T. Church era leader, vividly demonstrates this macro lesson throughout his ministry. In 1,2 Ti his prayers for Timothy are touching. His urging of the leaders to pray stands out. And it is clear in both epistles that prayer is foremost for him as he faces his last big crisis in his personal life.

52. Prayer Macro Lesson

Samuel makes a strong statement in his last public ministry act, his farewell address, 1 Sa 12:1-25.

> 23 Moreover as for me, God forbid that I should sin against the LORD in ceasing to pray for you: but I will teach you the good and the right way: 24 Only fear the LORD, and serve him in truth with all your heart: for consider how great [things] he has done for you. 1 Sa 12:23,24

At the heart of this statement is the fact that Samuel feels responsibility to pray for his ministry. And he sees this as a responsibility coming from God (note sin against God). Such a gracious attitude, Samuel is being eased out of leadership by these people, becomes this great leader. From this context, also verified strongly in Abraham's leadership (Gen 18) and Moses leadership (Ex 32) a macro lesson emerges, an observation on leadership and responsibility to pray.

Leaders called to a ministry are called to intercede for that ministry.

This macro lesson occurs in many leaders' ministry across the six leadership eras. It is seen most fully developed in Jesus' ministry and Paul's ministry. This macro lesson appears on the far right of the *Leadership Truth Continuum*, most likely an <u>absolute</u>. Written in value language it becomes,

A leader must pray for the ministry he/she is responsible for.

How a leader does this, actually praying and/or taking responsibility for it and making sure it is done is unclear in the Bible. But it should be done. It is this macro lesson which forms the underlying value for the *Intercession Philosophical Leadership Model*.

See **Articles**, *36. Macro Lesson Defined; 37. Macro Lessons, List of 41 ...; 25. Jesus—Five Leadership Models: Shepherd, Harvest, Steward, Servant, Intercessory; 46. Paul—Intercessor Leader; Vulnerability and Prayer.*

Relevance of the Article to 1,2 Timothy
When a leader deliberately models to influence people, as Paul did, it is imperative that he has gone through a *life power gate* experience. He must exhibit Union Life—victory in Christ. And when a leader corrects church situations like Paul did at Corinth and at Ephesus then he must also exhibit power that can only come via a *gifted power gate* experience. Paul knew the powerful presence of God in his life and ministry—the essential ingredient of leadership, i.e. the Moses Macro Lesson known as the *Presence Lesson.* This article explains those powerful paradigm shifts. Usually one or the other experience dominates a leader's life. For Paul both did.

53. Power Gates—Experiences That Renew and Enable Leaders

Introduction
One of the great macro lessons seen in Moses' life, and which runs throughout all leadership eras is stated as,

Presence Lesson   The essential ingredient of leadership is the powerful presence of God in the leader's life and ministry.

This macro lesson applies to all leadership, whether power gifted or not.[378]

Our studies of leaders' lives has pointed out that all leaders at one time or another come to a point in their ministry in which they know they must have the power of God.[379] As we have studied the power experiences comparatively we have been able to identify two major categories of power needs. One of the needs focus around *life power*, that is, the enabling power of God to live the Christian life--modeling a victorious which is essential for certain ministries. A second need focuses around gifted power--the ability to minister, usually publicly, with great power. The experiences which reflect God's meeting these needs are then labeled as power gates, that is, the opening of the person to the power from God to meet their need.

The passage through a power gate usually requires a paradigm shift. Before the shift, there is the need for power. The person knows it is there but can not break through to get it. The experience with God opens the person to the perspective that allows the receiving of that power. That is a paradigm shift.[380]

---

[378] The three clusters of spiritual gifts include word gifts, power gifts, and love gifts. The power gifts are a category of spiritual gifts which authenticate the reality of God by demonstrating God's intervention in today's world. These include: tongues, interpretation of tongues, discernings of spirits, kinds of healings, kinds of power (miracles), prophecy, faith, word of wisdom, word of knowledge. They demonstrate power. but what we are talking about here is more than power gifts. It involves demonstrating God's power in ministry no matter what the gifting. Love gifts need to be validated by God's powerful presence and working. Word gifts need to be validated by God's powerful presence and working.

[379] Such books as Edman's **They Found the Secret** or Choy's **Powerlines** are dealing with leaders and their appropriation of power.

[380] The *life power,* paradigm Shift is one of most important paradigm shifts taught in the Gospel of John. It is taught three times in John 4:14, 7:37-39, 15. John uses right brain techniques to present *life power*. He prefers to teach in terms of pictures: 1. Artesian well. John 4 What Jesus is to you will satisfy your inner self. 2. Life giving spring. 3. John 7:37-39 what you have will overflow to others. Productive Vine. John 15, its source a shared life with Christ—fruitful.

Entering Into Power--Life Power

Life power refers to the enabling grace of God in a life to enable a leader to walk above the controlling authority of sin in a life and to demonstrate in an ever increasing way the fruit of the spirit. Comparative studies of these experiences revealed a pattern.

Life Power Pattern
+Need + Surrender + Appropriation by Faith +or- a validating experience.

The symbol + means that it was always there. The symbol +or- means it may or may not be there. Those seeking this power always had a need. The shift always required some sort of surrender to God which opened the possibility of the need being me. After the surrender there was the realization that the power is available already; it must simply be appropriated by faith. Sometimes after this moment of accepting by faith thee was some sort of validation by God in some unusual way. Often this did not occur.

Entering Into Power--Gifted Power

About half of the leaders in Edman's book, **They Found the Secret**, went through the life power pattern as described above. But the other half went through a different pattern, the *Gifted Power Pattern*.

Going through the gifted *power gate* involves a seeking for power in ministry. Public rhetoricians, like D.L. Moody Charles Finney and for example, usually needed this kind of paradigm shift.

Gifted Power Pattern
+Need +or-Surrender+ Unusual Validating Experience + appropriating faith.

All going through this paradigm shift evidenced a strong need for the power. Sometimes, but not always, this involved a surrender to God for that power. Almost always the breakthrough for the paradigm shift came with some unusual validating experience. It was the experience, not a cognitive understanding of it, that made the difference in the paradigm shift. And then afterwards there was the step of faith to believe that God had empowered and that the experience was the authentication of God's validation. The leader then learned to use faith repeatedly to see God's power in ministry.

The Ideal Power Leader

The Gospel of John presents Jesus as the ideal leader with regard to power. Jesus demonstrated gifted power both in Word Gifts, Power Gifts and Love Gifts. And his teaching on abiding was foundational for those wanting to have life power.

Conclusion

Going through a power gate does not ensure that a leader will operate in power the rest of his/her life. It simply opens one up to God's power working. There must be the continual appropriation by faith.

Recognize that you will need power. And you will most probably come to a crisis point in your leadership where you must have power--either life power or gifted power.[381]

I have just one word of exhortation for you. Do not be satisfied with a powerless life or a powerless ministry. Seek God as Moses did for His Powerful Presence.

> Exodus 33:15 15 And Moses said unto God, If your powerful presence does not go with me then I am out of here as a leader.

And so must it be for all of us who are leaders.

See *ultimate contribution; public rhetorician, saint*, **Glossary**. See **Articles**, *Paradigms and Paradigm Shifts--Biblical Examples; 18. Focused Life.*

---

[381] One symptom of which power gate you will need hinges on your *ultimate contribution* categories. Folks with a *public rhetorician ultimate contribution* will usually be driven to a *gifted power gate*. Those with a *saint ultimate contribution* will usually be driven toward a *life power gate*.

Paul specifically alludes to principles of truth which are foundational to him in 1,2 Ti. See: 1 Ti 3:6,12; 4:2; 5:19,21; 6:11,12; 2 Ti 1:12; 2:2; 4:18. See also his truth asides in 1Ti 1:17; 2:3-6; 3:16; 4:9,10; 6;13, 15,16; 2Ti 1:9,10; 2:8, 11, 18, 19: 4:1. Paul was a person for whom the following two finishing well characteristics were important and well demonstrated: *1. A leader who finishes well maintains a learning posture and can learn from various kinds of sources—life especially. 2. A leader who finishes well demonstrates that Truth is lived out in his/her life so that convictions about God and His truth and promises from God are seen to be real.* This article describes my own approach to drawing out principles of truth from the Scriptures.

54. Principles of Truth

Introduction

Leaders who finish well are described by six characteristics.[382] Two of these claim that,

> **They maintain a learning posture and can learn from various kinds of sources—life especially.**

> **Truth is lived out in their lives so that convictions and promises of God are seen to be real.**

How does a leader get truth from the scriptures—one of the sources for learning? How does a leader get truth, form convictions, and arrive at promises from God?

Further, this leadership commentary has described a Bible centered leader.

> A <u>Bible Centered leader</u> refers to a leader whose leadership is being informed by the Bible and who personally has been shaped by Biblical values, has grasped the intent of Scriptural books and their content in such a way as to apply them to current situations and who uses the Bible in ministry so as to impact followers.

How does one get informed by the Bible on leadership? How does a leader get values which shape him/her?

This article suggests perspectives that help answer these questions. It details my own framework—the perspectives that have guided me as I comment on the Scriptures, suggest observations, guidelines, values, principles of truth, macro lessons, etc.

Principles

Observations of truth provide one useful result of leadership studies. These truths help us understand other leadership situations and predict what ought to be. They also help us in the selection and training of leaders since they give guidelines that have successfully been applied in past leadership situations. These truths are usually seen first as specific statements concerning one leader in his/ her situation. They are then generalized to cover other leaders and like situations. The question of how generally they can be applied to

---

[382] Six characteristics of a good finish include the following. Leaders ho finish well have: (1) a vibrant personal relationship with God; (2) a learning posture; (3) Christ-likeness in character; (4) lived by Biblical convictions; (5) left behind ultimate contributions; (6) and fulfilled a sense of destiny.

others is a genuine one. The certainty continuum and screening questions provide cautions about this.

Definition   Principles refer to generalized statements of truth which reflect observations drawn from specific instances of leadership acts or other leadership sources.

God's processing of leaders includes shaping toward spiritual formation, ministerial formation, and/or strategic formation. Analyzing formational shaping, serves as an important stimulus for deriving principles.

A few examples will help clarify. Analysis of God's use of the integrity check, word check, and obedience check to develop spiritual formation in numerous young leader's lives led to the following three principles.

Integrity is foundational for leadership; it must be instilled early in a leader's character.

Obedience is first learned by a leader and then taught to others.

Leadership gifts primarily involve word gifts which initially emerge through word checks

Analysis of Samuel's final public leadership act in 1 Sa 12 (see especially vs 23) led to the following truth.

When God calls a leader to a leadership situation he calls him/ her to pray for followers in that situation.

The Certainty Continuum and Related Definitions

Attempts to derive statements of truth from leadership studies meet with varied success. Some people seem to intuitively have a sense of generalizing from a specific situation a statement which apparently fits other situations. Others are not so good at this skill. This part of leadership theory is in is infancy stage. In the future we hope to delineate more structured approaches for deriving statements and for validating them. But for now we need to recognize that these statements often can not be proved as truth (in the sense that physical science can prove truth) hence we, as researchers, need to be careful of what we say is truth. Below is given the certainty continuum and the major generalization concerning the derivation of *truth* statements. These are an attempt to make us as researchers cautious about applying our findings.

Principles of truth are attempts to generalize specific truths for wider applicability and will vary in their usefulness with others and the authoritative degree to which they can be asserted for others.

description   The certainty continuum is a horizontal line moving from suggestions on one extreme to requirements on the other extreme which attempts to provide a grid for locating a given statement of truth in terms of its potential use with others and the degree of authority with which it can be asserted.

The basic ideas are that:
1. Principles are observations along a continuum.
2. We can teach and use with increasing authority those principles further to the right on the continuum.

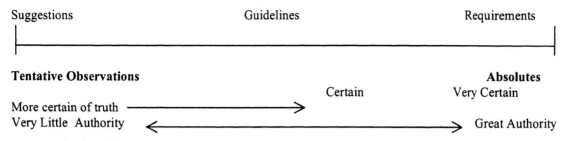

Figure 1,2 Ti 54-1. The Certainty Continuum

I am identifying principles as a broad category of statements of truth which were true at some instant of history and may have relevance for others at other times.

There is little difference between *Suggestions* and *Guidelines* on the continuum. In fact, there is probably overlap between the two. Some *Guidelines* approach *Requirements*. But there is a major difference from going from *Suggestions* to *Requirements*—the difference being *Suggestions* are optional but *Requirements* are not. They must be adhered to.

Definition   Suggestions refers to truth observed in some situations and which may be helpful to others but they are optional and can be used or not with no loss of conscience.

Definition   Guidelines are truths that are replicated in most leadership situations and should only be rejected for good reasons though their will be no loss of conscience.

Definition   Absolutes refer to replicated truth in leadership situations across cultures without restrictions. Failure to follow or use will normally result in some stirrings of conscience.

Absolutes are principles which evince God's authoritative backing. All leaders everywhere should heed them.

Suggestions are the most tentative. They are not enjoined upon people. They may be very helpful though.

Remember that a *Suggestion* or *Guideline* may move to the right or left if more evidence is found in the Bible to support such a move. If a *suggestion* or *guideline* identified in one place in the Scriptures is found to be abrogated, modified or somehow restricted at a later time in the progressive flow of revelation then it will move most likely to the left. However, if later revelation gives evidence of its more widespread usage or identifies it more certainly for everyone then it will move to the right.

Six Assumptions Underlying Derivation Of Principles

Principles are derived from Biblical leadership situations as well as from life situations. Several assumptions underlie my approach to deriving principles of truth. The following six assumptions underlie my approach to getting truth.

1. **Truth Assumption:** All truth has its source in God.
   I need not fear the study of secular material (social science materials, leadership theory, present day situations, etc.). If there is any truth in it I can be certain it is of God. For there is no truth apart from God. I don't have to limit truth to the Bible. The Bible itself shows how God has revealed truth by many different means. These means were certainly not just limited to ancient written revelation. The problem then lies in how to discern if something is truth.

2. **Source Assumption:** All of life can be a source of truth for those who are discerning.
   The central thrust of Proverbs 1:20-33 and in fact the whole book of Proverbs is that God reveals wisdom in life situations. The book of Proverbs is more than just content for us to use; it is a modeling of how that content was derived over time and in a given society. We can trust God to

reveal wisdom in the life situations we study (whether from the Bible or today). Truth that evolved in Israeli history came to take on at least guideline status and much of it became absolutes.

3. **Applicability Assumption.** Just because a statement of truth was true for a specific given situation does not mean the statement has applicability for other leaders at other times. Wider application must be determined via comparative means.

A statement of truth is an assertion of fact drawn from a specific situation. The dynamics of the situation may well condition the statement. That is, the truth itself may apply only in situations which contain the same dynamics. The fact that the truth did happen means it is at least worthy of study for potential wider use. Because of the consistency of God's character we know that the truth can not violate His nature. But its happening is not sufficient justification for its use anywhere at anytime by any leader.

4. **Dogmatic Assumption.** We must exercise caution in asserting all truth statements as if they were absolutes.

Fewer truths will be seen as absolutes if screened with applicability criteria. The use of applicability criteria, especially that of comparative study, will force one to identify a higher level function behind a given principle. Thus a statement of truth at some lower level when compared with other situations and similar statements of truth might lead to a higher order generic statement of truth. These higher level statements of truth, though more general in nature, preserve the function intended rather than the form of the truth. Such statements will allow more freedom of application. Statements which do not carry wide applicability or have attached to them dynamics of situations which can not be fully assessed will most likely have to be asserted with less dogmatism.

5. **Dependence Assumption.** We are forced more than ever to depend upon the Holy Spirit's present ministry to confirm truth we are deriving.

Because of the sources (life as well as Biblical) from which we are drawing truth, we will need more dependence upon the ministry of the Holy Spirit. That is, we will be forced to situationally rely on and become more sensitive to the Holy Spirit's leading and voice. We will need to recognize giftedness in the body and learn to trust those who have spiritual gifts which expose, clarify, and confirm truth (discernings of spirits, word of knowledge, word of wisdom, teaching, exhortation, etc.).

6. **Trust Assumption.** Because we are following Biblical admonitions (Heb 13:7,8; 1 Co10:6,11, Ro 15:4) in our attempts to derive truth we can expect God to enable us to see much truth.

God does not command us to do things that are impossible. God's commands contain within in them the promise of enablement. Because there are great needs for more and better leadership and because we need leadership truth to develop that leadership and because God has told us to study leaders to learn from their lives, we can expect God to lead us to truth that will greatly affect our lives. By faith we can trust Him to do this.

Conclusion

For each of the **Key Leadership Insight** sections for individual books I have listed statements called observations, principles, values, lessons. Each of these will need to be assessed on the certainty continuum to determine their level of applicability.

See *integrity check, word check, and obedience check, spiritual formation, ministerial formation, strategic formation,* **Glossary**.

Relevance of the Article to 1,2 Timothy

Paul demonstrates how an apostolic leader should confront heretical problems in a church setting in his intervention in the Ephesian situation. See especially the Leadership Topics in 1 Ti: Topic 4. Discipline; Topic 5. Complexity—Leadership Problems; Topic 7 Leadership Guidelines. This article was originally written for 1,2 Co, hence the emphasis on those books. But note the 4 heresies mentioned in 1,2 Ti. Leadership is complex, especially in stage 3 of Apostolic ministry.

55. Problems—The N.T. Church

Introduction

The final macro lesson identified summarizes what is seen about leadership across six leadership eras.[383]

> **Leadership is complex, problematic, difficult, and fraught with risk—which is why leadership is needed.**

Because there are problems, there is a need for leaders. And there will always be problems in ministry. I have frequently heard leaders say, "If we could only get back to the N.T. church. That would solve our problems." I always smile and ask, "Which one?" Cause all of the N.T. churches had problems. Which problems do you want to deal with? The N.T. Leadership Era was filled with problems. As Jesus' initiating work broke forth from a movement into an institution that could be transferred into multi-cultural situations, problems arose. The book dealing most comprehensively with church problems is 1Co. This article will simply list some church problems as seen in the N.T. Church Leadership Era.

My basic assumption is that awareness of problems is a first start toward avoiding them or solving them in one's own situation. And awareness of the N.T. church problems with possible N.T. advice about them goes a long way toward solving these problems. Knowing that problems can be solved is a great encouragement.

Problems With the Corinthian Church

Table 1,2 Ti 55-1 Summarizes problems in the Corinthian church.

Table 1,2 Ti 55-1. Problems in the Corinthian Church

Problem	Ch	Explanation/ Paul's Advice
Wisdom	Ch 1,2	*Problem*—over emphasis on secular wisdom. *Advice*—wisdom is centered in Christ; appropriate it. God reveals wisdom. Avoid tendency to want esoteric knowledge and to get it in unhealthy ways.

---

[383] See *macro-lesson*, **Glossary**. See **Articles**, *36. Macro Lessons, Defined; 37. Macro Lessons—List of 41 Across Six Leadership Eras; 26. Leadership Eras in the Bible—Six Identified.*

Divisions	Ch 3,4	*Problem*—over emphasis on following different leaders causing divisions and cultic like groups; claims of having more of whatever Christianity is because of belonging to one group and leader. *Advice*—disunity is a symptom of an immature church; Grow up; recognize different leaders are gifted by God for different functions in the church; Respect all of them. But do not become divided over them. Paul introduces stewardship model to describe responsibility of a leader.
Toleration of Immorality	Ch 5	*Problem*—in the surrounding culture there was moral laxity; The church had a couple living in immorality—involving at least an in-law relationship and maybe even. *Advice*—excommunicate the offending party for discipline sake, hoping to bring about repentance.
Lawsuits Among Believers	Ch 6	*Problem*—Christians were bringing lawsuits against Christians. *Advice*—Christians should settle legal matters before wise Christians in the church rather than in secular law courts.
Marriage	Ch 7	*Problem*—sexual passion and illicit sexual activity; separation and divorce. *Advice*—Singleness is good but marriage may be necessary because of physical needs. Concerning singleness or divorce, the basic rule is to stay together and try to work out one's situation. Staying together can allow for one partner to influence the other partner toward God. But separation is not forbidden. A person can operate as a Christian from the background that he/she was called in, whether married or single, circumcised or not, slave or free. A person is free to marry or not marry but be aware of the pressures of a marriage in the present situation. Time is short it must be used well. There is an advantage in serving the Lord in being single. One can marry and it is all right. If one can stay single it is better. Widows are free to remarry but staying single has its advantages.
Disputed Practices	Ch 8-10	*Problem*—Disputed Practices, Christian lifestyle, and Christian freedom. *Advice*—A Christian should recognize that some lifestyle practices are legitimate but may cause problems for other Christians who do not see them as legitimate. On the one hand, a Christian should be willing to forego these practices so as not to cause the Christian not having freedom to violate his/her conscience. But on the other hand, the Christian not having freedom can mature and recognize the other's freedom.
Worship Practice	Ch 11	*Problem*—Two specific disturbances included defiance of tradition among women—refusing to war head coverings as they pray publicly (strong cultural implications about this) and improper participation in the Lord's supper. *Advice*—Tradition has its place but remember public worship should not be upset because of cultural practices regarding head coverings or lack of for women. Common practice in churches has women praying in public using head coverings but it isn't worth arguing over. The Lord's supper should be a sacred remembering of the Lord's death and a reminder of his return. Do not participate in the Lord's supper in an improper manner but do so meaningfully or be judged by God.
Spiritual Gifts	Ch 12-14	*Problem*—tongues; Lack of order in public worship gatherings like multiple tongues without interpretation and inappropriate talking and questions, all causing confusion and not communicating to unbelievers visiting these services. *Advice*— There is a God-given diversity of gifts. Each has its place in the body. None should be highly exalted over others. Do things decently and in order. Let your gifts demonstrate your love for one another. Revelatory gifts should be controlled by those having them. Tongues should be done one at a time and interpreted. Prophecy should be done one at a time and evaluated. Communicate to bring about growth and to reach those needing to know the Gospel.

Doctrinal—Resurrect-ion	Ch 15	*Problem*—false teaching which denied the resurrection. *Advice*—Paul refutes the false teaching that there is no resurrection of the dead by showing such a doctrine also denies Christ's resurrection and invalidates the Gospel message. Christ has risen from the dead and will triumphantly return again to rule and to raise up those who belong to him. A resurrected body which is immortal is necessary in order to share in God's kingdom. At the return of Chris our bodies will be transformed into immortal bodies—demonstrating Christ's victory over death.
Financial Support—Relief funds; Christian workers	Ch 16	*Problem*—the Corinthians lack of recognition of, respect for, and supporting of Christian workers; need for relief fund. *Advice*—The Corinthians should systematically put aside money for the relief fund. They should send off the Christian workers with finances.

Problems In Other Churches

Table 1,2 Ti 55-2 lists in very brief form problems implied in other churches.

Table 1,2 Ti 55-2. Problems in Other Churches

Church	Possible Problems
At Rome	Understanding of Gospel both for initial salvation and for growth / Sovereign working of God—Jews and Gentiles; Giftedness; Disputed Practices.
Galatian Church	Understanding of Gospel—fundamental work of Cross/ legalism; strategic level spiritual warfare; work of Holy Spirit in a life; recovery of those who sin;
At Ephesus	At least 4 heresies—two of which are not clear (see Leadership Insights for 1,2Ti); improper conduct in worship; heretical teachings given by women; improper leadership selection criteria; acceptance of Timothy in this church setting; problems in Timothy's own life; social problem—how to help widows in need; lack of discipline of leaders falling short; conduct of slaves; rich people and their use of money; conscience; heresy causing arguments and dividing; social pressure toward negative character traits.
At Phillipi	Reaction of a leader under persecution and pressure; lack of unity in the body; specific disagreement of two women; need for joy as an expression of Christian reality.
Colosse	Seeds of Gnostic heresy—legalism in church; understanding of strategic level warfare/ place of the Cross in it; maturity issues for the body.
Thessalonica	Doctrinal problems about the second coming; misunderstanding of spiritual gifts of prophecy; lack of respect for leaders; failure to work.
On Crete	Lack of understanding of fundamental Biblical truth; in appropriate lifestyle behaviors by men and women; need for leadership selection criteria; understanding of 2nd Coming and its impact on present behavior.

Conclusion

Let me summarize and give a challenge. A major macro lesson occurring across all the leadership eras can be simply stated as: *Leadership is complex, problematic, difficult and fraught with risk—which is why leadership is needed.* Leadership is complex. Paul deals with a whole range of problems including moral issues, philosophical issues, practical everyday issues, social issues, theological issues, conceptual issues, methodological issues. Problems in a leadership situation are a main reason for the existence of leaders. Leaders must see problems not as hindrances to leadership but as the warp and woof of leadership responsibility. Problems actually can become challenges to those who can carry a positive attitude. It is in the midst of problem solving that much creative thinking emerges. Two observations are worth meditation.

a. Problems are opportunities for creative leadership to take place.

b.   Problems are part of the responsibility of leaders. They come with the territory. If you are a leader you must expect to constantly deal with problems.

Here is the challenge! Paul had a burden for the churches.

> 28 Then besides all this, daily, I am burdened with my responsibility for the churches. 29 I feel for them when they are weak. When someone falls I'm really upset. 2Co 11:28,29

So rather than be daunted by the many problems in these churches, he did three things:
1. He sent advice to help solve problems.
2. He sent people to them to help out.
3. He prayed about them regularly.

I will comment on all three.

On sending advice—note the theme of 1Co. This alone should be encouraging to us who face complex problems in our leadership.

Theme	**Church Problems, In Corinth,**
	• involve multiple/ complex issues: Problem about wisdom; Problem About Divisions; Problem on Toleration of Immorality; Problem of Lawsuits Among Believers; Problems About Marriage; Problem on Disputed Practices; Problem on Worship Practices; Problems About Spiritual Gifts; Problem About Resurrection; Problems in supporting Christian workers.
	• were dealt with by Paul in highly directive leadership styles, and
	• are seen as solvable if people respond to God's revelation about them.

But further, study the Pauline epistles from this perspective: What were the problems being dealt with and how did Paul deal with it?

On Sending People to Help Out—study especially Titus and Timothy's ministries.

On praying—note the following.

> First, I **thank** my God through Jesus Christ for you all, that your faith is spoken of throughout the whole world. Ro 1:8

> I **thank** my God always on your behalf, for the grace of God which is given you by Jesus Christ. 1Co 1:4

> Cease not to give **thanks** for you, making mention of you in my prayers. Eph 1:16

> I **thank** my God upon every remembrance of you. Php 1:3

> We give **thanks** to God and the Father of our Lord Jesus Christ, praying always for you. Col 1:3

> We give **thanks** to God always for you all, making mention of you in our prayers. 1Th 1:2

> We are bound to **thank** God always for you, Christian friends, as is appropriate, because your faith is really growing and your love reaches out all toward each other. 2Th 1:3

It is not enough just to pray about the needs and problems in churches. As leaders we must have a real note of thankfulness for these churches, which have many problems. My final word on problems in N.T. churches is, be thankful for these churches.

Relevance of the Article to 1,2 Timothy
My hermeneutical system involves 7 General Laws. The first one, labeled *Book and Books* is stated as, **In the Spirit, Prayerfully Study The Book As A Whole In Terms Of Its Relationship To Other Books in The Bible** (i.e. the Bible as a whole) **TO INCLUDE**: a. its place in the progress of redemption (both as to the progress of revelation, what God has said, and also the notion of what God has done in redemptive history) b. its overall contribution to the whole or Bible literature (i.e. *its purposes --why is it in the Bible?*) and c. its abiding contribution to present time. Five of the six laws study the book as a whole (*Book and Books, historical background, structure, theme, context*). One other law deals with the grammatical relationships within a given context. The final one involves studying *words* within a given context. Before one can comment on leadership findings in a book, due diligence, must be done in terms of a given book's reasons for being included in the Bible (i.e. studying it hermeneutically). Having done this, one can then comment, with due regard for the interpretation of the book, on its implications for leadership. This article takes the first principle, *Book and Books*, and traces throughout the Bible, when each book occurs and its basic contribution to the redemptive flow of God's working.

56. Redemptive Drama, The Biblical Framework

Introduction

In each of the overviews on the various individual books in the leadership commentary series I have a section called **Where It Fits**. In that section, I try to deal with the application of my first general hermeneutical principle,[384]

Language Principle 1 Book and Books
In The Spirit, Prayerfully Study The Book As A Whole In Terms Of Its Relationship To Other Books In The Bible (i.e. the Bible as a whole) **TO INCLUDE**:
  a. its place in the progress of redemption (both as to the progress of revelation, what God has said, and also the notion of what God has done in redemptive history)
  b. its overall contribution to the whole or Bible literature (i.e. *its purposes --why is it in the Bible?*) and
  c. its abiding contribution to present time.

I seek to find **Where It Fits** using two basic overall frameworks:

1. *The Unfolding Drama of Redemption*—that is, telling the story of what God has said and done in the Bible.[385]

2. *The Leadership Framework*. Since this is a leadership commentary series, I want to trace the contribution of a book to leadership. The leadership era it fits in helps inform us as to how to interpret its leadership findings.

This article is concerned with the first of these two frameworks: *The Unfolding Drama of Redemption*. I have previously dealt with the second framework in several articles.[386]

---

[384] See Appendix G in **Having A Ministry That Lasts** for the whole hermeneutical system I use.

[385] I am deeply indebted to a teaching mentor of mine, James M. (Buck) hatch who introduced me to this framework in his course, Progress of Redemption, given at Columbia Bible College. I have used his teaching and adapted it in my own study of each book in the Bible in terms of the Bible story as a whole. I have also written in depth on this in my handbook, **The Bible and Leadership Values**. This article is a condensed version of that larger explanation.

I will first introduce the overall framework with a diagram. Then I will give a brief synopsis for each chapter of the redemptive drama. Finally, I will list the Bible books in terms of the chapters of the redemptive drama.

Overall Framework--Redemptive Drama Pictured

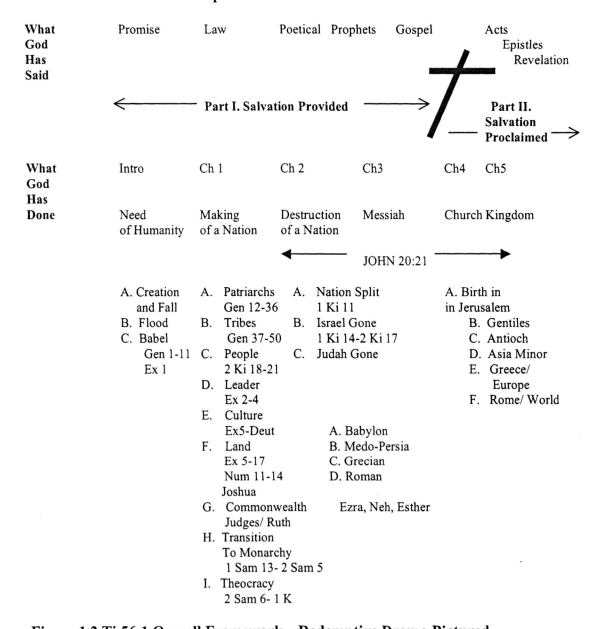

Figure 1,2 Ti 56-1 Overall Framework—Redemptive Drama Pictured

---

[386] See **Articles**, *26. Six Biblical Leadership Eras--Overviewed; 36. Macro Lesson Defined; 37. Macro Lessons--List of 41 Across Six Leadership Eras.*

The **Time-Line of the Redemptive Story** contains six sections,
         Introduction,
         Chapter 1. The Making of A Nation,
         Chapter 2. The Destruction of A Nation,
         Chapter 3. Messiah,
         Chapter 4. The Church, and
         Chapter 5. The Kingdom.

This story is briefly explained in a Running Capsule of the Redemptive Story. The story traces **what God does** and **what He says** throughout the Bible. And it shows that there is a progressive revelation of God throughout the whole drama. The Bible is unified around this salvation history. Once this is recognized then the notion of intentional selection becomes important. Each book in the Bible is there for a purpose and contributes something to this salvation story.

It is this framework which provides the macro context for studying each book of the Bible. Where is the book in the progress of redemption time-line? What does it contribute to it? Why is it there? What would we miss if it were left out? Understanding each book in terms of its own purpose is a preliminary first step that must be done before we can interpret it for leadership findings.

The Running Capsule for the Redemptive Story

I will first give an overview and then give more detail from each part of the redemptive drama.

Overall

At the center of the Biblical revelation is the concept of a God who has intervened in human history. He created the human race. He has revealed himself to that race. That race rebelled against His desires. In its fallen state it continually rebels against His wishes and desires and for the potential that it could accomplish.

So He started again and selected specifically a people through whom He could reveal Himself to the world. God moves unswervingly toward His purpose which is to redeem people and relate to them. He moves toward His purposes whether or not the people He has chosen follow them or not. They can willingly be a part in which they enjoy the blessings of God or they can be by-passed and He will find other ways to accomplish His purposes. He patiently works with them to include them in His purposes. But when all is said and done He moves on with or without them.

All the time He is increasingly revealing more of Himself and His purposes to His people. They come to know Him as a mighty God, all powerful and controlling, yet allowing human beings their choices. He is a holy God, that is, a being of perfection. He reveals His purposes as that of having a Holy people following Him. People who are becoming Holy as He is holy. They learn that to fall short of His demands or standards is to sin against Him and is deserving of retribution if justice is to be satisfied.

Part I of the redemption drama, **SALVATION PROVIDED**, is His selection of a people, which will prove foundational to accomplishing His purposes. Out of that people will come one who is central in the decrees of God. Not an afterthought but mysteriously beyond our thinking, known to God. Look at Revelation 13:8, the Lamb slain before the foundation of the world. In terms of what we know of God today, we see this Part I as revealing to us, God the Father, that is, the God who is source of all that we are and to whom we relate, infinite, eternal, powerful, a spirit.

God protects that line through which He will come over a period of many years and in times of failure on their part to know Him and obey Him as they should.

His incarnation into the world begins Part II of the Redemptive Drama, **SALVATION PROCLAIMED**. Galatians 4:4, in God's time. That incarnate God, manifest in the flesh, to communicate directly with the human race, to be a part of it, to share in its joys and sorrows, finally pays the supreme price of rejection, by a world who wanted to call its own shots, the death of the Cross, perfection paying the perfect price to satisfy God's Holy just demands. The great dilemma was solved, how God could be absolutely just and yet lovingly receive to Himself, those for whom justice demanded the harsh penalty of death. That time in which Jesus lived and walked and taught and did so many things to reveal God to us is the time, as we now know it of God the Son, God revealed to a human race as one of that race. Having accomplished the first portion of His work, the Cross, He ascended to heaven and will yet come again.

Having ascended, He sent the Holy Spirit into the world, the intimation of what is to come, the Spirit who indwells those people He has chosen.

In the meantime while we wait we are involved in Part II **Salvation Proclaimed**, which shows that this message was more than just for the Jews but for a whole world. And that is what we are about today, the proclamation of that reconciling message, that God has provided a way in which sinful human beings can be rightly related to Him and progress to live a satisfying and fruitful life, in harmony with His purposes. And as they live this purposeful life, demonstrating the power and presence of God in their time on earth, they know that God is going to make all things right someday--there is a justice coming; the Lord Jesus, now a risen Savior, a life-giving Spirit will return to claim His own. There will be a time of His reigning on earth and then there will be eternity. And we who have been called out, as a people to His name, will reign with Him for all eternity. In terms of what we know today, this is the Age of God, the Spirit.

Introduction

Genesis tells us of many beginnings. It tells of the beginning of the creation, the human race, of sin in the world, of the spread of the race, of judgment on the race and a new beginning for the race. It does not satisfy all our questions. We would ask more and want more. But it does give us the backdrop for the salvation story. Humanity is in need. It can not get along with itself. It has alienated itself from God. Left to itself it will be destructive at best. There is a need. And the salvation story which begins in Genesis chapter 12 will give God's response to meet that need.

Chapter 1. The Making of a Nation

God's basic plan is to choose a people and to reveal Himself and His plans for reconciling the world to Himself through that nation. Chapter 1 tells of the story of God's building of the nation.

If I were to pick out the most important events in the making of a nation, Chapter 1 of the redemptive drama I would say the following would certainly be a part of it.

1.   The call of Abraham--the Abrahamic Promise
2.   The renewal of the covenant with Isaac
3.   The renewal of the covenant with Jacob
4.   The deliverance of Jacob and sons through Joseph
5.   The call of Moses
6.   The power encounters in Egypt and the Exodus
7.   The Red Sea deliverance
8.   The Spies in the Land/corporate failure of a faith check
9.   The Giving of the 10 Commandments/covenant
10.   Moses' failure--striking the rock
11.   Moses' outstanding leadership in the desert years with a rebellious followership and his transition of Joshua into leadership
12.   Crossing of Jordan
13.   Circumcision at Gilgal
14.   Joshua meets the Captain of the Hosts
15.   Capture of Jericho
16.   Failure at Ai
17.   Success at Ai
18.   Gibeonite deception
19.   Capture of Land (lack of total obedience)
20.   Repetitive Failure--moving from dependence to independence. The Cycle of the Judges (need for centralized influence)
21.   Samuel's unifying influence
22.   Saul's anointing and failure
23.   David's anointing and success
24.   David's failure and discipline
25.   David's preparation for building the temple

Lets examine some of the Bible books which present these events.

From Genesis

From the introduction we know that humanity is not in good shape and is in need of intervention by God. And God has a plan thought out in eternity past.

God chooses one man, Abraham, and Promises (*The First Great Revelation--The Promise*) to make of him a great nation and to give them land and to bless the world through his offspring. (Gen 12:1-3, 7; 15:4,18, et al) Now God plans to use the nation He will bring forth to be a channel of redemption and revelation of Himself. So He begins to build a nation. For a nation you need people (including numbers) a coherent culture, a land, and a leader.

God begins to work on these things--the people first (the land has people on it who will be judged eventually when they are too evil to be redeemed). From this one man, who exemplifies faith in God's promise, comes a son, Isaac. Isaac has two sons, one of whom, Jacob, becomes the successor of the family line through which God will work--the 12 heads of the tribes: Reuben, Simeon, Levi, Judah, Zebulun, Issachar, Dan, Gad, Asher, Naphtali, Joseph, Benjamin.

Joseph, a son of Jacob's old age and his favorite, is sold into slavery by his jealous brothers (Acts 7:9 Because the patriarchs were jealous of Joseph they sold him as a slave into Egypt. But God was with him and rescued him from all his troubles. He gave Joseph wisdom and enabled him to gain the goodwill of Pharaoh king of Egypt; so he made him ruler over Egypt and all his palace.) Joseph, a person of proven integrity, rises to power through a series of providential appointments in which he shows wisdom from God upon several occasions. God gives some dreams to Pharaoh, the ruler of Egypt, which predict some good years followed by famine years. Joseph gives a wise plan to Pharaoh on how to prepare for it. He is put in charge and is right on target to protect his own family when the famine hits. The family comes to Egypt and rides through the famine years. It stays and expands in the land. Joseph , never losing sight of God's promise, exacts a promise from his brothers and fellow Israelites that they will take him back into the land when God takes them back. That is how Genesis ends.

From Exodus

Exodus opens many years later. There are many Israelite descendants, so many in fact, that the Egyptian King is fearful of them so he subjugates them. They are slaves and being ill-treated. Persecution takes the form of enforced labor and attempts to cut down the population (executing the boy babies).

God, having fulfilled the first part of his plan, getting a people, now works on the second part--getting a leader. Moses, an Israelite baby is preserved providentially and taken into the palace and educated as an Egyptian royal class person. As he reaches adulthood he recognizes that his people by blood relationship are in great bondage. So he wants to free them. His first attempt to help them is a disaster. He kills an Egyptian and has to flee Egypt. He goes to Midian, settles down, marries a Midianite woman, and has a family. After forty years, God selects him via a miraculous revelation, to go back to Egypt to lead God's people out of Egypt and into the promised land. Moses goes back and after 10 major confrontations with the Egyptian ruler (in which God-given power is seen--Moses certainly has spiritual authority) the people are freed to leave. But on the way the Egyptian ruler has second thoughts and pursues with his military. The military should overtake the Israelites who will be trapped by the Red Sea. God miraculously intervenes and they escape across the Red Sea on dry ground. The sea moves back as the military forces start to cross and they are wiped out. This is the heart of *the Exodus*.

From Exodus and Leviticus

God next begins to build the people culturally into what He will need. He gives them the LAW, the second great revelation and reveals more of Himself, His standards, and His purposes. The tabernacle which He gives the plans for reveals more of who God is in terms of access and revelation. The rest of EXODUS is given to that, revealing who G ·d is as is the whole of LEVITICUS. It is especially in Leviticus that the holiness of God is developed--an understanding of sin and its implications; what atonement is (that is, being made right with God by making up for wrong against Him).

From Numbers

After disobedience and a lack of faith prevent the people from going in to the land (see NUMBERS) they wander for 40 years in the Sinai desert until the older rebellious people die off. During the desert years they learn to trust in God's provision. God reveals Himself primarily through his leader Moses. Near the end of the 40 years they are again ready to go into the land. God has a people, a culture, a leader, Moses, and a leader to take his place, Joshua. Moses prepares them for that push into the land by giving them a series of addresses (DEUTERONOMY—second law). These messages, his final words to them, reflect warnings drawn from their desert experience, remind them of standards of obedience which reflects what they have learned of God, and gives encouragement in the form of expectations as they enter the land. He closes his final words to them with songs of warning and blessing that portend the future. And thus we are ready for the third part of God's plan to build Himself a people--getting them into the land.

From Joshua

Joshua transitions into leadership with some sterling miraculous interventions by God which give him the spiritual authority he will need to follow Moses (a hard act to follow) as leader. Joshua seizes Jericho, after following a supernaturally revealed plan for its capture. He proceeds after an unexpected failure, which teaches an important corporate lesson on obedience, to the people, to split the land in two militarily and then begins to mop up in the north and south. The land is allotted. Each tribe has a portion, just as Moses had planned. They decentralize and begin to settle into their spots--with much trouble. After having been so long in a centralized authoritarian mode, they enjoy being decentralized and having autonomy. But this decentralization eventually leads to spiritual deterioration. This brings us up into the times of the judges.

From Judges

For a long period of time, longer than we in the United States have been a nation, the twelve tribes live scattered. There is frequent civil war in specific locales and much fighting with various surrounding nations and peoples who were not totally destroyed when the land was taken.

In short there is an oft repeated cycle: the people deteriorate spiritually getting far from God, God brings judgment upon them, they finally recognize that their problem is relationship with God--they repent and cry out for God's help. He sends along leaders, very charismatic who usually lead a volunteer army to defeat their enemies. There are at least 13 of these including: Othniel, Ehud, Shamgar, Deborah (Barak), Gideon, Abimelech, Tola, Jair, Jephthah, Ibzan, Elon, Abdon, and Samson. Some of these are more well known than others. Gideon and Samson for example. These are evil times and few there are who follow God.

In a section of the Judges (Judges 2:7) the writer sums it up well, "After Joshua had dismissed the Israelites, they went to take possession of the land, each to his own inheritance. The people served the Lord through out the lifetime of Joshua and of the elders who outlived him and who had seen all the great things the Lord had done for Israel." And then again in the closing portion a repeated phrase haunts us-- Judges 21:25, "In those days Israel had no king; everyone did as he saw fit." These are the pre-kingdom years. Corporately the people are negatively prepared for the kingdom which will come.

From Ruth

There is a spark of life during those dreadful times. Ruth introduces us to that life by showing that there were some people of integrity who honored the Lord. This little romantic book shows how God provides and also allows us to see how the line through which the redeemer will later arise progresses.

The Judges and Ruth are pre-kingdom times. They prepared the Israelites to want a centralized structure after so much independence and autonomy. The Israelites were dependent upon voluntary armies raised up in times of crisis. Many times, other of the tribes than the one threatened, were not interested in their local squabbles and would not fight for them. Thus the entire commonwealth of tribes comes to the place where it needs, wants, and will accept a kingdom. Again God steps in and provides a transition leader--Samuel.

From 1 Samuel

The first thirteen chapters show how Samuel was providentially raised up as a leader. His ministry as judge was not just a momentary deliverance but a continual one. He visited the different tribes and judged them--that is, established law and justice for them. Samuel paves the way for a centralized kingdom. Crises around the people spur the need; Samuel's own sons are not able to replace him. The people demand a king--showing their need for one but also showing that they basically did not trust the unseen King. God gives them one king, Saul, who outwardly is what they would expect. But he fails repeatedly to follow God. His kingdom is spiritually bankrupt. God replaces him with David, whom God describes as *a man after my own heart.* The last part of 1 Samuel describes Saul's fall and David's early pre-kingdom years, in which David is gaining military expertise as a guerrilla warfare leader with a para-military band.

From 2 Samuel and 1 Chronicles and the Psalms

2 Samuel and 1 Chronicles give David's story--one written earlier to it and one written later. David is a long time in getting the kingdom as Saul's descendants try to hold on to the kingdom. After seven years of civil war, David is ruling a smaller part of Israel, the kingdom is united. God gives a covenant to David concerning his descendants. The poetical literature, particularly the Psalms, emerge more solidly from this era. David is an artistic person who spends time alone with God in worship. Many of the Psalms come out of those times alone with God, many spurred on by crises in David's kingdom. The kingdom is established under David and expands. In mid-life David has a major sin which tarnishes his lifetime. He has one of his military leaders killed in order that he might take his wife for himself. It and failure to manage his family well lead to a rebellion by one of his sons Absalom. David is deposed briefly but comes back winning a strategic battle. He is reinstated. Most of the rest of his kingdom is downhill. David's son, Solomon, after some manipulation and political intrigue succeeds David.

A number of the Psalms are ascribed to David. They reveal something of the personal touch--what that great leader was feeling during some of the more important times of his kingdom. They particularly show his need for God and why God calls him a "man after my own heart."

From Proverbs and Ecclesiastes

Solomon has the best start of any king in all the history of Israel. There is peace in the land. The borders have expanded almost to the full extent of God's promise. There is money and resources in the kingdom as well as a good military. Times are stable. Solomon builds the temple for God--a symbol of the centralized importance of religious worship in the capital. Solomon's early years are characterized by splendor. Most likely during the early and middle part of his reign many of the Proverbs were collected. These sayings embody truth that has been learned over the years (times of the Judges, times of the kingdom) about how to live harmoniously with others. Toward the end of his reign, he slips and falls away from following God. In this latter part of his reign, he writes Ecclesiastes which sums up much that he has learned over his lifetime. Its cynical tone shows need for an intimate relationship with God that is missing.

The nation is there. There are people. They know of God and his desires for them. There is a land. But they continually fail to live up to what God wants. During the reigns of David and Solomon the kingdom reaches its zenith. And thus ends Chapter 1, the making of a nation. In it all, God is seen to weave His purpose all around a people who frequently rebel against Him. They freely choose to live as they do, whether following after God or not. But even so He manages to move unswervingly forward to His purposes.

Chapter 2. The Destruction of a Nation

The story-line of chapter 2 hinges around the following major events:

1. Solomon goes away from the Lord, great warning--had the best start of any king yet did not finish well.
2. Rehoboam (1 Kings 12) makes unwise decision to increase taxes and demands on people-- kingdom splits as prophecy said. 10 tribes go with the northern kingdom, Judah with the southern.
3. The northern kingdom under Jereboam quickly departs from God. Jereboam is used as the model of an evil king to whom all evil kings are likened; He had a good start also--God would have blessed him.
4. The southern kingdom generally is bad with an occasional good Kings and partially good kings: Asa, Jehoshaphat, Joash, Amaziah, Uzziah, Jotham, Hezekiah, Josiah. But the trend was always downward. The extended length of life of the southern kingdom more than the northern kingdom is directly attributed to the spiritual life of the better kings. Spiritual leadership does make a difference.
5. During both the northern and southern kingdoms God sent prophets to try and correct them-- first the oral prophets (many--but the two most noted were Elijah and Elisha) and then the prophets who wrote.

Now in order to understand this long period of history you should know several things:
1. The History books that give background information about the times.
2. The Bible Time-Line, need to know when the books were written.
3. Need to know the writing prophets: northern or southern kingdom, which crisis, direct or special.

<u>The History Books</u>

The history books covering the time of the destruction of a nation include 1, 2 Samuel, 1,2 Kings, and 1,2 Chronicles. The following chart helps identify the focus of each of these books as to major content.

Table 1,2 Ti 56-1. The History Books--Major Content

1 Samuel	2 Samuel 1 Chronicles	1,2 Kings 2 Chronicles
Samuel, Saul, David	David	1,2 Kings: Solomon to Zedekiah 2 Chronicles exclusively on line of Judah

There are four categories of prophetical books. Prophetical books deal with three major crises: the Assyrian crisis which wiped out the northern kingdom; the Babylonian crisis which wiped out the southern kingdom; the return to the land after being exiled. There are also prophetical books not specifically dealing with these crises but associated with the time of them. The prophetical books dealing with these issues are:

A. Northern--Assyrian Crisis
    Jonah, Amos, Hosea, Nahum, Micah
B. Southern--Babylonian Crisis
    Joel, Isaiah, Micah, Zephaniah, Jeremiah, Lamentations, Habakkuk, Obadiah
C. In Exile
    Ezekiel, Daniel, Esther
D. Return From Exile
    Nehemiah, Ezra, Haggai, Zechariah, Malachi

In addition, to knowing the crises you must know that prophets wrote:

A. Direct to the Issue of the Crisis either Assyrian, Babylonian, or Return To The Land
    Amos, Hosea, Joel, Micah, Isaiah, Jeremiah, Ezekiel, Haggai , Zechariah, Malachi
B. Special
    Jonah, Nahum, Habakkuk, Obadiah, Zephaniah, Daniel.

The special prophets, though usually associated with one of the crisis times, wrote to deal with unique issues not necessarily related directly to the crisis. The following list gives the special prophets and their main thrust.
1. Jonah--a paradigm shift, pointing out God's desire for the nation to be missionary minded and reach out to surrounding nations.
2. Nahum--vindicate God, judgment on Assyria.
3. Habakkuk--faith crisis for Habakkuk, vindicate God, judgment on Babylon.
4. Obadiah--vindicate God, judgment on Edom for treatment of Judah.
5. Zephaniah--show about judgment, the Day of the Lord.
6. Daniel--give hope, show that God is indeed ruling even in the times of the exile and beyond, gives God's plan for the ages.

The Destruction of A Nation--The Return From Exile (see page 32)

Several Bible books are associated with the return to the land from the exile. After a period of about 70 years (during which time Daniel ministered) Cyrus made a decree which allowed some Jews (those that wanted to) to return to the land. Some went back under Zerrubabel, a political ruler like a governor. A priest, Joshua, also provided religious leadership to the first group that went back. This group of people started to rebuild the temple but became discouraged due to opposition and lack of resources. They stopped building the temple. Two prophets, after several years, 10-15, addressed the situation. These two, Haggai and Zechariah, were able to encourage the leadership and the people to finish the temple.

Another thirty or forty years goes by and then we have the events of the book of Esther, back in the land. Her book describes the attempt to eradicate the Jewish exiles--a plot which failed due to God's sovereign intervention via Esther, the queen of the land and a Jewish descendant going incognito, and her relative Mordecai.

Still another period of time passes, 20 or so years and a priest, Ezra, directs another group to return to the land. The spiritual situation has deteriorated. He brings renewal.

Another kind of leader arrives on the scene some 10-15 years later. Nehemiah, a lay leader, and one adept at organizing and moving to accomplish a task, rebuilds the wall around Jerusalem. He too has to instigate renewal.

Finally, after another period of 30 or so years we have the book of Malachi which again speaks to renewal of the people. The Old Testament closes with this final book.

A recurring emphasis occurs during the period of the return. People are motivated to accomplish a task for God. They start out, become discouraged, and stop. They must be renewed. God raises up leadership to bring renewal.

Preparation for the Coming of Messiah--The Inter-Testamental Period

I do not deal with this in detail, that is in terms of the various historical eras.[387] Some 400+ years elapse between the close of the Old Testament and the Beginning of the New Testament. There are significant differences in the Promised Land. Table 1,2 Ti 56-2 highlights these differences.[388]

Table 1,2 Ti 56-2. Differences in Palestine--Close of O.T., Beginning of N.T.

The End of the Old Testament	The Beginning of the New Testament
1. Palestine was part of a Persian satrapy, since Persian, an eastern nation was the greatest governmental power in the world at the time.	1. Palestine was a Roman province, since the entire world had come under the sway of the western Nation of Rome.
2. The population was sparse.	2. One of the most dense parts of the Roman empire.
3. The cities of Palestine as a whole were heaps of rubbish.	3. There was general prosperity throughout Palestine.
4. The temple of Zerubbabel was a significant structure.	4. The temple of Herod the Great was a magnificent building.
5. There were no Pharisees or Sadducees, although the tendencies from which they developed were present.	5. The Pharisees and Sadducees were much in evidence and strong in power.
6. There were no synagogues in Palestine.	6. Synagogues were located everywhere in the Holy Land. There was no hamlet or village so small or destitute as to lack a synagogue
7. There was little extra-biblical tradition among the Jews.	7. There was a great mass of tradition, among both the Jews of Palestine and those of the dispersion.

---

[387] In **Leadership Perspectives**, I do deal more in a detailed way with the various historical sub-phases of this period of history. A number of books in the Catholic canon occur during this period of time.

[388] These notes are adapted from material studied with Frank Sells at Columbia Bible College in his Old Testament survey course.

8. The Jews were guilty of much intermarriage with the surrounding nations.	8. There was almost no intermarriage between Jews and non-Jews.
9. Palestine was under the rule of a Hebrew.	9. Palestine was under the rule of an Edomite vice-king, Herod the Great.
10. The Hebrew governor was regarded by the Jews as their spiritual leader.	10. The scribes and priest were regarded by the Jews as their spiritual leaders.

In addition to differences, there were some similarities between end of O.T. times and beginning of N.T. times.

1. **Freedom from idolatry.** God had used the Babylonian Captivity to free His people from their oft-repeated tendency to idolatry.
2. **Israel in two great divisions,** the Jews of the Homeland (Isolation) and the Jews of the Dispersion (who were scattered throughout the world). In the time of Malachi a relatively small proportion of God's chosen people was located in Palestine, while by far the larger part was still in exile. Although Palestine was much more thickly populated in the time of Christ than in the time of Malachi, the same general situation prevailed as to the two-fold division of Israel into Palestinian Jews and Jews of the Diaspora (Dispersion), with a far greater number in exile than in the land of Canaan.
3. **Externalism and dead orthodoxy.** A comparison of Malachi (the last prophetical book of the Old Testament) and Nehemiah (the last historical book of the Old Testament) with the Gospels indicates that the outward conformity of the Pharisees to the law which they inwardly revolted from, was but an advanced step of the hypocritical conformity which had marked many Israelites at the end of Old Testament days.

It was during the inter-testamental period that these changes occurred. Daniel had foretold of the various empires that would emerge after Babylon: the Medo-Persian, the Grecian, and the Roman. Each of these were used by God to prepare the way for the coming of Messiah, the next chapter in the redemptive drama.

Galatians 4:4 states that Messiah came at the "fullness of time." That is, the time was ready. Some have suggested a fivefold preparation for Christ's Coming.

1. Religious Preparation--both negative and positive
2. Political Preparation--world at peace
3. Cultural Preparation--lack of meaning; cultural vehicle through which to spread the Gospel
4. The Social Preparation--great needs; life under bondage
5. The Moral Preparation

Chapter 3. Messiah

At the right moment in time--Jesus was born. His miraculous birth attested to his uniqueness.

He was the fulfillment of the Old Testament as to many of its prophecies, types, symbols. He was the seed of the woman who dealt a fatal blow to the seed of the serpent (Genesis 3:15); he was the tabernacle who lived among us (Exodus 25-40); he was the arch type of the brazen serpent, lifted up that people might look, see and be healed (Numbers 21); he was the arch types of the Levitical offerings , the perfect sacrifice (Leviticus 1-5); he was that prophet like unto Moses (Deuteronomy 18); he was the ultimate fulfillment of the Davidic covenant (2 Samuel 7); he was the Mess.∵nic Sufferer (Psalm 22); he was the one who was anointed to preach good news to the poor, to proclaim freedom for the captives, and release from darkness those who are prisoners, to proclaim the year of the Lord's favor (Isaiah 61:1ff) and the Suffering Servant (Isaiah 53); he was the righteous branch from David's line (Jeremiah 23); he was the one shepherd, the servant David, the prince of Ezekiel (Ezekiel 37); he was the one greater than Jonah, the sign after three days he arose (Jonah 21); he was the proper leader coming out of obscure Bethlehem (Micah 5:2); and we could go on.

Matthew showed he was the Messiah King, rejected. Mark showed him to be vested with divine power, a person of action and authority. Luke showed him to be the perfect representative of the human race: one of courage, ability, social interests, sympathy, broad acceptance. And John showed him to be Immanuel, God with us, revealing God to us and acting to demonstrate grace and truth, the heartbeat of the divine ministry philosophy.

The bottom line of the story line is given in a quote taken from John, "He was in the world, and though the world was made through him, the world did not recognize him. He came unto his own, but his own did not receive him. Yet to all who received him, to those who believed in his name, he gave the right to become children of God, children born not of natural descent, nor of human source but born of God. The Word became flesh and made his dwelling among us. We have seen his glory, the glory of the One and Only, who came from the Father, full of grace and truth." (John 1:10-14).

The story of this chapter of the redemptive drama ends abruptly. But there is a postscript. Each of the Gospel stories and the Acts tell us of Jesus Christ's resurrection. After His death He arose and was seen for a period of about 40 days upon various occasions. During those days He gave the marching orders for the movement He had begun. The great commissions repeated five times, Matthew 28:19,20, Luke 24:46,47, Mark 16:15, John 20:21, and Acts 1:8. Each of these carry the main thrust which is to go into the world and tell the Good News of salvation, that people can be reconciled to God. Each also carries some special connotation. It is these marching orders which set the stage for Chapter 4, The Church, in the redemptive story.

Chapter 4. The Church

The essence of the story line of chapter 4, is contained in the book of Acts. Its central thematic message is the essence of the story line.

Theme:　　**The Growth Of The Church**
- which spreads from Jerusalem to Judea to Samaria and the uttermost parts of the earth,
- is seen to be of God,
- takes place as Spirit directed people present a salvation centered in Jesus Christ, and
- occurs among all peoples, Jews and Gentiles.

This basic phenomenon reoccurs as the Gospel spreads across cultural barriers throughout the world. Though the message of the book of Acts covers only up through the first two thirds of the first century its basic essence reoccurs throughout the church age until the present time in which we live.

About half of the book of Acts tells of the formation of the church in Jerusalem and its early expansion to Jews, Samaritans, and finally to Gentiles. The latter half of the book traces the breakout of the Gospel to Gentiles in Asia and Europe. The structure of the book highlighted by the linguistic discourse markers (the Word of the Lord grew) carries the notion of a God-given church expanding.

Structure: There are seven divisions in Acts each concluding with a summary verse.
The summary verses: 2:47b, 6:7, 9:31, 12:24, 16:5, 19:20, 28:30,31

I.	(ch 1-2:47)	The Birth of the Church in Jerusalem
II.	(ch 3-6:7)	The Infancy of the Church in Jerusalem
III.	(ch 6:8-9:31)	The Spread of the Church into Judea, Galilee, Samaria
IV.	(ch 9:32-12:24)	The Church Doors Open to the Gentiles
V.	(ch 13-16:5)	The Church Spreads to Asia Minor
VI.	(ch 16:6-19:20)	The Church Gains a Foothold in Europe
VII.	(ch 19:21-28)	The Travels of the Church's First Missionary To Rome (The Church on Trial in its Representative Paul)

As to details there are many important pivotal events in the Acts, many of which have similarly reoccurred in the expansion of the Gospel around the world and throughout church history. Acts begins with Jesus' post resurrection ministry to the disciples and his Ascension to heaven. Then the disciples are gathered at Jerusalem praying when the Pentecost event, the giving of the Holy Spirit to the church, as promised in Luke's version of the Great Commission, happens and Peter gives a great public sermon which launches the church.

Early church life is described. Peter and John imbued with power heal a lame man at the temple gate and are put in prison. They are threatened and released. An incident with Ananias and Sapphira shows the power and presence of the Holy Spirit.

Stephen an early church servant has a strong witness and is martyred for it. General persecution on the church breaks out. The believers are scattered and preach the gospel where ever they go. Phillip, another early church servant leads an Ethiopian palace administrator to Christ and has ministry in Samaria.

Saul, the persecutor of Christians, is saved on the road to Damascus. Peter demonstrates Godly power in several miraculous events. Peter is divinely chosen to preach the Gospel to a Gentile, Cornelius. Herod kills James and imprisons Peter. Peter is miraculously delivered.

The story line now switches to follow the missionary efforts of Barnabas and Paul (formerly Saul) to Cyprus and Asian minor. It then goes on to follow Paul's efforts which go further into Asia minor and Greece. Paul makes a return visit to Jerusalem where he is accused by the Jewish opposition in Jerusalem. Eventually after several delays and hearings he is ordered to Rome. The book ends with the exciting journey to Rome, including a shipwreck.

The books of the New Testament were written to various groups during the church chapter. Many were written by Paul. These generally were letters to the various churches which had resulted from his missionary efforts. Each was contextually specific--written at a certain time, written at a certain stage of Paul's own development as a leader, and dealing with a specific situation--either an individual in a church or to a corporate group, some church at a location or in a general region.

Other New Testament books were not written by Paul. The book of Hebrews, author uncertain, John's three letters, Jude's one letter and Peter's two letters all are of a general nature. With the exception of possibly 2nd and 3rd John, these letters were written to believer's in general in scattered regions--probably Asia minor.

All of these, Paul's letters, and the general books, deal with the church. They give us insights into church problems, church situations at that time, and the essence of what the church is and how Christians ought to live. These New Testament books are filled with leadership information. Each of them represents a major leadership act of a leader seeking to influence followers of Christ. Many of them have actual details that reflect leadership values, leadership problem solving, and leadership issues. All of them have important modeling data.

We would have an unfinished story if we were left only with *just these* New Testament books. We would have a task. And men and women would be out and about the world attempting to fulfill that task. But where is it leading. What about those Old Testament prophecies yet to be fulfilled about *that day*. Our story is incomplete. We need to know how this redemptive drama is going to end. And so the Revelation.

<u>Chapter 5. The Kingdom</u>

The final book of the Bible is aptly named. The Revelation (unveiling, revealing, making clear) of Jesus Christ (the unveiling of Jesus Christ) brings closure to the redemptive drama. This final book in the Bible has among others these purposes:

1. to reveal future purposes of Jesus Christ and graphically show the power He will unleash in accomplishing His purposes, which include bringing about justice and bringing in His reign,
2. to show those purposes and power to be in harmony with His divine attributes, and
3. to bring a fitting climax to the redemptive story developed throughout Scripture.

The theme statement of the book of Revelation highlights the fitting climax of the redemptive drama.

Theme: **God's Ultimate Purposes For His Redemptive Program**
- center in the Person of His Son,
- involve His churches,
- will take place in a context of persecution and struggle--as described cryptically by many visions,
- will focus on the triumph of Jesus and his judgment of all things in harmony with his divine attributes, and
- will be realized in final victory for His people and ultimate justice accomplished in the world.

God's intent from the first of Genesis on has been to bless His people with His eternal presence. Ezekiel closes his book with that thought in mind. Numerous of the prophets point to a future day in which things would be made right and God would dwell with His people. The plan has had many twists and turns but through it all God has sovereignly moved on to His purpose.

Some have followed hard after God and were included in His purposes. Others refused to follow God. They were cast aside. God moved on.

In the New Testament God prepares a way where He can reveal Himself in justice and love and reconcile all people unto Himself. The Cross climaxes all of God's preparation to bless the world. The message of the Cross is seen to be for all. The church goes out into all the world. It has its problems. But always it seeks to be part of God's future purposes looking forward to Christ's return. Were there no Revelation, the Redemptive Story would be incomplete. The Revelation brings to a fitting climax all of God's working to bless the world. There is an ultimate purpose in history! Justice is meted out! And then a final blessing--God's eternal presence of with His people.

Suggested Chronological Writing of New Testament Books

When we study a given book of the bible we should know where it occurs in the redemptive drama. We should be familiar with what God has revealed to that point in time and what God has done redemptively up to that time. Table 1 below list each book of the Bible in terms of the Chapter in the redemptive story in which it falls. I have attempted to list each book in chronological order though there is not scholarly consensus on when some of these books were written.

Table 1,2 Ti 56-3. Bible Books Related To Chapters of the Redemptive Drama

The Bible Books: Chapter 1. The Making of a Nation

Exodus	Joshua	2 Samuel	Ecclesiastes
Leviticus	Judges	1 Chronicles	Song of Songs
Numbers	Ruth	Psalms	
Deuteronomy	1 Samuel	Proverbs	

The Bible Books: Chapter 2. The Destruction of a Nation

1,2 Kings	Hosea	Zephaniah	Daniel	Nehemiah
2 Chronicles	Micah	Jeremiah	Haggai	Malachi
Jonah	Isaiah	Lamentations	Zechariah	
Joel	Nahum	Obadiah	Esther	
Amos	Habakkuk	Ezekiel	Ezra	

The Bible Books: Chapter 3. Messiah

Matthew   Mark   Luke   John

The Bible Books: Chapter 4. The Church

James	2 Corinthians	Colossians	Titus	2 John
Acts	Galatians	Philemon	2 Timothy	3 John
1 Thessalonians	Romans	1 Peter	Hebrews	
2 Thessalonians	Ephesians	2 Peter	Jude	
1 Corinthians	Philippians	1 Timothy	1 John	

The Bible BOOK Chapter 5. Kingdom

Revelation

Relevance of the Article to 1,2 Timothy
It is clear from Acts 20 that the leadership in the Ephesus church involved a plurality of leaders. What is ·
not clear is whether or not there were regional churches (as in Corinth and Crete), which were also part of
this church. This article discusses the concept of regional churches and plurality of leadership and the
relative freedom of structures in different settings.

57. Regional Churches and Plurality of Leaders

Introduction
The New Testament gives lots of room for various forms of leadership structures in churches. A plurality of
leaders was one form of leadership. Consider the following verses which show a plurality of leaders.

Titus 1
5 The reason I left you in Crete was that you might straighten out what was left unfinished
concerning church leadership. I directed you to appoint church **leaders** in every town.

Acts 20
17 And from Miletus he sent to Ephesus, and called the **elders** of the church.

1 Timothy 3
1 This is a reliable saying, "If anyone aspires to leadership oversight, that one desires a good
work." ...

8 Similarly a lesser church leader should have good character, ...

11 Similarly, women leaders[389] should have good character,...

1 Timothy 5
17 Church **leaders** that are exercising good leadership should be evaluated as worthy of double
pay—especially the ones who are working hard teaching the word. ...
20 Those **leaders** that are sinning rebuke before all, that others also may fear.

Philippians
1 Paul and Timothy, the servants of Jesus Christ, to all the saints in Christ Jesus which are at
Philippi, with the **bishops** and **deacons**.

Plurality is well established. But the extent of leadership exercised by plurality is not so clear: plurality in a
house church? plurality in a local church? plurality in a regional church? plurality worldwide? Nor is the
relationship between a group of leaders serving as a plurality specified. How do they relate to one another?

---

[389] I have not dealt with the issue of female leadership in this article except to note that they exist in this
passage in Timothy. Priscilla, listed in this verse, was most likely a Bible teacher. Phoebe, listed in Ro 16:1
was serving as a leader also. For detail on this see **Article**, *20. Gender and Leadership*. See also
Leadership Topic 6 in 1 Ti.

But note also the notion of a strong leader, though unnamed here, even in a situation with plurality of leadership.

> Philippians
> 4: 3 And I intreat thee also, true **yokefellow**, help those women which labored with me in the gospel, with Clement also, and [with] other my fellow laborers, whose names [are] in the book of life

The New Testament also allows for various structures of the groups these leaders influenced. Note the following verses which seem to indicate very small groups of believers meeting in homes--that is, house churches.

> Philemon
> 2 Hello also to our beloved Apphia, and Archippus our fellow soldier, and to the church in your house.

> Romans 16
> 3 Greet Priscilla and Aquila my helpers in Christ Jesus…5 Likewise greet the church that is in their house.

> 10 Salute Apelles approved in Christ. Salute them which are of Aristobulus' household (indicating a group of believers, most likely).

> 11 Salute Herodion my kinsman. Greet them that be of the household of Narcissus, which are in the Lord household (again indicating a group of believers, most likely).

> 14 Salute Asyncritus, Phlegon, Hermas, Patrobas, Hermes, and the brethren which are with them (again indicating a group of believers, most likely).

> 15 Salute Philologus, and Julia, Nereus, and his sister, and Olympas, and all the saints which are with them (certainly indicating a small group of believers).

The New Testament also recognized larger groups of believers who met, probably in a city wide grouping.

> Philippians
> 1 Paul and Timothy, the servants of Jesus Christ, to all the saints in Christ Jesus which are at Philippi, with the bishops and deacons.

Further, there were groups, probably associated with a city wide base which were in a region (probably made up of house churches and local churches scattered about).

> 2nd Corinthians
> 1 Paul, an apostle of Jesus Christ by the will of God, and Timothy our brother, To the church of God which is at Corinth, with all the saints who are in all Greece.

> Galatians
> 1 Paul, an apostle, not of men, neither by man, but by Jesus C rist, and God the Father, who raised him from the dead; 2 And all the believers which are with me, unto the churches of Galatia:

What are we to make of these notions, plurality of leadership and various size groups over which leadership was exercised? My position is, we should be clear as the Bible on them: nothing less, nothing more, and nothing else. That will allow lots of freedom for different forms of leaderships and structures. Certain things happened historically and tradition has played a strong role in how we look at leadership today. But Biblically, we most likely have lots more freedom that is seen today.

Various Size Groupings: Small to Large

Probably it will help to define various size groupings of believers as seen in the New Testament.

definition	A <u>house church</u> was a small group of believers which met in someone's home with undetermined regularity and uncertainty as to leadership.
Example	The church that met in Philemon's house (Phm 2). The groups that met in the various homes in Rome (Romans 16:3,10,11,14,15).
Example	The host, person in the household in which the group met, probably exercised some kind of leadership (Priscilla and Aquila; Aristobulus; Narcissus; Asyncritus, Phlegon, Hermas, Patrobas, Hermes; Philologus, Julia, Nereus, and Olympas--all in Rome). Archippus probably led the church that met in Philemon's house.
Definition	A <u>local church</u> was a group of believers which gathered together usually on Sunday to sing, share truth from God, and partake in the Lord's supper.[390] There was appointed leadership consisting of elders and lesser leaders, deacons.[391]
Example	Phillipi, Ephesus
Example	Php 4:2 yokefellow. Rom 16:1 Phoebe
Example	The lesser leaders, which we call deacons, probably did service type of tasks in the local church (Acts 6, 1 Tim 5). This was a responsibility in which to grow and prove faithfulness. Such faithfulness could lead to becoming an elder, a recognized higher leadership level in a local church.
Comment	A given local church would probably have a plurality of leadership including multiple elders and multiple deacons. See Phillipi and Ephesus where the leaders are spoken of in the plural. (Php 1:1; 1 Ti 3:1-13; Acts 20)
Comment	Elders did two basic functions: 1. looked out for the spiritual welfare of the believers by teaching the word that is, truth from God to help the believers grow (oral tradition first and then later as the canon grew taught it); and by praying for the people, 2. led the local church—set its direction and helped it function as a group. They probably baptized folk and led the Lord's supper.
Definition	<u>Regional churches</u> consisted of a group of house churches or local churches in a given larger geographical situation
Example	Churches of Galatia—Paul addresses them as a group (Gal 1:2). Churches in Greece— Paul addressed them as a group (2 Co 1:1); Colosse—definitely a local church and most likely a regional since Laodicea believers and Philemon's house church read the circular letter sent to Colosse. Crete—believers were located in the various towns. Individual towns were to have a leader(s).

---

[390] See 1 Co 11 for regularity and verse 20 especially for Lord's Supper. See 1 Co 14 as a whole to show that the body participated in sharing revelatory truth from God. See 1 Co 16:2 which indicates regularity. See 1 Co 14:23 which shows the notion of a local church gathering. Col 3:16 which gives indication of a gathering and what they did. See 1 Ti 5:17 showing dual functions the leaders did—teaching and ruling. Note Php 4:2 for example of a ruling—solving problems.

[391] See **Article**, *50. Pauline Leadership Terms in the New Testament*. Also note 1 Ti 3 and Tit 1 where apostolic leaders like Timothy and Titus appointed leaders. See also Acts 14:21-23 where Barnabas and Paul apostolically appoint leaders in the fledgling churches begun on their first missionary journey.

Example   Leadership in regional churches is unclear. However, the Ephesian letter describing gifted leaders such as apostles, prophets, evangelists, pastors, teachers probably referred to regional leaders who traveled about ministering to more than one local church or house church in a region.[392] Paul has been describing the church universal in chapters 1-3. It appears in Eph 4:12-17 that he is applying this leadership to the broader size of structure rather than just a local church.

Definition   The <u>worldwide church</u>, sometimes called the universal church is composed of all the believers everywhere (and probably of all time) who make up the body of Christ.

Having defined the notion of plurality of leadership and also allowing for a strong leader over a group and the various sizes of groups we can probably give some observations which speak to the freedom we have in leadership today.

Conclusion

Here are observations that are drawn from the cursory treatment I have given about plurality and structures of churches.[393]

1. The New Testament house churches, local churches, and regional churches certainly allowed for a plurality of leaders. And this plurality could operate with or without some stronger leader to guide it (one among many concepts).

2. There could be a strong leader who dominated the leadership in a house church, local church, or regional church. Traditionally the term bishop came into being historically to describe a strong regional leader to whom all local churches related.

3. Leaders were appointed by apostolic types: Paul, Timothy, Titus. This function should happen today as well.

4. As to selection criteria for leadership, probably more important than *how many* leaders there are either in a house church or local church or regional church is *what kind* of leaders. At least this is true for house churches or local churches. The selection criteria focusing on character is paramount. For regional churches, the character issues would be a pre-requisite. In addition, the gifting would be important: apostleship, prophet, evangelist, pastor, teacher.

5. Eph 4:12-17 probably refers to regional leaders. A given local church may or may not have had the whole spectrum of leaders (apostles, prophets, evangelists, teachers, pastors)

6. Lesser leadership roles (deacons) provide experience for growth into more responsible leadership roles (elders/bishops).

7. Elders/bishops could be remunerated for their ministry. Paul, the exemplary apostolic leader for the church era, had freedom to accept remuneration or not. He would not if accepting it might thwart his ministry effort.

8. Spiritual authority, not positional authority, seems to be the major criterion on leadership at the various levels: house church, local church, regional church.

Let me restate some of the above observations in terms of leadership guidelines or values:

---

[392] John validates the notion of these traveling ministers (see 3, 5-9, 12 for veiled references to traveling ministers). Paul raises money for several of them (among which is Stephanus and Timothy).
[393] See also the **Leadership Topic 6, Leadership Guidelines** in 1 Ti, where I give observations flowing from Paul's advice to Timothy in the Ephesus situation.

<u>Leadership Principles/ Values Suggested by this concept:</u>
    a.   Character is crucial to leadership and must be the basis on which leaders are selected.
    b.   A Spirit-controlled conscience should be the norm for a leader.
    c.   Varying levels of church leadership and differing roles (probably based on giftedness) should be expected in local churches. The varying levels should be part of an overall leadership selection process.
    d.   A plurality of leadership can be used in a local church.
    e.   Plurality of leadership does not mean a lack of strong leadership. Plurality is not identified with consensus.
    f.   A foundational emphasis underlying leadership selection is the identification of integrity, character, and traits of exemplary being and behavior in a culture. Leadership in a local church should be above criticism (as to character) by the surrounding culture.
    g.   Lower levels of leadership should be allowed for a time of testing of younger leaders.

I close where I began. There is much freedom concerning leadership. While our traditional forms most likely fall into applications of this freedom, we as leaders need to be aware that there is probably much more freedom for how we view leadership today, than is the case in most of our leadership situations.

Relevance of the Article to 1,2 Timothy

Of all the things that Paul modeled for his followers, and yes, us too, the concept of *sovereign mindset* stands out as representative of what he meant in his Ro 8:28-30 sanctification concept. Paul viewed the happenings in his life through a God-lens, which always saw God's shaping activity involved. Such an attitude allowed him to make the best of his situations and to persevere on to a good finish. We do well to understand this concept—a sovereign mindset. If we do, we will find ourselves asking more *what questions* (what is God doing?) and fewer *why questions* (why me?) when deep processing comes our way. Hence, deep processing, difficult as it may be, will not blindside us. And we will have additional experiential resources (2 Cor 1:3,4) to help others out as they go through deep processing. 1,2 Ti demonstrates Paul at his very best in terms of maintaining a *sovereign mindset*. He knew God was in control of his life and ministry and had committed it back to God (2Ti 1:12; 4:18). He finished well. Sovereign Mindset was a major contributing factor to that great finish.

58. Sovereign Mindset

Mindset burst upon our English language scene in the mid-eighties. So it is a relative newcomer to English speakers. Not all English speakers even know it. But its definition is as old as the Bible itself. What is a mindset? A mindset is a fixed mental attitude or disposition—formed by experience, education, prejudice, or the like—that predetermines a person's responses to and interpretations of situations. One of the great Bible leaders, Paul the Apostle, demonstrated a special kind of mindset. I call it a sovereign mindset. A sovereign mindset represents one leadership value[394] that can make the difference for a Christian leader.[395] And I want to suggest that if you do not have this mindset you probably won't make it in ministry—at least not as an effective leader who will finish well.

A leadership value is an underlying assumption a leader holds which affects how the leader acts or perceives in leadership situations. It is a mindset, an underlying controlling force, which gives meaning to ourselves and explains why we do things or think things. It can relate to a belief. It can relate to personal ethical conduct. It can relate to personal feelings desired about situations. It can relate to ideas of what brings success or failure in ministry. It can be rooted in personality shaping. It can be rooted in heritage. It can be rooted in the critical shaping activities that describe our personal history of leadership development.

Paul models this leadership value, a sovereign mindset, more than any other New Testament Church leader.[396] Quickly glance through the two passages below to catch the flavor of this important leadership insight. Pay special attention to the boldfaced words.

---

[394] See also the **Article,** *51. Pauline Leadership Values,* which touches on 19 important leadership values derived from the book of 2Co. Values are desperately needed today in our world of tolerance for anything except absolutes. This article describes one important Christian leadership value.

[395] It can for a secular leader too. A Christian leader believes that God is involved in the events of life and therefore looks to learn what God has for him/her in the happenings of life. A secular leader who does not believe that God is or is involved in life's events can still also profit greatly from the happenings in life if that leader has a learning posture and believes that life's experiences can be used to teach lessons. The learning posture needed is simply, All of life is preparing us for all of the rest of life. We can be better leaders if we learn from life's experiences and let that learning inform our leadership. See also the **Article,** *29. Leadership Lessons—Seven Major Identified,* one of which deals with learning posture, "Effective leaders maintain a learning posture all of their lives."

[396] Paul is a major model for a Christian leader in the N.T. Leadership Era. We have more biographical information on Paul than any other Church leader. He himself recognizes the importance of modeling. See Php 4:9 and other cross-references.

> 3 Blessed [be] God, even the Father of our Lord Jesus Christ, the Father of mercies, and the God of all comfort; 4 Who comforts us in all our tribulation, **that we may be able to comfort them which are in any trouble,** by the comfort wherewith we ourselves are comforted of God. 5 For as the sufferings of Christ abound in us, so our consolation also abounds by Christ. 6 And whether we **be afflicted, [it is] for your consolation and salvation,** which is effectual in the enduring of the same sufferings which we also suffer: or whether we be comforted, [it is] for your consolation and salvation. 7 ¶ And our hope of you [is] steadfast, knowing, that as you are partakers of the sufferings, so [shall you be] also of the consolation. 2 Corinthians 1:3-7

> 8 For we would not, brethren, have you ignorant of our trouble which came to us in Asia, that we were pressed out of measure, above strength, inasmuch that we despaired even of life: 9 But we had the sentence of death in ourselves, **that we should not rely on ourselves, but in God which raises the dead: 10 Who delivered us from so great a death,** and does deliver: in whom we trust that he will yet deliver [us]; 11 You also helping together by prayer for us, that for the gift [bestowed] upon us by the means of many persons thanks may be given by many on our behalf. 2 Corinthians 1:8-11

Once you know what a sovereign mindset is, you can easily see it in the two previous quotes. But this sovereign mindset just leaps out from the pages in the following quotes.

> For this cause I Paul, the **prisoner of Jesus Christ** for you Gentiles, Eph 3:1

> I therefore, the **prisoner of the Lord**, implore you to walk worthy of your Christian calling. Eph 4:1

> So that my **bonds in Christ** are manifest in all the palace, and in all other [places]. Php1:13

> Don't be ashamed of the testimony of our Lord, nor of me **his prisoner**: but share also in the afflictions of the gospel according to the power of God; 2Ti 1:8

> Paul, a **prisoner of Jesus Christ**, and Timothy [our] brother, unto Philemon our dearly beloved, and fellow laborer, Phm 1:1

> Yet for love's sake I rather implore you, being such an one as Paul the aged, and now also **a prisoner of Jesus Christ**. Phm 1:9

Paul don't you have that wrong? Aren't you a prisoner of the Roman empire? Why do you say a prisoner of Jesus Christ? What a strange way to make your point! It's all in how you see it. Yes, Paul was a prisoner of the Roman Empire. But no matter what they intended, Paul knew God would use it for God's purposes. For you see, You Paul operated under a sovereign mindset.

Definition   A <u>sovereign mindset</u> is a way of viewing life's activities so as to see and respond to God's purposes in them.

Remember, a mindset is a fixed mental attitude or disposition that predetermines a person's responses to and interpretations of situations. Paul had a fixed mental attitude toward the things that happened to him. He saw God in them. Or as he says in 2Ti 3:11, "...out of them all God worked."

God was sovereignly and providentially working through all of life's circumstances to shape Paul, guide him, and make him the great leader he became. Four keys to Paul's sovereign mindset include:

1. Paul recognized God's hand in life happenings—no matter who or what the immediate cause.
2. Paul submitted to God's deeper purposes in life happenings.
3. Paul learned and used the lessons derived from these life happenings.
4. Paul shared those lessons (and God's provision in them) with others.

His deep experiences with God were at the heart of the spiritual authority[397] he had with followers.

Let me come back to the two passages I first cited as indicating a sovereign mindset. I want to draw out some leadership observations that directly apply to Christian leaders.

From 2Co 1:3-7:

1. God will meet us in deep processing.
2. We are helped in order to help.
3. Deep processing tests our own value in the sufficiency of Christ.
4. Our own development through processing gives us hope that our followers can also know the sufficiency of Christ in their deep processing.

From 2Co 1:8-11

1. We really trust in God when we come to the end of our own resources.
2. Deep processing is meant to be shared.
3. Deep processing shared brings partnership in prayer.
4. God receives much more praise when our situation is solved.

A leader with a sovereign mindset recognizes that at the heart of all God's shaping activities is the idea that processing is never just for himself/herself alone. Leaders are shaped by critical incidents and shaping activities for our development, yes! But our processing is also for our followers. It is this confidence in God's meeting us in deep processing that gives us confidence in His sufficiency. And a by-product of that confidence is spiritual authority, the dominant power base of a Christian leader.

Stated as a leadership value, the sovereign mindset strikingly challenges us.

Value   **Leaders Ought To See God's Hand In Their Circumstances As Part Of His Plan For Developing Them As Leaders.**

Paul had a sovereign mindset. He kept it till the end. It was one of the secrets of his finishing well. This leadership value is fundamental to a Christian view of the development of a leader.

See **Articles**, *51. Pauline Leadership Values; 29. Leadership Lessons—Seven Major Identified; 71. Value Driven Leadership.*

---

[397] See also the **Article**, *59. Spiritual Authority...*, which describes a major power base for a Christian leader.

Relevance of the Article to 1,2 Timothy

Paul had no positional authority with the Ephesian church. He had released that church to its own leadership in Ac 20. At the time of the righting of 1,2Ti Paul depended on spiritual authority—he had no positional authority with them. If his spiritual authority wasn't to be honored then he was in deep trouble. As you read through these six characteristics, think of whether Paul does or does not demonstrate them in the Ephesian situation. See also **Article** *21. Influence, Power, and Authority Forms* as you ascertain how Paul used his power base to influence the Ephesian church. Note also that Timothy had no positional authority there also. He was an outside consultant, representing Paul and being sponsored by him, coming in to help solve some major problems in the church. His ministry was that of an itinerant apostle. Spiritual authority was critical to Timothy too.

59. Spiritual Authority- Six Characteristics

A Biblical leader is a person with God-given capacities and with God-given responsibility who is influencing specific groups of God's people toward God's purposes for them. To influence, a leader must have some power base. I am indebted to Dennis Wrong[398] for helping me identify a taxonomy of concepts dealing with power. Wrong has influence as the highest level on his taxonomy, power next, and authority third. Influence can be unintended or intended. In terms of leadership we are interested in intended influence. Intended influence can be subdivided into four power forms, the second level: Force, Manipulation, Authority, and Persuasion. All of these are important for Christian leaders with the final two being the most important—authority and persuasion—since spiritual authority is related to both. Authority, the third level, can further be sub-divided into coercive, inductive, legitimate, competent, personal. A leader will need to use various combinations of these power forms to influence people. However,

Effective leaders value spiritual authority as a primary power base.

This is one of seven major leadership lessons that I have identified from comparative study of effective leaders. This article defines spiritual authority and gives some guidelines about its use.

Spiritual Authority—What Is It?

Spiritual authority is the ideal power base for a leader to use with mature believers who respect God's authority in a leader. A simplified definition focusing on the notion of maturity of believers is:

Definition   Spiritual authority is the
- right to influence,
- conferred upon a leader by followers,
- because of their perception of spirituality in that leader.

---

[398] See Dennis H. Wrong, **Power—Its Forms, Bases, and Uses**. 1979. San Francisco, CA: Harper and Row.

An expanded definition focusing on how a leader gets and uses it is:

Definition   Spiritual Authority is that
- characteristic of a God-anointed leader,
- developed upon an experiential power base (giftedness, character, deep experiences with God),

that enables him/her to influence followers through
- persuasion,
- force of modeling, and
- moral expertise.

Spiritual authority comes to a leader in three major ways. As leaders go through deep experiences with God they experience the sufficiency of God to meet them in those situations. They come to know God. This experiential knowledge of God and the deep experiences with God are part of the experiential acquisition of spiritual authority. A second way that spiritual authority comes is through a life which models godliness. When the Spirit of God is transforming a life into the image of Christ those characteristics of love, joy, peace, long suffering, gentleness, goodness, faith, meekness, temperance carry great weight in giving credibility that the leader is consistent inward and outward. A third way that spiritual authority comes is through gifted power. When a leader can demonstrate gifted power in ministry—that is, a clear testimony to divine intervention in the ministry via his/her gifts—there will be spiritual authority. Now while all three of these ways of getting spiritual authority should be a part of a leader, it is frequently the case that one or more of the elements dominates. From the definitions and description of how spiritual authority comes you can readily see that a leader using spiritual authority does not force his/her will on followers.

What Are Some Guidelines—To Maximize Use and Minimize Abuse
The following descriptive characteristics about spiritual authority sets some limits, describe ideals, warn against abuse and in general gives helpful guidelines for leaders who desire spiritual authority as a primary means of influence.

Six Characteristics And Limits Of Spiritual Authority
These six descriptions were derived from my own observations of leaders and from adaptations made from several writers on power such as Watchman Nee, R. Baine Harris, and Richard T. De George. Nee was a Chinese Christian leader. The other two are secular authorities on power and authority in leadership.

Table 1,2 Ti 59-1. Six Characteristics of Spiritual Authority

Characterization	Statement
1. Ultimate Source	Spiritual authority has its ultimate source in Christ. It is representative religious authority. It is His authority and presence in us which legitimates our authority. Accountability to this final authority is essential.
2. Power Base	Spiritual authority rests upon an experiential power base. A leader's personal experiences with God and the accumulated wisdom and development that comes through them lie at the heart of the reason why followers allow influence in their lives. It is a resource which is at once on-going and yet related to the past. Its genuineness as to the reality of experience with God is confirmed in the believer by the presence and ministry of the Holy Spirit who authenticates that experiential power base.
3. Power Forms	Spiritual authority influences by virtue of persuasion. Word gifts are dominant in this persuasion. Influence is by virtue of legitimate authority. Positional leadership carries with it recognition of qualities of leadership which are at least initially recognized by followers. Such authority must be buttressed by other authority forms such as competent authority, and personal authority.
4. Ultimate Good	The aim of influence using spiritual authority is the ultimate good of the followers. This follows the basic Pauline leadership principle seen in 2Co 10:8.

5. Evaluation	Spiritual authority is best judged longitudinally over time in terms of development of maturity in believers. Use of coercive and manipulative forms of authority will usually reproduce like elements in followers. Spiritual authority will produce mature followers who will make responsible moral choices because they have learned to do so.
6. Non-Defensive	A leader using spiritual authority recognizes submission to God who is the ultimate authority. Authority is representative. God is therefore the responsible agent for defending spiritual authority. A person moving in spiritual authority does not have to insist on obedience. Obedience is the moral responsibility of the follower. Disobedience, that is, rebellion to spiritual authority, means that a follower is not subject to God Himself. He/she will answer to God for that. The leader can rest upon God's vindication if it is necessary.

Remember,

Effective leaders value spiritual authority as a primary power base.[399]

See *power forms* (various definitions), **Glossary**. See **Articles**, *22. Influence, Power, and Authority Forms; 29. Leadership Lessons—Seven Major Identified.*

---

[399] They also know that it will take varied forms of power including coercive, inducive, positional, personal, competence and others to influence immature believers toward maturity. But the ideal is always there to use spiritual authority with mature believers.

Relevance of the Article to 1,2 Timothy

When Titus arrived with the news of the Corinthian response to Paul's letter, you can rest assured that it was a spiritual benchmark. It brought great rejoicing for Paul and reassured him of God's continuing miraculous work in his life. We do not know the response of the Ephesus church to Paul's letters to Timothy. We can guess that it turned around (since John years later in the Revelation does not mention any of the problems Paul dealt with). If so, that is a good response, like at Corinth—then this too was a marker event for Paul—even if he did not live to personally see it. This article points out the importance of spiritual benchmarks in a leader's life (and also by implication in a corporate group's life; see Joshua's stones of remembrance incident). All leaders need spiritual benchmarks to remember, especially as they move into and through deep processing.

60. Spiritual Benchmarks

A benchmark provides a point of reference from which future measurements can be made. A spiritual benchmark represents a point of reference for a leader. It refers to something that happens in the life of the leader which serves as positive proof of God's activity in that life. It is something that a leader can look back upon and thus be encouraged to continue when confused or in a discouraging situation. Because it is foundational, sure and certain, and had the distinct imprint of God's Hand on the life.

Joseph's two dreams when he was 17 years old were spiritual benchmarks. Over the next 22 years he clung to them through thick and thin. Finally, they were realized when Joseph was 39 years old. But it was Joseph's remembering them and trusting God because of them that made them noteworthy spiritual benchmarks.[400]

Isaiah's encounter with God in the year that King Uzziah died was a spiritual benchmark that forever shaped his ministry.[401]

Paul's experience on the road to Damascus and the subsequent encounter with Ananias was the spiritual benchmark which shaped Paul's whole life purpose. He referred to it several times along the way to validate his ministry.[402]

Spiritual benchmarks usually represent destiny events. They are reminders of God's intervention in a life. Spiritual benchmarks serve several functions:

1. they frequently serve as encouragement later in ministry when things are tough,
2. they often are prophetic and hence help give perspective later in ministry,
3. they usually are key to understanding destiny shaping (destiny preparation, destiny revelation, destiny fulfillment).

All leaders need one or more spiritual benchmarks that they can look back to in order to remember God has worked in their life; He will continue to work just as he did at that benchmark time.

See *critical incident; sense of destiny; destiny processing; leadership committal;* **Glossary.** See **Articles:** *42. Paul—A Sense of Destiny; 8. Destiny Pattern; Divine Affirmation in the Life of Jesus.*

---

[400] See Ps 105:19.
[401] See Isa 6.
[402] See Ac 9, 22, 26.

Relevance of the Article to 1,2 Timothy

Note Paul's strong statement in 1 Co 9:24-27. "I am serious about finishing well in my Christian ministry. I discipline myself for fear that after challenging others into the Christian life I myself might become a casualty"—Clinton Paraphrase. At that stage of his life, probably early 50s, he was aware of the need for willful choices of discipline in his life. In the letters to Timothy, he is probably in his 60s and he still advocates spiritual disciplines as being important. Notice his advice to Timothy (1 Ti 4:8). As you read through this article clarifying various kinds of spiritual disciplines—think through the record of Paul's ministry, not only with the Corinthians, but others. Which of these disciplines do you see in Paul's life? Disciplines are one of the 5 Major Enhancements frequently seen in leaders' lives, who finished well. Leaders who want to finish well do well to deliberately choose needed spiritual disciplines in their life.

61. Spiritual Disciplines—And On-Going Leadership

Introduction

Comparative study of effective leaders who finished will unearthed five factors[403] which enhanced their perseverance and good finish. One of those was the presence of spiritual disciplines in the life

> Leaders who have disciplines in their lives are more likely to persevere and finish well than those who do not.

Leaders need discipline of all kinds. Especially is this true of spiritual disciplines.

Definition   Spiritual disciplines are activities of mind and body purposefully undertaken to bring personality and total being into effective cooperation with the Spirit of God so as to reflect Kingdom life.

When Paul was around 50 years of age he wrote to the Corinthian church what appears to be both an exhortation to the Corinthians and an explanation of a major leadership value in his own life. We need to keep in mind that he had been in ministry for about 21 years. He was still advocating strong discipline. I paraphrase it in my own words.

> I am serious about finishing well in my Christian ministry. I discipline myself for fear that after challenging others into the Christian life I myself might become a casualty. 1 Co 9:24-27

Lack of physical discipline is often an indicator of laxity in the spiritual life as well. Toward the end of his life, Paul is probably between 65 and 70, he is still advocating discipline. This time he writes to Timothy, who is probably between 30 and 35 years old.

---

[403] The list of five enhancement factors includes the following. Enhancement 1—Perspective. Leaders need to have a lifetime perspective on ministry. Effective leaders view present ministry in terms of a lifetime perspective. Enhancement 2—Renewal. Special moments of intimacy with God, challenges from God, new vision from God and affirmation from God both for personhood and ministry will occur repeatedly to a growing leader. Enhancement 3—Disciplines. Leaders who have disciplines in their lives are more likely to persevere and finish well than those who do not. Enhancement 4—Learning Posture. The single most important antidote to plateauing is a well developed learning posture Enhancement 5—Mentoring. Leaders who are effective and finish well will have from 10 to 15 significant people who came alongside at one time or another to help them.

7 But avoid godless legends and old wives' fables. Instead exercise your mind in godly things. 8 For physical exercise is advantageous somewhat but exercising in godliness has long term implications both for today and for that which will come. 1Ti 4:7,8

Certain practices are assumed in the Scriptures as valid for developing spirituality and have been proven empirically in church history to aid development of spirituality. The scriptures do not define most of the disciplines that have come to be accepted but do mention most of them.

Three Major Categories of Disciplines

The following two categories have proved helpful in describing spiritual disciplines.

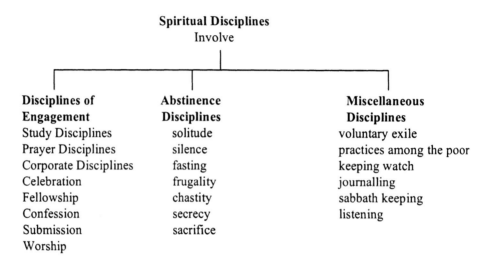

Spiritual Disciplines
Involve

Disciplines of Engagement	Abstinence Disciplines	Miscellaneous Disciplines
Study Disciplines	solitude	voluntary exile
Prayer Disciplines	silence	practices among the poor
Corporate Disciplines	fasting	keeping watch
Celebration	frugality	journalling
Fellowship	chastity	sabbath keeping
Confession	secrecy	listening
Submission	sacrifice	
Worship		

Figure 1,2 Ti 61-1 Spiritual Disciplines

Most leaders are somewhat familiar with the disciplines of engagement. I will define the abstinence disciplines since less is known about them.

Table 1,2 Ti 61-1 defines the disciplines. Table 61-2 lists purposes/applications of them.

Table 1,2 Ti 61-1. Abstinence Disciplines Defined

Discipline	Defined
solitude	The discipline of Solitude is a purposeful abstention from interaction with other human beings and the denial of companionship and all that comes from interaction with others with a view toward focusing on spiritual things.
silence	The discipline of silence is the practice of not speaking and closing oneself off from all kinds of sounds.
fasting	The discipline of fasting is the deliberate abstinence from food and possibly drink for a period of time.
frugality	The discipline of frugality is the abstention from using money or goods at our disposal in ways that merely gratify our desires or our hunger for status, glamour, or luxury.
chastity	A chaste person (whether married or single) is one who manifests the qualities of sexual wholeness and integrity in relationship to oneself, to persons of the same sex and to persons of the opposite sex.
secrecy	The practice of secrecy results from disciplined activities in which one seeks to abstain from causing ones good deeds and qualities to be known.
sacrifice	The discipline of sacrifice is the abstention from the possession or enjoyment of what is necessary for our living and involves forsaking the security of meeting our own needs with what is in our possession.

Table 1,2 Ti 61-2. Abstinence Disciplines—Some Purposes

Discipline	Defined
solitude	to free us from routine and controlling behaviors in order to gain God's perspective—to hear better; teach us to live inwardly; teach us to slow down; gain a new freedom to be with people.
silence	to cause us to consider our words fully before we say them so as to exercise better control over what we say; to listen to people more attentively; to observe others and other things; to allow life-transforming concentration upon God.
fasting	teaches self-denial; physical well being—cleanse body; releases power; increased sense of the presence of God in intercessory prayer; increased effectiveness; revelation from God; increase of spiritual authority; guidance in decisions; deliverance for those in bondage; increased concentration; brings intensive focus in Bible study.
frugality	frees us from concern and involvement with a multitude of desires; frees from the spiritual bondage caused by debt; teaches us respect for responsible stewardship; lessens the importance of things as essential to life; teaches us empathy for those who do not have resources; can lead toward simplicity as a way of life—the arrangement of life around a few consistent purposes, explicitly excluding what is not necessary to human well-being.
chastity	as an aid to total concentration while having extended times of fasting and praying; in marriage, bring proper focus so that sexual gratification is seen not to be the center of a relationship; recognize the importance of persons as persons; point out the power of lust in a life; teach positive relationships with those of opposite sex.
secrecy	to help us control a desire for fame, justification, or the attention of others; to help us center on God's affirmation; to learn to love to be unknown and even accept misunderstanding without the loss of peace, joy, or purpose; experience a continuing relationship with God independent of the opinions of others; teaches love and humility before God and others; help us see our associates in the best light; to help us see our egocentricity; help us appreciate a breadth of ideas related to competition; teach us to trust God in a deeper way.
sacrifice	learn to trust in God and not our own means of security; enables us to meet others needs; teach us the risk of faith.

Table 1,2 Ti 61-3. Abstinence Disciplines—Applicational Ideas

Discipline	Defined
solitude	1. Learn to take advantage of little solitudes during the day. 2. Find places that are conducive to solitude and deliberately set out to spend time in them. 3. Have special repetitive times during the year which you set aside to be alone for evaluation and reorientation of life goals. 4. If you go on a retreat for solitude remember the basic outline of such a retreat: entry, listening time, closure. Entry may require an unwinding. Sleeping may well be in order. The actual time of solitude will force inward reflection. Finally, seek to understand what has happened.
silence	1. Arise for a time alone in the middle of the night in order to experience a period of silence. 2. Go away to a retreat center for a day or so of silence. Some retreat centers are set up for silence. 3. Refrain from turning on the radio or TV or CD or whatever at times you usually do so. Instead observe silence. 4. When riding in your car do not turn on the radio but instead meditate. 5. Buy some earplugs or "Jet ears" to use to shut out sound when you study or meditate or read or pray. 6. If you go on a retreat for silence remember the basic outline of such a retreat: entry, listening time, closure. Entry may require an unwinding time--sleeping may well be in order. In your silence learn to listen for God. Seek when you finish to understand what happened in the time of solitude.

fasting	<u>Kinds of Abstention in terms of what denied</u>: absolute—without water and food (up to three days); no food, water only—up to 40 days; no food, some liquids other than water (no stimulants)--up to 40 days. <u>Kinds of Abstention in terms of purpose</u>: *Working Fast*—a fast done secretly while maintaining regular working habits. This usually has some goal attached to it. *Isolation fast*--a fast done in which the faster isolates himself/ herself from others concentrating wholly on God and spiritual matters. This usually has some goal. o *Power Fast*—a fast done primarily to increase awareness of spiritual warfare and to release God's power to accomplish victory in power encounters. *Discipline Fast*—a fast done in obedience to conviction from God that it should be done even though there is no apparent goal. *Apostolic ministry Fast*—a fast which has as its major goal the beginning of some new ministry. This can be done solo or in concert with some team.
frugality	1. Learn to eat simply (fewer meat meals). Healthy eating usually leads to less expense for medical and dental care. 2. Learn to opt for leisure activities which do not cost (reading, walking, etc.). 3. Walk instead of riding when feasible. 4. Make knowing choices in buying for home (don't have to choose top of line). 5. Respect the environment (like saving water, preserving plant life, trees, etc.). 6. Pass on clothing to others (that you no longer use). 7. Learn to get by without amassing the latest technological gadgets. 8. Learn to say no to advertising which promotes things you do not need. 9. Learn to budget and stick to it. 10. Recycle whatever you can. 11. Exercise discipline with credit cards (never charge what you can not pay off) or get rid of credit cards altogether. 12. Learn to depend on and utilize fully the resources you do have. 13. Practice "community" thinking (without living in a commune): covenant with one or two other families and/or singles for mutual accountability and encouragement in living responsible life-styles; own jointly some of the more expensive items—lawn tools, shop tools, books, journals; shop in bulk together and share; car pool whenever feasible. 14. Think homegrown: more letters, fewer long distance phone calls; purchase/make inexpensive gifts and then add a home-made personalization to give it a special touch; hand-made or hand-adapted clothing and furniture. 15. Churches and responsible living: our churches can purchase less than "top of the line" organs or other items and use the extra to share generously to the building fund of a 3rd world church. less focus on expensive entertainment and recreation at church outings; learn to get excitement and re-creation from outreach, evangelism, work projects for the needy. Occasionally go without coffee and snacks at group fellowships; use the time to talk about the hungry and give the usual expense money to the hungry. 16. Occasionally fast. 17. Hospitality—invite other to eat at your home rather than eating out; open home to out-of-towners and stay in homes when you are traveling.
chastity	1. Learn to value highly your own personhood and sexuality. 2. Learn to value highly the personhood and sexuality of others--male or female, young or old. 3. Guard thought life. 4. Abstain from any form of entertainment which might indulge improper sexual thoughts. 5. If married, abstain from sexual activity (with consent of partner) for extended times of praying and fasting. 6. Deliberately develop positive relationships with those of opposite sex which are healthy and do not focus on sexuality. 7. Deliberately seek the good of those of the opposite sex that you come in contact with in daily life. 8. Don't allow yourself to be put in potentially compromising situations with an individual of the opposite-sex.
secrecy	1. Refrain in the presence of others of discussing your accomplishments or good qualities. 2. Accept compliments graciously without much ado. 3. Recognize inwardly when accomplishments come of God's grace in giving you abilities or opportunities to accomplish. 4. Do not defend when you are attacked. 5. Trust God to both vindicate character if that is needed or to promote character if that is needed.
sacrifice	1. Respond to some other person's need by giving that which you had allocated to meet that same need for yourself. 2. After paying off all your bills at the end of the month give whatever is left over away to some needy cause. 3. Save all your loose change for a month and give it away.

Conclusion

Examples abound in the Scriptures for most of these disciplines. But what do we gain from these disciplines.

Writers on the disciplines often see the discipline of **solitude** as primary and prior to other disciplines. Its lessons are frequently necessary in order to insure profit from them.

We do not realize how much we depend on noise around us to shield out loneliness and to keep us from dealing with the distortions we have of our inner self. **Silence** helps us to separate out the false self from the true self. The practice of silence enables one to deal with loneliness in a constructive way that builds up the interior life. Silence forces evaluation of ones inner self. It helps one learn inward concentration. It will teach us to think before speaking and to choose our words well.

Fasting is a practice which many Christian's are discovering is for today and not relegated to the Bible or historic Christianity. Not to be practices by all, this abstinence almost more than any of the others teaches the value of discipline itself.

Debt is one reason that some Christians are not available to God for service. In II Timothy 2:4 Paul warns Timothy not to become entangled in the things of the world. In Romans 13:8 Paul admonishes Christians at Rome to owe no person anything save love. **Frugality** helps one learn the discipline of wise control of finances and other resources.

Sexuality is one of the most powerful and subtle forces in human nature. Its abuse can be destructive. Discipline in the area of sexuality can be foundational to other disciplines. Some distortions of sexuality are fornication, adultery, lusting, obsessive sexual activities, homosexuality, pornography and sexism. **Chastity** helps one learn about these things.

Proverbs 27:2 cautions a person about praising oneself. "Let other people praise you—even strangers; never do it yourself. The natural tendency of the heart is to be recognized for qualities and good things done. The proverb "tooting ones own horn" occurs in numerous languages and shows the recognition of this desire. **Secrecy** as a discipline counters this natural desire.

Sacrifice goes beyond frugality. Frugality is the careful stewardship of what we have. Sacrifice uses some of what we need for others. It is a discipline which focuses on giving beyond ones means.

Leaders who have disciplines in their lives are more likely to persevere and finish well than those who do not.

Relevance of the Article to 1,2 Timothy

Paul was strongly word gifted. But from time-to-time he saw power gifts demonstrated in needful situations. In the Ephesian ministry his word-giftedness abounds—apostolic, prophetic, teaching, exhortation. As you read through these important descriptive concepts think through the 1,2 Ti letters and observe Paul's use of his giftedness-set.

62. Spiritual Gift Clusters

Introduction

All Christians have at least one spiritual gift.

Definition   A spiritual gift is a *God-given* unique capacity imparted to each believer for the purpose of releasing a Holy Spirit empowered ministry via that believer.

While this is true for the body in general, leaders usually are multi-gifted. Over their time of ministry experience, at any one given time, they will be repeatedly exercising a combination of gifts. The set of gifts that a leader is demonstrating at any given time is important. It has a special label

Definition   A gift-mix is a label that refers to the set of spiritual gifts being used by a leader at any given time in his/her ministry.

Just as most leaders are multi-gifted and have a gift-mix, so too churches as a whole and Christian organizations as a whole corporately reflect gift-mixes. One way to assess this corporate gift-mix is to use a three fold category of giftings. These categories originated out of a study of Paul's affirmation to churches (corporate groups) for their impact on their surrounding communities. These affirmations occurred in an almost formula-like way in many of his salutations in his epistles. His full affirmation formula included faith. love, and hope. With some churches he would give partial affirmation. And with one church, with which he was extremely displeased he gave no affirmation at all. A study of these affirmations led to the identification of the functions implied in them: faith—the ability to believe in the unseen God (the function of the POWER gifts) , love—the manifestation of the reality of the unseen God in the lives of those who know Him (the function of the LOVE gifts), hope—the expectation of what He is doing; that is, the clarification of who He is, what He desires and what He is doing.(the function of the WORD gifts).

The identification of clusters of gifts that did those functions followed as did the actual naming of them as **WORD, POWER,** and **LOVE** clusters. This identification of clusters led to the correlation between Word gifts and leadership. *All leaders we had studied always had at least one word gift in their gift-mix; many had more than one.* This idea is a powerful implication for the selection and development of leaders.

The notion of spiritual gift clusters provides a special perspective, in fact a tool, that can aid strategic planning for a corporate group.

Three Corporate Functions Of Gifts: Word, Power, Love

These three crucial corporate functions were called power gifts, word gifts and love gifts and are described and illustrated as follows.

description   Power gifts demonstrate the authenticity, credibility, power and reality of the unseen God.

examples	miracles, kinds of healings, word of knowledge
description	<u>Love gifts</u> are manifestations attributed to God through practical ways that can be recognized by a world around us which needs love. They demonstrate the reality of relating to this God.
example	mercy, helps, pastoring
description	<u>Word gifts</u> clarify the nature of this unseen God and what He expects from His followers. People using these gifts both communicate about God and for God.
example	exhortation, teaching, prophecy

Pictorial View of the Three Corporate Functions: Word, Power, Love

Below in Figure 1,2 Ti 62-1, given in pictorial form,[404] are the three clusters, along with the individual gifts that aid these functions. Notice some gifts operate in more than one cluster.

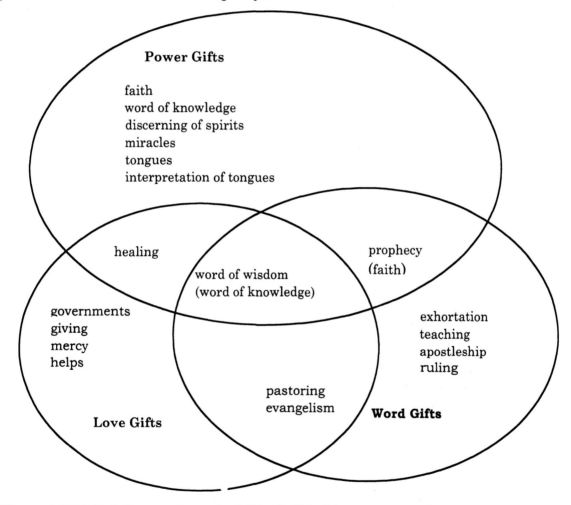

Figure 1,2 Ti 62-1. Power, Love And Word Gifts Pictured

---

[404] This is technically called a Venn diagram. All of the gifts listed in a circle belong to that circle. Where there is overlap, it means that the gifts in the overlap belong to both circles involved in the overlap (or all three circles as the case may be).

Power gifts =   faith, word of knowledge, discernings of spirits, miracles, tongues, interpretation of tongues, healing, word of wisdom, prophecy. These all help demonstrate the reality of the unseen God.

Love gifts =   governments, giving, mercy, helps, pastoring, evangelism, healing, word of wisdom, word of knowledge. These all demonstrate the beauty of that unseen God's work in lives in such a way as to attract others to want this same kind of relationship.

Word gifts =   exhortation, teaching, apostleship, ruling, prophecy, faith, pastor, evangelism, word of wisdom, word of knowledge. These all help us understand about this God including His nature, His purposes and how we can relate to Him and be a part of His purposes.

The Notion of Balance

Balance describes a proper relationship between manifestations of love, word, and power clusters operating in a given context so that God's witness in that situation can be adequate. Balance does not mean equality or equal amounts of gifts. Balance means having the appropriate mix of word, power, and love gifts for God to accomplish His purposes through the group to the people of its geographic area.

In the three profiles shown below an oval labeled with **A** means a **Word cluster**. An oval with **B** means a **love cluster**. An oval with **C** means a **power cluster**.

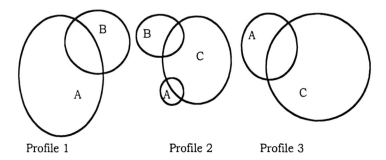

Profile 1   Profile 2   Profile 3

Figure 1,2 Ti 62-2. Three Examples of Corporate Mixes of Word, Power, Love

Profile 1 represents a church with a strong word ministry—since there is absolutely no power it means dominantly teaching and exhortation gifts. This would be a typical Bible Church. It has some compassion ministry but it is clear that it is dominantly a classroom type of church. The love cluster is about half within and half without the church. This means that there are probably a number of helps and governments gifts operating in the church doing service ministries and a number of mercy, helps types reaching out of the church. This church could use some power gifts in order to break through and reach new people for Christ. Its leadership gifts are probably pastoral and teaching. There could be some evangelism. No apostolic or prophetic types would probably be welcome here.

Profile 2 is church which has strong power gifts. Since it has power gifts there will be some word ministry through the prophetical, word of knowledge, word of wisdom gifts. It has very little word gifts which means that for the most part there will be little teaching and any exhortation would be in terms of the power gifts. It also has some love gifts working both in and out of the church—more outside than in. But its minimum word gifts means probably no Sunday School ministries so it probably doesn't need as many helps and governments inside the church. The question is how to get word gifts in here. There will probably be a big back door in this church. The leadership gifts in this church are probably apostolic, maybe evangelistic, maybe prophetic. There is probably a need for pastoral ministry and certainly a need for a teaching/ discipleship ministry.

Profile 3 is a church dominated with power gifts but one which has some ministry in the word. This means the leadership gifts in the church are probably apostolic and prophetical with possibly some teaching and a little pastoring. What is probably missing is an evangelistic thrust—no love gifts working. This church probably is having a hard time getting people to do ministry jobs in the church.

If I were to ask you how would you assess balance in each of the three profiles? What would you say? You could say it is unfair to ask. Balance determines whether or not the cluster fits the situation. You would need to know the contextual situations. For example, if Profile A was in the highlands of Papua New Guinea it would extremely out of balance—for power gifts are needed to get a hearing. But if it were in an early start-up church plant in a bedroom community of middle to upper middle class business types it would be appropriate. Profile 3 might be appropriate for early ministry in an inner-city location since power is needed to get breakthroughs. But later on this church will not keep its members till it develops a teaching/ discipleship thrust which need word gifts.

Conclusion

Spiritual gift clusters provide a tool for assessing development in a church. A church should know its people in terms of their gifts. Strategic planning will need this kind of assessment.

See *giftedness set, spiritual gift, various gift definitions*, **Glossary**. See **Article**, *9. Developing Giftedness.*

Relevance of the Article to 1,2 Timothy

The emphasis in the Pauline teaching on spiritual gifts is not so much the identification of them as the use of them for the church. This article gives an overview of giftedness (using a stewardship approach) which includes not only spiritual gifts, but natural abilities and acquired skills. Whatever we have entrusted to us should be used for God and not buried as in the talents parable. Development of what God has entrusted to us in terms of giftedness and its use to and for the body of Christ is the thrust of this article, not identification of spiritual gifts.

63. Spiritual Gifts, Giftedness, and Development

Introduction

All Christians have at least one spiritual gift.

Definition   A <u>spiritual gift</u> is a *God-given* unique capacity imparted to each believer for the purpose of releasing a Holy Spirit empowered ministry via that believer.

While this is true for the body in general, leaders usually are multi-gifted. Over their time of ministry experience, at any one given time, they will repeatedly exercise a combination of gifts. The set of gifts that a leader is demonstrating at any given time is important. It has a special label

Definition   A <u>gift-mix</u> is a label that refers to the set of spiritual gifts being used by a leader at any given time in his/her ministry.

My research on leaders and giftedness and my Biblical studies on *The Stewardship Leadership Model* resulted in the concept of the giftedness set.

Definition   The <u>giftedness set</u> describes natural abilities, acquired skills, and spiritual gifts which a leader has as resources to use in ministry. Sometimes shortened to giftedness.

Ministry flows out of beingness. Beingness describes the inner life of a person and refers to intimacy with God, character, personality, giftedness, destiny, values drawn from experience, gender influenced perspectives. The axiom, ministry flows out of being means that one's ministry should be a vital outflow from these inner beingness factors. Giftedness is a strong factor in beingness.

Out of my study also emerged also emerged the following observation,

> **When Christ Calls Leaders To Christian Ministry He Intends To Develop Them To Their Full Potential. Each Of Us In Leadership Is Responsible To Continue Developing In Accordance With God's Processing All Our Lives.**

This article deals with the notion of the giftedness set and suggests that a leader can develop himself/herself over a lifetime—a strong value flowing from the Stewardship model.[405]

---

[405] Stewardship values which relate to giftedness include: 1. Leaders ought to build upon abilities, skills, and gifts to maximize potential and use for God. 2. Leaders should recognize that they will be uniquely gifted both as to gifts and the degree to which the gift can be used effectively. 3. Leaders should know that

Giftedness Set

God endows a leader with natural abilities and later spiritual gifts. Along the way leaders pick up acquired skills. Comparative studies[406] resulted in a time-line which describes how the process develops over time. Figure 1,2 Ti 63-1 shows this.

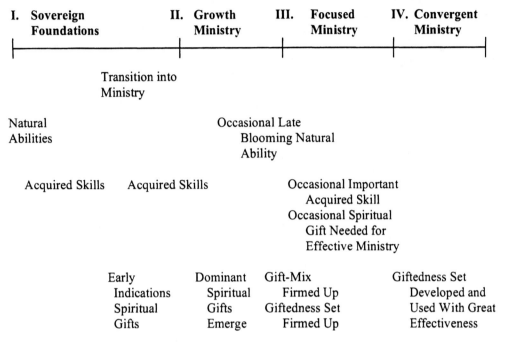

I. Sovereign Foundations	II. Growth Ministry	III. Focused Ministry	IV. Convergent Ministry

Transition into Ministry

Natural Abilities

Occasional Late Blooming Natural Ability

Acquired Skills   Acquired Skills

Occasional Important Acquired Skill
Occasional Spiritual Gift Needed for Effective Ministry

| Early Indications Spiritual Gifts | Dominant Spiritual Gifts Emerge | Gift-Mix Firmed Up Giftedness Set Firmed Up | Giftedness Set Developed and Used With Great Effectiveness |

Figure 1,2 Ti 63-1. Giftedness Development Over Time

As the giftedness set begins to emerge, a leader soon finds that one component of the set dominates the others. The other two components supplement or synergize with the dominant element.

Definition   The dominate component of a giftedness set—either natural abilities, acquired skills, or spiritual gifts is called the <u>focal element</u>.

About 50% of leaders studied in the research have spiritual gifts as focal. Another 35% have natural abilities as focal. About 15% have acquired skills as focal. This is important self-knowledge for a leader who wants to develop and wants ministry to flow out of beingness.

It is toward the notion of giftedness set developed and used effectively that I am talking when I say that Christ intends to develop a leader to full potential.

Development—What Does It Mean

A leader cannot develop natural abilities. These are givens, innate with their personhood. Though a leader may discover some latent natural ability later in life due to circumstances of ministry. Can a leader develop a spiritual gift? The answer is not certain from Biblical evidence. But certainly a leader can develop acquired skills and can develop synergizing issues related to spiritual gifts.

---

they will receive rewards for their productivity and for zealously using abilities, skills, gifts, and opportunities for God. See **Article**, *25. Jesus—Five Leadership Models: Shepherd, Harvest, Steward, Servant, Intercessor.*

[406] For almost 10 years,1985-1995, I studied leaders with a focus on giftedness analysis. The heart of this article flows out of that research. See **For Further Study Bibliography**, Clinton and Clinton, **Unlocking Your Giftedness—What Leaders Need To Know To Develop Themselves and Others**.

Definition   Development of a leader means an increase in efficiency and effectiveness in ministry due to addition of skills or other issues which enhance the leader's use of natural abilities, acquired skills, or spiritual gifts in ministry.

My research studies show that leaders develop their giftedness due to programmatic means (designed training), happenstance (day-to-day learning in the normal course of life's activities and processes), and by deliberate development (disciplined self-initiated learning).

Deliberate development takes place through formal or informal apprenticeships or other mentoring relationships, personal growth projects, and/or some identified plan of growth. Deliberate development ought to be the norm for a leader who has a developmental bias.

Studies into each of the leadership gifts[407] (Apostleship, Pastoral, Evangelism, Teacher, Prophecy, Exhortation) from a developmental perspective have resulted in numerous suggestions for development for each of the gifts.[408]

Conclusion

Leaders can develop over a lifetime. It happens. But with an awareness of how development can happen, a leader can much more efficiently develop, when self-knowledge and self-initiative are taken.

---

[407] These are the primary gifts in the Word Cluster. All leaders have at least one of these words gifts and usually are multi-gifted. See **Article**, *62. Spiritual Gift Clusters*.

[408] See **For Further Study Bibliography**, Clinton and Clinton, **Unlocking Your Giftedness,** ch 10, pages 251-280, where suggestions for developing spiritual gifts of the Word Cluster are given. It is beyond the scope of this article to give these suggestions since the suggestions run to 30 pages by themselves.

Relevance of the Article to 1,2 Timothy

Paul applies spiritual warfare tactics very carefully and not in a showy way. At first glance, you may not notice much of Paul's activity in terms of *Spiritual Warfare,* as seen in his epistles. You do see it in his activity as described in Ac in several situations. However, careful scrutiny of the Pauline epistles uncovers lots of implications of Satanic tactics in *Spiritual Warfare.* See the table below for instances and note that in 1,2 Ti at least 4 strong statements are mentioned about *Spiritual Warfare* (1Ti 1:20; 3:6; 4:1; 2Ti 2:26). A leader must be aware of Satanic involvement. This article seeks to expose issues involved in spiritual warfare. Not all conflict and opposition can be attributed to *Spiritual Warfare,* but neither can it be overlooked as a possible cause. Discernings of Spirits is needed.

64. Spiritual Warfare—Satan's Tactics

Introduction

A simple listing of times when Paul refers to Satan or the Devil and or demonic work is instructive. Seeing these kind of verses in their weaving context suggests tactics used by Satan in spiritual warfare. And to be aware of such tactics allows a leader to combat them.

Pauline Passages on Satan, the Devil or Demons

Table 1,2 Ti 64-1 lists some Pauline passages dealing with spiritual warfare instigated by Satan and lists some suggestions as to tactics involved.

Table 1,2 Ti 64-1. Spiritual Warfare—Satanic Tactics

Passage	Satanic Tactic
Ro 16:20	Satan upsets Christians' inner life attitudes, taking away peace due to divisions in the church. **Antidote**: Strive for unity and maintain inward peace as God works through the relationships.
1Co 5:5	Satan can destroy a life by controlling a person through immoral sexual addiction. **Antidote**: Avoid situations that can lead to sexual addiction.
1Co 7:5	Satan can gain inroads into the life of a married person when sexual needs are not being met. **Antidote**: Keep lines of communication open in a marriage relationship, concerning sexual needs.
2Co 2:11	Satan can use lack of forgiveness and failure to receive one who repents to control a church situation. **Antidote**: Accept those back who God has forgiven and who have shown genuine repentance.
2Co 11:14	Satan can counterfeit good things that attract believers (e.g. apparent good teaching; false apostles). Satan can appear like a messenger from God to deceive Christians. **Antidote**: Get discernment on apparent good teaching, apparent dynamic leaders. This may involve having to depend on people with revelatory gifts (discernings of spirits; word of knowledge; word of prophecy; word of wisdom etc.).
2Co 12:7	Satan can use a physical sickness or disability to prey upon a believer and instill doubts about God and His enabling grace. But God can also use these things to prevent abuse of power and pride in a leader's life. **Antidote**: Don't let sickness rob you of your trust in God. Seek His enabling grace (whether or not He chooses to heal you).

Eph 4:27	Satan can use anger in a life to gain inroads into a life and eventually control that life through the anger. **Antidote**: Get help if anger controls you. This may require inner healing. Also recognize the benefits of anger.
Eph 6:10-20	Satan uses lies or half-truths to trick believers and give unreliable perspectives on their lives and situations. Satan uses lack of righteousness (on-going unrighteous things in a believer's life) as an inroad into the life. Satan uses lack of presentation of testimony in a believer's life to weaken that believer's stand. Satan causes a believer to doubt God (character, dealings, truth, etc,). Satan robs believers from the impact of salvation in their lives. Satan keeps believers from using the Word of God in their lives and in combating his tactics. Satan keeps believers from praying in the Spirit as they confront him in his tactics. Satan keeps people from being alert to his tactics and from discerning his involvement. **Antidotes**: See the imperatives in the Eph 6:10-20.
1Th 2:18	Satan can block a believers guidance. So closed doors are not always clear guidance. **Antidote**: Get certainty guidance. Let all of the major guidance elements give weight to your guidance: God's Voice in the Word; God's Voice in the Heart; God's Voice in Circumstances; God's Voice in the Church.
2Th 2:9	Satan can do signs and wonder through a leader so that the leader looks as if he/she is empowered of God (apostolic workers also do signs and wonders). **Antidote**: Get discernment on apparent good teaching, apparent dynamic leaders. This may involve having to depend on people with revelatory gifts (discernings of spirits; word of knowledge; word of prophecy; word of wisdom, etc.).
1Ti 1:20	Satan can use a lack of responsiveness to one's conscience to eventually destroy a leader and take them out of ministry and further cause them to blaspheme what they once believed. The antidote, keeping a clear conscience and holding on to the truths of the Christian faith. **Antidote**: On the one hand, don't go against your conscience. On the other hand, allow God to impact your inner life and correct wrongly held ideas that affect your conscience.
1Ti 3:6	Satan can take a young leader out of ministry due to pride. **Antidote**: Potential young leaders should not be placed into leadership responsibility too soon.
1Ti 4:1	Satan use demons to influence teachers to give false doctrines that appeal to people. They are actually described as seducing spirits, hypocritical liars with no conscience. **Antidote**: A Bible centered leader like Timothy should teach the truth about these evil doctrines countering these heresies.
2Ti 2:26	Satan blinds people to truth. **Antidote**: Gently persuade people winning them over by manner as well as truth.

Conclusion

I have only barely touched on Satanic tactics. I have limited myself to Pauline input since the Handbook on touches on Pauline epistles. Each of the passages above should be studied in a detailed way in their context. And the other passages in the N.T[409]. need to be comparatively studied along with these.

---

[409] Some 89 passages mention the Devil or Satan. Other passages talk about demonic influence. But at least the above form a core of truth to start with in observing Satanic tactics.

Relevance of the Article to 1,2 Timothy

Paul walks the balance presented in this article concerning the two extremes to avoid. It is clear in his epistles that he was constantly aware of spiritual warfare and dealt with it when needed. But it is also clear that he did not attribute all conflict and opposition to spiritual warfare. He operated with discernment. He models for us how to maintain a balance with regard to these two extremes.

65. Spiritual Warfare—Two Extremes To Avoid

Introduction

Did Paul ever engage in spiritual warfare? Oh, yes! But when you read his epistles there is very little up front information, i.e. direct teaching, on doing spiritual warfare. There is Eph 6:10-17 and Col 2:13-15. But for the most part, spiritual warfare is incidental and remarks about it are asides simply woven into the fabric of a letter.[410] In my opinion, you can draw implications from them but not solid models that can be passed on authoritatively as to how to do spiritual warfare. And herein lies a model—two basics—that can help us approach spiritual warfare.

Two Extremes To Avoid

From a comparative study of all of Paul's epistles looking for spiritual warfare information I have drawn the following implications for leaders.

1. Spiritual warfare exists.
2. The spirit world is real and impinges on our world.
3. Leaders should be aware of spiritual warfare and their strengths[411] and limitations about it.
4. Paul is a model for how leaders ought to approach spiritual warfare in their ministries.

Paul deals with many problematic situations and people in ministry. Occasionally he will assert something about spiritual warfare as being involved in a problem or as the source of some person's situation. But for the most part Paul avoids two extremes:

Extreme 1.   **Overemphasis on Spiritual Warfare**
                    Paul does not assign blame for everything that happens on spirit beings, demons, and spiritual warfare.

He sees the human side of things as being heavily involved in many of the problems.

---

[410] For example if you trace spiritual warfare content through 1,2Ti you will see only several asides: 1Ti 1:18-20; 3:6,7; 4:1; 2Ti 1:6. You will see little or none in most of Paul's epistles. The omissions speak loudly.

[411] See especially the **Article**, *66. Spiritual Warfare—Two Foundational Axioms*.

Extreme 2.   **Under Emphasis on Spiritual Warfare**

Paul does recognize that some problems and issues have at their heart spiritual warfare. Demonic influence must be countered.

Yes, there is spiritual warfare and it must be discerned and dealt with. But, no, not everything is spiritual warfare. Paul has a healthy balance.

Conclusion

In most of the evangelical world I have dealt with (Bible teaching ministries), **Extreme 2** is the norm. And most of those ministries do not discern or deal with spiritual warfare, even when most needed in their people or situations.

In a little, but not as much, the charismatic or Pentecostal circles I deal with, **Extreme 1** is the norm.

When **Extreme 2** is the norm—great needs go unmet. When **Extreme 1** is the norm, abuse of power can abound. Frequently such a leader involved will fall by the wayside (many due to overpowering from the demonic world; many due to the power and pride barriers.)

Balance! How much we need it as leaders. Consistency in maintaining a middle ground and heeding both these dynamic extremes at the same time is needed. And Shakespeare said it well, "Consistency, thou art a jewel!"

See **Article**, *17. Finishing Well—Six Major Barriers.*

Relevance of the Article to 1,2 Timothy

Having acknowledged that spiritual warfare is real in the previous two articles and that a careful balance must be maintained as we deal with our leadership situations, nevertheless we will face these situations in which spiritual warfare must be dealt with. These simple but clear truths from Scripture will under gird us as we do so. And John realized it. Both of these axioms flow directly from John's ministry/teaching. You will note that Paul certainly rested on them—at least implicitly.

66. Spiritual Warfare—Two Foundational Axioms

Introduction

Spiritual warfare is real. All leaders engage in it, knowingly or not. Spiritual warfare was introduced in the book of Da.[412] There we learned some initial truth about spiritual warfare.

1. The unseen spirit world is real and does affect a leader's world.
2. Leaders seemingly unanswered prayers may be delayed because of spiritual warfare in the unseen spirit world.
2. Leaders can know that God does protect them with supernatural beings.
3. Some renewal experiences can be via supernatural beings who will affirm, encourage, give physical strength and reveal God's working to leaders.
4. Progressive revelation[413] is needed before spiritual warfare in the heavenlies and our participation in it can be understood. That is, Daniel does not give the full picture or information about human leaders intervening in spiritual warfare.

Definition   <u>Spiritual warfare</u> refers to the unseen opposition in the spirit world made up of Satan and his demons and their attempts to defeat God's forces angelic beings and God's people, today called believers. It also involves the response by believers to these attempts.

This articles identifies two fundamental axioms concerning spiritual warfare which are part of the progressive revelation given in the N.T. An axiom refers to a maxim widely accepted on its intrinsic merit. It is a statement accepted as true as the basis for argument or inference. It is an established rule or principle or a self-evident truth. To engage in spiritual warfare without these fundamental axioms is to

---

[412] Leadership commentary on Daniel. In the Bible spiritual warfare is introduced in Gen 3 with Satan's influence over Adam and Eve. It is explained further in Job which points out how the unseen spiritual world can influence the seen world. There are occasional allusions to it in other books (see 2 Kings 6:8-23; Note especially vs 16). Spiritual forces on God's side are mentioned throughout the Bible (Angels). And Da gives more information on spiritual warfare.

[413] Progressive revelation is a concept noted in the O.T. and N.T. that God is a God who continues to communicate and over time clarifies earlier revelation, expanding on it, filling in more details, helping later leaders see the relevance of it, etc. See especially prophetic ministry. Example: Daniel's prophecies in ch 2, 7, 8, 9, 10-12. There is progress in both content and methodology as observed in various genre in Old and New Testaments. See Job for further references to spirit world intervention in human affairs. See also Eph 6:10ff for basic teaching on spiritual warfare, particularly what human leaders can do. See also Jn 16:11 and Col 2:15 for the strategic basis of spiritual warfare.

invite defeat. To engage in spiritual warfare with these fundamental axioms lays the foundation for victory over those unseen spiritual forces representing Satan.

Axiom 1. Strategic Warfare

Jesus makes an unusual statement in Jn 16:11 as he looks forward to the Cross.

> 11 Judgment is certain, because the ruler of this world is judged."[414] Jn 16:11

Removing the figurative language and expressing the meaning in a powerful statement we have the foundation for Axiom 1 on Strategic Warfare.

> **11 At the Cross I will defeat Satan and his forces; this judgment on them is sure. Jn 16:11**

This aside on spiritual warfare concerns an aspect of the Cross not usually stressed. Besides dealing with sins, sin and righteousness, the Cross also was a strategic victory over Satanic forces. This is the single most important truth for leader's using power ministry in spiritual warfare.

Paul gives the basic teaching on this foundational axiom in Col 2:13-15.

> 13 And you, Gentiles, were dead in your sins. God gave you life through Jesus' death, having forgiven you all your wrongdoings; 14 All our failures to meet the law's demands were taken care of at the Cross. 15 At the same time He openly triumphed over those spirit beings which powerfully oppose God. They are defeated. Col 2:13-15

Axiom 1.   Strategically, Jesus Has Already Defeated All Spiritual Forces Opposed To God. The War Was Won At The Cross. It Only Remains That This Strategic Victory Be Appropriated And Won Tactically.

This is fundamental to any believer's spiritual warfare. It is a truth that must be believed and acted upon.

Axiom 2. Tactical Warfare

Though the Commander-in-Chief has declared the overall war won there are still battles going on all around us. It doesn't always appear won. A defeated army can still inflict many casualties. So it is in spiritual warfare. Satan has not acknowledged defeat and still fights on. A fundamental axiom basic to this continued warfare is introduced by John.

> 1 Beloved, believe not every spirit, but try the spirits whether they are of God. Because many false prophets are gone out into the world. 2 But here is how you can know the source is by the Spirit of God: Every spirit that affirms that Jesus Christ is come in human form is of God: 3 And every spirit that does not affirm that Jesus Christ came in human form is not from God. Such a source is a spirit against Christ and already is in the world. 4 You are of God, little children, and have overcome these spiritual forces, **because greater is he that is in you, than he that is in the world.**

In a context dealing with spiritual warfare (trying the spirits) John gives the encouraging statement which enables tactical victory.

Axiom 2.   A believer has within himself/herself, the Spirit of God which is much more powerful than Satanic forces.

---

[414] This is a certainty idiom, the *prophetic past*. A future event is spoken of as if it had already happened (the **TEV** and **NLT** translate—*has already been judged*) because it is so certain, in this case the Cross and one result of it. *Captured: At the Cross I will defeat Satan and his forces; this judgment on them is sure.* See *capture, certainty idiom,* **Glossary**. See **Article,** *13. Figures and Idioms in the Bible.*

Conclusion

Victory is certain, it was potentially won at the Cross. It will be won totally in history. In the meantime, a believer has the indwelling Holy Spirit who will enable victory in everyday skirmishes over spirit forces. Count on these axioms.

See **Articles**, *64. Spiritual Warfare—Satan's Tactics;65. Spiritual Warfare—Two Extremes to Avoid; Daniel—Supernatural Beings and Spiritual Warfare.*

Relevance of the Article to 1,2 Timothy

Paul deals with gender and leadership in 1 Ti. (See 1 Ti 3:1—notice the *anyone* not man as in KJV). This article details the process by which God changes a situation from a less ideal (e.g. like a male dominated culture with regard to leadership) taking it to a more ideal position (leadership based on call and giftedness regardless of gender). See also **Article 20.** *Gender and Leadership* and **LEADERSHIP TOPIC 6. LEADERSHIP GUIDELINES** (Item 7; Note my paraphrase of 1Ti 2;13).

67. Starting Point Plus Process Model

The book of Philemon suggested some principles under the label social issue. In that book, the whole social institution of slavery was being undermined by Christian values. The two principles about social change that were listed include:

a. One means for overcoming a social evil is to undermine it at value level. Many Christian values speak to social issues.

b. Major social change will take a long time to implement. One of the reasons for this is the way God works to bring about change in a culture. The starting point plus model seeks to identify God's methodology for changing cultures and cultural practices.

The Starting Point Plus Process model, outlines 4 major assertions suggesting how God brings about change in cultures and cultural practices. The basic motif is that *God begins where people are and progressively reveals Himself and applicable truth to move them toward supracultural ideals.*

Four Major Assertions

1. Assuming a valid faith-allegiance response,[415] God allows for a range of understanding of Himself and His Will for people, for He starts where people are rather than demanding that they immediately conform to His ideals.

2. This range of understanding of God can assume a variety of potential starting points anywhere from sub-ideal toward ideal perception of God and His ways.

3. God then initiates a process which involves a revelational progression from a sub-ideal starting point toward the ideal.

4. This process of beginning with a range of sub-ideal starting points of perception and behavior and moving by revelational progression from the sub-ideal toward the ideal can be applied to any doctrine of Scripture and any Scriptural treatment of behavioral patterns.

---

[415] By a faith-allegiance response is meant a valid decision to place God as top priority in a life — a trusting response for God's salvation and work in a life.

Marriage Example

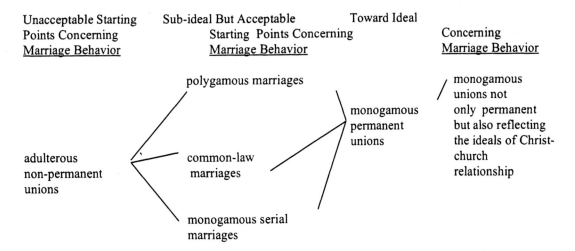

Unacceptable Starting Points Concerning Marriage Behavior

Sub-ideal But Acceptable Starting Points Concerning Marriage Behavior

Toward Ideal Concerning Marriage Behavior

polygamous marriages

monogamous permanent unions

monogamous unions not only permanent but also reflecting the ideals of Christ-church relationship

adulterous non-permanent unions

common-law marriages

monogamous serial marriages

Figure 1,2 Ti 67-1. Starting Point Plus Process Model-Marriage

As can be seen above, God works in a cultural situation to move toward the ideal on the right. Assuming that a group within a culture has come to Christ and are giving allegiance to Him above all else, God will begin to work. But assume they are at the far left. God will reject the starting point and immediately move that group toward a sub-ideal position. God will move them over time further right toward the sub-ideal and eventually toward the ideal. This is actually the Biblical record of how God worked on marriage in the Old and New Testament. God does not expect immediate attainment toward an ideal but movement toward it. It took hundreds of years to move toward the ideal of monogamous unions not only permanent but reflecting the ideals of Christ-church relationship.

Slavery—A Typical Example

This same *starting point plus process model* can be applied to many kinds of issues and doctrines in which a given culture or society fall short of Biblical ideals. For example, consider the slavery issue. This is a sub-ideal position with regard to the view of a human being made in God's image. So God begins by accepting the viewpoint of slavery but works to improve the conditions under which it takes place. Then He works to eliminate it in its varied forms (actual slavery; pseudo-slavery like Mexican immigrant workers illegally in the United States, child slaves sold into sexual prostitution in Asia, etc.). Then He works to eliminate ethnic prejudice, a subtle form of corporate slavery. And so on, until He obtains the ideal of interdependency between various ethnic groups with respect for all individuals and groups as made in the image of God.

Women in Leadership—Another Example

Or consider gender and leadership. I believe that *the starting point plus process model* is seen at work again as God moves from sub-ideal positions on females in some cultures where they are only slightly better than chattel all the way across to the ideal where men and women are equal in standing before God and others (at least due to gender alone) and where men or women are leaders depending on calling and gifting.

Conclusion

We must not expect immediate perfection on some truth in the Scriptures by groups new to this truth, especially when it has taken years to bring the church to this position. And what is true with corporate groups like churches and parachurches is true of individuals. We should expect to reject positions that are less than sub-ideal. But we should be willing to patiently work to move people from sub-ideal to ideal.

Acknowledgment

This model was first identified by one of my colleagues, Dr. Charles H. Kraft in his book on ethnotheology, entitled **Christianity in Culture**. The above description of his model is my adapted version taken from my doctoral dissertation.

See **Article**, *20. Gender and Leadership*

Relevance of the Article to 1,2 Timothy
This article describes the methodology for synthesizing a time-line for a biblical character. It is helpful when studying the Pauline epistles to know where in the developmental time-line, Paul was. This article gives the time-line for Paul. You should note that Paul was probably in his 60s and had around 30 years of ministry experience when he dealt with the Ephesian situation.

68. Time Lines- Defined for Biblical Leaders

A major leadership genre is the biographical source. Below is given 12 steps to use for studying this source. Notice step two in Table 1,2 Ti 67-1 below.

Table 1,2 Ti 68-1. 12 Steps For Doing Biographical Study

Step	General Guideline
1	Identify All The Passages That Refer To The Leader.
2	Seek To Order The Vignettes Or Other Type Passages In A Time Sequence
3	Construct A Time-Line If You Can. At Least Tentatively Identify The Major Development Phases In The Leader's Life.
4	Look For Shaping Events And Activities (technically called process items, or critical incidents).
5	Identify Pivotal Points From The Major Process Items Or Critical Incidents
6	Seek To Determine Any Lessons You Can From A Study Of These Process Items Or Pivotal Points.
7	Identify Any Response Patterns Or Any Unique Patterns As You Analyze The Life Across A Time-Line.
8	Study Any Individual Leadership Acts In The Life.
9	Use The Three Overall Leadership Categories To Help Suggest Leadership Issues To Look For (leadership basal elements, leadership influence means, leadership value bases).
10	Use The List Of Major Functions (task functions, relationship functions, and inspirational functions) to Help Suggest Insights. Which were done, which not.
11	Observe Any New Testament Passages Or Commentary On The Leader. Especially Be On The Lookout For Bent Of Life Evaluation.
12	Use The Presentation Format For Findings On Bible Leaders To Help You Organize Your Results.

This article briefly describes step two. A time-line is the end result of applying step 2. Time-lines provide an integrating framework upon which to measure development in the life, to organize findings, and to pinpoint when shaping activities occur in a life.

Important Definitions for Time-Lines

Definition   The time-line is the linear display along a horizontal axis which is broken up into development phases.

Definition   A unique time-line refers to a time-line describing a given leader's lifetime which will have unique development phases bearing labels expressing that uniqueness.

Definition   A development phase is a marked off length on a time-line representing a significant portion of time in a leader's life history in which notable development takes place. Example Below has 4 development phases indicated by Roman Letters I, II, III, IV.

Definition   A sub-phase is a marked off length on a time-line within a development phase which points out intermediate times of development during the development phase. In the Example below Development phase III. has 3 sub-phases indicated by A, B, and C.

All leaders can describe a time-line that is unique to them. A unique time-line is broken up into divisions called development phases which terminate with boundary events. Development phases can themselves be subdivided into smaller units called sub-phases which have smaller boundary terminations.

Below is given the Apostle Paul's time-line with several findings about his life displayed. Paul's life, ministry, and development. I have also numerous other findings about Paul's life, ministry and development located on his time-line. Such things as; pivotal points, mentoring, development of life purpose, development of major role, isolation processing, other process items such as—paradigm shift, leadership committal, double confirmation, divine contact, conflict, crises, ministry conflict, word, obedience, integrity check. Time-lines are very useful to give perspective and force one to see across a whole lifetime of development.

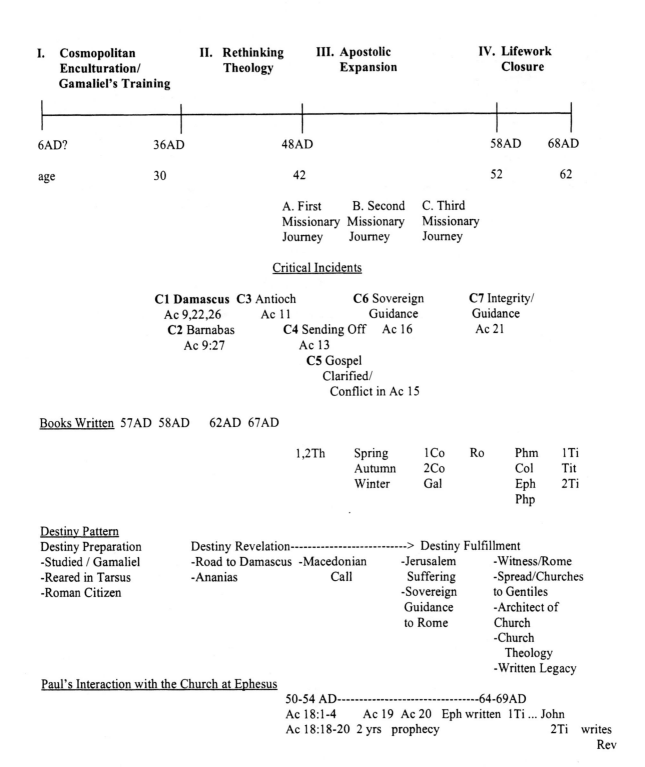

Figure 1,2 Ti 68-1. The Apostle Paul's Time-Line

For **Further study**: See paper, *Getting Perspective by Using Your Time-Line* listed in the **LET READER.PDF** at my web site. See also **Article**, *28. Leadership Genre*; **See Section Time Lines of Biblical Leaders.**

Relevance of the Article to 1,2 Timothy

Paul's use of mentoring is probably best illustrated with his training of Timothy. His on-going and deliberate training of Timothy remind one of the tremendous example in the O.T. of Moses tandem training with Joshua. This article points out that Paul allowed himself to come close relationally to his mentorees. In fact, three are called sons. One of those is Timothy and one is Titus. Both were involved in the Corinthian ministry. It is surprising that the other is Onesimus. That should alert us to the importance of the Philemon epistle. But it is in the 1,2Ti epistles that we see Paul at his best in mentoring—Timothy is the mentoree—a special beloved son in the faith.

69. Timothy—A Beloved Son in the Faith

Effective leaders view relationships in ministry as both a means and an end.

This is one of seven major lessons that I have derived from comparative study of effective leaders. Probably in no leader in the Bible, other than Jesus, is this seen any plainer, than in the life and ministry of Paul the Apostle. Paul was a strong task oriented leader. But he knew the value of relationships. In his epistles he lists almost 80 people by name whom he had personal relationships with. Paul believed that he ought to personally relate to those around him in ministry. It was good in itself. It was good to accomplish ministry too. Paul indicates this notion of a strong relationship when he uses the phrases: *my own son in the faith, my beloved son, as a son with the father, son, dearly beloved son, my son, own son after the common faith, my son.* For three—Timothy, Titus, and Onesimus—it meant strong intimate relationships.

Table 1,2 Ti 68-1 lists the instances and uses of these strong, special, intimate relationships by Paul.

Table 1,2 Ti 69-1. Paul and Intimate Relationships

Reference	Phrase	Who	Use
1Co 4:17	Who is my beloved son	Timothy	Sponsoring Timothy to the Corinthians so they will receive him with respect as Paul's representative.
Php 2:22	as a son with the father	Timothy	Sponsoring Timothy to the Philippians so they will receive him with respect as Paul's representative.
1Ti 1:2	[my] own son in the faith	Timothy	Greeting of encouragement to Timothy personally.
1Ti 1:18	son	Timothy	Exhortation to Timothy to boldly act as a leader in a tough situation remembering the prophecies and operating with a clean conscience.
2Ti 1:2	[my] dearly beloved son	Timothy	Greeting of encouragement. The most intimate of all the phrases.
2Ti 2:1	my son	Timothy	An exhortation to go on, drawing on the enabling grace found in union with Christ
Tit 1:4	[mine] own son after the common faith	Titus	A word of encouragement; a word sponsoring Titus before the Cretian believers.
Phm 1:10	my son	Onesimus	Sponsoring of Onesimus to Philemon. Shows how strongly Paul believed in him.

Let me suggest an exercise for you. Go back and read each of the references listed in Table 68-1. Read the surrounding context as well. And imagine you are Timothy hearing those words or Titus or Onesimus.

How would you feel to hear such words? Paul knew the motivational importance of affirmation. And a personal strong intimate relationship expressed openly to the person not only affirms but motivates them.

Table 68-1 shows that Timothy was Paul's closest associate. He was a beloved and true son in the faith. Leaders need to pass on their heritage. They need to leave behind ultimate contributions. One sure way of doing this is to have relationships with those to whom they minister and with whom they minister. Values are passed on. Ministry methodology, though adapted lives on. Vision is caught and lives on.

Effective leaders view relationship as both a means and an end in ministry.

Paul did. Who are your true sons and daughters? Who will carry on your values, ministry philosophy, and vision?

Relevance of the Article to 1,2 Timothy

Throughout all of Paul's epistles and especially in Ro, 2 Co and Php, he emphasizes that his living of the Christian life involves a unique relationship with the living Christ. It is this relationship, and an ever progressing realization of it that eventuates in practical sanctification in everyday life for Paul. I use the term *union life* to express the notion that Christ lives in us and through us uniquely in terms of who we are personality wise, our giftedness, and our values that He has instilled in us. This article seeks to give an overview of my understanding of union life. Note the tremendous passages in 2 Co, which reveal Paul's understanding of union life—especially the clay pot illustration and the transformation from one degree of glory to another. 1,2Ti show that Paul's Union Life relationship with the Lord Jesus sustained him in the triumphant conclusion to his life.

70. Union Life- Intimacy With God

Introduction

One of the most famous union life verses appears in Col 1:27.

> 27 To whom God would make known what is the riches of the glory of this mystery among the Gentiles—**Christ in you**, the hope of glory. Col 1:27

Note the phrase **Christ in you**. Paul uses this concept of being **in Christ**[416] many times in his epistles. It is the essential phrase describing union life. What is union life?

Definition   Union life is a phrase which refers both to the fact of the spiritual reality of a believer joined in spirit with the resurrected Spirit of Christ and the process of that union being lived out with Holy Spirit power so that the person is not dominated by sin in his/her life.

In essence, it the life of a believer who is living above the controlling authority of sin in a life, not a perfect life, but also not controlled by sinful habits, tendencies, sinful addictions, the sinful self. It is a believer walking sensitively to the Holy Spirit's leading and moving inexorably to being conformed to the image of Christ. That is the life of Christ in and through the believer—in fact, it is not too strong to say Christ in the believer as that person. Christ in me as me.

Today, with our modern emphasis on dysfunctionality, thousands are bound by a past which will not allow them to live freely. Without wanting to negate the complexities of these foundational shaping events and people in our pasts I do want to say that there is provision for victory in Christ. That is what union life is all about. Union life is certainly part of the answer to that need and maybe perhaps the answer.

Throughout Christian history people serious about their Christianity have longed for a more zealous life-style expression of it. They have longed to have a deeper walk with God. They have sought to appropriate that walk with God. Union life has been the experience of many a saint who has sought this deeper walk. Different names have been used to describe this mystical union and its effect in life. Such terms as the exchanged life, replaced life, deeper life, victorious life, normal Christian life and life on the highest plain can be found in the literature. Various methodologies have been tried to attain that "more committed" expression. Numerous movements have sprung up. The phrases listed above convey rather esoterically what these various believers have discovered.

Paul comprehensively explains this kind of life in Ro 1-8. He models it in Php. He also shows its power in his own life in 2Co. John treats the concept in metaphorical fashion—living water, vine and branches. The Bible also deals with the concept using the term, *New Covenant*. This article will give an

---

[416] Paul uses the phrase *in Christ* 74 times, *in Jesus* six times and *in him* eight times referring to aspects of union life.

overview of this important concept.[417] I as a believer living in Union Life can know this beautiful union—Christ in me as me. It is entered into simply by faith by knowing and appropriating what Christ has already done at the cross.

Bible Passages Dealing With the Union Life Concept

Union life is promised in the O.T. God reveals the New Covenant in the O.T. and then points to its realization in the book of Heb. Essentially the New Covenant, a promise made to corporate Israel becomes individualized in its N.T. application shown in Heb.

> 31 Behold, the days come, says the LORD, that I will make a new covenant with the house of Israel, and with the house of Judah. 32 Not according to the covenant that I made with their fathers in the day [that] I took them by the hand to bring them out of the land of Egypt; which my covenant they brake, although I was an husband unto them, says the LORD. 33 But this [shall be] the covenant that I will make with the house of Israel; After those days, says the LORD, **I will put my law in their inward parts**, and **write it in their hearts**; and will be their God, and they shall be my people. 34 And they shall teach no more every man his neighbor, and every man his brother, saying, Know the LORD: for they shall all know me, from the least of them unto the greatest of them, says the LORD: for I will forgive their iniquity, and I will remember their sin no more. Jer 31:31-34.

Heb applies union life to the N.T. church as part of what Christ has done.[418]

> 8 For finding fault with them, he says, Behold, the days come, says the Lord, when I will make a new covenant with the house of Israel and with the house of Judah: 9 Not according to the covenant that I made with their fathers in the day when I took them by the hand to lead them out of the land of Egypt; because they continued not in my covenant, and I regarded them not, says the Lord. 10 For this [is] the covenant that I will make with the house of Israel after those days, says the Lord; I will put my laws into their mind, and write them in their hearts: and I will be to them a God, and they shall be to me a people: 11 And they shall not teach every man his neighbor, and every man his brother, saying, Know the Lord: for all shall know me, from the least to the greatest. Heb 8-10

Paul describes union life by the phrase in Christ, in Jesus, the supply of the Spirit of Jesus or joined unto the Lord. Some of his most famous union life verses include the following:

> 15 But when it pleased God, who separated me from my mother's womb, and called me by his grace, 16 To **reveal his Son in me**, that I might preach him among the heathen. Gal 1:16

> 20 I am crucified with Christ: nevertheless I live; yet not I, but Christ **lives in me**: and the life which I now live in the flesh I live by the faith of the Son of God, who loved me, and gave himself for me. Gal 2:20

> 26 [Even] the mystery[419] which hath been hid from ages and from generations, but now is made manifest to his saints. 27 To whom God would make known what is the riches of the glory of this mystery among the Gentiles—**Christ in you**, the hope of glory. 28 Whom we preach, warning every person, and teaching every person in all wisdom; that

---

[417] Theologically we are dealing with the notion of sanctification when we talk about union life.

[418] Thematically, Heb is teaching that **God's Redemptive Revelation in Christ** is superior to any other, is final, and therefore demands a continued faithful allegiance. Part of its superiority is the realization of New Covenant through Christ.

[419] A mystery, in Pauline language, means something not previously revealed by God but now revealed by God and opened up so people can see its truth. Union life is such a concept.

we may present every person grown up and mature in Christ Jesus: 29 Whereunto I also labor, striving according to his working, which works in me mightily. Col 1:27

17 But he that is joined unto the Lord is one spirit. 1Co 6:17

Peter describes the foundation for union life in breath taking language.

> Whereby are given unto us exceeding great and precious promises—that by these you might be **partakers of the divine nature,** having escaped the corruption that is in the world through lust. 2Pe 1:4

Most believers can read these verses and still not know anything about union life. What does it look like? Paul models it for us in all of his epistles. But it is most clearly seen in Php.

What Does Union Life Look Like? See Philippians.

Whereas Paul teaches conceptually about union life in the book of Ro, he demonstrates it in the book of Php. Table 1,2 Ti 69-1 describes seven characteristics of union life as modeled by Paul in Php.

Table 1,2 Ti 70-1. Seven Characteristics of Union Life Modeled By Paul in Philippians

Characteristic	Vs	Explanation
Christ-centered	1:20-22	Paul's daily life involved a centeredness in Christ and a desire to have this Christ impact his everyday testimony.
Inner Resources	1:19; 3:9,10; 4:13.	Paul knew that the Spirit of Christ indwelled and that Spirit was his source of power. It was the same kind of power as that which raised Jesus from the dead—resurrection power.
Joy	1:4, 25, 26; 2:2, 17, 18, 2:29; 4:1.	Joy in the midst of hard, shaping life experiences, should be the hallmark of a believer in union with Christ. Joy is a fruit of the Spirit that distinguished a believer from an unbeliever, particularly in distressing circumstances. Joy is referred to throughout Php. Paul uses five different words for joy.
Relationships	2:1-3; 4:2 and general tone throughout	A believer in union with Christ recognizes also that he/she is related to every other believer in the body. Such a recognition longs for unity with them—like mindedness, good relationships.
Sovereign Mindset	1:12; 2:17; 4:11,12.	Sovereign mindset refers to an attitude demonstrated by the Apostle Paul in which he tended to see God's working in the events and activities that shaped his life, whether or not they were positive and good or negative and bad. He tended to see God's purposes in these shaping activities and to make the best of them. A person in union life sees God's activities through life's experiences (Ro 8:28-30) as shaping toward the image of Christ.
Destiny/ Growth To Maturity	3:10-14; 15-16.	Paul has a driving goal to move toward maturity in Christ. (see also Ac 20:24 and 2Ti 4:7,8). A believer in union life presses on toward growth an maturity.
Peace	4:6,7.	Paul speaks of the God of peace and the peace of God. A believer can know this fruit of the Spirit, this aspect of victory in the life, in the midst of pressing life circumstances. In fact, it like joy, is a hallmark of a believer in union life.

Explanation—The Left Brained Approach —Logical Presentation Given in Ro 1-8.

Until a believer fully enters into the notion that Christ has indeed paid the full penalty for all his/ her sins, those committed in the past, those being commuted in the present (known or unknown), and those to be committed in the future, it is very unlikely that that believer will enter into and experience *Victory* in the Christian life. The Ro 3:21-31 passage (dealing with justification—that is, God's means of justifying a sinner deserving of punishment by the sacrificial death of Christ for him/her—technically called the vicarious atonement) is the foundation for believing truth about *Victory in Christian living.* Some will by faith accept this truth without any preamble and enter into it, forever being freed from guilt. Others will perhaps need deliverance from some past dysfunctional hold as a preamble to seeing guilt forever gone.[420] In any case, a guilt free past is a pre-requisite or co-requisite to moving on to *Victory.*

The Christian life from beginning to end, Ro 1:16-18, is by faith. We accept what Christ did for us on the **Cross** to pay for our sins and make us guilt-free before a just God. We must also accept by faith what He has provided for *Victory in our lives*—that it is true that we can live increasingly knowing that sin does not control our lives. We do not claim perfection but we can live knowing we do not have to be dominated by some controlling sin in our lives. And we can experience this so as to encourage us as we move toward Christ-likeness in our lives.

The second look at the work on the **Cross** provides us with the revelation from God, the factual basis, which we accept by faith just like we did forgiveness of sins. We **KNOW** (Ro 6:6,7) it to be true, that we were mystically included with Christ in his death so as to break the controlling authority of sin in our lives and to be raised with him to know a resurrected life, free from this controlling authority of sin. It is a done deed.

We habitually **COUNT** (Ro 6:11) on it both implicitly and explicitly, moment by moment, as we sensitively follow the Spirit's leading. We know we can count on it. We give ourselves to this kind of life. It is by **FAITH** that we totally **SURRENDER** ourselves to this process, longing and wanting it in our lives.

And we know that it will take **SPIRIT FREEDOM**. But just in case we think it is us doing it we come face to face with the reality of the power of sin in our lives. And we are driven by deep need to want the **SPIRIT FREEDOM** and to know without it we are helpless and hopeless to experience that Victory in our lives.

And **SPIRIT FREEDOM** is there—again we know guilt free exposure before God and we recognize that without it we are helpless and hopeless to experience that *Victory* in our lives. And **SPIRIT FREEDOM** can be. We are assured within our **Adoption** into the family—heirs with Christ. We will grow up to be like Christ. The Spirit stands ready always to point out our need and take care of giving us *Victory* in that need. It is a process over time for the total full perfection to be. But it will happen. It is an inevitable process moving forward to completion. We will become Christ-like. It is so certain that the whole process is **spoken of in the past** (prophetic past idiom). We were saved, we are being perfected, we will be totally perfected. Or another way of saying it: we were saved from sins, we are being saved from sin's control, and we will be freed forever from its presence. We were saved. We are being saved. We will be yet totally saved.

Summarizing, Paul teaches logically that a believer's sins were taken care of at the **Cross**. Such a believer can be freed of guilt for those sins. But not only were sins dealt with at the **Cross** but also the controlling authority of sin in a life, the sin principle, was dealt with. A believer can accept this provision of enabling power to live above the controlling authority of sin in a life simply by faith. And a believer can continue to count on this enabling power. It is the Holy Spirit who will sensitively lead that believer to experience the power of the inward Christ life over sin. Such a believer, walking sensitively with the Holy Spirit will increasingly know more of this enabling power over time. Such a believer, in this life, will inexorably move toward experiencing this Christ life. It is an on-growing, ever increasing, process of growth.

Conclusion

Throughout this leadership commentary I have used the notion of,

Ministry flows out of being.

I have described being as comprised of at least the following: intimacy with God, character, personality, giftedness, destiny, values drawn from experience, gender influenced perspectives. Now I want to take it

---

[420]Inner healing in which God miraculously provides knowledge about something enslaving from the past and breaks that hold or the Catholic approach of mediated authority (confession, penance, absolving) are two approaches I have seen effective in breaking past holds. For others, the Good News of the Gospel alone is sufficient. The passage in 1 Corinthians 6:9-11 shows experientially that such holds can be broken.

one step further. Ministry flows out of what being? I want to suggest that in addition to these characteristics ultimately I am talking about being involving the *union life being*—a person's beingness is complete when that person realizes intimacy as union with Christ.

Have you discovered this mystery, Christ in you as you—union life?

See **Articles**, 58. *Sovereign Mindset, Abiding—Seven Symptoms.*

Relevance of the Article to 1,2 Timothy
In **Article** *51. Pauline Leadership Values*, I identified 19 values emphasized in 1,2Ti that Paul either explicitly or implicitly utilized in his ministry with the Ephesian situation. Paul was a value driven leader.

71. Value Driven Leadership

A leader's ministry is said to be <u>value driven</u> if that leader consciously attempts to identify, make explicit and explain leadership values that under gird his/her ministry and deliberately operates his/her ministry based on these values. A <u>leadership value</u> is an underlying assumption which affects how a leader perceives leadership and practices it. Most leaders operate with underlying implicit values. To identify such values allows for several advantages: 1. The leader can have an increased effectiveness and consistency in his/her use of them by proactively applying them. 2. The leader can adapt or change or discard those which are not so good—as long as they are implicit, this can not be done. 3. The leader can better teach these values to others. 4. The leader can pass on the values to selected leaders who will carry them on as part of his/her heritage. Jesus and Paul are the prime N.T. examples for explaining values underlying their ministry. See all the Gospels where Jesus is constantly explaining why he does what he does and why he says what he says. I have especially studied the Sermon on the Mount for values underlying Jesus authoritative teaching. See especially 1,2Co and Gal where Paul explains the motivational reasons (values) behind his leadership behavior. I have identified and made explicit 19 Pauline leadership values from 2Co. See the **Article** *51. Pauline Leadership Values*.

Relevance of the Article to 1,2 Timothy
This article describes my own pilgrimage in discovering a paradigm that has under girded my life long study of the Bible. Today we need *Bible Centered Leaders*. Paul demonstrates this king of leadership—he was a *Bible Centered Leader*. This is my own journey toward grasping what Paul advocated and modeled.

72. Vanishing Breed- Needed, Bible Centered Leaders

The concept of a vanishing breed is a relatively modern idea. For example, in the latter third of the 19th century, the buffalo became so hunted as to become an endangered species—a vanishing breed. As applied to the Christian scene the concept of a vanishing breed, in one sense, is a modern concept but in another is quite old concept. Until the mid 19th century and the proliferation of printed materials only a relatively few leaders were very familiar with the entire Bible. But with the Bible becoming a perennial best seller as has been the case in the 20th century, you would expect that many leaders would be Bible Centered leaders. But actually that is not the case. And it is growing worse, relatively speaking, because a rising generation of leaders is basically a non-reading group of people. But the notion of being a *Bible Centered Leader* is as old as the N.T. Church Leadership Era. Paul, the Apostle, stressed it to Timothy his younger co-worker. His two epistles, 1Ti and 2 Ti fairly bristle with Bible Centered Leadership insights. I suppose that you are not really surprised when I say the endangered specie I am concerned about is a little known animal—*A Bible Centered Leader*. Let me stress some ideas about that concept that I want to cover in this article:

We need Bible centered leaders.
You can become one.
Here are some helpful suggestions to become a Bible centered leader.

Shortly I will define for you a Bible centered leader. Let me first give my credentials.
I have been studying and using the Bible for 34 years. I have some deep convictions about that Bible. And I have learned some things about how to habitually ground oneself in this Bible. Three of my fundamental convictions are simple. They are captured in the following Biblical references.

A Lasting Source

> The grass withers, the flower fades; but the Word of our God will stand forever. Isaiah 40:8

Fads, helpful as they may be, will come and go.[421] Effective leaders will recognize and use fads which are appropriate to the times and situations in which they lead. But there is more. My personal conviction about lasting effective ministry flows from the following two verses.

2 Timothy 3:16,17 The Guarantee About That Source
Every Scripture inspired of God is profitable for teaching, for setting things right, for confronting, for inspiring righteous living, in order that God's leader be thoroughly equipped to lead God's people.

---

[421] I consider a fad as a fashion that is taken up with great enthusiasm for a brief period of time; a craze. Frequently, behind a fad is some dynamic principle. If we can identify the dynamic underlying principle we can re-engineer other *fads* which will work later after the original fad dies out (e.g. seeker sensitive churches, various church growth fads, etc.) But the Word of God will always be eternally fresh for any time if its dynamic principles are unlocked.

2 Timothy 2:15 The Proper Response to the Guarantee
Make every effort to be pleasing to God, a Bible Centered leader who is completely confident in using God's Word with impact in lives.
The grass withers, the flower fades; but the Word of our God will stand forever. Isaiah 40:8

In my opinion we have only one guarantee for an effective life time experience as a leader. We must be people of the Word. Seminaries are good. But a seminary degree does not guarantee an equipped leader. Short term training in leadership institutes are good and helpful. But institutes that offer various leadership emphases can not guarantee equipping. Retreats, workshops, seminars, and conferences, all good in themselves and helpful in our development, can not guarantee equipping. But God does guarantees it. He insures us that this unfading Word which will stand forever can equip us. If we center our lives and ministry in the Word we have a guarantee from God that it will equip us to lead. Our job is to respond and make every effort to please God in our mastery and use of this Word for our own lives and for those we serve. Let me suggest then, that,

> Effective leaders should have an appropriate, unique, lifelong plan for mastering the Word in order to use it with impact in their ministries.

I want to share with you four discoveries I have personally learned in my own thirty-four year pilgrimage of mastering the Word and using it with impact in my ministry.

1. A Guiding Paradigm Helps

Few leaders master the Word without a proactive, deliberate approach which plans to do so. I was challenged early on, shortly after my *Lordship committal* in 1964, to begin a lifelong mastery of the Word of God—an overwhelming task I thought at that time. Pastor L. Thompson, the challenger, had been in the Word almost 30 years at that time. He was my model that it could be done. My Navigator trained friend, Harold Dollar, gave me my first paradigm for doing that. The Navigators were using an illustration called *The Hand* to challenge people to study and use God's Word. The little finger represented listening to God's Word. The ring finger stood for reading God's Word. The middle finger indicated studying God's Word. The index finger reminded of memorizing God's Word. The thumb represented Meditating on God's Word. I immediately set out to use this paradigm. I learned to listen well (using *Sermon Listening Sheets*). I started to get tapes from Bible teachers. I started my yearly read through the Bible program. I began to memorize three verses per week. I set a goal to study one book thoroughly each year (if a long book or more if shorter books). I learned techniques for analyzing verses and doing word studies which helped me learn how to meditate. In short, I made this paradigm really work for me. I used this paradigm for 15 years with one or more of the components having more prominence from time-to-time.

During the next 10 years I found that not all the components were important to me. By this time I was well into my leadership research and was not actively teaching the Bible in a local church context. I did continue to use several of *The Hand* components as guidelines. Essentially I was struggling for a better paradigm that both fit me and my ministry.

During the last seven years I have been working from my new paradigm. And that is what I want to share with you. It has given me new life. Every where I go I try to share it—one on one, in groups, in seminars, and in classes. I find that people really respond to it. They react with a fresh new excitement about studying the Bible. I know that some of my readers have really plateaued in their mastery of the Word. I know that some of you are not seeing the Word impacting your leadership. Some of you are probably seeing impact, but are looking for m re. Maybe what I have found may help you.

But even if my new paradigm may not work for you, I still contend that you need some plan to move toward life long mastery.

2. The Breakthrough Insight—The Notion of Core

I stumbled on to this new paradigm as I studied giftedness of leaders.[422] In my research of leaders developing over a lifetime, I found that:

(1) all leaders have at least one word gift; most have a set of word gifts. Word gifts include teaching, exhortation, prophecy, pastoring, evangelism, apostleship, and ruling (leadership). Sometimes either word of knowledge, word of wisdom, discernings of spirits or word of faith functions as a word gift.

(2) all leaders have core items in the Bible which are important to them.

It was this last item that was the *breakthrough insight*. This observation can prove extremely valuable to one who has a desire to establish a life long habit of mastering the Word and wants to use it impactfully in ministry. The observation, expanded a bit:

> **Leaders usually have favorite Bible books, or special passages, which God has used mightily in their own lives to spur their growth or solve their problems or otherwise meet them. It is these books or special passages which form the basis for much of what they share with others in their ministry.**

And they usually do so with added impact since these core items have meant something to them personally. This interest in and repetitive use of core items suggests a selection criterion. We can limit what should be mastered in-depth over a life time to our core items. These core items provide a definite starting place for mastery of the Bible. From this observation I have drawn two important definitions.

Definition   A <u>Core Set</u> is a collection of very important Bible books, usually from 5-20, which are or have been extremely meaningful to you in your own life and for which you feel a burden from God to use with great power over and over in your ministry in the years to come.

Definition   A <u>Core Selection</u> refers to important passages, important biographical characters, special psalms, special values or key topics which are or have been extremely meaningful to you in your own life and for which you feel a burden from God to use with great power over and over in your ministry in the years to come.

It is this breakthrough insight which makes mastery of the Bible a realizable potential for word gifted leaders. The *Equipping Formula* suggests one paradigm a leader can use to focus his/her mastery of the Bible.

3. The Equipping Formula—four components

My new paradigm, which I call the *Life Long Bible Mastery Paradigm*, has four components.

Component 1. **Mastery** of one's Core Books or other core material,
Component 2. **Devotional Input** (from Core Books and other Bible portions as well)
Component 3. When needed, **Familiarity Reading** of weak Bible Portions.
Component 4. **Situational Study**

The first two components are obligatory and should be going on all the time. The next two are contingent upon need.

All leaders need to be working on mastering core material continually. All leaders need to have God speak to them personally through the Word. All leaders need to have some minimum familiarity with the whole Word, even though they are moving toward mastery of a limited number of core items in the Bible. From time to time leaders will have situations in their leadership setting which demand a searching study of the Bible for special findings. These will come and go as prompted by situations. The *Equipping Formula*

---

[422] These first three observations which follow came as a result of 10 years research in giftedness among contemporary leaders at the School of World Mission. See **Unlocking Your Giftedness** from Barnabas Publishers which gives the results of studies of giftedness among leaders.

takes in to account these various needs. Its four components form the basis for planning, short term and long term.

4. Impact Communication—Studying for Ideas that Change Lives

Core items are important to a leader. They have already impacted that leader personally. Because of this, a leader can usually use the core items in ministry to impact others. I teach those who want to use this *Life Long Bible Mastery Paradigm* to identify the key ideas in a core book, a core Psalm, a core passage, a core topic, core biographical characters or core values. Then as part of the plan of mastering that core item, I teach them to design communication events to present these key ideas.

Effective leaders should have an appropriate, unique, lifelong plan for mastering the Word in order to use it with impact in their ministries. We need Bible centered leaders. The *Life Long Bible Mastery Paradigm* is simply one of many that can be used. You may use others. I am happy if you do. The real questions are, "Do you have a Bible centered ministry? Are you a Bible Centered leader." Well, I promised earlier to define this endangered specie.

Definition   A <u>Bible Centered leader</u> refers to a leader whose leadership is informed by the Bible, who has been shaped by Biblical leadership values, who has grasped the intent of Scriptural books and their content in such a way as to apply them to current situations and who uses the Bible in ministry so as to impact followers.

Join the *Save the Bible Centered Leaders Association*! At least save one of them. You! Be a Pauline fan and appropriate 2 Ti 3:16,17 for your life and ministry. Don't *let Bible Centered Leaders* become a vanishing breed!

Relevance of the Article to 1,2 Timothy

Paul usually followed the epistolary format of his times. He opened his letters with a salutation. The important thing about this is that Paul usually foreshadowed what he wanted to deal with in the epistle by carefully worded, sometimes almost cryptic phrases. I have studied comparatively all of Paul's salutations to see what are the functions he carries out in them. I have identified seven functions. In the epistles to the Ephesians Paul touches on five of the seven. Functions 1, 3, 4, 5, and 7 are easily seen in the Timothy letters, 1,2Ti.

73. Variations on His Theme- Paul's Salutations- Harbingers of His Epistles

Introduction

I distinctly remember in my eleventh grade English class when I first ran into the word harbinger. It was in a poem by now long forgotten,

A robin is the harbinger of spring.

I had learned from my eighth grade English class to look up new words I encountered, a habit I am now very grateful for. So I looked up harbinger. Here is my simplified paraphrasing of its definition.

definition   A <u>harbinger</u> is one that foreshadows what is to come.

Usually it refers to a person. But I am applying it in my title of this article to a thing--Paul's salutation.

I think it was in my study of Romans, years ago, that I first noticed the connection between special phrases in the salutation[423] and thematic treatment of topics in the book.

Over the years as I have continued to study more and more of Paul's epistles as core books I have been very aware of Paul's salutations. A careful reading of his salutations puts you well on the way to focusing on important thematic ideas in his books.

Paul's Salutations

In our world, salutations in letters are very brief and contain only a few words or two like Dear Mom, Dear Sirs, To Whom It May Concern, etc. Not so with epistles in Paul's time. And I am thankful for the very wordy difference.

definition   A <u>salutation</u> is the opening line of a letter which describes to whom the letter is addressed.

definition   A <u>Pauline Salutation</u> is the opening paragraph in any of Paul's letters which follows the form of from /to with some greeting words thrown in and some qualifying phrases tucked here and there.

---

[423] Alford specifically identifies the doctrinal inserts in Paul's salutations and calls them fore-announcements. See bibliography for Alford entry.

definition   A <u>Pauline salutation extension</u> refers to the immediate   paragraph which follows the salutation and which often links the salutation to the body of the letter as well as leads into the body itself as part of the body of the epistle. It functions to extend the thematic intent of the salutation.

Paul's salutations are intriguing. Comparative study of them identifies several functions that Paul accomplishes in his salutations.

Function 1.   He claim's apostolic authority;
Function 2.   He qualifies, in a terse explanatory way, his ministry;
Function 3.   He foreshadows (a good motivating technique) some major concept(s) he will deal with in the epistle;
Function 4.   He does sponsors mentorees;
Function 5.   He identifies the recipient(s)--usually with a unique name or phrase if a church;
Function 6.   He sometimes gives his own personal state;
Function 7.   Greets, usually with some form of a blessing.

Not all of these occur in every salutation. But all of them do occur in some salutation or salutation extension. A recognition of these functions can alert us to read the rest of the epistle with a focus.

Paul's Salutations Displayed

Glance quickly through each of Paul's salutations. I will highlight some important features. I will then identify the functions accomplished by each and will identify the foreshadowing phrases. Finally I will try to correlate between the foreshadowing phrases and the overall theme of each book.

Romans 1:1-7

1 Paul, a servant of Jesus Christ, called to be an apostle, separated unto the gospel of God, 2 Which he had promised before by his prophets in the holy scriptures, 3 Concerning his Son Jesus Christ our Lord, which was made of the seed of David according to the flesh; 4 And declared to be the Son of God with power, according to the spirit of holiness, by the resurrection from the dead: 5 By whom we have received grace and apostleship, for obedience to the faith among all nations, for his name. 6 Among whom you are also the called of Jesus Christ: 7 To all that are in Rome, beloved of God, called to be saints: Grace to you and peace from God our Father, and the Lord Jesus Christ.

1 Corinthians

1 Paul, called as an apostle of Jesus Christ as God willed it, and Sosthenes, our brother, 2 To the church of God which is at Corinth, to those who are especially set apart in union with Christ Jesus, to live holy lives, with all who in every place call on the name of Jesus Christ our Lord, and theirs too. 3 Grace to you and peace from God our Father and the Lord Jesus Christ.

2 Corinthians

1 Paul, an apostle of Jesus Christ by the will of God, and Timothy our brother, To the church of God which is at Corinth, with all the saints who are in all Greece. 2 Grace to you and peace from God our Father and the Lord Jesus Christ.

Galatians

1 Paul, an apostle, not of men, neither by man, but by Jesus Christ, and God the Father, who raised him from the dead; 2 And all the believers which are with me, unto the churches of Galatia: 3 Grace be to you and peace from God the Father, and [from] our Lord Jesus Christ, 4 Who gave himself for our sins, that he might deliver us from this present evil world, according to the will of God and our Father:
 5 To whom be glory for ever and ever. Amen.

Ephesians

1 Paul, an apostle of Jesus Christ by the will of God, to the saints which are at Ephesus, and to the faithful in Christ Jesus: 2 Grace be to you, and peace, from God our Father, and from the Lord Jesus Christ.

Philippians

1 Paul and Timothy, the servants of Jesus Christ, to all the saints in Christ Jesus which are at Philippi, with the bishops and deacons. 2 Grace be unto you, and peace, from God our Father, and from the Lord Jesus Christ.

Colossians

1 Paul, an apostle of Jesus Christ by the will of God, and Timotheus our brother, 2 To the saints and faithful brethren in Christ which are at Colosse: Grace be unto you, and peace, from God our Father and the Lord Jesus Christ.

1 Thessalonians

1 Paul, and Silvanus, and Timotheus, unto the church of the Thessalonians which is in God the Father and in the Lord Jesus Christ: Grace be unto you, and peace, from God our Father, and the Lord Jesus Christ.

2 Thessalonians

1 Paul, and Silvanus, and Timotheus, unto the church of the Thessalonians in God our Father and the Lord Jesus Christ: 2 Grace unto you, and peace, from God our Father and the Lord Jesus Christ.

1 Timothy

1 Paul, an apostle of Jesus Christ by the commandment of God our Savior, and the Lord Jesus Christ, which is our hope; 2 Unto Timothy, my own son in the faith: Grace, mercy, and peace, from God our Father and Jesus Christ our Lord.

2 Timothy

1 Paul, an apostle of Jesus Christ by God's design, to proclaim the promised life which is in Christ Jesus, 2 To Timothy, my dearly beloved son. May you have Grace, mercy, and peace, from God the Father and Christ Jesus our Lord.

Titus

1:1 I, Paul, am ministering as a servant of God and an apostle of Jesus Christ to help mature God's own chosen followers. I want them to know the truth that leads to godliness. 2 I want them to have a faith and a knowledge grounded in an expectation of eternal life. God, who can not lie, promised this eternal life before the beginning of time. 3 At His appointed time, He revealed His truth about this. God our Savior entrusted me with this task and commanded me to preach it. 4 I write to you, Titus, one who is like my very own son because of our common faith.

Philemon

1 Paul, a prisoner of Jesus Christ, and Timothy our brother, to Philemon our dearly beloved, and fellow laborer. 2 Hello also to our beloved Apphia, and Archippus our fellow soldier, and to the church in your house. 3 Grace to you, and peace, from God our Father and the Lord Jesus Christ.

Table 1,2 Ti 73-1 Functions Identified in Paul's Salutations

Book	Fn 1	Fn2	Fn3	Fn4	Fn5	Fn 6	Fn7
Rom	√	√	√		√		√
1 Co	√		√	√	√		√
2 Co	√		√	√	√	√	√
Gal	√		√		√		√
Eph	√				√		√
Php		√		√	√		√
Col	√			√	√		√
1 Th				√	√		√
2 Th				√	√		√
1 Ti	√		√	√	√		√
2 Ti	√		√	√	√		√
Tit	√	√	√	√	√		√
Phm		√		√	√	√	√

Table 1,2 Ti 73-2 Foreshadowing Phrases

Book	Phrases
Rom	1....gospel of God, ... 2. promised before by his prophets in the holy scriptures, 3. Concerning his Son Jesus Christ our Lord, ... the seed of David according to the flesh; 4. declared to be the Son of God with power, according to the 5. spirit of holiness, by the resurrection from the dead: 6. ...obedience to the faith among all nations, for his name. 7...called of Jesus Christ: ...called to be saints:
1 Co	1. set apart in union with Christ Jesus, to live holy lives (Paul is going to deal with immorality problems) In the extension: 2. Grace of God (by metonymy the notion of spiritual gifts, which he will deal with in depth, especially the problems regarding projection of the tongues gifts on all) 3. enriched in everything (dealing both with the wisdom problem and the projection of certain gifts as being more important) 4. not lacking any spiritual gift (projection problem again foreshadowed) 5. without fault (dealing with the whole immorality problem and other problems—From a confidence that God can solve them) 6. day of our Lord Jesus Christ (they will be held accountable for their beliefs and actions) Note: Paul prays for the Corinthians.
2 Co	1. saints who are in all Greece In the extension: 2. with all the Saints who are in all Greece (reminds them of their needed holy behavior and that the church is bigger than their little groups in Corinth) 3. you will indirectly benefit (uses maturity appeal as well as gives expectation for the shaping activity of God through deep processing) 4. unshakeable hope (using Goodwin's Expectation Principle).
Gal	1. apostle, not of men, neither by man, but by Jesus Christ, and God the Father, 2. who raised him from the dead 3. Who gave himself for our sins, 4. that he might deliver us from this present evil world, according to the will of God and our Father:

Eph, Php, Col, 1,2 Th, Phm	none; extension yes
1 Ti	which is our hope
2 Ti	to proclaim the promised life which is in Christ Jesus
Tit	1. to help mature God's own chosen followers. 2. I want them to know the truth that leads to godliness. 3. I want them to have a faith and a knowledge grounded in an expectation of eternal life. 4. God, who can not lie, promised this eternal life before the beginning of time. 5. At His appointed time, He revealed His truth about this. 6. God our Savior

When you do detailed study of each of the books and are aware of these foreshadowing elements you will see them reflected in the theme of the book as a whole, in various parts of the structure of the book, and the emphasis of small contextual units as well as even larger contextual units.

Conclusion

I want to suggest 4 ways that an awareness of Paul's salutations and his use of them can help us as we read and study his epistles.

1. We always read better when looking for things. In our study of effective readers[424] we uncovered the basic principle that when you read looking for something you read much more alertly and discover much more than if you are reading just generally looking for things.
2. In his salutations, Paul stresses some important things to him. If they are important to Paul we want to know why.
3. It should make us aware of the basic principle of intentional selection. The Spirit of God superintended the writing of the inspired word and has not given us all that could be given but has selected that which we need. So we should recognize the importance of words. They are there not by happenstance but for reasons. This should also make us more conscious of our own words. We should use words that count.
4. Paul's use of phrases to describe God is important. He uses phrases to describe God in terms of God's revealing Himself to Paul to meet certain needs Paul faced. When we experience God, we should use language that describes God in terms of those experiences.[425] As leaders our language describing God will influence our followers. We should use our titles and phrases for God proactively so as to affect our followers.

Paul's salutations foreshadow what he will deal with in his epistles. We should read them with extra care, knowing that they will help unfold truth in the epistles.

Final Comment:

Paul introduced—not all the problems in the Corinthian church that he would deal with—but certainly some very important ones.

---

[424] See my booklet, **Reading on the Run.**

[425] The archetype of this in the Bible is Daniel. His use of names and phrases to describe God captures who God was for him.

Relevance of the Article to 1,2 Timothy
More than in any other of his Epistles, Paul stresses the importance of the Word of God in a leader's life. His admonitions to Timothy, especially in 2 Ti 2:15 and 3:16,17, stress just how important it is for a leader to do due diligence in his/her study of the Word and also that that same Word of God will equip a leader for ministry. Timothy had seen the importance of the Word of God in his grandmother and mother. He saw it in Paul's life. And he knew, from Paul's own challenges just how important it must be for his own life.

74. Word Disciplines and Bible Centered Leadership

Introduction

Paul, in the book of Titus, made some powerful demands upon Titus concerning ministry in Crete. It was clear that Titus had to know God's Word (part of that was in process; involved knowing Paul's oral teaching).
Note the demands on Titus.

Titus 2:
1 Your teaching must be solid, through and through. 2 Teach the older men to be temperate, worthy of respect, self-controlled, and solid in what they believe. They should demonstrate love and endurance.

**3 Likewise, teach the older women to be reverent in the way they live.
... No one should be able to malign the word of God because of their daily behavior.**

6 Similarly, encourage the young men to be self-controlled. 7...Teach with integrity. Show that what you teach is important. 8 What you say should be irrefutable. Those who oppose you will have no grounds to condemn you. In fact, they will be embarrassed, because they can not deny what you have said and done.

9 Teach slaves ...

15 These, then, are the things you should teach. Encourage and rebuke authoritatively.   Don't let anyone put you down.

Titus had to teach all age groups. He had to teach cross-gender. He had to teach with power. His teaching had to be irrefutable. It is clear that Titus needed to be a Bible Centered Leader.[426]

definition   A Bible Centered leader refers to a leader whose leadership is significantly informed from the Bible and who personally has been shaped by Biblical values, has grasped the intent of Scriptural books and their content in such a way as to apply them to current situations and who uses the Bible in ministry so as to impact followers.

---

[426] See **Article**, *5. Bible Centered Leader*, for more details on this.

There are two central components and two complementary concepts in this definition.

1. Essential Component: A leader whose leadership is being informed by the Bible,

2. Necessary Credibility Component: A leader who personally has been shaped by Biblical values,

3. Necessary Contextual Component: A leader who has grasped the intent of Scriptural books and their content in such a way as to apply them to current situations and

4. Essential Component: A leader who uses the Bible in ministry so as to impact followers.

In my classes dealing with leadership studies in the Bible I have a series of Bible tests to help folks assess their Bible knowledge. The longest of these is rather detailed--a 300 question test that takes 6-8 hours. Its purpose is to let students know their strengths and weaknesses in the Bible. It also helps them identify their core material.[427] I want them to know the information in the Bible. But understand this. *Knowing the facts of the Bible does not guarantee that a leader will be a Bible Centered Leader.* But **not knowing the facts of the Bible will guarantee that you are not a Bible Centered Leader.**

So I stress that emerging leaders need to establish habits of life long mastery of their core material. The following are some word disciplines that I have identified that can make the difference in a leader moving toward becoming a Bible Centered Leader.

Word Disciplines Needed

Our studies of leaders today reveals that a number of them became Bible Centered Leaders because they had good word disciplines in their lives. Here are some word disciplines that can prove useful.

Table 1,2 Ti 74-1 Some Word Disciplines

Discipline	Purpose	Where to Go for Help[428]
Devotional Habits	Learn to hear from God so as to move the heart and will; forms basis for impacting others with the Word	See **Having A Ministry That Lasts,** ch 4, p 83-93. See also **Fellowship With God.**
Analytical Habits—Synthesis of Large Portions of Scripture	See the overall perspective on what God is doing using a book of the Bible. Helps one to recognize dynamical equivalence between Bible and modern day application.	See the **Bible and Leadership Values** for the application of this to each book in the Bible. See Appendix G in **Having A Ministry That Lasts.** The first three hermeneutical principles deals with this kind of study.
Analytical Habits—detailed exegetical skills with small units of Scripture,	Enables one to identify observations, guidelines, principles and values from Bible material. Such material has the potential to be transferable to today's situations.	See Appendix G in **Having A Ministry That Lasts.** The last four hermeneutical principles deals with this kind of study.
Analytical Habits—word study skills	Allows one to do thorough, good Bible study. Gives credence to exegetical work.	See **Interpreting the Scriptures: Word Studies.**

---

[427] All leaders are *word gifted.* Word gifted folks have special material in the Bible which God has used in their lives and which they in turn use in their ministry. We call this material, core material. Leaders should continually be mastering and using their core material over their lifetimes. Their core material will also be expanding as the develop over their lifetimes. See *word gifted, core material,* **Glossary.**

[428] All of the items listed in this column are my own publications available through Barnabas Publications, my own publishing arm.

Analytical Habits--special hermeneutics	Gives skills to interpret unusual language in Scriptures. Gives evidence of thorough knowledge of word and credence to study as well as pointing out emphatic issues from Bible.	See Appendix G in **Having A Ministry That Lasts** for special language principles which outlines the special language forms you should be able to study. See also **Interpreting the Scriptures: Figures and Idioms; Parables— Puzzles With a Purpose; Hebrew Poetry**.
Perseverance--On Going Study of Core Material (principle of base + advance)	The Base + advance principle provides a guiding value toward being a person of excellence.	See **Having A Ministry That Lasts**, chapters 4 and 5, note especially p 128-132 and 135 for Base + Advance concept.
Impact Communication	It is not the knowledge of the Bible which makes one an effective Bible Centered Leader, it is the use of the Bible to impact lives.	See **Having A Ministry That Lasts**, chapter 7 communicating with impact.

The Equipping Formula

Few leaders master the Word without a proactive, deliberate approach which plans to do so. So then, I suggest that life long habitual study of the Bible is done best if a leader has some framework for approaching the study of the Bible. All of the above word disciplines fit well into the equipping formula, a framework for guiding one into life long study. Notice, it is made up of 4 components. Two of them are obligatory (+) and need to be in place all the time. Two are optional (+or-) and need to be in place when required by you ministry situation.

Mastering the Word
for Gifted Power
includes   =   +   **regular devotional input**
                                   +   **progress on mastering your core set (material)**
                              + or –   **familiarity reading in all of Word**
                              + or –   **situational study**

definition   Regular devotional input means a disciplined quiet time in which you use the Word to feed your own soul and your intimacy with God and His ways.

definition   A Core Set is a collection of very important Bible books, usually from 5-20, which are or have/been extremely meaningful to you in your own life and for which you feel a burden from God to use with great power over and over in your ministry in the years to come. (Core materials include core passages, core Psalms, core parables, core topics, core bios, core values)

definition   Familiarity reading means a regular reading program through the whole Bible or various portions of it to keep up familiarity with the Word.

definition   Situational study is the study of a concentrated portion o˜ the Word for some personal reason, or for direct use in a ministry setting.

You need to plan around the Equipping Formula always heeding obligatory and also using optional when needed. The base plus advance will guide you as you continue to master your core material. It will force you to work on your impact communication as well since on-going mastery involves developing communication events delivering results of your study to others.

Conclusion

Desire to be a Bible Centered Leader is not enough. You will need a major commitment of the will toward becoming a disciplined student. of the Word. Remember the challenges to Titus? Why not make them your own.

Titus 2:
1 Your teaching must be solid, through and through. .

7...Teach with integrity. Show that what you teach is important. 8 What you say should be irrefutable. Those who oppose you will have no grounds to condemn you. In fact, they will be embarrassed, because they can not deny what you have said and done.   .

15 These, then, are the things you should teach. Encourage and rebuke authoritatively. Don't let anyone put you down.

Glossary—Leadership Definitions

The following leadership related definitions occur throughout this book. They are listed here alphabetically for convenience in referencing. SRN stands for Strong's Reference Number. These numbers can be used to look up the definitions of these words in the Strong's Exhaustive Concordance containing Hebrew and Greek dictionaries. These numbers are now also used by many other Bible study aids.

Item	Definition
accountability	a term used to describe the fact that a leader will answer to God for his/her ministry. Paul has a major leadership value concerning this. See Ultimate Accountability.
apostleship	one of the 19 spiritual gifts. The gift of apostleship refers to a special leadership capacity to move with authority from God to create new ministry structures (churches and parachurch groups) to meet needs and to develop and appoint leadership in these structures. **Its central thrust is Creating New Ministry.**
bench marks, spiritual	this refers to something that happens in the life of the leader which serves as positive proof of God's activity in that life. It is something that a leader can look back upon and be encouraged to continue when confused or in a discouraging situation. Because it is foundational, sure and certain, and had the distinct imprint of God's Hand on the life. See also destiny processing.
Bible centered leader	a leader (1) whose leadership is being informed by the Bible and (2) who personally has been shaped by Biblical values, (3) who has grasped the intent of Scriptural books and their content in such a way as to apply them to current situations and (4) who uses the Bible in ministry so as to impact followers.
capture	a technical term used when talking about figures of speech being interpreted. A figure or idiom is said to be captured when one can display the intended emphatic meaning of it in non-figurative simple words. e.g. not ashamed of the Gospel = captured: completely confident of the Gospel.
certainty idiom	refers to one of three different idioms which have as their intent the emphasizing of something to the extent that it can be counted on with certainty: The three certainty idioms include: 1. Double certainty—a negative and positive statement (in either order) are often used to express or imply certainty; e.g. 1 Ki 18:36. 2. Fulfilled— in the fulfillment idiom things are spoken of as given, done, or possessed, which are only promised or proposed; e.g. Gen 15:8. 3. Prophetic Past— in the prophetic past idiom the past tense is used to describe or express the certainty of future action; e.g. Jn 13:31.
church era	shortened form of Church Leadership Era. The leadership era associated with Peter, Paul, and John and to the present. Ushered in at Pentecost. It is a time of spiritual leadership exercised around the world in many cultures.

conscience	the inner sense of right or wrong which is innate in a human being but which also is modified by values imbibed from a culture. This innate sense can also be modified by the Spirit of God.
contemporary model	one of nine mentor types. A *mentor contemporary model* is a person who models values, methodologies, and other leadership characteristics in such a way as to inspire others to emulate them.
contextualization	the process of taking something meaningful in one context and making it relevant to a new context. e.g. the Christian movement which began in a Jewish context had to be reinterpreted by Paul to a non-Jewish context, the Gentiles.
destiny fulfillment	the third stage of the destiny pattern. The destiny pattern usually follows a threefold pattern: destiny preparation, destiny revelation, and destiny fulfillment. This stage refers to the completion of some destiny for a leader.
destiny pattern	a leadership pattern. The development of a sense of destiny usually follows a three fold pattern of destiny preparation, destiny revelation, and destiny fulfillment. That is, over a period of time God shapes a leader with experiences which prepare, reveal, and finally brings about completion of destiny.
destiny preparation	the first stage of the destiny pattern. The destiny pattern usually follows a threefold pattern: destiny preparation, destiny revelation, and destiny fulfillment. In the preparation stage, the leader receives hints of a destiny to come.
destiny revelation	the second stage of the destiny pattern. The destiny pattern usually follows a threefold pattern: destiny preparation, destiny revelation, and destiny fulfillment. In the revelation stage, the leader receives clarification or further word of a destiny to come.
developer	a concept seen in Paul's life. A developer is a person with a mentoring bent who readily sees potential in an emerging leader and finds ways to help move that emerging leader on to becoming an effective leader.
disciplines, spiritual	one of five enhancement factors seen in the lives of effective leaders. <u>Spiritual disciplines</u> are activities of mind and body purposefully undertaken to bring personality and total being into effective cooperation with the Spirit of God so as to reflect Kingdom life. Three categories are frequently used to describe spiritual disciplines: <u>abstinence disciplines</u> like solitude, silence, fasting, frugality, chastity, secrecy, sacrifice; <u>engagement disciplines</u> like study, worship, celebration, service, prayer, fellowship, confession, submission; other <u>miscellaneous disciplines</u> like voluntary exile, keeping watch, sabbath keeping, practices among the poor, journaling, listening.
divine affirmation	a concept from leadership emergence theory. The shaping activity of God whereby God makes known to a leader his approval of that leader. This is a major motivating factor to keep one serving the Lord.
divine appointment	a Pauline leadership value seen in 2Co. *Leaders ought to be sure that God appointed them to ministry situations.*

entrustment, leadership	the concept of a lifetime of leadership ministry viewed as a gift from God which is entrusted to the leader to manage as a stewardship. Paul is strong on this concept both in 1 Timothy and 2 Timothy. Viewing leadership this way, requires a strong sense of destiny. It also heightens the responsibility a leader feels for carrying out that ministry so as to give an account of it on *That Day.*
enhancement factors	comparative study of effective leaders who finished well has identified five things that enhance their perseverance and ability to finish well. These include: 1. Seeing present day ministry in terms of a life time perspective and in terms of God's perspective for the ages; 2. Experiencing repeated renewals throughout their ministry—some sought, others serendipitous; 3. Maintenance of disciplines in the life, especially spiritual disciplines; 4. Having a learning posture throughout their whole ministry; 5. Having mentors from time-to-time, who enable them in various ways.
evangelism	one of the 19 spiritual gifts belonging to the Word Cluster and the Love Cluster. The gift of evangelism in general refers to the capacity to challenge people through various communicative methods (persuasion) to receive the Gospel of salvation in Christ so as to see them respond by taking initial steps in Christian discipleship. **Its central thrust is Introducing Others To The Gospel.**
exhortation	one of the 19 spiritual gifts. It is a spiritual gift belonging to the word cluster. The *gift of Exhortation* is the capacity to urge people to action in terms of applying Biblical truths, or to encourage people generally with Biblical truths, or to comfort people through the application of Biblical. . **Its central thrust is to apply Biblical truth.**
figure	the unusual use of a word or words differing from the normal use in order to draw special attention to some point of interest. The more important figures (100s used in Bible) include: metaphor, simile, metonymy, synecdoche, hyperbole, irony, personification, apostrophe, negative emphatics (litotes and tapenosis), rhetorical question. See individual definitions for each of these. See **For Further Study Bibliography, Figures and Idioms** by Dr. J. Robert Clinton.
focused life	A focused life is a life dedicated to exclusively carrying out God's unique purposes through it, by identifying the focal issues, that is, the major role, life purpose, effective methodology, or ultimate contribution, which allows an increasing prioritizing of life's activities around the focal issues, and results in a satisfying life of being and doing.
giftedness set	a term describing natural abilities, acquired skills, and spiritual gifts which a leader has as resources to use in ministry. Sometimes shortened to giftedness.
gifted power	refers to the empowerment of the Holy Spirit when using giftedness; 1Pe 4:11 gives the basic admonition for this to the use of word gifts. It is naturally extended to other areas of giftedness.
gift-mix	refers to the collection of spiritual gifts that a leader demonstrates repeatedly in ministry over time.

Goodwin's Expectation Principle	Bennie Goodwin in a small booklet on leadership published by InterVarsity Press (see bibliography) identified a social dynamic principle which is helpful in developing leaders. In my own words, *Emerging leaders tend to live up to the genuine expectations of leaders they respect.* The challenge embodied in the expectation must not be too much or the young leader will not be able to accomplish it and will be inoculated against further challenges. The challenge must not be too little or it will not attract. It must be a genuine expectation. Paul uses this with Timothy several times (see fn 1Ti 6:11; 2Ti 1:5).
grace	carries essentially the sense of freedom; when used in a context describing salvation from God it implies that God freely gave us salvation without our earning or deserving it; when used to exhort continuing in the Christian life it carries the sense of the enabling presence of God in a life so as to free (enable) one to persevere victoriously. Paul uses it especially this way in his last epistles 1Ti, 2Ti, Tit. Peter does too 2Pe 3:18. And John also, Rev 22:21. It is interesting to observe that the three great church leaders in their closing words stress the importance of grace and its value in continuing in the Christian life. It is also used by Paul as a metonymy (Corinthians and Romans) standing for spiritual gifts given freely by God.
harvest model	one of five philosophical leadership models introduced by Jesus and one which focuses on a leader's responsibility to extend the Kingdom by reaching out to those not in it and challenging them to enter it. See **Article**, *Five Philosophical Leadership Models in the Gospels.*
helps	one of 19 spiritual gifts occurring primarily in the Love Cluster. The <u>gifts of helps</u> refers to the capacity to unselfishly meet the needs of others through very practical means. **Its Central Thrust Is The Attitude And Ability To Aid Others In Practical Ways.**
heresy	refers to deviation from a standard, whether in belief (orthodoxy) or practice (orthopraxy). e.g. See 1Ti where both are present in the Ephesian church (as prophesied in Ac 20:30).
heritage pattern	refers to the early development of a leader in the foundational phase; a foundational pattern which describes the background situation out of which a leader grew up and which describes at least a nominal understanding of God and his ways. Timothy is a positive example of one who had a good heritage. He was grounded in the Scriptures and saw faith modeled by his mom, Eunice, and his grandmother, Lois.
indigenized church	a church which has its own leadership from its own people and which is organized to survive independently of outside leadership from other cultures and operates with appropriate forms, rites, and ministry fitting to its own culture. According to Allen it will be self-supporting, self-governing, and self-propagating. Others, however, see a combination of these three items along a continuum moving from dependency to interde ·endency where differing levels are appropriate for different times in the life of the church. Timothy in 1 Timothy is coming as an outside consultant to an indigenized church having its own leadership.
indirect conflict	one of 10 Pauline leadership Styles. A highly non-directive style. The <u>indirect conflict leadership style</u> is an approach to problem solving which requires discernment of spiritual motivation factors behind the problem, usually results in spiritual warfare without direct confrontation with the

parties of the problem. Spiritual warfare is sensed as a necessary first step before any problem solving can take place. Matthew 16:21-23 illustrates this style.

integrity	the top leadership character quality. It is the consistency of inward beliefs and convictions with outward practice. It is an honesty and wholeness of personality in which one operates with a clear conscience in dealings with self and others.
invincibility principle	protection of a leader by God till He is finished with that leader; this principle was derived because of the observed confidence that Jesus and Paul asserted based on their relationship with God and their understanding of their destiny and an awareness of timing in their lives such that they sensed that God would protect them until their accomplishment of their destiny was completed. See Jn 7:30; see Paul's shipwreck in Ac 27.
last days	a term used by Paul to describe the end times before the coming of Christ.
leadership committal	a special shaping activity of God observed in leadership emergence theory which is usually a spiritual benchmark and produces a sense of destiny in a leader. It is the call to leadership by God and the wholehearted response by the leader to accept and abide by that call. Paul's Damascus road experience, the destiny revelation given by Ananias, and Paul's response to it as a life calling provide the New Testament classic example of leadership committal.
leadership selection	the life-long process of divine initiative and human recognition whereby a leader emerges. The process is punctuated with critical incidents, as viewed from a two-fold intermeshing perspective—the divine and the human. God selects a leader as indicated by various kind of shaping activities and human leadership affirms that selection, recognizing the shaping activities of God and working with God in that processing.
leadership style	the individual tendency of a leader to influence followers in a highly directive manner, directive manner, non-directive manner, or highly non-directive manner. It is that consistent behavior pattern that underlies specific overt behavior acts of influence pervading the majority of leadership functions in which that leader exerts influence. The style is the means that the leader uses in influencing followers toward purposes. I identify 10 Pauline leadership styles. See Clinton **Coming To Conclusions on Leadership Styles.**
leadership value	an underlying assumption which affects how a leader behaves in or perceives leadership situations. Usually when explicitly identified and written the statement will contain strong forceful words like should, ought, or must to indicate the strength of the value. e.g. A specific Pauline leadership value—*Paul felt he should view personal relationships as an important part of ministry, both as a means for ministry and as an end in itself of ministry.* Or generalized to all leaders—*Leaders should view personal relationships as an important part of ministry, both as a means for ministry and as an end in itself of ministry.* Stronger would be the word ought and even stronger the word must.
learning posture	an attitude of willingness to learn even though what may be learned may differ and expand or even contradict what has been previously learned.

Such an attitude reflects what has been noted as a major leadership lesson: *Effective leaders maintain a learning posture all of their lifetimes.*

list idiom

an idiomatic use of a list of items. The initial item on the list is the main assertion and other items illustrate or clarify the primary item (1 Ti 3:2-7). An alternate form, usually introduced by a list indicator idiom [these (number) things, no these (number) things] has the last item on the list emphasized (Prov 6:16-19; Ro 3:10-18).

litotes/tapenosis

a negative emphatic figure of speech. It is used quite a bit by Luke and also by Paul. Something is diminished in order to emphatically stress just its opposite. e.g. not ashamed of the Gospel in Romans 1:16 means emphatically—completely confident in the Gospel. While technically different, I group litotes and tapenosis together as a class of negative emphatics. They essentially emphasize the opposite of what is denied.

love gifts

a category of spiritual gifts which are used to demonstrate the effects of God's transformation of lives and His care for people. Love gifts demonstrate the beauty of the unseen God's work in lives in such a way as to attract others to want this same kind of relationship. These include: pastoring, evangelism, gifts of healings, governments, helps, giving, mercy, (word of knowledge, word of wisdom sometimes).

Luke 16:10 Principle

an application principle drawn from Luke 16:10. An emerging leader who is faithful in small tasks will be faithful later in larger tasks.

macro-lesson

is a high level generalization of a leadership observation (suggestion, guideline, requirement), stated as a lesson, which repeatedly occurs throughout different leadership eras, and thus has potential as a leadership absolute. Macro lessons even at their weakest provide at least strong guidelines describing leadership insights. At their strongest they are requirements, that is absolutes, that leaders should follow. Leaders ignore them to their detriment. Example: *Prayer Lesson: If God has called you to a ministry then He has called you to pray for that ministry.*

mentor

in a mentoring relationship the person helping the mentoree. This is also a label given to the ultimate contribution of a Christian leader whose has a major focus in ministry of personal ministry to individuals as opposed to public ministry. e.g. Jesus, Paul the Apostle. Mentoring is also one of the five enhancement factors enabling effective leaders to finish well.

mentor counselor

one of nine mentor types. A mentor counselor is one who gives timely and wise advice as well as impartial perspective on the mentoree's view of self, others, circumstances, and ministry. In a corporate sense (that is, given to the group as a whole and not an individual mentoring situation) Paul is a mentor counselor for the Corinthian and Ephesians situations.

mentoree

in a mentoring relationship the person being helped by a mentor.

mentoring

a relational experience in which one person, the mentor, empowers another person, the mentoree, by sharing God-given resources. See the 9 mentor roles: mentor discipler, mentor spiritual guide, mentor coach, mentor counselor, mentor teacher, mentor sponsor, mentor contemporary model, mentor historical model, mentor divine contact. e.g. The apostle Paul demonstrated many of these roles in his relationships with team members and others in his ministry. See Stanley and Clinton **Connecting** for a popular treatment of mentoring. See Clinton and Clinton **The Mentor Handbook** for a detailed treatment of mentoring.

mentor spiritual guide

one of nine mentor roles. A spiritual guide is a godly, mature follower of Christ who shares knowledge, skills, and basic philosophy on what it means to increasingly realize Christ-likeness in all areas of life. The primary contributions of a Spiritual guide include accountability, decisions, and insights concerning questions, commitments, and direction affecting spirituality (inner-life motivations) and maturity (integrating truth with life).

mentor sponsor

one of nine mentor roles. A mentor sponsor is one who helps promote the ministry (career) of another by using his/her resources, credibility, position, etc. to further the development and acceptance of the mentoree.

mentor teacher

one of nine mentor roles. A mentor teacher is one who imparts knowledge and understanding of a particular subject at a time when a mentoree needs it.

mentor model (contemporary)

one of nine mentor roles. A mentor contemporary model is a person who models values, methodologies, and other leadership characteristics in such a way as to inspire others to emulate them.

mercy

one of 19 spiritual gifts occurring primarily in the Love Cluster. The gift of mercy refers to the capacity to both feel sympathy for those in need (especially the suffering) and to manifest this sympathy in some practical helpful way with a cheerful spirit so as to encourage and help those in need. **Its Central Thrust Is The Empathetic Care For Those Who Are Hurting.**

metaphor

a figure of speech which involves an implied comparison in which two unlike items (a real item and a picture item) are equated to point out one point of resemblance. e.g. The Lord is my shepherd. These can be simple (all elements present) or complex (verbal metaphor, some element may be missing and has to be supplied). 2Ti 1:6 stir up the gift is complex, a verbal metaphor. Gift is compared to a flame which has gotten low. Timothy is urged to develop and use with power that gift.

metonymy

a figure of speech in which one word is substituted for another word to which it is related. This is to emphasize both the word and call attention to the relationship between the two words. e.g. Philemon 6 communicate your faith = communicate what you believe and on which you have strong convictions.

ministry task

one of 51 process items that God uses to shape a leader. A ministry task is an assignment from God which primarily tests a person's faithfulness and obedience but often also allows use of ministry gifts in the context of a task which has closure, accountability, and evaluation. e.g. Barnabas trip to Antioch; Titus had 5 ministry tasks.

modeling

a means a leader can use to influence followers; it involves openly demonstrating in one's life the attitudes and actions desired in others. It counts on the followers admiring and wanting what the leader has in their own lives.

pioneer

a label given to the ultimate contribution of a Christian leader who starts apostolic ministries. e.g. Paul.

power gifts	a category of spiritual gifts which authenticate the reality of God by demonstrating God's intervention in today's world. These include: tongues, interpretation of tongues, discernings of spirits, kinds of healings, kinds of power (miracles), prophecy, faith, word of wisdom, word of knowledge.
power ministry	refers to use of the power gifts to demonstrate God's intervention and often to validate or vindicate a leader's spiritual authority in a situation.
promoter	a label given to the ultimate contribution of a Christian leader who effectively distributes new ideas and/or other ministry related things so as to inspire others to use them. e.g. Jesus, Paul.
prophetic past	see certainty idiom.
role enablement	a pattern observed in leadership emergence theory concerning giftedness. A leader in a situation which warrants it may be given a spiritual gift needed for that situation. After completing or leaving that situation the leader in a new place or ministry may not see the gift in the new situation. That is, it was a temporary enablement for a specific role which needed it—a non-vested gift. See vested gifts. Probably the case with Timothy (2Ti 4:5).
saint	a label given to the ultimate contribution of a Christian leader who models a Godly life in such a way as to demonstrate Christ-likeness, the fruit of the Spirit, union life and which draws others to want to emulate it. e.g. Paul the Apostle.
sense of destiny	an inner conviction arising from an experience or a series of experiences in which there is a growing sense of awareness that God has His hand on a leader in a special way for special purposes. See destiny pattern.
shepherd model	one of five philosophical leadership models introduced by Jesus and one which focuses on a leader's responsibility to relate to, protect, care for and develop those being ministered to. See **Article**, *Five Philosophical Leadership Models in the Gospels.*
sovereign mindset	a Pauline leadership value seen in 2Co. *Leaders ought to see God's hand in their circumstances as part of His plan for developing them as leaders.* See **Article**, *Sovereign Mindset.*
spiritual benchmarks	see benchmarks, spiritual—for a description of foundational events which are touchstones or watermarks for a lifetime of ministry.
spiritual gift	a God-given unique capacity which is given to each believer for the purpose of releasing a Holy Spirit empowered ministry either in a situation or to be repeated during the Church Leadership Era. I identify 19 such gifts from a comparative analysis of the 8 major and 16 minor passages about gifts in Scripture. I categorize these 19 in terms of major purposes for the hurch as Word gifts, Power gifts, and Love gifts. The 19 include: teaching, exhortation, pastoring, evangelism, apostleship, prophecy, ruling, word of wisdom, word of knowledge, faith, miracles, gifts of healings, governments, helps, giving, mercy, tongues, interpretation of tongues, discernings of spirits. All leaders have at least one word gift. See word gifts. See Clinton and Clinton **Unlocking Your Giftedness** for detailed explanation of leadership and spiritual gifts.

spiritual warfare	refers to the unseen opposition in the spirit world made up of Satan and his demons and their attempts to defeat God's forces, including believers. It also involves the response by believers to these attempts.
stewardship model	one of five philosophical leadership models introduced by Jesus and one which focuses on a leader's responsibility to recognize, develop, and use resources given to that leader. See **Article**, *Five Philosophical Leadership Models in the Gospels*.
stylistic practitioner	a label given to the ultimate contribution of a Christian leader who models a unique ministry style that others want to emulate. e.g. Peter, Paul.
superlative idiom	the Hebrew superlative is often shown by the repetition of a word. e.g. Hebrew of the Hebrews. See Php 2:27, 3:5; 1Ti 1:18; 6:12, and others.
teaching	one of the 19 spiritual gifts. It belongs to the Word Cluster. A person who has the <u>gift of teaching</u> is one who has the ability to instruct, explain, or expose Biblical truth in such a way as to cause believers to understand the Biblical truth. **Its central thrust is To Clarify Truth.**
ultimate contribution	a focused life concept; one of 4 focal issues; <u>An ultimate contribution</u> is a lasting legacy of a Christian worker for which he or she is remembered and which furthers the cause of Christianity by one or more of the following: setting standards for life and ministry; impacting lives by enfolding them in God's kingdom or developing them once in the kingdom; serving as a stimulus for change which betters the world; leaving behind an organization, institution, or movement that will further channel God's work; the discovery of ideas, communication of them, or promotion of them so that they further God's work. 13 categories have been identified. Paul indicates a 14th—that of giving to the poor. See **Article**, *A Focused Life*.
union life	a phrase which refers both to the fact of the spiritual reality of a believer joined in spirit with the resurrected Spirit of Christ and the process of that union being lived out so that the person is not dominated by sin in his/her life. Synonym: exchanged life, replaced life, deeper life, victorious life, normal Christian life. Paul comprehensively explains this kind of life in Romans 1-8. He models it in Philippians. He also shows its power in his own life in 2 Corinthians.
vested gifts	a concept from leadership emergence theory. Leaders operate repeatedly over a lifetime with certain gifts. These are called vested gifts. There is the implication of development and use of the gift (see 2Ti 1:6 fn 8). Most of the word gifts are vested gifts. See also role enablement—i.e. non-vested gifts.
word gifts	a category of spiritual gifts used to clarify and explain about God. These help us understand about God including His nature, His purposes and how we can relate to Him and be a part of His purposes. These include: teaching, exhortation, pastoring, evangelism, apostleship, prophecy, ruling, and sometimes word of wisdom, word of knowledge, and faith (a word of). All leaders have at least one of these and often several of these.
writer	a label given to the ultimate contribution of a Christian leader who captures ideas and reproduces them in written format to help and inform others. e.g. Paul, Luke, John.

Bibliography- For Further Study

Alford, Henry
  1871 **The Greek Testament in Four Volumes, Vol III.** 5th Edition. London: Deighton, Bell, and Co.

Bertelsen, Walt
  1985 *When God Gives A Sense of Destiny—A Biblical Study on Motivating Leaders.* Pasadena: Unpublished paper in the School of World Mission of Fuller Theological Seminary.

(Bratcher Robert G. et al)
  n.d. **Good News Bible- Today's English Version.** New York: American Bible Society.

Bruce, A B.
  1929 **The Training of the Twelve.** 3rd Edition. Garden City, N.Y.: Doubleday, Doran & Co.

Butt, Howard
  1973 **The Velvet Covered Brick: Christian Leadership in an Age of Rebellion.** New York: Harper and Row.

Clinton, Dr. J. Robert
  1977 **Disputed Practices.** Redone in 1994. Altadena, CA: Barnabas Publishers

  1977 **Interpreting the Scriptures: Figures and Idioms.** Altadena, CA: Barnabas Publishers

  1986 **A Short History of Leadership Theory.** Altadena, CA: Barnabas Publishers

  1986 **Coming to Conclusions on Leadership Styles.** Altadena, CA: Barnabas Publishers

  1987 **Reading on the Run- Continuum Reading Concepts.** Altadena, CA: Barnabas Publishers.

  1988 **The Making of a Leader.** Colorado Springs, Co: Navpress.

  1989 **Leadership Emergence Theory.** Altadena, CA: Barnabas Publishers

  1989 *The Ultimate Contribution,* Altadena, CA: Barnabas Publishers

  1993 *Getting Perspective- By Using Your Unique Timeline.* Altadena, CA: Barnabas Publishers.

  1993 **Leadership Perspectives.** Altadena, CA: Barnabas Publishers.

  1994 **Focused Lives- Inspirational Life Changing Lessons from Eight Effective Christian Leaders Who Finished Well.** Altadena, CA: Barnabas Publishers

  1995 **Strategic Concepts That Clarify A Focused Life.** Altadena, CA: Barnabas Publishers

  1998 **Having A Ministry That Lasts.** Altadena, CA: Barnabas Publishers.

Clinton, Dr. J. Robert and Dr. Richard W.
  1991 **The Mentor Handbook- Detailed Guidelines and Helps for Christian Mentors and Mentorees.** Altadena, CA: Barnabas Publishers

1993   **Unlocking Your Giftedness- What Leaders Need to Know To Develop Themselves and Others.** Altadena, CA: Barnabas Publishers.

Choy, Leona Frances
1990   **Powerlines: What Great Evangelicals Believed About the Holy Spirit, 1850-1930.** Camp Hill: Christian Publications.

Doohan, Helen
1984   **Leadership in Paul.** Wilmington, Del.: Michael Glazier, Inc.

Edman, V. Raymond
1964   **They Found the Secret: Twenty Transformed Lives the Reveal a Touch of Eternity.** Grand Rapids, MI: Zondervan

Foster, Richard
1988   **Celebration of Discipline: The Path to Spiritual Growth.** San Francisco: Harper and Row.

Goodwin, Bennie
1978   **The Effective Leader.** Downers grove, IL: InterVarsity Press.

Graham, Billy
1997   **Just As I Am: The Autobiography of Billy Graham**. San Francisco, CA: Harper.

Hall, Clarence W.
1933   **Samuel Brengle, Portrait of a Prophet.** New York, NY: Salvation Army.

Hersey, Palul and Ken Blanchard
1977   **Management of Organizational Behavior- Utilizing Human Resources.** Englewood Cliffs, N. J.: Prentice- Hall.

Kinnear, Angus I.
1973   **Against the Tide: The Story of Watchman Nee.** Eastbourne, England: Victory Press.

Kraft, Charles H.
1979   **Christianity and Culture.** Maryknoll, N. Y.: Orbis Books.

Leupold, Herbert Carl
1969   **Psalms.** Grand Rapids, MI: Baker. (This is a reprint of an earlier publication.)

Machiavelli
1950   **The Prince and Other Discourses.** New York: McGraw Hill.

McNeal, Reggie
2006   **Practicing Greatness—7 Disciplines of Extraordinary Leaders.** San Francisco, CA : Jossey-Bass

Nee, Watchman
1972   **Spiritual Authority.** New York: Christian Fellowship Publishers Inc.

Peterson, Eugene H.
1993   **The Message- The New Testament in Contemporary Language.** Colorado Springs, CO: Navpress.

Skinner, Betty Lee
    1974   **Daws: The Story of Dawson Trotman, Founder of the Navigators.** Grand Rapids, MI:
            Zondervan

Stanley, Paul and J. Robert Clinton
    1992   **Connecting- The Mentoring Relationships You Need to Succeed in Life.** Colorado
            Springs, Co.: Navpress

Strong, James
    1890   **The Exhaustive Concordance of the Bible (with Dictionaries of the Hebrew and
            Greek Words).** Nashville: Abingdon Press.

(Taylor, Ken did original version; other Bible scholars the new version)
    1996   **Holy Bible- New Living Translation.** Wheaton, Il: Tyndale House Publishers, Inc.

Willard, Dallas
    1988   **The Spirit of the Disciplines: Understanding How God Changes Lives.** San
            Francisco: Harper and Row.

Wrong, Dennis
    1979   **Power- Its Forms, Bases, and Uses.** San Francisco, CA: Harper and Row.

BARNABAS PUBLISHER'S MINI CATALOG

Barnabas: Encouraging Exhorter — Dr. J. Robert Clinton & Laura Raab

Connecting: The Mèntoring Relationships You Need to Succeed in Life — Dr. J. Robert Clinton

Fellowship With God — Dr. J. Robert Clinton

Figures and Idioms (Interpreting the Scriptures: Figures and Idioms) — Dr. J. Robert Clinton

Having A Ministry That Lasts: By Becoming a Bible Centered Leader — Dr. J. Robert Clinton

Hebrew Poetry (Interpreting the Scriptures: Hebrew Poetry) — Dr. J. Robert Clinton

A Short History of Leadership Theory — Dr. J. Robert Clinton

Isolation: A Place of Transformation in the Life of a Leader — Shelley G. Trebesch

Joseph: Destined to Rule — Dr. J. Robert Clinton

The Joshua Portrait — Dr. J. Robert Clinton and Katherine Haubert

Leadership Emergence Theory: A Self Study Manual For Analyzing the Development of a Christian Leader — Dr. J. Robert Clinton

Leadership Perspectives: How To Study The Bible for Leadership Insights — Dr. J. Robert Clinton

Coming to Some Conclusionson Leadership Styles — Dr. J. Robert Clinton

Leadership Training Models — Dr. J. Robert Clinton

The Bible and Leadership Values: A Book by Book Analysis— Dr. J. Robert Clinton

The Mentor Handbook: Detailed Guidelines and Helps for Christian Mentors and Mentorees — Dr. J. Robert Clinton

Parables—Puzzles With A Purpose (Interpreting the Scriptures: Puzzles With A Purpose) — Dr. J. Robert Clinton

Reading on the Run: Continuum Reading Concepts — Dr. J. Robert Clinton

Samuel: Last of the Judges & First of the Prophets–A Model For Transitional Times — Bill Bjoraker

Selecting and Developing Those Emerging Leaders — Dr. Richard W. Clinton

Starting Well: Building A Strong Foundation for a Life Time of Ministry — Dr. J. Robert Clinton

Strategic Concepts: That Clarify A Focused Life – A Self Study Guide — Dr. J. Robert Clinton

The Making of a Leader: Recognizing the Lessons & Stages of Leadership Development — Dr. J. Robert Clinton

Unlocking Your Giftedness: What Leaders Need to Know to Develop Themselves & Others — Dr. J. Robert Clinton

A Vanishing Breed: Thoughts About A Bible Centered Leader & A Life Long Bible Mastery Paradigm — Dr. J. Robert Clinton

Webster-Smith, Irene: An Irish Woman Who Impacted Japan (A Focused Life Study) — Dr. J. Robert Clinton

Word Studies (Interpreting the Scriptures: Word Studies) — Dr. J. Robert Clinton

(Book Titles are in Bold and Paper Titles are in Italics with Sub-Titles and Pre-Titles in Roman)

BARNABAS PUBLISHERS

Unique Leadership Material that will help you answer the question:
"What legacy will you as a leader leave behind?"

"The difference between leaders and followers is perspective. The difference between leaders and effective leaders is better perspective."
Barnabas Publishers has the materials that will help you find that better perspective and a closer relationship with God.

BARNABAS PUBLISHERS
Post Office Box 6006 • Altadena, CA 91003-6006
Fax Phone (626)-794-3098

Printed in the United States
70720LV00001B/127